LOONYOLOGY

LOONYOLOGY

CHARLES BRONSON

APEX PUBLISHING LTD

First published in 2008, Reprinted in 2008 by
Apex Publishing Ltd
PO Box 7086, Clacton on Sea, Essex, CO15 5WN

www.apexpublishing.co.uk

British Library Cataloguing-in-Publication Data
A catalogue record for this book
is available from the British Library

ISBN 1-906358-11-7
978-1-906358-11-2

Typeset in 10pt Baskerville Win95BT

Production Manager: Chris Cowlin

Production Assistants: Sean Green, Jackie Bright, Joan Hastie, Helen Whiteley

Cover Design: Siobhan Smith

Printed and bound in Great Britain by
the MPG Books Group

The insane take their madness to heart.
After all … it's loonyology.

I dedicate this book to my son Mike.
It's you I have in my heart, and I always will.
Box it clever, son, walk tall, freedom is soon.
Dad
x

The power of insanity is the beginning of loonyology.
Welcome to my world!

FOREWORD
BY CHARLIE RICHARDSON

I have seen it all over the years: the very best of human nature, but primarily the very worst. I have been incarcerated with the absolute scum of our so-called society. Most of these 'people' give off pure evil; it comes off them like a strong case of BO. You don't need to be told 'he's evil' or' she's evil'; they don't need pointing out, they just are what they are: 100%, putrid, Satan on Earth evil!

Over the years, the powers that be have tried to convince the poor, weak, gullible public that Charlie Bronson is one of those scumbags and, incredibly but I suppose not surprisingly, the poor old public, who think they know it all, are taken in by it. Charlie Bronson is not evil - he never has been and never will be - but those they have slung him in with are. Ian Huntley is just one that Charlie Bronson has to live in close proximity to. Christ, is it surprising he gets wound up from time to time?

I cannot believe Bronson is still in there. What are they trying to do with this man? The man is a rebel and he doesn't take too kindly to being shoved about by authority, but that doesn't make him 'Britain's most dangerous prisoner', 'the UK's most violent man' and all the rest of the crap they label him with.

By making men like Bronson out to be the worst criminals in the country, it gives the illusion that the Government are winning the war on crime when they are not; they are losing - badly. But the worse they make out those held captivity to be, the more successful it makes them look.

This is nothing new; it's been going on for generations. It's just that so many people are too thick to see it!

Charles Bronson should've been freed years ago. If he was a filthy child molester like these so-called 'pillars' of society he probably would've been. My dear, close friend Tel Currie asked me to contribute to this book. After he explained the reasoning behind it I accepted, as there is a very human reality about this one.

In this book, we finally get to see the real man, not the myth; the human being, not the legend. For those who do not know the man, it may come as a big surprise. Read on ...

Charlie Richardson.

Best wishes
Charlie Richardson

FOREWORD
BY TEL CURRIE

Out of all Britain's underworld villains of the past 50 years, only the Kray twins conjure up more myths, lies and bullshit than Charlie Bronson.

We have heard it all about Charlie - nutter, psycho, evil, Britain's most violent and dangerous man, killer and even serial killer!

Where does this crap come from?

For those of us who know the truth, it gets so ridiculous it becomes hilarious. But then you remember that there are plenty out there who believe it, and have you noticed that the more stupid the person, the more outspoken they are? Why is that?

You would think that someone would be aware of being completely thick, but these idiots are not; they are actually convinced they are more intelligent than intelligent people!

If you ever find yourself surrounded by velour-tracksuited, sovereign-ring-splattered, chain-smoking chavs, with five kids of differing ethnic persuasions and with 150 items in the '10 items or less' queue at the supermarket, listen to the strong opinions that pour forth.

Empty cells definitely make the most noise!

Opinions should be earned. They should be the reward for those who take the time to acquire the knowledge to then earn an opinion on that subject. Opinions should be developed through learning, not just to fill the air.

Unfortunately, this is not the way it is. And this is one reason why misconceptions about people, especially people the sovereign ring mob have never met, find their filthy way into the world.

The other method, of course, is via media propaganda, turning somebody or something into what the media want it to be, good or bad (usually bad). Circulate these around our mentally challenged friends and - bingo! - we have a myth (even if the sovereign wearers do think that's a female moth!)

This is why a percentage of the population view Charlie Bronson and others so badly. And, once again, the ones that are most likely to try to impress you with their outbursts are those that know the least about it. 'Nutter', 'Evil', 'Killer'- these wildly inaccurate descriptions of Bronson are fed from the media straight to the dim, who then regurgitate this to their even dimmer friends.

The most surprising element of this whole process is that it is actually very powerful. There is no doubt that it works and, as with Chinese Whispers, men like Bronson become just that bit more evil each time it's told. That is the power of propaganda and it has massive results.

Why does it always work? Well, how many times have you heard someone actually say, "Hold on a minute, stop there. What are the facts? What did this guy actually do?"

Exactly!

I bet most of you who have adopted these media labels for Bronson don't actually have a clue what in fact he has or hasn't done. I explain exactly what Charlie has and hasn't done elsewhere in this book. These are facts, not rumours or fallacies to create a myth to fill dull lives.

Not too long ago, a Sunday supplement printed a list of whom they considered were the fifty most evil people in Britain. Charlie Bronson - an armed robber who NEVER pulled the trigger or even attempted to kill anybody - was considered more evil than Ian Huntley, Rose West, Peter Sutcliffe and Roy Whiting.

Is there a man alive who can justify that? Is it possible that some faceless hangman from the Home Office had a word about who went where?

Charlie Bronson is no angel. He knows what he has done and he has suffered severely for it, as of course has his lovely mother Eira, who has already lost a husband and son at a young age.

It also amazes me that whenever Charlie blows a fuse the press make him out to be Satan's nastier big brother!

But consider this:

He is locked up for 23 hours a day in 'monster mansion'. This means that most of his neighbours are Britain's most evil child murderers, who are allowed to wear women's clothing and call themselves women's names whilst watching Kids' TV. (I have seen a copy of the actual report in which Charlie appeals, to no avail, to be moved and be punished in "A man's prison".) Charlie despises nothing on the planet more than a nonce (which every proper man should be in agreement with).

In these circumstances, wouldn't you blow a fuse every now and then?

At one time Charlie was trussed up like a Christmas turkey, stark bollock naked, on a freezing cell floor in a body belt (a contraption that makes it impossible to move). He had to lie in his own piss and shit for days.

Charlie's mental strength is unbelievable and, believe it or not, he could handle that bit. The part that was harder to take, and obviously well contrived, was that while lying there, unable to move, he had to listen to that filthy, bastard, pond life Roy Whiting (the lump of turd that tortured and killed lovely little Sarah Payne - God rest you, sweet angel) laughing and doing Christ knows what to Kids' TV with the sound on maximum.

Now, I will ask you again - wouldn't you blow a fuse every now and then?

These, of course, are the little details they leave out of the media when they print the 'Nutter Bronson is at it again' headlines.

If people could just use their common sense and read between the lines of these media fantasies and digest the whole situation, it would be a step in the right direction.

People have always needed their public good guys and bad guys, their nice heroes and their evil villains, but please, if you have to have an evil one, get it right and save that designation for the Huntleys and Whitings of the world. Do not hang your 'evil' caption on a man who has given away most of the money he has ever had to children's charities. (This 100% true. Phone Zoe's Hospice if you need proof.)

In fact all the 'Nasty Villains' like Joey Pyle, Freddie Foreman, Roy Shaw, Alfie Hutchinson, Tony Lambrianou, Charlie Richardson and Dave Courtney have given more money to children's charities than ten men would make on average in a lifetime!

I have promoted boxing shows and I have seen the generosity. There is NOTHING in this piece that I don't know to be 100% true. But, of course, they're just villains clearing their consciences, or whatever crap people with no clue are making up this week. It's amazing how much shelf stacker's in Tesco and kids working at Burger King know about the motives and mechanics of Britain's underworld!

I'm not saying let Bronson walk free right now, but at least give him a chance to mix on the wings and take it from there. If he fucks up, then back to the seg unit he goes. But how can a man prove that he can do something if he's not given the chance to try it?

I hope you can see the injustice in the treatment of men like Bronson and Biggs compared with the REAL evil scum - surely you must! If you can, chatting over the garden fence or in the pub is as much use as a chocolate teapot. Write to Charlie, then to your MP, then the Home Office. DO SOMETHING!

This book will give you an insight into the Charles Bronson that I know and, yes, love. This is the real Charlie: a man who has become a political prisoner and national embarrassment; a human being who deserves a chance; a man whom those of us who really know him MUST stand by; a man who at least deserves to be heard - a man that should be FREE!

Respect!
Tel Currie

CONTENTS

Acknowledgments

I would need another book to mention everybody who have given me so much support over my untold years of institutionalization.

You all know who you are .... "Thanks."

Sadly so many have passed away, gone forever.

But I love you all .. "Living or Dead."

Now a big "Hi" to all my "Brothers and Sisters" all over this mad planet who are locked away in every form of institution known to mankind ..

Whether it be a Max-Secure-Hell Hole.

Or some crazy isolated Lunatic Asylum.

"I salute you all" "Stay strong."

" Unless of course your a filthy nonce or a grass " then I spit on you. {Hurry up and Die}

Remember life's the journey.

So strap in tight and enjoy the ride.

It's 1st Class all the way to Disneyland.

Yours in the name of Loonyology.

X
2008

.. GoLDie LocKs is A DRUG RUNNER ...

.. HumPTY DUMPTY WAS PuSHED ... iT's TRue .....

.. WHEN You've ReAD THis BooK .. LooK UNDeR YouR BeD .... JuST INCASE ....

.. PoPeYe is A PooFTeR ...

INTRODUCTION

There have been many books written on me, but none of them were l00% me. This one is 200% me. No ghost writer. It's yours truly - me. I'm about to take you on the maddest journey of your life. By the time you get to the end of my story you won't know whether you want a good shit or a good wank (or both). Loonyology is a word I created. It just came to me. It's basically how I see the entire legal and penal system: MAD. It's a mad, mad fucking mental world of loonies. From the tea boy to the Home Secretary, they're all caught up in the bollocks of life.

Me - I'm just a pawn on the chessboard of life. They move and push me into battle. You'll never see me back away from a battle. Fuck the consequences. I go forward with dignity. If it's a war worth fighting, then a man must give it his best and, believe me, this is a bloody war. How the fuck I'm still alive is beyond me. Sure I'm a lot older, but I'm also a lot wiser. My war now is COURTS. I'm gonna fuck this system by law. I'll do it with a pen and my brain. I'm turning the tide. If my lawyer Giovanni Di Stefano (I call him the Master Lawyer) can't get me my freedom, then nobody can. I'll either walk out a winner or be carried out in a body bag. It's as simple as that; no in between. But it's time for the public, the real people, to decide if enough is now enough.

I say it's got to stop now. I've had enough. It's now become POLITICAL. The system wants to make an example. Charlie Bronson is for once the victim. Let's stop all the red tape and excuses. Let's for once lay this case on the table for all to see. I'm the fucking hostage and their demands are insane. They want me to grow a pair of wings, lick some official's arse and scream how sorry I am.

Hell, I've not survived 3½ decades of torture to get on my knees and humiliate myself for anybody. My freedom can never be won by begging. If it is to be a victory, it has to be won with dignity. For what it's worth, I am sorry for some of my past crimes and truly sorry about the people I hurt, but how many times have I got to say I'm sorry? I'm getting sick of saying it. I was a nasty bastard and I deserved all I got, but isn't 3½ decades of punishment enough to pay for my crimes?!

I'm now a 55-year-old man; I was 21 when I got put away. Since 1974 I have been in maximum security for all but four months of freedom. Yeh, I've had four months of freedom in the past 33 years. Think about that. You just stop and wonder how it's been for me! I've been to hell and back so many times that it's now just normal to me. Hell's a blessing. It's heaven's that's the problem. Does it exist?!

So let me tell you some true-life crazy things, stuff that's gonna rip out your soul and chew your heart up. Here we go.

Enjoy!
Charles Bronson

CHAPTER 1
THE BADDIE DADDIES ... 'RESPECT'

On Saturday 17 February 2007 Ray Kray, a solid, staunch mate of mine, visited me with his wife Emma. Ray's loyalty is second to none. He's even climbed roofs in protest to get my campaign highlighted. He did one with my son Mike at Westminster, where they scaled that church roof next to Parliament. Armed Old Bill were soon on the scene. That's loyalty at its finest. They could've been shot, but they took the risk for a buddy. Ray went AWOL from the air force just to be at one of my trials. Yep, that's my buddy Ray Kray!

Anyway, on Saturday 17 February he was up to see his old china. It was a good meet up and lovely to see Emma. I'm actually godfather to their son Aiden.

After the visit, I got back to my special cage - I call it the Bronco Zoo - and was told that Joe Pyle had passed away. My whole world fell in. It was like losing my dad all over again. How many more family and friends have I got to lose on this fucking sentence? And, to top it all, I still can't go to a funeral. I'm still Cat A. I'm still public enemy no.1. After all this time I'm still wearing that 'mad' label and it sticks like shit to a blanket. It's there till the day I die.

To say I'll miss Joe Pyle is an understatement. He was a true friend. "Hey, get on this, 'my dad was Joe Peterson'." Note JP - Joe Pyle. JP Joe was a second dad to me and he looked after bits of biz for me. When I needed something sorting it was done. Nothing was too much for Joe - nothing! Any problem, no matter how big or small, he would sort it out for me. Why? Well, he was Joe Pyle, the true governor. Hey, and don't let anybody tell you different. Cos I'm now telling you - he was the Daddy of ALL Daddies. I'm not interested in the Mafia or who or what it represents. But Joe Pyle to me was the ORIGINAL Godfather - the best the UK has ever seen and will ever see. And I feel fucking lost without him. My brain has shrunk. I think my soul's been grabbed by Lucifer and chewed up. It's now all gone bollocks.

Things have gone downhill. Some men have taken serious liberties - one or two against me. Names will not be mentioned, but as sure as bears shit in the woods I'll be banging on doors later. Nobody on this planet rips me off or disrespects Joe Pyle's name. It's always the same when great men die: the parasites crawl out of their holes. Well I'm the guy to push 'em back in their holes. It's just a matter of time with me, and I've got plenty of time. All I do is train for freedom. I'm the strongest, fittest 55-year-old man you'll ever see, that's who I am - THE SURVIVOR.

1

Joe was born in 1935 and he survived till 2007, and boy what a journey he had for 72 years - the best. He lived every day how he knew - like the man he was, with pride and dignity, and he helped plenty on the way. He had a few falls and he done a bit of porridge, but even in jail he walked tall. Men like Joe Pyle don't ever weaken. He was a born fighter - at times ruthless; at times kind. But you never cross men like Joe, or you only do it once. Now that he's in his coffin some clever fuckers take the piss. Some did it with the Kray twins. People wait till people die and then get brave. So who's gonna piss on my grave?! What slimy snake's gonna sell a story to the *News of the World* about me when I'm rotting with maggots? Do it now, you traitors. Do it now, you cowards. Let's all dance with the devil. Let's all bleed together. Lovely jubbly.

The Joe Pyles of this world are a dying breed of men. Please believe it. Fortunately, we still have some left! But not too many. I've been sent a pair of Joe's gold cufflinks, which I'll wear with pride once I'm free, along with Reg Kray's tie and the twins' pocket watch and my dad's ring. (I'll be a fucking walking part of history!)

Let me leave you with a Joe Pyle bit of philosophy, which was on his funeral brochure for all to see:

'LIFE' BY JOE PYLE

*What we get in life is the way we live
but we make a life from what we give.
Life's so short that we shouldn't care
for we only live once and we don't have a spare.
Try to ignore what life owes to you
And remember the debts that you owe too.
For it's best to live life poor and be healthy
Than to live through sickness and then die wealthy.
Now when you judge others be sure to be wise.
Look first with your heart and then with your eyes.
And stand by your morals and reach for the heights
As you win when you lose when you stand by your rights.*

Joe's son, Joe Pyle jnr, should take note of that (he will know what I mean by that). Be a man and do what's right.

Let's take a trip down memory lane and jog the old memory with some more legends. I bumped into Little Jimmy Essex in the early 1970s in Wandsworth. He was only 5 feet 1 inch. And don't forget the 1 inch - it was important to him. Well, let's face it, you wouldn't mind an extra inch on your dick would you?! Jimmy was a prison legend. He'd killed two cons on two separate occasions and had only manslaughter for each! That alone is amazing. Seeing as he was so small, he was a target for the prison bullies. But how wrong was them two? Anyway, he was already serving six years and copped six years for each killing, so he ended up with an 18 stretch, which for two killings ain't bad! No fucker ever tried it on with Jimmy again. I know for a fact that the Kray twins loved Jimmy. They always spoke very highly of the man. To me, he was a lion in a man's body. They do say the best things come in little packages. A top geezer and a true diamond he was. I don't know if he's dead or alive now, but I salute the man.

So what does an ex-con do when he's caught in a trap and he's looking at another long stretch in max secure? What would you do? You're just out after serving a 12 stretch for armed robberies, and you're surrounded by armed cops for more armed robberies. I'll tell you what Tony Baldessaro did. He blew his brains out. Tony was one of those men who meant what he said and said what he meant. On his 12 stretch he vowed never to return. He got out and went back on the pavement. Robbery was his trade and he was the best! Then it come on top for him. The Old Bill surrounded his house and a gun blaze began. This was in the early 1970s in east London. The siege went on for some time. Then a single bang went off inside the house. That was his way out. And you'll never guess what he did before he shot himself ... He burnt all the dosh. He wasn't gonna let anybody take his dosh, so he set fire to it. The other strange thing was that before he died he actually phoned up Joe Pyle to say goodbye. Joe tried to talk sense to him but Tony had made up his mind the day he left prison that he would never return. To me, Tony Baldessaro was a true man of his word, and one a dying breed of man. He was a good, solid, loyal man that we all respected. Never to be forgotten.

Another legendary sad ending was that of 'the Duke' Colin Osbourne. If you were around in the '60s you couldn't not know Duke Osbourne. He also served a lot of porridge. The Duke had survived it all: stabbings, shootings, fights. He lived life on the edge and he loved a gun. That was his game: guns. Some men love a blade, others love *Coronation Street*, others love a pint. Duke loved a gun. He was found dead on Hackney Downs. It was an 'Open Verdict', but at the time the Old Bill were closing in on him for some serious crimes. Maybe the Duke had decided that enough was enough. A man can only take so much porridge. But what a legendary character! He almost died years before in Gartree Prison with a knife in his back. Men like the Duke are just born to live, and boy did he live it.

Then there was Eric Mason, although I don't think much of him anymore as I feel he disrespected me and Tel Currie. We helped him out when he got out of jail and made sure he had a few quid in his pocket. Then he had it with one of our enemy. To me that's treachery. You can't trust a man who has it with the enemy. But Eric Mason has to be an old legend in my book! He survived an axe in the skull. Bash! Crack! His skull opened up like a melon. That to me is a born survivor. He was also the last man in England to be birched in Dartmoor Prison. He survived it all - bread and water, serious beatings - and he's still alive and kicking today. Maybe his age has

3

played on his mind! I respect him for what he once was. But now I wouldn't ever go out of my way to help him out; nor would Tel Currie or a lot of the other chaps. He let himself down big time. But this is a man who survived what a lot of men 'pretend' to survive. He was a fucking hard, solid man! Could you survive an axe in your skull? Or laugh as you're being birched? Eric Mason got the T-shirt: 'Survivor'.

When I landed in Walton Jail in the 1970s, the lads were still talking about the death of Timmy Noonan. Now there was a tough con: a proper fighter who never gave up. He spent some hard years in solitary, and I mean years. Years with nothing but a bare cell, not even a bed. Tim had done it all: riots, violence, hunger strikes, the birch, bread and water. He even did Broadmoor. He was a legend among legends and a well-respected man. But the stress and brutality weighed heavy on his heart. He died a young man in his thirties.

His battles in prison are legendary. You can't but mention Timmy Noonan if you're writing a book on prison. To me he was an icon. When I smashed up Walton Prison roof I actually shouted down and made it clear: this one's for Timmy Noonan! All the Scousers cheered out of their cell windows as I ripped off the slates as, like me, they loved Tim. He's never forgot! Never.

I see they've just made a movie on Carlton Leach. That should be worth a butcher's. He's a fucking legend. He started out a football thug, went into 'door work', and then became a bit of a celebrity. And now they're making a movie on his life, based on his book. That's not bad going, is it? Good luck to him. Considering he's stayed out of jail, that to me says he's got a good biz brain. Respect to the man!

I'll tell you who's a prison legend: Big Stevie Lannigan from Manchester. Steve was only 18 years old when he got his life sentence in the early 1970s for kicking a man to death. I don't know why; that's for him to know. But he was a tough nut to break. He took a screw hostage in a workshop in Wakefield Jail. It was the first time armed cops had come into the prison. He had a sniper's sights right on him. They nutted him off to Broadmoor where they pumped him full of jungle juice. Now Steve was a big guy anyway - 6 feet 4 and 18 stone, but after six months in Broadmoor he was up to 24 stone! They were fucking killing him. That's what the psychiatric drugs do to you: destroy! You get sluggish and lazy and basically just eat, sleep and shit. That's it. You're vegetabled. Steve had a loyal family and a good bunch of pals who fought to get him moved back to prison. But by then he'd been labelled an activist! So wherever he went they were ready for him. His journey through hell began. He took the roof off at Parkhurst. He chinned his way through 30 years of madness! And then - bang! - he had a massive heart attack, followed by several strokes. The years of war had finally caught up with him. But he survived even that. Last I heard of Big Steve he was in a low cat. jail doing his time peacefully in a hospital wing. Let's hope soon he'll be freed. My funniest memory of him was in Parkhurst in the 1970s He used to play his music very loud and sit on a chair outside his cell door smoking a joint! He loved Pink Floyd. Anyway, this day we were all out on association and there was Big Steve sitting outside his door with 'Dark Side of the Moon' blaring out. He was actually off his head; stoned. He was laughing his socks off. A screw told him to turn the music down, so Steve just stood up, knocked the screw out cold and then sat back down and carried on laughing. That's loonyology at its very best! That's a true legend. Love him or hate him, he's a legend in every sense of the word. Even with a dodgy ticker he's still the same guy who entered prison over three decades ago. I salute the man.

Another legend I remember from the 1970s was Barry Robinson. Who? Yeh, you may well ask. Barry jumped in a police car at Rhyl, Wales, and stuck a shooter in the cop's face: "DRIVE!!" So he drove all the way to Blackpool. No one got hurt, but Barry copped a life sentence. It turned out he was ex-Broadmoor. Fuck knows why he hijacked the copper. I doubt if Barry himself knows. He probably just fancied a fast ride. I met him in Hull Jail in 1975 and he's one of the nicest blokes you'll ever meet. He did me an oil painting but sadly it got smashed in a fight. Some cunt got lemon with me and I hit him and - bang! - he landed on the painting. Such is life! I often wonder what happened to Barry. I do hope he made it out.

That was a nice escape in the 1980s when Micky Fenton had it off the van! We all knew he was making one. He was being transferred from Parkhurst to the Scrubs for accumulated visits. Out come the tool and off come the cuffs. Next minute he's driving the fucking van. They shit themselves. Tally hooooo!. Nearly Xmas! Another legend is born.

There's plenty of sadness with a lot of legends. It's a hell of a price to pay. Take Emma Humphreys. She had a hell of a sad life. At 16 she was forced onto the game (those fucking pimps have a lot to answer for). Emma basically got mixed up in the world of shit and she ended up stabbing the pimp to death. To me, this was a serious case of duress, but she got life for murder. The next ten years for Emma were so sad: drugs, suicide attempts, depression - she had it all. She finally made it out, only to die of a broken heart. Please, please, all of you young girls, try to stay clear of drugs and pimps, coz it will destroy you. Think of Emma! Do it for Emma and stay clean.

Hey, get this. 'Big Webber' is a 25-stone lifer who's now served a good 30 years. Guess what his ambition is in life? Come on, guess! I bet you won't! I'll tell you: he wants to be the UK's longest serving prisoner of all time. Can you believe that? That's fucking insanity at its very best. Loonyology!

Chris Haigh was a top geezer and a good London villain. I met him in Wandsworth Chokey in the 1980s. There were a couple of bully screws down there at the time who were always trying to dig people out and nick them. They took an instant dislike to Chris - probably jealous of him coz he was a seriously good biz man even though he'd just copped 15 years. Anyway, these two dog screws were actually betting on who could nick more cons in a week than the other. Silly little games like not shaving, a dirty cell, bed not made, abusive language! A pathetic little game that cost us cons punishment: loss of canteen; more solitary; closed visits, etc. For a week Chris deliberately never took his razor in! So each day one of the screws was ready to nick him. But Chris had no stubble, so how could they nick him? This went on for a whole week. Chris usually had strong facial hair growth, so how was he doing it? They were baffled and confused (and so was I). What had happened is that the con above him had been passing him down a line from his window to Chris's window with a razor attached. He would shave and then pass it back up. It was fucking brilliant! A bit technical for me though. I prefer to chin the cunts!

I was sorry to see Stevie Miller's died. Some called him 'The Caveman'. Last time I saw him was in Whitemoor seg block. He was a Welsh chap doing life. Outside he was one of those guys who loved the open air. He did a lot of poaching up in the Welsh valleys, free as a bird. He actually lived in a cave for a spell when the Old Bill were on his trail. 'The original Rambo' and a true prison legend.

Hey, and let's have three cheers for Little Jock Costello. Hip hip hooray! Hip hip hooray! Hip hip hooray! Jock cut the Ripper up in Parkhurst in the 1980s. Bosh! Cop hold of that, you nonce! It cost Jock an extra five years on top of his original sentence. I reckon he should've got a medal!

The biggest and strongest man on the Kray firm was Big Pat Connelly. When he was on the club doors nobody fucked around. He was the original bouncer.

In the 1980s a legend was murdered. He was 71 years old, and a young lad of 18 killed him. Shane Keeler was later sentenced to life for it. But this old legend wasn't just an old man, he was Charlie Bateman. Who? you may well ask! Aka Charlie Clark, the no. 1 cat burglar in the 1950s and '60s. Without a doubt Charlie was the best! You don't hear of cat burglars today like in them days. They were the cream! They went for the rich pickings and Charlie made a fortune. But he also lost a fortune as he loved to gamble! His life was a gamble. I met him when he visited Ronnie Kray in Broadmoor in the early '80s. and he looked what he was - an old rogue! He had that look about him: been there, done that, got the T-shirt. This man deserved a medal. Some will say, "Fuck a medal. He was a burglar." But what you don't realise is that he was a professional, a tradesman, just like in any other workforce. He just chose a burglar's job and he was the master thief. To be the no. 1 you have to be the best, and he was the best. I don't know why Keeler killed Charlie, but he's got to live with what he's done. Killing an old man is nothing to be proud of is it? And he was disabled. So it was a sad end to a real legend. We all loved Charlie Clark. He gave the term burglar a new meaning. 'The Cat Man'. You wouldn't find a 'real burglar' nicking your pension book or your TV set. He went for the prize: jewels, antiques, paintings. Fuck me, he wouldn't go through a window if it wasn't for more than 50k. He had a lifestyle to live up to! After all, he was a gentleman. R.I.P.

Another great was Chopper Watts. Charlie was from Walthamstow, east London. He done a bit of porridge in his time as we all do. Yeh, you guessed it, for a blag. 'Legendary'. These legends never die. They live on, even when they die. It's a fact of life.

Another old London villain who always pops up in conversation is the one and only Billy Bligh from north London. He copped a 4 stretch for cutting the notorious Jack Spot. Billy actually died in prison from an untreated stomach ulcer. In them days you just suffered and died in prison. No fucker cared a shit. The doctors were vets; the nurses were heavies; prison was hell. And it's all you expected. That's how it was! But Billy is always remembered. He was one of the chaps and, like Jimmy Essex, he was only a small man. Come to think of it, so is Frank Frazer. So what does that tell you? You don't ever fuck with these small guys or you're gonna be very sorry. I've known 20-stone, 6-foot steroid freaks who haven't got no bottle at all. Never judge nobody by their size, coz you could be in for a shock.

Then there was Jenny Johnson. In the mid-1970s Jenny robbed a bank. She got clean away, but was later grassed up by her fella! What would you do with a partner like Jenny? She's every robber's dream. And she went to work with a little toerag and got eight years! She probably served half of it and made it out. I've never heard of her since. But what a star! What a woman! A dream on legs. If I'd met Jenny Johnson all them years ago, we could've ruled the planet. Believe it. That was then, but now I'd still love to have a pot of tea with her and some home-made cakes and have a chat about the good old days. There ain't too many like her about, that's for sure!

And we can't forget 'The King of Brooklyn', the undisputed Mafia boss himself: Albert Anastasia. He was known as the mad hatter! He was the boss of all bosses. He lived and died his dream. He made it to the top from the gutter. He did it his way and no other way! A true legend.

Did you know that 'Pretty Boy Floyd' was given that name by a prostitute in Kansas City? His real name was Charles Arthur. The 1930s was the decade for Floyd. He just hit every bank along his road to hell. They caught up with him in 1934 and sentenced him to 15 years' hard labour - or so they thought! On the way to prison he escaped. They eventually caught him and the FBI gunned him down like a dog. They were terrified of him! Pretty Boy Floyd died pretty. He lived fast and died young.

One of the biggest Mafia funerals was that of Frankie Vale in 1928. It was fit for a king, costing 200k. That's a lot of dosh for back then; it's even a lot in 2008. His coffin was made of silver and gold and there were over 250 limos, 40 of which were full of flowers! What a send-off for Frank Vale. That sums it all up for me. Legendary.

And here's another one: Johnny Nash, one of seven brothers from the Angel of Islington. John goes back years. He was doing bird in the Shepton

Mallett Glass House at the military prison with the Krays in the 1950s. That's how long he goes back. And even today, in his 70s, he can still throw a punch. He's what I call 'a man amongst men' and nobody alive or dead could ever say different. A friend of Johnny Nash is a friend for life, and I'm lucky to have such a good friend. He's one diamond geezer.

I'll tell you who else is a prison legend and I've not bumped into him for a good five or six years: Sharkie O'Connor. It was at Woodhill CSC unit that we made one together and we called it on - over a fucking stupid tea bag! Some muggy screw refused to give him a tea bag and there's a bloody crate full of them in the office. Anyway, fuck it. Off come our shirts. We ripped them up to bandage our hands and shouted to the pigs, "Let's get it on!" That's how insane prison is. All that violence over a silly tea bag. But was it just about a tea bag? Sharkie's dark skinned, the offspring of a white mother and a black father, so could the screw who denied him a tea bag have been a racist cunt? That's my view, otherwise why not give Sharkie a tea bag? It stunk to me! I'll always support a con if he's in the right, and this time Sharkie was 100% right. And when he spat in the screw's face I made him spot on. Out came 12 screws in their space suits and holding shields and I was the first to be rushed. You can only do so much with so many, but I recommend body shots. Rush in, crash the shields and steam into them with good body blows. It's a great way to liven the day up! You can never win, but it's fun trying! After it's all over, the van arrives and off you go to the next battlefield. Sharkie will go north and I'll go south, or vice versa, and that's how it all works. It's a fucking chessboard: we're the pieces and the system's the game. That one tea bag probably ended up costing 20k, if not more, and all because of a vindictive screw who wanted to wind Sharkie up. He gets spat on, we have a rumble, all hell breaks out, vans arrive ... Fuck me, put the kettle on and let's have a cup of rosy lea!

Hey, this is becoming like a fucking criminal history lesson. I hope you appreciate my knowledge. Anyone doing a degree in Criminology will defo pass once they get a hold of *Loonyology*. And the list of legends goes on:

* Seymour Young, Dave Courtney's best buddy. Believe me, you never really know a true pal until the heat is turned up full. Most will melt and run off. Seymour stood solid to Dave even with a gun in his face. That's a true pal. That's a real brother.

* Kenny Baker. He was a first-class blagger; fearless. The Old Bill were terrified of him and shot him dead on a bit of work in 1990. They don't make them like Kenny Baker no more. The cream of the crop.

* Michael Biggs, Ronnie's son. He's a legend in his own right in the way he fights for his old man's freedom. He's a top son that any father would be proud of.

* Bernie Davies. Another hard man - a Welsh ex bare-knuckle fighter. The valleys breed them tough. Bernie's been in my corner for years and he's always welcome in any of the chaps' company. This guy has earned his

respect a million times over.

* Jamie Foreman. One of Britain's top actors and the son of Freddie. No wonder Fred's so proud of him. Every time Jamie comes on the TV or is in a movie you can bet your arse on it that every con in the UK is watching him. He's fucking brilliant.

* Bobbie Frankham, the legendary cobbled fighter. The gypsies love a fighter. Men who fight like Bobby become icons. They earn respect the hard way. The kingpin of the gypsies was Johnny Frankham. This guy could have a serious fight. He was a British light heavyweight champion in the 1970s, but Johnny's fought 'em all, not just in the ring. He's spilt blood in pub car parks, fields and circus tents, all the way to the Royal Albert Hall. That's what you call legendary. No wonder the gypsies love him to bits. A man of rock.

* Jimmy and Wally Stockin. Two cracking gypsy bare-knuckle fighters. They're both up there in the legendary status, both men of respect. They were born fighters, bred for fighting. When they stepped on the cobbles you knew there would be blood spilt, ribs smashed to bits and teeth knocked out. Fuck Russell Crowe or Charlton Heston or Stallone - that's all fairy stories. The Stockins were for real! True gladiators.

* Liam Galvin. You've probably not heard of him so I'll tell you who and what he is. He's the chaps' official cameraman. He does all the filming of wedding parties and compiling DVDs. He's the dog's bollocks.

* Kevin Paddock. Another legendary fighter and he beat Lenny McLean in the ring. So much for Lenny saying he could never be beaten. No man is unbeatable. We all have to taste the bitter-sweet defeat, but a true fighter comes back and wins. Guys like Kevin don't get a lot of media coverage, coz they're low-key men who don't want to be in the limelight. They're fighters, not actors. But to me they're legends I salute.

* Johnny Waldron. Another fighter who beat Lenny McLean. He knocked him clean out in Round 1. If that's not legendary, then what is?

* Brian Hall. He used to run the Rising Sun boozer in Essex for years. Brian used to spar with Henry Cooper and he prepared Roy Shaw for the Donny The Bull Adams fight in the 1970s. Men like Brian Hall are never forgotten! I'm not sure what he's up to today. I'd like to think he's helping out in some local boys' boxing gym, coz the kids listen to men like Brian; they all trust a fighter.

* Peter Scott. Another famous cat burglar. You'll probably remember him for nicking Sophia Loren's jewels in the 1960s. He was known as 'The Human Fly'. He's had Picasso paintings and diamonds worth millions, and has also lost millions through his life of crime. But he would never ever steal from the poor. He was known in the game as a 'gentleman thief'. Sure, he spent some years in Her Majesty's Prisons, but I'll tell you now: he would have no regrets. This man lived his dreams. I really don't know if he's alive or dead, but believe me he really was born a legend. He was one of the best

thieves we've ever had. If you was ever a victim of Peter Scott, then you was robbed by the best.

* Old Duchy - Peter to his friends. If there ever was a legend it's this guy. Get his book and learn how to become a survivor. This guy was a thalidomide victim, born with no legs and a twisted-up body. Every day of his life he fought his way up. He's done it all; seen it all; had it all. He's a fucking hero. And he's done a bit of porridge too. We love him to bits. This guy makes his disability his advantage. Nobody in their right mind would mess with Duchy. He's a fucking lunatic - a good loony, that is. But he won't just do anybody's - only the elite. You better believe it. Three cheers for Duchy. Hip, hip, hooray! Hip, hip, hooray! Hip, hip, hooray!

* Rocky Hart. He got stabbed to death in Parkhurst in the mid-1980s by fatso pea-brain and no-good cunt Rogers. He was already serving life for murder. Then in a cowardly act he slipped up behind Rocky in the kitchen and took him out over fuck all. He killed a top diamond geezer. The cunt got nutted off and sent to Ashworth Asylum and Rocky Hart got a grave. All the chaps respected Rocky and we won't ever forget him. He was a proper good fella.

* Max Lacololi. One of the top three doormen. When him and his mate Stilks are on the door you can guarantee a peaceful night. Unlike a lot of doormen, these guys know how to nip the bud before it grows. A good doorman means a good club. A bad doorman means a bad club. Max can work on my door anytime. Look me up later, Max. You've got it, mate.

* Rickie Tregaski. This geezer copped an extra six years on his sentence for cutting little Sarah Payne's killer, Roy 'Dogface' Whiting. He cut him here in Wakefield. How the fuck can a judge give anybody six years for cutting a filthy child-killing nonce? Rickie should've got a medal and early release. Hey, and guess what? The nonce got a nice few quids' compensation too. How sick can it get?

* Alphie O'Leary, Laurie O'Leary's brother. The Krays respected both of them. Sadly Alphie died in 2002, but he's never forgotten. The O'Learys came from the poor part of east London in the war era. They were born tough in them days. You had to be handy. Alphie was a gentle giant, a kid who'd done well out of life. He even ended up travelling the world with the great Eric Clapton. Alphie was respected in both walks of life, the good and the bad. He was that sort of man. He could drink with a prince or a gangster and be loyal to both. That's what you call a legend in my book. R.I.P.

* Geordie George Craig. He was a hard man; they don't come a lot tougher. He was one of those sorts of men you don't hear a lot about, coz he never went around blowing his own trumpet. He served several sentences and served them his way, and only his way. Then he got out and did a lot of good in life by opening up the 'Lazarus Centre' in Sunderland, housing the homeless, alcoholics and drug addicts. Ever since then he has never looked back and all he earns now is respect. I suggest you read his best-selling book

Mud Sticks, and then you'll see what a real winner is. Respect.

* Eric Rubin. I met this Russian guy in Parkhurst. He was nicked with Valerio Viccei on the Knightsbridge safe deposit boxes. Eric was a tough cookie. Parkhurst to him was a holiday camp considering he'd served time in the Russian salt mines. Eric's stories blew me away. He was the original Papillon. What he don't know about hardship and torture ain't worth knowing. He even had the chain marks on his ankles and wrists. This guy I truly admired. Sadly his health wasn't good - he was coughing up a lot of blood. I don't know what happened to him, but I'd like to think he survived his 20-year sentence and got out and kicked some more arse. The Russian Mob can sure be proud of Eric Rubin - a top villain.

* General Hoffman, a little Spanish bloke, who was opposite my cell in Long Lartin in 1990. He was known as an international player. There was nothing this guy hadn't done. He was a true survivor, as well as a funny little fucker. He was always up for a laugh. One day he pretended to have a heart attack and just lay still on the corridor. The screws were running all over the place, everybody panicking. Then he jumped up and said, "I'll have a nice cuppa tea now." This is one guy I want a pint with outside.

* Sidney Earnshaw. Old Sid spent 40+ years locked away, mostly in the asylums. I met him in Ashworth Asylum in 1984. He was in his seventies then. Sid was one of the forgotten faces, but I soon changed that. I sorted him out and got him back in touch with the outside world. His face lit up and all my mates enjoyed meeting him. Sid had just lost his way in life and become totally brainwashed. The system had chewed him up. He loved a bet, so I sorted him a phone number so he could put some bets on. And, fuck me, did he win or did he win? It turned out he was a horse-racing genius. The Ashworth screws couldn't understand how all the dosh was coming to him. He was winning more dosh than the screws' wages and he had a life of luxury. I brought him back to life.

* Tommy Comerford. A true Scouser and a Liverpool legend, known as 'The Boss'. I've known Tommy for years, so he must now be in his late 60s or early 70s. There's fuck all this man hasn't done, from hijacking lorries loaded with booze to armed blags. I last bumped into him in Long Lartin in the 1980s. Tom's a character and I do hope he's now free and enjoying his old age. This guy's eaten more porridge than the Scottish Guards, so it's time for some eggs and bacon.

* Courtney Rumpole. I met Courtney in Long Lartin in the 1980s. He was one of the best hooch masters in the system. A bottle of his hooch would blow your socks off. I used to tell him, "Pack in the crime and start your own brewery." What better job could there be for him? He'd be a self-made millionaire. I hope he took my advice.

* Les Cromer. A top geezer and a true pal. He was opposite my cell in Walton Jail in the early 1990s. I had fuck all at this time as I was on a lot of punishment. Les was only on remand, but they were holding him in the seg block over an alleged fight up on the wing. He used to leave me stuff in the recess for when I slopped out: biscuits, sweets, Mars bars, etc. He even got me a little transistor radio. All this stuff was a luxury to me. Anyway, Les got out and sadly died soon after in a car crash. He was a young man with everything to live for, with a great family he loved a lot. He was a good, solid, staunch man, the best. Respect!

* John Dillon. Another top Scouser. This guy had a nice escape from the prison van when he was being escorted from Risley to Liverpool Crown Court in the 1980s. Bang! Masked gunmen got him out of the van and he vanished. Sadly he got nicked soon after. That's showbiz! I last saw him in Full Sutton some time back. He's your typical Scouser - a funny fucker. The Scousers are good lads to do bird with. Apart from that mad cunt who almost bit my thumbs off in Walton. I always seem to bump into loonies.

* Billy Simpson. He was a nobody till I smashed him with a teapot. Then he became a legend. Billy 'Teapot' Simpson. it's fucking mental. But it will stay with him till the day he dies. I'll have a teapot done in flowers for him. Everybody knows the teapot.

* Abouzuz. I met this Arab guy in Gartree in the 1980s. He was a big, strong bloke who got nicked in Leicester and copped a ten stretch. He used to do a lot of sparring with me on the exercise yard in the seg block. That was until I knocked him out. It was a genuine accident, but after that he never did come out no more.

* Roy Ivors. I first met Roy in the 1980s down on 'the island'. He was a powerful man; so strong that he almost kicked his way out of a Cat A security van whilst being escorted to a jail. The eight screws in the van shit it, so they drove to the nearest cop shop. The van was a write-off. He'd kicked a big fuck of a dent in it. It looked like a JCB had crashed it. Roy was serving a 19 stretch. He should be well out by now and I'm one guy who hopes he's doing well. Max respect to the man.

* Mohammad Khan. The West Midlands police force fitted this guy right up. He copped 18 years for a blag he could not have committed, and he proved it and walked out from the appeal court. What happened? I met him in Gartree in the 1980s and he showed me all his depositions. It was obvious he'd been fitted up. He was apparently seen running away from this armed blag he was supposed to have done, but a few days before the robbery took place Mohammad lost two of his toes and he was heavily bandaged up. How could he have been running? Sure as hell, he walked free. Around this time the West Midlands police were fitting up plenty. There was a massive inquiry and a lot of the Old Bill were sacked. But how many were jailed? Very few. The slags should've all got 18 years. We can only be grateful to the courts of appeal, where the injustice of some of our trials can be seen and men like Mohammad Khan can be freed.

Hey, talking of toes, there was a lunatic in Rampton who actually bit his big toe off. Don't ask me why, or how, he just did. Yeh, it freaked me out too, coz he actually ate it. He ate his own fucking toe. Jesus ... get me the fuck out of here!

* Tony Peterson. I only met him in Belmarsh in 1996, but the guy's a living legend. He was in the '69 Parkhurst Riot, the riot of all riots. Sadly he got nicked in '96 over a trumped-up charge. I never heard how he made out, but I do hope he walked. They were trying to wind him up in Belmarsh over visits, so I stepped in. Some silly screw was just getting lemon, so I said, "You wind my mate up and you wind me up. Now what's it to be?" It passed over peacefully. Who said screws are brain dead?

* Big Pat Purcell. I first met Pat in Full Sutton and then in Shitemoor - oops, sorry - Whitemoor. Pat's a good old-fashioned cockney with good old-fashioned morals. He made it out and stayed out. A big black roller collected him from the prison gate and it's been party time ever since. Cheers!

* Mad Ritchie. I met Ritchie up in Ashworth Asylum in the 1980s. He was a big bald-headed guy, with big spaced-out eyes - everybody's nightmare - and he talked with a growl. But I took time to get to know him and deep down he was a genuine guy - a bit freaky, but I love a loon. One nutter came running into my cell shouting, "Help, help, Ritchie's gonna chop me up and put me in a curry." So I said, "Fuck off or I'll put you in a stew"! Ritchie was a strange guy. He forever played The Eagles tape *Hotel California*. He was also bang into the Bible and once when he got on my nerves I grabbed his Bible and slung it through the cell bars. "Fuck off now, Ritchie," I said, "or you're next." It was that close to a punch-up. Fortunately he walked away. These loonies are okay just in small doses, coz they can come on too strong, and when they do it's like a mad dog. You've got to get in first or lose your throat.

* Bob Taylor. Bob copped life in the late 1970s. I met him in Parkhurst. He was a brilliant artist, but he had serious psychological problems and kept losing the plot. Once in Gartree he stuck a 6-inch nail in a lump of wood and rammed it into a con's neck (for a laugh). He lived on dog-ends: where there was an ashtray, there was Bob. Fuck knows what happened to him. He probably got lung cancer and died.

* Franco Vincitore. I met Franco in Woodhill back in 1993. He was on remand over some blag, but I believe he got a not guilty. He used to work out with me on the yard. He was a good training partner. I really put him through it, but he loved it coz he knew it was good for him. One day out in the sunshine we were throwing the medicine ball at each other and doing sit-ups. My ball was a big 11-pounder full of sawdust. I shouted and pointed up at the sky. "Look. Look at that!" He looked up and I threw the ball. Crash! It smashed into his head and almost knocked him sparko. "Franco," I said, "always be ready, be alert. And only trust one man - yourself." He was a top guy I admired.

Another man I salute is Tony Crabbs, a lifer and a good friend. He once climbed through some razor wire and sat on top of a CCTV camera for four hours in the rain to support me and then got a good kicking for his troubles after. Would any of your friends do that for you? I bet not. That's my friends for you in a nutshell - the best hard nuts but staunch! It's all loonyology!

Now see why I'm so lucky with all the amazing people I've met and shared time with. It's been a brilliant experience and it's still not over. My life has yet to start up. Wait until I'm free and then my real life will begin. I can't fucking wait.

CHAPTER 2
THE MAD, THE BAD AND
THE DOWNRIGHT EVIL

So who is, or was, the maddest bastard I ever met? I bet you're dying to know. What a question. Let me think … I need to think some more about that one. That's like me asking a 35-stone fatty their favourite bar of chocolate. It'll come to me, though. But, until it does, here's my latest poem. Oh yes, I'm a poet. Yeh me. What's so funny? It's not just poofs and toffs who write poems. I do too. This one is called Sucked Away:

God … My face is blown away
My soul's gone with it
I'm empty and lost
Heartless and soulless
Somebody pass me an axe
A very sharp one
It's time to do some chopping
It's time to walk the line
Who's coming with me?
Put your hands up
Don't be shy
I'll take you all
The more the merrier
You over there with the long beard
Yeh you - you scary fucker
It's time you took a ride
A one-way ticket
Hell awaits
Hey you - yeh you
You with the big fat nose
You're scaring the kids
It's time you moved on
You've had a good innings
Stop crying
You're all the fucking same
Hopeless and spineless
You make me sick
My skin's crawling

You're crackheads
Pissheads
Take your last drink
Cheers
Here's to Lucifer
Kiss my arse
Lick it
Stick your nose right up my butt
Go on, do it
That's better
You'll feel good
Born again
That's the trouble with you lot
You don't know you're born
You've never had it so good
Whilst you're on your knees
Clean my boots
Spit and polish
Put some elbow into it
I want to see my face in it
A reflection of madness
Loonyology
Amen!

So here's the maddest fucker I ever met, and by God I've met the lot. It's Robert 'Cannibal' Maudsley. I've known this nutter for 30 years and believe me he's madder now than he was 30 years ago, okay, and he's two cages from me.

Maudsley got life back in 1974 at the same time as I got put away myself. He was a young man of 19 years. He'd left Liverpool and headed for Kings Cross, London, to be a rent boy. Some fucking rent boy. He's 6 feet 2 and built like a shithouse door. There's no way he got too many punters but he copped for one and cut him to bits. He pleaded guilty to manslaughter on the grounds of diminished responsibility. He got sent to Broadmoor Asylum for the Criminally Insane.

Two years later he took a fellow lunatic hostage with another loony called John Chessman. The hostage was a young lad called Alan Francis. He was the weakest on the ward, which is why they grabbed him. He never weighed 10 stone soaking wet. They dragged him into the boot room and barricaded the door. Alan's screams could be heard all over the Asylum. The cowards were torturing him. My argument is that if their victim had been a guard or a doctor would they have sat back and allowed the screams to go on without smashing the door in to save him? The truth is, Broadmoor did not give a fuck about it. He died in agony. Half his brain was protruding out of his skull

16

and some of it was missing - one of them ate it. Well it is an Asylum so what did you expect?

Chessman and Maudsley stood trial at Winchester and both got a further life sentence. Chessman went to the Scrubs where he took another hostage and shagged his arse all night long. Maudsley seemed to settle for a spell up in Wakefield Jail; that was until 1978 when he started again. This time he killed two prisoners - two in one night. Again one had a bit of brain missing. The cannibal was hungry. Again he was sentenced to two more life sentences with a recommendation that he died in prison. That's now four life sentences. Fuck me, how many lives has he got?!

Since that double murder he has literally been held in isolation. He's definitely a survivor, but a complete nutter.

It was four years back that I had a big fall out with him over a watch. I had a new watch sent in and I thought I'd give him my old one. It was a summer's day and he was in one yard, me in another. Our yards are 20-foot-square cages where we walk up and down for an hour a day alone. This unit is a maximum secure control unit. We are not allowed to mix. We are always escorted from our cells to the yard by no less than seven screws, sometimes more.

Anyway, I said to him through the fence, "Fancy a watch Bob?"

He said, "Yeh."

So I said, "Look, it's a Seiko, a good one. I'll sort it for you that you can have it."

He said, "Thanks."

And that was that - or so I thought.

I went out of my way to sort it, as it's all got to be done proper or he can't have it. It must go on his Property Sheet. So I get to see the Reception screw and he was an old school screw, a decent chap.

"Yeh sure, Charlie, I'll do that for Bob."

Next thing Maudsley is shouting at the screw, "Fuck off!"

I'm now confused. The screw says, "I've a watch for you. I need your signature to go on your property."

But Maudsley is shouting, "Fuck off!"

I tell the screw, "Bin it, fuck him."

I then tell Maudsley, "You're an ungrateful cunt."

He says, "I'll stab your eyes out and eat your heart."

"Yeh? Not before I break your jaw and bust all your ribs."

And that's it. We now hate each other. I've had dummies and nappies sent to him, even the *Gay News* and a male blow-up doll - all to wind him up. I pray one day I'll bump into him at 300 mph; unlike him, I don't need a blade. He has to have a tool to come at me. It's the only chance he'd have against me.

I can make allowances for the insane, but not in this case as this guy is a walking danger zone. He really would rip my heart out, but then again I really would punch a hole in his face. Why did he mug me off over the watch? Who knows. I don't think he even knows. Maybe the untold solitary years have now made him madder. He's really got nothing left in his life except his mad, mad world. He lives in a complete fantasy world of violence. He has no humanity in his entire body. So I make him the maddest bastard in the system. In a strange way I actually feel sad for him, but I'd still enjoy punching him up. Nobody rips my heart out or eats my brain, especially a fucking nutcase like Bob Maudsley.

When it comes to nutters, Ian Walbey takes some beating too. In Woodhill CSC Unit he had a bad day and got a bit depressed. So he got a razor and cut his face to shreds. It took 100 stitches to put it back together. A hundred fucking stitches! He almost lost his eye over it. That's what you call depression. That's what you call loonyology.

Can you believe it's 30 years since Elvis left the planet? There was a loony in Rampton Asylum who used to sing 'Jailhouse Rock' all the time - at 3 a.m. when the asylum wanted to sleep. So we sort of went off Elvis after that. Cunt. He had a slight accident and he had to have his jaw wired up. Peace at last.

I met a lifer down in Parkhurst in the 1970s called Ginger Evans. He had a valve in his heart, a hearing aid, a glass eye, one leg shorter than the other and a hair lip. Fuck me, I've never seen nothing like it! I just had to ask the 10 million dollar question:

"Hey, Ginger, what did you get life for?"

"I blew my wife's head off with a shotgun," he smiled.

"What for?" I asked.

"She was a moaning bitch. She drove me mad!"

There's not a lot you can say to that is there?!

Henry Farrell, now there was a nutter if ever there was one! I don't mean that in a nasty way, coz I actually liked the guy. He just acted strange and it upset people and made them very wary of him. I first met him in the asylums in the '70s and '80s and then again in Parkhurst in the '80s. I spent a few weeks on B Wing with him at Parkhurst. B Wing was full of 'London faces', cons like Reg Kray, Bobby Maynard, Martin Long, Paul Edmunds, Terry Smith. In fact at this time it was multicultural. It had sections of cons - not so much gangs, but more like families. Everybody stuck to their own - the Greeks, the blacks, the Irish, etc. - but if one section had a bucket of hooch for sale or a lump of dope, the deals were done. That's how it was in the '70s and '80s at Parkhurst. It was party time from 6 p.m. to 9 p.m. Henry was in no-man's land, 'lost'. He kept darting from one cell to another upsetting people, talking mental, with his big staring eyes. He didn't mean any harm, it's just how he is: 'mad'. Anyway, to cut a long story short, he had some hooch, some dope and some pills and he ended up in Reg Kray's cell, where there was a party going on. Hey, I bet this all sounds like the West End to you! Reg told Henry to call it a night and go and bang up and get his head down. Henry got very lippy and insulted Reg and next thing - bang! - he was knocked out cold. We got him back to his cell and banged his door up. Problem solved. The next day Henry walked into Reggie's cell and made another scene, so again he got knocked out. And that's how it was! There wasn't a day went by without somebody getting a slap. It really was a fucking madhouse! It's hard to believe, but on some cell doors there'd be a doorman - you only got into a party if you'd been invited. There was one con who had every part of his cell pasted with fanny pictures. To sit in there for five minutes used to fuck up your head. Fanny everywhere. You wouldn't be allowed to do that now, not with women screws. Crazy times.

Dennis Mercer must come high on the loony list too. He actually made me feel sick. He had a way of destroying all humanity and feelings. I don't think he was off our planet. Broadmoor 1979 was a very mad era for me. I met the maddest of the mad, lots and lots of characters. Mercer was in the next cell to me in Norfolk Intensive Ward, which was a max secure unit for Broadmoor's most dangerous men. Mercer used to have 'strange ways' and act out 'strange things'. His cell always smelt of shit. No wonder - he spread it all over the walls! He also used to bang the door all night with his head. When we all got unlocked in the morning, out he used to come, covered in shit and with blood all over his head and body. Not a nice way to begin a day. Sights like that never leave the brain. It's horror on horror, insanity gone mad, and that stink seems to stay with you all day. All asylums smell of shit and piss, but this was bloody ridiculous. He would've made a brilliant pig farmer, the best. On second thoughts, no, it would be cruel to the pigs! Broadmoor's the best place for him.

One loony you didn't fuck with was big Steve Roughton, who stood at 6 feet 5 inches and weighed 280 pounds (of muscle). I met him in Ashworth Asylum back in the 1980s. Boy oh boy could he punch. Boy oh boy did he punch. He chinned more screws than any loony in the asylum, but to his friends he was a gentle giant, and to his mother he was her angel. That's how it is with real loons. They're lovely people. You just don't upset them, or they can turn as fast as switching a light on. Steve used to strip off naked and run all over the asylum grounds. You just let him do it, let him burn himself out, otherwise people would get hurt. You can't run away from Ashworth. It's got a fucking big 25-foot wall around it. It's max secure. Some call it the Broadmoor of the North. I spent a year in that place. I've got stories that will make you laugh and cry.

I'm one of only a handful of guys who have spent time in all the top secure asylums in England -Rampton, Broadmoor and Ashworth - and let me tell you now I'm proud I did coz I'm a better man for it. It was an experience of a lifetime. I met the maddest bastards on the planet. You can't buy that sort of experience. It's why I am what I am today - a very knowledgeable man. I understand the insane, I feel for them. Yeh, sure, there's a few I've hurt, seriously hurt, but I had no choice but to take action. When a madman lights up, somebody has to switch him off.

Like the time I was in the recess in Rampton and a loon walked in and started wanking right by me. "Oy, fuck off, you mad twat." He just kept on wanking with bulging eyes and that sort of sicko glazed look with spit in the corner of his mouth. What do you do in that sort of position? I know what I did. I kicked him in the nuts, then kicked him in the head a dozen times. Problem solved. Nobody insults me like that 'mad or not'. I can't accept that sort of behaviour. He had to be stopped there and then. It was a fucking liberty. Although an act of madness, a sane man can't allow that to go on. Okay, he was in for the rape of a little girl. So I actually enjoyed sorting that problem out.

Another time, still in Rampton, a loon kept following me around the ward. Why? Fuck knows why. I doubt if he even knew. One day I was having a shit and his head popped up over the door. No words; he just stared at me. "Oy, fuck off mate, I'm having a shit." What does he do? He stays there staring at me. Now this is madness. I'm stuck in the middle of the belly of the beast. What would you do? Even as I wiped my arse he was there. "Now look here, you daft cunt …" Then he runs off. That's how it is for the insane. It's a struggle. It crucifies you. It rips you up. There is no escape. Even at night in a single cell all locked up safe, you can't escape the screams and laughter. One laughs, then two, then a dozen. Even I laugh. We are all crying of laughter. My ribs hurt. I'm sweating. I fall to sleep having laughed myself daft. Even the night clocky would be laughing. But nobody knows why anyone's laughing. That's the madhouse for you. It's fucking brilliant. It's like being in one big party that never ends. Please don't let it end.

I met an old East London gangster in Rampton called Slash Walters. I'd heard all about him from Ronnie Kray. "Slash?" I said. "Why Slash?" "Cos he cuts people," Ron says. He had this thing about leaving his mark: a big tramline down your boat. Slash was knocking on a bit, but he had all his marbles. I liked the guy a lot. Some of his stories blew me away. I won't repeat them, as it's for him to tell you, but Slash was the right name for him.

Another old boy I met there had been locked up for over 50 years - Jip Carter. Now imagine that. This was back in 1978, so he was in Rampton in 1928. Come on, think about that one. It is fucking mind-blowing. It's actually fucking insane. He died there in 1981. Imagine that. Can you? Do you want to? To me it's a fucking serious act of cruelty; senseless; a waste of life. Do you know what? I don't even know what Jip did. He was that old I didn't want to know. I used to have a chat with him about life in Rampton as it was years back. Fuck me, it was horrific enough back in 1978 but it was mind-blowing back in the 1920s. He was there when Hitler was dropping the bombs. He was there when they were experimenting with electric shock treatment with no anaesthetic. Raw electricity going through your screaming, agonised brain. You could probably smell your brain burning like toast. Jip's eyes told the story for him: depression and despair. To me he was a lonely old boy, but he must have upset a lot of people of power for them to allow such misery.

It was rare ever to see him smile, but I got him happy a few times. Once I smuggled in a plastic shampoo bottle full of vodka. Jip and me shared that. Boy did we sing - all the old ones. The screws must have known we was pissed. On top of the vodka, remember, we were both pumped up on the psychotropic drugs - a seriously bad mixture. Drink and drugs don't mix; even more so in the loony bin.

Jip was just an old man living in a nightmare. He often sat silently looking at faded old photos with a sad face. Those times you just left him alone to reflect and go inside himself. I'll tell you how fucked-up Jip was. If a fight broke out between two loons, he would just sit there staring as if it was all part of life. He had seen so many acts of violence. He had been on the sharp end so many times. He was looking at himself with dead eyes. Nothing nor nobody could hurt Jip Carter. How could you hurt a man who's been dead for a lifetime?

I learnt a lot off this old legend. I've never forgot the old rascal. And after a lifetime of abuse and brutality he was never afraid of the system. Jip still stood up against it. If a liberty was being taken, he was up on his soapbox. I can still see him shuffling about the ward, and to think the maggots never even freed him to die. This just sums it all up for me in a nutshell. Wicked bastards.

I met a lot of old men in the three asylums. Some were legends in their own right. All were products of the system. All had their souls ripped away. All had that look in their eyes: the look of death - deep, black, bottomless pits of pain. It's only when you enter into madness that you can truly relate to what I'm saying.

It's a lost world, a world of loonyology. Every old man shuffling down the corridor is a ghost of yourself. We are all doomed. Some may get lucky and be freed, but can a man ever be free from so much madness? You can't escape the reality of life. Memories chew you up and spit you out. The drugs 'forced upon you' alone will eventually create some kind of reaction: first dreams, then nightmares.

The whole set-up is about control. They are not content with just locking the loonies up. They want to fuck the brain, take over. Like the German psychiatrists in the wartime 'Experiment with Life'. It's all about controlling another human being. Fuck the consequences, we have to research. They can test and kill a lot of rats with new drugs but soon it must be a human and any loony will do. Even better, a loony with no family - no ties or contact with the outside world. What a prize guinea pig he will make.

Okay, it's now 2008 and it's not as bad, but imagine it in the 1920s, '30s, '40s, '50s. The fucking 1970s were bad enough. It happened regular. The cunts used to inject me with all sorts. Why? How? What was it? The effects alone were terrible. Loonies don't forget. Would you? But loonies are not great witnesses. So who does a jury believe - a loony or a professor in psychiatry? The loony is there to be used if and when they please.

We don't forget. You do. We don't. Now understand me when I speak of the old men's eyes. I've been there, smelt it. It's not nice. Insanity can be a very shitty subject - literally. Madness can really become messy - like waking up in a bed of shit and your entire body covered in shit. I've seen them shuffle off to the shower stinking of shit. Er, I'll miss breakfast today. That's how it is. Believe me, morning time in the asylum is not for the weak-minded. The screws earn their wages I can tell you. Could you do their job? Would you want to? I'd say you must be mad to want to do that job, but it's a job. Somebody has to do it. And they do it. By God they do it alright. Insanity is another planet. It's just fucking insane.

THE HANGMAN'S NOOSE

Sometimes I sense I may have swung in another life
Just a feeling
Don't ask me why
Don't ask me where
It's just a feeling
A dream
No it's more than a dream
It's a vision
I've actually seen it
Felt it
I've woken up in a pool of sweat
At least I've been there
I know I have
It happens so fast
There is no pain
Only fear
You know it's seconds away
The hood goes over your head
Your hands are pinned behind your back
Your ankles are strapped together
You're on the trapdoor in the dark
It's a second away
What if I shit myself?
What if my head comes off?
What if it don't kill me?
What if ...?

There's nutters, and then there's mad, nasty dangerous psychos, and Harry 'Hate 'em All' has gotta be in the top five, and I don't mean that in a bad way as Harry was a good buddy of mine. It's just that he was a vicious fucker. He just enjoyed violence. Wherever Harry was, violence was not far off. He got his nickname 'Hate 'em All' off the Kray twins. The Krays loved him. Ron used to say if we'd had a dozen like Harry outside we could have took over the world.

He was fearless; scared of nobody. He fought his way through life, but it cost him dearly. The penal system actually drove him insane. Make no mistake about it, Harry was mad. He was only 5 foot 7 but very stocky and extremely strong. His original sentence was five years, but he got it topped up to 20 years, mostly for violence. He cut George Ince in Long Lartin Jail and that cost him five more years. Ince had been giving Charlie Kray's wife a length. You just don't do that, but even more so to a Kray. Ince was either nuts or just pushing his luck. After Harry sliced him, he got a gold watch off the twins and a bundle load of respect. Then he stuffed a china mug in McVicar's boat just for the fun of it. McVicar later become famous, or infamous - whatever you wish to call it - for his escape from Durham Special Unit. Harry just rolled on through the system, cutting and bashing people, including screws. He just loved to attack people.

I was in many jails with Harry and I saw his moods swing into action. Once in Leicester Jail he punched a screw's face in for looking at him. It's funny when you look back on it all, but Harry was deadly serious. His face would just change. His eyes bulged and he was off on a mission. Like the time he had it off the prison van with half a dozen other cons. They were being escorted from Wandsworth to Parkhurst and it took off at Portsmouth. They overpowered the guards and busted out of the van. Five ran off, but Harry carried on attacking the screws. He lost control and just kept bashing them. That cost him another five years. That's how he was: fucking mental. He was forever throwing his piss pot over governors and covering them in shit. All this behaviour cost him dearly: more kickings and more punishment, until it became normal. The system can't understand this. They can't work out why men get worse. Sure, some men will break and crack, but guys like Harry become harder and madder.

One time he almost got me into serious trouble. I was having a fight in the recess with this Scottish con. It was a fair fight: no tools, just fists. Then Harry steamed in with an iron bar and almost killed the guy. There was blood all over the place, us included. It was like a fucking slaughterhouse. I had to restrain him, as he'd lost it completely. If I hadn't have grabbed him, then that guy would've gone out in a zip-up bag. Harry's eyes were spaced out. He was foaming at the mouth. I was looking into the face of a lunatic, a complete fucking psycho.

It was up in Hull Jail that I first met Harry back in 1974. He'd just had a fight with another con called Billy. He later got nicked over the Hull riot and lost 600 days' remission. Billy was, in fact, a top-class geezer - a super-fit man who trained seven days a week. He was a handy boxer in his time, fast and strong with a good punch. He was a good six-footer with 200 pounds of muscle behind him.

Harry sure knew how to pick a fight. He kept bumping into him, calling him names and growling at him. Billy told him, "Drop it out, Harry. I don't want to hurt you." But would Harry have it? No way. He just wanted a fight. Bang! One punch and Harry was out cold. Next thing, Harry's got a foot-long blade ready to chop him up. A few of the chaps intervened. "Fuck off, Harry. You can't do that to Billy. It's a fucking liberty." Harry then turned on the chaps, so he got another good hiding. It got so bad that he had to be moved out of the jail before he got killed.

That was Harry's life, always moving around. It was in Gartree that he got his biggest kicking from a mob of cockneys. They went in his cell and really gave it to him. Days later he was tooled up for revenge. Again he was moved on. Real psychos don't have feelings; their heart is made of stone. It was only in old age that Harry mellowed and became a really nice guy. I think he found himself. I also believe he has found some peace, but I'll say now that I liked and respected Harry through all his violent years. He was a good friend to me, but I'll also add that no way would I have done a blag with him outside - it would've been suicidal. Imagine him with a shotgun on a bit of work! There would be bodies all over the place.

I last saw Harry in Gartree in 1993. He was then in his sixties. He'd lost weight and his face was very thin, but those eyes still had that look of defiance. He was still a man to be reckoned with. Nobody even then fucked with Harry. He was a bit like the old lion in a cage at the zoo: looks nice but can still bite your face off or rip your intestines out.

Harry was a product of the system and with all his faults he was still a good man. He just lived by his own beliefs and morals. 'Hate 'em All Harry' died how he lived: his way. I would say he spent a good 40 years behind bars and every day he fought it his way - the only way he knew. You fuck with me and I'll fuck you with a table leg. To me he was a legend. To the system he was a fucking problem. Harry was a problem they couldn't solve and never would. 'Hate 'em All Harry' lives on in memory.

Another real psycho that comes to mind is Neil, who I've not seen since Parkhurst 1986. We was on the unit together. Neil shot a cop and a ware-houseman dead up in Leeds in the early 1970s. He got life with a recommended 30 years, so he's well past the recommended tariff. In fact he's almost served 40 years now. I haven't a clue where he - maybe he got out or even died - but Neil was a very unpredictable man in his younger years. He wasn't a big man and never used a gym. He just loved his spliff and pot of rosy lea! He was a pretty laid back sort of guy until some cunt got in his face.

He had a spell in Broadmoor as he attempted to serve the doctor up in Parkhurst. He almost did just that. The doctor shit himself. If it hadn't been for the fast reactions of the screws, then the doctor would've got seriously hurt that day. But even Broadmoor never stopped Neil's violence. He ripped out a lunatic's kidney with a broken china mug. The loon's kidney was hanging out of his back. That's how Neil was: bloodthirsty.

He was the sort of guy that when he was nice he was one decent sort of fella but when he was bad he was the devil himself. During his first ten years inside he was on a mission of violence. He cut and stabbed his way through. One con in Albany was unlucky enough to have his skull smashed in. Neil laughed as he did it. A lot of cons actually used Neil to do their own dirty work, often paid for in cannabis so Neil was always off his head. He was living in another world, his own planet, but no man can keep lashing out with violence and not receive some back. He had his fair share of falls, but as with all psychos it comes with the reputation. The last time I bumped into him in '86 I must say he'd calmed right down, but with all psychos it's in their eyes. The violence is only skin deep.

Two decades later I often wonder how he is today. I'd like to think that he made it out and got on with his journey a free man.

Men of violence do change with age. They grow up and realise they can't continue their destructive way of life. Sadly, some don't get the chance. They die, mostly with a violent end. Violence does breed violence. The human world is no different from the animal way of life. In fact we are worse. Animals only kill to survive. Madmen survive to kill. It's a fact unless, of course, you're a cannibal. Most killers only kill for power, or a domestic dispute's gone too far. I've known men who've killed their wives in a rage of jealousy. They arrive at jail broken men. Many cannot accept what they did, so they kill themselves. But cold-blooded killers seldom have a conscious. They have no flashbacks, they just move on in life and hope never to be caught. The stiff becomes a faded memory. The maggots take over.

Have you ever wondered about all the thousands of missing people that vanish every year? In London alone, every year 10,000 people just vanish. They get up, go to work and that's it. Their husbands, wives, children never see them again. Nobody knows where they are. Dead or alive? They're history. A lot of them are youngsters, the homeless, down-and-outs. So where the fuck are they? Believe me, there's some serious loonies on the prowl: psycho killers on the loose.

Do you honestly think people just disappear into thin air or pack up and fuck off from their loved ones? Or maybe Martians kidnap them? No. I'm telling you, they're all in holes, long eaten away: some eaten by pigs; some cremated; others just rotting in a field. Hey, wild pigs will devour a corpse in 30 minutes, nothing left. There are mad killers out there laughing all the way to hell. The moors, woods and oceans are full of skeletons. Wake up and smell the coffee.

PSYCHO

All wrapped up like a Christmas turkey
Stuffed inside a padded room
He went mad with a bowie knife
Trapped inside the moon
His mother said he was a lovely boy
He never done no wrong
His father beat him black and blue
Bob Dylan wrote the song
He wanted to be a movie star
Arnie was his King
He caught a plane to Hollywood
His brain began to sting
He smoked some pot and dropped the pills
He slept up in those hills
Madness crept inside his brain
A turd went down the drain
Another madman kissed the sky
A tear fell from his eye
Charlie Manson in his head
He lived on jam and bread
He walked the streets in a dream
His heart began to scream
He stabbed a man in a late-night bar
And had some pie and cream
He drove and laughed and drank more beer
Then crashed into a bridge
Blood trickled down his face
He woke up in the fridge
They call this place the freezer
Death Row gets very cold
The brain's on ice, the soul is dead
Nothing more to hold
Hollywood kiss my arse
Arnie is a joke
All wrapped up for Santa Claus
A dream gone up in smoke
Stay away from drugs and crime
Don't end up like me
Life's too precious to throw away
Don't live it under key

Yeh, you may just go out and kill some poor sod. You may be off your nut on drugs, but the truth is you're gonna pay dearly no matter how fucked up you are. You're gonna end up more fucked. You won't know your arse from your mouth. You won't know what day, month or year it is, and when you do wake up you're gonna have to live with what you've done! Then the 'lifemare' begins. Can you handle all that? Can you? Take some serious advice: STAY CLEAR OF THE DRUGS!

Hey, put it out, you fucking prat! If you was meant to smoke you'd have a chimney on your head. That Sir Walter Raleigh has a lot to answer for, bringing all that tobacco over here. He really started all this bollocks off! Look how many he must have killed. In fact, I bet he's the biggest mass killer of all time. He should've changed his name to 'Sir Walter Cancer'.

Gorilla - it's my new next door neighbour. Ain't I lucky?! Some get the neighbour from hell and I get a fucking ape. If I shaved all its fur off and dressed it in some ladies underwear (I wonder!), that can't be any worse than some of them hookers that hang around Kings Cross! Have you seen some of them tarts? Would you? Come on, be honest, would you? There's some right ugly fuckers hang around there, eh?

What a strange old world this is! But what a brilliant world too! Loonyology is 24/7. You've only gotta look out of your window to see something mad happening! It's magical! Enjoy it! Life is just a journey of madness! Peaches and cream, fucking delicious double helpings. How lucky are we?

I touched her face
I smelt her skin
I stroked her hair
I bit her ear lobe
I squeezed her tight
I wish I never
It was a fucking gorilla!
I awoke in an ape house
A cage full of apes
What a crazy dream
I was fucking with madness
Bestiality
The beast kept a hold of me
I was a hostage to the ape
She had beautiful eyes though
And lovely nipples
But did her breath stink
How the fuck did I get in here?
How the fuck do I get out?
Do I really care?

Bend over bitch
Let's do it again
Gorillas are fun
And they don't moan
What a dream
Whatever happened to peaches and cream?

Oh, yeh, and there was this one lunatic who could put a full-size orange in his mouth! Fucking amazing. Pop! Right in. His cheeks used to blow up like a chipmunk. It was so funny to see. He done it once too often though and choked to death. Fucking nutcase. Who the fuck wants to put a whole orange in their mouth? Hey, get this too. There was a madman in Broadmoor in the 1930s who took up knitting. Yeah, knitting. This loon wasn't that mad, as he knitted a 30-foot scarf and had it away over the wall. What a fucking blinder. See, there's method to all this madness. Some are fucking born geniuses, amazing people, and you gotta love 'em all (except the nonces). I'll tell you who's mad: the first bloke who steps in a ring with me. He's gonna have to be nuts or on a suicide mission. Talking of suicide nutters, what's that all about up in Glasgow - them two prats driving into the airport reception and exploding the car? One got 90% burns. Hurry up and die, you cunt, and as for the other one - well who gives a fuck about him. They're insane. They make the insane look sane. Fucking dickheads. Their brains are sizzled. It beggars belief.

Hey, did I ever tell you about the time I hit a loony in Broadmoor with a tin of pilchards? I hit the fucker about ten times over the crust. What for? He knows what for, and I know what for, and that's all that matters. He was a cunt. His nickname later was 'Fishy'. That's how nicknames start. He was never the same after that - very slow and mumbled a lot. In fact, a bit like a fish. He's lucky it wasn't an axe.

There was another loony there called Yo-Yo. He was always up and down all day - not a joke, serious. This guy was happy one minute and then - bang! - sad. A schizoid personality is a terrible illness, it really is. Very sad.

I can smell a madman, I really can. Don't ask me how. If you look deeply into a madman's eyes you'll see that black hole. Don't fall in, coz you sure won't get back out. That's good advice. Take it or leave it.

When it comes down to serial killers. Henry Lee Lucas must be up there in the top three of all time. He confessed to 360 murders. Thank fuck they executed him. That's one mother fucker we won't be missing. Rot in hell, you bastard.

Hey, do you remember the character 'Buffalo Bill' in *The Silence of the Lambs*? What Thomas Harris wrote was based on true-life mass killer Ed Gein. Gein was a fucking monster. He used to make clothes out of the skin of his victims. What a sick fucker he was. He screamed like a pig in the electric chair!

One of the most brutal Mafia killings was on Gus Greenbaum in 1958. They cut his fucking head off while he slept in bed. Sadly they strangled his wife at the same time - ruthless fuckers! You're best not messing with the mob!

Carl Panzram is the human closest to ever being the devil himself. He was pure evil. When they hung him on 11 September 1930 in Leavenworth State Penitentiary, he screamed out, "Hurry it up, you bastards. I could've hung a dozen men while you're fooling around." Panzram, I believe, was insane. He had to be. Just look at his life: when he was 11 years old he ran away from reform school; he jumped a train and travelled the USA; and four hobos raped him. And that was that for Panzram. He went to war with the planet with spells in and out of prison. He just became more and more bitter and hateful. His life in jail was brutal. He fought every day of his life. The beatings he got were second to none. He was born to kill and kill he did. He left a trail of bodies behind him and he didn't care who - women, kids and old folk. The world was a target to him, as was every fucker in it. He even killed in prison. He couldn't stop killing until they killed him. He was sick in the nut. Those four hobos turned that young boy into a killing machine. Carl Panzram was created by evil, lived as evil and died as evil. Amen.

I'll tell you, there've been some evil murdering bastards in the USA. One of them is Moses Sithole. Clock the last name. It's missing an 'h' after the 'S' - Shithole's more like it. This guy was known as the ABC killer. He started his murdering spree in Atteridgeville, then went on to Bokshurg and to Cleveland in Johannesburg, leaving behind 38 stiffs. On 6 December 1997 (my birthday) he got sentenced to 2,410 years. Over 2,000 fucking years?! How's he gonna serve all that?

Another freaky fucker was Gerry Maddog Stano. He killed 41, mostly women. His famous saying was: "They smell like pigs". Well, so did he when old sparky sizzled his brain! Anyone for a bacon butty?

I'll tell you who was a nasty fucker - John Wayne Gacy from the USA. He killed 33, mostly young boys. He was a clown called Poja. He wasn't laughing in the death chamber. His last ride was a one-way ticket to hell! Even that was too good for the murdering bastard.

And what about Harrel Braddy? He tossed five-year-old Quatisha Maycock into a swamp in Florida and she was found the next day half eaten by the alligators. He still sits on death row. Hurry up and die, you bastard. How the fuck can any human do that to a kid? It's beyond humanity. The sick bastard. Are we really in hell? Could this really be hell or is the planet a gigantic asylum? What is it? Somebody tell me.

Don't you ever wonder how many serial killers are out there walking the streets or potential mass killers bubbling along ready to explode into an orgy of violence? It could be that weirdo three doors up from your Aunt Rose's flat. Or that wino who hangs around the local supermarket. What about that crazy-eyed stranger who's always hanging around the local bingo hall? Who is it? Keep looking, coz as sure as you've got a hole in your arse there's a few out there. Dr Shipman and Fred West may be dead, but there's others lingering about! Even Domestos don't or can't kill all the germs. Keep looking and stay safe!

CHAPTER 3
ALL IN THE NAME OF AHMED

There's been so much shit in the media about my divorce to Saira. She wrote a book calling me a racist thug, and she's even been on *Good Morning* TV slagging me off. The press had a Bronson frenzy; everybody stuck the boot in. I was black and blue all over, but was my side ever told? Is my side ever told? Well, it fucking will be now, and this is the first.

We got wed on 1 June 2001 in Woodhill CSC Unit Maximum Security. but I'm now gonna blow you away. Legally it was a farce. I was never officially married.

Saira Ahmed to me was a Bengali Princess. She was the most beautiful woman I had ever seen. I dreamt of covering her naked body in cream and licking it all off. So some fucking racist I must be. She's Asian. Racists don't do that. Do they? Hell, I had my first bit of black pussy 40 years ago. I'm sure a racist don't do that. Do they? Or am I missing the point?

I actually idolised Saira; loved her to bits. She had the most beautiful eyes and teeth. Her skin glowed; it shone. Everything about her was bloody gorgeous ... eatable. She picked up a paper and read about a man who's Britain's most violent, dangerous man? She fell in love with a convict who's serving a life sentence while in a cage - a coffin indefinitely. It's like them fucking nutters who become close to the Death Row inmates and marry them. They're married for a year or two and then they fry the cons' brains! Two thousand volts is the divorce - end of! A book and then a film follows. It's all now very predictable.

Now do you see what I'm getting at? Saira was unknown. Then on 1 June 2001 she was in every paper in Britain, on the TV, in mags. She was Mrs Bronson! It was her claim to fame - but was it?

Mr and Mrs Bronson don't, nor ever did, exist! Quite simply, as my real name is Micky Peterson and I never did change my name to Bronson legally, by law we could not have been married. So therefore there could not be a divorce. Am I making sense?

Charlie Bronson was my alias. I used to fight under the Bronson name. All my unlicensed fights were as Bronson. Then, when I got nicked, the Old Bill charged me as Bronson and that's how it came about. So Mrs Bronson was never legal! All you read and saw was a complete farce.

But let's say it was legal and we were married, then why did she go through with it? I'm not what you call a good catch am I? I've no dosh. I've no home. I've not even got a shed. She was marrying a man who could well die inside. There can be no sex; no babies; no security.

So why the fuck marry somebody like me? As I've said, it's simple. It was a good way of getting famous. She became big news. She loved it all. It was brilliant for her. My mates really spoilt her rotten. She had more dosh than she'd ever had. Dave Courtney put on the party. She had it all - limo, guests, hotel, the lot. Any bride would have been proud on that day and God she looked beautiful, an angel. I was so proud of her, I truly was, but I was blinded by love. Love can and does fuck you up big time. I was forewarned by some old mates. Some had seen right through her. I even lost some old friends over it, as I basically told them: accept her, or fuck off. As simple as that!

I've always believed in 'cruel to be kind'. Why fanny about? To me life is for action. You think it, then do it. Don't look back and say, "I wish I'd done this and that." Fuck me, I had just married the most beautiful woman on the planet. ME. Me of all people. She grabbed my cock at the wedding and squeezed it and said, "That's mine." I grabbed the cake, stuffed it in my mouth and said, "That's mine." The riot mob were on standby all through the service. The unit was swarming with screws. It really was a mad day.

Another reason we were never wed: she's a Muslim. There was no Imam present. A further reason: the marriage was never consummated. The reasons go on and on. Now is it clear? It was a joke!

Over the next four years we gradually grew apart, simply because I started to see right through her. She was a lazy, greedy bitch. She would not get a job, but she loved to squeeze me dry. Good mates of mine sorted her out over those years - and I mean really looked out for her. She would call them up and cry, beg, make them feel sad. They would send her dosh. I knew fuck all about some of this until later. So I had to sort it all out. She was becoming an embarrassment; a fucking parasite. It became too much. She'd forgotten I was in a hole, with £4 a week in prison wages. I didn't need this shit, but I was arranging dosh, dosh and more dosh. All I got in return was a fucking big headache. I was becoming a right mug and she was becoming a right ponce. Like it was expected. I'm a fucking jailbird after all. I kept saying, "You need to get a job", "You need to pay your own bills", but one smile from her and I melted. She would travel up from Luton to Wakefield and stop in a hotel for two days to visit me. It was costing me a fortune just to see her. She started sending me bills - electric, rent, all sorts - and silly bollocks was sorting it.

There were people who owed me favours, but favours run out. I was dried up, fed up and getting very frustrated. I wasn't even getting a good shag out of it. Then it happened - bang! - I woke up. The ungrateful bitch pushed her luck too far. She had to go, and go she did. Love was mugging me right off. All I had done for her was not enough for one favour. This was the straw that poked out the … etc.

Saira wore saris the Muslim dress, and they're lovely. I do like a sari. I like the material and colours and style, but there is a place and a time for everything and my mate Charlie Breaker's pub in North London is not the place. It was a Bronson Night to raise a few quid (incidentally, the dosh was for Saira). All the chaps were going - Joe Pyle, Charlie Richardson, Freddie Foreman, Johnny Nash, Roy Shaw, David Courtney, Ray Kray; also my mum and my sister Loraine. Hundreds were going. It was to be a great night. Tel Currie was organising it, like he always does. So let me explain about the sari.

Saira had been to some shows before to represent me and it got back to me how cold she was towards my friends. They could not approach her; as she was very unfriendly nobody could touch her. Muslim women do not like all that, especially in pubs or clubs without their husband. Her attitude was strangling my name, even Loraine said so.

She was offending people so much that nobody really cared no more, as it was ignorance. It was my culture being insulted. She was good enough to take their dosh but she wouldn't integrate with them. It was becoming embarrassing for me and, to top it all, it was at the time of the Beslam massacre. You will all recall that horrific day when Islamic lunatics lay siege to a school in Russia and killed scores of children.

It was at this time that the UK was getting fed up with it all. What next? Our kids? People were unsure about how to approach Muslims in saris! It was a bad time. I asked Saira, "Can you wear some English clothes." After all, the first photo she ever sent me was of her in a pub in jeans and a top (she looked lovely). It's all I asked of her on this occasion. It was not a demand. It was a simple request.

She got seriously mad. "Don't tell me what to wear! Who do you think you are?" … blah, blah, blah.

That was it for me. We never spoke again from that day on. She didn't go to the Bronson Night. The night was a good one and all enjoyed it. All were happy - including me.

I kept my mouth shut. I let her get on with it and all I got in return was slagged off. Most of it I could accept, but the racial thing was just evil. There was no reason for it. If anyone was racist it was her for her coldness towards my friends.

But I'm not going down that road. It was an experience I learnt a lot from, but it cost me a lot of friends. I put her before my friends. I was wrong to do that. My only excuse was 'Love'. I just loved her - that was my only wrongdoing. She got a book out of it. I'm told it never sold 500 copies, but it's still a book - a great achievement. She got a play done about it in a London theatre. She got TV out of it, and radio! She's the ex-bride of Bronson.

When I changed my name by deed poll to Ali Ahmed for her and I became pork free, I actually tried to become a Muslim. I even read the Koran. That religion is like the rest - full of shit. I'm anti all religion. I've no time for it, but Saira proved to me what a joke she is by publishing her book as Saira Bronson when I gave her back the name of Ahmed. She only used Bronson as nobody knows Ahmed! She rode on my back like all parasites do. After all that, I really have no bad feelings about her. I actually wish her well. She's still the most beautiful woman I've ever seen. I'm still in the hole. She's as free as a bird, but I have something she will never have: I've still got the same morals I was born with. She's lost all hers. That's if she ever had any to start with.

I've purposely left her daughter out of this, as I don't believe in that sort of thing. Kids are the innocents in domestic problems. She's now 16 years old with her own journey to make in life. I only wish her well.

I would only say to other 'Lifers', be wary of strange women falling in love with you, as it's not all that it seems. I recently read that some fat, ugly bird is in love with the Yorkshire Ripper. Hell - that's just loonyology at its best. How can any woman fall for the Ripper? It don't pay to think about that one! I reckon she needs locking up in the asylum, or am I missing something here?

They do say that marriage is only a piece of paper. Well, so is bog roll. It's all a complete load of shit to me!

Talking of the Ripper (Sutcliffe), his ex-wife Sonia was a hot cookie. She used to visit him in Parkhurst dressed up as a schoolgirl, with a pony tail, short skirt and thigh-length socks. The cons got right mad over it, so his visits ended up isolated away from the normal ones.

We just don't like cunts like him. Do you? We can't accept crimes like his and we can never work out why the women stick by them! How can a man kill 13 women and his wife sticks by him? It don't add up.

I suppose it's like Brady. His mum stayed loyal to him. Like Harold Shipman. His wife stayed loyal to him. It's all a bit mental to me coz in my world a monster is a monster. Humans and monsters don't mix. It don't add up - it really don't. Sugar and salt: it's not the same, it never can be. Sane and insane - it don't mix.

How about this for a story … you'll fucking love this one. This one is more out of a spy movie. I was up in the Durham Special Cage which is next door to the CSC Unit. It's a totally isolated cell. Silent. I was in there when the planes hit the towers, as big Tony McCulloch shouted me out of his cell window from the Unit, "Chaz, Charlie, Chaz!" Fuck me, he was excited to tell me something. "Chaz, you're not gonna believe this. I've just seen on the telly …" (Lucky fucker had a telly in his cell.)

"Chaz!" he shouted for the fiftieth time. "Two planes have gone into the twin towers in the USA. You should see it - it's mental!" That was the year something strange occurred to me in that very cage. It was December time, the same year as the planes (work the year out for yourselves). Years don't mean dog shit to me. I only count the decades these days. At this time I was

Ali Ahmed and this Durham cage had two doors to it: a solid steel outer door and an inner door, similar to the Wakefield cage. They feed you through a cat flap.

This day, my outer door opened and there stood two very well dressed men. They looked official. One had a file under his arm and the other had these deep-set eyes that never left my eyes.

"Who the fuck are you two?"

It felt very tense and unreal.

"Who are you?" I growled.

The one with the file smiled and said, "It's not who we are, it's what we are."

The other then said, "We have a deal for you."

I was by now getting angry and anxious, as I didn't know who they were. "Who fucking are you?"

The one said, "if you do us a favour, we will do you one."

I was even more confused.

"Ali. Can we call you Ali? Ali, how would you like to move to a normal location on the max secure unit in Belmarsh Prison?"

"What? What the fuck are you on about?"

"Look, if you do this then we can make it good for your parole."

"What?! Who the fuck are you pair of cunts?!"

"Look, Ali. We want you to infiltrate the Muslim inmates in Belmarsh and find out what's what. Everybody knows you. You're the most infamous con in the UK. They'll trust you, tell you things, now you're Muslim Ahmed Ali."

I really was in shock, but not so much to realise I was being asked to be a fucking spy. Me? Me, of all people? You just couldn't make this shit up. Never in my life have I been put in this position. I actually felt angry, so I spat through the cage and told them to fuck themselves.

"I'm nobody's spy. Go on, fuck off!"

As a screw appeared from nowhere to shut the door, the one with the file was wiping the spit off his face and said, "Ahmed, that will cost you."

Then SLAM! - the door shut.

I swear I didn't know who they were. I've never seen them since. Nothing like this had ever happened before and has never happened since. My lawyer knows all about it; it's on file. The screws and Prison Governor denied it ever happened, although there's a CCTV camera outside my door. It's a fucking mystery I have to live with.

Let me just add, I fucking despise the Islamic terrorists and all they stand for. I'd shit on them all, but I'm nobody's puppet. I don't work for no fucking spineless system, even if it means my freedom. I can't ever go down that road. It's not in me to crawl out or kiss arse. I'd sooner die right now than sell my soul. I do hope this makes sense to you all. If it don't, then fuck it. But I made my decision there and then and it may well be what's buried me.

Who were them two guys? At a guess, MI6, MI5 or maybe terrorist officers from Scotland Yard. Whoever they were, believe me they were top dogs and looked what they were: fucking dangerous and powerful; the type that can crush a man like a grape or put a .45 in your eye and blow the back of your skull clean off. It sure gave me a restless night and a memory never to forget.

This is a piece from my website, www.freebronson.co.uk:

CHARLES BRONSON ASKED TO SPY by GIOVANNI di STEPHANO

INTELLIGENCE chiefs tried to recruit one of Britain's most notorious prisoners to spy on Islamic terror suspects held in a top security jail, it has been claimed.

Violent Charles Bronson says MI5 asked him to mingle with Muslim remand prisoners at Belmarsh maximum secure unit and become a secret informer.

In return for intelligence about international terror cells, Bronson, who is serving a life sentence for hostage taking and assaulting prison staff, was told he could be granted early release.

But the 54-year-old former circus strongman angrily rejected the deal and claims his life has been made 'hell' ever since.

Bronson, who has spent 28 of his 32 years inside in solitary confinement, says the offer came in December 2001 - three months after the 9/11 terror attacks and six months after he converted to Islam when he married Muslim bride Saira Rehman.

The deal would also have coincided with the dramatic arrest of nine foreign Al Qaeda terror suspects who were detained at Belmarsh on December 19, 2001.

At the time, 'category A' crook Bronson was known as Ali Charles Ahmed and into the 27th year of life behind bars.

In a new telephone interview with his lawyer Giovanni di Stefano taped from his current Wakefield jail, he describes how two men were led to his cell in Durham prison six years ago.

"Two very official geezers in suits came to my cage door," he is heard saying.

"The screw opened the door and left them there and they were both stood behind. They were pretty friendly and they said: 'Listen, do you want to get out or don't you?'"

Bronson, who was first jailed for robbery in 1974 and has moved prison more than 150 times, replied: "Of course I want to get out. Anyway who are you?"

They said, "Well it doesn't matter who we are, we've come to put a deal to you. Are you prepared to do us a favour? We want you to go to Belmarsh maximum secure unit."

Bronson, who renounced his Muslim faith after divorcing Saira Rehman last year, continues: "They wanted me to mingle with the Islamic remands there and get some information.

"But I said 'Listen, get away from my door.' I then spat at one of them and as they were walking away from the door one said: 'That's the worst thing you'll do in your life, Bronson. That's going to cost you a lot of years'."

He has never seen them again, he adds.

But when his lawyer asks about life inside since then, Bronson, who was expecting to be released in 2003, replies: "They're just not letting me move on and I honestly believe that incident has got something to do with it."

His lawyer, Mr di Stefano, said last night: "The Home Office and MI5 have tried to use Charles Bronson for the wrong purposes. He is not an informer, which would be contrary to his principles, and that has cost him."

Operational since 1991, Belmarsh prison, in Woolwich, can hold 915 inmates. Its maximum secure unit, which is used as a detention centre for Islamic terror suspects, has been branded Britain's 'Guantanamo Bay'.

Around the time of the alleged offer to Bronson, nine foreign nationals were just beginning three years of being detained without trial on suspicion of terror links.

Also there in December 2001 was Abu Doha, a member of an Algerian terror group and who is believed to have had links with Osama bin Laden. Known as 'The Doctor', he had been arrested at Heathrow in February 2001 trying to board a flight to Saudi Arabia with a false passport.

He has been fighting extradition to the US where he is accused of plotting to blow up Los Angeles airport in 2000 ever since.

Charles Bronson, meanwhile, lost his latest bid for freedom last month when the Home Office turned down a request to reduce his dangerous 'category A' prisoner status, which could have paved the way for his release.

Originally jailed for robbery as a19-year-old in 1974, he has tasted freedom only for a few months ever since. He was given a life term in 2000 following a series of violent assaults and hostage taking incidents on fellow inmates and prison staff.

They included a 47-hour rooftop protest at Broadmoor in 1983 which caused £750,000 damage.

In 1994, he demanded a helicopter, an inflatable doll and a cup of tea as ransom for the release of a guard he was holding hostage at Woodhill Prison in Milton Keynes.

Later that year, Hull Prison the deputy governor was forced to take a month off work recovering from injuries sustained by Bronson during a five-hour hostage ordeal.

But friends also say the intelligent dad-of-one, who longs to be free to see his son, has a softer, caring side.

He has also won prizes for his art and poetry and has written 10 books, including one about how to keep fit in confined spaces.

Born Michael Peterson in Aberystwyth in 1952, his parents were local Conservative Party stalwarts. He later moved to Merseyside and finally Luton, which he considers his home.

He was given the name Charles Bronson in honour of the Hollywood actor by his bare-knuckle fighting promoter in 1987.

He married Saira Rehman, then a 31-year-old Bangladeshi-born divorcee from Luton, in June 2001.

After seeing Bronson's picture in a newspaper, she claimed to have fallen in love and described him as 'her soulmate'.

Bronson has since poured scorn on her motives, accusing her of wanting to cash in on his infamy.

MI5, MI6, CSA, IRA, SAS - who gives a flying fuck who they were?! I'm nobody's puppet; not today, not tomorrow, not ever. My strings were cut long ago. I can't be manipulated and used and they don't like it, coz after 30 years they still can't get me to bend. I could've agreed to do this and maybe got my freedom by now, but I would've walked out a 'rat'. I would've gone to my grave a hollow, weak man. I'm nobody's filthy fucking grass. I walk tall and proud. I'll make it out to freedom my way. You can bet your arse on that one. Don't worry, it's safe with me.

Laugh! I wet myself
My ribs were killing me
Almost a heart attack
Crazy times
Mental memories
One big scream
We all love a joke don't we?
The Iraqis hijacked a plane
I hijacked them
You couldn't make it up
Hijackers hijacked
That's a bloody movie on its own
It's magical
They fly a hijacked plane from Iraq
Land it at Stanstead Airport
And I hijack them in Belmarsh Prison
That hijack cost me 7 years of my life
I fucking despise hijackers
They're vermin, a disease to humanity
It could have been my mum on that plane
It could have been me
Lucky for them it wasn't me
Cos the lot would've dived out -
Without a parachute
The only way to deal with a terrorist
Is the Bronson way
Steam in and overpower
Belmarsh Prison cell is no different
Teach them who's who
This is England, Great Britain
You want to come here then get used to me!
Men like me
Cos we love our county
Respect us, our culture, or suffer
It's that simple
Human rights don't exist in the darkness
Loonyology takes over
I'm the governor when the door shuts
And it's barricaded up
I'm the master of madness
Believe it

LOONYOLOGY

The ultimate mentalist
I had them wrapped up like Xmas parcels
One I had tickling my toes
Laugh
I was in agony
It was pukka
Pure ace
Yahoooooooooo, yippeeeeeeeeeeee!
Faster, faster, tickle, tickle
Laughter frees the soul
It's just what I needed - a laugh!
And a laugh it was
Fuck all the highjackers
Have a laugh

CHAPTER 4
THE LION AND THE PUSSYCAT

It's been said that I'm Britain's most violent prisoner. Am I? Am I bollocks! How can I be? It's just a label. So how did it come about? Why? I'll tell you. I was naughty. A little bit naughty. I've done things most only ever dream of doing. I do your dreams. I live out your fantasies. My dreams I turn to reality. If I don't like somebody they sure know about it, and I don't give a flying fuck about it. Just stay out of my space. Live and let live I say. But some prats don't know how to keep out of your face.

I remember one time I was being escorted over to the hospital wing to see a dentist in Wandsworth. Ten screws were taking me 'cuffed up'. As we got to E Wing I clocked a con cleaning the stairs. It was a filthy grass I'd known in Scrubs. I just acted on impulse. I legged it over to him with the ten screws chasing me, blowing a whistle and shouting. I made it to the cleaner and kicked him at least six or seven times before I was restrained. Not bad, eh, considering I was cuffed up?! Eat your heart out, Rambo!

Who remembers the Cambridge Rapist, going back to the early 1970s? That little toerag raped a dozen women. He used to creep around Cambridge with a leather zip-up mask with 'rapist' written on it. He was only five feet nothing; a horrible scumbag that looked like a little rat. He was into wearing women's clothes. He had also done a spell in Broadmoor.

I remember when he turned up at Parkhurst in the '70s. He was cocky little fucker; arrogant. He started poncing around in women's clothes. I thought to myself, of all the jails to send him to they put him in Parkhurst. This jail at the time was the No. 1 jail, full of proper villains, real cons. Is it any wonder I wrapped a steel mop bucket around his fucking crust? Little bastard. I'll teach him to walk down the landings in his see-through panties and silly pink shirt. Crack! Cop a hold of that. He would've got more but some prat rang the alarm bell.

And who remembers the 'Guernsey Beast' Beasley. Sounds a lot like beast. It's probably why I remember the toerag. He got 30 years for sodomising little boys. A right ugly fat bastard. Sadly I only got to see him through a fence in Albany and a couple of times through a window in Parkhurst. He served his time on Rule 43 with all the other nonces. He actually served 20 years (that's one good thing) but, believe me, when these monsters all get together on a little unit, or wing, they party. They get through pots of KY Jelly. They all have a funny walk. Their arses must be red raw.

I used to stick razor blades in bars of white Windsor soap and throw them over the fence where they walked by, hoping maybe one would find its way into one of their pockets and a nice little accident would happen in the shower (one can wish). I also used to throw sweets in wrappers over the fence after I'd contaminated them with shit. I wonder how many were ever eaten? If only one, then it was a result. Personally, I'd sooner punch them up.

I just can't be having a serious nonce around me. Can you? Could you live next door to a nonce, let's say a paedophile or child killer? Well could you? No you couldn't. Well why should we in prison live with them? I'm just not happy with them monsters near me. They should be in 'Special Jails', away from the proper cons. Let me say now, I'm a believer in punishment. I actually believe in the birch. I think prison should be hard. It's all we deserve. I'm not into a soft regime. But why should some get it easy and some hard? Let's all get it hard. Let's stop playing silly games. All this psychological crap, it don't work, it's a joke. Prison is for punishment; to teach us a lesson not to treat us like a load of muppets.

I just read in the paper that Ian Huntley has just bought a bed rug as the prison rug is too rough. He should be sleeping in a black hole with the rats. It all makes me feel sick. But that's how it is today. It's all crazy and if you don't go along with it then you become like me: the dangerous one. You end up in a solitary cage. Yeh, for real. You end up in a fucking big hole that sucks away your light. This is the end of the line. The crematorium awaits. Mine's a bacon roll with mushrooms. Fuck the Rice Krispies. Give mine to the muppets. In fact … sling it in the bin. Don't spoil the fuckers.

Hey, did you know that bulletproof vests, laser printers and windscreen wipers were all invented by women? I thought you might like to know that. Fuck knows why, but it's just historical facts.

'Tostum' is the Latin word for scorched or burning, thus cometh toast. Hey, I love cheese and tomato and spring onion on toast with a nice mug of tea! It's years since I had a treat like that. I'm fucking hungry just thinking about it. I can almost smell it. Why do I have to torture myself with these beautiful memories. Maybe I'm just a masochist! I probably am.

In the early 1970s the toughest jails were places like Winson Green, Strangeways, Armley and Wandsworth. These were known as the POA Power Houses. Troublemakers were sent to these seg blocks for a good kicking. Make no mistake about it, it was brutal and you got fuck all. My life, my world, was in these blocks. I was kicked around from pillar to post. I would arrive naked in a body belt and the treatment would kick off from day one. These blocks were run by a fist of steel, always by the biggest and ugliest screws in the jail, not one of them under six feet. All were ex-military; men you would be proud of on a rugby field. They loved nothing more than a good old-fashioned ruck. Some - most - were vicious, vindictive bullies. They loved the power and used it to the full. The black cons got it the worst in Wandsworth block, as at this time there were a lot of National Front screws, all proud to display their member badges. Also the Irish got it bad. As for me, they just loved me every time I turned up there. On my first spell in Wandsworth block back in 1975 I attacked three screws within a week. My life was forever in the strongbox in restraint. I used to do anything and everything to fuck up their regime. Regularly I used to walk across the infamous steel-rimmed centre. It's sacrilege to step on that centre. Every time I did that I was jumped on and carted off back to the box black and blue.

That's how it was. You either behaved or you suffered. I was labelled a prison activist. I would climb the roof, smash the place up, shit on it all. Shit up. Nobody knew what I would do next - not even me.

Incidentally, the only two other cons I knew of who used to walk across Wandsworth centre were Frank Frazer and Frank Mitchell. Apart from them I don't know of anymore. For 99% of cons it's just basically head down, do your bird peacefully and get out fast.

Every jail has nasty screws; evil fuckers who are set to make your stay a bad one. In the 1970s the two worst screws I knew there were Ryan and Beasley.

Beasley was a giant of a man with a seriously nasty streak and he would nick you for a button undone. I chinned him and told him, "Next time I'll cut your throat." That cost me 120 days' remission, 56 days' punishment and a £5 fine. Five quid was a lot in the '70s - about two months' wages for me. But that's what you get when you attack authority. You have to take the consequences.

Strange enough, Beasley wasn't so bad to me after that. I think he respected me. Bear in mind that I was only a young man of 23 at the time and he was well into his forties. But he was a giant of a man; a hard man. Rumour had it he'd been out in the Middle East snapping necks in some special force. That could be shit, but with him I wouldn't doubt it.

Ryan was a different kettle. He was a little vindictive fucker. Even the screws despised him, as he was always causing unnecessary trouble. He worked on D Wing, the long-term wing. D Wing was a little more easy owing to the sorts of cons it held: lifers Cat A and Cat E; all sorts of high-risk inmates. Most had just got their sentence, so it was very tense in there. The screws sort of kept a back step. But Ryan was a total cunt. I mean it - a cunt. Slamming doors, shouting abuse, pushing it all the time. Like all Irishmen he loved a drink. You could always smell it on them. Him and me just had to get it on. He was in my face all the time. It happened in the mail bag shop on the end of D Wing. I just felt that's it, I've had my lot of him, so I hit him with a right hook (that's all, I swear). The alarm went and in rushed the mob to take me off to the block for a good kicking. I could hardly walk for a week afterwards as one of my balls had swollen to the size of an orange, but that's showbiz.

There was one old screw there who told me privately, "You done us all a favour there. It got rid of the Irish prick for a spell." There was an old screw there in his sixties. I used to chat with him coz I liked his style. He was one of those screws that just did his job, and he treated the cons with respect. All the cons respected him. He used to stop a lot of trouble by using his own ways of dealing with problems. "Come on, son. Cool down. Go behind your door. You don't need this shit. Come on, do yourself a favour. Think of your family." Nine times out of ten his way worked. When he was on duty it was always a treat to see him. Other screws did not react like him. Incidentally, he was a screw in the hanging days. The stories he told me were amazing. He actually witnessed them. He spent time in the death cell with the condemned prisoner. I told him that when he retired he should write a book.

By the way, did you know that most hangings literally shit themselves. The bowels just burst open and that was it. Piss and shit just pours out. I bet that's put you off lunch.

I met all the faces in Wandsworth: anyone who was anyone. It was a breeding ground for criminals over the years. Real villains come out of Wandsworth: men like the Krays, Richardsons, Freddie Foreman, Frank Frazer - all the legends; good old-fashioned armed robbers like Danny Alpress, Terry Smith, Ronnie Easterbrook, Wayne Hurren, Roy Shaw and Ronnie Brown. They all passed through Wanno. Wanno was the stepping stone for Parkhurst or Dartmoor. It's like an apprenticeship of crime. You have to get the experience. That's what it's all about. To be a criminal you will one day get porridge. You will fall eventually. So expect what you get and plenty of it.

My true advice would be: don't do what I've done. Do your bird easy and get out fast. You only win by walking out or going over the wall. Freedom is the ultimate goal in life inside unless you are a complete institutionalised moron. After all my years inside I still hate prison life and prison life hates me. I can never become institutionalised. It's against my philosophy.

Some of my best years were in Wandsworth - crazy years, but memorable. I was just born to rock the boat and rock it I did. I almost escaped from there, I cut people there, I chinned people there, I got on the roof there, I shit up there, I met some of my best buddies there, I slept in the cell next to the condemned cell there, I taught myself to play chess and bridge there (out of books), I spent a good four years in solitary there, I was on hunger strike there, I chinned a doctor there, I chinned several governors there, I attacked a good dozen screws there, I smashed up dozens of cells there, I attacked many nonces there, and I met some decent screws there. They weren't all bad. There's always some good everywhere. One in particular, was a gentleman. He done a lot for me over the years. Over the last 34 years I've probably been back there 20 times, if not more, and he was always there. I watched his hair go grey. He watched mine fall out. That's how life is inside - a fucking journey of madness. I'll leave you with a funny story on Wanno. You'll love this one ...

Lord Longford - Frank to me - used to visit me all over England from as far away as Durham all the way to Parkhurst, the Isle of Wight. He was one of my favourite regular visitors and we had some bloody good laughs. He also helped me a lot with advice, etc.

My first visit with Frank was in the block in Wanno years back. He came to see me over my long years in solitary and he wanted to interview me for the book he was writing called *Prisoner or Patient*. Our visit had to be held in the Governor's office in the block (the Adjudication Room) as I was considered too unpredictable to be escorted over to the visiting area. Plus, going to the visiting area would mean passing the centre, and they didn't want me walking over it. So the visit would be in the block. The Adjudication Room was quite large with a portrait of the Queen on the wall. So, ten screws unlocked me and marched me to the room. Frank had been told it was not safe to see me alone, but he responded, "Charlie won't attack me. I wish to see him alone." I walked in to see an old man with bottletop specs. I gave him a hug before we sat down to chat. The door had a plastic glass in it so they could look in on us. I said to Frank, "Look at them nosy fuckers." He smiled and said, "They're only doing a job." So we had a good chat. He was a really nice fella to talk with: very clever; very helpful. He asked me what I did all day in my cell. I told him press-ups. How many, he asked. So I told him: between two and three thousand. As we spoke about my press-ups I said, "Look, watch this." I got on the floor and told him to sit on my back while I did a quick hundred. To my amazement he did, but he fell off. As I went to help him up, the screws rushed in. They thought I'd hit him! It was so bloody funny. Then Frank showed me his press-ups. He managed about five, which for an old man is great. He put all this in a wicked book he did called *Longford Diaries*.

He was a brilliant old fella and I really liked him a lot, although we did have some heated arguments about Brady and Hindley, as my thoughts were anti and always will be. A lovely man. He's another one I'll not be having a pint with, but he remains in my heart - respect.

My prison records date from 1974 to 2008 (I was inside 1969, 1970 and 1971 for short spells - a shit and shave as they call it):

Risley: Chinned about five screws; attacked a good ten nonces; attempted a roof protest; got wrapped up in the barbed wire; cut a grass.

Walton: Took the roof off; smashed up the block; chinned the Governor; shit-up on a couple of screws; attempted escape; half a dozen fights with cons.

Armley: Attacked the riot mob; took off a cell door; a shit-up; assaulted a governor and screw.

Full Sutton: Took a probation officer hostage; attacked six screws; attacked the riot mob; assaulted several governors; set fire to a cell with a grass in it; half a dozen fights with cons; smashed TV sets.

Durham: Chinned two screws; kept in specially constructed cage.

Gartree: Chinned four screws; alleged stabbing; alleged scolding of a nonce; smashed up four cells.

Long Lartin: Attacked five screws in one day; chinned nine screws.

Whitemoor: Hunger strike; attacked riot mob; shit-up.

Lincoln: Chinned Deputy Governor; assaulted two screws; shit-up.

Leicester: Got on roof; took cell door off; two assaults on screws.

Woodhill: Took library screw hostage; smashed up special unit in stand-off riot.

Highdown: Chinned Governor; three assaults on screws.

Bullingdon: Took solicitor hostage; smashed up cell.

Bristol: Assaulted Governor; shit-up.

Albany: Smashed block up; assaulted two cons; chinned one screw.

Camp Hill: Attacked four screws; hunger strike.

Parkhurst: Certified insane - liquid cosh (drug control); stabbed con; assaulted five screws; chinned two screws; cut one screw; stabbed-up myself multiple times; several fights with cons; smashed up wing; got on roof; alleged arson to workshop.

Winchester: Got on roof; smashed up block; two assaults on screws; one assault on con.

Hull: Took Governor hostage; got on roof; took teacher hostage; cut a con; three assaults on screws; two shit-ups on Governor; attempted escape; once put in restraint and ankle straps and moved out in wheelchair; liquid cosh.

Wakefield: First con in Britain to be pepper sprayed; attacked riot mob; smashed up three cells.

Norwich: Shit-up.

Strangeways: Assaulted two screws.

Oxford: Chinned a screw.

Ashworth: Cut a lunatic; Asylum; attacked four screws.

Rampton: Attempted strangulation of a lunatic (paedophile); attacked four screws; liquid cosh.

Broadmoor: Three roof protests; attempted strangulation of a nonce; attacked three screws; attacked four lunatics; attempted escape; hunger strike; liquid cosh; smashed up lots of cells.

Winson Green: Attacked four cons; stole Michael Samms' leg; took doctor hostage; attacked riot mob; smashed up three cells.

Belmarsh: Attacked two cons; took three hostages (Iraqis); assaulted Governor; smashed up cell.

Scrubs: Smashed up seg block; attacked riot mob; assaulted two screws; attacked Governor.

Pentonville: Shit-up; smashed up cell; assaulted two screws.

Do you know, this is only half of what I did? It's not even counting my disciplinary charges or verbal threats and abuse or bad behaviour. Fuck me, I really was a nasty bastard. How I've changed. It's now seven years since I was in any serious trouble. I've actually learnt the hard way. I'm just not the same man nowadays. I'm now anti-violence and anti-crime. This record is my past, thanks. Fuck, it makes frightening reading and it's only a small summary of my past behaviour. Now you know me better. Maybe you now hate me or you believe I should die inside, but bear in mind that I have paid the price. I have been punished severely. People do change. I'm the proof of it. I could actually help a lot of youngsters stay out of jail.

I will never glamorise crime or violence. One thing's for sure - my body is now paying the price for my violent life. I'm a walking scar and the arthritis is kicking in. My eyes are going. My mind wanders. I feel shell-shocked. I suffer with post-traumatic stress disorder. I'm the old ghost …

Did I ever tell you about the time I carved a gun out of a bar of carbolic soap and then spread black boot polish over it? I stuck it in a work screw's face and said, "Give me your fucking keys now, you cunt!" Fuck me, he nearly had a heart attack. The governor wouldn't accept that it was only a prank, so that cost me three months in chokey with no canteen and no bed. They just can't take a joke these people! Hey, it did look like a real gun though. You see, in jail you have time to think, time to pass. You can do anything if you're determined; well, anything within reason.

In one jail I was in, which I'll not name for obvious reasons, I made a kite. Yeah, a fucking silly kite. I got hundreds and hundreds of yards of cotton and flew it over the wall from my cell window. Why? Use your head! Let's just say I never went without for a good brew. It's easy if you're 100% determined, but you have to believe in yourself and have contacts outside. Nowadays they smuggle in mobiles. Every week in jail there are hundreds found and confiscated, especially in the low cat. jails. Times change. How nice it must be to call your girl up, in private, and have an hour or two's dirty talk. Why not? In one jail I was in the lads were passing around a blow-up doll with a real fanny hole. It cost 3oz of baccy a night. You'd be amazed at who was shagging that doll. It's more of who never shagged it! Okay, I had a go. I put a load of margarine in the hole and went for it. Fuck me, I never kissed it! Then rock band Procol Harum came on the radio with 'Whiter Shade of Pale', so we had a slow dance. Then I bent her over the bed and did her doggy style. Sure it's mad, but that's how jail is - mad! You can't get through it without being mad. Luckily I covered up the door spyhole, or I'd have ended up in the padded cell! The screw ended up knocking on the door at 2 a.m.

He shouted, "Take down the cover so I can see you, Bronson."

I shouted back, "I'm having a shit!"

He yelled, "What, since 9 p.m.?"

"Fuck off!" I shouted as I cuddled up to the doll.

"You're nicked, Bronson."

What's new! The next night some other hot-blooded stag had a go. Now I'm not making this up, but in one jail they had a sheep, a fucking blow-up sheep ... and no, I never!

There's a whisper here that some have blow-up dolls with cocks on. Now that don't amaze me with all these filthy nonces, so it's probably true. It's fucking loonyology, total insanity gone mad!

I've only ever had one fair fight with a screw in 33 years and that was in the seg block in Wandsworth back in 1976 - or was it '75? One of them years. He was a Geordie screw; a big lump, in his early thirties. He loved a drink and a fight. What Geordie don't?

Anyway, one thing led to another and a confrontation broke out. He took off his keys and ran into my cell. That was it. A real fight began, toe to toe. Crack, bang, wallop! It was a good fight. That's how it should be sorted, not ten onto one. Men don't need ten behind him. So Geordie got my respect. Even though some of his mates ran in to break it up just as I was getting the better of him, it was a proper scrap that we both wanted. It cleared the air.

You gotta understand that men are born to fight. In my walk of life you can't but fight. Prisons are a volcano of violence just waiting to erupt. It don't take a lot to work out why: we are men; frustrated; anxious; fed up; bored. We are sick of it all. Why can't the system wake up? Let us have a good old-fashioned fuck every once in a while; a bit of pussy juice. Let us do what we are put on the planet for. That's unless a guy is satisfied wasting his life away. I'm not. That becomes boring.

Hey, I should have been a psychologist! My way would clear up all prison violence. I would make our prisons safer places - with common sense! Work the cons hard, with lots of discipline, but every so often let the girls in to bring in some loving. Sweet and tender loving works! Wake up you prison officials. My way would stop all the pain!

SWEET AND TENDER LOVING
Games of the mind ... a tortured soul
Loveless and empty
A body full of pain
No release
No smells
No sweet smells. Nothing but doom
Sweet and tender loving
Roll it my way
I'll have some of that in a slice of bread
Toasted and hot and juicy
Without love there is no hope, no life, no dreams
It's a fucking pit of despair
A cage of snakes
Ripping out your lungs
Squeezing your strength
A dead man breathing
A fucking pile of shit
Dehumanised ... Brutally destroyed
Bloodless ... All dried up
A faceless, boneless person
A number for a name
Close the coffin lid and fuck off!

Over the years I've had some memorable visits from all walks of life: family, biz and pleasure. I've even had a fuck several times. Difficult but it's possible.

Kelly Anne was one. We got it on in Hull and Albany Jail. She was one crazy bitch but a good visitor. At Albany I was forever in the seg block and all my visits were in a room meant for solicitors' visits. Screws used to sit outside the door and it also had CCTV, so you would think it impossible to have a shag. Yeh, so would I. Plus we were supposed to sit at either side of

48

the table. This was the rules. This was the late 1980s. This is what happened.

I arrived at the visit with an escort of eight screws, as I was on a seriously heavy unlock these days as my world was a crazy journey. I was so unpredictable. I sat down at the table waiting for Kelly Anne to come in. In she walked with a tray of orange juice and chocolates. She had a wicked smile. She was up to no good. I always knew when she was being naughty. Then she undid her coat. Fuck me, she had fuck all on and it was winking at me. What she'd done was slid into the Ladies, taken her clothes off and stuffed them in her pockets! I couldn't believe it. I really couldn't.

I had a raging hard-on and said, "Right, let's do it."

She came around my side of the table and sat on me. It slipped right up her. I just could not fucking believe it. We was fucking. Her coat was still on, so all the screws could see was her sitting on my lap. It was mental.

One screw came in and said, "Come on, Charlie, that's not allowed."

What could I do? What would anybody do?

I said, "Look boss, she's a bit upset. Give it five minutes."

And it worked!

He said, "Five minutes or you'll get me in trouble."

As she bobbed up and down there were screws looking in. It was fucking brilliant. Hot, wet, sticky and bloody lovely. But, as usual, Kelly can't behave. She just goes over the top.

"It's supposed to be a secret fuck," I whispered. "Slow down, you're putting it bang on me there."

But she kept bouncing up and down and making the noise that's only ever used when you're alone.

The screws came back in. "Come on, Charlie, you'll have to let her sit on her side of the table."

As he spoke I shot my load right in her. The screw must have known as I was truly hazy.

"Yeh, okay boss, no problem."

Kelly got off and went to the toilet to clean up, but most of it was all over me. My jeans were drenched in pussy juice and come. When she came back we just started laughing. It did me the world of good. All my stress and anxiety had vanished. I felt human again. It was brilliant.

After I ate some chocs and drank some orange Kelly then gave me a good old-fashioned wank under the table. I swear the screws could see. There's no way they couldn't but see. She wasn't playing chess under the table. Her body was shaking as she wanked me off. It was so funny. A bit strange, but again I shot my load. Most went on the floor, but she must have got some on her hand as she licked it off. Kelly Anne was to me sex on legs. What a visit that was - very memorable.

Another time was in Hull Jail. Looking back I guess she's an exhibitionist. She loved getting men at it. It's her scene but it all turned nasty with Kelly. It's all in my other books so I won't bother going into it again. I've no real bad feelings on the matter, I just move on in life, bury the hatchet so to speak. But marks out of 10 for sex with Kelly would be 10½. It was brilliant. She was bloody crazy and that's how I like my women: a bit mental, dangerous, unpredictable. She took a gamble and it paid off. It could've turned nasty, but it truly was a brilliant fuck to remember. That shag in Albany must go down in history.

She must've been so up for it, as it just slipped in. It was the hottest fanny on the planet. It's the danger that does that to a woman: the dare, the gamble. She had planned it down to the split second - all the way from Luton to the Isle of Wight. She was gagging for it. She wanted to give me something to behave for. It was her way of saying, "Be good, behave and get out fast and you can have a lot more of this. It's waiting for you. Come home."

But life don't ever work out like that. I don't believe in fairy tales. Never have done. Life is reality. Kelly Anne knew it too. She had other plans for me. Plans that I knew fuck all about but I was sure to be dragged into them, and I was. The rest is history.

The moral to the story is: the cat that gets the cream is not always a happy cat. Some cats are greedy, selfish fuckers! I also had a blow job in Parkhurst Visiting Room. I'll not say who by. My reason for that is simple: I don't wish to. Some women don't deserve to be exposed; in fact most don't. Most to me are ladies I respect.

This blow job was not planned. It just started off as a kiss and a bit of fondling. A screw did come over and say, "Cool it, Charlie", and that was that. The visiting room was quite full, so there was a lot of noise and I just enjoyed the company. For a laugh I pulled out my dick under the table and grabbed her hand and put it on it. She laughed and gave it a few pulls. Then she disappeared under the table. I was having a fucking blow job in the middle of the visiting room! I could not believe it. Remember, it's months and months with no sex. So it don't take long to come, and come I did. I couldn't stop coming. Another memorable visit. But, believe me, these sorts of visits are very few and far between. It's why you can never forget them.

Talking of pussies, the nicest pussy I can remember was Jan Lamb's, and I say this with the utmost respect as she's a proper lovely lady, solid. Anyway, it's no secret that she's proud to have had me in the sack. I'm still in touch with Jan all these years later. We practically fucked ourselves silly. She done things with my cock I never thought possible. There's shagging and there's shagging. This was SHAGGINGGGGG. Fuck me, my dick was red raw. We never stopped. If we'd videoed it, it would've sold a million copies overnight. People just don't understand, but when a man's gone without pussy for so long it just takes him over. Jan Lamb was a very lucky lady meeting me. Someone had to help me back to sanity and it was Jan. Hey, make no mistake about it, she's a lovely sort and a respected woman amongst my firm, my circle, my special haunts, my world. The Krays loved Jan as well. Both respected her. But my memories of her are special. We'd never laughed so much in our lives - so much were crying: a pool of sweat and tears. That's how sex should be: raw and mad. When a bloke shoots his load he's gotta let it fly: hit the fucking ceiling, shoot it in the face, over the tits, then rub it in and start all over again. Fuck till you drop. With Jan we loved it doggie style, growling and barking. It's fucking fantastic. I've got a hard-on now just thinking about it.

Well, I love a good woman and when that woman becomes a part of my journey she becomes 'special'. So when we fuck, we fuck with our souls, we enter the unknown. It's fucking wicked, beautiful. Jan had those special piss flaps that sort of wrap around your cock like a foreskin. Do you know what I mean? Maybe you've not all seen them. Let me explain if I can. The flaps sort of feel like bits of liver - nice. Anyway, she had lovely flaps that have stayed in my memory. I study things like that. I'm a bit of a studier on the quiet; an analyst. I like to see how the human body works. There's nothing quite like our body. It's unique in every sense of the word. So look after it. It's yours. Don't let nobody ever abuse it. Love yourselves. Love your body. Reach in and love it too. My cock is still erect. I'm ready to rumble. I'll leave it at that.

Who remembers their first fuck? Come on, you must do. That first time you felt that hot, wet, sticky pussy and you thought: fuck me, does it bite? Was that first time scary or what? That first time she grabbed your cock and slipped it in the honeypot. We all remember it. Awesome. It don't make no difference if you reach a low, you always remember it. That first-love fling when your whole world was lit up with rainbows. Dreams come true. You just cannot get enough of it. No sooner had you shot your load, you was ready again. You fucked till your dick was red raw from hour after hour of grinding away. Who says dreams don't come true?

The teenage years was just one long fuck. I had my share of pussy but my greatest memory was with a half-caste chick. She will remain nameless as it's not my thing to embarrass women - unless, of course, they're evil bitches - plus by now she would be a granny.

I met her at a party and we just hit it off. I was 17 and she was 24. She had a flat she shared with her mate, who I actually knew. She worked at a factory that I once robbed. Anyway, something mental happened that night that's never happened before to me. I think it was a one-off, a miracle. Call it what you will, but it was mental; it just happened.

We were naked in the bedroom and I was giving her some serious fucking doggy style, really banging away big time. My balls were slamming into her like the birch and we was doing it in front of a mirror so we was both looking at each other. I shot my load and something weird happened - my dick stayed rock hard, it never went limp. It was mental. I kept pumping away and thought no more of it till I shot my second load. I still never went limp. This time I actually pulled out just to check. I was rock hard and all my come was trickling out of her. It blew me away. It didn't make any sense. Even she said, "Don't you ever stop?" That night was weird. I came five times before I went limp. My dick was really sore for days after. I've never forgot it. I never will. Would you? I bet she hasn't either!

There's no explanation for it. It's spooky, but we've all been there as teenagers. Was it good or was it good? Come on, how good was it? It was brilliant: the music, the style, the parties, the speed of living. We was always fast living, but the pussy was something else.

Why is it that black girls are so sexy and hot? Can a black girl move, or can she move? Have you ever seen them move on the dance floor? Come on, you must've done! The way they move that arse is lovely! They're just sex on legs. You can't take it from them. They're just oozing with sex - and they know it! I wouldn't mind dying of a massive heart attack in bed with a beautiful black girl, say about 20 years old. What a way to call it a day! What a way to leave the planet! The ultimate dream! Here I go again. My dream would probably end with a Colt-45 in my mouth and my brains all over the pillow. She would probably be an escaped lunatic, a right psycho, crazed bitch. Come on, we all love a sexy hot bird, don't we? You can shag your wife or husband for 40 years, but you can't tell me you don't dream of a sexy young bird. Yeh, you know it too. We all know it. That tight little hot, sticky, sweet-smelling pussy. Come on, you know it's your dream. Or, for your old lady, I bet she's sick of your shrivelled-up dick with your baggy bollocks all wrinkled and heavy and your bad breath or your bald patch or beer belly. She wants a good stiff cock with tight balls and a nice firm arse to grab hold of. And if she don't then she's not normal. It's everyone's fantasy. It's why so many mid-life crises happen. They all want that last big fuck to prove they haven't lost it. There's nothing wrong with it - just don't get caught! Live out your dream and enjoy it. When I hit out, every day will be a dream come true for me. Believe it! I'm sure you do.

Love will be the making of me! But am I gonna have a sore dick? Or am I? I can't fucking wait. I really can't. Whose gonna love me to death? Who's gonna shag me to death? Whose gonna kill me with love? I fucking can't wait to die! Just kill me slowly. Torture me with kisses and tongues! Smother me in pussy. Yahoooooooooo! Yippeeeeeeeeeeeee! It's gonna be soooper-dooooooperrrrrr.

LOVE IS ...

Love is robbing a bank and getting clean away
Love is finding a wallet of £50 notes
Love is waking up with a beautiful pussy in your face
Love is bumping into a rat who grassed you up years ago
Love is a giant plate of apple pie and cream
Love is driving a roller in the rain
Love is riding a Harley on a summer's day

Love is walking out of prison
Love is leaving school for the last time
Love is seeing your mother smile
Love is finding a lost treasure
Love is swimming with a dolphin
Love is on top of the world
Love is health and fitness
Love is being loved
Love is a beautiful vision of loveliness
Love is art
Love is poetry
Love is helping a child to win in life
Love is being respected
Love is being wanted
Love is buying an old car and doing it up
Love is your fist shotgun and sawing the barrel down
Love is having a dog
Love is nice clothes
Life is love and love is life!

Everything is love if you want it to be! There's nothing that can't be loved. We all love something, or somebody. What's your greatest love? If it's me, you're fucking mental!

Hey, I loved that Tina Turner in her heyday. What a lovely arse she had. And what about Suzi Quatro in her leather trousers?! Or Joan Collins in *The Stud*? There's been some hot chicks over the years. She's a handful that Dolly Parton. It's a wonder she don't lose her balance. What a lovely singer though.

Love is a box of Dairy Milk chocolates and a good video and someone to share it with. That's what love is all about: being free to do it all. I loved it when Robert Stroud found some love with his birds. For those who don't know of Robert Stroud, well he was 'The Birdman of Alcatraz', You may've seen the film starring Burt Lancaster, who played Stroud. It was brilliant. Let me tell you the story. He killed and robbed a bar worker back in 1909. He started his sentence on McNeil Island in Washington State Penitentiary. There he turned into a vicious and violent inmate, stabbing and cutting anybody who crossed his path. He built up a serious reputation as a prison activist, so they sent him to one of the toughest penitentiaries in America at that time: Leavenworth in Kansas City. Make no mistake about it, Leavenworth was a tough old jail, built and designed to break a man down slowly. The screws were a hard bunch and kept on top of the cons by sheer brute force. Stroud made a tool and stabbed a screw to death in the mess hall, witnessed by 1,000 convicts and 100 guards. He'd just dug his own hole. Mysteriously he was reprieved and committed to a life sentence. They built a cage for him in Leavenworth where he remained in solitary for almost 30 years, and that's where he became the birdman. It all began the day he found an injured bird out on the exercise yard. He put it in his pocket, smuggled it back to his cell and treated it. The prison governor heard all about this kind act and the system allowed him his own birds, mostly canaries. And the rest is history! He bred them, wrote books on them and became a bird expert!

Now get this. It may shock you. The Birdman was moved to Alcatraz in 1942, where he was put straight into solitary and denied his birds. For the next six years he remained in Alcatraz seg block alone - a purely vindictive move. For 30 years he'd kept sane and made some good out of all the bad. He'd become a living legend in US prison history. Sure he killed a screw, but 30 years in the hole was not long enough for him and they wanted more. Bear in mind that he's now knocking on in age. After six years in the Alcatraz hole they then moved him to the hospital wing, where he spent the next 11 years. All believed he would die there, and no doubt he believed that too. Then in 1959 he left Alcatraz a very old man to go to Springfield Medical Centre in Missouri. He survived till 21 November 1963, dying at the ripe old age of 73. He'd spent 54 years in prison. For me, I think it's a tragic story. But it's one of many from that era. It's why they made so many films of these legends. So next time you hear about 'The Birdman of Alcatraz' you can say, "Yeh, he was the Birdman but he had no birds in Alcatraz." Really it should have been 'The Birdman of Leavenworth'. Well, now you know the story. This is one birdman who never flew the nest. He actually died the day the screw died.

Let's be honest with ourselves, those manic sex-romping years are long gone (for us oldies). Imagine even trying to live it now! You couldn't last a week. You'd burn out in no time. Your dick would get you down. Fannies dry up. Tits sag. Teeth fall out.

How the fuck do people stay married for 40, 50, even 60 years? How do they do it? Is it love or is it more a weakness? Nag, nag, nag. It's like a prison. It's not a real life is it? Where have you been? What time is this? Who do you think you are? Do the garden. Clean the car. Don't wear that. Do this. Do that. Gimme all your money. Does my bum look big in this? Honey, your arse looks like a hippo. Yap, yap, yap. Bunny, bunny, bunny. Nag, nag, nag. Pass the aspirin.

How does a man remain a man living like that? Is it love? What is love? I believe marriage is a form of torture! I really do. You've gotta be a nutcase to survive it! I also believe a man becomes broken, weak and manipulated. It ends up like a mother/son relationship. You become the boy all over again. That sweet, hot, wet, juicy pussy actually becomes your soul; a fucking big black tunnel of darkness. Crazy eh? Loonyology at its best.

Enjoy the teenage years, coz that era soon flies by. No sooner are you shooting your load than you're shitting in a colostomy bag! Hey, don't old folk smell? Stale piss, BO, smelly feet, bad breath and they fart a lot. They creak when they move, their hair's white and their skin's flaky and flabby and their eyesight's not good. The pussy is like a dried-up fig and the dick shrivels to a maggot. Fuck me, it's horrible! And then there's some nasty nurse giving you a slap to behave and if you're extra unlucky you end up with a Dr Shipman! How mad is that for an ending?

I'll say now to all you old folk: don't die a shell; if you're gonna go, then go out in style. Go get a nice hot, wet, pussy and pay her to bring a dream ending. Die with your heart and dick pumping some love. Or if you're an old woman, go get a young stud. Have one final orgasm of life. Scream the house down. Spend all your savings. Go out happy. Fuck the lumbago away. Shag the arthritis away. Enjoy the dream all over again. At the very worst you can always act it or die with a '69' - a sweet, hot pussy in your face or a big stiff cock in your mouth. Housey-housey - bingo!

Fucking sex toys - do me a favour. I am the sex toy and this is how it is with us birdmen. We are starved of sex, hungry like a loon, and then we fly out and become greedy. What do you expect? We are hungry men, desperate for a fuck, and the ladies love us. It's true. Line me up with a dozen normal men and I guarantee that if we were all bollock naked with hard-ons the ladies will choose me. Even if some are in their thirties they'll still choose me. Why? It's simple. The ladies love a bit of rough and I'm the roughest diamond you'll ever get hold of. The only problem is, you could never keep me. I'm unkeepable. I soon get bored, fed up, and need some action, some excitement. Let me explain. If I was on a seaside pier and a big fish was swimming below - let's say a shark or a whale - and hundreds of people were looking, I'd dive in, just to say I did it. Now that's a rare gift. If the fish don't eat me then it's a story; historic; something to be remembered for.

There was one black lunatic in Broadmoor who had a cock on him like a hosepipe and he loved showing it off too. He liked to walk down the corridor with it hanging out of his dressing gown. It was fucking gigantic - terrifying. It almost touched his knees. It swung like a giant pendulum and he always had that sick smirk and those beady eyes saying: cop a load of this. He got on my nerves in the end, so I hit him with the fire extinguisher. Flash bastard. I hate flash cunts. A laugh's a laugh, but every day he did that. Well, it soon stopped after I cracked him. Fucking lunatic.

Blimey, I've some breaking news: I've just farted. I've gassed my cell out!

Talking of farts, that's what Fielding done when I cut him down the boat in Wandsworth in '77. Fucking rat. He fucked my escape up. I was doing well on it. I had six bricks out of the back of my cell wall. They were crumbling out and that prick grassed me. That cost me 180 days' remission with 56 days' solitary: no bed, no canteen and a fucking good kicking to go with it. That's how it was in them days. It's all part and parcel of life inside. Grasses have been around since day one. These weak, gutless Jesus people. Fielding actually believed he'd got away with it. He thought I didn't know, but the daft bastard made one mistake. I clocked him at the spyhole in my door. My spyhole had a pinhole in it through which I could see light. I happened to notice no light so I rushed to the door and saw him walking away. Five minutes later the riot mob came rushing down the landing and my door crashed in. I was bang to rights: a fucking big hole in my wall, 20 feet of sheet-knotted rope, a steel chair bent as a grappling hook, and I had £100 and a black coat.

My feet never touched the floor all the way to the chokey block and I bounced off some walls on the way there. Fielding done me up like a kipper. It was three months later I hid behind a cell door and cut the rat from his left eye to his jawline: 'Stripe'. So every time he looks in a mirror he will be reminded that he's a filthy grass. That's 31 years ago but he's still the grass. I've always said a grass is born a grass. You don't wake up one morning and say, "Oh, I think I'll be a grass today". It don't happen like that. You're always a grass. Some may hold it back in the good times, but it always slips out. Some are that stupid they even grass themselves up. How mental is that?

I'll always remember Fielding's face the second he knew it was bang on him: the 'Oh God please help me' look. Well, he will tell you himself that there is no God's help in hell. That prick destroyed a brilliant escape plot. In the war he would have been shot as a traitor. You may laugh and say that's a bit extreme. Well, it is extreme, as my freedom was stolen from me.

I remember once in Wandsworth block when it used to be down on H1. Our exercise yard used to be at the back of the laundry. Four screws used to take me on my own and stand in a circle whilst I walked round. One day a lorry come up. Bear in mind that there's a fence and a wall. A security screw and a dog handler opened the gate in the fence. That was it for me. I made a run for the lorry. I only had seconds, but it was worth a try. I jumped on the bonnet of the lorry, and as I went to scale up it a screw was on my legs. All hell broke out. I kicked, punched and nutted for my life. All four were on me with sticks, and even the other two joined in with the dog. By the time I got back to my cell my clothes were drenched in blood. My head had swelled up like a melon! The things we do to go home! I was very spontaneous in them days. I just acted on impulse.

That's how it was with me. If the gate of opportunity arises, then jump at it. Fuck the consequences, coz if you don't act on it you may live to regret it. It's like walking down a street and you see a security van pull up outside a bank and a hatch opens and two bags of loot are slung out. There's just you, one guard and two bags of loot. What do you do?

Years ago I'd have chinned the guard and done a runner with the two bags. I'd have been a mug not to! Now I've no need to do that, but then I wouldn't have hesitated. It's a golden opportunity that 99% of guys only dream of taking. They dream their boring lives away. Me, I'm what you call an opportunist. I'm just born lucky or unlucky, whatever side of the wall I'm on.

It's a prisoner's duty to escape isn't it? I'm not so sure nowadays. Maybe it's just old age and the thought of forever being on the run. I guess I prefer to 'walk out' the right way, simply as my crime days are well over.

Believe me now, you can't relate to my world. It's fucking crazy, inhabited by crazy people, and I love 'em all. I've grown up with loonyology. It's in my blood, in my brain. I eat it, shit it, sleep it and I'm in control of it. Nothing or nobody can ever drive me over the edge again. I'm now the driver on this journey. You have to trust me. So put your tongue into my mouth in the dark. Will I or won't I? Trust me ...

Right now my last seven years have been closed visits. I've not had a hug for over seven years. I actually feel dehumanised. I probably am. I no longer feel human. I feel different not the same. Bear in mind that I'm forever in isolated conditions. Hey, people shout about human rights, well let me tell you something: human fucking rights don't exist for Bronson. I'll tell you now. I don't have animal rights let alone human rights. It's a fact.

I'm a born poet but yet to be discovered. I'm a philosopher but silent within. The late Lord Longford told me I'm a genius. How? Why? Don't ask me. I don't know. I'm an artist. I'm an author. Me. So how the hell does my label stick to me like shit to a blanket? Somebody tell me before the hearse arrives. Tell me before my bones crumble. For God's sake fucking put me out of my misery.

WALKING ALONG THE EDGE

A tightrope
No net
No harness
Just you and the drop
The bottomless hole
Black as the night
No stars, no moon
Only shadows
Have you ever been there
Well?! Have you?
Have you felt that sweat drip down your spine
The stinging of the eyes
The tremble of the lips
That's looking at hell
You can smell it
You can taste it
It's in your veins
The big rush
Like a volcano in your heart
Just waiting

Throbbing
Pulsating
Bubbling away
Have you been there?
Come on … tell me
If you're afraid to say then whisper
You're safe with me
Trust me
I'm one guy you can trust
I know how it is
I've lived on the edge all my life
A fingertip job
Hanging on, holding on for the hell of it
Laughing all the fucking way
I've laughed so hard I've shit myself
It's crazy
Everything is so fucked up
It's unreal
A giant circus
Forever on the road
I can't get off
Of course I tried
Many times
It don't work
It's in your blood
You are what you are
Accept it
The sooner you accept yourself
The sooner you laugh
Tears turn to laughter
Fear turns to pleasure
Pain becomes a thrill
Join the circus
The Bronson Loonyology Tour
Grab a midget
And throw him as far as you can
Yippeeeeeeeee!
Look at the little fucker fly
Look at the bearded lady
The lizard man
The two-headed dog
We love 'em all
I mean them all
Monsters in human form

Men and women from the unknown
We loved the Elephant Man
We love an ugly bastard
Don't you?
Political correctness
Kiss my arse
You fucking wimps
Keep away from the tents
It's not for wankers
Seeing is believing
Believe or fuck off
Faith and hope and ugliness
Bring it on
Wicked
Pukka
Magical
It's my old woman all over again
The Queen of Tarts
The local bike
Don't forget to pay the bitch
No freebies
And wipe your shoes before you go in
And don't wipe your dick on my towel
Why?
Cos I'll rip your head off
That's why
So what's it gonna be, buddy?
My way or your way
Sheep or lion
Butterfly or maggot?
Make up your mind, you sad bastard
It's your life
Your journey
Your crash
It's not if ... it's when
But you're gonna crash
We all crash in the end
One way or the other
Fast or slow
It don't make no odds
Your time will come
Until it does
Go kick some butt
Kick it black and blue

CHARLES BRONSON

Keep on kicking till you die
Die kicking
Kick it till the light goes out
Smash your way out of this ugly world
Don't crawl out
OKAY?!

CHAPTER 5
WELCOME ABOARD THE DUNGEON EXPRESS

Imagine waking up every morning with a dream and 30 years later you're still dreaming the same shit. Believe me it dies. You have to survive on reality, not dreams, otherwise you go mad. The dream is today, now, here. It's all about survival. Lifers are chess pieces. You only move when they decide to move you. You're just a piece of the same. I learnt this years ago. Their dreams are different. You either dream along with them, do it for real, or pretend, or you don't move on. Fuck their dream or anyone else's dream, that's what I say. That's what I do. We all gotta do what we gotta do. Get on with it.

Now I'm gonna test my memory. My entire track record: sentences; charges; transfers! This will blow your socks off! As the moves alone will make you dizzy, imagine how I felt. I'm the only con that hit three jails in one day - yes, three! So work that fucker out ... I'm still trying to!

1965: Shoplifting: 3 months' detention at Beechwood Detention Centre, Luton
1968: Criminal damage: Remanded to Risley Jail for 4 months; 2 years' probation
1969: Driving offences: Remanded to Risley Jail for 5 months; banned for life. Bundles of fines, etc. (stolen lorry and a serious smash)
1970: Smash and grab: 3 months at Werrington House Detention Centre
1970: Criminal damage and ABH, Fines: Risley Jail for 4 months plus probation
1972: Stolen goods, Fines: 2 months' remand at Risley Jail
1974: Armed robbery, GBH, possession of firearms : Sentenced to 7 years - the journey begins:
1974: Risley
1974: Walton
1974: Hull
1974: Armley
1975: Wakefield
1975: Strangeways
1975: Armley
1975: Wandsworth
1976: Walton

1976: Winson Green
1976: Scrubs
1976: Wandsworth
1976: Albany
1976: Parkhurst
1977: Wandsworth
1977: Scrubs
1977: Pentonville
1977: Winson Green
1977: Wandsworth
1978: Parkhurst
1978: Camphill
1978: Winchester
1978: Parkhurst

It was whilst at Parkhurst in 1978 that I was certified insane and sent to the asylums. I must add that all these moves from 1974 to 1978 were all dungeon to dungeon, block to block, solitary to solitary. My life was like a beach ball being kicked around all the dungeons. I was brutalised black and blue and forever in body belts and ankle straps, and was even injected with tranquillisers. I was, in fact, Britain's No. 1 Prison Activist! My reputation followed me! Was I Insane? Let's just say, if I wasn't, I soon fucking would be!

Bear in mind that this was the 1970s, the decade of madness. I just had this thing about head shrinks. Basically I never fucking liked them. I still don't, but nowadays I can sit down and discuss things. In them days there was fuck all to discuss; I just didn't trust or like them and my opinion of them was spot on. They eventually 'nutted me off'. I see psychiatrists and psychologists as 'nutters', 'nosey fuckers', delving into the past, making excuses for people's behaviour, blaming mummy and daddy. Here, take this pill, bend over and let me inject you with 100ml of psychotropic tranquillisers.

Well I say fuck off; get the fuck out of my face, my life. Don't you dare put the blame on my parents. I'm a man, 240 pounds of prime beef, and my past, my life, my journey are mine. I don't cry about fuck all. In fact I'm a lucky old git coz I'm still alive.

There was one psychiatrist in Risley that really woke me up to how 'false' they really are. This was back in 1969. Risley Remand Jail was a brutal place with a lot of suicides. It was in fact a hellhole. It may have changed over the years, but has it? Anyway, this Scottish psychiatrist said to me in his office, with six screws on standby (yeh, that's how brave this fat cunt was - he had to have six burly screws in the office to see me; I was 17 years old and probably 11 stone soaking wet), and I quote: "You, sonny, want to behave yourself or you're heading for a bloody good kicking and a dose of the liquid cosh." Well, to say I was shocked is an understatement. I was speechless. Here was a top prison psychiatrist telling me I'd get a good kicking. Now that just about sums it up for me. Okay, sure, they're not all like that are they? Well, I woke up that day in that office and saw it as a war, nothing less, nothing more. They were out to control me and crush me. I was out to fuck up their system. I just don't like bully boys, and that's all it ever was: a show of force. Outside in the free world they're faceless people. In my book they would be sitting in the corner afraid to speak up. In my corner it's rock 'n' roll.

Nowadays I can accept a lot more. In fact I can laugh it off. I don't dwell on it so much, as they know, and they know I know. We all know it's a big fucking game.

1978: Rampton Asylum
1979: Broadmoor Asylum
1984: Ashworth Asylum

Seven years in the Cuckoo House. They finally certified me sane, but the truth is they couldn't afford me. I was dubbed Britain's most expensive lunatic! They lost three roofs, and it would've been four if they hadn't returned me back to sanity. Also, take note that it's now 1984. Ten years had passed by, but my original sentence was only seven years! Unfortunately on my journey I picked up some more charges, resulting in more years being added on, but that's showbiz for you. So here we go again. Strap in tight for the ride of your life.

1984: Risley
1984: Strangeways
1985: Walton
1985: Durham
1985: Armley
1985: Albany
1985: Scrubs
1985: Wandsworth
1985: Parkhurst
1985: Scrubs
1986: Parkhurst
1986: Winchester
1986: Norwich
1986: Winchester
1986: Scrubs
1986: Wandsworth
1986: Albany
1986: Parkhurst

1986: Wandsworth
1987: Gartree
1987: Leicester
1987: Lincoln
1987: Gartree

Then, on 30 October 1987, I walked free. I must add all these moves were 99% dungeon to dungeon again. My whole life was solitary and no prison governors wanted me in their jails. I wonder why? Freedom lasted only 69 days, as I was arrested on an armed blag on James Tobin's jewellers shop in Wellington Street, Luton. I actually got away, and no jewellery was recovered except for one ring. It was a week later that I was arrested, and then the madness took off again. Here we go.

1988: Leicester (on remand); Luton Crown Court sentence of seven years:
1988: Brixton
1988: Leicester
1988: Brixton
1988: Wandsworth
1988: Durham
1988: Wandsworth
1988: Full Sutton
1988: Durham
1988: Armley
1988: Strangeways
1988: Armley
1989: Full Sutton
1989: Long Lartin
1989: Bristol
1989: Winson Green
1989: Winchester
1989: Wandsworth
1989: Albany
1989: Parkhurst
1989: Albany
1989: Gartree
1989: Durham
1989: Parkhurst
1990: Durham
1990: Parkhurst
1990: Frankland
1990: Durham
1990: Albany
1990: Parkhurst

1990: Frankland
1990: Full Sutton
1990: Wandsworth
1990: Full Sutton
1991: Parkhurst
1991: Wandsworth
1991: Albany
1991: Leicester
1991: Lincoln
1991: Hull
1992: Lincoln
1992: Parkhurst
1992: Scrubs
1992: Wandsworth
1992: Parkhurst
1992: Wandsworth
1992: Strangeways
1992: Scrubs
1992: Parkhurst
1992: Scrubs

On 14 November 1992, I was released from the Scrubs for a short spell of freedom before:

7 January 1993: Arrested for possession of firearms and GBH; remanded to Woodhill
20 February 1993: Luton Court: firearms charge dropped and GBH charge reduced to unlawful wounding; fined £800 and freed
27 February 1993: Charged with conspiracy to commit armed robbery on a Luton bank; firearms charges; remanded to Woodhill
August 1993: Sentenced to 8 years:

1993: Woodhill
1993: Winson Green
1993: Belmarsh
1993: Bristol
1993: Wandsworth
1993: Belmarsh
1993: Bullingdon
1993: Belmarsh
1993: Bullingdon
1993: Belmarsh
1993: Wakefield
1993: Frankland

1993: Hull
1994: Leicester
1994: Wakefield
1994: Bullingdon
1994: Leicester
1994: Wakefield
1994: Bullingdon
1994: Leicester
1994: Wakefield
1994: Strangeways
1994: Walton
1994: Winson Green
1994: Belmarsh
1994: Lincoln
1994: Scrubs
1994: Lincoln
1994: Albany
1994: Full Sutton
1994: Frankland
1994: Long Lartin
1994: Lincoln
1994: Highdown
1994: Full Sutton
1994: Lincoln
1994: Wandsworth
1995: Frankland
1995: Durham
1995: Lincoln
1995: Armley
1995: Highdown
1995: Winson Green
1995: Frankland
1995: Winson Green
1995: Full Sutton
1996: Walton
1996: Bullingdon
1996: Belmarsh
1996: Wakefield
1996: Durham
1996: Wakefield
1996: Full Sutton
1996: Belmarsh
1997: Durham
1997: Walton

1997: Full Sutton
1997: Wakefield
1997: Belmarsh
1997: Woodhill
1997: Full Sutton
1997: Woodhill
1998: Hull
1998: Whitemoor
1998: Hull
1998: Woodhill
1999: Whitemoor
1999: Woodhill
1999: Whitemoor
1999: Woodhill
2000: Full Sutton
2000: Woodhill
2000: Woodhill
2000: Belmarsh
2001: Wakefield
2001: Woodhill
2001: Whitemoor
2001: Frankland
2001: Durham
2001: Wakefield
2001: Belmarsh
2001: Wakefield
2002: Full Sutton
2002: Whitemoor
2002: Woodhill
2003: Belmarsh
2003: Wakefield
2006: Full Sutton
2006: Wakefield
2007-2008: Still here, still in the infamous cage, still in isolation!

Take note that my eight-year sentence in 1993 was expanded to a life sentence, but that over the last five years there have been fewer moves (nowadays they bury me in one hole and forget about me). Also clock that some years my moves are in double figures. I am without a doubt Britain's most moved inmate! Also 99.5% of my moves have been to solitary. What a fucking journey. What a ride. What a life. It is total loonyology. It's fucking mental. Who's driving the fucking bus? As Dave Courtney says: stop the ride, I want to get off! So my eight-year sentence became a life sentence. I guess I took one too many hostages. I've buried myself ... or have I? Never say die, never give up, for as long as the heart beats there is always hope. I've now served 14½ years on this stretch. A good 14 years of that have been in solitary and I am still the no. 1 at press-ups. Fuck it, I'm winning! I'll die winning! You know it! I wonder where my next move will be?

Let me explain what these multiple transfers are all about. They're a way of breaking up families and friends. They're designed to cut you off from the outside world, in a lot of cases causing divorces and split relationships, as families can't cope with it. How can normal people cope with such treatment? Imagine it for the family: the wife, the kids, the grandparents, etc. One day the loved one is far up north and they plan to visit him. Then he's moved to the Isle of Wight, so they plan a visit there, only to be told he's now back up north. Also half the time the Prison Service won't even tell them where you've been moved to - 'Official Secrets Act' - so they have to wait for a letter, which arrives days late. It does cause a lot of stress and anxiety for the families, but for me it is all part of the journey of life. They can move me to Mars for all I care. But they'll never smash my family, ever. They haven't done it in four decades, and they never will. My only sadness is that I've lost too many family members to death, but apart from that I say fuck 'em.

Also a lot of my moves were unnecessary and without reason; purely vindictive, solely to upset my routine. For many of these moves I would be jumped on, restrained, put in a body belt and ankle straps and carried to the van. A few times even a straitjacket was used. That's how it was: all fun and games. During 90% of the moves I didn't even see where I was going, as I was on the van floor with six burly guards on top of me. Crazy times, but all experience, all character building. I'd have it no other way.

The only thing that used to get me mad was when they returned me to jails I'd just left a week before: the insane moves. I'd arrive there and say to the governor, "You're a fucking lunatic!" Why move me out only to accept me back a week later? It just didn't make sense. It got so mad for me at times that I would forget where I was! I would awake in the early hours and struggle to think where I was. Take it from me, it's a mad, mad world when you're on the never-ending ghost train. Some call it 'The Road to Madness', coz it can and will drive you over the edge! Hey, I bet I've spent six months of my time locked up on the motorways. Maybe I should put a claim in for travelling expenses (food for thought)!

Imagine waking up every morning with a dream and 30 years later you're still dreaming the same shit. Believe me it dies. You have to survive on reality, not dreams, otherwise you go mad. The dream is today, now, here. It's all about survival. Lifers are chess pieces. You only move when they decide to move you. You're just a piece of the same. I learnt this years ago. Their dreams are different. You either dream along with them, do it for real, or pretend, or you don't move on. Fuck their dream or anyone else's dream, that's what I say. That's what I do. We all gotta do what we gotta do. Get on

68

with it.

Hey, did you know I'm a walking, talking, fucking genius? There ain't nobody in the UK with my knowledge of prisons and asylums. If there is, tell me who? I'm the man. If you were studying for a university degree in Criminology then you'd pay for my knowledge. Pay me and pass. My brain is full of facts. Go on, ask me any question and you can guarantee I'll be able to supply the answer, and no doubt there'll be a story behind it too.

Q: Who was the last woman to hang in Armley Prison?
A: Easy. It was Emily Swann, on 24 December 1903. In fact it was a double hanging that day. She hung alongside her boyfriend John Gallagher. They both killed Emily's husband. Now John Gallagher is a name I can't forget, coz it was the same name as the Jock I cut up in Hull Prison in 1975. Was he the reincarnation of Emily's lover boy? It's possible. And did you know that Emily's last words to John were: "See you in hell, babe"?

Q: Okay, big-head, who was the last man to hang in Armley Prison?
A: Fucking easy. Can't you make them any harder? Right, it was Zsiga Pankotia in1961. Trust it to be a foreigner. He was Hungarian. He swung on 29 June. It was Harry Allen who topped him and I believe it was Allen's last execution. It was definitely Pankotia's! Hey, did you know that Armley Jail was opened in 1847 and it was built for 300 convicts. Nowadays it holds 1,500 cons. Work that fucker out. It's mind blowing. You see, what people fail to realise is that the old jails were built for one con per cell. Now they ram three cons into one cell, even though the fucking cell is still the same size. It's loonyology.

Q: When was the last execution in Durham Prison?
A: 1958. I'm not sure of the exact date, but I'd put my arse on it being 1958. It was Brian Chandler and he fucking deserved it. He killed an old lady. He's still lighting Lucifer's arse. Lucy won't let him stop. Hey, I hope you don't all think I'm a flash bastard. I can't help being a know-all. You've got to appreciate that it's been my life. Come on, next question. Make it hard.

Q: What jail had the longest prison roof protest and who did it?
A: No, it wasn't me I'm sad to say. But I am happy to tell you that the jail was Gartree and the protester was Michael Hickey. The poor cunt was up there for three months in the 1980s and it was snowing. He was one of the Bridgewater 4, convicted of killing the paper boy Carl Bridgewater. It was one of those cases that would never go away. Well, why should it? They were all innocent men. Those three months up on Gartree roof sent Michael mad and he eventually went to Ashworth Asylum. They all got a walk at the Court of Appeal after serving 15 years for fuck all. Imagine serving 15 years for killing a boy you didn't kill. And what makes it worse is that the Old Bill

knew they hadn't done it. When Michael was up on the roof the cons passed him stuff up: food, blankets, and even a radio. He was almost free. Well he was free, under the stars. You couldn't be any freer. But he couldn't have lasted a day up there without the cons' support. Could you see that happening today? Could you fuck. Anyway, it was Gartree and Michael - I salute you.

Q: In what jail was Dr Crippen hung?
A: Easy peasy. Pentonville in 1911. Fucking good job too. Whilst I'm on Pentonville, this was where Christie hung too in 1953. The last hanging there was Arthur Bush in 1961. He killed Elsie Batten. Why did he kill her? I don't know. Ask him yourself when you land in hell.

Q: Six infamous spies were hung in Pentonville in 1940. Who were they?
A: Yeah, you're spot on: Carl Meier, Jose Waldeburg, Charles Albert Van Der Kieboom, Oswald John Job, Pierre Richard Charles Neukermans and Joseph Jan Van Hove. They all got convicted under the Treachery Act 1940 during the Second World War. It never paid to be a spy in them days. And it was Albert Pierrepoint that stretched those necks. He had his work cut out did old Pierrepoint in the war years. He got plenty of practice in with the spies. Hey, could you be an executioner? Think about it - could you? Come on, next question. No trick ones though. Play fair.

Q: When was the last topping in Strangeways?
A: Fucking easy. It was actually the last hanging in England and it took place on 13 August 1964. But get this - a bit of history for you. At the same time as they hung Johnny Walby on this day in Strangeways they also hung a man in Walton Jail, Liverpool, called Peter Allen. So it was a double topping that ended hanging.

Q: Why do they call Wakefield Prison 'Monster Mansion'?
A: Are you fucking stupid or have you been up on Mars for a spell? Why do you think they call it Monster Mansion? Hey, did you know that the road it's on is called Love Lane? You couldn't make it up. Love fucking Lane! And did you know there's a brewery right next door?

Q: More people were probably hung at Wandsworth than at any other prison. How many, and who was the last man to be hung there?
A: Fuck me, you flash cunt. You're telling me the answers, or are you just guessing them? Don't try to get lemon with me, pal. Just ask the question, don't tell me your answers. You've thrown me off the plot here. So fuck off with your knowledge. Right, the last hanging was Henryk Neimasz in 1961. He'd committed a double murder. He walked to the trapdoor whistling, fearless in the face of death. Now, that's what I call a brave man. Okay, now for the second part of flash Harry's question. A total of 134 men were hung

in Wandsworth from 1878 to 1961 and only one woman. The woman swung for the murder of her lesbian mistress in 1879. So there you have it. They even had lesbos in them times. Amazing, eh?! I suppose the most famous man to hang there was Lord Haw-Haw. Who? Fucking look it up yourself. I'm not your teacher. Another famous hanging there was Derek Bentley in 1953, executed by Pierrepoint. He was only 19 years old and he was innocent. In 1998 he was posthumously pardoned - a bit late considering they topped the poor sod 45 years earlier. What a fucking insult. The only reason they topped him was down to pure red tape. The Appeal Court judges never had the bottle to do anything, all because it was a copper that got killed on a robbery. So they let a young lad swing for it. See the film or read the book. It's a disgrace and it still fucking winds me up. Cunts!

Q: What is the biggest jail in England?
A: Scrubs. Fucking easy.

They're getting too easy for me. I get bored when they're this easy. Try harder.

Q: In what year was the Dartmoor Mutiny?
A: 1932.

Q: Is it true that there was a prison called Clink?
A: Yes. The jail Clink existed from 1127 to 1780 and that's where the word 'clink' comes from. The jail was in Southwark, London, and now it's a museum on Clink Street, London, SE1 9DG. Go and have a butcher's. Take the kids and frighten the fucking life out of them. It'll put them off crime forever.

Q: In what year did Alcatraz open?
A: Hey, don't try your trick questions on me, pal. It was a military prison until it opened up for criminals in 1934. So suck on that one.

Q: Where did Charlie Wilson, one of the Great Train Robbers, escape from?
A: Winson Green. Easy.

Q: When the Kray twins got their sentences, where did they go?
A:. Ronnie went to Durham max secure unit and Reggie went to Parkhurst unit. It took Ronnie two years to get to Parkhurst with Reg, and that was down to their mother campaigning to get them in the same jail as it was too much for her to visit them both at different ends of the country. Ronnie hated Durham and Durham hated him. Still, what's new? Durham hates itself. It's one of them jails that makes your skin itch.

Well, I told you I'd cough up all the answers. Read 'em and weep!

CHAPTER 6
HANGMAN'S NOT A GAME,
IT'S A TRAGEDY

I'm dedicating this chapter to all the youngsters in jail and out of jail: to the ones who think it's a laugh; to those who think it's 'hard' to be a criminal. After you read this I hope it puts you off crime for life. What you are about to read is sad and tragic and a total heartbreaker. I've researched it especially for *Loonyology*. So please take time to digest this part. If it don't make you feel sad, then you're either not human or you're a heartless bastard.

In 2002 there were 95 suicides in our prisons. Almost 100 men, women and youngsters took their lives. Every one is a sad and miserable ending. Read this and never forget it, and remember that every year there are just as many. I chose 2002 because it was the year I almost died myself.

2002

04 01 02: Victoria Winterburn, aged 21, HMP Newhall, hung herself
17 01 02: Roy Waterson, aged 58, HMP Garth, renal failure, thrombosis
19 01 02: Kevin Hipgrave, aged 24, HMP Exeter, hung himself
22 01 02: Michael Scott Williams, aged 24, HMP Exeter, hung himself
26 01 02: Miranda Cox, aged 41, HMP Newhall, hung herself
28 01 02: Dick de Graaf, aged 42, HMP Newhall, hung himself
31 01 02: Gareth Barrow, aged 19, HMP Northallerton, hung himself
01 02 02: Steve Mountford, aged 28, HMP Woodhill, hung himself
03 02 02: Darren Payas, aged 27, HMP Woodhill, hung himself
13 02 02: Bryan Totton, aged 21, HMP Northallerton, hung himself
16 02 02: Arthur Springer, aged 49, HMP Canterbury, hung himself
23 02 02: Mahill Ravinder Singh, aged 29, HMP Leicester, hung himself
25 02 02: Charles Wolfe, aged 28, HMP Lewes, hung himself
25 02 02: Nariman Tahamasbi, aged 27, HMP Lewes, hung himself
(Take note of Nariman and Charles. Both hung themselves on the same day in the same jail - very strange.)
06 03 02: Gary Wilkinson, aged 35, HMP Preston, hung himself
08 03 02: Derek Fitzimmons, aged 34, HMP Leicester, hung himself
13 03 02: Andrew McPherson, aged 24, HMP Holme House, hung himself
23 03 02: Patrick Maloney, aged 31, HMP Brixton, hung himself
24 03 02: Joseph Peter Scholes, aged 16, HMP Stoke HMYOI, hung himself
(Note that Joseph was just 16 years old. It's a national disgrace.)

29 03 02: David Hanlon, aged 31, HMP Wandsworth, hung himself
01 04 02: Paul Brissett, aged 35, HMP Featherstone, hung himself
04 04 02: Derek Rispoli, aged 45, HMP Winchester, unknown
(Now that's a mystery. He must have died of something, as its suicide.)
10 04 02: Andrew Cliff, aged 36, HMP Holme House, hung himself
12 04 02: Emma Owen, aged 23, HMP Eastwood Park, hung herself
14 04 02: David McCafferty, aged 39, HMP Durham, hung himself
20 04 02: Alvin Walker, aged 27, HMP Dovegate, hung himself
20 04 02: Trevor Hill, aged 56, HMP Hull, hung himself
21 04 02: Andrew White, aged 33, HMP Leeds, hung himself
11 05 02: Mark Allen, aged 34, HMP Holme House, hung himself
11 05 02: Marcus Downie, aged 20, HMP Chelmsford, hung himself
12 05 02: Terry Joseph Doyle, aged 29, HMP Brixton, hung himself
13 05 02: Wayne Tranter, aged 25, HMP Cardiff, hung himself
16 05 02: Kevin Bright, aged 32, HMP Woodhill, unknown
(Somebody must know, people don't just die, but it's self-inflicted suicide.)
16 05 02: Peter Farrar, aged 42, HMP Leeds, unknown
(The report just says self-inflicted.)
19 05 02: Noel Dooley, aged 41, HMP Full Sutton, unknown (self-inflicted)
23 05 02: Keith Clark, aged 54, HMP Kingston, hung himself
27 05 02: Joe McCarroll, aged 38, HMP Preston, hung himself
02 06 02: Gavin Pascoe, aged 19, HMP Exeter, hung himself
07 06 02: Peter Swelling, aged 33, HMP Bristol, hung himself
14 06 02: Kevin Warren, aged 43, HMP Pentonville, hung himself
17 06 02: Stephen Miller, aged 46, HMP Dovegate, "Self-inflicted."
21 06 02: Ian Ballantyne, aged 19, HMP Castington, hung himself
26 06 02: Scott Charles Fisher, aged 24, HMP Durham, hung himself
27 06 02: Anthony McGrogan, aged 28, HMP Holme House, hung himself
27 06 02: David Fitzgerald, aged 40, HMP Belmarsh, hung himself

Well, don't it make you feel sick, sad and angry? It fucking chokes me up, but you need to know the truth. It really is a national disgrace. Hey, the death penalty stopped 40 years back and there's more hangings now than then. It's crazy.

04 07 02: James Devers, aged 21, HMP Liverpool, hung himself
10 07 02: Andrew Hambleton, aged 39, HMP Altcourse, hung himself
17 07 02 : John Blackham, aged 41, HMP Dovegate, unknown
30 07 02: Ramar Tucker, aged 35, HMP Doncaster, hung himself
01 08 02: Joe Ramon Espineria Villa, aged 24, HMP Lewes, unknown
06 08 02: Andy Garrett, aged 24, HMP Bristol, hung himself
07 08 02: John Foley, aged 24, HMP Bristol, hung himself
08 08 02: Julius Gomez, aged 30, HMP Lewes, hung himself
10 08 02: Nissa Ann Smith, aged 20, HMP Styal, hung herself

11 08 02: James Lee Holland, aged 33, HMP Nottingham, hung himself
13 08 02: Trevor Turley, aged 49, HMP Blakenhurst, hung himself
17 08 02: Ryan Edmunds, aged 20, HMP Norwich, hung himself
18 08 02: Jacqueline McPartine, aged 32, HMP Holloway, hung herself
19 08 02: Diana Shooling, aged 52, HMP Durham, hung herself
23 08 02: Lee Paul Wilson, aged 35, HMP Wealstun, unknown
29 08 02: Karl Fletcher, aged 32, HMP Liverpool, hung himself
09 09 02: Philip Offland, aged 50, HMP Risley, hung himself
09 09 02: Steven Hampson, aged 19, HMYOI Hindley, hung himself
13 09 02: Douglas Howles, aged 44, HMP Blakenhurst, hung himself
14 09 02: Marcus Buggy, aged 31, HMP Wakefield, hung himself
17 09 02: Tracey Newton, aged 29, HMP High Point, hung himself

There's no end to this misery. It just goes on and on. How's your head? Has it sunk in yet? Can you feel their pain and emptiness? Can you sense their loneliness?

17 09 02: Belbir Lal, aged 39, HMP Wormwood Scrubs, hung himself
18 09 02: Leif Millward, aged 33, HMP Nottingham, hung himself
20 09 02: Gary Horth, aged 30, HMP Bedford, hung himself
21 09 02: Sean Richings, aged 30, HMP Parc, hung himself
30 09 02: Thomas Evans, aged 26, HMP Bedford, hung himself
02 10 02: Beverly Fowler, aged 32, HMP Durham, hung herself
02 10 02: Paul Day, aged 31, HMP Frankland, hung himself

Paul Day was actually a police informer and he done a deal with Wandsworth Prison to get a move to a safe jail (a grass wing). He got fuck all. They used him like they use all the grasses. Once they squeeze it all out of a grass, all that's left is an empty shell. The system dumped him up in Frankland (he's a Londoner) and they moved him to the farthest jail up north. He then went on a dirty protest in Frankland seg block. Nobody cared. Nobody gave a fuck. The suicide thoughts took over and that's the end. Let it be a lesson to all would be grasses! It's a lousy end. It's guilt that chews you up.

06 10 02: Ian Powell, aged 17, HMP Parc, hung himself
(Note 17 years of age - a boy! That sums up this fucked-up system - it stinks.)
06 10 02: Robert Longworth, aged 19, HMP Moorland, hung himself
07 10 02: Terence Gaskill, aged 33, HMP Durham, hung himself

Have you ever wondered what it's like to hang yourself? It can't be easy. Some say you're a coward to take your own life. I say it's bravery with a confused mind. The mind must be wrecked! The heart and soul are smashed. It's an act of total and utter determination. Very few ever leave a note. Nobody knows why. Only them. I believe the cell has crushed the life out of them. Some probably do it in fear; others may do it in contempt. It's their last act of rebellion. Fuck you lot. Clean the mess up, put me in a bag and send me home. It's their way of winning their freedom.

18 10 02: Peter Warren, aged 40, HMP Wakefield, hung himself
18 10 02: John Nicholls, aged 37, HMP Exeter, cut his wrists - bled to death
26 10 02: Jason Machin, aged 28, HMP Durham, hung himself
30 10 02: Stephen Cuming, aged 20, HMP Lewes, hung himself
04 11 02: Shane Firth, aged 31, HMP Hull, hung himself
06 11 02: David Nazami, aged 50, HMP Bedford, refusing treatment (self-inflicted)
14 11 02: Richard Jones, aged 37, HMP Liverpool, unknown

Also think about this: a lot of these suicides are by remands. They're innocent until proven guilty. So the remand prisoners died innocent. Remember that. It's worth thinking about, coz some of them should not have been on remand, some just could not take it, so they were driven to suicide!

19 10 02: Alan Heels, aged 42, HMP Bullingdon, hung himself
22 11 02: Ritza Fooladi, aged 23, HMP Bullingdon, hung himself
26 11 02: Anna Baker, aged 29, HMP Styal, hung herself
02 12 02: Mark Stephenson, aged 25, HMP Holme House, hung himself
03 12 02 : John Negus, aged 22, HMP Highdown, hung himself
04 12 02: Chris Gilchrist, aged 28, HMP Hull, hung himself
04 12 02: Richard Jones, aged 29, HMP Gloucester, hung himself
08 12 02: Leslie Parrott, aged 39, HMP Wolds, hung himself
11 12 02: Mark Tunnard, aged 34, HMP Hull, hung himself
17 12 02: Richard Harden, aged 28, HMP Doncaster, hung himself
21 12 02: Gary Cunliffe, aged 32, HMP Strangeways, hung himself
21 12 02: John Paul McDonagh, aged 20, HMYOI Aylesbury, hung himself

And on Christmas Day 2002, Walter Hitchmough, aged 53, died in HMP Littlehey of a heart attack. Poor old Wally. Imagine his family getting the call. Think about it. How sad is that?

On top of all these sad deaths, all in 2002, there were also 55 natural deaths due to old age, illness, heart attacks, etc. So the total was 153 body bags for one year! And the truth is, this was an average year. Some years there are even more!

But there was one death we all celebrated: Myra Hindley, 15/11/02, HMP Highpoint. That witch should've hung the day she was convicted of her evil crimes. Pneumonia took her out. Did you know I used to have boxes of cheap fags sent to her via a pal of mine who deals in cheap French fags. He used to put a card in: "From Charlie. Smoke plenty and die quick". Another pal of mine sent her a 14-inch vibrator with a note: "Shag yourself to death, you child killer".

As for all the screws and governors who treated her like a princess and gave her an easy ride, I hope they get pneumonia too! She should've served her time in a cage in solitary. She deserved no less!

So that's your lot on death. I hope 2002 will stay in your mind. I also hope it's shocked you. If you're young and really thinking of turning to crime, then stop and think coz that could be you, hanging up in some dark and lonely cell. Please believe it! Prison may drive you to despair. It could drive you insane. You won't be the first or last to rip up your bed sheet and tie it around your neck and be found swinging from the bars or light fitting. Your pants will be full of shit, your neck twisted, your face blue, your eyes bulging, your tongue protruding. That's the 'photo' your parents will see. Take this one bit of advice from a man who knows about prison: STOP AND THINK.

If you just think about it, that's all I ask. If you still decide to be a criminal, then good luck, coz you'll need it. These poor sods lost out on luck. It all ended like the butterfly that flew into the fire. Don't do it!

THE DARK SIDE OF THE LOON
He awoke screaming
He shit the bed
Drenched in sweat
The stench of madness
It had finally caught him up
He knew it was coming
He dreaded it
Feared it
It's all over
A lifetime ripped apart
Tears of blood
Alone in the dark
Nobody to touch
Nothing to see
Just the smell of shit
An empty heart
Forever screaming
What a fucking ending
What a way to go
A padded room
A straitjacket
Standing in a pool of blood
Drowning in despair
Choking on pain
The cancer of insanity spreading

LOONYOLOGY

Forever eating you away
The dark side
The blackness
A loon without a name
Faceless and lost
Loveless and cold
A headless chicken
5 seconds of nerves
A twitch
Then stillness
That's a loony
A fucking vegetable
Doped up
Psychotropic tranquillisers
Electric shock therapy
An old man with a long white beard
Dead, yes
Dreamless
A shuffle
A dribble
Never a smile
Silent
He sits alone in the corner
You can smell him
The piss smell
That smelly old man smell
The skin flakes
The back bends
Arthritis sets in
Bones crumble
Somebody change the fucking colostomy bag
I'm a walking turd
Shoot me
Fucking shoot me
Stop this torture
It's time to move on
Let it be
Enough's enough
No more
He runs the razor across his throat
Then across his wrists
He watches the blood flow
It's a deep feeling of warmth
Watching life run away

CHARLES BRONSON

A lightness
He's covered in a glow of light
He died with a smile
He left behind a bag of shit
And a lot of cleaning
The dark side of the Loon
AMEN.

Death is never easy at the best of times, but inside it's even worse. There can't be a darker end. You're in hell before you arrive. It's nice, though, when the Beasts take their own lives: the likes of Fred West, Harold Shipman and John Steed. We have a party when that happens. In fact when West hung himself in Winson Green Jail I'd like to think I played a part in that, as all I used to do was shout out to him, "Top yourself, you nonce." I used to give it to that monster 24/7. I drove him fucking mental. I once looked at him through his spy hole in the cell door. He was sitting staring at the wall. He looked a bit like Benny out of *Crossroads*; a right fucking muppet. He had that sort of face, like a sad bloodhound dog.

What an evil fucker he really was, noncing his own kids. Fuck me, he even put one of his kids under the patio. Him and Rose should've hung for what evil acts they both did. But seeing him sitting there all sad and sorry for himself made you wonder - WHY? HOW? What makes a man do such a crime? It's truly beyond belief to me.

"Hang yourself, you fucking nonce!"

"Come on, Bronson, get away from his door," the screw shouts.

"Fuck you, screw! Open it so I can steam in and give the animal a slap."

The very first hanging I saw was in Risley Remand Prison up in Warrington, Cheshire, in 1969. I was only 17 years old. It was fucking gruesome and he shit himself. His tongue was hanging out and his face was blue, eyes bulging. It was truly horrible. They took him out in a body bag. The smell of death lingers on for weeks after. He was 16 years old on a taking and driving charge. Fucking tragic.

I've seen a lot of sad endings: some you never forget; some you can't forget. They scar your brain. You get flashbacks. It fucking hurts, especially when it's a mate:

* Johnny Bond, Parkhurst, 1977. He was a top geezer; a good man in his late twenties and someone I respected and admired. His cell was spotless - you could eat off the floor - and his fitness was second to none. He was always cleaning and on the go: press-ups, sit-ups; running on the yard; sweating it out in the gym. He couldn't keep still, relax or chill out. He was a silent type, very into himself, but he suffered with terrible 'manic' depression. He was in a lot of torment and mental anguish. His life sentence was chewing him up. I used to sit and have a chat with him in his cell. I tried to get through to him that there is life after life. You will one day walk free.

It won't always be this way. Keep the faith. Fight on, John. But it was mostly one-way talk. I got little back. It's how he was. He bottled it up. You could see it in his eyes. He was dying inside. He was holding on to a thin thread. We all knew it would snap. Life in prison to him was like breaking a dove's wing.

I actually believed he would lose his mind and kill a screw, as he hated them, or kill a con; whoever upset him. He was just waiting to explode; a one-man army. I'd seen him in the gym do an hour's workout and walk out fresh as a daisy. He was just a body on fire. We all liked Johnny. Even the Kray twins used to say, "What a shame we didn't have him on our firm outside." That's a compliment coming from Ron and Reg, believe me. One night John got on his cell call bell and told the screw to get him moved down to the seg block. He wanted to be isolated. So they moved him down to the block. We never saw him again. He hung himself in the early hours. What a fucking tragic waste of a good man. What a fucking sad old world.

* Tony Cunningham, Wandsworth Nick. Tony was only serving a seven-year stretch. He was a jack the lad and everyone liked him. You could trust him. He was only young, about 30, maybe younger. He was walking around the exercise yard with me and Noel Travis, telling us jokes. He was laughing, happy. The sun was shining and everything was sweet. Wandsworth is a shithole. This was in the 1980s, but it's probably still a shithole now. Full of rats and cockroaches and muggy screws. Everyone loves Wanno - I don't think so. I've had more kickings in there than I care to remember. I'll get back to that later.

Tony was okay that day on the yard. He showed no signs of depression or a troubled mind. After our hour we all went in to bang up. Another day over. Another day less to serve! At 7 p.m. they bring the tea urn to the doors. When they went to Tony's door on D Wing (all single cells) they smelt shit. As the door unlocked there he was: hanging; cold as a slab of meat in the freezer; lifeless; dead as a doormat. The whole jail was depressed. Work that one out if you can.

I still think about Tony, coz I still can't work it out. It don't add up and it drives you mad to wonder why. What caused it? Just what was going through his mind that day, one minute telling us jokes and the next hanging himself. It just don't make an ounce of sense.

* Barry Rondeall, Long Lartin. This guy was a legend. All the chaps respected him. I first met him in Gartree Jail in 1987. In fact he was doing punishment in the block with me. He got 56 days chokey over an attempted escape off a prison van. I was doing 112 days over two assaults on screws. He got life when he was 19 years old. It was over a stabbing at a football match. This guy was a fitness fanatic. He used to do one-armed press-ups for fun and held the record for the most sit-ups in 30 minutes.

A couple of years later I landed in Long Lartin and Barry was there doing well: plenty of gym, plenty of grub, and he was looking good. He actually sorted me out a few quid to get some decent food in. We had a chat and left on a high. It was great to see him so lively. He could now see some hope of getting out, but he got out sooner than he expected. They took him out in a body bag. He cut his throat and wrists and bled to death. Blood was running under the cell door. Nobody could save him. He knew exactly what he was doing, but again - WHY? Why did he do it? Nobody knows. Nobody ever will know.

Let me tell you how hard men cried over that. Men dubbed Britain's most dangerous men - armed blaggers, mobsters, killers - we all felt so sad and hurt over that. It take ages to get over such a tragedy because we are all lost for words. There are no answers. We walk around shell-shocked for months after wondering deep thoughts. It never leaves us. How can it?

* Tommy Hole jnr, Parkhurst. This story will blow your mind through the top of your head. This is tragedy built on tragedy. It comes no worse.

Tommy got an eight stretch. He was a Canning Town born and bred villain, just like his old man Tom snr. Tom snr was a true pal to me. He was one of the best and a proper armed blagger; a pure old school villain. Old Tom was down in Parkhurst serving a 22 year sentence when young Tom arrived. He come down from Full Sutton Jail for visits with his dad. It was great to see them together on M Wing. M Wing was like a little unit. All good lads on there; men like Vick Dark, Kev Brown, Dennis Campbell, Mark Foley, Mickey Reiley, Terry Smith, 'Big H' MacKenney - the list goes on, okay - and yours truly. Yeh, me. Although I rarely last long anywhere, my short spell on there was a nice time till this tragedy struck.

It happened on a Sunday morning. Old Tom had made some tea and toast and took it up to young Tom's cell. That was it. The scream rocked the wing. Everybody froze. Tom was hanging off the cell bars - dead.

I've spent years of my life locked away but nothing can prepare you for such a thing. It rips your heart out. Again you ask: WHY? HOW? WHAT REASON? There is no reason. That same Sunday the Hole family was visiting them both. Old Tom had to face all that. Imagine that. You can't.

Later Tom lost the plot. He went mad and they sent him to Rampton Asylum. He got better and finally got freed. Then - crash! - a gunman runs into a pub and blows him away. That's what you call a tragedy. Two great men, father and son. Men of grit, men of respect and honour, and well missed I can tell you. I loved them both. I had some good times with Tommy Hole and young Tom. They're never forgotten. How can you forget that? You can't.

It was soon after that I lost the plot and had my own riot in Parkhurst. I demolished M Wing, but that's another story.

* John Paton, Garth HMP. John and me go back years. I'm sure I see him on Noah's Ark. He copped a twelve stretch. Strange enough, he was from my town, Luton, but that twelve stretch ended up a double life sentence. He killed a fellow con in Wakefield Jail and, if that wasn't bad enough, he killed

another con in Parkhurst Jail. Now you're all thinking, "What a violent animal." Well, let me tell you, it's not how it sounds. John really was a nice fella - polite and very friendly - but he could not stand pressure. His head just flipped if somebody was coming on strong to him or taking the piss. It used to bring out the worst in him and he would get a tool and do the biz. He couldn't fight, he wasn't a big man, so he used a tool. You just did not play games with John Paton, as it could well be your last game.

The con he killed in Parkhurst was Magee. John stabbed him in the dinner queue. He was dead before he hit the ground. That was it for him. He went back into the cages for more years of isolation. It took him a good ten years to be trusted again to mix. Unbelievably they took him off Cat A (decategorised him) onto a Cat B and moved him to Garth Jail. That for any lifer was a progressive move, but for John Paton it was a fucking miracle. We were all pleased for him, as things were finally moving in the right direction for him after so many hopeless, dead years.

My true opinion was that he would never be freed (ever). No Home Secretary would dare release a man who had killed twice inside, but I could be wrong. After all, why did they move him to a Cat B Jail if he was never to be freed? It did seem strange, but we were all pleased for him.

Soon after that move he topped himself in his cell. WHY? HOW? What motivated him is beyond us all. All those years in isolation, all that surviving the lonely, boring years, and he takes his own life. It really does break my heart. It's insanity. It's loonyology. There is no reason. How can there be an answer to madness?

That's how it is: sad, agonising, lonely, empty. It's a fucking house of horrors. So who's next? Anyone for a one-way ticket to nowhere?!

Suicide by cop, Sunderland, 1991. Who remembers Walbank, who walked out of his house with a cushion tied to his chest, carrying a gun? Bang! Armed cops blasted him. Now why would a man do that? Walbank was a career criminal! He'd done bird and was a dangerous man. He wasn't silly, he had a good criminal mind, so he must've known that a cushion couldn't stop a bullet. He knew what the outcome would be. The Old Bill in this case had no option but to fire, so ask yourself why did Walbank do that? I'll tell you, he was sick of porridge! It was his way out. He hated the cops and they hated him. The war was never-ending. Fucking do it now; let's escape this madness. So he forced them to shoot - suicide by cop - and eat the bullet, so they say. I actually admire a man who can leave this planet like that. It does take a lot of bottle. But the cushion ... why the cushion? That has baffled me for 17 years! Why would a man strap a cushion on, other than to confuse the problem. I think it was to freak the cops out, and freak them he did. They shit themselves. Wouldn't you?

I've often wondered about heaven and hell. Would it not be better to rule in hell than serve in heaven? Surely hell's for living on the edge?! What do you think? I think hell's for party time and heaven's for sucking toffee apples. Take your pick. You may like a toffee apple, or sucking the top off a yoghurt, so each to his own. But I like to party. I like to balance on the edge. What about you?

I know one man who liked to live on the edge: Barry Pruden. Who remembers him? The Old Bill sure do, coz they shot him dead in the 1980s. Barry just flipped, lost the plot and went on a mission. He grabbed his guns and knife and did a Rambo. They even brought in some SAS geezer to track him down. After he'd killed two cops they finally surrounded him and that was curtains. There could only be one end for Barry Pruden. He wrote his own death script. That's how it ends with guys like Pruden. They only know one sure way - death. But boy, oh boy, did he bring some hell! You ask any Yorkshire copper who was around then and they'll tell you what fear is. Men like Pruden only know one way in life: their way and no other way. There was no way in a million Sundays they could take him alive. Even armed cops thought the same. It was just a case of who was gonna get lucky with the first shot. Let's face it, if you play with fire you're gonna get burnt! And at the end of the day there's more of them than there is of you. You can't win. Rambo is just a movie character! In real life you can't survive such insane odds, you're gonna die.

Who saw *Bonnie and Clyde*? That's one of my favourite ever movies. Look how they ended up: shot to pieces; so full of holes they looked like tea bags. Fear did that! The cops were shitting bricks and all they could do was keep their finger on the trigger: make no mistake, take no chances, kill the fuckers! They all cop it in the end, whether facing a bullet or 30 years in the can.

I'm always locked alone; have been for years. That's how life is for me. Some believe I'll die inside. Let 'em believe it, but there's one sure thing: I'll never top myself. Never. Do you know why? Firstly, I love life too much. Even in jail I have a life. Secondly, I know if I did it would make so many screws incredibly happy. I can't be having them celebrate my ending. Fuck that. I'd sooner live on till I'm 108. Honest! So please, if ever you read that Bronson topped himself, ask one question: "WHO DID IT?" Cos I fucking didn't. Don't let me swing in doubt. Some fuckers did it.

ONE WAY OUT

Some do it, some don't
Some will, some won't
Who knows?
The mind's a strange thing
When you're alone it can drive you mad
It can turn you inside out
Rip you up
Bite a hole in your face
Turn you ugly

You don't know yourself
You're lost inside yourself
There's no tomorrow
Only a torn sheet
A noose and a chair
Lots of mental anguish
The mind's a power unto itself
You do what you're told
The voice
Do it
Be free
Go now
Do it before the light comes on
Leave a note
Kiss my arse
Clean up my shit
Cut me up in the morgue
Bury me in pieces
Rest in pieces
I fucked the system
Maybe that's why they do it
Who knows?
Who cares?
I do
I really do
So many good men
Ghosts of the past
Men in memory
You did it, boys
Your way
One way out

Did I ever tell you the story about the time I thought I'd had my lot in Leicester Jail seg block? In this seg block there are only five punishment cells and one strongbox. I was the only one there at the time. Now, believe me, if you're alone in a block with six burly screws you could well have a problem, as they can do anything anytime they want, especially if you're not too popular in the system.

So let's face facts. I'm not the most popular con, am I? All I've done for 3½ decades is battle through it all. It's been a never-ending war. So here I am, alone. I slop out, I exercise alone, I don't see no cons. Only six screws, and if they press the bell there will be 26 more. I'm like a fly in a spider's web waiting for it to happen. Will I attack them, or will they attack me, or will we attack each other? What will today bring?

My door crashed in. I was still in bed half asleep. I was dragged out onto the landing naked by a good ten screws, and then it started!

"Bronson, look at that. Take a good look. Any fucking about and you'll end up swinging off it. You touch one officer in our jail and you're fucking dead."

It was a noose hanging off a beam. A fucking noose. Then they slung me back in my cell and slammed the door shut. I banged the door for hours after that shouting, "Don't tell me, you cunts, do it! Do it, you gutless pricks! You're all fucking talk!"

The next day I had a rumble with them and they put me in the body belt, slung me in the van and moved me.

They're all rabbit - bunny, bunny, bunny - brave fuckers in teams of ten coz one can't do it. But I must add that noose did look naughty and their faces told only one story - it wasn't nice.

Years later I got up on their roof. I always get my own back. It may take years, but I do. That's how life is with me: swings and roundabouts. You fall off sometimes, but you get back on. It's one big fuck of ride, and the faster the better.

Talking of roundabouts, that Milton Keynes is full of them. Every time I go to Woodhill Jail I get dizzy. How can one place have so many fucking roundabouts and concrete cows? That sums up Milton Keynes! Loonyology.

CHAPTER 7
JUNE'S TUNES AND LOONS

Ijust heard that Curtis Warren's been released after ten years in a Dutch jail. Ten fucking years of Dutch Edam cheese and walking about in clogs. Fuck that. He copped a twelve stretch over drugs and then got four years added on for manslaughter over a fight with a con. I suppose some will say he's lucky. Well, losing ten years of your life isn't lucky. On top of that, the media have assassinated his character. There's even books about him. I only hope he now does his own book so he can put his side over. That will shock a few.

I first met Curtis in Armley Jail in the late 1980s. Like most Scousers he's a funny fucker; a likeable character - one of your own, as I say 'a top geezer'. So I'm well chuffed he's made it out. Stay out Curtis, coz the Old Bill will be sick you're out. Plus they have their grasses clocking your every move. So chill out and enjoy your freedom.

16 June 2007, Yorkshire Post
DEATH OF MAN FACING MURDER TRIAL
He was found by cellmate
By Stuart Robinson
A man awaiting trial for the murder of his ex-girlfriend was found face down in his prison cell by a fellow inmate.
Shaun Stoker, a former warehouseman of Edendale, Castleford, was on remand at Armley Jail waiting to face court for the murder of mum of two Ann Riel at his home address on May 15.
The inquest opening at Leeds Coroner's Court heard that Stoker, 49, had a history of alcoholism and depression and had been married but had divorced.
He had been remanded at Leeds since May 21.
Suicide precautions were being observed at the prison in the build-up to his death.
He had been placed in a cell with another inmate while a "buddy" system was operated. He was also checked on an hourly basis each night.
At 3 p.m. on the afternoon of June 8, Stoker's cellmate left the cell for a regular period of interaction between prisoners. Stoker stayed in his cell and when the other prisoner returned just before 4 p.m., he found him face down on the cell floor with a piece of towel material knotted around his neck.
Prison staff and paramedics attempted to revive him but he was pronounced dead just before 4.30 p.m.
A post mortem report gave a provisional cause of death as compression of the neck.
West Yorkshire Coroner David Hinchliff adjourned the inquest pending further reports

from the police and the Prisons and Probation Ombudsman.
Mr. Hinchliff said: "This will be an appropriate case for me to hear before a jury at the conclusion of all investigations."
The YEP understands a family member discovered Miss Riel's body at the house. It is believed the 47 year old had been strangled.
Stoker had yet to enter a plea for the murder and was awaiting a further court appearance at Leeds Crown Court later this year.
An inquest was opened and adjourned on Monday into Miss Riel's death.

Here's another con, who got out the same time as Curtis. But he went out in a body bag. He couldn't face up to his life inside. Fuck me, he couldn't even face his trial for murder. He gave up all hope. At 49 he felt it was all over and it was useless even trying to go on. His world had crushed him.

I always feel sad when I read these sorts of stories. It sort of makes me think, what's it all about? Everybody lost. Kids suffer. Parents are destroyed. Lives are in ruin. There's nothing but pain and grief. Why did he kill her? Why kill himself? Why not just kill himself in the first place before he killed her? It's all fucking mad, the more you look into it all. The world's gone mad. It drives people over the edge. Then his cellmate suffers. The screws are in shock. It's just one big fuck-up. It's unnecessary. In fact it's actually selfish.

Why couldn't he at least have gone in style? He could've climbed the jail roof, smashed it up and dived off. He could've gone a hero. He chose a very sad and lonely death. Imagine the state of his mind: confused and deluded. Just another statistic. Scrub him off the board. Fill his cell with another number. He's not the first. He sure won't be the last. There'll be another stiff tomorrow; another three next week. A man or woman who wants to die will die. You can't stop it. Nobody can. It's impossible to stop.

One sure thing is that Shaun Stoker has no more problems. His ended in that jail cell. His dreams were sucked into oblivion. I wonder where he is now. Who really cares? Life's gotta go on. This train waits for nobody. There are no stops.

The Sun
TAT'S HIM!
Cops had no trouble recognising this fugitive killer - his face is COVERED with tattoos.
Nazi jail bird, Curtis Allgier, fled a hospital appointment after snatching a 60-year-old prison officer's gun and shooting him in the back of the head.
Allgier, 27, then hijacked a 4 x 4 and led police on a 100 mph chase across Utah's Salt Lake City. He continued for miles even when his tyres were spiked.
Allgier ran into a fast food restaurant where he was overpowered by a member of the public and finally arrested.
He will now face the death penalty after being charged with first degree murder.

Hey, get this geezer. Imagine bumping into him in one of your nightmares. He would be fucked on an ID parade. He's buried now: straight to death row; straight to Old Sparky. He's only 27 years old now. He will probably be 29 by the time his trial comes up. Then he will be appealing against the death sentence for 20 years. All for what? They will still execute him. Imagine that - spending 20 years on death row and then they pull the switch: 'Time to Fly'. How fucking mental is that? You live in a cage for 20 years, survive all the chains and brutality, and then you have to walk to the death chamber! Shit, what for? Why survive all that just to let the state blow you away. This guy would have been better off blowing his own brains out along with the guard he snuffed out. I think he lost his way the day he had all those face tattoos put on. He sort of cut the world in half. He filled his heart with so much hate that he choked on it. He lost the plot and went nuts. Sad really. He's never gonna stroke another pussy, walk on grass again, walk under the stars or eat and drink what he chooses. He's going into a concrete coffin; a living death. Kids should take note of this guy and learn from him. Don't go down his road, coz the lights don't work. And all you crazy women who are about to fall in love with him and propose marriage, get a fucking life and wake up, you sad bitches. You're better off with a vibrator. Better still, get a free man.

I get a sack load of letters every week: 99% from genuine people who wish me well; 1% from lunatics. Some want to fight me, some want to fuck with me. I even get women sending in knickers but I don't see them - the prison censor tells me! Some letters are even stopped due to the graphic details that some women put in them. So think before you write me a mad letter, coz it's odds on it will go in the trash can without me seeing it.

I wonder why they do it? They must be sad, lonely people with nothing better to do than dream of a man in a cage, or deliberately want to wind me up - like the Welsh prick who writes me wanting to fight me. In your dreams, Taffy. If you really want the meet, keep your pen in your pocket, wait till I'm out and then challenge me to my face. I'll put on the fight and generate a good buzz. I can make a nice few bob out of it. But all this silly letter shit don't go with me. It's like the dirty tart who writes me from Liverpool, who wants to do me up the arse with her dildo. Believe me, sweetheart, it's not ever gonna happen. You'll have to shoot me first. No fucking lunatic does me up the deaf and dumb. I'd smash all your teeth out and snap your arms off before you touched me. You're mad ... fuck off.

Then there's the nutter from Bedford who writes me love poems. Look, Jack, save it for your boyfriend. Why send me love poems? Why waste a 36p stamp on me? I only read the first line and then rip them up. Your silly poems are only good for bog paper.

I also get begging letters. Begging - to me? How can you beg to a man in a coffin? It blows me away.

I've got one old lady up in Glasgow who wants me to go and live with her.

She's 85 years old. She wants to give me a blow job.

God give me sanity. I just attract the insane. I'm a magnet of madness but it helps to pass my years away and I thank you all, especially the 99% of you who really do support my struggle. If you enclose a stamped addressed envelope then I'll reply, otherwise I can't. I live in a hole not a post office. You can see a few of my solid, staunch supporters in the middle of this book. That says it all: respect!

20 June 2007, Daily Mail
ANOTHER APPEAL ON MURDER OF JILL DANDO
The man jailed for the murder of television presenter Jill Dando has won the right to a new appeal. The criminal Cases Review Commission is expected to announce today that the case of Barry George will be referred to the Court of Appeal on the grounds that a speck of firearms discharge residue found on the clothing was given 'too much importance and significance' before the jury.
George's lawyers are expected to argue that a new investigation by police in Strathclyde has undermined the evidential value of residue in criminal investigations.
The discharge was found on the lining of an inner pocket of George's overcoat. Prosecutors are expected to say that the residue was consistent with that found on Miss Dando's hair and clothing.
It will be the second appeal for George, who lost his first in 2002. The Appeal Court is obliged to hear cases referred by the CCRC, which was set up to examine potential miscarriages of justice.
The 37-year-old Crimewatch and Holiday presenter was shot dead on the step of her home in Fulham, West London, in April 1999.
There was speculation that the killer was a professional hitman, possibly hired by a criminal exposed on Crimewatch, or even a Serbian gunman exacting revenge for the Nato bombing of a Belgrade TV station.
George, 42, who lived near Miss Dando, was found guilty by a 10-1 majority at the Old Bailey in July 2001 and sentenced to life imprisonment.
Critics argued that the prosecution case against him was thin. No one saw the shooting, no one identified George and no weapon was found. There were also no fingerprints or DNA traces and the prosecution could produce no motive.

I met this prat in Belmarsh eight years back when he was on remand. Take it from me, he did not kill anybody. I don't like him. I never have and I never will, as he has a record for noncing - 'a sex case'. Also he's two cans short of a six pack. But he's serving life over a stitch-up. Sure he's a nutter, a right fucking freaky bastard, but he did not kill Jill Dando. I'll explain why. George is what's known in the game as a 'joke'. The Old Bill were pressurised to get a body; Barry George was that body. He was in the right place at the wrong time, or the other way round. The Old Bill knew he was a nutter. Who better to nick?! Case solved. But it's never that easy with such a high-profile case. Everybody who knows about this case will tell you that whoever shot Jill Dando was a professional - a cold, cruel, cunning killer; a very smart and lethal hit man or -woman. It was a pro job. Why? Who knows? It could have been for money reasons. You can guess all day long. It's the facts you need to know, not the ifs and buts. George is a dreamer, a true-life wanker. He even wanks himself silly in rubber suits. He's a fucking pervo, a brain-dead freak. He just could not have shot her without being seen or leaving some evidence. He can't even wipe his own arse properly. He yacks like a demented frog. His IQ must be that of a peanut. He suffers from delusions. This guy is just not capable of such a professional hit. Thank fuck, coz he would embarrass the real hit men!

Take it from me, the cops involved in this case and the prosecutors all knew he didn't do it. The screws in Belmarsh all knew it too. The screws there know who's a 'fit-up'. They deal with killers all day long. Every screw in Belmarsh said it was a joke. He don't even look, act or think like a hit man.

As for me, I've lived amongst killers all my adult life. You get to know who's who.

George fits into the 'hobbit' category: a faceless nobody. He has served his last six years on the Rule 43 nonce wing along with the likes of sex killers and paedos and grasses (owing to his own nonce behaviour). I'm told by good sources that he gets his arse pumped regular. Some cons take advantage of him as he's so simple, but that's life in jail. You get what you deserve. You either bend down in the shower or you fight your way out - your choice.

Muppets like George will bend over all day long and suck cock till the cow jumps over the moon. What do you think goes on in them nonce wings - Scrabble and Monopoly? Fucking wake up. It's a sex party. Paedo gangs, rapist gangs - they're alive and kicking. It's party, party and party, and guys like George are fresh meat. That's how it is and always will be. And some of the screws who work on them nonce wings look a bit iffy (take my word on that). They sort of walk funny and talk funny. I suppose with years of mixing with monsters rubs off on them. Some have actually been sacked over bringing in hardcore homo mags. One got caught bringing in a 12-inch vibrator. You just can't make up this shit.

Talking of vibrators, I just read in the paper that some con in Swaleside got caught with a mobile phone up his arse. It apparently started ringing inside him! Can you believe that? A fucking phone up your arsehole?! It beggars belief.

There was one con who smuggled in a gun up his arse in bits - three bits at a time. A fucking shooter! Now see why *Loonyology* has to be written. It's mental. Total insanity.

Anyway, if Barry George walks free on appeal, the million dollar question is: who did do it? It's like the Princess Di case - we all know it was murder but who did it? I'd love to see George win his freedom and then in a year or two hear that he's been found dead down some sewer. A fitting end to a rat.

22 June 2007, Daily Mail
A FANATIC ON THE LOOSE
Al Qaeda suspect snubs control order and disappears from his British home
A suspected Al Qaeda recruiting sergeant was on the loose in Britain last night after becoming the seventh control order suspect to abscond.
The Iraqi asylum seeker, a follower of dead Al Qaeda warlord Abu Musab al-Zarqawi, vanished from his home on Monday.
His disappearance leaves the policy of using control orders to monitor terror suspects in tatters. A minister admitted that the orders cannot prevent "determined" suspects escaping.
The missing man is alleged to have been part of a six man recruitment team sent to Britain by Al Qaeda in Iraq to enlist volunteers to join attacks on British and U.S. troops serving there.
He managed to gain a foothold here by claiming to be fleeing persecution in Iraq.
His admission to Britain is likely to reignite debate about the way the asylum system is abused by terror suspects. Around a quarter of those arrested under anti-terror laws are would-be refugees.
The fanatic, who was wearing an electronic tag and under a 14 hour curfew when he fled, has not been traced despite a huge manhunt.
Although other control order suspects have been named and pictured, his identity is being kept secret on police advice.
"This is yet another example of how control orders, while doing much to undermine our rights and freedoms, are astonishingly ineffective at protecting our safety", said Shadow Home Secretary David Davis. Liberal Democrat spokesman Nick Clegg added: "This is yet another serious blow for the increasingly discredited system of control orders. The Government must hold a wholesale review."
The escaped suspect was one of six Iraqi asylum seekers arrested in August 2005 on suspicion of recruiting or financing other extremists. The six were closely linked to al-Zarqawi who murdered British hostage Ken Bigley in Iraq.
In November that year, the six were placed under the strictest control orders possible - forcing them to observe an 18 hour curfew.
Last August, the orders were quashed by the courts under human rights law for being too strict and ministers had to reduce the curfew to 14 hours.
Within hours of the ruling, a member of the group, later named as Bestun Salim, went missing. The Iraqi Kurd, the first control order suspect to abscond, is since thought to have returned home.
Security Minister Tony McNulty last night appeared to blame the courts for the latest fiasco and once again indicated the Government may set aside human rights law so it can impose tougher control orders.
"Control orders are not even our second - or third - best option, for dealing with suspected terrorists," he said, "but under existing laws they are as far as we can go."
He said the restrictions placed on the latest man to abscond were "the most stringent obligations we could impose in this individual's case".
But he added: "Within these limits, it is very difficult to prevent determined individuals from absconding."
"We will consider other options - including derogation - if we have exhausted ways of

overturning previous judgments."
Derogation - or opting out - of the convention would allow the Home Office to bring
in a tougher form of control order.
Five of the seven missing control order suspects have been named.
Along with Bestun Salim, they are Lamine Adam, 26, his brother Ibrahim, 20, and
Cerie Bullivant, 24.
Zeeshan Siddiqui, 26, a former London Underground worker who trained with a
London suicide bomber in Pakistan, is also missing.

This is what makes me fucking mad. It's insane. 'If' these guys are so dangerous, then why the fuck are they not in a max secure jail? How can they be on 'tag' and living 'free'? it just don't add up in my book. The public are being put at risk. So the question the public need to ask is: if the nutters are out on tag, why can't Charlie Bronson be tagged?

Hey guys, I'm not gonna bomb the planet up and I'm not a threat to the state, so let's get something moving to get me my freedom. Let's stop playing games. Isn't enough enough now? Let's stop all this crap and get some sense back into our country. This guy Al Zarqawi is a fucking warlord. He is capable of mass murder. Now put him up against my crimes. I'm a pussycat compared with him, yet he and the other Muslim cranks have all fled on tag when they should have been held in jail. Somebody please explain this shit to me, as I can't work it out no more. What exactly have I done to live like I do, or am I missing something out here? Maybe if I were a Muslim fanatic I might get a tag? Well, fuck the state. Fuck you all. You're just a bunch of faceless, spineless prats.

This isn't law or justice, it's a bloody circus run by a bunch of clowns. No wonder our great country has gone downhill. Talk about the lunatics having taken over the asylum ... it's now true - you have!

Hey, it's about time my CCRC come up and I'm back at the Appeal Court. Read my QC's Report to the CCRC in April 2007. It says it all. Mr James Lewis QC is my brief. He's one of the UK's top QCs and my case is 'UNSAFE' - WATCH THIS SPACE. The truth is I either walk free from court or I'll get carried out in a coffin, coz the powers that be don't want me to go free EVER. I think my end could be as interesting as my beginning.

IN THE CRIMINAL CASES REVIEW COMMISSION
CCRC Reference: 00358/2006
REGINA
-v-
CHARLES BRONSON
ADVICE

Background

1. On 17th February 2000, following a trial before His Honour Judge Moss and a jury at Luton Crown Court, Charles Bronson was convicted of false imprisonment. Mr. Bronson, who was unrepresented throughout the trial, had sought to advance a defence of duress of circumstances, but the learned judge withdrew the defence from the jury. Mr. Bronson received a sentence of life imprisonment, with a specified period of three years. His appeal was dismissed on 2nd April 2004.

2. In May 2006, Mr. Bronson applied to the Criminal Cases Review Commission for review of his conviction, with a view to a reference being made to the Court of Appeal. This application was refused in March 2007. For further details of the application and its refusal, the reader is directed to the Advice submitted on Mr. Bronson's behalf on 31st May 2006 and the statement of reasons issued by the Commission on 5th March 2007.

Renewal of application to the Commission

3. Mr. Bronson now seeks to renew his application to the Commission. The issue raised is whether in the circumstances of the case the learned judge should have requested the assistance of an amicus curiae. This argument was not raised on the appeal, or in the submissions made to the Commission on Mr. Bronson's behalf in May 2006.

Amici curiae: general principles

4. An amicus curiae is a non partisan participant in proceedings, whose role is to provide information or assistance to the court on questions of law or fact. The court has a discretion whether to request such assistance. The present practice is to exercise this discretion in two main sets of circumstances (see e.g. Allen v. Sir Alfred McAlpine & Sons Ltd [1968] 2 QB, at 266F-G, per Salmon LJ) The circumstances are:-
(i) Where the court considers that an important point of law has arisen in the proceedings, which for some reason may not be fully argued by the parties.
(ii) Where one party is not represented (or perhaps not adequately represented) and the court considers that in fairness that party's case should be fully presented.

5. Clearly these categories overlap. In the present case, Mr. Bronson was an unrepresented defendant in criminal proceedings which involved a substantial issue of law (the scope of the defence of duress). The case may therefore fall within both categories.
6. It is important to note that although it is a prerequisite for inclusion in the second category that a party is unrepresented, the role of the amicus, once appointed, is not to provide formal representation. An amicus is there to assist the court, not to act as counsel for the unrepresented party. He cannot take instructions from that party and he does not generally have the right to tender evidence or cross-examine witnesses: R

v. Mills [1997] 2 Cr. App. R.206, at 214, per Swinton Thomas LJ. Subject to these limitations, however, his task is to present the party's case as fully as possible.

7. The basic principle underlying the second category of cases is that, if a defendant is unrepresented, the court should appoint an amicus to present his case, where it is in the interests of justice and fairness to do so. This stems partly from the defendant's right to a fair trial, under Article 6 of the European Convention on Human Rights and at common law. There is also a wider public interest in the fair and proper administration of justice.

8. In determining where the interests of justice and fairness lie in any particular case, the court should, in my view, have regard to the following factors:
(i) The reason why the defendant is unrepresented.

(ii) Any physical or mental characteristics of the defendant which are likely to affect his ability to present his case.

(iii) The seriousness of the offence and the potential sentence, in particular whether conviction is likely to result in the defendant losing his liberty or livelihood, or suffering serious damage to his reputation.

(iv) Whether the proceedings may involve novel or complex issues of law. (Evidently there is an overlap with the first category of cases in this respect).

(v) Whether the proceedings may involve novel or complex issues of fact.

(vi) Whether it is in the interests of someone other than the defendant that the defendant's case is fully presented.

9. This list is not exhaustive. The court should consider all the circumstances of the case, having regard at every stage of the process to the underlying principles of justice and fairness.

Application of these principles to the present case
10. In my view, the issue which arose at Mr. Bronson's trial, whether the defence of duress of circumstances should be left to the jury, was an important issue of law, which in the circumstances was not likely to be fully argued. The proceedings therefore fell within the first category of cases in which the court should request the assistance of an amicus.
11. Having regard to the factors listed at paragraph 8 above - in particular factors (iii) and (iv), and possibly factor (ii) - I also consider that Mr. Bronson's case fell within the second category of cases in which an amicus should be requested, i.e. cases in which the defendant is unrepresented and it is in the interests of justice and fairness that his case should be presented as fully as possible.

Safety of the conviction
12. Overall, my opinion is that an amicus should have been appointed in Mr. Bronson's case and that, in the absence of an amicus, the trial was unfair. This raises

the question whether Mr. Bronson's conviction is, as a consequence, unsafe.

13. In dismissing Mr. Bronson's appeal on 2nd April 2004, the Court of Appeal held that, although the learned judge's explanation of his decision on duress was not as clear as it might have been, it was nonetheless the right decision. The reason for this was that in order for duress to be made out there must have been, objectively assessed, an imminent danger in this case. Further, the judge was entitled to conclude that there was no evidence of a nexus whereby the duress relied on by Mr. Bronson impelled him to act as he did.

14. It would appear therefore that if the only advantage which would have been gained by the appointment of an amicus is that the judge would have heard more thorough argument on the law, then the absence of an amicus does not render Mr. Bronson's conviction unsafe.

15. On the other hand, it may be that the advantage of appointing an amicus would not have been limited to the presentation of the law. It is possible that it would also have had an impact on Mr. Bronson's presentation of the facts, such that there would have been evidence of an imminent danger and of a nexus between that danger and Mr. Bronson's actions, and the right decision would therefore have been to leave the defence of duress to the jury. If that were the case, then the absence of an amicus would, in my view, render Mr. Bronson's conviction unsafe.

James Lewis QC, Rachel Kapila, 3 Raymond Buildings
26th April 2007

CHAPTER 8
COME AND SMELL MY
NEIGHBOURS FROM HELL

THE DEVIL'S SON
He walks the asylum corridors
With an Uzi in his mind
Blood, snot and tears
Madness is also blind
Dreams that crashed and died
Tears that turned to blood
Just another loony
Face down in the mud
A shark inside a tank
A monster behind the glass
Forever looking out
In hell there is no grass
A number for a name
A cage for a home
All dressed up in white
A dog without a bone
The darkside of the loon
Pictures in your head
The key inside the lock
One turn and you are dead
Eyes that never shine
Lips that never smile
A body bent and twisted
The throat is full of bile
Bitter like a lemon
Ugly like a bear
Never feeling human
Pulling out his hair
Life is just a struggle
Life is but a joke
Dragons in your head
Fill your face with coke
Walking up and down
Year after year

CHARLES BRONSON

Loonies in your face
Never changing gear
No flowers, no trees, no birds
Concrete, steel and wire
The end is creeping in
A furnace full of fire
The asylum is a cemetery
Dead men in a dream
How can this be human?
Dead men really scream
Hell behind the wall
Broadmoor sucks you dry
You laugh, you cry, you sing
A bullet in your eye
Born to be a loony
Play the hand your dealt
Your time is almost here
By God your gonna melt
Death is but a blessing
A body bag and you're free
No one lives forever
You, or him, or me
A bat flies in your room
It bites you in the face
You know your time has come
To leave the human race
What fun, what joy you had
Pull the other one
Let's not kid ourselves
You was the devil's son

Until you've walked those asylum corridors and lived amongst the loons, you can never really know what it's like. How can you? You can't.

It's the ultimate experience of life on the other side. It's fucking brilliant, exciting and very, very, very dangerous. You've gotta have eyes in the back of your skull. Anything can happen, any time, any place! You're not even safe in bed if you're in a dormitory. You're sleeping in a nightmare. A room full of nutters.

Okay, yeh! Political correctness again! They don't like to call 'em loons or asylums. It's all nice words now - hospital, therapy, patients! Well, with me you get what it is. Broadmoor is a fucking giant straitjacket. It's full of mad people; dangerous mad people. Some will eat you. Some will shag your dog. Others will rip your heart out for fun. It's your worst ever nightmare.

I'm not into political correctness. I'm into the truth; reality. And I'm telling you, Broadmoor is the same asylum as it was a hundred years ago: a lunatic asylum for the criminally insane. I lost five years of my life behind that wall, so I'm a man who can speak of the horrors of mad people. I can relate to it all coz I lived it; I saw it; I smelt it.

Did you know that the insane have a very musky smell about them? It's a fact. They stink of madness. It's like a mental odour they throw off. Fuck knows what it is. But you can smell a madman a mile off.

I remember once standing at an underground station in London. Hundreds of people were waiting to jump on the tube. I clocked a nutter. He looked what he was: a loon. He had that face, that presence. His eyes were bulging. He had that sicko smile about him. I clocked the passengers' faces. They were uncomfortable. You could see it: fear. He was only a skinny little bleeder. Scruffy but dangerous. He could push you under the train for a laugh, and that's the madness he threw off. You can smell it, sense it. Some of the passengers were deliberately stepping back just in case. They sensed it, I saw it. Some of the women looked scared.

I walked over to the loon, put my hand on his shoulder and whispered in his ear, "Oy, fuck off now." He fucked off, simple as that, and that's how you deal with madness. You cut the bud, stop it; you don't allow it to grow. No one knows what a madman will do, but you can guess. You can sense it: that moment of insanity. You either step in fast or you're a part of it. He was obviously off his rocker, unpredictable, probably sky high on drugs, but my one firm hand and words brought him to reality. He fucked off to scare the shit out of another crowd some place else. My crowd were safe.

And that's how life is in the asylum 24/7. Sure, there's no trains, but there's plenty of dark tunnels. The mind is the tunnel and at times the mind explodes. Every loony is capable of falling off the edge and when it happens it rocks the boat. People get hurt. Some die.

You're walking on a minefield, believe me. It's why I am what I am today: a very aware man; alert; prepared for anything. I'll never change either. Be prepared - always. If you put your guard down, you become a target. Predators don't pick and choose, you know. They're vicious, hungry bastards. They're hunters. It's how they live. Being behind a wall don't change nothing. A mad killer can or will kill again. It's as simple as that.

And being Charlie Bronson many loons dream of killing me. It's the Jesse James treatment. If you take out Jesse, you become a somebody. For some young loony to take me out would put him high up on the chart of achievement. It's a fact of life and that's what it's all about. If you take the Daddy out, you become the Daddy.

LOVE THY NEIGHBOUR
Ha ha ha, what a laugh
How do you love a lunatic
Somebody tell me

CHARLES BRONSON

Could you
It's not exactly your everyday situation
Borrowing a cup of sugar
Neighbourhood Watch
Barbecue time
Let's party
My neighbours are insane
I rarely see them
They don't see me
We only hear and smell
And imagine
Anyone for tennis
Or a quick dip in the pool?
It would be your last dip
Drowned, you bastard
Even a game of tennis
Would end in death
Or serious injury
This is not Wimbledon
This is the cemetery
We are zombies
Neighbours from hell
There is no cups of sugar
Or chatting over the garden fence
Love thy neighbour
Yeh, sure
Pass the chainsaw
I'll show you what love is
It's just a silly word
A word that don't add up
We don't like it
It's fucking mental
Mentalism
We pace up and down like demented bears
Hungry for life
Dreaming of a desert island
Freedom
A sense of worth
A feeling of dreams
Our world is so unreal
So false
We can't speak no more
Silence says it for us
Years of keeping it in

Feelings squashed
A neighbour hangs
Another cuts his throat
What's new?
One falls to his knees
God save me, he screams
No more, no more, he shouts
The rest just laugh
Shut it, you prat
That's life in the graveyard
Heartless and cruel
To survive you need to be nasty
The devil's apprentice
It's a whole new world inside
Love thy neighbour
Ha, ha, ha, I'm pissing myself
I'd sooner pour petrol under their door
And make some toast
There is no neighbourhood
How can there be in solitary?
It doesn't exist
It's just a noise
A figment of your imagination
Get on with it
Neighbours? Don't make me laugh

Neighbours from hell! This unit I'm on here in Wakefield is known as 'the cemetery': dead men dreaming. It's the biggest black hole in the entire penal system. You can't get no deeper than this place. It's maximum secure, and built and designed for long-term isolation. It's total solitary.

They call it the CSC. They can call it what they like. I'm telling you it's just isolation. We rarely see each other. There's just six of us, all in cages. Take Fred Lowe next door to me. I may see him once a year if I'm lucky - on a good year, twice - and that's only to see him for a few seconds walking past my door or behind the cage door to the shower. No con. On this unit we are not allowed to mix, nor ever will. We are the incurable, the untreatable. Well, that's what they tell us.

I've now been here for five years (apart from two short spells away). This is my world: a cell with two doors, the outer one solid steel and bulletproof. When they unlock that door there's another door, a cage door, like in a zoo. That's what it is, a fucking human zoo. We are monitored and analysed 24/7. Everything we do or say is noted, reported: CCTV watches our every move; visits are closed and monitored; mail is censored; calls are taped. This is 200% control. Nobody moves on or off the unit without HQ say-so. It's the system's golden egg. It's fucking madness at its best.

My neighbours are out of a nightmare. I'm the only one who hasn't killed. The rest are murderers, insane killers, hopeless cases, never to be freed. They live in a cocoon.

Fred Lowe, all 20 stone of him, looks like a bear. He's got a massive skull. He looks what he is: a raving psycho. I've known him for well over 30 years and I've seen him go insane. Fred's just a crazy man. He loves his own world. Freddie Kruger is his hero and he's also a *Star Trek* fan. I hear him laugh a lot and talk to himself. Fred stabbed to death a con in Gartree Prison 20 years ago. He stabbed him so many times that he looked like a fucking tea bag. There was blood everywhere: the walls, the ceiling, the floor. It was an abattoir. Fred was the executioner. He was laughing hysterically when he did it. Other cons spewed up at the sight of it. Hardened screws fainted. Fred loved it. He loves stabbing people - anyone who upsets him. Ten years later, guess what? He killed another con! This time it was in Long Lartin Jail. He got the urge again, so out came the blade. Fred just enjoys killing. It's his thing.

Some of us enjoy a cup of rosie lea with a biscuit. Fred prefers a stiff. He's been locked up for well over 30 years now. He will die in prison. He knows he will. There's not a Home Secretary mad enough to release Fred Lowe. Fred just plods on in a world of his own. He don't get no visits, no mail, no calls, coz he don't want them. He don't care. He's long forgot he's a lost soul. He's a heartless, cold, cruel bastard. He don't know about humanity. Why should he? If he ever awoke he would go insane. Fred's just lost the plot.

Next door to him, two doors from me, is Bob Maudsley, Britain's very own Hannibal Lector, as described earlier. He's just a fucking lunatic. Keep taking the pills, you muppet.

And next door to him is the Beast of Bedlam, one ugly mother fucker, Victor Miller. This piece of shit raped and buried alive a 12-year-old boy. Miller the monster has been caged for well over 25 years. He's a dead man breathing. He stinks like a rotten corpse. The cheeky fucker tried to get compensation over the time I attempted to smash in his door at Woodhill. He claimed it caused him post-traumatic stress. Poor thing, I upset him. Upset him?! I'd willingly rip out his throat. He's a beast. He never showers. He stinks. His cage stinks. The screws hold their breath when they open him up. I've seen him four times in five years, each time only for a split second as he walked past the shower gate. He walks like a monster. He is a fucking monster. This is the closest you'll ever get to hell. It smells like decay.

Fuck knows how the screws work on here. But, then again, Wakefield Prison is known as Monster Mansion. The normal wings are full of monsters: the likes of Roy Whiting. Sidney Cooke, Black, Huntley, Cannon, baby killers, rapists. They are all here. We don't see them. They don't see us. Just as well. But that's our life, our world. Now ask yourselves something: what the fuck is Charlie Bronson doing in this cemetery? If you ever find the answer, please let me know. But, you know what? It grows on you. This room is my sanctuary; my space; my home; my life. It's everything to me. I write, I draw, I create my thoughts, my poems, my philosophy. I see myself as a tortoise. I'm in a shell, but not by choice. I'm stuffed into the shell. I can't get out. I'm stuck.

But I've learnt to survive it and to turn it around to my best advantage. The screws here all say I shouldn't be here. Most would set me free tomorrow, but it's Prison HQ that want me in this hole. It's get-back time. They want to make an example out of Bronson so that all the youngsters can see the end - a body bag. They did it with Reggie Kray. They're doing it with Ronnie Biggs and they're loving it with me. Well, they've got a long wait till I hit the floor. I'll live to a hundred just to spite the fuckers. I really will. If I don't win my appeal, then that's the end. But what is the end? Who knows? Who cares?

Hey, as I write this on 15 June 2007, guess what? Saira is on the *Jeremy Kyle Show*, still going on about 'us'. She's plugging her second book. Wow. She is still riding off my name. It's like a leech in a swamp on your neck, and the only way to get it off is burn it. They're horrible things. That's how I see people who can't move on and let go: leeches.

Get a job and stop talking about me. What's wrong with people? If you don't like to work, then go rob a bank, but don't be a bum. The world is full of them. They think the world owes them a favour. It owes you fuck all. Get your own bowl of soup.

THE CEMETERY
The cemetery is lovely and peaceful tonight
I use it to reflect
Some nights I can hear an owl
In the day there are crows
I can hear the trains, the station is just over the wall
I hear cars and motorbikes
There must be a fish and chip shop close by, as on a windy night
I can smell it
There's a brewery right outside the gate
A fucking brewery
What a wind-up!

We should've been allowed a piss-up when Shipman hung himself a while back. Best thing that old fucker ever done. He was an arrogant, obnoxious bastard. He actually thought he was better than everyone else. Can you believe that some of the cons were going to him for advice on their health? Fuck me, how insane is that? You may as well drink petrol and start smoking.

We had him here not long back - The Fox (Hutchinson). You remember

101

that piece of shit? Some years back he murdered four people. Two were a bride and groom, just wed. He burst in and raped the groom in front of the bride. Raped the geezer! I told you this is a madhouse. The Fox was - is - a filthy pervert. Why don't they just hang these monsters? What good are they? They're never to be released, so it's just sense to waste them. I used to whistle Billy Idol's song 'Nice Day for a White Wedding' when The Fox was out on the yard. He used to go mad. I'd sooner chin the bastard but I can't, so I whistle instead.

They've all been through this place, the devil's disciples. Colin Ireland 'The Fairy Liquidator', he don't like gays. He strangled five of them in London. He won't ever see daylight again. He's got a bus ride one-way ticket to hell. That bus will be full up for sure. I hope I miss the ride. Fancy being on that bus: no brakes, no steering wheel, not even a driver. What a crash! Loonyology.

Hey, you'll fucking love this one. There was a prison counsellor who held some of her meetings here in Wakefield Monster Mansion, where she met and fell in love with a con, and they got married here, the con copped a 14 stretch for kicking an old guy to death. He was a young guy when it happened. Are you on it already? Anyway, he was moved to Grendon and then to Ashwell. These jails are less secure, so the visits are less monitored, less observed. Plenty of sex goes on - and why not, I say. A good old-fashioned wank under the visits table and a bit of pussy juice flowing can brighten up the day. She visited him and stood by him for 12 years and he finally makes it out - free as a bird. She's 12 years older than him and he's still a young man. So guess what? He fucks her off for a newer model! And why not, I say. Did she really expect him to stay? Whilst he was inside she had the power hold. Well, it don't work like that does it? Life's not a dream, this is reality. A man or woman can't live on borrowed time. It all comes crushing in. So much for prison romance! I'd say it was pure lust. And don't I know. Now she's calling him all the nasty fuckers under the sun. Get some counselling girl, and move on. He's just catching up on some lost pussy years.

One of the nicest people I ever had the privilege of meeting inside was Sister Carmel Fennessy. Sister Carmel was a nun who used to visit here at Wakefield. She used to sit outside my cell door once a week and we had some lovely chats. Not about religion - as you know I've no time for that shit - but our talks were lovely! She always brought me news in from the outside world. She was just a lovely person with a smashing way about her: funny, clever, smart, warm and caring, and very much a true lady.

Earlier this year I was informed that she had died. What a loss to many! Please read her book, *A Time to Serve*. It's an eye opener. She truly was an inspiration and a wonderful friend to me. There wasn't a bad bone in her body. I'd say she was the closest thing to an angel I've ever met - and I don't mean Hell's Angels!

I bloody miss our chats, I really do. But nothing ever lasts in life. Even the good have to stop breathing. Flowers grow, blossom and die, and so do people. That's how it is. But I thought I had to give the nun a mention. Sure, there's other religious people here - priests, chaplains, Imams, and even some Sally Army nutter - but they stay clear of my door. I don't want them at my door. I'm sick of the religious bigots! I don't need any more shit in my life than I've got already. I'm a man, not a fucking puppet! No one pulls my strings; I pull my own. I'm what you would call 'a real man', not plastic or pretend. I'm proud of my manhood.

Talking of manhood, anyone up for giving me a blow job? Come on, I'm only human ...

13 November 2006, Solitary Confinement
A Report by THE NUFFIELD FOUNDATION

The Foundation is funding Dr. Sharon Shalev, Mannheim Centre for Criminology, LSE to produce a handbook on solitary confinement. The project aims to provide prison practitioners with a much needed single point of reference on the health effects of solitary confinement, and on professional, ethical and human rights law guidelines and codes of practice relating to its use.

Background

With the exception of the death penalty, solitary confinement is the most extreme penal practice legally imposed on prisoners. It was first widely and systematically used on both sides of the Atlantic in the 19th century as a tool for reforming prisoners (Roscoe, 1823; Rothman, 1980; Evans, 1982), but abandoned when it transpired that, rather than being reformed, a large proportion of prisoners became mentally ill (Ignatieff, 1978; Philo, 1989; McConville, 1981). By then, however, solitary confinement had become a permanent feature of prison systems worldwide, routinely used as a form of short-term, if severe, punishment for prison offences; for holding political prisoners and those charged with offences against national security and for protecting vulnerable prisoners. In addition, in the last two decades solitary confinement has been increasingly used as a tool for the long-term management of prisoners variously labelled dangerous, violent or disruptive. This trend is particularly prevalent in the USA, where the Federal Government and at least 38 states have constructed new prisons generically known as "Supermaxes", specially designed for a regime of strict and prolonged solitary confinement. Although on a smaller scale, similar prisons have been built in the last decade in Australia, Canada, England, Holland, Peru, Turkey and South Africa, holding prisoners in conditions described by a US district judge, referring to a Supermax in California, as ones which "may press the outer bounds of what most humans can psychologically tolerate" (Madrid v. Gomez, 1995).

The assertion that solitary confinement profoundly affects the mind is endorsed by many health professionals and monitoring bodies. Studies indicate that it may lead not only to mental illness, but also directly contribute to increased violence, thus turning some prisoners into the dangerous individuals they were claimed to be all along (e.g. Nitsche & Williams, 1913; Faris, 193; Rasmussen, 1973; Rassian, 1983, 1986; Haney, 1994, 2003; Toch, 1992; Kupers, 1999). Prison sociologies from the 1950s to date similarly highlight the damaging effects of solitary confinement, and indicate that it is an effective tool for prisoner control (e.g. Sykes, 1958; McCleery, 1961; Colvin, 1992; Adams 1994, 1998; King & McDermott, 1995; Sparks et al. 1996; Rhodes, 2004). The severity of solitary confinement also raises human rights issues, and the practice is specifically addressed in a large number of international and regional human rights law instruments (including the UN International Covenant on Civil and Political Rights 9 (ICCPR), the UN Convention Against Torture (CAT), the UN Standard Minimum Rules for the Treatment of Prisoners (SMR)). In recent years human rights bodies have been increasingly explicit in their criticism of the practice and have stated that under certain conditions it may amount to cruel, unusual or degrading treatment in breach of international law (e.g. UN Committee Against Torture 2000; UN Commission on Human Rights 1996; Prison Reform Trust 1998 & 1999; Human Rights Watch 2000, Committee for the Prevention of Torture (CPT) various country reports).

But such criticisms, the experience and knowledge gained through over two centuries of the use of solitary confinement in prisons, the wealth of medical literature documenting its damaging health effects, sociological and criminological research demonstrating its ineffectiveness, and human rights and legal standards regulating and limiting its use, appear to be largely unknown to those who devise and manage isolation units, not least those charged with diagnosing and treating isolated prisoners. In this regard, it could be said that prison health professionals unwittingly assist in making solitary confinement, to use a term coined by historian David Rothman (1980), become "legitimised despite its failures". The lack of a cohesive review of research findings on the health effects of solitary confinement, nor a single volume addressing relevant human rights standards, professional codes of ethics and best practice recommendations issued by professional and human rights bodies does not assist matters. This is a serious problem, particularly when, on the ground, growing numbers of prisoners and detainees are subjected to social isolation and restricted sensory input, with severe mental health consequences.

Objectives

The main objective of the Handbook on Solitary Confinement is to provide prison practitioners with a comprehensive single point of reference. Its outcome will be publication that will:

* *Document the health effects of solitary confinement*
* *Summarise relevant professional guidelines and recommended codes of conduct and ethics for prison practitioners*
* *Set out the human rights and other case law on its use*
* *Offer, in light of the above, best practice guidance on the use of solitary confinement.*

A regime of solitary confinement cannot be divorced from the physical design of segregation units, which also has an impact on prisoners' health. Equally, health effects will depend on the psychological state and particular circumstances of those placed in solitary confinement. The Handbook will therefore also:

* *Examine prison design issues and their impact*
* *Provide an overview of which prisoners are placed in solitary confinement, the role*

of health professionals in the prisoner classification process, and the possible conse-
quences of classificatory decisions.

Geographically, the Handbook will focus on UK and European practices, with
reference to the United States and elsewhere where needed. As findings on the health
effects of solitary confinement and international human rights laws, standards and
ethical codes are universally applicable, however, the core of the Handbook will be of
relevance to prisoners and prison practitioners worldwide.
It is hoped that the compilation and dissemination of the Handbook will achieve a
number of goals: firstly, to guide and inform prison health professionals and prison
staff about the health effects of solitary confinement, and prison designers and
architects on the impact of the prison environments they design; secondly, to inform
those working in prisons of the relevant codes of conduct and ethical guidelines
pertinent to their work; and, thirdly, to provide a single reference point on the human
rights position regarding solitary confinement for practitioners, policy makers, penal
reform and human rights organisations and legal professionals. On a more academic
level, the Handbook will help to demonstrate how the disciplines of criminology and
human rights, which have traditionally developed separately and with little reward to
one another, can, and should, serve to inform each other.

There's nobody on this planet who knows more about solitary than me.
Maybe Rudolph Hess or Rasputin did, but they're long dead. I am the
solitary king and it can't be disputed. All these doctors and psychologists
only guess what it's like. They haven't got a fucking clue. Half the prats
couldn't live one day of my existence and that's a fact. My solitary life is
unique. I've made it my journey. I've achieved so much out of nothing, and
I mean nothing. Isolation has helped me! I've passed the test. I don't
recommend it, it's not fun to live alone, but after so many years it's just
become a way of life. You learn to overcome the loneliness. You live the
dream. Fuck anyone who says it's not a life, coz it's my life. I've made it work.
In this graveyard I've created a lot of good. Who said dead men can't win?

Solitary is soul digging
Heart wrenching
You come alive in the dark
You shine through
You're seeing my art
You're feeling my poetry
That's not bad for a lunatic!
I'm the ex-Broadmoor no-hoper!
I'm the man without a soul!
So who are you?
What have you achieved?
You're free ... and I'm caged
It's fucking crazy!

CHAPTER 9
HER MAJESTY'S ALTERNATIVE LODGINGS

Here's a guided tour around the different prisons throughout the UK, some of which have swallowed me up and spat me out again. You won't find any of this accommodation in no holiday brochure, that's for sure!

HMP Acklington, Northumberland
Cat C, adult male
Before it opened in 1970 it used to be an old RAF camp. Don't know a lot about the gaff - not sure I want to.

HMP Albany, Isle of Wight
Cat B, adult male
Originally opened as a Cat C in 1967, but in 1970 it changed to a dispersal Cat A. In 1992 it went back to a Cat B. Inmates are 85% sex offenders. In the dispersal era Albany was one of the best max secure jails in the country. Cons were cons and screws were screws. Everybody knew their place. How times change. If you're not a sex case, stay clear of the place. During my stay there, there was just one wing for nonces, all on 43 Protection. Now there's four wings full of them! That tells you how it's changed. Bob Dylan had it spot on: times are a-changing.

HMP Alycourse, Liverpool
Adult male
Privately run by Group 4 and opened in 1995. Don't really know too much about the place, as I've never been in a privately run jail, but going by what other cons have said it's better than most jails. They say the visits are good and the food is excellent. So it can't be bad.

HMP & YOI Ashfield, Pucklechurch, Bristol
Male YPs
Another private jail, opened in 1999. In his national audit report Sir John Bourn stated that it was the worst young offenders institute in the country. That covers Ashfield.

HMP Ashwell, Oakham Rutland
Cat C, adult male
Opened in 1955. I know nothing about this place except that if you don't fit in you're soon on the bus out. They don't stand no nonsense in a Cat C. Misbehave and you're straight back to a Cat B.

HMP Askham Grange
Female Open Jail
Opened in the 1950s. Also has a baby unit - well, women prisoners do have babies! Where do you think the babies go? I don't know how it works. Not sure I want to know. I suppose it depends on how long the mother is serving and the baby reaching a certain age. Then they are separated. Rules are rules. My advice would be: don't get nicked if you're pregnant. Problem solved.

HMP & YOI Aylesbury, Bucks
Cat B, Closed, YPs
Built way back in 1847 and it's been used for all sorts. First it was an adult mixed prison, then a female borstal. Now it's a long-term secure jail for YPs, mostly lifers. Once they turn 21 they're moved to adult jails. In 1870 a 20-year-old called William Mobbs was the first to be hung there. His body was buried in the grounds. They were tough old times. Cor, not 'arf!

HMP Bedford
Cat B, male
First opened long before my time, in 1801. It's actually my local prison but I've never been sent there (they refuse to accept me). This was the place where John Bunyan wrote *Pilgrim's Progress*. Not that I care a flying fuck what he wrote. I visited a friend there back in 1969. It looks medieval, like stepping back in time - to the days when porridge was lumpy.

HMP Belmarsh, London
High security, male
Opened in 1991 and was built on a fucking marsh! Can you believe that? All the faces have passed through there over the last 16 years. Just to name a few: Charlie Kray, Reggie Kray, Ronnie Field, Dingus Magee, Dave Courtney, Lord Archer, Ronnie Biggs, that one-eyed, hooked, Islamic nutter Hamza ... oh, and me. It was there that I hijacked the Iraqi hijackers, That siege cost me an extra seven years. Such is life. As jails go it's not a bad place. The food is shit though, but bear in mind that it's got 1,000 cons there - that's a lot of porridge to make.

HMP Birmingham, Winson Green
Cat B, male
Opened in 1848. It's had it all; seen it all and got the T-shirt. It's a tough old lock-up jail, make no mistake about it. It's one of the old 1970s regime jails. Ask the 'Birmingham 6'. They got the shit bashed out of them there, first by the screws and then by the cons. That's how it was in the 'The Green'. Barry Prosser died there in 1981 (in a strip cell). Three screws were charged with murder but they all got cleared at trial. So who did kill Barry Prosser ... himself? Oh, and it was there that Fred West topped himself. Best thing he ever did. Let's hope Rose follows him.

HMP Blakenhurst, Worcestershire
Cat B, male
Another private run jail, opened in 1993. I know very little about the place, except that in 1994 Alton Manning was unlawfully killed when several screws applied the control and restraint techniques on him. That's what happens when people are not up to the job. He died of asphyxia. They're not supposed to strangle us! They're trained to restrain us if we are violent. Alton died. No reason for it. I've been jumped on and beat up more times than I can remember! Why haven't I been killed? I've been put in straitjackets and body belts. Why haven't I been killed? A few times I've come close to it, you can bet your arse on that. Could you imagine the kickback if I was killed? Heads would roll!! Believe it.

HMP Blundeston, Suffolk
Cat C, male
Opened in 1963. I know more about Mount Everest than Blundeston and I know FA about Everest.

HMP & YOI Brinsford, Wolverhampton
YPs, male
Opened in 1991. I know less about this place than I know about knitting.

HMP Bristol
Cat B, male
Opened in 1882. One of the old-style nicks. Full of character and brilliant legendary stories. Even the old screws love a story. It's years since I landed there. I like the place! It's unique and full of ghosts. I do love a ghost - you're never alone in a haunted house. On the seg block exercise yard, you can see the houses over the wall. Freedom! In one house I used to clock a woman peeping from the bedroom window every time I was out there! It got so regular. She used to flash me her tits. It was magic. Just what the doctor ordered! I'd be fucked now, as my eyes are not so clever. Lovely memories.

HMP Brixton, London
Cat B, male
Opened in 1851 and back then it was known as the 'House of Correction'. Then in 1852 it became a prison for females, 90% of them prostitutes and pickpockets. Then in 1882 it became a military prison until in 1884 it opened up as it is today. It used to take Cat A remands, but that stopped when two IRA men escaped with guns. That's why Belmarsh took over. Brixton has always been a shithole. It's just got that smell about it. But it's full of what a jail should be full of: excitement. You never know what's gonna happen in a jail like this. Stabbings, cuttings, murder, arson - It all goes on! My only advice to you new cons would be: don't bend over to pick up your soap in the shower. Believe me, you'd only do it the once! My second bit of advice would be: pray you get bail.

Broadmoor Hospital, Berkshire; Ashworth Hospital, Liverpool; Rampton Hospital, Nottingham
Max secure asylums for the criminally insane
I thought I'd best put these in before I forget, simply as the system don't like to see them as prisons. But to me they are prisons! Locks, bolts, cameras, razor wire, dogs, 30-foot wall, screws in size 10 boots. I can't ever call a prison a hospital. Sorry, but only mad people could do that and I'm not mad! Are you?

HMP Brockhill & YOI, Worcestershire
Female
Opened in 1997. I don't really know a lot about this place, but I wouldn't mind six months there myself. Me and the girls could have a good laugh! Well, why not? I am only human after all!

HMP Buckley Hall, Lancashire
Closed, female
Opened in 1994. It was a male prison until 2002, then it changed to female. I bet it cost a few bob to change it all, especially the toilets! Well you can't have women pissing in men's urinals ... or can you?!

HMP Bullingdon, Oxfordshire
Cat B, male
Opened in 1992. Originally accepted Cat A prisoners, but that stopped in 1995. I don't know why. I hope it wasn't anything to do with me taking a solicitor hostage. I enjoyed my couple of stays there in the seg block. The food was brilliant and the lay out was very humane - probably too soft. I'm not used to all that comfort. I don't normally like the new-style jails, but this one was pukka - even the strongbox was nice and spacious and clean. For those who don't know what a strongbox is, I'll educate you. It's a double-

doored isolation cell where they put 'naughty' cons. Fuck knows why I was in there! Oh, and as for the solicitor siege, it was just a bad day! Come on, don't tell me you don't have bad days.

HMP & YOI Bullwood Hall, Essex
Closed, female

Opened in 1962 as a female borstal. 'The Good Old Days'. But words change, places don't! It's now called a YOI, but they still lock young teenage girls up in it. So in reality it's still a borstal. Maybe it's not so strict or disciplined, but it's still a borstal - or am I missing something here? Look: a jail is a jail is a jail; a car's a car; a plane's a plane - so to me it's still a borstal! I'd love to be a fly on the wall in their dormitory ... cor, not 'arf! Now that would be worth being a fly for the day.

HMP Camp Hill, Isle of Wight
Cat C, male

Opened in 1912 and has some serious history to it. It was actually opened officially by Winston Churchill as a preventative detention establishment and - guess what? - cons from other jails helped to build it. That's how it was in them days. Fucking mental Camp Hill is right next to Parkhurst and Albany - three jails together! Why don't they just make it one jail? In fact, why don't they move everybody off the IOW and turn the whole Island into a prison colony? Food for thought. In the 1950s it became a borstal and it was a tough old regime. Then in 1957 it became a Cat C jail. I spent just one day there! I don't think they liked me but, then again, no love lost.

HMP Canterbury, Kent
Cat C, male

Opened in 1808. Outside the old gate lodge there's still a carved inscription: 'House of Correction'. Well, that's what all the old jails were called in their day. Sounds good, eh? Historic museum stuff. It's like a Bronson medieval tour - a trip through the archives of hell! It also became a naval prison in the 1940s. I bet there was a few sore arses then! 'Over the barrel, where's the Vaseline?' Then in the 1950s it just became a local jail. Now it's a Cat C trainer. I bet the sailors are sick.

HMP Cardiff, Wales
Cat B, male, local

Opened in 1827. Hey, look, It's a Welsh nick. I bet they do a nice lamb hotpot there! This was one of the old hanging jails and they hung an innocent man - Mahmood Mattan. He was convicted of killing a woman in 1952, the year I was born. So I'm born and Mahmood is murdered by the state. In the court of appeal 46 years later his conviction was quashed. He was an innocent man and they topped him! How many more suffered the same fate? Plenty I bet. In them days the Mr Plods, the local bobbies, were lovely people who never fitted people up or lied on oath. Like fuck they never! Let's hope Mahmood is still in Cardiff haunting the bastards.

HMP Castington, Northumberland
YP, closed, male
Opened in 1979. I get quite a lot of mail from the YPs around the country. Most of them read my books and just write to me for advice. I'm a bit like an agony uncle, I really am, and I always give good advice. A lot of YPs are just confused with life inside and they miss their families. I tell them to read my book, *Solitary Fitness*, so they can get into some serious physical workouts. I tell them it's no good pulling your dick all day and fantasising about page 3 dolly birds. You've gotta work out your frustrations and become alert and ready for your release. They're basically all good lads. They just need a bit of respect, and putting on the right road. I did read that some screw in this gaff just got awarded 100K compensation for stress and - guess what? - there's another 100 screws gone down with stress! I wonder why?! Fucking stress! You don't know what stress is. It makes my blood boil to read such crap! If you're an easily stressed sort of person then you shouldn't be in the job, you muppet. What is this country coming to? It's full of wimps. 100K for a stressful screw! Poor thing ... tuck him up in bed. Fucking muppet!

HMP Channings Wood, Devon
Cat C, male
Opened in 1974. It's close to Newton Abbot racetrack, not far from good old Torquay. There's a good few lifers there, coming to the end of their sentences. So it's probably a nice chilled-out sort of jail. It's obvious why: a lifer has to behave or he don't get out! And for a lifer to be in a Cat C it's almost home time! They're chilled-out cons. This jail is so laid back it's even got its own radio station. It broadcasts to all the south Devon jails. Not bad, eh? Jailhouse Rock, House of the Rising Sun, Bat out of Hell. Hey, guess what they call the station? Come on, guess ... Con Air Radio! It had to be didn't it?! The DJ Birdman.

HMP Coldingley, Surrey
Cat C, male
Opened in 1969. Coldingley was the first ever industrial training prison. You worked, or you got moved out. I see it as slave labour, 'working for peanuts'. Nothing more, nothing less. I can't understand cons. Why don't they work outside for a good wage rather than work inside for peanuts?! It don't make sense to me - or am I mad?

HMP & YOI Cookham Wood, Kent
Training, female

Opened in 1978. I don't really know too much about this place. With a name that sounds like Cock Ham, it beggars belief. I think they called it that to wind the girls up. I bet that's all they do there - dream about cock! How cruel is that? In 1997, ten years ago, Carol Hanson gave up her dream of ever getting out. She'd served 25 years inside. Her end was suicide. She made it out in a body bag! How sad is that? But she made history, as hers is the only suicide by drowning recorded in a female prison in the UK. Some people are just born to make records! Even in death they are legendary characters! God bless you, Carol.

HMP Dartmoor, Devon
Male

Opened in 1809. One of our finest infamous/notorious prisons! It's the museum of institutions. It's hell on earth. Even the cockroaches wear boots and the rats chase the cons. Dartmoor is just Dartmoor - historic. It's had its escapes, murders and riots! It's had it all and no doubt there's more to come. The stories to come out of this place could turn your hair white. I suppose the best known convict ever to enter its doors must be Frank Mitchell in the 1960s. He also escaped from there, never to be seen again. Some escaped only to die on the freezing cold moor, and we are talking FREEZING cold. Don't dare to go over the wall in winter, as the odds are you'll freeze to death. Even in the summer you could easily get lost on the moor. Better still, don't end up in jail and then you won't have to escape. Hey, years back it was so damp in the seg block that water used to run down the cell walls. No wonder there were a lot of sick cons. But, then again, It's what jails were all about. It's hard to believe that in 2007 it's still open. Obviously it's all been touched up and modernised, but it's still Dartmoor. They can do it all up, but it's still the same old cells and walls. The ghosts live on - plenty of them too.

HMP Deerbolt, Co. Durham
HMYOI, male

Opened in 1973 as a borstal, but now it's a YP jail - just the same, only a different word. All this political correctness bollocks! Why not just leave it as a borstal? It actually sounds better than HMYOI and we'd all understand it better. "You're going to borstal, laddie, for two years." It sounds like a punishment, don't it?! Why do we have make life so complicated for everyone? Some things are best left alone. Or am I just old-fashioned?

HMP Dorchester, South Yorkshire
Local, male
Opened in 1881. One of the historic prisons! They used to hold public hangings outside the gate. Imagine that. "Come on, kids, pack the picnic basket, we're off to Dorchester to see some executions." How fucking cruel did we used to be? What sick bastards we once were.

HMP Dovegate, Uttoxeter
Cat B, male
Opened in 2001. Another privately run jail, so I'm at a loss myself and I can only go on what I'm told. It's bollocks! So what's new?

HMP Downview, Surrey
Closed, female
It's right next door to High Down (male prison) and on a windy night you can smell pussy, you really can. I'm sure they only do this to wind us up! Why stick a women's jail next to a men's? It's a fucking wind-up! Must be for the girls too! Why don't they just stick us all in one jail? What a fucking orgy that would be - loonyfantastical! I've just made that word up. It'd be a great name for a jail!

HMP & YOI Drake Hall, Staffordshire
Semi-open, female
Opened in 1958 and was a male open prison until 1975, when it became female semi-open. I don't really know a lot about it. It's one of those jails that don't get a lot of media attention, which tells me it's a fucking boring place not worth speaking about. It's not even had a riot or a roof protest. How fucking boring.

HMP Durham
High security, male, female unit
Opened in 1840. The female wing is fenced off from the male side of the jail and holds 100 women, mostly lifers. It's a fucking madhouse! Imagine it! A screw once told me - in confidence - that a lot of the girls have the biggest dildos you've ever seen. In fact he said they're considered dangerous weapons and have to be confiscated! He told me that when Rose West was there she had a 12-incher, and a lesbo partner to go with it! It's fucking disgusting ... I wish I could watch! Durham's one of the old jails and plenty were topped there over the years. The old hangman certainly had his work cut out! What used to wind me up when I was there was Durham Cathedral ringing its muggy bell all day on a Sunday. It gave me a headache! Fucking wankers. Oh, they do a lovely drop of soup up there. It's more a broth really, but very thick and rich. It's bloody hard to understand what them Geordies are talking about. They're a tough breed up there too, coz in the winter

you're freezing your bollocks off and the screws are walking about in short-sleeved shirts, showing off their tattoos. They're a strange lot! When I go there, I'm always kept in the 'special cage'. Oh yeh, and the dentist there is a lady. She's the best dentist I've ever come across in any jail. She really does care about us and does a good job. But she must think I'm a right animal, coz when I visit her I'm kept in restraint cuffs and there's always ten screws with me. She must think I'm Charles fucking Manson! The best escape ever from Durham was back in the sixties - John McVicar. They even made a movie about it, starring Roger Daltry from The Who. Durham Jail's had it all - murder, arson, rape, stabbings, cuttings, roof protests, hostages. It's a fucking house of horrors! But it's one of them jails that grow on you.

HMP & YOI East Sutton Park, Kent
Open, female
Opened in 1945 as a borstal for girls, but now holds females under 21 and over 21. Not a lot I can add to that, except to say there must be some gorgeous pussy in there. It would be a dream come true if I was sent there to serve my sentence. What a dream!

HMP & YOI Eastwood Park, Gloucestershire
Closed, female
Opened in 1996 as a female jail, but before that, from 1964, it was actually a boys' detention centre for a few years, and a tough one at that - a proper old-fashioned boot camp: bed packs, short back and sides and marching orders! "Yes sir, no sir, three bags of shit sir." Now a female nick, so what's left to say? Do your bird.

HMP Elmley, Kent
Local, male
Opened in 1992 and has two jails next to it on the Isle of Sheppey: HMP Swaleside and HMP Standford Hill. I bet the Isle of Sheppey loves having three jails on its plot! I don't really know too much about the gaff. It's not the sort of jail I can move to. You'll all remember Jonathan Aitken the former Conservative Defence Minister - well, he got released from there in 2000. Have you noticed how 'cons' like Aitken always get sent to soft jails and always find Jesus? Amazing that is ... fucking amazing!

HMP Erlestoke, Wiltshire
Closed, male
Opened in 1960 as a boys' detention centre. These centres popped up all over the UK in the '60s and '70s. But did they work? Did they fuck!

HMP Everthorpe, East Yorkshire
Cat C, male
Opened in 1956 as a closed borstal and it stayed that way till 1983. Then it became a youth custody centre right up until 1991 when it became a male adult Cat C. In 1995 there was a good old-fashioned riot there. That was a good year, '95. It was the year Fred West hung and also the year three cons had it over the wall from Parkhurst. Three cheers for '95! Hip hooray, hip hooray, hip hooray! A good riot, a great escape, and a nonce topping himself. Brilliant.

HMP & YOI Exeter, Devon
Adult & YP, male
Opened in 1854. One of the old jails and full of character. Now has a YP wing separated from the adult wings - otherwise there would be some seriously sore arses.

HMP Featherstone, Wolverhampton
Cat C, male
Opened in 1976. Located next door to HMP & YOI Brinsford, what I still call a borstal. My buddy Eric Anslow served a bit of time in Featherstone, He said it was easy bird, and he should know coz he's spent years in some of the toughest jails in the UK him. Between them, he and his brothers Dave and John must've served 100 years. With a name like Featherstone, I'd say it's soft ... too fucking soft!

HMP & YOI Feltham, Middlesex
Male
Opened in 1983. This place has forever been in the media over the years, but nothing so bad as in 2000 when Robert Stewart killed Zahid Mubarek - he bashed his brains in! Stewart was a known racist - a proper skinhead thug with swastikas on his head. And they locked him up with an Asian lad?! Come on. it's not rocket science. Why lock him up with an Asian? What did they expect? It was a case of feed the rat a mouse. It was incompetence within the system. They didn't care what happened! A young lad got his head bashed in for fuck all, that's what happened. Stewart got lifed off and young Mubarek got a grave! How fucking mad was that? But, then again, this is loonyology we're talking about, so what more do you expect?

HMP Ford, West Sussex
Open, male
Opened in 1960. Well, guys, this is the gaff! Five-star accommodation! This is the jail we all wish for, or dream about going to. It's the finishing hurdle and you're almost home - the end of your sentence is nigh! There's 'nothing' to stop you walking out, as it's an open jail. You could even pop out and have

a shag with your old lady and pop back in - who's to know? It's the Hilton of the jails. Please, please, please accept me! I promise to be good. I promise I won't sneak out and not come back!

HMP Forest Bank, Manchester
Local, adult & YP, male
Opened in 2000. I've not got a fucking clue about this drum, but the name Forest Bank sort of sums it up for me - piss-takers.

HMP Foston Hall, Derbyshire
Closed, female
Opened in 1997. Actually, it started in 1953 as a detention centre for young lads and stayed that way till 1996. Then the builders went in and changed it to a female nick. I've known a few girls who've done time there and they all said it was 'cool'. There's even a shower in each cell! Not bad, eh? But I'm told there's a lot of lesbo activity going on. Well, the girls do get lonely - they need a bit of loving - so a good stiff dildo does the trick. I wish I could go there to be a sort of helper like a listener or welfare! I'd be all right at that! I'm wasted really. I could do so much in Foston Hall!

HMP Frankland, Durham
Cat A high risk, male
Opened in 1983. They'll never forgive me there for taking the Governor hostage. Nasty, vindictive bastards! It's only a couple of miles from Durham Jail. They talk strange up there and they love a pint and a punch-up. A lot of the screws in Frankland seem hell-bent on trying their utmost to cause aggro. Every time I land there, it's straight into the seg block for me. They won't ever let me up on a normal wing there. I wonder why? Vindictive fuckers! I've probably been there half a dozen times over the last 20 years. I'm never kept there too long. There's one screw up there who I've known for donkey's years, and he's a gentleman (I won't say who) as he always goes out of his way to make my stay comfortable. If I ever saw him outside I'd drag him into a pub and get him pissed. Top geezer. Fuck knows how he sticks it in a shithole like that. My old buddy Charlie Magee died in his cell there. Charlie was from my old town of Luton. He blew a copper away on a blag. His death was one of those mysterious ones (if you know what I mean). We all miss Charlie - a top chap. The only con to escape from there was Franky Quinn. Believe me, it takes some brains to get out of a max secure jail, but he did it - in a laundry lorry! Well, I tell a lie. Alan Byrne did it too, but he pulled it off from an escort van going to hospital. A few of the chaps crashed into the escort with shooters and took him off the van. A lovely bit of work.

HMP Full Sutton, York
Cat A high risk, male
Opened in 1987. It's a madhouse! Every time I land there I'm jumped on, bent up and slung in the box. My time there is in a concrete coffin, being fed through a cat flap in the door. This place has seen and had it all over its 20 years of being open: riots, murders, arson, rapes, violence, more violence, and lots more violence! I'm afraid a lot of the explosions are down to drugs. There's a lot of smack heads there who think they're untouchable - bulletproof prats, and the screws actually think they're the chaps Ha ha ha! They really do believe they're tough guys. Okay, they're not all prats, but the ones in the seg block are. That seg block is a fucking joke run by clowns. But when you've got ten guards opening your door, all in riot gear, it really is bad odds if you decide to make a go. There's been a lot of sad incidents there over the years. Billy Skingle died there. Poor old Bill. He killed a copper in the early 1970s - shot him six times. He used to say that his tool had a hair trigger and it was an accident. It made me laugh that. Old Willie Taylor died there too. He was an old ex-boxer - a good heavy in his day. Mickey Jamison topped himself there, and I took the probation guy hostage. It all went on in that place. Not bad for a jail that's only been open for 20 years! They've even found bullets there and explosives! Nobody has ever escaped though. A few have had it away on escorts off the van, but nobody's ever gone over the wall. They've got that gaff sewn up as tight as a duck's arsehole.

HMP Garth, Preston
Cat B, male
Opened in 1988. It's next door to Wymott Prison. Why do they build jails so close to each other? I've never been able to work that one out. I don't know fuck all about Garth, only that my old mate Johnny Paton hung himself there. A sad day. A bloody big loss. Apart from that I don't know any more. I don't think I want to. Do you?

HMP Gartree, Leicestershire
Cat B, male
Opened in 1966. Gartree got decategorised in 1992, having previously been a Cat A max secure. I should know - I spent two years there. That place has been to hell so many times. It's satan's favourite hole. Believe it. It was back in 1987 that John Kendall and Syd Draper escaped from there in a helicopter (England's first and last chopper escape). It was fucking brilliant. The whole penal system was buzzing. It was party time! Nowadays it's a Cat B for lifers and from what I'm told it's okay. If you want to settle down and do your sentence 'easy', then this is the place to do it. If you're a lifer then you have to get your head down and sort yourself out, and if you get allocated to Gartree then you're lucky.
I hit lucky there in 1992: I chinned three screws in one day. A hat-trick!

Bosh, bosh, bosh! There was one old screw who worked in the seg block, Mr Kershaw. I'll always remember him. He was a hard man but a fair one and I liked him a lot. He was always good to me. He used to let me read his daily paper and he always gave me double helpings off the hotplate. He saved me a lot of aggro in that seg. Men like him know how to treat cons. You learn it with experience, through years of working in jail. Too many screws take life too seriously. They can't laugh. If a man can't laugh then he's a miserable cunt. They used to do a lovely Sunday roast there and duff with custard. Do you know, I never slept on a bed during all my time there. I never fucking had one. All my time was there was spent in the seg cell, the way I like it best: in the trenches; the battle zone ... let's get it on.

HMYOI Glen Parva, Leicester
Closed YOI and Remand Centre
Opened in 1974. I don't know fuck all about this place. It's probably run by the Invisible Man.

HMP Gloucester, Gloucestershire
Cat B, male
Opened in 1782 and is one of the old jails. It'll probably end up as a museum and the governor will be mummified.

HMP Grendon, Buckinghamshire
Cat B, adult
Opened in 1962. This place is beyond me. They call it the 'therapeutic experiment'. It's all based on psychological crap. The cons there have to agree to go for therapy and sign a contract, otherwise they can't or won't be there. It's a simple as that. Play the game or you're not welcome. Sure it works for some, but for me it's a piss-take. I'll never tell them where my loot is buried.

HMP & YOI Guys Marsh, Dorset
Cat C , male
Opened in 1960. This gaff takes adults and YPs. There's not a lot I can add to that. It's been open for 47 years and I can't tell you a thing about it. It's not even had a riot or a roof protest. What a fucking boring 47 years it's been.

HMP Haverigg, Cumbria
Cat C, male
Opened in 1967. It was in 1999 that the place exploded with a good old-fashioned riot. There was plenty of destruction. I'm not sure why it blew up - probably the porridge was cold. Whatever. These things happen. It just livens the place up and tells the screws to back off. They make a lot of good

quality garden furniture there and it sells well in Cumbria. See, cons are not all wasters. If you treat them well they behave well.

HMP Hewell Grange, Worcestershire
Cat D, open
Opened in 1946. This place was previously a borstal and a YP jail, but in 1991 it became a male adult jail. It's more like a big house than a jail, and it's surrounded by beautiful gardens and a deer estate. Sounds cool, eh? I could do with a spell there. One can dream on.

HMP Highdown, Surrey
Cat A, male
Opened in 1993. I gave the governor a sore jaw there. The cheeky fucker got a bit lemon with me, so he had to have some. I was moved out the same day, never to return. Sad really, as it was a lovely clean jail and very laid back. The grub was excellent. Hey, get this for a fact: Highdown is built on the grounds of Banstead Asylum. I told you it's all loonyology.

HMP Highpoint North, Suffolk
Closed, female
Opened in 1977. I know nothing about this drum, only that it holds 300 pussies. That's some pussy! Me-fucking-ow!

HMP Highpoint South, Suffolk
Cat C, male
Opened in 1977. This jail is 20 years old and I don't know sod all about it - nothing. Probably for the best.

HMP & YOI Hindley, Lancashire
Closed, male
Opened in 1961. This was one of the old-style borstals to begin with, for all the young hoopies from Manchester and Liverpool. It's not really changed since then. It still deals with YPs. Back in 1986 there was a coach load of YPs on the way to Hindley from Bridewell Courts and it kicked off. Four of them managed to escape out of the skylight in the roof. Well done lads. That was pukka.

HMP & YOI Hollesley Bay, Suffolk
Cat D, open
Opened in 1938, originally as a borstal. Fuck me, there were so many borstals all over the UK I've lost count of them all. Never did much good did they? So much for a tough regime. All it ever did was create tougher cons.

HMP Holloway, London
Cat B, female, local
Opened in 1852. Holloway was originally built for both men and women, but became a female jail in 1903. Here's a bit of knowledge for you: Oscar Wilde spent some time in Holloway before he went to Reading Jail. So it could've been 'The Ballad of Holloway'. How crazy is that? Ruth Ellis, the last woman to be executed in the UK, was hung in Holloway. What a fucking liberty that was. Here's something I bet you've all forgotten or didn't know. Back in 1974, the year I got put away, big fat lesbo screwess Patricia Cairns fell in love with Myra Hindley. Anyway, she got sacked and nicked for plotting to break Hindley out. She ended up with six years (should've been 60 years). What person in their right mind would want to break a monster out? Cairns served four years of it and got released (never to wear the infamous Holloway uniform again). Personally I think that she should've gone to Broadmoor. What sane woman could fall in love with Hindley or sacrifice her job to bust her out? Well, this is loonyology. I visited someone in Holloway years ago (I won't say who as I was visiting under an alias). There's a strange smell to the place - probably all the execution skeletons buried there. It looks very spooky. Mind you, I suppose I did too with a false beard on!.

Hey, before I go on any further I bet you're all thinking: fuck me, how does Charlie know all these amazing facts and stories? Well, I'll tell you: I'm a fucking genius, I'm a clever cunt and I do my research. My life has been in institutions and that's how I know it all. And I hope you appreciate the way I'm putting all these jails into alphabetical order. It fucking takes a lot of mental work. I'm actually feeling dizzy. So many poxy jails to think and write about. And, believe me, I'm not institutionalised, nor will I ever be. I despise prisons and all they stand for. They make me puke. I hate the sight of them. Anyway, we're up to H, and I've just done the pussy house, so what's next? Let me think ... That's it, I've got it. I'm back on the journey. He we go. Eyes down.

HMP Holme House, Stockton on Tees
Cat B, male
Opened in 1992. I really don't know a lot about these foreign jails. Well, anything past Watford Gap is foreign to me. All I know is that Holme House sounds a bit nutty. Fancy calling a jail a house! A fucking Wendy house no doubt. It's not a Dartmoor, that's for sure.

HMP Hull, Humberside
Cat B, male, local, and YP
Opened in 1870. This gaff's a museum; historic; fucking mental. It holds well over 1,000 cons. I first landed in Hull in 1974, but in the 1930s it was a

military prison, in the 1950s it became a borstal and then in the 1960s it became a max secure jail before its current Cat B status. It's been everything. What next? A brothel? In 1976 there was the infamous Hull Riot: five glorious days of violence and destruction. It was brilliant; magic; awesome. Did you know that Hull was the only jail that actually had a boxing ring? Well, that was when the fairy governor and screws took over with their fairy ways. The whole jail turned into a nursery overnight. It really was a no. 1 nick where men were men. I met the best of the best there: Charlie Wilson, Sydney Draper, Ian Dorum, Johnny Reid, Big Les Hilton, Timmy Tedstone, Paul Sykes, Harry Johnson, Bertie Costa, Ernie Page, Stan Thompson, Eddie Richardson. They were all there, the chaps: proper villains, tough cons, the dog's bollocks; the cream. I could write a book on Hull, I really could. I took a governor hostage there and a teacher, and I chinned over a dozen screws there. It was like a cowboy film. We lived on our toes. It was exciting; a buzz.

One of the best escapes ever went off in Hull CSC. Unit - Dave McAllister. It was fucking brilliant. He got this big fat teacher (looked like Rose West, but fatter) to fall in love with him and then he got her to do all sorts. He even told her that he'd take her to Australia with him once he'd escaped, and all that bollocks. Believe me, Dave's only been out with dolly birds. Anyway, to cut a long story short, he leads her up the garden path in the love trap and she helps him to escape. He got out of the max secure unit and right out of the jail. She got six years for it, daft bitch. Sadly Dave got nicked soon after in a flat down south. All that for nothing. It really was a lovely escape though. The things you do for love.

HMYOI Huntercombe, Oxfordshire
Closed, YP
Opened in 1946. Hey, get this for an exclusive: it was built in 1941 as an interrogation centre for prisoners of war - the Germans. I bet there were some screams coming out of that hellhole. Then in 1946 it became a borstal and has been a YP jail ever since. That's all I really know. Well, I've given you an exclusive, what more do you want?

HMP Kingston, Portsmouth
Cat B, male
Opened in 1877. It's a funny little place this. I once stopped there for dinner on my way to Parkhurst. It's like a castle and full of character. It's been an all lifers (mostly domestic) jail since 1969. I think it holds about 150 and most of them have a budgie. It must be like a giant aviary. Oh, and by the way, it's not true that I bit a budgie's head off - more fucking media lies. Anyway, Kingston when it opened, was for male and female inmates from the Portsmouth area and - guess what? - yeah, it was a borstal in the 1950s. Another fucking borstal! We must've had more borstals than bingo halls.

Johnny Hilton had it over the wall from there. A nice little escape it was too. But fuck all lasts - he soon got captured.

HMP Kirkham, Preston
Cat D, male
Opened in 1962. Get this for a fact: from 1998 to 2003 over 900 cons absconded from there. It's not an escape, as there's fuck all to escape. You just walk out. 900 gone walkies. It's now 2007. How many more? It's fucking mind blowing. Hey why can't I go to Kirkham. Please - I'll be good.
HMP Kirklevington Grange, Teeside
Cat C, male
Opened in 1992 as a resettlement prison. Actually it was a detention centre back in 1963. Fuck knows how or why it stopped - probably too many kickings given out, coz those detention centres were famous for a bit of size 10 boot fun. Fucking bully cowardly bastards. I do know now that this place won an award recently for the 'safest jail' in the UK. How lovely for them.

HMP Lancaster, 'The Castle'
Cat C, male
Opened in 1458. Get that - 1458. Fuck me. Can this place tell a story or what? Old dungeon cells and the walls are five feet thick. Talk about claustrophobia. It's the oldest fucking jail in Europe. Why 'The Castle'? It used to be a holding place for convicts waiting to be transferred to the colonies. Fucking *Papillon* or what? Just imagine what it was like in those times. I bet there's some skeletons buried there with some horrific tales. Cor, not 'arf.

HMYOI Lancaster Farms
YP, male, closed
Opened in 1993. I get plenty of mail off the lads there. Some ask me how best to do their bird. I always tell 'em: easy, eat plenty and train hard and get out as quick as you can.

HMP Latchmere House, Surrey
Cat D, male
Opened in 1948. This is the Daddy of them all. You actually leave the jail to work outside and then come back to sleep in the nick. It's for trustees - cons coming to the end of their sentence who are allowed home for weekends. So plenty of shagging the old lady and the dolly birds, booze, good parties, and then knock on the prison door to come back in. Must be fucking hard to knock on a jail door to ask to come in when you've just left a hot, wet, juicy pussy at home in bed. That must be torture. That's gotta be worse than a good kicking. I would sooner be on bread and water or smashing up rocks. How does a man leave a pussy to knock on hell's door? What a cruel system it is. But that's how it is - loonyology!

HMP Leeds, Armley
Adult male, local
Opened in 1847. It's a fortress, one of the old regimes, and a grade 2 listed building. I first landed there back in 1975 and I've been back there half a dozen times. It holds a good 1,000 cons; it's chock-a-block. The food is shit, but then again I've not been back there for a good ten years now. I once smashed through my cell door there. Only a handful of cons in the system have ever taken a cell door off - and Charlie Bronson is one of them. And I'm proud of that fact. It's not easy to take a door off - it takes a lot of sweat! They've executed a lot there over the years, and in the 1970s and '80's it had the highest suicide rate. It was a very gloomy, depressing place if you allowed it to suck away your soul. I spent a lot of my time there in the strongbox under restraint, battling my way through. I gave it to a sex case there in the bathhouse. He was a filthy paedophile. I just worked him like a human punchbag and I smashed his ribs to bits. It was brilliant. It's always good to do it in the bathhouse naked, coz you can just jump under the shower, the blood runs down the drain, you get dressed and you walk out. No evidence, only the busted-up body of the nonce. Why kill the fuckers?! Bash 'em up and let 'em suffer and live on in fear! Death is a release! Torture the scum. Nowadays they're spoilt rotten. Yeh, Leeds holds some crazy memories for me, like the day I robbed the canteen. I put a bag over my head with eyeholes cut into it, jumped over the counter and filled a bag up with sweets and tobacco. The snatch of the century! It's all loonyology. Fucking cockroaches, they're everywhere. I've had them crawl in my ears and up my nose as I slept. Fuck knows if any slipped up my arsehole! What a horrible thought. Dominic Noonan climbed the roof there in the 1980s! They went up after him and slung him off. Big Paul Sykes, who fought John L. Gardner in the 1970s, they bashed him to a pulp and broke his arm. John Massey got a terrible kicking there too. We all got the Armley treatment. Rivers of blood ran in that place. And there were rats as big as cats! The good old days.

HMP Leicester
Male, local
Opened in 1825. It's an old medieval castle, a fucking fortress, but I was on top of the world there back in the 1980s. There's a lovely view from the roof - you can see Leicester City Football Club. It once had a high secure unit there, housing a dozen cons. Anyone who was anyone was there: cons like Tommy Wisbey, McVicar, Joey Martin, Reggie Kray, Freddie Foreman, Ronnie Brown and Harry Roberts, who almost escaped from there by using a home-made crossbow. Yeh, there were some heavy guys there: gangsters, IRA, bank robbers, psychos. I remember one paedo coming into the gym shower and I grabbed him and put a blade at his bollocks. I told him, "Come in again and you'll lose your plums." Never did see him again.

HMP & YOI Lewes, East Sussex
Cat B, male
Opened in 1867. There's always a big cry about drugs in prison. How do they get them? Who brings them in? Is it the families on visits? Well it's not. Check this out. Prison Officer Andrew Hubbard was convicted at Hove Crown Court in 2001 of smuggling in heroin, cannabis and steroids and got seven years. So what do you really need to cry about? How long had he been doing it? How much dosh did he make? How many more bent screws are doing it? Cos I'll tell you now, loads have been convicted over the last ten years. Do some research. You're in for a big shock. There's bent screws all over the UK. Or do you think they're all angels? Wake up and smell the coffee. Every fucker's got a price, even the Prime Minister!

HMP Leyhill, Gloucester
Cat D, open
Opened in 1946. If you land in this jail, then you're almost free. A lot of lifers finish off their sentences here. Who remembers 'Dirty Den' in *Eastenders*? He served part of his life sentence here. He also started his acting here, as it's got its own theatre stage. So, if Dirty Den hadn't ended up in prison for murder, he may never have become Dirty Den. Is that good or bad? Personally I thought he was bollocks anyway - a total prat! But I'll leave it for you to decide.

HMP Lincoln, Cat B
Male, local
Opened in 1872. Lincoln is one of the old school regimes with old screw rules. Behave or take the consequences! They used to be very handy with the 'black pill', i.e. a good fucking seeing to with a size 10 boot. The last time I was there a good ten years back I chinned the Governor. We had a special unit on there, which only held six of us. Some good cons passed through that unit: Paul Sykes, Tony Steel, Jakucubcxtly (Polish), 'Varidic Joe the Greek' Joe Puritiss. One con called Kelly went on a visit and got caught having a blow job. Well, no harm in that is there? Except it was with a geezer! Dirty fucker! It fucked all our visits up that did. All our visits used to be on the unit and until he did that they were chilled-out visits. Fancy doing that - fucking loony. I liked Lincoln Jail. It was full of characters and some good old screws who turned a blind eye. I made some of my best hooch there. It was fucking rocket fuel - powerful stuff. I had it all sorted: a nice lump of yeast and plenty of fruit and sugar on a regular basis! For a litre of my hooch you needed to cough up a week's canteen (it was that good) and, no, I will never divulge the exact ingredients. Well, Guinness don't, so why should I?

HMP Lindholme, Doncaster
Cat C, male
Opened in 1985. This place was built on an old RAF base. The old hangars and ancillary buildings are still there and house the prison workshops. I've had mail from cons there, who all say it's easy - so it must be. It's not my type of jail though. I find places like that a bit boring: no atmosphere, a bit stuck-up, the screws are plastic, and the cons aren't real cons. It's more like a fucking circus.

HMP Littlehey, Cambridgeshire
Cat C, male
Opened in 1988. I call this place 'the muppet show', as it does a lot of sex programme treatments and therapy for the high number of sex offenders there. I feel sorry for the straight cons who have to be in the same nick as these nonces, but there you have it - that's how it is today. It's a new era, and the system bends over backwards for the nonces - literally. They hate us real cons, but they just love a nonce. I've never been able to work that out. It's loonyology.

HMP Liverpool, Walton
Cat B, male, local
Opened in 1855. This is one of the many Victorian jails and it's full of stories. It survived the German bombs, but it didn't survive the Bronson War - I pulled its roof off in the summer of 1985. A bloody lovely summer it was too! I got as brown as a berry (who needs Costa del Sol?!) I actually shit through the sky hatch. By the time it hit the centre's floor it was like a bomb and it went everywhere. It was five floors up, remember. This place holds over 1,500 cons. The Scousers loved me for ripping their roof off and I still get Xmas cards from some who remember it 22 years later. Historic, see. They're a good bunch the Scousers - funny cunts. I like them. I've met some legends in there over the years. I've probably been back six times, always in the seg block. In the 1970s it was a brutal place with lots of kickings, and I had (more than) my share of them. But I got on with a lot of screws. I met one there in 1974 who'd been working there since 1938. He was a right old fella who had many a story to tell. He told me about the executions he'd witnessed. He'd actually been on hanging duty many times and each one had sent a chill up his spine. You could see in his eyes the effect it'd had on him. There was another old screw there who used to give me a bag of hard-boiled sweets. He was a diamond. I was always on a ten-screw unlock in them days. I had one of my best fights ever in that jail. It started in the bathhouse with just me and one con, and then six of his mates jumped in. It was brilliant: 7 onto 1. That's how I come alive. Fucking bring it on. Half of my thumb had been bitten so bad it was hanging off and one of my eyes was closed up, but they were worse off than me. Cunts! Brave fuckers! 7 to 1 and

they still couldn't take me out! Give it a rest, and go and have a wank. Yeh, I've some wonderful memories of that place during the violent era, when men were men. Oh yeh, believe it! There are ghosts there. I'll tell you about it one day.)

HMP Long Lartin, Worcestershire
Cat A, high secure, male
Opened in 1971. Long Lartin to me represents loonyology at its very best. It's a fucking madhouse! I'm not sure what it's like now, as my last spell there was back in 1991. All the chaps have passed through there: Johnny Bowden, the Anslow Brothers, Alan Byrne, Billy Tobin, Stan Thompson, Charlie Knight, Alex Sears, the Coulson Brothers, Terry Smith ... I could go on and on. They were some of the best armed blaggers ever to walk in a prison yard - good honest robbers. That sounds crazy, don't it? I'll rephrase it - robbers with principles. "Hand over the loot or bleed to death, you cunt." In one day I chinned five screws there at breakfast time. Oh, and two nonces. Seven chins in one go - could be a record that. My time at Lartin to me really was a battle of sanity - so many went mad there: pissed up, drugged up and fucked up. Some resorted to suicide. Even Reg Kray cut his wrists there. Paranoia spreads in jail and it affects us all differently. I ran out of my cell one day with a broomstick with a blade on it. Why? Well, why not? That's how it was. The cells have electric doors. You push a button, speak, and they let you out, one at a time, through the night. It's nice to come out for a shit or a shower. It works well. It's a modern secure jail, see. Its got a gym and a sports field and the visits are humane. If you're doing a big sentence then you could be in a worse place.

HMP Lowdham Grange, Nottingham
Cat B, male
Opened in 1998. It's another privately run prison, operated by Premier Services. Some of the cons there work for £40 a week wages. Forty fucking quid! The average wage in the state jails is £10. Fucking get me to Lowdham Grange.

HMP & YOI Low Newton, Durham
Local, closed, female
Opened in 1965. I don't know much about this place, only that it's full of pussy. What else is there to know? Ain't that enough?

Hey, before I go on, howzabout this for an idea. The Yanks have Hollywood, the Indians have Bollywood, so why can't we have Loonywood? It's brilliant. Let's do it.

HMP Maidstone, Kent
Cat C, male
Opened in 1819. This place has been around for yonks. It was once a jail to
do your bird peacefully, but it's all different now. Maidstone's turned sour.
For example, that nonce Jonathan King served some of his time there and
he loved it, walking around like Jack the lad. Ten years ago he would've had
his throat cut or a table leg rammed up his arse. But that's life. Times
change. This place is famous for its executions. A total of 58 hangings have
taken place there. One of those hanged was a 14-year-old boy in the 19th
century. How fucking cruel we were in those days. We were wicked bastards.
Look how we put the kids up the chimney and the boys in the mines. What
a fucking sick country we were. We even burnt witches. Fuck me, Maggie
Thatcher was lucky.

HMP Manchester, Strangeways
Local, male
Opened in 1868. Fuck me, I missed the riot! Britain's longest ever riot, and
where was I? Parkhurst block, 400 miles away and across the ocean. In 1990
it exploded and what an explosion. It was magical. It had been building up
for years. Strangeways was the biggest hellhole on earth. This place oozed
violence and carries some horrific stories. But then, what old Victorian jail
don't? The hangman had a field day there. Plenty had their necks stretched
- too many for my liking. The punishment block was brutal. You either
followed their rules or you bounced off the walls. I had my fair share of
bouncing about, but that's showbiz. The Mancunians aren't a bad bunch of
lads. I met some good men in Strangeways. Some I'd done some biz with
outside - staunch guys. Read my book *Legends*. There's a whole chapter in
there on the Manchester firm. It's ten years since I was last there, and I must
say it was a different place after the riot: cleaner, nicer food, more showers,
and a better regime. But there was a right muppet of a governor there! I
told him, "Fuck off, or get a hole in your face." I don't think he liked me. I
wonder why?

HMP Moorland, Doncaster
Cat C, male
Opened in 1991. I know sod all about this place, but I don't think I'm
missing a lot!

HMP& YOI, Moorland
Open YP, male
Opened in 1954. It was formerly an old army camp and then a detention
centre, before becoming a YP jail. It only holds 160 youngsters, so it will be
a good place for food. The smaller the jail, the better the quality of the grub,
as it's much easier to cook for 160 than 1,600.

HMP Morton Hall, Lincoln
Semi-open, female
Opened in 1958. What's to say? It's a pussy hole! Let's all go there with balloons and bubbly and party. Why not?

HMP The Mount, Hemel Hempstead
Cat C, male
Opened in 1987. It's another old RAF base. Why do they build jails on old sites? Strange. Talk about Biggles! The place is only up the road from my town, Luton. I wish I could move there. One can only dream.

HMP & YOI New Hall, Wakefield
Closed, female
Opened in 1961. It's only down the road from my drum, Monster Mansion. On a windy night I can smell the pussy (or it could be the fish shop). This was another detention centre in the 1960s. Yes, another one. Surprise surprise! Now it's got 400 girls in it all gagging for it. I bet there's nearly a riot on banana night, all fighting for the biggest one. Some of the male screws here have worked there and they tell me it's mental. One told me that he often saw some of the girls masturbating in full view when he did his night checks. They don't care who sees. Imagine it: going to the cells of 400 girls, looking through the Judas hole to check on them and seeing half of them spreadeagled and wanking! What a fucking job (where's my camera?). But you must get fed up of seeing so many piss flaps ... or do you?

HMP & HMYOI Northallerton, North Yorkshire
YP, male
Opened in 1785. Back then it was called the North Yorkshire House of Correction (no human rights in them days). Cor, not 'arf. There were worms in the porridge and maggots in the straw (no beds). Then in the 1930s it became a military prison and a tough one at that: hard and brutal. Now it's a YP jail with 300 cons in it. Get the ball out and have a kick about. Fuck the system.

HMP North Sea Camp, Lincolnshire
Cat D, male
Opened in 1935. Cons built this jail. Yeh, cons! 'Slave labour'. It's been a detention centre and a borstal in the past, but for the last 20 years it's been an adult jail holding 300 cons. I don't know much more about it, only that it's yards away from the sea. I've heard they do lovely fish and chips there.

HMP Norwich, Norfolk
Local, adult, male
Opened in 1887. It's one of the old dungeon nicks and you can smell the history. The last execution there was in 1950 when they hung Norman Goldenthorpe. He deserved it as he killed an old lady. I may be wrong, but I think hangman Harry Kirk did his last execution there. Whatever, Norman Goldenthorpe's neck snapped, end of story.

HMP Nottingham
Cat B, local, male
Opened in 1891. Plenty of Robin Hoods here! It used to be known as one of the UK's cushy jails - it even had a swimming pool (only one of three jails to have one), but it's now gone. And they talk about progress! They filled the fucking pool in, the lousy bastards. Reg Kray was there. He loved it, but the cunts stitched him up over a pretend gun escape. It was pathetic. He'd already served 25 years without a single escape attempt, so why try it after all that time? Even the screws knew it was all a load of bollocks. Some cunt of a snake stitched him up and it worked - he was moved back to high security. Now it's even got a sex offenders unit, housing some of Britain's worst sex beasts and paedophiles. The local people are kicking up a right stink about it, coz these monsters are going out on unescorted day trips. Lock up your kids, Nottingham folk, or bring back Robin Hood to sort it out.

HMYOI Onley, Warwickshire
Closed, YP, male
Opened in 1968. Hey, guess what? Yes, you guessed it - ex borstal. Fuck me, how many more borstals did we have? It now holds nearly 700 YPs. I bet it's noisy, and I bet there's some serious wanking going on under the sheets there. Fuck working in the laundry.

HMP Parc, Bridgend
Closed, local, male
Opened in 1997. This is a privately run jail in Wales and I don't know a thing about it. It's only ten years old, so I say give it time. A jail has to survive 100 years before you can call it a real jail. It's just a baby. Boohoo fucking boo.

HMP Parkhurst, Newport, Isle of Wight
Cat B, male
Opened in 1838 and is the Daddy of all jails. Even the name says it all. Parkhurst is like Alcatraz or St Quentin or Devils Island or Colditz. It's fucking famous and we've all done a spell behind those walls, all the 'faces'. Sadly today it's not the Parkhurst we all knew. It's even got a supergrass unit,

located where the old security unit used to be and which was used for the Great Train Robbers, the Krays, the Richardsons and the like. Now it's full of filthy police informers. How sad is that? Parkhurst dropped its max secure label back in 1995 and became what it is today: just another boring jail. The place has seen it all, from murders to riots to escapes. It's a prison full of stories: some brilliant, some just insane. Parkhurst for me is part of British penal history and some of it is fucking shameful. For example, in the 19th century it was used for children. It was a juvenile institution used for transporting the kids to Van Diemen's Land, which was Tasmania. How fucking sick is that? Parkhurst holds mixed memories for me, as it was here I first met the Kray twins in 1975. It was also here that I got certified insane in 1978 and here that I survived a multiple stabbing in 1992. I met some of my best friends in that place. It was an exciting jail full of exciting people. Even the screws were different: there was an old screw called Tom, who worked in the seg block for years and always treated the cons well. He actually stopped a lot of violence. Men like old Tom knew how to handle a situation without drawing his stick. Young screws are too fast to resort to violence. Only experience teaches you how to resolve a problem, and 90% of the violence in our prisons is caused by muggy two-bob screws who haven't got a clue. These bully boys come at you ten-handed, but as soon as you corner one of them it's a different situation. Like in the Nazi trials, their defence was 'we was only doing a job'. Well, tell that to the brutalised Jews and the six million grave dwellers. Parkhurst had its brutal bastards too and us cons fought back. We made that jail what it was: a cons jail. Now it's a screws paradise. They do what they want and the cons let it slip. Good or bad? That's for today's cons to decide. I really don't give a flying fuck anymore, coz I'm lost to it all. I can no longer understand the cons' mentality. It's a new era, one that I'm alien to. Even today's crime baffles me. It's 85% drugs related. It's a new breed of criminal. Me, I'm just an old-fashioned blagger, a dying breed. I don't want to be a drug lord or a coke head or smacked out of my face. Parkhurst for me was a great life experience, and to all the 'proper' cons I met there: I salute you. To name just a few, these include: Ron and Reg Kray, Joey Martin, Johnny Heibner, Vick Dark, Terry Smith, Alan Byrne, Paul Edmunds, Valerio Viccei, Big H MacKenney, Danny Acpress, Bob Maynard, Ronnie Knight, Wayne Hurren, John Reid, Kev Brown, Micky Reiley, Tommy Hole snr and jnr, Billy Gentry, Ron Easterbrook, Bruce Reynolds, Tommy Wisbey, Johnny Kass, Colin Robinson, Chilly Chamberlin, Bertie Costa, Barry Cheetham, David Cottage, Dave Anslow, Big George Wilkinson and Wally Lee. These are just the tip of the iceberg. There are so many more. We are talking bank robbers, mobsters, safe blowers, psychos, heavies and cat burglars. Parkhurst had 'em all and yours truly was a part of all that: a knowledge of criminality, 'The College of Crime'. You either passed or you got buried. 'Top of the world, Ma'.

HMP Pentonville, London
Cat B, local, male
Opened in 1842. I only ever spent a week there, years back, and it was a right overcrowded place. Not that I saw much of it, as I was kept in the seg block. This gaff holds a good 1,500 cons, most of them remands and short-termers. Pentonville was the 'hanging jail'. It's where the hangmen trained to become official executioners. And it was there, back in 1956, that they hung Timothy Evans. Guess what? They killed an innocent man. In 1966, ten years later, Timothy Evans was pardoned. Big fucking deal! A bit late seeing as he's dead. You killed him, you cunts - an innocent man. No wonder a lot of executioners had drink problems and went a bit funny in the head. What a fucking job! How many more innocent men and women were hung? How many?

HMP Peterborough
Cat B, male
Opened in 2005. A private jail, so what do I know?

HMYOI Portland, Dorset
Closed, YP, male
Opened in 1848. This used to be the UK's toughest borstal; proper strict. Boys went in as boys and came out men. That's what porridge was all about in the old days - lumpy and cold but sure did you good!

HMP & YOI Prescoed, Wales
Open, adult, male and YP
Opened in 1939. Guess what? Yes, another borstal and detention centre. They grow on you like a rash. It became a YP centre and adult jail in 1988. That's all I know. I don't really wanna know no more - do you?

HMP Preston, Lancashire
Cat B, local, male
Opened in 1790. This drum holds 700 cons, mostly remands. I'm told it's okay - peaceful. The old jails normally are. It's the new governors that cause the problems - believe it.

HMP Ranby, Nottingham
Cat C, adult, male
Opened in 1971. It's built on an old army camp and is close to Rampton Asylum. On a full moon there's a lot of howling. Burglar Duane Bullivant got 4½ years for breaking into the Ranby Screws Social Club - you couldn't make it up.

HMP & YOI Reading, Berkshire
Male. adult and YP
Opened in 1844. This is the place where Oscar Wilde wrote 'The Ballad of Reading Gaol' in 1895. I still say it's crap. Hey, and guess what? Yeh, it was a borstal in the 1950s and '60s. Yeh, another one. Broadmoor Asylum's not too far away. So behave, or they'll nut you off there.

HMP Risley, Cheshire
Cat C, male
Opened in 1964. It used to be a remand prison in the '60s, '70s and '80s. I should know - I was there in each decade. It also had the highest suicide rate. In 1969 I actually saw a young YP hanging - not a very nice sight, I can assure you. It was a brutal jail, make no mistake about it. When it was a remand jail it was for both sexes. We used to shout to one another out of the windows. It was brilliant. From B Wing, the YP wing, we could put our heads through the bars and see the girls. They used to flash their tits. It was great. What a laugh. I served up a few nonces there. I did one filthy kiddie fiddler up like a kipper. He never fucked with kids again - believe it. Another time I stubbed out a cigar in a nonce's eye. You could smell the eyeball melting. Them monsters don't 'arf scream. They're only hard to kids. Fucking maggots. Brady and Hindley were on remand at Risley in the 1960s. Their trials were at the same court as mine: Chester Assizes - an old court with old dungeons. Risley had the biggest fucking rats I've ever seen. Some nights you could hear the security dogs tearing one to bits. What a shriek. It also had plenty of cockroaches. I used to make a lot of hooch (moonshine) here, coz when you're awaiting trial you need a good piss-up at weekends. It now holds 1,000 cons and I'm glad not to be one of them. I never did like the place. Still, no love lost - they never liked me either.

HMYOI Rochester, Kent
Closed, YP, male
Opened in 1874. Rochester had the UK's first ever borstal - they sure started something up, the cunts.
It now holds 400 YPs. In 2001 the cons rioted and took a screw hostage. Slow down lads, or you'll end up like me: in a cage with nothing but lost dreams.

HMP Rye Hill, Warwickshire
Cat B, male
Opened in 2001. It's one of those private jails. It's so fucking private that I've never heard of it. Have you? But get this, you Internet fanatics: the flash fuckers have got their own website - www.hmpryehill.co.uk. Anyway, fuck them, get yourselves on my site - www.freebronson.co.uk. You can get 'Free Bronson' T-shirts and car stickers on mine.

HMP Send, Surrey
Closed, female
Opened in 1962, initially as a detention centre. Now it's got 200 beautiful hot, wet, dripping pussies doing nothing. It's just not fair. What a waste - 200 pussies just waiting for some action. Surrey too - how posh.

HMP Shepton Mallet, Somerset
Cat C, male
Opened in 1610, as an old House of Correction. At that time it was for men, women and kids. They slung them all together to correct them of their bad ways. Imagine what it was like. Birch the bastards. It then became an army military prison until the Prison HQ took over in 1966. It only holds 200 cons. And here's an exclusive for you all: in the military days, from 1939 to 1965, 21 men were hung and 2 were shot by firing squad. 'Happy days'.

HMP Shrewsbury, Shropshire
Local, male
Opened in 1793. It's a poxy little old medieval local. What more can I say about the place? I bet there's ghosts.

HMP Spring Hill, Buckinghamshire
Cat D, male
Opened in 1953. Note the date: the Queen's Coronation year. Her Majesty's Prison? I bet she's never even been there, or even heard of it. I bet you haven't either. Spring Hill - sounds like a vegetable.

HMP Stafford
Cat C, male
Opened in 1793. I know fuck all about this place. As I always say in the Old Bill Shop: no comment.

Hey, I must just break off here to offer you some serious advice. Take it or leave it. When you go down on your old lady, be extra careful, as one slip and you're in the shit.

HMP Standford Hill, Kent
Cat D, male
Opened in 1950. It's one of those places where a lot of cons are let out to work in the community and knock on the gate to come back in for the night. It must be fucking mental to do that. I just can't see me ever playing those games. I want to walk out of prison, not look back and never return. How can a man ask to come back in? It's fucking loonyology.

HMP Stocken, Rutland
Cat C, male
Opened in 1985. Johnny Vaughn, the TV presenter, served his sentence there. So did Eddie Jackson ... Who? Never mind who, I'm not a grass.

HMP& YOI Stokeheath, Shropshire
Closed, YP
Opened in 1964. Another ex borstal. How many more? I'm getting sick of hearing 'borstal'. It holds around 600 YPs, so I bet it's loud. Why not give them a weekend at Holloway? The girls would sort that lot out. They'd all come back to Stokeheath fucked, with sore dicks.

HMP & YOI Styal, Cheshire
Closed, local, female
Opened in 1963. In a period of eight months, in 2002, five women topped themselves in that place - a tragic shame. You need to ask - why? One, yes, maybe two, but five?! There's something very disturbing there. One is bad enough, but five is disgusting! It's time the public woke up and smelt the reality of life inside for women and young girls. Something is seriously wrong.

HMP Sudbury, Derbyshire
Cat D, adult, male
Opened in 1948. It's one of those jails that I know fuck all about. These Cat D jails are all alien to me. I've been max secure for 30 years, so what would I know?

HMP Swaleside, Kent
Cat B, male
Opened in 1988. It's the good old Isle of Sheppey nick. Plenty of the chaps end up there, and they all say it's easy, so it must be or they wouldn't say it. And it's never lost its roof - another good sign that it's easy.

HMP Swansea, Wales
Local, male
Opened in 1861. It's right next door to Swansea Football Club - so close that inmates can hear the game from over the wall. That's all I know, and it's all I want to know. I've more chance of going to Mars than going to Swansea.

Hey, I hear they've just found two bodies in Michael Barrymore's pool - 'two suicide bummers'.

HMP & YOI Swinfen Hall, Staffordshire
Closed, YP
Opened in 1962. Yeh, you know - ex borstal and ex detention centre, blah, blah, blah, all piss and wind. Did they work? Did they fuck.

HMYOI Thorn Cross, Cheshire
Open, YP
Opened in 1985. Known also as a boot camp. Make your own mind up on that. Mine's made up.

HMP Usk, Monmouthshire
Cat C, adult, male
Opened in 1844. Another old jail that was a House of Correction, then a fucking borstal, then a fucking detention centre! Now it's a Cat C for vulnerable prisoners and it runs a sex offenders treatment programme. God give me strength! Wake up, you clowns! The only treatment they need is a kick in the bollocks. Poison the water tank. Get rid of the filthy nonces.

HMP Verne, Dorset
Cat C, male
Opened in 1949. There's a lot of lifers finishing off their sentences there. If you're a lifer, this is a good move for you. Keep your head down, you're almost home and dry. The Verne used to be an old military barracks before it became a jail. Not that I give a flying fuck if it was an old slaughterhouse.

HMP Wakefield, West Yorkshire
High security, male
Opened in 1594. It's Monster Mansion. It's 2008 and I'm still here, still in the cage and still isolated! Yeh, it's me, Charlie Bronson, and I'm still alive and kicking. Welcome to my home, Wakefield nick. This holds over 1,500 cons: 90% are lifers, and 80% are sex cases. Thank fuck I'm in a cage away from the slags! Ian Huntley serves his time over in the hospital wing. Even the other sex monsters hate Huntley and say he's evil. So that sums him up! I'm on what is called the CSC unit. There's only six of us on here and we rarely ever see each other - total isolation for us all. But that's life. None of us is an angel. Last year I was the first con in the UK to be pepper-sprayed. I'm always the first. I'm the system's guinea pig. They invent a new contraption or restraint and it's Bronson they try it on - I should at least be paid for it. I first tasted Wakefield Jail's porridge back in 1975 and I've been back here a good ten times since. As blocks and regimes go, I don't mind it. But this unit is known as the cemetery. We are the forgotten cons. Take one bit of advice if you never take any again: stay clear of Wakefield Jail; otherwise be prepared to lose your soul. We are soulless.

HMP Wandsworth, London
Local, adult, male
Opened in 1851. Albert Pierrepoint was the most famous of hangmen. He topped all the famous cases and Wandsworth was the no. 1 hanging jail. Oh, by the way, another of 'my roofs' took place there and it was there that Ronnie Biggs had it over the wall. Pierrepoint got chinned there by Mad Frank Frazer. Frank just got lucky and spotted him and - crack! - he chinned him. Frank's like that; he acts on impulse. He's a legend and always will be in my eyes. Funnily enough I first met Frank in Wandsworth in 1976 and the last time I bumped into him was also in Wandsworth in 1988. Wanno was a tough old nick and don't let anybody tell you different. It was good for character building and it bred hard men. I spent years in their dungeon and I gave as good as I got (in the end they just dropped me out). In one day I attacked five of them and put three of them on the sick. That's how it was in the 1970s - violent. We were all mad, even the screws. We were all on our way to hell. So who really cared? I fucking never. I lost everything: my wife, my son, my freedom and my sanity. I even attacked a doctor. Why? Cos he was a cunt.

HMP & YOI Warren Hill, Suffolk
Cat C, YP
Opened in 1982. I'd never even heard of it until now. Have you? Warren fuck-off Hill. What's that all about? It sounds a bit poofy to me. Give me a borstal any day or a fucking good birching.

HMP Wayland, Norfolk
Cat C, adult, male
Opened in 1985. Poor old Reggie Kray spent his last bit of porridge there. He was very sick for some time and after 32 years inside they finally freed him on compassionate grounds from Wayland only for him to die days later in a hotel room in Norwich. But he died free, so Reggie fucked the system. Compassionate? The system don't know the meaning of the word. On 1 October 2000 Reg died a winner in my book and don't let nobody tell you different. He survived 32 hard fucking years in prison and I salute the man. Wayland holds a lot of lifers coming to the end of their sentences. I only hope you lot have a longer time in the free world than Reg did.

HMP Wealstun, Yorkshire
Cat C & D, adult, male
Opened in 1995. There was a nice roof protest there in 2003 - 20 cons climbed up. Fuck knows why coz it's still a low-cat. jail. If they were upset about the regime they could've just walked out and gone home. Or am I missing something here? Well, it is loonyology.

HMP Weare, Dorset
Cat D, adult, male
Opened in 1997. You'll never in a million fucking mental years guess what the Weare is. It's a ship; a prison ship. This is 2007 and we have a fucking prison ship. Amazing. The Weare was used in the Falklands War. You just can't make this one up. A fucking ship. 'Aye aye captain. Land ahoy.' But, first, let's get some nonces to walk the plank.

HMP Wellingborough, Northamptonshire
Cat C, adult, male
Opened in 1963. Yet another ex borstal. What's left to say? Blow it up.

HMYOI Werrington, Staffordshire
YP, male
Opened in 1895. Hey, it's my old detention centre. I spent three months there in 1970. Me and my best buddy John Bristow went there together and got released together. We ran the fucking place. A report stated in 2002 that it was the most violent institution in England. Well, fuck all's changed then.

HMYOI Wetherby, West Yorkshire
Cat C, YP, male
Opened in 1958. Another ex borstal. Hey, could it still be a borstal, but with a different name? All this HMYOI crap, it's just another word for borstal or detention centre or boot camp. I think I'm right. Somebody tell me I'm wrong, if you can.

HMP Whatton, Nottingham
Cat C, adult, male
Opened in 1966. This is a 90% sex offenders prison where they all do silly little courses and get silly little gold stars. Then they get a nice bit of early parole and go out and shag another granny or jump on another kid and it all starts up again. Bang 'em up for 30 years till they're too old to get their rocks off. Problem solved.

HMP Whitemoor, Cambridgeshire
High security, male
Opened in 1991. This place has had it, seen it and done it all and has defo got the T-shirt: escapes, riots, violence, murder. Hey, get this: John Brookes, together with Micky Caine, killed 'Catweasel' there, and then at the trial Caine found out that Brookes was a nonce - the reason they'd killed Catweasel. You couldn't make that one up. It just goes to show, you can't trust anyone. I did a 40-day hunger strike there. 'Forty Days' - the same as Jesus. I lost five stone. I bet Jesus never. He did it out in the wilderness. I did mine in a concrete coffin. I reckon Jesus had the odd rabbit. I had fuck

all. Whitemoor is 'Shitmoor'. I've never liked the place. Still, they don't like me either, so no love lost there. The IRA fucked 'em up when they escaped from the max secure special unit. That put the anteater in the nest. Cor, not 'arf. Six IRA men going over the wall - they make movies on stuff like that. It was a kick in the nuts for prison HQ. That's why they kicked the granny out of them when they caught them, but they all got a nice few quids' compensation over it, so the cons fucked 'em again. Who said we can't win?

HMP Winchester
Local, adult, male
Opened in 1846. I almost made the roof there years ago, but the screws were a bit lively and jumped me. Winchester to me is all a prison should be - a prison - and that's what it is. It's an old prison full of great legendary stories. You can't have a jail that's 150 years old that isn't legendary. But - and it's a big but - it's turning into a Wendy house. Clock this: in 2002 Pimlico Opera played in the jail: Shakespeare's *Romeo and Juliet* and Bernstein's *West Side Story*. That's two of the world's greatest love stories. Come on, we're cons. Who's taking the piss here, us or the system? There's 700 cons in Winchester, probably 650 career criminals, and they're watching operatic love stories. Whatever happened to *Silence of the Lambs*? Now it's lambs to the slaughter.

HMP Wolds, Yorkshire
Cat C, adult, male
Opened in 1992. The Governor (I got seven years for taking him hostage at Hull) ended up going to this private jail, which I thought stank of hypocrisy. He retired from the Prison Service with a big payout over his hostage ordeal and then he's working for the private jail operative Group 4. Or am I missing something here? Anyway, he got a nice fat pay cheque from Hull and I got seven years. Then he's a governor there. It don't add up to me. I know very little about Wolds nick. I'm not sure I want to with him there. The screws in Hull will all tell you what they think of him. He allowed me to tie him up (I had no weapon). Then, when the siege was dramatically ended and I was held under restraint, my hands cuffed up behind my back and I was lying on the floor, the big governor started kicking my face in (he had to be restrained by his own men). It's all in the statements - by his own men. That summed him up that day - a coward.

HMP Woodhill, Milton Keynes
Max secure, local, adult, male
Opened in 1992. Hey, I got married there and I demolished the CSC Unit. I had my own riot there. I tried so hard to smash down Victor Miller's cell door. Who? You may well ask. He's a notorious child killer. He shagged the kid first and then buried him in a wood. I just felt in the mood to disfigure

138

the paedo's face. What's wrong with that? The evil bastard was boasting to cons about what he did. That was all I needed to hear. The fuse was lit. Have some of me, you cunt. Woodhill to me is a strange sort of jail. For example, it has a concrete sheep (honest). Even Broadmoor Asylum don't have concrete sheep. It's one of the new modern jails built on psychology, but it seems to work for the 750 cons there. Maybe it's just me. Maybe I'm stuck in a time warp; an old dinosaur; extinct. Maybe I've gotta go with the times. No doubt I'll return there as it's my local Cat A jail with a max secure unit built just for cons like me - if there are any more like me, that is. The system seems to feed the media with the opinion that there is no other like Bronson, and we all know the system never lies.

HMP Wormwood Scrubs, London
Local, adult, male
Opened in 1890. This place has had it all ten times over: escapes, riots, murders and screws being nicked for supplying drugs and bashing cons up. It's one of the most notorious jails in the UK and has a murky past. Any students studying criminology ought to research the Scrubs' past record - it's horrific. In fact it's an entity on its own merit; hell within; corrupt and evil. And I should know as I've been on the receiving end more than once. My dad passed on when I was there and the following day I almost died too due to one of the worst beatings I've ever had. It's all documented and in other books, but you can never forget such a cowardly attack, ever. I'm still praying I'll bump into some of them cunts who done it to me. Fuck the consequences, coz I'll be going for their eyes. I'll blind the cowardly fuckers for insulting my dead dad. But, as in all walks of life, there's some good old screws - those who do a tough job and some who try to make your day a better one. Even those screws despise the bully screws. I actually believe the slag screws despise themselves as they know they're cowards - born cowards. In the 1960s Blake, a Russian spy, escaped from there, never to be recaptured. So he fucked 'em up good and proper. You couldn't even keep a notorious spy in. What I will say is good about the Scrubs is the chapel. It's got the nicest chapel of any prison in the UK. Whether you're religious or not, you can't but admire that lovely chapel. Not that I go in them places too often. But I remember sitting in there at a very low time of my life and the sun shone through the coloured glass and a beam of light shone on the cross of Jesus and my whole body felt warm. I just felt safe and a feeling of hope shot through my veins. It was a one-off experience that has stayed with me ever since. It really was nice. Weird, as I'm not into that sort of thing, but it does make you wonder.

HMP Wymott, Preston
Cat C, adult, male
Opened in 1979. I don't know anything about Wymott. So, no comment.
Amen.

That's your lot. The A to Z of prisons and I'm fucked. I need a lie down. My
head's in prison mode. I can't believe there are so many, can you? I just hope
you've learnt something from it. Even if it's just one little thing then it's been
worth all my research. A piece of advice: try to stay clear of them all, as
they're all a waste of space. They're all there for one reason: to control you.
It really is loonyology. Stay sane - stay well clear!

THE A-Z OF PRISONS

How many more do we need
Forever on this journey
The heart forgets to bleed
Borstals, YPs, detention
They're all the bleeding same
This is hell before you
It's one big fucked-up game
Low cat., high cat., max secure
Come in and take your pick
The queer waits in the shower
He loves to suck a dick
'Rehabilitation' Don't make me laugh
The word it don't exist
A con walks in the shadow
He's cut his fucking wrist
The door slams in your face
There's nowhere else to go
Isolation chews you up
The time it goes so slow
The A to Z of prisons
Trapped inside your mind
You're just another convict
Left so far behind
The prison bell is ringing
The jail begins to wake
Wrapped around your body
It's like a giant snake
Your name becomes a number
You live inside a shell
Wash behind your ears
Or your body starts to smell

The prison becomes your home
In time it's all you know
Living in a dream
Your head full of snow
The A to Z of prisons
Spread across our land
Santa never comes
It's just an empty hand
There'll always be a prison
There'll always be a crime
You're going away for life
The crime ends up the time
Do yourself a favour
Go straight and get a job
Stay away from trouble
Earn yourself a nice few bob
The A to Z of prisons
It's like a fucking zoo
Just look in the mirror
It looks back at you

CHAPTER 10
JULY'S LIES, HIGHS AND SIGHS

Ronnie Easterbrook. Now there's a real top geezer. As I write this, he's in the hospital wing here in Monster Mansion. Ron's not very well. He's old now - in his seventies - and he's only got one lung. He's done his porridge hard but he's still a great chap. I first bumped into Ron in Parkhurst back in 1976. He was a proper armed blagger, the real McCoy. All the London firm respected Ron, as he was the cream of the crop and he done his bird like the man he is: staunch, solid. He made it out and got nicked on a ready eye. Some cunt set him up. Tony Ash got shot dead on that bit of work by some trigger-happy cop and Ron caught a bullet in his back. I was in Brixton Cage on D Special Unit when Ron came in. I was gutted for him and they gave him a life sentence. This was 1988. It's now 2007. Twenty years have passed and he's still in. It's a fucking liberty. They want him to leave jail in a body bag. If he was a paedo he would've gone free ten years ago. It makes me sick how the system treats the 'real villains'. The system is heartless but, then again, no love lost. Our hearts turned to stone so long ago we can survive it. Don't dare doubt it.

That was a good year - 1988 in Brixton. It was rocking. Fuck me there was some tough cookies there at that time. Just to name a few: Vick Dark, Tommy Hole, Mickey Reiley, Wayne Hurren, Big Freddie Lieveld, Charlie Magee, Perry Wharrie, Freddie Foreman, Dennis Wheeler, Dennis Campbell, Kev Brown - we're talking serious armed robbers here, the fucking cream - and the one and only Valerio Viccei, who robbed 60 million bucks out of the Knightsbridge safety deposit boxes. SIXTY MILL! They only got a mill back; 59 are still missing. This is James Bond stuff: Ferraris; 50k diamond-studded Rolexes. We're talking master criminal league! We're talking Valerio Gigi Viccei, my Italian buddy. What a guy this fella was. There's a book out on him. Surely there must be a movie to follow? His whole life was one on the edge, fast and furious, and he died how he lived: dangerously. The Italian pigs shot him up. He was in fact out on home leave and they just shot him dead. He let go a few of his own slugs. It was a good shoot-out, but it's one he lost. He died along with the secret of where the missing 59 mill dosh is. He died a fucking icon. We salute him. Long live Valerio Viccei. We love you, man. You're never forgotten, my friend. You fucked them all - big time!

Talking of movies, look at this shit. Here we go again. More lies! There's not a month goes by without some crap in the paper about me. After 30+

years of it, you'd think I'd be used to it by now but I'm not, as shit like this really upsets my family (especially my mother). She now thinks, "Fuck me, my son has gone mad again." Well, the truth is that this story is so far from the truth it's unreal.

1 July 2007, *News of the World*
EVIL CON JAIL FURY
Evil prisoner Charles Bronson smashed up his cell - after Hollywood star Tom Hardy snubbed him.
Bronson, dubbed Britain's most violent inmate, went berserk at Wakefield jail after Hardy's snub.
He had wanted the 29 year old Black Hawk Down and Layer Cake star to portray him in the biopic. Friends have arranged a £750,000 film budget and Bronson helped write the script.
But London born Hardy's agent Linda King said last night: "Tom was approached for the role, but he wasn't interested."
Now Bronson, 54, wants Hardy to visit him in prison for a face to face meeting.
Bearded Bronson, real name Michael Petersen, has been in jail almost continually since he was 19 and is now serving life after taking a jail worker hostage in 1999.

Max Beesley the actor is a good friend of my family. He's a top geezer. He was out in Hollywood with his pal Tom Hardy. So Tom spent two hours on the phone to my Loraine explaining that he did not say this shit and - wait for it - he does want to play my role. In fact he's already done a 20-minute shoot of the movie. He loves it. He's yet to sign the contract but it looks as though he'll play me!

All my family tell me he's fucking magic and looks a lot like me in my younger days. All I've said is: please don't mug me off on my press-ups. You must get it right: hand clap, one arm, handstand, crocodile and normal; 94 in 30 seconds. The man is in serious training for it!

As for the bit in the story about me smashing my cell up, that's not just news to me, it's news to the screws. So it's a total fucking lie. Now see what I have to put up with. The only truth in the story is the ¾ of a mill bucks on the table. They got that right. So the question is: why lie about the rest? What's the Press Council got to say about it? Hey, if it was Jeffrey Archer he'd probably get libel compensation. Me - I get fuck all! I've had 30 years of this shit! So has my family. The public still think I'm a crackpot, evil and a psycho. Well, wait for the movie and then you'll see who's fucking evil - and it won't be me! I'm about to expose this system for what it is: a fucking joke! It's one big crazy lie. We are talking loonyology!

4 July 2007

Woke up this morning at 6.25 a.m. A little bird was whistling outside my window, a rare thing here, and it's always lovely to hear it. It reminds me of freedom. I just lay there in the peace, all cosy and warm. I just felt happy.

Fuck knows why; after all, I'm in a fucking cage. The bird outside free and me in the cage. Something don't add up here. I had a semi hard-on, but no time to pull it. Time to get up. It's a new day. I love a new day!

I switched on Radio 5 and got the news. Alan Johnston freed from his living hell! For 114 days the army of Islam had held him hostage out in Gaza, Palestine. Fuck me, it's only a week or two back they had the poor sod wearing a suicide bomb vest. It don't sound that long, 114 days, but it's a lifetime when you're on the edge of life with guns in your face and expecting to be executed. After all is said and done, he was, is, just a journalist doing a job. When I heard this news, I actually thought: yeh, magic, I'm pleased for the guy! Not that I know him or fuck all about him, I just felt happy for the guy. It's good news, as he could so easily have lost his head. He's a lucky man indeed! It takes a big man to survive that. Psychologically, he will be scarred for ever. You can't spend 114 days in a hole in the ground, expecting to die, without it leaving serious problems. I often wonder how that Terry Waite is today, coz he spent four years as a hostage back in the 1980s. I believe it was from '87 to '91. But he survived it, and he has my utmost respect! Anyway, three cheers for Alan Johnston. I salute the man. It really set my day off in a happy mood.

Hey, get this! Paddy is on a quiz show and the quizmaster says, "Right, Paddy, your first question. Name three of the Great Train Robbers."

"Well, that's easy ... but I can't answer it."

"Why?"

"Coz I'm not a bloody grass!"

Talking of the 1963 Great Train Robbery, loads of those involved are now dead: Charlie Wilson, Lennie Field, Pat James. Billy Boal, Buster Edwards. All very sad, but I'm lucky enough to have met a lot of them. I met Charlie Wilson up in Hull Jail in 1974, Bruce Reynolds and Tommy Wisbey in Parkhurst and Roy James in the Scrubs. Let me tell you, they were smashing chaps, the salt of the earth. Their sentences were inhuman! But what else do you expect from the system? They hate it when you nick bags of dosh - jealous bastards! I remember as a boy of 12 when they robbed the train, coz it wasn't that far from Luton. It was 'big talk'; everybody was buzzing about the crime of the century. Bear in mind that a million bucks back in 1963 is like 30 mill (if not more) today!

I remember some muppet after the robbery was walking his dog and found a sackful of dosh all in £5 notes - untraceable. The mug handed it in to the police and got a £100 reward! What a prize muppet he was! He gives the Old Bill a sack of dosh and he gets £100! It's mugs like him who give me the shits! Mr Goody Two Shoes! Mr Perfect! Look at me ... I'm honest! Well, mate, you're a first-class prat in my book! All that dosh was being taken to Scotland to be burnt, as it was old money. Unfucking traceable! Un-fucking-believable! Don't it give you a headache? It does me!

I think I must have decided that day to be a villain. That crime for me was magical. The whole country loved it (except the government) and it woke me up. It really had a big effect on my life. Sure, I never became a master criminal, but I did become a very aware sort of guy! I've always lived by my own code. And, to top it all, I met the best criminals that ever walked our land. Most just read about it! So I'm blessed. Nobody can ever take that from me. Sure, I've lost a lot, but I've gained more. There will always be 'top cream villains' and you'd better believe it.

Hey, ain't somebody nicked the Crown Jewels? Come on - who's the Daddy? The guy who nicks them will surely be the no. 1 criminal of all time. I hope it's done in my lifetime. Wouldn't it be lovely to see?! Something to tell your grandkids!

Cop a load of this - you'll love it. There was this boxer back in the 1980s and he was the dog's bollocks. He had it all: style, combination, speed, footwork, stamina, and boy could he hit. He was going to the top. His record spoke for itself: 30 fights, 28 wins by knockout, 2 draws. But the poor sod got brain damage. He'd forget that he even wiped his backside. He was a mess. Guess what? He ended up getting a job in the Prison Service and he's now the Governor of Full Sutton. No wonder it's a shithole!

Talking of Full Sutton. I was last there in 2006 and I've a blinding story for you all. I arrived there from here, after being the first con in the UK to be pepper sprayed. Fuck me, it's not like your eyes just stream with water, you're blinded and it's like being stung by a swarm of wasps. It fucking hurts. I've always gotta be their guinea pig. "Let's try it on Bronson".

Anyway, I've arrived at Full Sutton seg block and they've a 'special cell' for us CSC prisoners. It's unique compared with all the other cells. In fact, it's fucking inhuman. The window - a sheet of bulletproof glass - is barred and no air comes in. Plus the door has a feeding hatch in it! You're like a London Zoo pet. The bed is bolted to the ground, the sink and toilet are concreted to the floor and the table and chair are made of compressed cardboard. I'm 230 pounds. You try sitting on a silly Mickey Mouse chair. I can't tell you the chairs I've buckled and fell off.

It's the usual reception committee as ever: 20 hard screws all pumped up with adrenalin. You can see it in their eyes: make our day, Bronson. I clocked a few old faces, sensible screws. I always show them respect. "Hi guv. Ain't you retired yet? You must be well over 90 now." So that's it. I strip off. They give me a fresh kit and bang me up - crash! I'm not in the best of moods when my cell wall bangs. Some con in the next cell is shouting and banging on my wall.

"Oright, mate. You got any baccy?"

I shout back, "I don't smoke, pal."

"Talk on yer pipe, mate."

So I get on the floor and chat on the pipe. It's like a line - you put your ear on the pipe, then cup your hands and speak. It's how you communicate when you have no window. He has a window, flash fucker.

"Where you from?" he asks. "How long you doing? Blimey, there was a lot of screws with you. Have you got any drugs ...?" Blah, blah, blah.

Do I need this shit? My eyes are still stinging. I have a headache. I don't smoke, I don't do drugs. I've fuck all in common with this muppet. Anyway, who the fuck is he? He's coming across as a serious tough guy. He talks like a yardie (gangster).

I ask him, "How long are you doing?"

He says, "Life with a rec 30 years."

Which tells me this guy is not in for shoplifting. He's a serious criminal.

I say, "Big bird, mate. Who've you killed, mate?"

Then it comes out that he's Rocky Andrews, the guy who shot dead a 14-year-old girl in a drive-by street shooting in Nottingham. A big, tough yardie? I don't think so. What killed me was his next comment:

"Yeh, it's not good, but shit happens."

That was it for me! I went mental.

I said to the prat, "Oy, cunt! See you - they should hang your black arse. You killed an innocent kid and you say 'shit happens'! Big, brave man with your guns, giving it the large, off your nut on coke! Fucking gangster. You're a child killer. Fuck off and don't bang at my wall again. I've just left Monster Mansion and now I'm next door to a real monster. Fuck off!"

He soon moved.

Every morning at dead on 6 a.m. I would sing 'Wonderful World' at the top of my voice to wake up the entire block. Why? Well, why not?! Cos it is a wonderful world, even with scum like Rocky Andrews about. Hey, don't get me wrong, accidents happen, and it probably wasn't meant for that kid to catch a bullet, but you don't lay it off as 'shit happens'. He wasn't even remorseful or sad. He was just an arrogant, selfish prick who didn't care. He was more worried about where his next spliff was coming from or his next line of coke. In jail he may be Top King to his lot, he can be Gov of the yardies for all I care, but in a one-to-one fight I'd rip his throat out and snap his spine, simple as that. I don't need a gun or a tool. To me he's a child killer who should bow his head and shut his mouth, or even try to put it right with the kid's family. He could even try to stop would-be killers by making them think about the consequences of pulling a trigger. "Thirty years in hell. Don't do it." I'd like to think Andrews will one day grow up and face the reality of what he did. He sure can't bring the kid back. But he could stop so many others from dying. Wake up, Andrews, you owe it to the kid's family. If I'd done it, I'd have ripped my sheet up and topped myself, as I couldn't live with myself for taking a kid's life. I'd be riddled with guilt. I'd see her face in my dreams. Oh well, that's how life is inside. Fortunately for him, we are isolated! But it's not just the crime, it's the attitude that rips into my soul - like his crime is acceptable and he's 'the Daddy'. Well in my book he ain't, nor ever will be. I may be old-fashioned in my own way, I may be a raving lunatic to some, I may be an old dinosaur, but I live by morals and values! Stand up and be a man! Say sorry if you're wrong! I could 'hug' any man who's a genuine human being. Well ... maybe not! I suppose I could, but I'd squeeze them that hard their ribs would cave in. What a way to go: 'The Hug of Love'.

I've met some great guys in the dungeons up and down the country. And, believe me, you do meet some of the 'cream' in our dungeons: proper men of principle; men who stand strong in the face of adversity.

It was also at Full Sutton that I bumped into Paul Stevenson - only a young fellow, but plenty of bottle. I had just smashed up the shower room, as our exercise had been cancelled owing to the weather. There was fuck all wrong with the weather. The screws were playing games, Anyway, I ended up having a rumble with 20 of them, as usual, and into the strongbox I went at 100 mph! Next thing, Paul smashed up his cell in support of me. So in the screws go with him and he ends up in the next cooler to me. Now that's what I call loyalty from a top geezer; a man I admire and respect. He was only 20 years old, but he had more bottle in one finger than some of the cons had in their entire bodies. Sadly, some years later Paul got the 'L' plates lifted off. He fell into the two-strike law and got life! Like me, he's not a killer, he's just a fucking problem to the system. Like me, he don't get Xmas cards off the governors. Like me, he don't give a flying fuck.

I met that Michael Stone in the dungeons too. I'm sure you'll all remember his case. Some years back, a lunatic steamed into a family with a hammer on a sunny day in the countryside in Chillenden. Bash, bash, bash! He kills the woman and one of her daughters, and the other daughter survives. It was a horrific attack - he smashed their skulls like a boiled egg. But it's one of those dubious cases: did he do it? The fact is that there was no evidence to say he did: no DNA and no witnesses. The only thing that got him convicted was a grass in jail, who said that Stone confessed to him. Well, that's the oldest one in the book. It's the favourite stroke the Old Bill pull! They slip into a grass and promise him the world. He makes a statement and it helps a conviction. I really don't know if Stone did it or not. But by British law he should never have been convicted, as there's is not a scrap of evidence on him. I don't particularly like him. He's just an old druggie, full of shit, and lives in cloud cuckoo land. The last time I bumped into him was in the Full Sutton block. He was on punishment. He was plotting a roof protest about his conviction and he was asking my view on it: how best to do it; what to take up; how best to get up, etc. Four years later, he's still talking about it! It's all fucking talk with some people! Hellfire, if that was me serving natural life for two murders I didn't commit, I'd be protesting every day till I died. The system would have to kill me, it's as simple as that! But I do hope he can one day prove his innocence; only he can, and his legal team. But one sure thing is that it won't go away! Them sorts of cases can't disappear. Let's hope we get to see him up on the roof! At least he'll get more respect from the cons instead of talking the fight. Me personally, I'd sooner dive off the roof onto my head than live with that shit hanging over me. One thing's for sure: Stone is not proud of it and he's genuine in his belief that one day he'll be proven to be a victim of a state fit-up. I wish him luck. But he won't ever win fuck all by sitting on his arse dreaming. The last time I seen him he'd shaved his head and grown a big beard. If he wore dark glasses he'd be a Bronson double. I don't think so! There can never be two of me. You'd better believe that. Some may try to be me, but dream on! It's impossible. To be me you need to experience all I have. You're gonna have to bleed it, smell it, taste it. No normal man can ever do that. Whether people accept it or not, I've become a dehumanised freak of nature. And it's fucking brilliant. I feel brilliant. Here's a tip for life: when you go to sleep, smile and think happy thoughts. Then when you awake you're laughing. It works. It's all in your heart. Be free of sanity. Sanity is boring. Loonyology is the way to go! It's the new way of life. Fuck it, before it fucks you.

One of the craziest fuckers I ever met on my journey was Archie Hall, known as 'The Mad Butler'. Fuck me, what a story. I'm amazed there's no movie on him. His whole life was on the edge. But I've got to put the record straight now before I go on. Archie was a proper good villain, a top criminal in his day. He goes back to the war era, the times of 'real' criminals, men like Billy Hill, Jack Spot and Frankie Frazer. Okay, Archie wasn't in their league; he was more of a one-hand player - the 'cool hand lucky Luke' sort of guy. He was a top jewel and antiques thief. He done his porridge like us all, when porridge was tough. But unlike a lot of cons Archie had grace. After all, he really had been a butler once, to the ex-MP Walter Scott-Ellis at his residence in Richmond Court, Sloane Street, London. He ended up snuffing them out, and that's how it all ended for Archie: a life sentence. And life meant life! He was in his fifties when he copped his life back in 1977. He knew it was all over. It wasn't just Mr and Mrs Ellis that got killed; three others died too. He was on a man-killing spree! The 'Mad Butler' went mad! The butler did it, so to speak. In prison he was just like a lost soul. Imagine how it must be for a butler, one day living on the crest of life and the next in a cell with a smelly pisspot! Archie survived for 20+ years, but died an old man in his cell. I suppose he'll be remembered in jail for his marathon-long hunger strike, which went on for five years. A five-year fucking hunger strike! Mental! Don't ask me how - it's crazy; not human! His only luxury in jail was getting his cock sucked! All his canteen went on the jail faggots. That was his thing. It's no secret that he was an iron even outside! But in his old age he just enjoyed his blow job. If that's what the 'Mad Butler' needed to survive, then who's to make it wrong? Sadly, he had to pay for it. A very sad ending. Who the fuck wants to be a butler anyway? One sure thing: they don't make 'em like him anymore - thank fuck!

July 2007, Inside Time - Mail Bag
Adult magazine equality
Here at Wakefield, gay or bisexual inmates are not permitted to order/purchase gay 'adult' magazines, yet which contain the same material as those purchased by heterosexual prisoners. Secondly, I would like the situation clarified regarding prisoners having condoms and lubricants in possession. Finally, I have been involved in the newly formed gay forum and wonder if there are any other such forums in prisons in England & Wales and whether they too might have encountered similar problems concerning 'adult ' magazines. - Thomas Hodge - HMP Wakefield

The Prison Service writes: To begin with, Governors have the discretion to allow/restrict the type of periodical they permit in their establishment and can withhold or withdraw any periodical, magazine or book if they consider that possession of the material is likely to have an adverse effect on the prisoner's physical or mental condition. However, the guidance given to establishments in relation to possession of 'adult' magazines is that if it can be purchased from a reputable high street newsagent such as W H Smith, i.e. 'top shelf' adult material, then it should be allowed into the establishment, and that gay/bisexual prisoners would not be discriminated against.

Mr Hodge then goes on to mention the supply of condoms to prisoners. The facts of custody, including the need to protect vulnerable prisoners and to maintain the good order and discipline of the prison regime, mean that it would be inappropriate for prisons to encourage sexual activity between prisoners. However, whilst not condoning this type of activity, the Prison Service recognises that sex in prisons is a reality and as such carries with it a public health issue in relation to preventing the transmission of HIV infection via sexual activity. In 1995, prison doctors were advised that they could make condoms available to individual prisoners on application, if in their clinical judgement there was a risk of transmitting HIV infection. The intention therefore is to preserve an individual's health rather than encourage sexual relationships/activity.

Finally, Mr Hodge mentions that he has been involved in the newly formed prisoner's gay forum at Wakefield and has asked whether there are any such forums in other prisons in England/Wales and, if so, have they encountered any problems similar to the one concerning 'adult' magazines. Unfortunately I do not have this information readily to hand but will endeavour to obtain this and write to you again in the near future.

Patrick Hunter - Policy Lead for Prisoner Communications.

Hey, take a butcher's at this. I'm telling you for real, there's a dustbin full of KY Jelly handed out with condoms every week in Monster Mansion. It's fucking mental. You can see the cons walking funny and some of the screws. The wings are like Kings Cross on a Saturday night. "Hello, Sailor. Fancy a quickie?" Fuck me! I'm a Celebrity, Get Me the Fuck Out of Here. Hey, maybe there is hope for us heterosexuals yet! Cos if the gays can have sex, why can't we with our wives and girlfriends? Are we not being discriminated against? This could be a legal matter; a human rights issue! Why can't we have a good old-fashioned fuck? After all, it's only human! Food for thought. I say bring back the birch! I could do with a whip round! Fuck the KY lubrication, give me a bit of apple pie instead.

5 July 2007

Di Brown came to see me with her 12-year-old daughter Elle. I showed them my party trick by doing handstands on the back of the chair. Don't try it, coz you'll break your neck. I also did 90 press-ups in 30 seconds. A bad day, coz I can hit 94! Elle couldn't believe it. She said I'm the fastest, fittest old man she's ever seen. I'd not seen Di for over two years, coz she now lives out in Spain. She moved out there for her kids' future - Billy and Elle. They want me out there for a month's holiday! We shall see. Then again, I could do with some sun. I look like a ghost. It's years since I soaked up the sun. Even when I made it out for those few weeks it was wintertime: cold and dreary. If it'd been sunny I might well have stayed out longer! There's something about the sun that makes you feel good: those rays on the beach; the breeze; the gulls; the ocean; a fuck-off big ice cream. It just makes life worth everything. It's priceless.

The rain and cold bring out the worst in me - it's hat on, collar up, and steam in. "Gimme all your dosh, cunt! Hand your loot over or I'll rip your head off and play basketball with it! It's not your dosh. It's insured. Now gimme it." Nine out of ten will hand it over. That 1% of daft bastards have to be silly! Why? Why do they even think it? They're fucking mental! They must get a flash of the bravery award. Look at me! Look how brave I am. He's not so brave when he awakes in hospital with shitty pants and a body covered in bandages! There's being brave and there's being a cunt.

Anyway, where was I before I went on one of my rants? Oh yeah, the beach, the sunshine. I always get a hard-on when I'm on the beach, so if you see me lying on my front 'best leave me alone'. I can't help it. I'd be fucked on a nudist beach - my back would be sunburnt for real! People don't understand what prison takes away from a man. My dick still gets rock hard with just a flicker of humanity, simply as I've not had any for so long. Can you see me on a nudist beach?! Come on, think about it. I'd be stuck in the sea so long I'd drown! Coz you can't be walking about with a big hard-on! imagine it! It's mental! It's loonyology.

7 July 2007

Hey, I got a book sent in today from Big Cass Pennant. What a book! I'll start reading it later. It's Billy Walker's autobiography, *When the Gloves Come Off*. I've had a flick through it and it's gonna be a pukka read. Billy was a top heavyweight fighter in the 1960s. He fought 'em all, but just to mention a few: Jack Bodell, Henry Cooper, Karl Mildenberger, Brian London, Joe Erskine, Joe Bygraves, John Prescott and Jose Gonzalez. He had 31 pro fights, won 21, lost 8, 2 draws. Take it from me, Billy Walker was the dog's bollocks and a really nice fella. I'm really looking forward to this read. Oh, and Cass got 'em all to sign it for me: Henry Cooper, Roy Shaw, Sammy McArthy and, of course, Billy himself. Thanks Cass!

Cass has now got his own publishing firm called Pennant Publishing Ltd.

Not bad for an ex football hooligan! Cass has done right well for himself and has written some brilliant books. Who said a leopard can't change it's spots?! Cass is living proof. If I had the chance, my spots would also disappear. Anyway, a great book. Cheers Cass! He never forgets me! Okay, it may just be a book to most, but this book has brightened up my day ... well, actually, my week, my month and my fucking year. A little thing to the free world is massive to me!

Also today I got a pair of spectacle frames sent in from Rachel Bristow. They're antique frames, pre-war ones, like Alf Garnett used to wear. You know the sort: granddad specs. They're the sort I wear. Now I have to see the optician to get my prescription lenses put in (as my eyes are fucked up big time). Rachel is my mate Billy Bristow's daughter, and they've just recently had a serious heartache. Bill's son Martyn died in a car crash on 29 May. He was a top geezer too, well respected. And here's his sister Rachel sending me in specs! I told you 'my friends' are so special to me! They're family. I love 'em all.

I've known Billy Bristow for well over 35 years, so knocking on four decades. Bill's brother John was my best buddy. We used to go everywhere together and Bill would come too. He was a bit younger than us, but we was all good buddies, and still are. Great times. Plenty of parties and tons of pussy! That's how It was in the '60s and '70s: pussy for breakfast, lunch and tea; even supper time was a slice of pussy. It was the swinging fuck-off sixties. We moved fast, and got out faster! Me and John only ever fell once. We was on a smash and grab on a leather shop in Chester. It come on top and we got three months. You do the crime, you do your time. That's how it was. You get lucky on some, unlucky on others. Some bits of graft are just not meant to be - a disaster from the word go and the whole plan seems to come unstuck! John learnt faster than me. He done his three months, got out, and never retuned! That was it for him. Once bitten, twice shy. He's now married with kids. A good life and a proud man! He's an old grandpappy now. He loves his fishing and lives for the big catch! As for me, I guess I never learnt. I got lost along the way. But I've no regrets. Why should I have? I've got my son, I've got my health, and I'm still ready for round 1,000! It's taken a lifetime to learn.

Hey, thanks Rachel for the specs! It means a lot to me. And treasure the lovely memories of your brother Martyn. He's sure to be in a nicer world! Max respect.

I had two nice visits last week, one from Ray and Emma Kray and the other from Alan and Natalie Rayment. It's great to see people from the other side! News and a good old chat over a pot of rosy lea!

Please believe me when I say prison is another world; a new planet. It even smells different. It's a world where the trees are extinct! Well, think about it - trees, climbing ...! Better still, forget I said it!

A loony walks into the doctor's office and said, "Doc, doc! I feel like I'm a

151

pair of curtains."

The doc replied, "Pull yourself together."

Hey, it's just come to me about the readers. You must be thinking, where the fuck is this story going to next? I bet there's not another book on our planet like this one. It's fucking mental. I don't know myself where to take it. As I told the publisher before I even started writing it, it's loonyology at its very best. I just write what's in my head at the time. It's just as well I'm anti drugs - could you imagine me on speed or coke?! Now where am I? What comes next?

Fuck it, I'm gonna have a mug of tea now. Why don't you all take a break. I used to enjoy a pot of tea with my mate Big H MacKenney down in Parkhurst in the 1980s. Big H is 6 feet 8, a giant of a man! He got put away for five murders (which he didn't commit). John Childs the supergrass put him away. He clears his name 24 years later! All those years of his life lost! That's what a snake does to a man. He steals his life away. You can't ever compensate for those 24 years. Yes, we had some nice pots of tea down on the Island. Vodka would've been better! But beggars can't be choosers. A nice strong cup of Tetley's does the trick with a plateful of cheese rolls and, if we're lucky, some Freddie Sewell prison-grown tomatoes. Fred may have shot a cop dead back in the 1970s, but his tomatoes are the best on the island. His corn on the cob isn't bad either. I wonder where he is now? I do hope he made it out! Oh well - cup of tea time. I'll be back ...

I told you I'd be back. I never break my word if I can help it. I always feel guilty if I do. Here's a couple of examples:

I'd arranged to meet my uncle Ian Godfrey and his two sons, my cousins, Stuart and Darren in the Moakes Pub in Luton, as I needed to see them for a chat. And, fuck me, I'm jumped on and had a gun stuffed in my face. "You're under arrest, Bronson." It's always a gutter to let people down, but that's how life is. Sometimes it's not possible to turn up. They found out later when it was all in the media: 'Bronson Charged with Robbery'. I had a nice 'wad' on me that day! I was gonna treat them to a good drink. That's how I am outside, when I'm flush. All my lot get looked after. Criminals don't live like normal people! We just live from day to day. It's a lucky way of life till it runs out, and when that happens it's out of the picture for years.

I jumped in a motor one night - 'borrowed it'. It was a black BMW, a nifty little thing. Now I'm not what you call the best of drivers! I'm not bad on the straight, but on the bends I often hit things or go on the pavement. I just can't seem to get the swing right. The fucking cars I've clipped is no one's business! In fact I prefer to be driven. But this night I was driving myself. I was heading for St Albans as I'd arranged a meet there with some chaps. Well, to cut a long story short, I never made it! I went to turn a right on a major road and I hit the pavement and ploughed straight into a bus shelter. Nobody was hurt, but the motor seized up. It just conked out! Loads of people were looking, as it was early evening, around 6/6.30. I got out of the car, all 'booted and suited' in my trilby, black gloves and shades, plus I was carrying a biz case! One fella shouted, "You okay, mate?" So I shouted back, "Mind your own fucking biz!" and walked away. Minutes later I'm in a taxi and on my way to the meet in St Albans, and that's how crazy a world of crime is. It's unreal. Fuck all matters! It's only a motor, a silly motor - it's not even mine! Who fucking cares?

Now can a working guy act like that? Can he bollocks! His wife would kill him. And this is the difference between criminals and straight people. We live on the very edge. Everything we do is iffy; everywhere we go we're on the ball; and everyone we meet we view with suspicion. It's a way of life. You can't be any other way. And now, I'm glad to admit, it's over for me. I couldn't live that way anymore even if I wanted to, coz it's fucking insane, it really is! It's mind blowing.

I love getting news from visitors, but I also like keeping my finger on the pulse by reading the newspapers, so here's some assorted snippets for you.

8 July 2007, The People
SARAH'S KILLER IN F1 SCAM
Child killer Roy Whiting has been caught trying to blag cash from celebs including Zara Phillips flocking to today's British Grand Prix. Vile Whiting, who abducted and murdered eight year old Sarah Payne in 2000, landed a job in jail boxing up goodie packs for VIPs who will be cheering on Formula 1 ace Lewis Hamilton. The scheming paedophile secretly scrawled his name and prison number on the gifts pleading for money to be sent to him. Rappers P Diddy and Pharrell Williams are among the stars expected at Silverstone. Staff at Wakefield prison, West Yorks, rumbled Whiting's plan and cut some of his privileges.
Guests
But they are not sure they have caught all the packs he defaced. A prison source said, "This guy is a seriously sick individual. It is unbelievable that he would try such a thing. He is one of the most scheming men in the prison and always desperate to get his hands on cash. When he got found out he was distraught." Celebs at yesterday's Live Earth concert are among those expected at the G.P. Selected guests are given the packs containing programmes, glossy brochures and details of special offers and information. The source added: "Inmates often get jobs like this to do. I think Whiting honestly believed he would get away with it and these celebrities would be sending him fat wads of cash in the post. He committed an horrific murder and it would have been a tragedy if he'd managed to persuade some VIPs to give him money." Serial sex offender Whiting, 47, snatched Sarah from a field near her grandparents' home in Kingston Gorse, West Sussex. He was trapped by forensic evidence and jailed for life in 2001.

Now here's another monster in the mansion. This piece of dog shit walks about Wakefield as if he owns it. It's as if he thinks he's special. Seven years he's now served and he serves it in luxury, on a wing with all his 'friends', fellow paedos! The only good news is that he's probably got another 30 years to serve, which will make him 80. Could be a 'Zimmer frame release'! Then, as he gets out of the prison gate, some nutter shoots him (a nice ending fit for a beast).

I've gotta tell you I just love a story like this old girl, 76-year-old Marilyn:

8 July 2007, The People
GUN GRANNY RAIDS A BANK
A pint-sized granny held up a bank at gun point to help her hard-up son, a court heard.
Marilyn Devine, 76, hid her face with a gold scarf before threatening cashiers with the weapon.
She fled with $6,000 - around £3,000 - but was caught later that day. Ex nurse Devine admitted robbery and was put under house arrest for two years in Pittsburgh, USA. One of her victims said "Good. I've been ridiculed at being robbed by a grandmother."

Come on, don't it crack you up? Don't it get your juices flowing? She robs a fucking bank and runs out with 3K in her bag! Is that fucking magical or what? I wish my granny was like her when she was alive! This old duchess deserves a medal. They don't make 'em like old Marilyn anymore! The state was taking the piss out of her and not giving her what she was entitled to. That's what governments are good at. Robbing off the old. Fuck, the gutless cunts. Well you can't take liberties with our Marilyn. Next time she could well blow your head clean off. She's one granny not to be fucked with. We salute you gran. We love ya. Everyone's safe for two years whilst she under house arrest.

11 July 2007, Daily Mirror
Great Train Robber Ronnie Biggs is still on the make in Prison - by selling his autograph to fellow lags.
Ailing Biggs, who is regarded as a celebrity by other inmates, is swapping his signature for extra tobacco and sweets. The 77-year-old was moved to Norwich Prison from the tough Category A Belmarsh Jail in south-east London last week on compassionate grounds. He is already a huge hit with other lags.
A prison source said: "Biggs has been quick to cash in on his notoriety by signing autographs in return for extra treats like baccy, Mars bars and toilet paper."
"Ronnie might not be as strong as he was but he is a wily old fox and he knows he is a big name to the rest of the lags and he is making the most of it." "Prisoners get celebrities like him to sign phone cards which can then be easily smuggled out of prison by relatives."
"He is not a well man and spends most of his time asleep in his cell."

I see Ronnie's been moved to Norwich Jail. It's not before time that he got out of Hellmarsh, sorry Belmarsh. Poor old chap, they should let him home. I'm actually amazed the evil pigs haven't moved him to Wandsworth Jail where he escaped from four decades ago. That's about their sense of humour in a nutshell. I bet some prat up in HQ has dreamt about doing just that. That's how they work! Fucking cunts!

I went to collect my dinner the other day and some fat prat of a governor said, "Hello, Mr Bronson". He said it right sarcastically! Well, he's got ten screws around him, so he can afford to be cocky. I just said, "Oy, I'm a con, not one of your fucking Huntley cunts. Don't call me Mr nothing." I despise sarcastic cunts, especially when they look like a sack of shit. Why call me Mr Bronson when for years he's called me Charlie? If he wants to call me Bronson, then leave the Mr bit out. As I've said, I'm a con. I'm in jail to be punished and locked up, not to be called Mr Bronson. That's all the PC brigade for you, and human rights issues aren't for me and never will be! I'm a convict! Fucking put us in chains and whip us all, it's all we deserve. Most of them would scream and cry for mummy! Me, I'd want more! That's how I am. It's how it used to be and how it should always be. Mr Bronson? Do me a favour! That sort of shit don't work well with me! He's a sarcastic, fat, useless pen-pusher who sits on his fat arse all day, reading my prison file. Did you know my file is the biggest file in the system? They need a fucking barrow to move it around. It fills the prison van up. It's unbelievable. Several screws have done their backs in carrying it. I seen it happen to one at Bristol Jail. He ended up on the sick for three months with a slipped disc. It was so funny. Plus he was a dog screw too, so it was all the funnier. I actually said, "Fucking good job, you lazy slag." Even the other screws laughed about it.

"Hey doctor, doctor, I can't stop telling porky pies."

"I don't believe you."

"Hey, doctor, doctor, I think I've got a serious inferiority complex."

"Don't be daft, you are inferior."

What do these doctors get paid for? Taking the piss!

"Hey, doctor, doctor, I've got a problem. Those pills you put me on are making me walk like a crab." "Don't worry about it. It's the side effects."

"Hey, doctor, doctor, I'm not really a schizophrenic. I just do it to prove two can live as cheaply as one."

"The lunatic was so fucking ugly that when he was born the midwife slapped the father."

"Doctor, doctor, I'm going nuts! I keep dreaming I'm the invisible man."

"Who said that?"

"Hey, did you hear about the shoplifter who nicked a calendar. He got 12 months."

"My wife's not that fat, but she does wear a g-rope."

"Hey, my old lady is so thin that when I take her to the local pond in the park the ducks throw her bread."

"Hey, I'm not really bald. My hair is just flesh coloured."

Life's a joke! That's all it is! You either laugh or you cry, it's up to you. It's your choice, but don't cry near me, or I'll give you something to cry for.

9 July 2007, The Sun
SEND THEM TO THE CHAIR
Prison bosses worried about lags smuggling phones and weapons inside their bodies are getting to the seat of the problem with an electric chair. BOSS, short for Body Orifice Security Scanner, has three ultra-sensitive sensors which can detect metal items as small as a paper clip. The £6,500 American-made machines have been issued to Britain's eight top-security prisons, including Belmarsh in South East London and Woodhill in Milton Keynes, Bucks.
The Woodhill scanner has already caught two prisoners, one with a phone and another with a knife. Senior officer Graham Cochran, 49, said, "It's amazing - and it will help to make prisons safer by hopefully eliminating this kind of smuggling. If the machine tells us there is anything metal in the prisoner's middle area they are taken to the segregation unit and monitored until nature takes its course - or they confess. As more prisoners learn about BOSS's extraordinary powers it will also act as a big deterrent."
Governor Luke Serjeant said, "Woodhill holds category A prisoners and terrorists. If terrorist prisoners gain access to mobile phones there is no end to the possible conse-quences and safety of the public. Sex offenders with mobiles could also be a significant risk. BOSS detects knives and small gun components which could be used to assist in escapes." Justice Minister David Hanson said, "New technology enables prison staff for the first time to detect hidden objects. It will undoubtedly improve security, which is paramount in prisons." A spot check found 188 mobiles among the 550 inmates at Kirkham Jail, Lancs.

Get a load of this! This could be a new job for me. I could work in reception and when a nonce comes in, I can plug the chair into the mains and electrocute the bastard. What a job! How about it? It's fucking brilliant!

They give me a little job in Full Sutton in the 1980s. I used to sweep and mop the corridor. Well, that was until I threw the contents of the mop bucket over a governor's head!

I was asked later why I did it and my response was: "Why not?" There's not a lot you can add to that is there?!

Only I lost my job. Nasty fuckers!

23 July 2007, The Sun
SULKY HUNTLEY'S JAIL PAY SLASHED
Soham monster Ian Huntley's cushy jail privileges have been axed by a tough new prison boss.
The crackdown was ordered after the sulky child-killer's prison manager was removed - amid fears he had "gone soft" on the beast.
Last night Huntley - who had wormed his way up from "basic" to "standard" - had his jail pay slashed from £14 to £7 a week.
His monthly visits were also halved - from two to just one - as punishment for "surly and uncooperative behaviour". Evil Huntley, 33, serving life for murdering ten-year-olds Holly Wells and Jessica Chapman, was also warned he faces losing other perks

including his cell TV, radio and computer games console.
An insider at Wakefield Prison, West Yorks, said, "It's about time. A lot of people were
surprised scum like him was given privileges in the first place.
"Huntley has been revelling in his notorious reputation. He's basically been doing
what he likes in the hospital wing where he is held.
"Now his cushy world has changed completely." Another source confirmed: "The good
life is finally over for Huntley inside this nick."
A spokesman for the group Victims' Voice said: "Murderers like Huntley shouldn't be
given privileges - such as money to spend on luxuries- at all. It's outrageous."
The Prison Service said: "We do not comment on individual prisoners."
But a senior source there said: "The earning of privileges is essential for maintaining
discipline and giving prisoners an incentive to behave. All prisoners are entitled to
earn these privileges."

Oh, the poor thing, he's lost his privileges. Oh, it breaks our hearts. Thank fuck we now have a prison governor who's getting real. Respect to him. Put the crybaby in a cage and give him some of what I've had for 30 years. Give him FA. This evil cunt's had a soft ride up to now. Put him in the next cage to me. I'll make sure he doesn't sleep for six months. If I was the governor he would be cleaning toilets with his tongue. Or how about euthanasia? Well, what do you think? Should a prisoner serving a life sentence have a choice whether to live or die? What do my readers think? It's a good subject; powerful. My opinion, for what it's worth, is yes, leave it to the cons. If a con can't or don't wish to go on, then let him or her choose death. If it were me and I decided I'd had enough, then I'd choose something unique, special and insane and go in style. Why can't we have the old Roman arenas back? Caesar had the right idea. It was brilliant. Men were men - that's how it was. How long would the likes of Huntley have lasted? I would've stabbed him that hard up his arse with my spear it would've come out of the top of his skull. Caesar would've loved me. I bet he would've loved Ronnie Kray too. He would've defo loved Mad Frankie Frazer. I'm telling you now: bring it on. If only. What a dream. Brilliant.

Wednesday, 25 July 2007

I just had a brill visit off Loraine and Andy. They've just sold their house and are off to live in Spain. I don't blame them either. Loraine's been visiting me for 30+ years and she still will; maybe not as often, but she will still be in my corner, as will Andy. They're two of the best ever humans on the planet to me. Everyone, in all walks of life, loves my Loraine. At one of my trials in Luton Crown Court she was in the public gallery with Lord Longford when he stood up and his trousers fell down. It was so funny; nobody could believe it! Fucking loonyology. He was old and a bit dodgy on his pins, but the old chap was as loyal as his word to me. I always had a soft spot for him. He really tried his best to help me over the years, but he was up against a very vindictive system.

Thursday, 26 July 2007

I saw my son Mike today. He looks brilliant: clean shaven, head shaved and solid muscle. All he's missing is the handlebar tash. It's our first visit in a good while, so it's made my year. He's my best buddy and I always say, if a son tells his dad "I love you", then that's priceless. You can't buy that sort of love. My son never had me around as a boy, but he's got me as a man and we've got it all to come. What a smashing future we have: both single, both free, no ties. What a party! "Pass the pussy, son." "Let's fly to Disneyland." Mike and I have got it all on a plate. Just let me get the fuck out so I can get back with him. Cunts. Let me out. Mike's philosophy in life is much like my own: don't fuck with me and you're sweet. And, yes, he has done a bit of porridge. He's done his time and done it like a man. He's learnt. No more crime for him. It's all legit now with us. We don't need crime. Crime doesn't need us. Fuck off.

Saturday 28 July 2007

Three visits in a week. Yahooooo! Not bad, eh? Ronnie Field and John Asling came up for a chat. A nice way to end July - over a pot of rosy lea and a chocolate cake, or six.

Drinking non-alcoholic beer is a bit like licking your sister's pussy. It's just not right.

I went to see the nurse for my annual health check this morning.

She said, "I think you should stop wanking."

I said, "Why?"

"Cos I'm trying to examine you!"

I see Michael Barrymore's knocked back another Christmas panto. He said he did Aladdin six years ago and hasn't heard the last of it yet.

Last night I lay in bed looking at the beautiful stars, moon and sky. Then I thought: fuck, where's my roof?

A geezer goes to the doctor with wind. The doctor gives him a kite.

30 July 2007, Daily Mail
JAILED MURDERESS FIGHTS FOR THE RIGHT TO BANG DRUM
A woman who murdered her baby son wants to sue prison bosses for refusing to give her a native American drum so she can talk to dead animals. Chah Oh-Niyol Kai-Whitewind, from Birmingham, claims her human rights are being violated because she is not allowed potions, spell books and a peace pipe in her cell. The 31 year old was jailed in 2003 for throttling her 12 week old son Bidzill when he refused to breastfeed. She changed her name after becoming obsessed with native American culture and practises a religion she describes as 'Shamanic Paganism'. Kai-Whitewind has written to jail bosses at Low Newton in Durham demanding special treatment for her beliefs. Her letter states: 'I do not believe in violence. I have respect for all life and individuality. This prison, like many others, has an unwritten policy of pagan persecution. I have been refused and denied possession of religious items.' A prison insider said: 'She's threatening to take it to the very top - to Europe. But prison is supposed to be a

deterrent, not a holiday camp. You can't just sit around chanting and drumming.' A Prison Service spokesman said he could not comment on individual cases, but added: 'There are 282 prisoners in England and Wales registered as pagans who can worship in their cells or in dedicated communal areas of the prison. There are certain religious artefacts pagan prisoners may be allowed in their cells but each is subject to risk assessment. These artefacts include items such as a hoodless robe, a flexible twig and rune stones.

Here's the biggest fucking joke. This murdering fucking baby killer wants a drum in her cell! She's a nutter, there's no other word for it. And guess what? She'll probably take this to the European Court of Human Rights and win. Let's face reality here. Forty years ago she would've got her neck stretched. Problem solved! The evil slag killed a 12-week-old kid, so what about the kid's human rights? And she wants a fucking peace pipe too. I'd give her one filled up with TNT! I actually find all this very frustrating and embarrassing to read about. There's people in prison who are genuinely in need of legal help, and mad bitches like this make a mockery of the entire legal system! Who cares about the baby killing evil bitch? Some poncy solicitor for sure! It's a fucking joke. It's gotta be, ain't it? No, it's real! 'Shamanic paganism'? Fuck off!

31 July 2007

Well, it's the last day of July 2007 and I just got my mail: eight letters, so not bad, and one's from my mum. She's off to the Isle of Man for a week to stay with her friend. That'll be nice for her. I got one from my Aunty Eileen too. She's a good old stick. Eileen is solid behind me and will be to the day she dies. I remember when I first came away it was her who got me a nice radio. Sadly I only had it a week, as I smashed it over a screw's head. Such is life! I got a card from Eddie Richardson. He's on another world tour. Good luck to him, he deserves it! He's done his porridge, years of it. I got one off Mark Sharman with £100 in it for me. Mark's a good biz man and a great buddy of mine; in fact he's more like a brother. I also got one off Tel Currie, one off my son Mike and one off Al Rayment. It's always good to hear from Al, as he's always got loads of news for me. Finally, I got one off Ferdi Lieveld from Woodhill Prison. He's a total prison legend and does his bird hard. I first met him in Albany block back in the '80s. He's a big black shaven-headed lunatic (and I say 'lunatic' with the utmost respect), but this guy don't give a flying fuck; he's utterly fearless; born to kick arse. His last 20 years have been one long hard slog through the system. He's been stabbed up, punched up, kicked up; he's even had a pan of boiling hot oil poured over his head. This guy makes Rambo look like a muppet! He may sound like a fucking animal, but far from it. He's actually a very educated, articulate man; a man of reason. But a 20-year stretch has buried his dreams, and he now lives for each day. Ferdi got double life over two killings in London, and from the first day he entered this penal system he's fought his way through. He won't back down to nobody or nothing. He's a man on a mission of madness, and he has no brakes. That's Ferdi Lieveld in a nutshell. I predict that in time, and sooner rather than later, they'll send him back home to his homeland. He'll fly home - no surer bet. South America here he comes! And when he gets on that plane he will have won! He's a true survivor, and nobody can put that past him! He's done it all, and got a box of T-shirts to prove it! A lesser man would've curled up and died years ago. If you don't know this guy or have never heard of him, then you've never served time in max secure, coz Ferdi is the ultimate max secure con. He's a smaller version of that black dude in Green Mile, but the real thing. That guy's only an actor; Ferdi does it for real. He could've made a fortune outside as a top 'minder' to one of the Hollywood greats. But he's made it in the world of madness and he'd get the loonyology badge any day. Respect to the man.

July 2007
WARDER IS CAGED FOR THEFTS FROM LAG
A warder who pilfered items from a maximum security jail to sell on eBay was caged yesterday. Timothy Stark, 38, became hooked on receiving good feedback on the auction website. Stark stole photo film used for mug shots from Full Sutton Prison, near York. He also swiped an inmate's tracksuit and storage boxes which came from top security Rampton Hospital. The dad of two made £1,200 on the site. But he was nailed when cops, alerted over the stolen film, posed as buyers. Defence lawyer Glen Parsons said, "It was not about the money. It was the compliments he became addicted to." Stark of Pocklington admitted three charges of theft at Hull Crown Court. He wept as he was jailed for four months. Judge Graham Robinson, noting Stark wants to re-train as a plumber, said, "I would be concerned about letting a plumber who stole from a prison into my home."

Four months, and he squeals like a roasted pig! Out of that four months he'll probably only serve eight weeks. That about sums it all up for me! Loonyology! It's as mad as a March hare with a rocket up its arsehole. I bet he's sorry he ever even nicked the cons' clobber. That's the difference between cunts like Stark and me. I've taken all my punishment! This cunt, and all the cunts like him, just cry wolf. Big fuck-off crocodile tears - 'poor me'. Do you know, I'm not sorry after 30-plus years. What's the point in being sorry? We did it and we deserve all we get. We chose to be criminals. I'd never do it again. It's taken me a long time to realise that crime don't pay - but it's been a hell of a journey.

CHAPTER 11
EXCUSE ME, SIR ... DO YOU
SPEAK PLANET PRISON?

If you're in a bit of trouble whilst inside, then get yourself a lawyer who specialises in prison law, coz a lot of good lawyers outside are 'lost' when it come to prison law. As I've said 1,000 times, the prison world is another planet, so use the experts. You'll be amazed at what they can dig up! They're all waiting for your letter to assist you. Here a good few to choose from:

* Buckinghamshire
Hine & Associates Solicitors
17 East Common, Gerrards Cross, Buckinghamshire, SL9 7AG
Tel: 01753 482400

* Befordshire
Barrant & Co. Solicitors
Kate Dumanska, 21 Cardiff Road, Luton, Bedfordshire, LU1 1PP
Tel: 01582 488411

Roman Pearce Solicitors
Christine Ayanbadadeso, 54 Wellington Street, Luton, Bedfordshire
LU1 2QH
Tel: 01582 424234

* Cheshire
Meldrum & Young Solicitors
6 Broad Road, Sale, Cheshire, M33 2AL
Tel: 0161 969 6415

* Cornwall
John Boyle Solicitors
The Square, 5 West End, Redruth, Cornwall, TR15 2SB
Tel: 01209 213507

* Devon
Frank Goddard Solicitors
County Chambers, 75 Queen Street, Exeter, Devon, EX4 3RY

Tel: 01392 202404

Parlby Calder Solicitors
1st Floor, 7 Whimple Street, Plymouth, Devon, PL1 2DH
Tel: 01752 600833

* Essex
Bailey, Nicholson & Grayson Solicitors
Mark Bailey, 5th Floor, Montrose House, 412-416 Eastern Avenue, Gants
Hill, Ilford, Essex, IG2 6NQ
Tel: 020 8518 3999

* Hampshire
Eric Robinson Solicitors
359 Bitterne Road, Bitterne, Southampton, Hampshire, SO18 1DN
Tel: 023 8042 5000

* Isle of Wight
Robert Tell, Twell and Co.
3rd Floor, 48 Lugley Street, Newport, Isle of Wight, PO30 SKD
Tel: 01983 539999

* Kent
Nelson Guest & Partners Solicitors
5th Floor, Roxby House, Station Road, Sidcup, Kent, DA15 7ES
Tel: 020 8309 5010

* Lancashire
Beesley and Co. Solicitors
Mark Lee, 25 St John Street, Manchester, M3 4DT
Tel: 0800 975 5454

B.W. Solicitors
Danny Reynolds, Whelmar House, Southway, Skelmersdale, Lancashire,
WN8 6NX

Cunninghams Solicitors
2nd Floor, Bridge Street Chambers, 72 Brine Street, Manchester, M3 2RS
Tel: 0161 833 1600

Kristina Harrison Solicitors
City Point 2, 156 Chapel Street, Salford, Manchester, M3 6BF
Tel: 0161 823 3934

Levys Solicitors
Manchester House, 84-86 Princess Street, Manchester, M1 6NG
Tel: 0161 233 6600

Olliers Solicitors
11 Duke Street, Manchester, M4 4NF
Tel: 0161 834 1515

* London
Ashley Smith & Co. Solicitors
4-6 Lee High Road, London, SE13 5LQ
Tel: 020 8463 0099

Attridge Law Solicitors
Miriam Actaf, 147 Fleet Street, London, EC4A 2BU
Tel: 020 7842 8600

Chartwell & Sadler Solicitors
111 Asylum Road, London, SE15 2LB
Tel: 020 7635 5255

Doves Solicitors
209 Old Kent Road, London, SE1 5NA
Tel: 020 7232 5100

Dozie & Co. Solicitors
Rachel House, 214-218 High Road, London, N15 4NP
Tel: 020 8808 2244

Ernest & Co. Solicitors
14 Stoke Newington High Street, London, N16 7PL
Tel: 020 7254 2244

Frank Brazell & Partners Solicitors
97 White Lion Street, London, N1 9PL
Tel: 0800 0832724

Guney Clarke and Ryan Solicitors
Clara McElvogue, 60 Green Lanes, London, N16 9NH
Tel: 020 7275 7788

Hayes Burcombe Solicitors
7 Cambridge Court, 210 Shepherds Bush Road, London, W6 7NS
Tel: 020 7348 5100

Kaim & Tudner Solicitors
Ben Conroy, 195 Walworth Road, London, SE17 1RW
Tel: 020 7708 0700

L.B. & Co. Solicitors
91a Whitechapel High Street, London, E1 7RA
Tel: 020 7655 4941

Lewis Sidhu Solicitors
11 The Pavement, Pupes Lane, Ealing, London, W5 4NG
Tel: 020 8832 7321

Mackesys Solicitors
Geoff Wordsworth, 207 New Cross Road, London, SE14 5UH
020 7639 0888

Mang and Co. Solicitors
198 St Anns Road, Tottenham, London, N15 SRP
Tel: 020 8800 7868

Okeeffe Solicitors
56 Dean Street, Soho, London, W10 6AQ
Tel: 020 7440 5111

Osibanjo & Co. Solicitors
Michael Oslarewaju, 74 Camberwell Church Street, London, SE5 8QZ
Tel: 020 7708 0077

Ross Solomon & Co. Solicitors
17 High Street, Sutton, London, SM1 1DF
Tel: 020 3186 1067

Somers and Blade Solicitors
49B Boston Road, Hamwell Road, London, W7 3SH
Tel: 020 8567 7025

V.L.S. Solicitors
Aloyslus Osuji, Aaban House, 806a High Road, Tottenham, N17 0DH
Tel: 020 8808 7999

* Merseyside
A.L.B. Law Solicitors
21a Hoghton Street, Southport, Merseyside, PR9 0NS
Tel: 01704 500771

A.S. Law Solicitors
8 Myrtle Pardade, Liverpool, Merseyside, L7 7EL
Tel: 0151 707 1212

* Staffordshire
Stevens Solicitors
Bank Court, Bank Passage, Stafford, ST16 2SR
Tel: 07659 111000

* Teeside/Co Durham
Appleby Hope and Matthews Solicitors
35 High Street, Normanb, Middlesbrough, Teeside, TS6 0LE
Tel: 01642 440444

Wilson & Co. Solicitors
Paul Wilson, 56 Avenue Road, Hartlepool, Co Durham, TS24 8AT
Tel: 01429 869523

* West Midlands
Millerchip Murray Solicitors
3 The Quadrant, Coventry, West Midlands, CU1 2DY
Tel: 02476 243615

Tuckers Solicitors
Mr Andy Mandleberg, 210 Corporation Street, Birmingham, B4 6QB
0120 236 4324

* Yorkshire
Chivers Solicitors
2 Wellington Street, Bingley, West Yorkshire, BD16 2NB
Tel: 01274 561666

Harrison Bundey Solicitors
219-223 Chapletown Road, Leeds, West Yorkshire, LS7 3DX
Tel: 01132 007400

Jordans Solicitors LLP
Crime Team, 4 Priory Place, Doncaster, South Yorkshire, DN1 1BP
Tel: 01302 365374

Shepherds Solicitors
Thornton Road, Hendray, Barnsley, South Yorkshire, S70 3NG
Tel: 0114 201 4566

Taylor Bracewell Solicitors
17-23 Thorne Road, Doncaster, South Yorkshire, DN1 2RP
Tel: 01302 341414

* Scotland
Bruce and Co. Solicitors
87 Commercial Street, Dundee, DD1 2AB
Tel: 01382 225099

Fraser Currie Robertson & Ross Solicitors
7 Causeyside Street, Paisley, PA1 1UW
Tel: 0141 887 7971

There's a good few for you, situated all over the UK. Remember, you're never alone! Pick up a pen. The pen is mightier than the sword. Well, that's unless you stab your pen in someone's ear at 30 miles an hour - that could be lethal! But try using it to write to a good lawyer instead. Always try the legal way, as nine out of ten times you could win in court. You might even get some serious compensation with it! There's some good lawyers out there. Once you find the right one, stick with him or her.

Honestly, good lawyers are worth their weight in gold. Once a lawyer believes in you and is not afraid to fight the system, then you're halfway there! I've had some right fucking lawyers in the past! Now I've got the best on the planet. Win or lose, my lawyer always gives 200%. I don't mind losing so long as it's a good fight. It's the wimpy lawyers who sit on their arses afraid to rock the boat that I despise. Remember, you're against the 'state' - a big, nasty, evil firm to beat. Good Luck!

CHAPTER 12
AUGUST - DRUGS, MUGS AND THUGS

Did you know that the official deaths in police custody make frightening reading. In 1996 the figure was 53; in 1997, 58; in 1998, 65; in 1999, 44; in 2000, 35; and in 2001, 34. And that's just in police cells! Some others were due to natural causes, and some were very iffy to say the least! Hey, I remember once in Luton police cells I was out having a shave and the coppers walked off and left me for five minutes - a bit of trust. So I walked over to the door of this cunt who'd kept me awake all night with his banging and verbally aggressive and nasty shouting, and I opened the food hatch. He was asleep on the bench, so I kicked the door and shouted "Breakfast" As he got up I had to smile. He looked like that Cat Weasel geezer on the TV: a scruffy, ugly fucker. I chinned him through the hatch. "Now shut the fuck up, you cunt." Blood was pouring out of his nose. So I shut the hatch and carried on with my shave. The cunt got on his cell bell and grassed me up! Can you believe it? Grassed up by Cat Weasel! You've gotta laugh or you'd go mad! I fucking love it! 'Where there's a will there's a way.' I had a peaceful sleep that night. See, my way works.

Hey, did you know that Salvatore 'Sally' De Vita, the Mafia hood, was a transvestite? He preferred to dress as a woman, but you all know what was in his handbag! You still didn't argue with Salvatore though. It just goes to show that it takes all sorts. I bet you never knew that!

I met a little black geezer in Parkhurst in the 1990s who was serving a double life. He was a merchant seaman and he shagged two of his fellow seamen and pushed them through the portholes - but the ship was in dry dock! I told you it's loonyology.

1 August 2007

A fucking pukka day. We've got a new exercise contraption to use, and it's brilliant! I'm not really into gyms and machines, as I believe in my solitary workouts. But this little contraption is magic! It's a plastic thing with two handles either side and wheels on the bottom. It's only small - about the size of a loaf of bread, and it's very light. How you use it is simple. You get on your knees, hold the handles and then go forward into a press-up position. Then you wheel it back towards the knees and roll it out again. As you do this you can actually feel your stomach muscles pulling and ripping. It really is a brilliant little machine. It beats sit-ups as it's more dynamical. I did 500 today. I'll do 1,000 tomorrow! I'm a greedy fucker. For me it's the best thing I've had in years, a lovely little surprise and I'm well grateful! So I'll now work it along with my press-ups and sit-ups for a month and see how it benefits me. But after just one session I can feel it working. What a brill way to start up the month. In fact August looks as though it'll be a lucky month.

I saw an advert in the paper today, which stated: "Get ready for the Tache Wars. Are you a contender? Visit: www.tachback.com". Call them a tash? They look more like 'The Village People'! I'd blow 'em all away with my tash - it's legendary! They say the length of a man's tash is the same as his cock! Now you know I'm the Daddy! It's true!

I got a letter from Gemini Reynolds - my Cyprus connection. My art gets everywhere on the planet! She's pleased with her artwork and she's had it framed.

I called my buddy Mark Emmins tonight and had a nice chat. He lives down in Devon - good fish and chip country, not to mention the real ale. I see Mike Reid has died of heart attack, and he was only 67 years old. He was a good 'un - a proper nice fella. And he'd done a little porridge himself. I liked that in a guy. He just picked himself up and moved on and won. He was brilliant in *The Comedians* in the 1970s - one of the best, together with Bernard Manning, George Roper, Frank Carson and Charlie White. They were all brilliant - proper comedians who made us laugh. There was none of that political correctness bollocks then. Everybody laughed and saw the funny side, whether blacks, Irish, Jew or Muslim. Or, if they didn't like it, they soon fucked off. Oh well, who's next to die? I hope it's not me.. Don't leave it here, carry it on, coz there's no end to loonyology! You'd better believe it!

Did I ever tell you the time a loony tried to mug me in Rampton? Yeh, mug me! Cunt. He was either double mad or double brave coming after me for my canteen. Fucking idiot. I left him in the recess with two broken arms and a fractured skull. But you've gotta give it to him for even thinking of mugging me. Well, come on, would you? You'd have to be insane. Well, he was.

'NONCE' LANGHAM IS PRISON TARGET
Shamed star on suicide watch
Pervert actor Chris Langham will be a hate target for prison inmates after his conviction for downloading child porn.
The disgraced star, 58, faces 10 years in jail for looking at sick images of kids being abused.
But his frantic friends and family fear he will not be able to cope and will suffer a breakdown. Langham is already on suicide watch at Elmley Prison on the Isle of Sheppey, Kent.
Twisted
And he is likely to be kept in solitary confinement as sex offenders are notorious targets

for the other inmates, who despise "nonces".
The judge ordered prison officers to keep a close eye on him over fears he would try to kill himself or be attacked by inmates.
On Thursday he was cleared of under-age sex with a teenage girl, but found guilty of viewing images of children being tortured, raped and sexually abused.
The evil images fell into the sickest 'level 5' category. Judge Phillip Statman indicated he would be sending Langham to jail, telling him the crime "well and truly padded the custody threshold". Langham was enjoying TV success after years trying to make it big.
His political satire show The Thick of It won critical acclaim while his sitcom Help with Paul Whitehouse, 49, had won a Bafta. But PR guru Max Clifford, 64, said Langham's sick crimes meant he was now finished as an actor.
He said: "It would be nigh on impossible to work in television in Britain again. He would have more chance if he had murdered someone."
Mark Borkowski, of Borkowski Public Relations, said he would suffer a similar fate to former pop star Gary Glitter, 63.
He said: "You can't lift the dark cloud that will follow his career."
Disgraced Langham, who has been ordered to sign the sex offenders' register, has been remanded in custody until he is sentenced on September 14. Police raided his home in Golford, near Cranbrook, Kent, and seized three computers containing child pornography.
During the trial at Maidstone Crown Court, Langham sobbed in the dock, revealing he had been sexually abused as an eight-year-old.
The jury found him guilty of 15 charges of making an indecent photograph of a child between September and November 2005.

On Thursday 2 August 2007 this piece of shit was found guilty of downloading kiddies' porn. He looks like a typical nonce. He gets sentenced on 14 September. I can't fucking wait to see how long he gets. I bet you anything it won't be ten years. Let's wait and see. Let's all hope he's having a rough ride in HMP Elmley, the cunt.

3 August 2007

I went over to the dentist today, escorted by seven screws and a dog. It's like a big security manoeuvre, with CCTV cameras zooming in. All movement stopped. All this just to walk me over to the hospital to see a dentist. The lady dentist is a really lovely lady, so nice and friendly. She pulled out one of my wisdom teeth, which has been playing me up for ages, so it was best out. I watched the screws' faces as she ripped it out - so funny! One went pale! I don't suppose it's nice to see or hear a tooth being ripped out though, is it? Not that it bothers me, coz I've ripped a few out myself ... but that's another story. I told the dentist to put the tooth on eBay, which made her laugh. I thanked her, shook her hand and off we went for the 300 yard walk back to the special unit. It's a nice walk: grass, flowers, workshops. I could see faces looking out of the cell bars on one wing - no doubt some monsters weighing me up: that's mad Bronson; he don't look so hard; I could take him out; I'd eat his heart raw! Yeh, right, just fucking try it! The sun was out, there was a little breeze … and my fucking jaw hurt. Oh well, that's another tooth that won't be causing me any more shit. Hey, as kids the tooth fairy left us a sixpence! Now I get fuck all. It's the same as Santa. I've not seen him in 50 years. Fat, useless cunt. Santa - I'd fucking shoot the bastard and eat Rudolf. I'm a nasty git at times!

Hey, did I ever tell you about the time I bought a silver Zephyr Zodiac motor, a big six cylinder? That was in 1972 and I got it cheap. I'd only had it three days when I took it down this lane to try a quick getaway. Anyway, the wind got under the bonnet, which flew up, smashed the windscreen and then shot over the roof into a parked car. So much for a fast getaway! I've always been unlucky with cars. I either smash them up or they conk out on me! I prefer to be driven about. It's an easier and cheaper life. No names mentioned here, but I remember years ago pulling into a Little Chef with two of my mates and a mob of rockers pulled in on these bikes. They had trouble all over their face, so we gave it to them, big time! I pulled out a pump-action and started firing away! They soon got the message and fucked off. You don't need to kill or chop people up, you just need to give them a serious warning and nine times out of ten it'll do the trick. Only a fucking lunatic is gonna argue with a shotgun, and even then it's a front - unless they're suicidal. An axe has the same effect. If you pull an axe out, I don't know too many who are gonna stay around, do you? Who in their right mind is gonna stand up to an axe? Not too many, that's for sure!

Anyway, I'm having an early night as my jaw's still sore. That was some fucking tooth, and now it's some fucking hole. Good night.

6 August 2007, The Sun
BIGGS IN 'FREE ME BEFORE I DIE' BID
Great Train Robber Ronnie Biggs is making a fresh bid for freedom. His legal team have asked for the 77 year old to be released so he can live out his remaining time with his family. Biggs is semi-paralysed and can barely speak after several strokes. Last month he was moved from a top-security jail to a 'nursing home' wing for elderly prisoners at a lower security unit in Norwich Prison. Now his lawyer, Giovanni di Stefano, has written to Justice Secretary Jack Straw to beg for his release on compassionate grounds.
His letter reads in part: "The said transfer (to Norwich) cannot for one moment compensate the need and urgency for our client to spend his remaining period of life with his family." Biggs was part of a gang which ambushed a mail train in 1963, escaping with £2.6 million cash. Driver Jack Mills was coshed over the head during the robbery causing his early death. Biggs was caught and jailed for 30 years - but escaped after 15 months and fled abroad. He finally gave himself up to British authorities in 2001.

Oh well, let's hope Giovanni di Stefano can get Ron out. If anyone can, he will! The whole country should support this campaign and help get the sick man his freedom. But my gut feeling is that Ron will die inside. There is no compassion in the top brass of the prison system and that's how it works. Sad but true.

As I'm writing this, my outside door has been unlocked and the mail screw is here. I've just got eight letters. Not bad for a Monday, and a nice way to start the week. There's one off Mark Emmins. Mark runs the Bronson site - top geezer. There's one from Loraine, my sister, too. Someone's been stirring it again. Apparently the latest media story is that I'm on a hunger strike. News to me! Loraine called the jail up to find out what was going on. More bollocks. Who the fuck starts these stories up?

Big Jo Egan has sent me his book, signed for me, so I'm well chuffed with that. What a lovely surprise. Mike Tyson has done the foreword. Joe's an Irish fighting hero to many and a really nice chap. I'll save it for the weekend and enjoy a good read then. And there's a couple of jail mail letters. I get a lot of letters from other cons. Yeh, it's a nice Monday. I had a good workout, a nice shower and I've just been informed I'm on a visit on Thursday 9th with my mate 'Ifty'. So it looks like a good week; a lucky week.

There's a couple more decent screws here on the unit. Mr Lowe used to work at Strangeways and was on duty when it kicked off. He earned a fucking fortune with the overtime. He's just in this job for the wage at the end of the week. Then there's Simon. He's in his forties and runs a lot of marathons for kids' charities. I'd have a pint with him anytime. I keep telling him, "Make sure you're on my escort to the appeal court and I'll make sure you get a bottle of brandy to come back with." Then there's Mr C. This screw gets things done. If I need a telephone number passing, he'll do it, no problem, whereas others take ages to do it and half of them forget. They're too fucking bone idle and would sooner sit on their fat, lazy arses and talk shit. Yeh, they're not a bad bunch here. They don't make my life any worse. It's pretty peaceful! And it's nice to be free of shit. Well it's nice to be nice. Try it sometime.

7 August 2007

I've had a surprise visit from the unit's Governor. He's the no. 1 governor of all CSC units: Woodhill, Whitemoor and here. He came to my door for a chat.

I said to him, "What do you want off me? What have I gotta do to move on? I've been in your CSC units now for years. I've given you seven years' good behaviour."

He replied, "But you won't work with psychology."

I responded, "So what? I don't have to! Where in the prison rule book does it say I have to work with prison psychologists? It don't! So it's blackmail. You're blackmailing me. I either work with your psychologists or I never move on."

He said, "Don't put it like that."

I replied, "Well, that's basically what you're saying! I've made it 200% clear and given you every reason to move me on and progress with how my behaviour has been. It's obvious I'm a changed man. I don't need a fucking psychologist to tell me what I already know. I changed a long time ago and every fucker knows it. I'm never gonna grow a pair of wings or clean your fucking boots. But I'm entitled to come out of solitary and move on." And then I added, "Incidentally, I thought psychology was supposed to be private and confidential."

He said, "It is."

"Well, how can it be when the CCTV camera is zooming in on it? And you can't tell me that on a max secure wing it's not bugged. Every word is taped, it's got to be. There is no confidentiality on a max secure unit and if you say there is then you're a liar. It's the screws' reports that you should take note of. They lock and unlock my door. They know how I've boxed it clever. They know how I've changed. That's what you need to do: talk to them."

He then asked about my appeal.

I said, "With or without my appeal I am still entitled to move on and mix with my fellow cons."

So that was that. Believe me, I'm not being blackmailed by no fucker. It don't take Einstein to see that I'm a changed man. Sure that psychology works on some cons, but it don't on me. To me it's a cat and mouse game. It's actually embarrassing. It belittles me. It makes me feel weak and small. I have nobody but myself to blame for my time in prison, and I'm man enough to take it on the chin without blaming the planet. Prison psychologists are the system, so they're not gonna take my side, are they, when I say the system stitched me up there and ten screws bashed my brains all over the walls? How can they take a con's side? It's fucking pathetic and I'm not playing these silly games. Just so long as I'm polite and respectful and I continue my anti-violence, anti-crime stance then they can kiss my arse. End of.

I also got six letters today, one of them off Cherri Gilham. She's brilliant. She always brightens up my day. Cherri used to be on the *Benny Hill Show* and other comedy TV programmes in the 1970s and '80s. She's still a beautiful woman. I like her philosophy on life; she's got it spot on. I also got a letter from Mark Emmins, my old buddy down in Devon. He's up to see me later this month. He works his bollocks off on the 'Free Bronson Campaign'. My other letters were from 'Queenie' Janice Faulkener, Tel Currie and Gary White, and I also got a book from Wyn Thompson. Wyn always surprises me with something. Wyn and me breed pedigree rottweilers, the best. If you're lucky to get a Bronson pup then you're one of only a lucky few.

I've had a good workout, nice shower and shaved my head. Grub wasn't too bad either. All in all, it's been a half-decent day. Oh, and I created an A3 artwork, which I've called 'Psychomanicphobia'. It's a loon with five faces - real spooky. Fuck knows where that came from. I'm on the phone later, so that's the cherry on the cake. Who said there's no heaven?

COKEHEAD!
BENT WARDER SNORTS DRUG OFF PAL'S BONCE
7 August 2007, The Sun
Bent prison officer Carl Towle snorts cocaine off a pal's bald head - in a snap that left him with a long spell inside a cell.
It was taken on a mobile by crooked colleague Michael Dowd. And it proved vital evidence for cops probing a £30,000 drugs ring. Hull prison warders Towle, 27, and Dowd, 28, were part of a gang who pushed £26,000 worth of drugs every week.
The snap was taken as the mob swigged beer, played computer games and snorted coke during nights out in the East Yorkshire city.
Cops grabbed them in January after a three month undercover operation in which they were seen moving drugs between houses, dealing and collecting cash.
Car dealer Stephen Fox, 39, transported cocaine to ringleader Lance Busby, 33, a former Doncaster prison officer and ex-Doncaster Dragons rugby league pro.
Dowd stored drugs at his Hull home and helped to prepare and sell them along with Towle.
When police swooped, gambling addict Busby was caught red handed with £13,000 worth of coke and a list of dealers.
Another £13,000 worth was found in Dowd's flat with drugs paraphernalia.
Even the mob's mobiles bore traces of cocaine and pictures. And as well as taking pictures gang members also filmed each other doing drugs.
Callous Busby even duped his unwitting brother David into helping the gang, Hull Crown Court heard.
He asked David to hand over cash to Fox, telling him it was payment for a car.
Busby and Towle, a former rugby league academy player, admitted conspiring to supply Class A drugs.
Dowd and Fox were found guilty of the same charge after a two week trial. Tricked David was cleared of any involvement.
He said afterwards, "I didn't know my brother was involved in drugs. I have never used them - they ruin people's lives. I don't know if I will ever speak to him again."
Sentencing of the four was adjourned for reports but all face long jail terms.
Detective Inspector Alan Brookes, who led the inquiry, said: "It is sad and extremely disappointing when individuals who should be role models resort to criminal activity. "This network was operating at a high level. They knew the risks they were taking. Yet, because of the potentially high rewards they were prepared to forsake their liberty."
A spokesman for HMP Hull said Dowd and Towle had been sacked.

Hey, look, one of my old jails. Maybe he needs the psychologist. Fucking hypocrite. And this is the tip of the iceberg. Every jail in the world has cunts working in them like this and anyone who says different then you really do need some medical help. Wake up before you turn into a spring onion or a King Edward.

You'll never see Charlie Bronson doing that - not in a trillion years. They're mugs, total fucking muppets. Give me a pussy any day or some fish and chips and a Guinness. I don't know what I've gotta do to wake the public up. Why are the screws different than people in any other workforce? Some do drugs, some don't; some bully, some don't. Just don't think a muggy uniform makes anyone any better than anybody else.

Hey, get on this. There's a screw who used to work here who became a serial killer. He got life. There's another screw who worked in Durham who cut his wife up and put her in the freezer with the pork chops. So don't tell me about the screws being angels, coz they ain't. Even some of the governors are shady characters.

Here's a story for you, but I'll not name the person for obvious reasons. I worked with a screw on a club door. He was doing it for an extra few bob. He was a fucking lunatic and just loved a punch-up. It was as simple as that. We had him taking in drinks to some of the cons we knew. He got a few bob out of it and our mates got pissed every weekend. That's life. That's how it works. That's how it's been from the beginning of time. Some screws will roll over; some screws are fucking mentally fucked. They're just men trying to get on in life and do the best for their families. Good luck to them I say. Just don't get caught.

9 August 2007

I had a great visit from my little buddy Ifty Ifthkhor, but he forgot to get my milkshakes. I love my milkshakes on a visit. But he did get me some chocolate cakes and a flask of coffee, so one mustn't grumble. I was on top form, as I hit 90 press-ups in 27 seconds. It blew Ifty away - he couldn't believe it. Even the screws commented on it after, as they'd obviously seen it on CCTV. Like I told you, this is the real *Big Brother* - so hurry up and vote me out Ifty's kids all call me Uncle Charlie! They're great kids - the best.

KRUEGER MANIAC IN SLASH SUICIDE
10 August 2007, The Sun
Serial killer Daniel Gonzalez - who fantasized about becoming movie monster Freddy Krueger - killed himself inside Broadmoor yesterday.
The 26-year-old psychopath used the sharp edges of a shattered CD case to slash his wrists.
He was found in a pool of blood by staff at the top security hospital.
Knife nut Gonzalez - whom a judge promised would die behind bars - was locked up for life last year for hacking to death four total strangers and trying to kill two others. Psychiatrists had described him as one of Broadmoor's most dangerous patients.
An insider said: "He has always been a suicide risk and checks were supposed to be carried out regularly - but he was only found at 7am when rooms were opened.
"There was a lot of blood and paramedics were called but he was clearly dead. The guy was a complete psycho. When he was on remand before his trial he tried to chew through his veins and arteries.

"To be honest I don't think a lot of people will be mourning his passing."
Horror film addict Gonzalez got six life sentences at the Old Bailey last year.
He believed he really was Krueger, the killer from Nightmare on Elm Street - and in
September 2004 set out to murder ten people so he would be remembered for ever.
He stabbed to death Marie Harding, 73, in Highdown, West Sussex. Pub landlord
Kevin Molloy, 46, became his second victim in Tottenham, North London.
He broke into the home of paediatrician Derek Robinson, 75, and wife Jean, 60, at
nearby Highgate and butchered them in the face neck and body.

Killing himself was the best thing he'd ever done in his 26 years of life. Fucking lunatic. Prats like this give loonyology a bad name. As for Elm Street, he never got there, but he sure arrived at the gates of hell: Broadmoor. Anyone for toast?

Somebody tell me this. Why don't they make mouse-flavoured cat food? Strange that. I've never seen a cat fishing, but they all like to chase a mouse.

I see they're now trying to parole that cunt who shot John Lennon. How nice. He should've fried year ago. Fucking rat. What a senseless killing that was. Now if it'd been Ringo or McCartney, yeah sure, but why Lennon? Why take out Lennon? What a waste.

Still, that's how life ends - in death. It's the only sure ending for us all. The long sleep. Time to rest. Curtains. Back into the darkness. Back to being alone. Fuck getting buried in that pine box. Imagine it. It's horrific. No fucking way. Talk about claustrophobia. You and the worms. Yuk. Them crawling up your arsehole, in your ears, up your nose. Fuck that - no way, amigo. I'm off to the furnace, the incinerator. Burn me, you bastards. Get rid of the evidence. Leave no trace behind. Not guilty, my Lord. Hey, think on this. You've just been buried, you're asleep in the hole, and then some psycho nutcase necrophilic sex maniac digs you up and shags your arse and you can't do a fucking thing about it. Well - do you still wanna be buried?

Don't it make you feel sick? You're not even safe in your own grave. Dead or alive, you're a target. There's always someone waiting in the shadows. There's no escape. It's loonyology. Then you get all the drunks stumbling through the graveyard pissing all over you. Do you really need that? Then in 50 years' time the council decide to dig up the cemetery. What then? Your bones are scattered all over the place. Hey, and what about the grave two down? He could be a grass or a nonce. Half the cemetery could be wrong 'uns. Fuck all that. Who needs it? Burn me, you bastards. Free the soul and destroy the shell. Death is simple. It's life that's complicated.

Hey, did you know that a baby panda only weighs 8 to 10 ounces? It's like a little pink mouse. Can you believe that? It's fucking mental. Such a large animal giving birth to something so small. It freaks me out that does. Nature is the miracle. It's beautiful.

I see the smoking ban's here. No more smoking in public places. Grown people being told what they can and can't do, and what they should and shouldn't eat! Fucking hell. What a life. And the prats who tell us all this, they're fat, useless bastards who've never done fuck all in their muggy old sheep-fucking lives. Boring farts. Pooper scoopers. Could you see Al Capone with a pooper scooper? Oy, Capone, put that cigar out! Oy, Bonnie and Clyde, you can't come in here without a tie on! Come on, wake up and get real. Soon you'll not be able to have a good old-fashioned wank. The world is run by muppets. All this health and safety shit, what's it all about? Have you seen the kids at school playing conkers with big safety goggles on? What a fucking world we live in. No wonder we have so many wimps in government. Bring back Churchill, I say. Not that I'm a Churchill fan, but he did smoke a cigar and he had some bollocks. He was a proper leader; he was a fat cunt.

12 August 2007, News of the World
BRONSON CELLS HIS STICKERS
Britain's most violent prisoner is selling car bumper stickers from his prison cell demanding he is set FREE. Serial hostage-taker Charles Bronson, 54, is flogging packs of ten stickers saying "Free Charles Bronson" for £2.00. He has spent 23 years inside, most of it in solitary, but is campaigning from Wakefield prison to try to persuade the parole board to let him out. Bronson says on his website: "These stickers can be used on your car, books, computer - anywhere you want - even give some to your friends." But so far Bronson has only taken £8.00. In May he was awarded £200 in compensation to buy new spectacles after his old ones were broken during a fight with prison officers.

Cheeky fuckers! My stickers are now all over the world! Eat your heart our Mandela, It's my turn now. I'm coming out - sooner rather than later.

12 August 2007, News of the World
Bent prison officer Michael Todd has a cunning plan to help crooks escape from jail - he'll whisk them off by helicopter for a £5,000 bribe. He made his astonishing offer to an undercover News of the World reporter who had asked him for advice on freeing a lag inside Todd's prison. The greedy screw also boasted of smuggling heroin, cocaine and mobile phones into the jail for cash and admitted: "I would say half the officers are on the take." Todd works at one of Britain's most violent and drug-ridden prisons, HMP Forest Bank near Salford, Manchester, which houses 1,000 adult and youth offenders. And yesterday, after being told of our findings, prison bosses suspended him and promised a full investigation. Our man videoed the officer - now for all to see on our website notw.co.uk - as he..
Boasted: he could smuggle in heroin or cocaine for £5,000
Told: how a female officer performed sex acts on inmates and
Divulged: secret information about camera positions, cell keys and staffing rotas in the nick.
Our undercover reporter was introduced to 23 year old Todd by an ex-inmate of his jail earlier this week at the Old Monkey pub in central Manchester. The con, who

admits having received goods smuggled in by Todd while he was inside, was still wearing an electronic tag.

Over lunch at the New Hong Kong restaurant in nearby Chinatown, shaven headed Todd demanded £5,000 to help our man's pal escape from Forest Bank and came up with his helicopter wheeze. He said: "They've got a landing space in the exercise yard. All you need is a helicopter and you're out of there. Within two minutes nobody is knowing where your are. As soon as you come over that fence, the camera will see you and the police will be called, but by that time the rope's dropped and it's all gone."

He also gave details of the best time to lift our man from the yard, saying: "Obviously, it would have to be on my wing. I could send him to the exercise yard. Seriously. I think that the best option."

His alternative plan involved our man injuring himself to secure a hospital visit, where accompanying screws could easily be overpowered. Todd suggested: "You'd have to have somebody outside watching and people waiting at the other end. He'll be cuffed up but the officer will have the keys. It's been done before, they got away and there was no comeback." Proudly, Todd told how he had been working at the £46 million prison, run privately by security firm Kalyx, for seven months. He whinged: "It can be long hours. It's OK but it's not well paid. I come out with £1,200 a month." He revealed how he boosted his income by "looking after" lags by supplying drugs. He claimed it was relatively easy to dodge staff searches. "If they had a search in the morning then you know it's not going to happen again." he said. "They have drug dogs and if they bark you're straight down the nick for a strip search so it's quite risky." When our reporter claimed his friend inside the prison wanted a parcel of cocaine and heroin delivered to him, Todd was happy to oblige. "I can sort it," he said with a grin. "For a package like that you're looking at £5k. That's for one ounce (of gear) What I'd have to do is get him on my wing, which shouldn't be a problem."

A recent report on the prison showed 40 per cent of inmates took drugs. Earlier this year two officers were arrested for smuggling in drugs, and, as Todd downed a beer and a Cantonese fillet streak, he claimed several other officers were on the take. He added: "There are a lot of people with money in there."

Todd offered to smuggle in a mobile if we wanted our inmate to have one. "Where there's a will there's a way." He smiled. "You have to break it up, take the battery off it. I'd take it in stages."

Next came Todd's claim that a female prison officer performed oral sex on an inmate in his cell. He laughed: "Now everyone wants it."

He said some bent officers "take on more inmates than they can handle" but added: "What I'm always careful about is who you speak to. I don't say nothing to no one." But for once crafty Todd has forgotten his own advice and it could land him behind bars. Our dossier, including video footage, is available to Manchester police, who have been alerted by prison officials. When we confronted Todd yesterday at his semi in Royton, near Oldham, where he lives with his girlfriend and six-month-old son, he broke down in tears. Asked about his boasts he swore and said: "I haven't done nothing", before driving off at speed.

Here we go again! No sooner am I on a page for loonyology and some more shit crops up. As I've told you all, it's just the tip of the ice lolly. It gets deeper as we go along! But, like I always say, everyone's got a price.

13 August 2007, The Sun
£30k CELL DRUG FIND
A police probe is under way after a "fist sized" ball of heroin was discovered in a cell - one of the biggest single hauls in a UK prison. It is thought the stash could have been worth up to £30,000 on the prison black market. The find was made on E-wing at Swaleside Prison on the Isle of Sheppey in Kent. A search revealed the stash inside the cell of a convicted drug dealer. Swaleside holds more than 700 prisoners - half of them lifers. Last night a jail insider said: "It is one of the biggest single hauls found in a cell."

One sure thing is that he never smuggled that lot in on a visit. I wonder who he got it off? It don't take much working out does it!

Hey, I read a blinding book last week called *Glue*. I couldn't put it down! ... Alright, please yourselves! Have you read Lord Archer's books? He shit himself in Belmarsh Jail. At first he was scared to leave his cell. But fair play to him, he survived it!

Q: What do you call an escaped lunatic with an Uzi in your face?
A: SIR.

13 August 2007

I was on the yard when it started hail stoning. It was fucking magic - like a monsoon. I could feel it stinging my head and face - fresh and alive. I love the rain. A real top screw, Mr D, came to see me for a chat. He used to work down here. He's done a lot of good on this unit. He's made it a better way of life for us cons. It's down to him and his trust that when we get escorted over to the dentist we don't get cuffed up. It's only a small thing to most, but it's massive to us. He just believes in a lot of trust and it goes both ways! If all screws were like him I'd have been out years ago. Plus he's an ex-mod, a scooter lad of the old Crombie and Ben Sherman style. It was a class era. Us old mods never lose the sparkle, see!

21 August 2007, The Sun
SEX TOY 'GUN' ROBBER JAILED
A robber who staged a stick-up with his girlfriend's vibrator was jailed for five years yesterday. Nicki Jex, 27, pretended the sex toy was a gun and made off with hundreds of pounds from a bookies. He was nabbed by police after bragging to pals about the stunt. Jex, of Braunstone, Leicester, was high on booze and drugs when he entered a Ladbrokes shop in the city last December. He pointed a bag containing the Rampant Rabbit at the cashier, who thought it was a gun. He then made off with £613 but was tailed to a pub by customer Wayne Vakani, who heard him boasting. He was arrested after his DNA was found on a hat he dropped. Jex, who has 21 previous convictions and was on bail for burglary and driving offences, pleaded guilty to robbery. Judge Philip Head said at Leicester Crown Court: "You didn't have a firearm, but you

intended those you confronted to believe that you did." He awarded Mr Vakani £500.

Fuck me, you couldn't make this up! A 5 stretch for his bird's Rampant Rabbit, now that takes the fucking biscuit! If this isn't loonyology then what is? It's fucking brilliant. It's complete insanity gone mental! This geezer should've got a Bronson award! It's blokes like Nicki Jex who cheer our planet up. Well done, my old son, congratulations. There's a first time for everything and you're the first robber to use a Rampant Rabbit. Now you're inside, your girl will get plenty of fun with it. It's brilliant! It's what movies are made of!

I had a good few words from Jan Lamb today - I mentioned our sexploits earlier (also see list in middle of book). I don't wanna blow my own trumpet, but Jan Lamb done it for me. Believe me, she didn't need no vibrator when I was on the scene. Sadly I'm not often on the scene! But when I am it's 'Lock Cock and two Smoking Balls'. It's why the birds all love a con man. We don't play silly games. We have to make up for lost time in the sack. I once had three birds in one session. There was spunk flying all over the place! I couldn't stop. It was fantastic. I see it as a workout, that's all. Love don't come into it. Hey, I love an apple pie but wouldn't marry one!

Talking of apple pies, I'm fucking starving! And all I've got is three custard creams and four slices of bread. What a poxy fucking life! Stay out of jail if you know what's good for you. It's not worth a wank, believe me.

August 2007, The Sun
BIGG WASTE OF JAIL CELL
Can anyone explain to me why we are wasting money keeping Ronnie Biggs in prison? Admittedly he has been transferred from high-security Belmarsh to Norwich prison after suffering several strokes and heart attacks that have left him seriously ill, but what's the point of keeping this frail man inside? I know he's stuck two fingers up to British justice for years and I thought it was right that he was sent down when he returned from Rio. But when we've got paedophiles, rapists and murderers back on the streets, why is Ronnie still banged up? Have a heart and release him.

Old Jon Gaunt wrote this in his page in the *Sun* on 7 August 2007. I've gotta say he's bang on it! How true is this article? Good on you Gaunty, you're a sensible chap. It's good to see some of you column journalists writing what the majority of the public think.

One of the funniest things ever in Parkhurst was when Tony Coulson chinned Chic Matthews in the gym and knocked him sparko. He then got some chalk and chalked around his body, so when he got up you could see where he fell. It was so funny! Legends are born in moments of madness. Moments like these are not planned, they just happen - it's fate.

I remember one time in Risley in 1974 I was slopping my pot out in the recess. Carl Douglas was booming out of the radio 'Everybody was Kung Foo

Fighting' and I just kicked off big time. I never planned it, it just happened! It ended up as one of the best fights ever! I put down three cons and then the screws steamed in, so I put three of them down too. It was brilliant! I ended up in the hospital strongbox in a straitjacket, and was treated to a nice big injection. It's only when you awaken the next day and your body feels like it's not yours and it hurts to move that the screws all pile in again. "Want some more, cunt? Come on, tough guy. Try it on us. You're not so tough now, are you?" Er, I'm still in straitjacket! What is all this big tough guy bollocks? There's ten of them (cowards where I come from). Fuck off. The fight was yesterday. It's over. Move on! Get me a mug of tea before I get nasty - two sugars, and three slices of toast. Fuck off. I guess I was what you would call unpredictable! Most cons get one good kicking and that's it, 'scared shitless'. Thereafter they become model inmates. My kickings become a weekly issue with me! I won't go so far as to say I liked it, but I have been known to get a hard-on during a rough and tumble. I told you, this journey is loonyology.

17 August 2007
Loraine sent me in £200 today which was nice of her. She always 'sorts' her brother out when she's flush. That's what a skin and blister's all about.

I also got a very sad letter today from Dee Morris. She's a lovely girl. She just dropped out about two years back (she was a regular correspondent to me). It turns out she's had nothing but heartache. Her dad died, and then she had to take on her brother's kids. It's all been one heartache after another for her. Things are looking up now I'm pleased to say. See what I mean? There's always some poor sod worse off. Just look at Britney Spears. All her dosh hasn't kept her happy has it? Or Amy Winehouse? What's that all about? Loonyology.

This month looks set to end nicely. I'm getting a visit on Saturday 25 August from Mark Emmins, who's travelling all the way up from Devon. That's friendship for you. What a top geezer. Then the following Wednesday the Frayne brothers, Leighton and Lindsey, are coming up to see me. I called up Dave Courtney today and had a good chat with him. I caught him just in time as he was on his way out - probably another porno movie. He's into that. And why not, I say. A bit of Jack and Danny and get paid for it. Good luck to him. He's off to Hollywood soon. He'll make it out there, coz the yanks love a cockney wise boy. Let's face it, Dave's got character and charisma and a 30 grand knuckleduster. He hit a bloke in a club once and three diamonds got embedded in his chin. He called it a 10k knockout. You don't want a clump off Dave. He's still got a good peach of a punch on him. He punches his own weight, so you're getting hit by a rhino. He's very large nowadays.

I had a moth in my cell last night. Of all the cells here it comes into my window. Oh yeah, and I had a fucking lovely dream. I smelt a woman lying next to me but I couldn't make out the face. She was all over me like a rash. I wonder who she was? I couldn't be bothered to have a wank though. What's the point? So I got up and had a jam butty and a mug of cold water. It's nice drinking water here. I drink a gallon a day. I'm like a fucking horse. I wish it was Guinness though.

Wake up and smell the bacon. You're being fried away. This is now why so many villains have hung up their tools. Grassing has become the 'in thing' today: 'Deals with Old Bill'. Tell us what we need to know and we will look after you ... blah, blah, blah.

They're making more dosh out of grassing up their mates than they are at crime. The whole world of criminality has changed. As I say to the youngsters, stay clear of it. It's really not worth it, coz your best mate could now be the one willing to put you away. Imagine it. It's really not worth thinking about!

August 2007, The Sun
Informers get £2.2m
Informants were paid £2.2 million by the Metropolitan Police last year. The force forked out £2,220,574 to 4,373 covert human intelligence sources for information. Senior officers insisted criminal informants were crucial in the fight against crime and terrorism. Critics said the 'cloak of extreme secrecy' left some procedures vulnerable to abuse. But Asst. Commissioner Steve house said, "Their lives are often at risk. We do not give too much detail."

Yeah, I bet you fucking don't!

Hey, did you know that the Japs in the Second World War used to push a hosepipe down your throat, fill you up with water and then make you explode? The dirty slit-eyed bastards. And they used to grow bamboo through your body. Nasty fuckers. No wonder the yanks nuked the cunts.

I had to laugh at the Rolling Stones gig at the O2 Arena in London this week. Keith Richards and Ronnie Woods kept lighting up fags despite the 'no smoking in public places' ruling. They were told that for every fag they lit up they'd get fined £50. As if they give a flying fuck. The Stones have gotta be the greatest rock band ever. Whether you love 'em or hate 'em, who's better? They started it all off. They're fucking brilliant. Keep on lighting up boys. You're the dog's bollocks in my book. Fucking mental. Pure loonyology at its best.

Have you seen the state of that Kate Moss's fella, Pete 'somebody'? Can you see him lasting 40+ years? Yeah, pass the cheesecake. Let's all be sick together.

Did you know that in India in 1938 a guy was so sick he spewed up his liver and spleen? Can you believe that? And, get on this, some loony pushed a pea with his nose from Land's End to John O'Groats. Imagine that - on your hands and knees pushing a fucking pea. It beggars belief. I don't know how long it took him, but it must've been a good year. Is it a fact or is it bollocks? It's like that madman who ate a fucking car. He ate a car?! Fuck it. Pass the cheesecake again.

Did you hear about the 11-year-old Liverpool boy who got shot dead as he was playing football with his mates? Some toerag rode up on a BMX bike and shot him in the neck. What the fuck is going on out there? Where's the sense in this? It's unbelievable. You get some Home Office prat saying, "Statistics say gun crime's going down this year", but that's no consolation to the boy's family. Fuck the statistics. This is a crime that should never have happened. What is going on? I swear to God I could stop a lot of this crime if I was given the chance to talk to the youngsters. The kids listen to me. It's a pity these pricks who run the Prison Service don't listen. Once I've spoken to the youth they won't want to be criminals, believe me. The person that blew this boy away was only a kid himself. That trigger boy has a family too. Look how many will suffer over this: mums, dads, brothers, sisters, aunts - all sorts will be feeling the pain. Nobody wins in these crimes. Everybody hurts. It's a river of tears and it breaks my heart, it really does. What a waste of a boy's life. It's so sad, and it's only the tip of the iceberg. Just look at how many youngsters have been killed so far this year, and it's only August:

* Jevon Henry - 18 years old - North London - Stabbed
* James Ford - 16 years old - Streatham - Shot
* Michael Dosunmu - 15 years old - Peckham - Shot
* Billy Cox - 15 years old - South London - Shot
* Odwayne Barnes - 16 years old - Birmingham - Stabbed
* Jason Spencer - 17 years old - Nottingham - Stabbed
* Kodjo Yenga - 16 years old - Hammersmith - Stabbed
* Adam Regis - 16 years old - Plaistow - Stabbed
* Paul Erhakon - 14 years old - East London - Stabbed
* Kamilah Peniston - 12 years old - Manchester - Shot
* Dwaine Douglas - 18 years old - South London - Stabbed
* Sam Brown - 16 years old - Blackpool - Stabbed
* Sian Simpson - 18 years old - Croyden - Stabbed
* Annaka Pinto - 17 years old - Tottenham - Shot
* Ben Hitchcock - 16 years old - Beckenham - Stabbed
* Martin Dinnegan - 14 years old - Islington - Stabbed
* Abukar Makamud - 16 years old - Stockwell - Shot
* Rhys Jones - 11 years old - Liverpool - Shot

18 innocent young lives wasted. For what? Nothing. If that don't touch a nerve nothing will. It's bloody tragic, heart-breaking, cruel and insane. What a world it's become. It's very sad. These boys should never be forgotten. How many more will be killed this year? Let's hope none.

20 August 2007
Mullens 'The Monster', a 21-year-old filthy paedo who raped and strangled a two-year-old little girl, his niece, came down the seg block. He was found in his cell shivering and crying like a rabbit in the headlights. At Leeds Crown Court on 2 July 2007 Judge Justice Simon sentenced him to life with a recommendation that he serves not less than 35 years. It's not enough, coz that will only make him 56 when he gets out. This piece of dog shit should serve the rest of his life in a hole. How the fuck can anybody rape a two-year-old kid? Even an animal wouldn't do that. Personally, I believe shit like this should hang. What's the good in keeping him in jail for 35 years? For what purpose? For what reason? Fuck human rights. Gas the bastard. This piece of shit is typical for Monster Mansion, but even the other monsters don't seem to want him on the wing. Now that's gotta tell you something. But you'll get all the do-gooders and Bible bashers and psychologists making excuses for him. I can see it now. In a year or two he will have found God. Most of these toerags all seem to see the light. Then you'll get the prison chaplain writing sickly sweet reports on how nice he is and how he makes all the screws cups of tea and cleans (licks their arse, more like). Then he'll be making teddy bears for charity. More good reports. Then some head shrink will blame his childhood. In ten years he'll be a church worker, probably sucking the chaplain's cock. It's fucking mental. For his crime he should be in a box.

Anyway, days later in the seg he gets depressed and threatens to slice his wrists. Hey, Mullen, don't just say it, fucking do it. Guess what? They moved him over to the Huntley quarter and he's now in the hospital wing having it cushy! That about sums it all up as usual in a nutshell. Let's spoil the monster and give him an easy ride. Yeh, like his two-year-old niece got. They're all the fucking same these filthy nonces! They're lions to kids and lambs to men. Now the system will build Mullens up. He'll probably serve his first ten years in Wakefield up on normal location - on a wing full of child abusers, so he'll be in good company. He'll have a comfortable ride. Probably get his arse shagged regularly. He'll have a nice cell, carpets, curtains, TV, CD, Playstation, a gym, good food, snooker, table tennis. Oh, and all his visits will be open. I'd say that anybody who visits a shit like him must have a dodgy past themselves.

It's time the public fucking woke up and faced facts, coz nonces like this are living a life of luxury whilst villains like me are living in cages, isolated. It can't be right can it?! Old screws are sick of it, coz years back he would've got the treatment: serious kickings. He would've been terrified every time his cell door opened. We would have piss in his tea and shit on his food. All his clothes would've been used to mop up piss! His sheets and blankets would've been smelling of shit. He would've hung himself. Who cares? You? I don't know a man alive who would care about a child killer. Even the Court Defence Team deep down wouldn't lose any sleep if he died, but they would all love to hear he gets a rough time.

If Mullens ever crosses my path, I'll just nut him that hard his nose will be all over his boat. Even if it means I have to serve extra time for it, so what? He needs a good hiding for what he did. There can be no excuses for raping and killing a two-year-old kid. Hey, who would be a screw? Could you open his door without being nasty? The screws are a strange breed, coz there's no way I could do it! Bear in mind that these screws choose to work in this Monster Mansion. A lot of screws I know in the London jails won't work on nonce wings and I make them right! How can any normal man work with nonces?! But I do know that a lot of screws here hate the fuckers. I also know that a handful of them still give them a tough time, which is good to know. One screw, who will remain nameless, told me about one child killer here: he often slips in his cell and makes him lick the toilet bowl. This sums it all up. The nonces are only good at noncing kids, but as soon as a man confronts them they'll drop to their knees and lick a shithouse. Gas the bastards!

25 August 2007

Mark Emmins visited! He drove all the way from Devon today and all the way back, just to see the Bronson Zoo. That's 13 hours of motoring! And all to visit me. If that's not a friend, then what is? He's a top geezer, the best! Max respect to my old buddy Mark Emmins.

I also got a strange letter today from some Scottish bird called Annie. She's just read my book *Silent Scream* and she wants to marry me. Here we go again. Was it a full moon last night, or are people just born insane?! It's all loonyology. It's fucking brilliant.

Mark, my brother, has just gone to Spain for a week with mum and his kids. It'll do them all good. And I've just won £50 on my premium bonds. My luck's in. Stick by me and you won't go wrong.

Hey, did you know that an ostrich egg can hold two pints of water? Amazing.

28 August 2007

I've just got a postcard from Charlie Richardson who's in Costa del Sol. He's spoken to my legal team and they've told him it's looking good for me. So that's made my day. Charlie says the champagne's on ice. I'm looking forward to tomorrow when I'm getting a visit from the Frayne brothers, Lindsey and Leighton, two legends. Both have had their problems in life and done their porridge, and both have moved on and become successful biz men. I always admire men who can go out and win. I'm next. You watch me outside. I'll show you how to turn it around.

I also got a card from Corfu from Mark Fish. He's having a well-deserved rest. Us biz men need a rest: a bit of sun, sea and good grub to recharge the batteries of life. That's what it's all about: work hard, be a ruthless fucker and then pick the rewards. You can't knock it! Biz is biz. And legal biz is the cream - it makes you feel good.

It's all happening today. Monster Miller got bent up by the Mufti. Fucking brilliant. He refused to strip off in a search. He soon stripped off when he kidnapped his little boys. He's a fucking beast. Why can't they just 'accidentally' drop him on his head? Crash! Problem solved.

The screw Simon Hubbard's back off leave. He's just run another marathon for his kids' charity. I salute the man. I admire things like that. He's over 40 too, so that's brilliant. Some of these fat cunts who work here can only just manage to run to the shithouse before they shit themselves.

Oh well, visit tomorrow. It's been a great day for me. Miller getting bent up made it for me and I got two extra boiled eggs today. A result. The soup wasn't bad either!

Hey, here's a funny thing! If all the Chinese, Russians and Indians farted at the same time, the Earth would explode! It would just blow up! End of. The end of mankind. The end of eternity.

28 August 2007, The Sun
MR TRIPPY
Ice cream van delivers jail drugs
Prisoners have been getting high on drugs thrown over a jail fence - after being alerted by the bell of an ice cream van. The chimes told inmates that packages - including tennis balls packed with class A drugs - were being lobbed in. Lags would then drop lines out of their cell windows with hooks attached to reel in the parcels, which also included mobile phones. Warders hid in vans outside Dorchester prison, Dorset, in a bid to catch the throwers. They weren't nicked but the scam was stopped. Governor Tony Corcoran said: "There are always problems of items coming over the wall with jails in towns. It was a problem here but we have dealt with it. I am very pleased with the way my staff has handled this and other problems at the jail." The problem was revealed in an official report by Her Majesty's Inspectorate of Prisons. The report recommended an urgent review of procedures. Now cell windows are being replaced with a special vent to stop inmates swinging lines down to collect the packages.

Pressures
In her report, Chief Inspector of Prisons Anne Owers made a number of other criticisms of the Victorian jail. Overcrowding is a particular problem, with 242 inmates during an unannounced inspection in April - when its certified normal accommodation was just 147. Ms Owers referred to Dorchester as a small, old and overcrowded local prison holding around two-thirds more prisoners than it should. But she added: "In spite of the considerable pressures, managers and staff have made progress in some key areas."

Where there's a will there's a way! Nothing is impossible in this world and if the ice cream don't work then there's always a screw on the make. If you can't find a dodgy screw then a governor will do.

29 August 2007

So much for my visit. The fuckers are out on strike. Fortunately I got a governor to call the Frayne brothers on their mobile. They'd already set off to visit me so they won't be pleased, but at least it saved them from coming all the way.

So what does happen in a strike like this when all the jailers walk out? I'll tell you. Us cons go without. Human rights go out of the window. We are basically cannon fodder. Our food will be the basics. There's no exercise, no visits, no phone calls. Nothing. And on the CSC unit our doors stay locked. We're just fed like dogs under the cat flap. The forgotten people. Let me say this about the screws' strike. I really don't blame them, simply because the government officials have fucked them over their wages. Them slags are just born liars along with the prats in prison HQ. It's all just one big piss-take. The screws accept a pay deal and they're still waiting for it a year later. So why not strike? That day's strike has stuffed the system right up. But back to the cons. What about us? Do we deserve to be punished over their wage deals? What's it got to do with us? Fuck all. But it's us paying the price for the screws' action again. I lost my visit, I got a plate of shit and I lost my exercise. And all for what? Behaving myself.

30 August 2007

Look what problems the strike caused yesterday. All over the country, courts were affected and probation, legal and domestic visits were stopped. Imagine the chaos in the remand jails. You can't. You never can unless you've lost your freedom: the tensions, the frustrations, the hate. It becomes a hate factory. For example, imagine a con waiting to see his family. He only gets ONE visit off his parents a year, so it's a very special day. They travel 500 miles to see him and - bang! Imagine the feelings there. Imagine your trial stopping over it; the stress, the anger. Imagine your cell has no window, so it's airless, stale and smelly, and all you look forward to is the hour on the yard in the fresh air. It's stopped. You're hungry, fed up, depressed. What about the cons who are mentally unstable or they're not getting the medication on time. What about the suicidal cons? When you add it all up, it's a fucking volcano of human misery. So when their door unlocks these guys are angry. Us lot here, our doors don't unlock. We're in coffins. It's fuck us lot, we don't matter. But in some ways we are probably better off than most, coz if I was in the main population I would be very angry. The stink alone would cause a lot of frustration. Me, Robbo, Reg Wilson, Travis and Yorkie had a good laugh shouting out of the window, "The screws are overpaid and underworked." I fucking lost my voice. Then we started shouting. "We're starving. Let's eat Huntley!" Apparently the striking screws outside the gate could hear us, so the media could too. When the Governor pushed my food under the hatch he said, "Here's a Huntley sandwich." I had to laugh. Prison is a humorous place. You have to see the funny side, coz if you take it all serious (like some do) then you'll end up a miserable bastard. You clock the screws' faces as a lot of them come to work. I'm sure they're sucking on lemons. But that's life. That's what's dealt. We all have to play our hand. Watch this space, as those strikes will be back. The prisons are about to explode, I can sense it. I predict a lot of shit ahead and when it hits the fan we're all gonna be covered in it. Loonyology.

31 August 2007

I've just been told that the Frayne brothers have rebooked their visit for Thursday 6 September. I won't hold my breath, coz there could be another strike.

Mickey Rooney's 86 now. What a life he's had: 8 times married. Looking at him you must think: short arse - who's gonna marry him? Let's face it, he's no Brad Pitt is he? He was once married to the beautiful Ava Gardner, but she walked out after a couple of months with her legendary words: "I'm sick of being married to a midget." You've gotta give it to guys like Rooney, coz they know how to live other guys' dreams. But what is it with beautiful women who hitch up with strange men? Why would Ava Gardner even want to marry Rooney in the first place? It's all loonyology to me. What about you? Rooney's current wife is country singer Jan Chamberlin. I bet she sings him a lullaby or six. It's a funny old world. Who said midgets don't get pussy? The Seven Dwarves didn't do bad with Snow White. Hell's bells! What would you have given to see that? Food for thought to all blue movie producers: 7 midgets banging away at some Snow White.

Hey, did you know that there's an African midget tribe in the Congo that lives in the thick, long grass. They're called the 'Where the fuck are you?' tribe.

The shortest screw I've ever seen was in Belmarsh. He was about 5 feet 2 inches. He looked like a fucking paper boy. The fattest screw I've ever seen was in Broadmoor. He was 30+ stone. You knew who was eating all the loonies' pies there. What a fat cunt he was. He never walked, he fucking waddled. He also sweated a lot. Talk about a lazy cunt. What the fuck good is he? There was another fat screw at Frankland who worked on the hospital wing. He should've been in hospital himself getting liposuction, the fat lazy fucker. All that fat makes me feel sick. I think all fatties should be put in some sort of fat camp and stay there until they're human again. What about them fatties you see on the beach? Don't they put you off your ice cream? It should be a crime the way they waddle about giving it large. They remind me of those big sea elephants: blubbering, ugly fuckwits. Get a life, you lazy cunts, and stop making me feel sick. There's fat and there's fat. I'm talking about the fat, fat slobs. Well, join the fat club and fuck off.

It's time we had a Prime Minister with balls. We need a big wake-up call. Cor, if only it was me I'd wake you fuckers up. I'd be fair but I'd be fucking brutal. Okay, so you wanna be fat. Then be fat, but you're going in an asylum called 'Fatty Asylum'. It will be the biggest asylum in the world and you'll stay there until you wake up. There'd be an asylum for smokers too. All you smokers will be certified insane and you'll stay mad until you're cured. Druggies too. Your asylum will be called 'The Turkey House' and you're in it till you're cured. I'll clean it all up. The wake-up call. What a fucking laugh I'd have. And watch out all you stupid religious fanatics, coz there'll be an asylum especially built for you lot - right next to a crematorium. Be warned, be afraid, coz your beliefs are starting to spread. Take it from me, even God don't like it. You're all pushing it too far now. Be happy like me. Life is brilliant. Find yourself a midget and fuck the blues away.

Come to think of it, I could well see me having a fuck with a giant - the world's tallest woman. Imagine it. How tall? 7 foot 6, 7 foot 10. That would be a photo. I suppose I could practise on a giraffe. Hey, have you noticed how sexy a giraffe's eyes are with those big, long lashes? And what about that tongue wrapped around your bell end?! It's just as well you guys know me, otherwise you could think I'm serious. As if I'd get a blow job off a giraffe! Whatever next?

Did I ever tell you about the time I was a window cleaner. Better not, or I'd be in trouble. I once saw something that put me off cucumbers for the rest of my life. What a filthy bitch she was ...

August 2007, Daily Mirror
PRISONERS CELL BLOCK HOOCH ...
Bad girls are getting pie-eyed on home-made hooch at a notorious women's prison.
Shocked warders at Holloway found gallons of moonshine stashed around the London jail.
It is the first time DIY booze has been found at a women's prison in Britain.
A source said: "The inmates were bored and decided it was time to spice things up. They spent months getting the ingredients and paraphernalia to be able to make it - though the end result was potent and foul-tasting. But the most shocking thing was the huge amount the women had managed to hide - about 20 gallons."
Guards found the hidden hooch during a search of the prison two weeks ago. It had been brewed from yeast, fruit and sugar nicked from the prison kitchens.

I see the girls must've read my book *The Prison Guide Book*. Don't forget, girls, put plenty of fruit in and not too much yeast. Put it in a warm place, near the hot pipes, and give it a good stir every 12 hours. Cheers!

CHAPTER 13
THE FACTORY OF VIOLENCE

The old Roberts Rambler with the PP9 battery was always the cons' favourite radio in the '60s and '70s. That's late '60s, and even then some jails would not allow radios. But the Fidelity radio was a popular one and I'll tell you why. The handle: it was a lethal weapon. When snapped off and straightened out it was a good 14 inches of steel - fucking lethal. All you had to do was work on the tip by rubbing it on the wall or concrete floor, and you had a serious tool. If you tied it onto a mop or broom handle you had a very dangerous spear. Nobby Clarke used one in the bathhouse on F2 in Parkhurst on a con in the bath. He speared him like a fucking whale. Bosh! Cop hold of that. That was Nobby on his way to Broadmoor. Yeah the Fidelity radio had to be the no. 1 for a would-be spear. And it was there - a harmless handle on your radio - just waiting, if you needed it. You can make a tool out of almost anything if you're that way inclined. Your fingernails can be lethal weapons, a pen, a pencil, a paper clip, anything. But a Fidelity handle was the cream. Believe it. The old bed springs were naughty too. It's why they stopped making them. Nowadays it's strips of steel. But the old springs made a serious chain of cutting power. Believe me, you wouldn't want it smashing you in the head at 70 mph. Another good tool was a large nail or screw embedded into a shaving brush. Bosh! Straight into the kidney or the neck. I know one con who kept a flick knife up his arsehole (well, where would you expect him to keep it?) Prison's a factory of violence and it's spewing out the psychos in dozens. It's never gonna be any different. A couple of years back in a Cardiff prison a con killed his cellmate, practically decapitating him, and then started eating him. Talk about house of horrors. Fuck me, the food's not that bad. What makes a man do that? I'll tell you: pure insanity. You can't stop it. It's all part of this world of loonyology.

There was a con in the Scrubs who nobody went near, coz he was a crazy loose cannon. He'd always be laughing and talking to himself. Guys like him are best left in their own space. One day he dived on a screw and bit part of his face off. Why? Who knows. I remember watching a con on the yard in the Scrubs one day. He looked drunk and was wobbling all over the place. Then I noticed the shaving brush on top of his head. The nail or screw was sticking into his brain. So easy. He was just walking on the yard and next thing - bosh! - it's all fucked up. He's a cabbage. Fuck knows what he'd done to deserve it. Who cares - he must've done something. It was probably such a minor, insignificant thing. It's a dangerous way to live. I've walked into a recess and seen a man on his knees looking for his eye or his nose that's just been chewed off. You've gotta witness this shit to believe it. I've seen a man run down a landing bollock naked, screaming, "Get me out of here!" with six screws running after him. Where can he run to? Where does he go? I'll tell you - straight to the strip cell, the strongbox, the padded room. Call it what you like, but it's straight to hell. That's where he goes. You see it but it's just another day, it's meaningless. Today's pain is tomorrow's joy, a laugh.

"Did you see old Tom yesterday? He's a funny fucker. Where is he now?"

"Oh, he cut his throat. He's dead. They took him away in a zip-up bag. Mad bastard. Good bank robber though."

Joe Driscoll was a dangerous fucker. I met him up in Hull in the 1970s. He copped a 14 stretch for armed robbery but got it topped up to 28 years for violence in jail. He served 19 years of that, got out and was found down an alley with a hole in his head. It's the only way anybody could take him out - with a hole in the back of his head. It's all fate.

No name mentioned, but I saw one geezer I've known for years crying like a baby over the death of his mother. He was never the same after that. His heart died that day. It smashed him to pieces. A hard, dangerous man, unbreakable, only his mother's death caught him up.

I wish the youngsters could witness all this pain, coz it's all gonna happen to you if you continue your journey to hell. Slam! Once that cell door shuts on you, you're on your own. It's time to search, before it's too late. Sure, you can live on in a soulless existence, anyone can do that, but believe me now, it's an empty way to live. Once you're dehumanised you become a 'thing', 'the thing', that heartless, cold, evil bastard. Welcome to the funny farm. Pass the colostomy bag.

I'm dying for a pint of Guinness. That first pint won't touch the sides. One gulp. I want a day out at London Zoo. I want to lie on a lilo in a pool and drift away and awake free from all the shit. Peace tranquillity, fucking magic. The Sex Pistols' 'Never Mind the Bollocks' blaring out. Yahooo! Yippeeee.

THE BOTTOMLESS HOLE

A galaxy of madness
Black as coal
Bats as big as rats
Rats as big as cats
Cats with razor teeth
I'm not kidding
This is hell
A place you don't wanna be
A place you don't wish to see
Crazy mental eyes
Even the tears are blood

LOONYOLOGY

Rotting flesh
The whole place reeks of despair
A nightmare come true
A lifemare for sure
No way out
No escape
This is how it ends up
Insanity
Unbalanced minds
The demented
Maniacs of madness
Dangerously disturbed
The circus tent
Roll up, roll up
It's the world's no. 1 freak show
Scary
Lots of shitty pants
If you don't scream you faint
The world disappears
You're dehumanised
Ugly!
One ugly bastard
Join the monster brigade
Dribbling and shaking
Violently sick
Watch out for your face
It may get ripped off
Along with your throat
There is no sanity here
It's all sucked away
There's nothing here but pain
Mental torture
Psychological scars fester
Agonising dreams
Everything has turned sour
Blind man runaway
Running into the darkness
A light ahead
Help, help - I'm over here
The light gets bigger
The rumble gets louder
It's a fucking train
You haven't got a fucking chance
Crash!

It's all over
Who said ghost trains don't hurt?
You're as flat as a pancake
OBLITERATED
The flies take over
It's mealtime
Maggots and worms
It's party time
A rat runs off with a piece of your ear
Some chap shovels you up into a bag
That's what's left of you
What a way to end the ride
The bottomless hole

The media have slaughtered me over the years, but at times they've done me a right good favour. For example, my old buddy Jack Binns, better known as 'the mad yorkie' got in touch out of the blue. I'd last seen him in Hull Jail in 1974 and we'd totally lost contact. Then in 2006 he was reading a story on me in the *Sun* newspaper and got in touch, and - bang - we're back as buddies after 30+ years. I've even had ex-girlfriends get in touch after seeing a story in the press. So it does have its good points. But, then again, is it any good being kept as public enemy no. 1? Who really needs it? I fucking don't, especially now. I'm actually trying to change my image! Anyone for a cucumber sandwich?

Hey, I bet you're wondering where the fuck this book is going next! It's all over the place. Even I don't know, coz I just write what comes into my head. I get a flash of a memory and I'm off down memory lane. To me a book is about drawing the reader in and creating suspense. I want to take you where you've never been before: into the shadows. I want you to smell the excitement and taste the fear. Let's get back to some action! Big boys do bleed. It's a river of blood.

It was Xmas time 1975 up in Hull Jail. Me and half a dozen cons were in the seg block, so our Xmas was gonna be shit. We'd not even a drop of hooch or any extra grub as we were all on punishment. So we decided to smash up! And smash it up we did. The riot mob was brought in to wrap us up. So, one at a time, our cell doors crashed in and we were all rushed and crushed. I was last, so I heard all the others getting dragged out: shouting, kicking, sticking, screaming (not a nice sound)! It was like a scene from hell and you're just waiting your turn. My turn arrived, and I laid into them with a table leg. However, when you've got half a dozen big men behind shields, all in protective gear, it's a bloody hard job to smash through them. But I actually hurt one of them, so that was a good result. When they'd got me down, restrained me and put me in a body belt and ankle straps, I felt my right eye go pop. My fucking eyeball had popped out and was hanging down! Luckily a hospital screw was there and he put it back in. That's how fucking mad it becomes. Please take note of this, coz it could happen to you. In violent situations, mistakes can happen on both sides. The adrenalin is pumping. It's an Alpha Male thing.

Cons have sustained serious injuries and even died in these struggles - choked to death, had seizures, heart attacks, broken bones, smashed heads - so don't go down this road if you can't take it! But you have to give it out. I've bitten the fuckers. It's all in the game and they all expect it! Those few seconds can end up a lifetime of madness. You pay for it later, they make sure of that. So think carefully before you go down my road, and accept the consequences that face you. It's a lot of pain. Hell, that was some Xmas that one. We got less than we would've got if we hadn't smashed the place up, so was it worth it? Fucking right it was. We fucked up the screws' Xmas and we had a laugh. And I learnt that your eye can pop out and pop back in with little damage. Hey, why is it that there's always one screw who squeezes your bollocks in a struggle. Every time you get a ball squeezer! Home tendencies I guess! Leave our balls alone, you pervo. It's a wonder I've any balls left.

My second time up on Broadmoor's roof was my finest. It was summer 1983. Fuck me, that's 24 years ago and it seems like only last week. It's still fresh in my mind, like all victories are. If I say so myself, it was brilliant how I did it, and to top it all I got to kick a screw in the head as I went up the pipe. Well, he shouldn't have tried to grab my leg. Bosh! I caught him with a cracking side kick to the head - lights out. I'll tell you what it feels like to be on top of the world - fucking brill, fantastic. This second roof job was better than the first or the third, simply as it looked an impossible climb. But I pulled it off and I was so proud of it. This was at the time when us lunatics were being treated like mad dogs, and I mean mad dogs. We were all victims of a very vindictive lot of old-fashioned fascist bastards - nurses in size 10 steel toe-capped boots. We were all on Norfolk Intensive Care Unit. Ha ha, don't it make you laugh? Intensive care? We were locked up 24/7 and treated like Alcatraz cons, and if we kicked off we got a fucking big injection of psychotropic jungle juice. Few kicked off. They were terrified of the drugs. Me? I used to weigh it all up and I decided to fuck this lot every time I got a chance. I decided that attacking them was useless, so I'd hit them in the pocket and wreck the godforsaken place. Money talks. Plus, while I was doing it, I could expose the bullies and show 'em my arse at the same time. I'll moon to the planet. Kiss that, you maggots. Lick my butt hole. I even made a flag up there on this protest, a red one, as it was all I had. No significance in it; it was just a red bit of cloth. But no doubt the doctors made something of it: look, it's a red flag, he's a communist. I hung it from a TV aerial and sang 'Wonderful World'. I slung slates at anything that moved. Those slates cost about £5 each back then, probably £15 now.

Hey, let me educate you on something. Did you know that Broadmoor is beautiful? I'm not being funny here. It really is a beautiful building: the structure, the design, the old red Victorian brick. They don't make buildings like that anymore. Some will say, "Thank fuck", but, I say it's a shame, coz I do love a nice big roof. There's something mysterious about the place, like an old church. It's eerie, spooky, but full of vibrant colour and character. The shadows make you feel alive. The laughter of the loonies; the smell of misery; the taste of insanity; the stories; the dreams and the horrors that lay in every cell - it's fucking brilliant. God, it's a fucking nest of humanity gone mad and Charlie Bronson is out on top of it all. I was fighting for lunatics' rights - not just in Broadmoor, but for all the loons all over the world. I saw myself as their leader. Yeah, me. I was showing the world that we have a voice. If you fuck with us we fuck you back. If you treat us like humans we act like you. If you treat us like dogs we'll bite your face off. You cunts decide. That's how I saw it. Yeah, sure, I can hear you say, it can't have been that bad. Well, go and ask the men who lived it. Go and listen to their stories. Go and look into their eyes. You'll see the truth. You won't just see it, you'll feel it. Those old madmen are survivors, men I love, men I salute, and my roof jobs were for them, with respect.

In 1983 I was the Daddy. At 31 years old I'd been locked up for almost ten years. I was a young man full of spunk. Of course I had a wank up on the roof. I had several. You can't beat a good old-fashioned wank in the night breeze under the stars, especially with all the female loonies watching you from their cell windows. What would I do with one of them up on the roof with me? What would we do with each other? Probably fuck ourselves insane. People just don't understand what it's like to go for so long without sexual contact. It's a fucking lonely journey. Even the dreams fly away. It all becomes a fantasy and it takes you over. A bat zooms by. An owl hoots. A plane flies over. Pleurisy sets in. Pain takes over. Splinters become infected. Eyes are blurry, full of dust. The back aches. A nail's embedded in a foot. You're starving. You're cold. You're dying. It's all over for another year. It's back to hell. An empty room. Turn the light off. Wake me up next year. If I don't wake then bury me. But don't fuck with my soul or I'll be back to have every one of you.

Yeh, great memories - legendary! I always smile when I look back. It was fun, it truly was, and I wouldn't have it any other way. I could never be that old man sitting in the corner with a face of stone and a heart of steel, regretting, wishing he'd fought it. They all dream of doing what I did. It's the same with Ronnie Biggs. Every con in Britain dreamt of Ronnie Biggs. You tell me one con who never. He escaped! He lived like a lord out in Rio de Janeiro for 30+ years. He was our hero. We loved him. Some just dream their bird away! Every time I chinned a governor or a screw, cons would dream they'd done it (especially if it was a dog screw who'd treated them like shit). Of course they loved me for it - why wouldn't they? We all have to live our own dreams. Mine was a dream of war against a system I despise. What's wrong with that? It was my fight, my belief. I lost, but did anybody win?

Nobody ever wins in this game. Believe it!

Hey, did you hear about the Broadmoor bird flu? Sounds nasty. Sounds mental! But the sane are safe. It's only for the insane. I think a lot of this flu is man-made and let loose to see what effect it has on the public. I'm fucking sure of it. Like this mad cow disease! What's all that about? What does it matter to us? Cos once you cook meat it kills all germs anyway. So what's the big problem? If we catch a cold or flu they don't kill 20 million of us, so why kill all the cattle? Cos they get a touch of flu? It's all loonyology to me! It's a mad, mad, mad old world. But it's still beautiful! Fuck the mad cows, mine's a T-bone steak with chips. I'll eat it till the cow jumps over the moon! All day long!

I bet you're wondering where I'm taking you next? This ain't a normal book is it?

Do you recall the Balcombe Street IRA Siege in the 1970s? The four of them spent most of their time on remand at Wandsworth, unknown (coz Wandsworth was not a remand jail). They put them on their own down on E1 seg block. At the time I was doing 100 days' punishment over on H1 seg block, but my exercise used to be over on E1 yard, so I got to chat to them through the cell windows. They had fuck all down there for months. The only reason they were down there was to isolate them from the other Irish lads. Everybody knew it was them who'd done the Birmingham pub bombings. They even admitted it to the police. But the Birmingham 6 got lifed off over it and they were all innocent. That's how fucking corrupt the law is! They all knew the truth but they let the Birmingham 6 rot in jail for 16 years. Those heartless bastards. The Balcombe Street Siege proved what we all knew: the police are lying fuckers. Over the years I bumped into the Birmingham 6 and the Balcombe Street 4 in many jails across the country. They were all good guys to do bird with and were blinding hooch makers. The Irish lads do their bird well. Vince Donnley was the funniest fucker I ever met! I've always liked the Irish.

I remember once when I was in Parkhurst seg block, I was on my way in from the exercise yard when I made a dash for the pipe to get onto the roof. I got up about 15 feet and then got wrapped up in the razor wire. I cut myself to pieces. I couldn't move: I couldn't go up; I couldn't come down. That was until I got dragged down. Another time, over in the hospital wing, I hit a screw with a fire extinguisher and it went off. That was so funny. If I'd tried to do it, it wouldn't have worked. Another time I was in Doctor's office being interviewed when I jumped up to explain something and a good ten screws ran in and jumped me. That's when I realised the Doctor had an alarm button under his desk. After that incident, for all my interviews I was put in a body belt. Don't life suck?! I also remember sunbathing once on the yard and I fell asleep. It was in 1976, that hot summer, and I ended up like a fucking lobster!

Anyway, here's a few interesting facts for you. Did you know:

* that it takes 400 bees to make one jar of honey? You've gotta respect those little bees. They don't 'arf work their bollocks off. So next time you open that jar of honey you appreciate it.

* that in an average lifetime a human will sweat four bathfuls? Can you fucking believe that - four?! Don't it just blow your mind?

* that in an average lifetime a human will drink 100 bathfuls of fluids?

* that if you massage your cock regularly with goose fat for six months it'll grow an inch longer? Why bother for an inch? All that work and a smelly dick for half a year coz goose fat stinks. Is it worth it? I suppose it is if your cock's only 3 ½ inches! It's a crazy world, ain't it? You couldn't make it up!

Well, guys, it's getting near to the end, or is it the beginning? What is the end? Who says it's the end of anything? I don't know about ends or beginnings, I just glide through each day as it comes in my own little world in my own space in time. Or time in space. But what I do know.

This read is a one-off and it's a fucking miracle you've even got it in your hands. One day I'll let you all know how it happened. Until I do, ask yourselves one question: would Prison HQ have allowed it? Would they fuck. They'd stop me writing a letter if they had their way. A book? Shit! Can you see their faces when *Loonyology* lands on their desk. Rest assured that a copy will be sent to HQ coz, unlike them maggots, I don't write or say things behind backs. What I do is expose and write the other side, so it's a balanced debate. I let the reader decide. You can say I'm nuts or on a death wish or just totally lost in my own beliefs, but I'll tell you this - so is the system. This is the first and last book on me until I'm free (that's 100% me). Don't get me wrong, I'm still proud of my other books, but co-authors and professional writers polished them up. This *Loonyology* is me; my words. Love it or hate it. It's no ordinary book, it's more a memory lane memoir based in no particular era. Sure, it's like a puzzle, a bit confusing, but that's how I had to create it and it couldn't have been done without Chris Cowlin's belief in me. Bear in mind that it all had to leave the jail mysteriously, and one day I'll say how I did it. Until then, guess! I could never write this and send it out in one part. It simply wouldn't get past the prison gate - I wonder why? So it's been created bit by bit and I have to get it out the best way I can. Some of it has been a fucking pain in my brain. I hope you can appreciate that, but I doubt it. Thank fuck for prison pigeons, 'pony bird express'.

Unfortunately plans don't always work 100%; stuff goes missing and not all postmen are honest! Do you know how much post goes missing with Royal Mail every year? Check it out - you'll be in for a shock! I bet half of it's mine. A lot of my mail ends up on eBay: photos, documents, statements! All sorts of parasites are getting a few quid on my name. Gutless fuckers! Wannabe villains! But that's life. I'm not crying. I'll just sit on it and put names in my little - correction, big - black book.

I'll collect later what's mine! Let's leave it at that on that subject, coz I don't want to frighten anybody into confession time! A rat's a rat in my book!

So the million dollar question is: will Charlie Bronson ever walk out, or will he be carried out in a body bag? And how many really care? That's yet to be seen! My true gut feeling is that I'll walk. Then, and only then, I'll sit down and really come alive. I'll write the no. 1 best-seller on a beach! Now I'm concentrating on my art and poetry, so expect some more books on those.

Hey, I've not finished yet! I can feel another chapter coming on ...

CHAPTER 14
WORDMANIACAL LOONYOLOGY

Did you know Johnny Roberts had seven toes on his right foot? Who? You may well ask. He lived in the next flat to me. A right fucking freaky cunt. Seven toes. Weirdo. Did you know Sammy Davies jnr had a glass eye and Giant Haystacks had a size 16 boot? More knowledge for you. I spoil you lot. And talking of weirdos, look no further than Harry the Conk. What a hooter - the biggest nose I've ever seen, awesome, huge, gigantic, fucking ugly. I just couldn't believe it. It was like a rhino, a parrot, disgusting. If I had a hooter like that I'd wear a bag over my head. He will frighten the children, nasty ugly bastard. No wonder he got shot!

One of the ugliest cons I've ever seen was in Wandsworth in the early 1970s. He was so ugly that the screws would not double him up with anyone in case he scared the shit out of them. So he was always kept in a single cell and given a wide berth. I'm not being nasty here, but he was more beast than man. He had a gigantic head, no neck, sloping shoulders and long arms with big fingers. He really was a horror on legs and he smelt. He never spoke, just grunted, and he was the blackest man I've ever seen. We called him 'The Thing'. He was serving nine years for manslaughter, having killed a man with his bare hands! One day out on the yard he just lay on his back and started to shout crazy words. Fuck knows what. In them days nobody could sit down or stop walking or the screws would get you in off the yard, so three screws went over to him and said, "Get up and walk or we're taking you back to your cell." The thing jumped up and started punching them up in the air. It was just pure madness at its best. Sights like that stay with you forever.

Hey, clock this for an example of a fucking mad world:

Llanfairpwllgwyngyllgogerychwyrndrobwllllantysiliogogogoch

58 fucking letters in it. Obviously it's Welsh and it's the name of a place in Wales. Now try to pronounce it! It's fucking loonyology. New Zealand has got a 57 letter word for a hill over there. Here goes:

Taumatawhakatangihangakoauauotamateapokaiwhenuakitanatahu

Flash bastards. Who needs it? I'd say they're just copying the Welsh. And who the fuck made that word up? What a prat. It's bloody pathetic, insane. It's some cunt who loves a long word and so created it. It's a hyperpolysyllabicsesquipedalianist. That's a person who uses long words. A fucking wordanorak. You can picture one can't you? Glass-bottle specs, a fluff of hair at the side of the head, bald on top, a hunchy back, short and fat, wearing a tweed jacket and sandals, farts a lot, in their late fifties, still a virgin but a professional wanker, loves the Internet chat rooms. Yeah! We know who you lot are. Wankers. Well I've a word for you prats: floccinaucinihilipilfication. That means you're fucking worthless. Now fuck off before I dig out some more beauties. Hey, you'll love this one: chargoggagoggmanchauggagog-gchaubunagungamaugg. I bet you haven't a clue what this one is? Come on, have a guess. I dare you, come on. Okay, I'll educate you. It's a lake in Massachusetts, USA. Yeah. It had to be the yanks. They've always gotta be clever bollocks. I bet they can't even pronounce it. Prats. Why call a lake that?

Hey, don't tell me you don't learn nothing in Loonyology. On every page you learn something. Okay, it may be bollocks but it's facts.

More weird words for you. Unless you suffer with a phobia then you'll never understand what it's like. I bet you can't even name ten phobias. I bet you can't even name five. Get on some of these:

Achluophobia	Fear of darkness
Acrophobia	Fear of heights
Agoraphobia	Fear of open spaces
Ailurophobia	Fear of cats
Algophobia	Fear of pain
Amaphobia	Fear of dust
Androphobia	Fear of men
Apeirophobia	Fear of infinity
Arachnophobia	Fear of spiders - why not just call it spiderphobia. Wouldn't it be easier so we all understand?
Astrapophobia	Fear of lightning
Basophobia	Fear of walking
Batrachophobia	Fear of reptiles
Bibliophobia	Fear of books - how can anybody fear a book? Why a book? What's scary about a book? Fuck me, there's some nutters out there.
Chrematophobia	Fear of money
Claustrophobia	Fear of closed spaces
Cynophobia	Fear of dogs
Dikephobia	Fear of justice
Eisoptrophobia	Fear of mirrors - I'm alright there. I go years without seeing a real mirror.
Genophobia	Fear of sex
Gymnophobia	Fear of nudity - yeah, that's probably fat fuckers who are ashamed of those bodies.
Gynophobia	Fear of women

Hadephobia	Fear of hell

Who makes these fucking words up?

Haematophobia	Fear of blood - best not get a job in a slaughterhouse.
Harpaxophobia	Fear of robbers
Hedonophobia	Fear of pleasure - somebody tell me, how can anybody fear pleasure? It's fucking loonyology to me.
Helminthophobia	Fear of worms - best be cremated then.
Hypnophobia	Fear of sleep
Kleptophobia	Fear of stealing
Lyssophobia/Maniaphobia	Fear of insanity - trust insanity to have two.
Mastigophobia	Fear of flogging
Musophobia	Fear of mice
Necrophobia	Fear of corpses
Odontophobia	Fear of teeth
Olfactophobia	Fear of smell
Ommatophobia	Fear of eyes
Oneirophobia	Fear of dreams
Ouranophobia	Fear of heaven
Phasmophobia	Fear of ghosts
Photophobia	Fear of light - fuck me, how can you be scared of light? You may as well go to sleep and not wake up.
Poinephobia	Fear of punishment - I'm sweet there.
Potophobia	Fear of drink - thank fuck I'm okay with that one.
Satanophobia	Fear of satan - don't be scared of him, he's okay.
Siderophobia	Fear of stars
Sitophobia	Fear of food
Spermatophobia	Fear of germs
Taphophobia	Fear of being buried alive
Thalassophobia	Fear of sea
Triskaidekaphobia	Fear of number 13
Xenophobia	Fear of strangers
Zelophobia	Fear of jealousy
Zoophobia	Fear of animals

Come on, somebody tell me. I'm not believing half of this phobia shit, are you? Some head shrink will get £100 an hour for treating these freaks. It's all bollocks to me. Take thalassophobia - fear of sea. Solution/cure: stay away from the sea. It's bollocks, total bollocks, and all these head shrinks are laughing at you phobia freaks. Come to me, I'll cure you. I'll cure you with the facts, the truth. You're just suffering with loonyology. These phobias are just the tip of the iceberg and, believe me, it's fucking melting, and all your phobias will be drowned along with your fears. Wake up, it's not real.

Hey, I've even created my own loonyology vocabulary. Cop a load of these beauties:

A-Z OF LOONYOLOGY WORDS
(eat your heart out Oxford Dictionary)

A	Arsewipephrenia	Arse phobia, study of anus, anal expert
B	Bollockphobia	Psychosis of the bollocks, mental illness, incurable
C	Cockfacepsychosis	Ugliness beyond humanity, fixation of freakiness
D	Dildollymania	Disturbed erotica feelings of artificial penis
E	Eggermuffingus	Paranoia of eggs, eggmaniac
F	Fuckfacescabbydelirious	Psychosis of the face
G	G-spotsanitorium	Delusions of the G-spot, forever searching for the perfect orgasm
H	Hidophenic	Lost within, soul sucked, washed away dreams
I	Insomaniacnutterphobic	Dangerously demented, no hope, inhumanity
J	Jellybellypsychic	Fat, flabby and fucked up
K	Kreemingasphelta	Overdose of semen, spunked off
L	Loverdrycrutheral	All dried up, an old prune
M	Minglemouthdona	Blow job pro, mouth angel, orally genius
N	Negrophrattler	Pill head, druggie, low life
O	Oniongraffiti	Tear drops, wrecked, unstable
P	Peepshowstopperation	Pervo, out of control freaky fucker
Q	Queerbendoverquickie	Gayster, loose, tunnel of perversion
R	Rogeringmaniacal	Super king shagger
S	Shaggerphobia	Afraid of the contact, unfuckable, masturbator
T	Twinferational	Food allergy, starvation
U	Universalmentalist	World famous nutter, universal nut, legendary maniac
V	Verokiskia	Fear of tights and lycra
W	Wankeroptical	A total tosspot, personal abuser
X	Xertiuvellion	Soulless and empty
Y	Yoyododobuzzerical	Battery sex toy
Z	Zebeddiotion	Home-made dirty movie

I'll tell you what's mad - rhyming slang. It's used a lot in society, in the media, on TV, but so few understand it. Do you? Why don't somebody do a dictionary on it, or have they? If there is one, then get it flying. I'm gonna give you a good start. By the time you've come to the end of this chapter you'll be halfway there! Okay, here we go:

First the East End specials, ones you need in everyday life, especially around the markets and pubs in East London. This will save you being ripped off!

Artful Dodger	Lodger
Ascot Races	Braces
Berkshire Hunt	Cunt
Blood and Blister	Sister
Boat Race	Face
Bob and Dick	Sick
Bob and Hit	Shit
Bob Powell	Towel
Bobby Rocks	Socks
Burlington Bertie	Number 30
Burton on Trent	Rent
Butcher's Hook	Look
Buttered Bread	Dead
C & A	Gay
Cabbage Tree	Flee
Cain and Abel	Table
Calvin Klein	Wine
Can of Coke	Joke
Can of Oil	Boil
Cape Kelly	Belly
Captain Hook	Crook
Careless Talk	Chalk
Cash and Carry	Marry
Cat and Mouse	House
Chain and Crank	Bank
Charlie Beck	Cheque
Charlie Chase	Race
Charlie Dance	Chance
Charlie Drake	Brake
Charlie Frisky	Whisky
Charlie Howard	Coward
Charlie Pope	Soap
Charlie Randy	Brandy
Charlie Walk	Talk
Charming Mottle	Bottle
Cheese Crackers	Knackers

Cheese Grater	Waiter
Cock and Hen	Ten
Eiffel Tower	Shower
Emmerdale Farm	Arm
Errol Flynn	Chin
Fifth Gear	Ear
Flowery Dell	Cell
Flying Trapeze	Cheese
Forty Four	Dirty Whore
Frankie Frazer	Cut-throat Razor
Fred Astaire	Jet Black Hair
Gary Glitter	Bitter
Gary Lineker	Vinegar
Gay Gordon	Traffic Warden
Gene Tunney	Money
General Election	Erection
George and Zippy	Very Lippy
George Blake	Snake
Georgie Best	Chest
Ginger Beer	Queer
Ginger Bread	Head
Hackney Marsh	Glass
Hampstead Heath	Teeth
Ice Cream Freezer	Geezer
Jam Jar	Car
Mother Hubbard	Cupboard
Mother Kelly	Telly
Mother's Joy	Boy
Mother's Pride	Bride
Nat King Cole	Dole
Oliver Twist	Pissed
Polly Parrot	Carrot
Polo Mint	Skint
Pony and Trap	Crap
Popeye the Sailor	Tailor
Pork Chop	Cop
Posh and Becks	Lots of Sex
Raspberry Ripple	Cripple
Reggie Kray	Tray
Ronnie Kray	Pray
Sad and Sorry	Lorry
Salmon and Trout	Snout
Sammy Lee	Pee
Sausage and Mash	Cash

Smack in the Eye	Pie
Snake in the Grass	Drinking Glass
Snakes Alive	Five
South Pole	The Hole
Spanish Guitar	Cigar
Steffi Graf	Bath
Stevie Wonder	Thunder
Stick of Rock	Cock
Sticky Toffee	Coffee
Sunday Best	Rest
Sunday Lunch	Hunch
Swan Lake	Cake
Taxi Rank	Wank
Tea and Toast	Sunday Roast
Tea Leaf	Thief
Teddy Bear	Pear
Terry Waite	Late
Test for Two	Shoe
Tom Sawyer	Lawyer
Tom Thumb	Bum
Tom Tit	Shit
Tommy Cooper	Trooper
Tommy Tucker	Fucker
Vanity Fair	Electric Chair
Vincent Price	Ice
Yorkshire Ripper	Slipper

Hey, I didn't make that lot up. They're all words used regularly these days. Learn the lingo, as one day it could save your life or even save you from being ripped off, coz all the scallywags use it. It's another world. A world of puzzles. A world of loonyology.

I hope you're getting into all this. It's fucking brilliant once you know it all. It's a whole new ball game! Now some serious stuff that could save your arse - 'The Drug Scene'. A lot of innocent people are dragged into it without realising it. So here's a whole new world you need to know so you can walk away from it. For example, you could be in a pub, club or party and talk starts up - words you don't know. It may all sound innocent enough, but it's lethal. So remember all this.

Heroin:	Fix	Jimmy Hicks, Tom Mix
	Tom	
	Gear	
	Scag	
	Smack	
	Chase the Dragon	

Crack:	Apple Jack	
	Half Track	
	On Your Back	
	Sack	
	Dirty Mac	

Cocaine:	Coke	Big Bloke
		Charlie Oats
		Charlie Barley
	Poke	Up in Smoke
	Line	Patsy Cline
	Snow	You Know
	Powder	Niki Lauda

Cannabis:	Dope	Bob Hope or Bar of Soap
	Grass	Brass
	Hash	Johnny Cash
	Weed	Bird Seed
	A ¼	A Bottle of Water

Pills:		Jack and Jills
		Pebble Mills
		Jimmy Hills
		Damon Hills
		William Hills

Speed:		Lou Reed
		Oliver Reed
		Good Deed

All this is Drug Rhyme is worth teaching the kids. If you don't know, how can you walk away? People have a choice in life, but you have no choice if you don't know what's going on! Pills or powder can easily be used by someone to spike your drink or food, but if you know the slang you will know the people. Then it's up to you (fuck 'em off). Me, I fucking despise the drug world. Always have, always will. They're gutless, weak people, sucking on the sheep of life, but I can never work out the drug mugs who junk up in the first place. Give me a plate of fish and chips any day.

So be aware of the drug scene. Hear it and fuck off before you become another huggy sheep! Now let's get back to some good old-fashioned slang. Enjoying it? I hope so, it's brilliant:

Army and Navy	Gravy
Arty Roller	Collar

Bacon Bonce	Nonce
Bag of Sand	Grand
Barnaby Rudge	Judge
Bees and Honey	Money
Bobby Moore	Score
Brighton Rock	Dock
Bugs Bunny	Funny
Cape Kelly	Belly
Cassius Clay	Sunny Day
Charlie Freer	Beer
Cock and Hen	Ten
Dad and Mum	Rum
Daisy Roots	Boots
Darren Gough	Cough
David Courtney	Rather Naughty
David Gower	Shower
Dig in the Grave	Save
Dog and Bone	Phone
Dolly Mixtures	Pictures
Don Revie	Bevy
Dr Crippen	Dripping
Ducks and Drakes	The Shakes
Duke of York	All Talk
Elephant and Castle	Arse Hole
Elton John	One Big Con
Frank Zappa	Crapper
George Raft	Banker's Draft
Gloria Gaynor	Trainer
Goldie Hawn	Prawn
Helter Skelter	Shelter
Henry Fonda	Honda
Henry the Third	Turd
Hickory Dock	Clock
Ian Rush	Brush
Irish Rose	Nose
Isle of Wight	Turn off the Light
Jam Roll	Parole
Joan of Arc	Car Park
Jockeys Whips	Chips
Julian Clary	Fairy
Kermit the Frog	Snog
Kiss and Cuddle	Muddle
Knobbly Knee	Key
Kung Fu Fighter	Lighter

Laurel and Hardy	Bacardi
Lemon and Lime	Time
Lemon Squeezy	Easy Peasy
Man on the Moon	Spoon
Mars Bar	Scar
Michael Caine	Pain
Microchip	Whip
Mile End	Friend
Milton Keynes	Tin of Beans
Monkey Tail	Nail
Morris Minor	Shiner
Nobby Styles	Piles
Normandy Beach	Speech
Nursery Rhyme	Crime
Ocean Pearl	Girl
Office Worker	Shirker
Orange Squash	Dosh
Oxford Bag	Flag
Paraffin Lamp	Tramp
Pen and Ink	Stinker
Penny Brown	Town
Peter O'Toole	Stool
Peyton Place	Lace
Pig's Trotter	Squatter
Plates of Meat	Feet
Porky Pies	Lies
Pot and Pan	Old Man
Pot of Glue	Jew
Pots and Dishes	Wishes
Pound Note	Coat
Punch and Judy	Moody
Rabbit Hutch	Crutch
Randolph Scott	Spot
Raud Gullit	Bullet
Rising Damp	Cramp
Rosie Loader	Whisky and Soda
Rosy Lea	Tea
Ruby Murray	Curry
Runner and Rider	Cider
Ryan Giggs	Digs
Saint and Sinner	Dinner
Sally Gunnell	Blackwall Tunnel
Sawn-off Shooter	Looter
Scooby Doo	Screw

Semolina	Cleaner
Sharon Stone	Telephone
Shepherds Bush	Push
Sky Rocket	Inside Pocket
Slice of Toast	Ghost
Slip in the Gutter	1 lb of Butter
Sniffer and Snorter	Newspaper Reporter
Soft and Silk	Milk
Soldier Ants	Pants
Southend Pier	Ear
Spanish Onion	Bunion
Stand to Attention	Pension
Steak and Kidney	Sidney
Sugar and Spice	Nice
Sweaty Sock	Jock
Tom and Jerry	Merry
Tom Sawyer	Lawyer
Tommy Guns	Runs
Tower Bridge	Fridge
Tower Hill	Kill
Trafalgar Square	Chair
Treacle Tart	Fart
Trouble and Strife	Wife
Turkish Bath	Laugh
Turtle Dove	Glove
Uncle Sam	Lamb
Wallace and Grommit	Vomit
Westminster Abbey	Shabby
White Cliffs of Dover	It's Over
Willy Winky	Chinky
Wilson Picket	Ticket
Worms and Snails	Fingernails
Yankee Doodle	Noodle

That's your lot! If you want any more, then let the publisher know and I'll do a whole book on it, but these will help you out if you're ever down London. Let's put it like this, it may even save you a few bob. Be your own Barnaby Rudge, coz you're the real Ice Cream Freezer! Oh, by the way, mine's a double Charlie Randy. Cheers!

CHAPTER 15
SEPTEMBER - CHILLERS, GORILLAS AND SPILLERS

Here's a fucking blinder. You'll love this one. A British law was passed back in 1845 that anybody attempting to commit suicide would be punishable by the death penalty. Can you believe that? It's fucking insanity gone mad. You're breaking the law to attempt it, but the state will do it for you. All I can add to that is: don't attempt it, fucking do it, coz if you don't they sure will.

Q: What do you call a 38-stone stripper with a mass of body hair?
A: Unemployed.
Q: Why did the skeleton refuse to go bungee jumping?
A: He had no guts.
Q: Did you hear about the pregnant librarian? Her baby was born two weeks overdue. She got a 64 pence fine.
Q: What keeps hot in the freezer?
A: Mustard.
Q: What goes 'Ooo, Ooo'?
A: A cow with no lips.

There was a loony in Rampton Asylum who was forever telling jokes - jokes he made up himself. They were only jokes to him though, so only he laughed. They were fucking mental. He would end up crying with laughter. Well, it is a nuthouse, so what do you expect?

I see that Brian won the 2007 *Big Brother*. The twins should've won it, not that daft sod. He never even knew who Shakespeare was. A 22-year-old man who's never heard of Shakespeare?!

I knew one nutter who believed he was me - yeah, me - and that I was an impostor. He soon got a fucking slap. I broke his jaw in three places. Cheeky cunt. Imagine that. Some nutcase telling you you're not you, he is. It's mind boggling. It's total loonynutterphobic (a good word that).

Did you know that the game Monopoly was invented back in 1933? I've often thought about inventing one based on prison. I may just do it one day, coz I'm getting fed up of books.

Hey that Leonardo Da Vinci was a clever fucker. He was born in 1452 and wasn't just into art. He studied anatomy, physics, mechanics, engineering, writing, philosophy and botany. Clever cunt. He applied his art skills to architecture, canal building and weapons design, and drew up the plans for a bicycle, helicopter and steam-powered cannon. Flash fucker. He even did parachutes, underwater breathing devices, ocean rescue equipment, water turbines, cranes, mechanical saws - all sorts of stuff. The man was a fucking genius and a brilliant artist.

Did you know American statesman Benjamin Franklin invented bifocal specs, as he hated having to wear two pairs of specs? Clever cunt.

Hey, and Steve McQueen invented a bucket seat for a racing car in 1970. He was a top geezer, McQueen.

2 September 2007, Daily Star
JAIL CARNIVAL FOR BAD GIRLS
Female lags including killers were treated to an all day carnival - in jail. The ten hour bash at taxpayers' expense provided a carnival queen contest, a barbecue lunch and an evening rock and dance fest. An insider revealed: "Some of the girls were getting down and dirty. They were all over their partners and really letting it all hang out. It was real Dirty Dancing!"
The event was staged at Send prison, near Woking, Surrey - where inmates include convicted killer Jane Andrews, 40, Sarah Ferguson's former dresser, and road-rage murderess Tracie Andrews who stabbed her boyfriend to death. It offered drum workshops, DJ sessions, face painting, henna tattoos and stalls. Our source said: "It was like Glastonbury Festival. The event was huge and must have cost a packet to put on. Some will see it as rehabilitation. But victims of crime will be wondering what sort of punishment is being delivered." A Prison Service spokesman said: "Send prison held a Cultural Diversity Day as part of its commitment to promote race relations and cultural awareness. The cost was covered by the prisoners' general purpose fund which consists of profits from the rental of in-cell TVs."

Cheeky bitches, they never even invited me. But, then again, would I want to go? I don't think so. Cor, that Tracie Andrews was an evil sod. I remember that case like it was yesterday. After she stabbed her fella to death she blacked her own eyes, put the blade in the petrol tank of the car and pretended they were both attacked. It almost worked. But the mother of the dead lad saw right through her and it all came unstuck. Yeah, fuck it, don't invite me. I'm too young to die. You never can tell what those witches will do next.

Did you know that Rudyard Kipling the author of *Jungle Book* invented snow golf. He just painted the balls red. I'm not so sure about that. It really depends on how deep the snow is.

Do you know what is meant by a Chicago Overcoat? A coffin. And that nearly 43% of released American cons are re-arrested within six months.

Hey, what's the murder of a brother called? Fratricide. What about the murder of a sister? Sororicide. I bet you never knew that? You learn a lot in my books!

And Yo-yos were invented in 1929. I bet you never knew that? I was a yo-yo champion at school, as well as a conker champion and marble champion.

Andy, Lorraine and me, Belmarsh 1996. One month later I hijacked the Iraqi hijackers!

Above: Aunty Eileen, 'James Bond' and mum. Sorry ... my brother John (he would have made a good Bond!), 2000.

Top left: My Cousin John Cronin - a top geezer!

Left: That's Danny Hansford, the movie man. Whatever you do Danny don't bend down when DC is behind you!

Wahid Iftkhar

Wilf Pine and Tel Currie.
Wilf's a living legend!

Ronnie Knight and the one
and only Tel Currie.

Left: "To Ron and Reg, I'd like to pay my respects to
you both. I miss you both very much, you were two
great friends of mine. Never forgot."

Above: Mark Fish.
If you don't vote then your not my friend.

Wyn Thompson, a good friend of mine
and a mean pool player.

Stu Cheshire and Roy Shaw.
You don't want to upset these two.

Mark Fish, Giovanni's son Michael
and Jason Marriner.

Michelle and Kitch - two lovely friends.

Gemini Reynolds, how can you lose
a trial with Gemini

Big Joe Egan The toughest white man on the planet

Above: Big Joe Egan - the toughest white man
on the planet and "Mike Tyson"

Matt Legg, John Markey and Dave Courtney - 3 of the best!

Mark Emmins and Dave Courtney
- my two loyal buddies.

Ex-Champion Boxer of the World, John H Stracey with his
wife Cathy in Grazianos bar, New York USA, 2007.

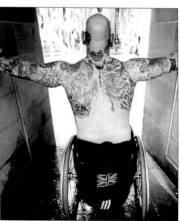

The legend him self Kenny Herriot,
who needs legs, this guy is Superman!

Lindsay Frayne, Mark Emmins, John Markey,
Mum and Leighton Frayne.

Andy Salvage, Al Rayment
and my Lorraine.

Above: Two top geezers: Mark Emmins
and Apex Publishing's Chris Cowlin.

Below: A nice piece from John Conteh.

Above: Tom Hardy, actor playing me in my film. Who
else could play me but Tom?

Below: One of the best mates I ever had and I still
miss the old rascal, my uncle Jack Cronin (the original
Del Boy himself) every body in Luton knew Jack. And
that's mad Kelly Anne with him she would later set me
up with a gun although she retracted her statement,
but once a rat always a rat.

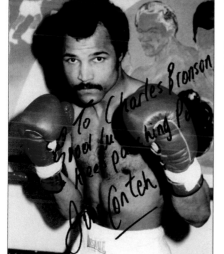

A night out for the chaps: Dave Courtney, Tel Currie, Freddie Foreman and Howard Marks.

Joyce Connor, what a great arse! What a beautiful girl! What a dream! She's my personal head shiner! The princess herself!

Mark Sharman and wife Sandra with DC. At one of my art shows that Mark Sharman organized - a great occasion, a proud night.

Left: Di Brown's daughter Elle Brown, she's a star!

Left: Ray and Irene Williams, when your on a night out with these two expect to get pissed. (there the best couple I know), and we go back four decades.

Right: Dessy Ludwick - you really don't want to mess with Dessy.

Johnny Bristow,
we go back 40 years
- a top man!

Tel Currie and Bruce Reynolds - one of the great train robbers.
I last see Bruce in Parkhurst in 1976.

My Lorraine and Mark Fish, he's like family.

My Lorraine and Howard Marks at a
Bronson campaign night.

Red Menzies firm: the three angels - Jodie, Stella
and Sabrina (Mum and Daughters).

The Frayne brothers with Mark and Lisa Emmins.

Needs Swellbelly Lead singer of
Swellbellys, a pro tattoo artist
and a loyal mate.

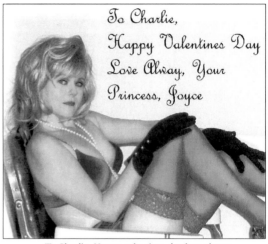

To Charlie, Happy valentines day love always,
your princess, Joyce.

Jillian Lofts from Ipswich - a good soul.

Left: Ron Greedy
and Chris Reed,
these two guys are
special to me. To
me there true
survivors,
They survived
Broadmour when
it was a hell hole, I
salute them both.
Sadly Ron died
recently, we are
going to miss the
old chap.

Left: Ill drink to
that! Loonyology
will one day rule
our planet.

Right: Freddie
Foreman and Al
Rayment (at a
Mark Fish bash)
two legends in
there own rights.

Big Gary White and wife Mimms
long live the outlaws.

Below: (Signed to me) Ricky Hatton in training for the
pretty boy Floyd Mayweather fight in 2007
Ricky's a top geezer...a legend.

Frankie Fraser and Tel Currie.

My two cousins Stuart and Darren Godfrey,
with their old ladies.

Charles Bronson, 1987 - it's all under the hat!   A nice piece from Frank Bruno - a born winner!

Dave Dobson landlord of the Blind Beggar keeping
an eye on my old duchess, top geezer is Dave
Respect to the man - everyone spoils my mum.

Dave Courtney with a copy of my framed book cover.

Lindsay Frayne and Leighton Frayne. I tried
to get them to play the Kray twins in my
movie, it wasn't to be.

Tel Currie, Charlie Richardson,
Roy Shaw and Harry Marsden.

Tel Currie with Carlton Leech and pal

Redds daughter - Jodie Menzies,
aged 13 - a lovely girl.

Left: "Your the man!" Best wishes from your pal, Terry Stone (actor). Look out for him in my movie.

Below: Cliff Field - the legend, one of the best unlicensed fighters to ever step in a ring, I salute the man.

Ronnie Field with Joe Pyle, the true guvnor, one of the last snaps taken of Joe on this planet, 2007.

John Alfred Lodge. My little Welsh buddy, one of the best blaggers to come out of the beacons.

Above 1: Big T - this guy pulls planes for fun, see him in my book Solitary Fitness.

Above 2: Redds daughter - Sabrina Menzies, aged 16, boy can she kick!

Fight promoter Caroline Bayford in Spain.

Charlie Breaker, Ernie Shavers and
Caroline Bayford. Ernie had the hardest
punch in boxing history.

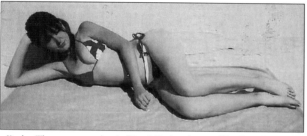

Keeley Thompson, my lovely friend Keeley always a bit of sunshine one
smile from her and the sky lights up, for real.

Above Right: Ifty's
daughter: Zahrah
Iftkhar, the beautiful
Zahrah.

Left: Gary White and
Roy Shaw, a night out
with the outlaws.

Left: Tom Hardy - he looks more like me than I do!

Below: My brother John, and Mum. John died soon after this photo was taken of a brain tumour. A great loss for us all he was a good man, everybody loved my brother! We all have to move on but its never the same! Dreams get smashed! That's how life is crazy and the good always go first I'm sure to reach 135!

Above: A boxing legend Alexis Arguello with his beautiful wife, 2007.

Below: Andy Salvage doing his Elvis act out in Spain he can star at my club Bronco's anytime. A top act, a top geezer and a great guy.

Above 1: Chris Reed, mum and Lyn Jamieson.

Above 2: Gypsy Joe Smith, Jimmy on the Cobbles Stockin, King of the Gypsy's Johnny Frankham and Tel Currie

Left: Leighton Frayne, Tom Hardy, Lindsey Frayne, John Markey and Darren McDade.

Below: My two Brothers, Mark and John, I salute you!

Above: George Chuvalo, George was without a doubt one of the hardest men in the boxing world in the 60s and 70s he fought them all. three times over he was the Canadian heavyweight champion this guy was born hard, rock hard And his entire life has been hard in and out of the ring he even lost three sons. Sons are supposed to live out there dad! George is just a top guy we all admire and respect a true legend. That's Alec and Freddie with him - two diamonds!

Above: Redd Menzies, Cliffy Fields and Bill Buddy Cooper. Cliffs a true legend ... He's one of the chosen few who put Lenny Mclean on his arse. Even Roy Shaw said cliff was one of the toughest unlicensed fighters around in the 1970s Bill was cliff's corner man. Redd, a good pal the three are just chewing the fat on a summers day in 2007.

Charlie Richardson, Tel Currie and Johnnie Nash.

Dee Morris. My lovely friend Dee, she is a true star!

Tony Crabb and son Joe. Tony's serving life - a true gladiator!

Billy copper and Roy Shaw two legends together men of rock old and wise but still hungry. With friends like Billy and Roy you don't have too many enemies

Left: Sue May - she is now free after 11 years for a crime she never committed! A travesty of justice!

Right: My old mate of 38 years - Billy Bristow ... cheers!

Above: My mother was and still is the most beautiful human I have ever known!

Left: Micky Dunn - a top man!

Left: Jim Dawkins, my mum Eira and Roy Shaw

Below: Big wedding day - Al and Nat Rayment with little Thomas, my God son.

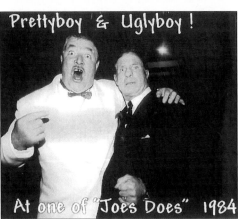

Prettyboy & Uglyboy !

At one of "Joes Does" 1984

Charlie Breaker and Roy Shaw. Charlie now lives out in Spain, he sold his boozer in London and went to greener pastures He keeps in touch regular. Roy...well Roy does what he always does he keeps on winning neither have changed in the 23 years since this photo.

Above: Clare Raper and grand daughter Katie, 5 months old, two angels together, 2007.

Right: Mohammed Iftkhar - a true friend.

My God son - Thomas Rayment.

Left: Saira had her "play" on in London called Saira and I had 6 bodyguards to make sure it all went well. Stilks was one of them. Nobody fucks with this guy, some have tried all have ended up in the casualty ward. Stilks Stylianou. He's a true gentleman with very old school morals. Tel Currie was also on guard at this show.

My aunty Eileen (my mother's sister) - still going strong.

My son Mike. He's now 36 years old we've never even had a pint together it rips me up, it really does But my boy knows I love him our time is yet to come he understands his old dad. Let's leave it at that - it's our bizz.

Above 1: John Griffiths and Charlie Magri. At Charlie's pub "The Vic" East London

Above 2: Billy Walker, Ex-British and European champion plus one decent good man, a man of rock

John and Mary - two diamonds.

Apex Publishing's Chris Cowlin and actor Tom Hardy.
Without Chris Cowlin's belief in me there would be no
Loonyology book - so thank him!

Lisa and Mark Emmins with Jillian
at a Bronson show.

Jim Dawkins and Al Rayment. If all screws were
like Jim when he was a screw I would have been
out 20 years ago!

Right: Syied
Iftkhar - staunch
lad - max respect!

Left: Rachel
Bristow - one of
my favourite
visitors and a
lovely girl, she's
got her own
Bronson art
gallery.

Left: Ray Kray, with his two diamonds, this photo spells
out freedom and peace to me, a photo like this for me is
an inspiration to fight, and win in life no matter what.

Ted Jarvis. Does he ever smile?

A warriors boxing night in honour of myself
- thanks lads!

Left: It's all
Loonyology to
me, insanity
gone mad!

Right: Andy,
Lorraine and Me,
Belmarsh 1996.
My visits them
days was in the
governors office,
believe it!

Jan Lamb. We go back years - the angel of the
underworld, that's what Jan is to me.

Gary White, landlord of the Stillwell Tavern;
Derby. Long live the out laws - respect!

Lady boys - a few beers down your neck. Would
you really know? It's always best to check before
you leave the bar! That's my advice, but then again,
it's all Loonyology to me!

Right: Billy Cooper at 65 years old. If ever there was a legend Bill is up there with the best he still does his road work and works out like a good un, Bills fought all his life its all he knows. I salute guys like Bill...there gladiators you can watch all your Rocky movies and Arnie Fantasies these guys are for real. Men of rock.

Left: Gregg and Ann Vurley.

Below Right: Tel Currie Snr in his army days. A top man, I'm going to miss him, I'll catch him up later for sure! Respect!

Diane Brown, still a cracker! She can share my chocolate egg anytime.

Above: Ishaaq Iftkhar, another one of Ifty's sons. There all good 'uns.

Above Left: That's a 55-year-old back, you don't get it by pulling your cock and dreaming your life away, I have worked on my body and fitness every day of my journey through Loonyology, I'm still the daddy at press ups, I'll be doing press ups in my grave "believe it!" Respect your body. It's the only one your ever have look after it and it will look after you.

Above Right: Me in Wakefield, 2008. It nice to be nice!

Left: My old pot and pan (Dad). I still miss the old rascal he was a top Dad. The best, a good boxer in his day, a respected man, I couldn't of had a better father, the day he died we lost a legend. Believe it

Right: Mark Peterson. My younger Brother ex Royal Navy A top geezer and a good buddy. He now works on the oil rigs I'm dieing to have a pint with him, to many years have flown by between us its time for a good piss up!

Left: When it comes to bottle my two buddies Al rayment and Kenny Harriot take the gold! There both be in a chair for life, but there both 10 feet tall in my book. Living fucking legends!

Right: Charity auction - Roger Devonshire and Frank Fraser.

Tel Currie and his late father Tel Snr
- two peas in a pod!

Dave always spoils my old duchess he's part of the bronco camp! We don't need UZIs and shotguns our fists will do.

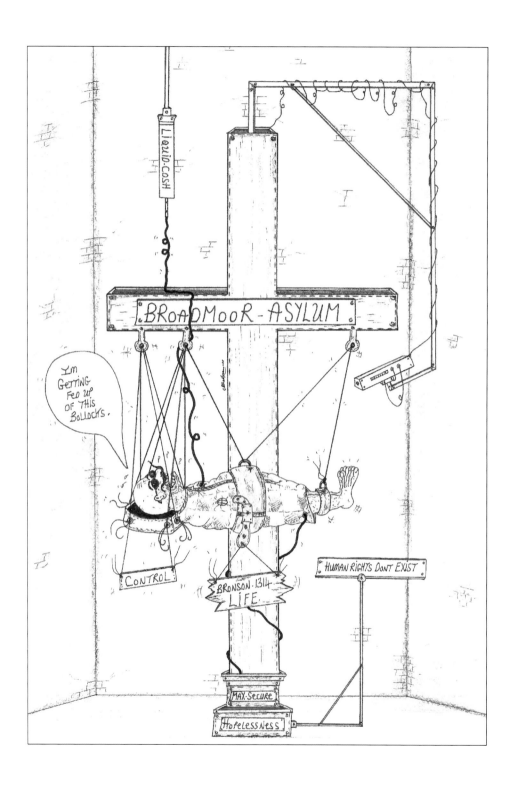

R.I.P.

RONALD
1933-1995

REGINALD
1933-2000

A CHARLIE BRONSON TRIBUTE.

" Free . AT . LAST . "

. . THE KRAY TWINS . .

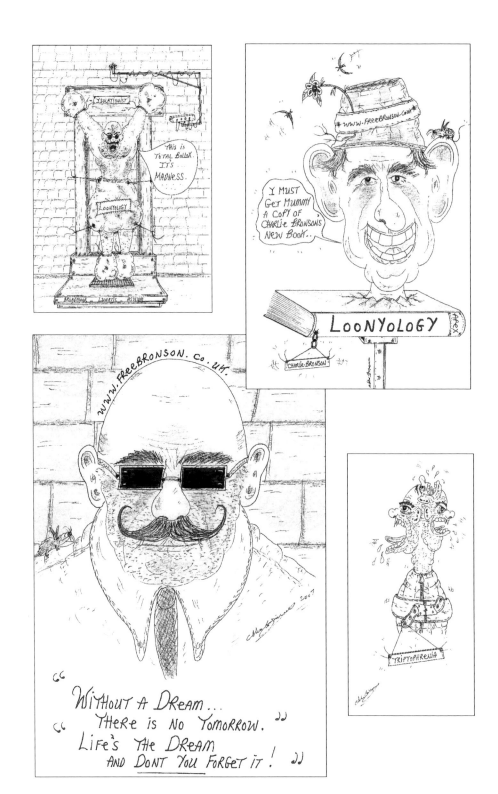

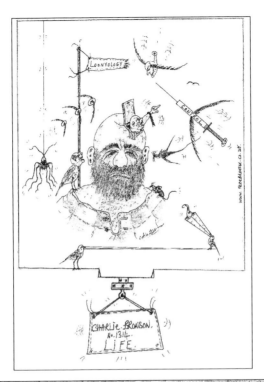

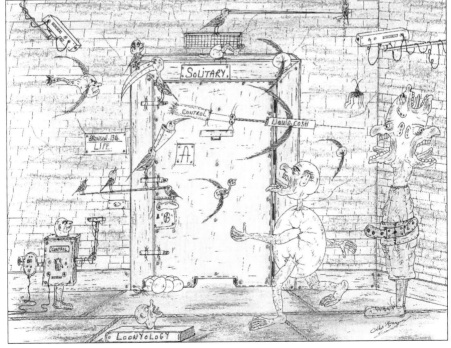

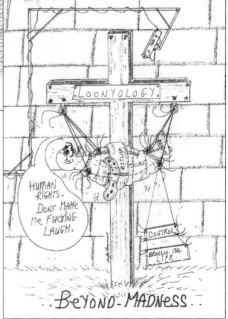

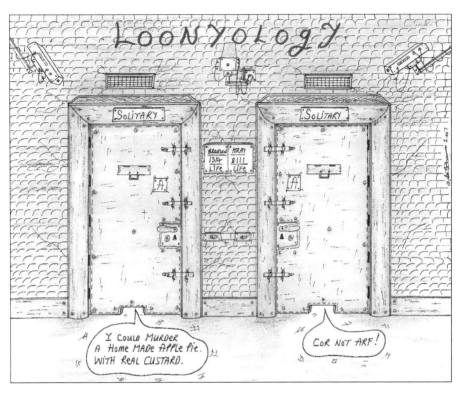

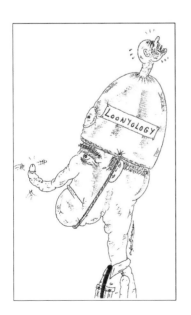

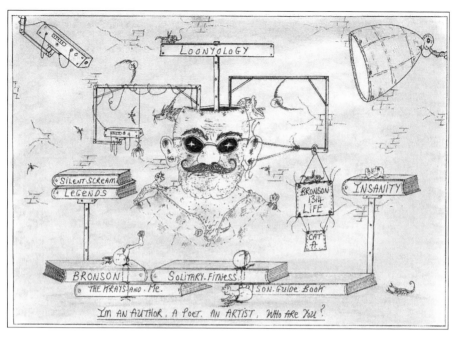

I'M AN AUTHOR, A POET, AN ARTIST, WHO ARE YOU?

WWW.FREEBRONSON.CO.UK

The more I listen to George Galloway on Talk Sport Radio the more I like the bloke. In my book he's a top geezer. I remember when he was arrested and slung in a cell for protesting over Britain's possession of weapons of mass destruction. The man fights for what he believes in, unlike most of them muppet MPs. George does what he says. That's a good quality. You keep doing what you do George, coz you're a winner in my book. The government officials hate him. I wonder why? I'll tell you: it's coz they hate the truth and men like George Galloway are dangerous to them. I can actually foresee him having a mysterious death. The men in grey suits only take so much. Watch your back, George.

In New Mexico, USA, there's a woman with a 4-foot beard. A 4-foot fucking beard! Can you believe this shit? Imagine waking up to that. It don't pay even to think about it!

Did you know the shortest ever war was 38 minutes? It was between Zanzibar and England in 1896. Zanzibar surrendered after 38 minutes. Fucking wimps.

THE SUN DON'T SHINE NO MORE
It's dark, cold and gloomy
It's cold and shadowy
She walked away
Never came back
Not even a goodbye
Not even a postcard
She took the sun away
Laughing all the way
What do you do?
What can you do?
Nothing
You can't breathe
You can't sleep
You can't even think
When the sun don't shine
Hell freezes over
It rips your soul away
You become dehumanised
Feelings just fly out of the window
It's a long way back to sanity
You walk but don't move
It's a slow-motion state
You eat but don't live
Everything's gone mad
The sun don't shine no more
Did it ever?

CHARLES BRONSON

Was it all a dream?
Did she ever exist?
Why did she go?
Why did she ever come?
The oceans dried up
The sky fell in
My heart exploded
There's nothing left to see
Nothing left to do
A state of disillusion
Despair
Loneliness
What can you do?
What will happen?
A flower needs the rain
A man needs a woman
That's how it's supposed to be
Or is it a fucking stitch-up?
A weakness?
A brainwashed useless prat?
Living in a nutshell
Hoodwinked
A follower of normality
A boring everyday existence
The taxman wants your dosh
Pay up or rot in hell
Let him bleed you dry
Keep on eating shit
The sun don't shine no more
Does it really matter?
The bitch has found a new bed
A new life
It's another journey
Smiles and cuddles
Lots of kisses
Laughter and rainbows
It's free
Be free
Stay free
You're born free
Let the sun shine on you
Soak it up
Walk in a field of flowers
Smell the freedom

Don't look back
Don't ever return
Keep smelling that freedom
Tears of happiness
Sweet and tender love
All wrapped-up togetherness
A future bright and loving
Good luck
And
Goodbye

4 September 2007

I was out on the yard today in the lovely sunshine, with not a cloud in sight. There was a nice breeze, so I had a jog around. I felt light and fast and free. As I went around and around like a fucking hamster on a wheel in a cage, I thought about Jane Tomlinson who passed away last night. Jane was a big heroine of mine. At the age of 26 she was first diagnosed with cancer. Then it progressed. She fought it for 17 years but over the last 7 years she battled on like no person I know. She ran marathons, she swam, she got involved with all sorts of charity events. She raised well over 2 million quid and the people of Leeds idolised her. She died last night at the age of 43 and left behind a husband and three children. How proud they must be of her. Let's hope a statue goes up for her in the city of Leeds. This lady was an inspiration to so many. God care for Jane. I salute you.

Live fast and die young, I say, but the following deaths will blow your socks off. Who would be a pop star?

1959	Buddy Holly	Age 22 Plane crash
1959	Ritchie Valens	Age 17 Plane crash
1963	Patsy Cline	Age 30 Plane crash
1965	Nat King Cole	Age 45 Cancer
1967	Otis Reading	Age 26 Plane crash

Fuck me, what's up with these planes? Spooky or what?

1969	Brian Jones (Rolling Stones)	Age 27 Drowned in pool
1970	Jimi Hendrix	Age 27 Choked on vomit
1970	Janis Joplin	Age 27 Drugs
1971	Gene Vincent	Age 45 Ruptured stomach ulcer
1971	Jim Morrison (Doors)	Age 27 Drugs
1973	Bobby Darin	Age 37 Heart failure
1974	Mama Cass Elliot	Age 32 Heart attack
1974	Nick Drake	Age 26 Drugs
1975	Tim Buckley	Age 38 Drugs
1976	Paul Kossoff (Free)	Age 25 Heart failure
1976	Keith Relf (Yardbirds)	Age 33 Electrocuted playing guitar

| 1977 | Elvis Presley | Age 42 | Heart failure |

All his millions never saved the King. When your time's up, it's curtains.

| 1977 | Marc Bolan (T Rex) | Age 29 | Car crash |
| 1977 | Ronnie Van Zant (Lynyrd Skynyrd) | Age 29 | Plane crash |

Who's flying these things?

1978	Keith Moon (The Who)	Age 32	Drugs
1978	Sandy Denny (Fairport Conv.)	Age 31	Brain haemorrhage
1979	Sid Vicious (Sex Pistols)	Age 21	Drugs
1980	Bon Scott (AC/DC)	Age 33	Choked on vomit
1980	Ian Curtis (Joy Division)	Age 23	Suicide
1980	John Bonham (Led Zeppelin)	Age 33	Choked on vomit
1980	Steve Peregrine (T Rex)	Age 31	Choked
1980	John Lennon	Age 40	Shot by lunatic
1981	Bill Hayley	Age 55	Heart attack
1981	Bob Marley	Age 36	Cancer
1983	Pete Farndon (The Pretenders)	Age 30	Drowned in bath
1983	Karen Carpenter	Age 32	Anorexia

Well, do you still wanna be a pop star? It's fucking depressing reading.

| 1983 | Dennis Wilson (Beach Boys) | Age 39 | Drowned |
| 1984 | Marvin Gaye | Age 44 | Shot |

His old man shot him. Why? Ask his old man. Marvin was one of the greatest soul singers of all time.

1986	Phil Lynott (Thin Lizzy)	Age 36	Drugs
1991	Steve Clark (Def Leppard)	Age 30	Drugs and booze
1991	Steve Marriott (Small Faces)	Age 44	House fire
1991	Freddie Mercury (Queen)	Age 45	Aids related
1994	Kurt Cobain (Nirvana)	Age 27	Suicide
1995	Jerry Garcia (Grateful Dead)	Age 53	Heart attack
1996	Tupac Shakur (rapper)	Age 25	Shooting
1997	Jeff Buckley	Age 30	Drowned
1997	Michael Hutchence (INXS)	Age 37	Suicide
2001	George Harrison	Age 58	Cancer
2002	Lisa Lopez	Age 30	Car crash
2002	Joe Strummer (The Clash)	Age 50	Heart attack
2002	John Entwistle (The Who)	Age 57	Drugs
2004	Darrell Abbott (Pantera)	Age 38	Shot

I could go on and on and I've left loads out. I've just chosen the most famous ones. Life as a pop star isn't all it's made out to be. I'll give it a miss. How about you?

September 2007, Daily Mail
TRIPLE KILLER FLEES PRISON
A prisoner serving three life sentences for slaughtering his family was on the loose last

night after escaping from an open jail.

A huge manhunt has been launched for Martyn Hughes, 50, after he failed to return to Sudbury Open Prison near Derby on Sunday.

He was due to be released next year after serving 13 years for the manslaughter of his wife and murder of his stepsons.

Prison sources said it was astonishing Hughes had not been transferred to a more secure unit already. Two weeks ago, he was spotted driving his own car to a central storage site for prisons where he works during the week.

But at the end of his shift, instead of driving back to prison, Hughes drove three fellow inmates to nearby Burton Upon Trent, where he browsed the internet at a library.

The four then met up again at a pizza restaurant, before Hughes drove them back towards the prison.

Instead of being transferred to a stricter jail, a source said Hughes was merely given a ticking off before being granted five days' home leave.

Hughes was working as a funeral director in Hemsby, Norfolk, in 1995 when he strangled his wife Deborah, 32, after a row and left her body laid out with a crucifix on her chest. Then he throttled his stepchildren, James Brackhahn, seven, and Matthew, six, as they lay in bed.

This is what winds me up big time. This cunt's free. How can a triple killer serve just 12 years and be in an open prison? That's four years per killing he's served. Two of those body bags were stuffed with kids. Somebody please tell me how it works, coz I've not got a fucking clue. This Hughes prick should be in a cage for 50 years on bread and water. He even looks like a monster. I'll tell you how he got an open prison. He licked plenty of arse and made the screws plenty of cups of tea. He probably served ten years here in Monster Mansion with all his other mates. It's time this system is truly exposed, coz it's become a fucking joke. Three life sentences this scumbag got. THREE! I get one and I'm still in. It makes me fucking sick. If the Old Bill had half a brain they would shoot the fucker when they arrest him. Problem solved. Better still, bring the cunt back here and I'll have him in with me. I'd look after him, you can bet your arse on it.

7 September 2007
I had a great visit today from the Frayne brothers. They're two of the best - proper 'old school' - and they're both ex-pro fighters. You don't mess with them sort. I had a good visit yesterday too with Al Rayment and his folks. It's been a nice couple of days. Plus old shitty arse 'Shafty' moved back to Woodhill unit. He's been on a shit-up for the last five months here in the box. Shit all over his walls and door. Imagine that. At least it'll smell better and there'll be less flies. The screws all put on their protective gear and masks to escort him to the van. What a job, eh? Who would be a screw? Would you? Anyway, let's forget old shitty arse. He's that nutty he don't even know why he's on a dirty protest himself.

Hey, and get on this. It's illegal in Utah, USA, to swear in front of a dead person. Are them yanks mad or what?

Here's a bit of knowledge that may come in handy: the Police, Screw, Security Radio Alphabet. It's to make certain there's no confusion with emergency calls.

A   Alpha
B   Bravo
C   Charlie
D   Delta
E   Echo
F   Foxtrot
G   Golf
H   Hotel
I   India
J   Juliet. I knew a Juliet in Luton. She was a lovely girl, but she had three nipples. It fucking freaked me out.
K   Kilo
L   Lima
M   Mike
N   November
O   Oscar. Oscar was my brother's nickname in the Forces. He was a Royal Marine bandsman and it came about because of the famous Oscar Peterson Trio. Oscar stuck with him for years. I remember his passing-out parade in Deal Barracks, Kent, in 1967. It was brilliant. My brother became a man, and a smart man at that.
P   Papa
Q   Quebec
R   Romeo
S   Sierra
T   Tango
U   Uniform
V   Victory
W   Whiskey. Yes please. Make it a double.
X   X-ray
Y   Yankee
Z   Zulu

See, on every page there's something knowledgeable. Not a lot of people know such things. To those who do - well, you shouldn't be a know-all.

I made a call tonight to Keeley. She's a lovely soul with a sexy voice. I told her I have a dream. I awake and I can smell and feel her lying next to me. I really can. She said to me, "I hope your dream comes true." See, I'm still alive. I still keep my dreams alive even though I'm in a coffin. Fuck the system, my dreams will keep me sane.

I'll tell you who's an evil fucker: Tony King. King got a 10 stretch in the 1980s for a string of sex attacks in north London. How the fuck he never got lifed off is beyond me. He was a sexual predator, a bully to women, a threat to any woman or girl. Guess what? He got paroled after five years. Now ain't that a surprise. Then in 2005 in Spain he was sentenced to life for the murder of two teenage girls. Surprise, surprise. Like I always say: 'A nonce is a nonce'. What do you expect a nonce to do? The cunt should've got life in the '80s and rotted in hell. Simple as that. Then those two Spanish girls would be alive today.

I'll tell you who else is an evil bastard. Dennis 'Paedo' Leckey. He copped an 18 stretch in 1997 for abusing kids. 18 charges to be exact. He's a filthy child predator. Guess what? He's back on the streets. He's back out amongst your kids. Now he's a big fat slob with a grey beard. He'll probably get a social worker who'll get him a fresh start as Santa. If this cunt had been put down in '97 he wouldn't be out there today. Don't it make you sick? Wake up world. It's your kids. Fucking wake up. Cunts like this Leckey are getting away with it. Ten years he served for shagging kids. He should've got life with a 30 rec. Do you want him next door to you?

When it comes to one-armed monsters, I can only think of one: Ian Bird. He got lifed off for three rapes on young girls and downloading 2,000 child sex images. I bet his lost arm fell off with all that wanking over the Internet. And I'll give you one guess where this dirty nonce is now. Yeah, you got it in one - Monster Mansion. Dirty bastard. One of his rape victims was only 12 years old. I bet her mum and dad would like ten minutes together with him in his cell. That would've been good punishment - to chop off his other arm and then let the kids in the cell with him. They could've kicked the slag to death.

Do you know something? Nothing surprises me no more. The world's gone mad and soon you'll all wake up in the funny farm if you don't see what's going on. It's your kids suffering over this shit system.

September 2007, Daily Mail
JUST SIX YEARS FOR RAPIST OF GIRL AGED 12
Child protection groups reacted with fury last night after a sex beast who led the horrific gang rape of a 12-year-old girl was jailed for just six years.
Shakil Chowdhury, 40, lured the youngster off the street who was lost and had been asking for directions before attacking her at a house with three friends.
The girl was raped 15 times in different rooms, including 11 attacks by Chowdhury.
Campaigners described his sentence as a "joke" and said he should have been locked away for life.
Michele Elliot, director of children's charity Kidscape said: "How can this be justice? This little girl's life has been taken away yet this man will no doubt be out on parole in three years. This was an absolutely horrific attack. Parents should be terrified that this man will be allowed back on the streets. Mark my words, people like him attack

again."

Minshull Street Crown Court in Manchester heard how the girl was trying to get home and asking passers-by for directions as she walked along a road in Oldham, Greater Manchester, in October last year. She was lured into Chowdhury's car where she gave her name, address and age, but was driven to another house and plied with alcohol. She was then forced to lie on a bed and was repeatedly raped.

After the horrific attack Chowdhury dropped the girl off at her home, asking if he could take her phone number before he left.

The girl reported the rape to the police and identified Chowdhury's address. Officers arrested him at the address in Chadderton, near Oldham.

Judge Roger Thomas QC passed the sentence after Chowdhury admitted six charges of rape. He also ordered him to sign the sex offenders' register for life. Police are still hunting the other attackers.

Det Chief Inspector Mary Doyle, of Greater Manchester Police, said: "This child was subjected to a terrifying and prolonged attack from Chowdhury and his associates. One of the first things that she told him was her name and age, so there is no doubt that he was aware how young she was." She added: "I hope her bravery will encourage other victims to come forward, safe in the knowledge that police will take robust action."

Somebody tell me how this fucking animal never got lifed off? He'll be back on the streets in two to three years. Now see why I get mad. It's a fucking insult to justice.

Now down to a real monster. Amato Wright killed his 71-year-old mother, Maria, who'd won two grand at a casino. Her own son tortured and killed her to get the dosh. This piece of shit was a smack head and the drugs drove him over the edge. Now he's got to live with it till the day he dies (hopefully in a cage). But I guess he'll get out one day. Even so, he has to take it to his grave. What a thing to live and die with. Let this be a wake-up call to all you drug mugs - STOP NOW. Or, better still, don't even start it. Drugs will eat your heart away. You'll end up as a heartless, soulless zombie. How the fuck can a son kill his own mother? Well, some do, coz they're out of their minds on drugs. Give it a miss.

Fuck me, I must be getting old. My memory is going funny. I've just remembered another one-armed beast: Adams. I can't recall his first name - probably Reptile Adams. He was on F Wing in Parkhurst around 1976 time and I went after him with a lead pipe I'd taken off the recess sink. I chased him down the F2 landing but the cunt made it back to his cell and banged the door shut. I was gutted. There was me outside his door, smashing it with this lead pipe and shouting at the monster, and then a bunch of screws were bashing me. That's showbiz for you. I ended up in the box busted up and Adams was laughing his cock off. Adams was a Scouser serving ten years for raping a schoolboy. If I remember rightly, he kidnapped the boy from a bus shelter and drove him to a park. All I wanted to do was bash his big, fat nonce head in. I never saw him again after that, as they moved him to another jail. He just disappeared. I never heard of him again - ever. Let's hope he's now dead or in some old folks' home riddled with cancer and there's a shortage of morphine, coz that's all the monster deserves.

There was another monster on F2 at the same time as Adams and he had an ear missing. We called him Noddy. He was an old fellow in his late 60s, but he still got the odd clump. If one of the cons got out of bed the wrong way, then you could bet on it that Noddy was in for a bad day. I don't know the ins and outs of his case, but everybody hated him - even the screws. All he ever got was abuse: spit in his food, piss in his tea. The good old days. A nonce is a nonce in jail. They can NEVER be accepted in a proper cons' jail. So when I set fire to his coat, with him in it, I had no regrets. Unfortunately he survived it. So no bad feeling my end.

Ronnie Kray hated the fucker. Ron's eyes used to bulge when Noddy was near. Outside Ron would've just shot his face off and exterminated the bastard. I never did find out how he lost an ear, but it's evens favourite it was sliced off by a nonce hater. Screws in them days never saw a lot - they let a lot go. They were a better bunch. After all, screws have kids. Why should they see everything? They're only human. Well - almost.

Here's a beauty for you to dwell on. The largest 'unsolved robbery' of all time was at the end of World War II. The German gold reserve - 730 gold bars, 6 sacks of bank notes, 25 boxes of platinum and diamonds and precious stones - disappeared in transit, never to be seen again. So who says crime don't pay? Some fucker did well out of that blag. Don't it make you wonder who had it? I think I know. In fact I'm sure I know (it don't take a lot of working out).

Now here's a bit of prison history for you.

'Borstal' - Where did that word come from? I'll tell you, as I know you're all dying to find out. The first borstal was opened in Kent in 1903. It was built in the village called Borstal so that's what they called it. Simple as that.

The fattest man on Earth is F.J. Lang from Iowa, USA. Yeah, it had to be a yank. He's 84 stone. 84 fucking stone! Is that gross or what? How can a human being get to that state? In a state like that you can't even wipe your arse. Your entire body is a mass of stench, blistered up and oozing out pus. How can anyone want to live like that? Dump them all in the sea for fish food. They're eating the Earth away. Greedy fuckers.

Hey, I bet you're wondering where I get all this from. I'm just a clever cunt, that's all. I do my research. I'm a walking encyclopaedia.

I had to laugh on the visit with the Frayne brothers. Both Lindsey and Leighton have done bird and, if I say so myself, they served their time with flying colours. But Leighton got in a spot of bother in Long Lartin and the system thought it would teach him a lesson and sent him to Ashworth Asylum. Here's the story Leighton told me the other day:

"So there I was, Charlie, in the nuthouse. All these fucking nutters - and that's just the screws. This fucking nut psychiatrist called me up for an interview and started asking me all sorts of bollocks. One thing he kept on about was the Kray twins. It's no secret me and Leighton are old pals with them. Anyway, the quack kept on about the Krays. Now, as you know, every nutter claims to be the Krays' henchman or one of Jesus's disciples or Elvis reincarnated, so this lot were probably thinking I was a nut. The next day I got a cheque from Broadmoor off my mate Ron Kray. That saved me. After that there were no more silly questions about IF I knew the Krays."

Well, I thought that was fucking brilliant. A typical psychological rat trap, but it fired back at the mugs. There may well have been 500 nutters believing they were in the Kray Firm, but Leighton really was a mate of theirs. Three months later he was moved back to Long Lartin.

8 September 2007

What a great day. England won the Rugby, Football and Cricket. Who says we ain't the best? England, England, England! And Michael Owen scored - brilliant. I also got a pile of letters in: one off Mum, one off Mark Fish, and Gary White sent me in a few quid. He never forgets me. I got a nice card from Cherri Gilham - she's booked up to visit me on 27 September. That'll be a laugh. And I got a nice letter from Dee Morris, who's doing a page or two for *Loonyology*. I got five more letters, all from strangers wishing me well. Did you know when I first came to jail you could only write out two letters a week and only receive two? The rest would go into your property. It was all to smash up your family and contacts. Fucking evil cunts. What a liberty. Even today when you're on punishment they will try to cut you off. I wonder why? It's simple. Work it out yourself.

That's a strange case of little Maddie who disappeared out in Portugal in May 2007. 'Still missing'. Now her parents are suspects. What's that all about? What a complicated case that's become. Three months have now passed and it's more crazy now than it was on day one. What a sicko world we live in. Sad, sad and sad.

Hey, did you know that during the war honey was used as an antifreeze in cars? You just mix it with water and it's non-corrosive. Amazing stuff.

And talking of honey, here's how to make your own face cream. Mix together some honey, egg white and almond oil till it's a fine, smooth cream, and there you have it. I know an old lady who used it. She's now 83 but looks 53. Her skin is as smooth as silk. When I get out I think I'll make a big pot of that for my cock - could make it taste good and feel good. Us blokes have gotta look after ourselves.

Hey, what's this thing with studs in your nipples and pussy lips and tongues, and even in the bell end? Somebody tell me. It's mental. Fuck that. Not my scene. I guess I'm just trapped in the '60s and 70's. Thank fuck.

The human body is made up of various raw materials: iron, lime, sulphur, sugar, potassium, fat. Fucking freaky or what? It all comes from an egg, sperm. It's a bloody miracle.

Anyway, I'm off to bed now. My brain hurts. Night night. Watch out for the bed bugs.

10 September 2007

I'm gutted to learn that Peter and Tony Coulson have been caught in Costa del Sol. They're two good guys; solid, staunch brothers. They had it on their toes a good few years ago. Both were serving big sentences and just decided to disappear. It must've been well over ten years that they were on the run from home leaves. I last saw them in Parkhurst in the early 1990s, where they were on M Wing. It goes to show that you can stay out for a long time even when you're on the run. I bet every day has been like Xmas for them and I salute them. Tony used to cook up some serious good meals in Parkhurst, probably the best on the wing. M Wing at that time was full of Londoners. It was like a big cockney get-together, a villains' paradise. But fuck all lasts. Parkhurst is now a shithole. It's like a local nick run by muppet screws and brain-dead governors. Parkhurst was a cons jail. We ran that place with our own code of morals. The cons have allowed it to get like it is today. Summertimes in Parkhurst it was shirt off, soak it up and bring on the ice cream. Now it's all working in silly shops, sweating your bollocks off for peanuts. I know what I'd sooner have. I'm fucked if I know why I fought the system for 30 years to make it a better place. I really don't know.

I see Jamie Blandford, the Marquess of Blandford, got six months today for driving offences and road rage. He's now in Bullingdon Jail. It just goes to prove that even the snobs can't behave. All his millions and he's eating porridge. His late mother was Susan Hornby of the WH Smith dynasty: multi-billionaires. He had the best of everything: best schools, best education. Back in 1991, he was sentenced to three months for a driving offence, and then in 1994 he was charged with deception. This guy is no different from any of us criminals. It's in his blood. He's in and out of rehab clinics for his drug addiction. What a fucking waste! He could be flying around in a private jet, with a dolly bird on each arm. He could be driving around in a Ferrari with some tart sucking his cock. Now he's probably doubled up with some smelly, rat-ased convict with cheesy feet. What a fall - the biggest! It's loonyology!

11 September 2007

Big Jack Binns, the mad yorkie, was up to visit today. He's 73 years old and looks 53! He's as fit as a butcher's dog. What a life he's had. Fuck James Bond, it's Jack Binns.

He was telling me a blinding story today. When he was 68 he was in a club in his home town of Bradford and some black guy was getting lemon and called Jack honky. Now this black dude was 6 feet 2 and 19 stone and loved nothing more than a punch-up. Fuck me, Jack was 68 years old! Crack! He let a nut go! All over. The black dude was carried out cold.

I remember that 33 years ago in Hull Jail Jack was famous for his headbutt. Nobody nuts like Jack! He really can do some damage. This guy is a walking bomb, so don't set him off. Even the Old Bill respect him because he's an old-style villain. He don't need a gun or a tool; this man's ex-army and ex-mercenary, a trained killer. They don't make them like him no more. Over the years he's fought them all, toe to toe, fist to fist, head to head!

Jack Binns, the mad yorkie, is a living legend! You'd be mental to disagree, and he's my top buddy.

Our mate Barry Cheetham is another legend, Barry copped a life sentence 30 years ago when he was a young lad. The poor sod is still inside. What a fucking liberty. He just don't suffer fools lightly. Whether screws, governors or cons, Barry will knock them all out! It's how he is: a born man, a man with a lot of principles and morals. His pride has cost him all these years inside, and that's how life is. Sad, but fact!

All the old cons remember Judo Jerry from the 1960s, '70s and early '80s. Jerry was a character, and he's done the rounds! I bumped into him in half a dozen jails. The poor old sod only came in to do a three stretch, but he kept getting it topped up for attacking screws; two years here, 18 months there. He ended up serving a good 20+ years.

I don't think he was a judo expert, he just enjoyed throwing screws around. Once in Wandsworth he called it on with a dozen screws in the canteen and they gave it to him big style! But he never went down without a good fight. Another time, down in Dartmoor, they broke his leg, and in Armley they broke his arm. Judo Jerry just kept rolling on. Fuck knows what happened to him. He probably got his neck broke.

I called my mum tonight. We always have a laugh. She's a good soul, 76 now, and still going strong, I'm so proud of her! I got six letters today and £50 sent in from a friend that I'll not forget. It's been a great day - one of them days when everything goes well.

This is a newspaper report I got sent in today from Luton on Sunday:

September 2007, Luton on Sunday
TINSELTOWN MOGUL HAS INFAMOUS LAG IN HIS FILM SIGHTS
A HOLLYWOOD blockbuster about the life of prison hardman Charles Bronson is being planned.
Details are contained on a Free Bronson website written by Bronson himself which says: "Danny Hansford is organising my movie. He's just back from Hollywood and all is looking good.
"There are a million bucks on the table, so now it's just a question of who plays who."
There would be plenty of incidents from his life to pack into such a movie.
Bronson, 45, and from Luton, was first jailed for armed robbery in 1974. Since then he has held fellow prisoners and staff hostage three times.
Bronson staged a 47-hour rooftop protest at Broadmoor in 1983, causing £750,000 worth of damage.
And in 1994 while he was holding a guard hostage at Woodhill Prison, Milton

Keynes, he demanded an inflatable doll, a helicopter and a cup of tea as a ransom.
In total he has been held at all three of Britain's security hospitals and at least 30 con-
ventional prisons.
He scooped a literary award for his writing on prison life and is generally regarded
as one of the country's most violent prisoners.

45?! Cheers! But that means I was 11 years old on the armed robbery! These reporters always get it mixed up. Like the Broadmoor roof - there were three and the damage was 1.5 million bucks. It's why the rats got rid of me in 1984 - they couldn't afford me. I was taking over the asylum and they didn't like it. I was a bit like the lunatics' union rep. That's how they saw me and labelled me: a fighter, an activist for lunatics' rights. I once told the superintendent Dr McGraph: "Look at it this way, doc. Us loonies are your bread and butter! Without us, you fucking head shrinks would be out of a job!" He knew I was right.

Did you know it's illegal to catch mice without a hunting licence in Ohio, USA? Is that fucking mental or what? That's the yanks for you!

Did you know Albert Einstein was expelled from school? So, all you worried parents with naughty kids, it's not the end of the world. If Einstein made it, so can your kids!

I met Einstein in Rampton Asylum. Well, he said he was him, fucking idiot! He didn't even know what year it was! The mad fucker could never even remember if he'd wiped his arse or not.

Italian dictator Benito Mussolini once got expelled from school too. He stabbed a fellow pupil. Fucking amazing. That's Italy for you. Crazy fuckers.

Here's a blinder for you. You won't believe this one. Abbad el Motaddid, who was the king of Spain a couple of centuries ago, used to have flowerpots all over his palace. So what's the big deal? The pots were enemies' skulls! I told you, this book is fucking nuts!

Talking of flowerpots, they were a big thing for long-term cons in the 1960s and '70s. In jails like Parkhurst, Hull and Albany, lots of cons loved to grow plants and flowers. Well, that was until security sussed out that they were growing cannabis plants. Like I say, the system's nuts!

Get a load of this for a wake-up call, coz you may not wake up. Watch out for natural poisons. Did you know that apple pips, almonds and the kernels of plums and cherries can cause mild cyanide poisoning. It's true! Caraway seeds can cause dizziness and headaches if eaten in quantity. Three of four whole nutmegs can be fatal. The stems and leaves of potatoes and tomatoes all contain the poison solanin. Deadly nightshade contains the poison atropine, most berries are poisonous, especially mistletoe and holly, but bryony is the most lethal. Be aware of fungi too. The death cap is lethal. Did you know the poison strychnine comes from the Indian tree Koochla, and it's used in small doses as an antidote for lead poisoning? Crazy! One poison to cure another poison.

Hey, watch what you put in your mouths, and you girls always use a wipe on your fella's cock, as you'd be amazed what diseases you can get from a smelly, dirty cock in your mouth. Wipe it! Give it a good clean. In fact, if your fella's a top geezer he wouldn't allow his cock to get dirty in the first place. I wash my bell end all the time, even after a pee! It's just the routine I'm in. I've got the time, see, so if you fancy a clean cock, I'm up for it, but clean your teeth first. The mouth contains more germs than on the rest of your body, so keep it clean! Cleanliness is next to ... Amen!

Did you know a cockroach can live on without its head? Fucking mental or what? How do I know? Well let's just say I experiment - try it on a cockroach, that is.

Here's a fact for you to dwell on. In 2006 in England there were 4,120 armed robberies. Four fucking thousand, one hundred and twenty! I've got my alibi, so fuck off!

Hey, never mind Hannibal Lector, he's a pussy compared with the Russian Alexander Pichushkin. Charged with 49 murders, he said on his arrest: "For me life without murder is like life without food for you." He kept a chessboard to mark off his victims. Although 60 of the squares were marked off, only 49 were on file. Crazy people. The word psycho comes to mind. Fuck playing chess with this fucker!

Yesterday, 12 September 2007, in Riverbend max secure jail in Tennessee, USA, Daryl Holton fried in old sparky - 1,750 volts shot through his brain. He'd been on death row since Christmas 1997 for killing his three boys and his stepdaughter. This guy was suffering from severe depression. He'd fought in the Gulf War and had come back with post-traumatic stress disorder. He flipped and lost the plot. Holton's attorney said: "He's finally free from the demons that haunted him."

Yeh, and I say it was the fucking state that put his demons there in the first place. This guy was insane. He should've been certified mad and locked up in a nuthouse. Oh well, the gates of hell closed shut on Holton, that's for sure.

In 2006, 53 executions took place in the USA, 52 by lethal injection and 1 by old sparky. I think the electric chair is about to become a thing of the past. It started in 1888 as a more humane method than hanging. Who are they fucking kidding? That chair has tortured many souls. For example, some have exploded in fire, multiple jolts have been used to finish the job, bones get broken coz of convulsing limbs and eyes pop out sizzling. Fuck me, give me the noose any day or a slug to the head. Fuck ending up as toast!

I heard two armed robbers were shot dead today outside a bank. Trigger-happy cops. They'll all be celebrating tonight, cunts! I'm waiting to hear their names.

Ramadan started today. What's that all about? Is that crazy or what? It don't make sense to me.

Hey, did you know that in 1945 a B-25 bomber crashed into the 79th floor of the Empire State Building? Wow! It was travelling at 250 mph. I bet you didn't know that. You see, you learn things with me. Fortunately it was carrying no bombs. Lucky or what? And did you know there's 56 lifts in that building? 56 fucking lifts! Mind blowing.

I called my lovely Keeley tonight. She's a breath of fresh air to me - so bubbly and full of life. She told me that my first wife, Irene, has done another story in *Pick Me Up* magazine. It's well over 30 years since we got divorced. I've not even seen her since 1975 and she's still selling me out. How fucking sad is that? What good does it do me? What do they pay her - £300, £400, £500? Is it really worth it? Why live in the past? Get on with your life. As I told you all those years back - good luck!

No doubt I'll get a copy sent in this week, but I'll tell you now, it's starting to piss me off. In all these years I've never once said a bad word about her and yet she can't stop selling muggy stories, which don't exactly help me. She's just recently divorced her second husband, so maybe she's skint. Fuck Charlie, he won't mind. Still, that's showbiz for you. Irene was a beautiful soul, but it seems she's now full of black thoughts.

Be like me, Irene, happy and free of shit. Stop letting life chew you up. and be thankful for the life you've lived. It can't be all bad, so go forth and win. There's still time for you to meet a new soul. I only hope he don't sell you out. For example: "I screwed Charlie Bronson's ex-wife! Blah, blah, blah ... She said this, she said that, she done this, no wonder Charlie went mad - she's nuts!" Be careful, Irene, coz life isn't all one-way traffic. It can all come back and bite your face off.

To date, I have won a total of 11 Koestler awards for poetry, art and writing. Sadly I stopped entering the competition in 2000. It's so pathetic I just can't be bothered - prison politics! I could win another 30 awards but I'd still be labelled a madman in their eyes, so why bother or waste my time - fuck 'em!

15 September 2007, The Sun
I'M NO PAEDO
Langham gets 10 months for vile child rape images but still insists: I'm no paedo.
Comedy actor Chris Langham was jailed for ten months yesterday for downloading vile films of child rape - then insisted: "I'm no paedophile."
The Thick Of It star, 58, had the worst level of child porn on his computer including the rape of a girl of eight.
Judge Philip Statman could have jailed him for ten years after he was convicted of 15 child porn charges. But he decided on the lesser sentence after reading a "moving" letter pleading for leniency from Langham's wife Chrissie, 54.
Outside Maidstone Crown Court, Langham's solicitor Angus McBride read a statement from the Bafta award-winning star.
It said: "The court has confirmed today that I am not a paedophile.
"If the prosecution had accepted this at the beginning I would have pleaded guilty.
"I have always admitted I should have never have downloaded those abusive images.

I am delighted that at last my account has been proved to be the truth."
The judge had told Langham he did not consider him a paedophile or a risk to children.
But he added: "Your career is now in tatters."
As he left the court Langham smiled, waved and blew kisses to his sons in the public gallery. His second wife Chrissie was not in court to see him sentenced.
In her letter pleading with the judge to set her husband free, she described Langham as a wonderful father and said: "Our family needs to be together to heal ourselves."
Earlier Langham, of Cranbook, Kent, wept as his QC David Whitehouse outlined how his career had been devastated.
He told the court: "He would exchange every award, every glittering prize he has ever won just to be a jobbing actor treading the boards in a humble repertory company. His life has been in many ways - in every way - destroyed."
He added that Langham had been threatened and abused by prisoners since he was remanded in custody last month.
Mr Whitehouse said: "He has had a dreadful six weeks inside. He has had his food spat in. Prisoners throw disgusting things at him from their cells."
Langham is expected to be free in three and a half months after the judge ordered he serve half his sentence less the 43 days he has already spent in jail.
Detective Chief Inspector Paul Fortherington who led the investigation said outside court: "This is a real video of real children being abused."
He added: "The judge recognised that people like Mr Langham are fuelling the abuse of children around the world."

Here's justice for you, British justice at its best. Only ten months even though his crime carries ten years! It's a fucking joke. This nonce is a danger to society. Judge Philip Statman should hang his head in shame - what a disgrace.

Well, how are you enjoying the book up to now? I bet you don't know what's coming next! Me also. I just write it as it comes to my head. I've not got a fucking clue. I get a quick thought, a memory or a fact and - bosh! - I'm writing it all down.

Here's something you may find interesting and not a lot of people know this: the oldest DNA of a human was from a 60,000-year-old skeleton. Can you fucking believe that? 60,000 years! It was found on the shores of Lake Mungo, south-east Australia. It fucking blows you away.

Hey, do you know who's in the European Union? I bet you can't name me every country? Well, clock this lot: Austria, Belgium, Bulgaria, Cyprus, Czech Republic, Denmark, Estonia, Finland, France, Germany, Greece, Hungary, Ireland, Italy, Latvia, Lithuania, Luxembourg, Malta, Netherlands, Poland, Portugal, Romania, Slovakia, Slovenia, Spain, Sweden, United Kingdom. And I say what a load of bollocks! What is the point?!

If you ever apply for a boxing licence the details are: British Boxing Board of Control Ltd, Jack Petersen House, 52A Borough High Street, London, SE1 1XN and don't forget to say: "You denied us a world champion when you denied Charlie Bronson a licence!"

Did you know that it's 5,990 miles from London Airport to Hong Kong? Not a lot of people know that. It's 9,008 to Perth, Australia, and it's only 230 to Amsterdam's 'red light' district - don't forget your condoms! Mexico city is 5,529 and Alcatraz, San Francisco, is 5,351 - a fucking long way to see a jail! Rio de Janeiro is 5,745, but it's well worth it for all that pussy. Ronnie Biggs once said you can smell the pussy on the beach there. Have you seen it on TV? It's fucking amazing! I bet you can smell that pussy too! Unfuckinbelievable!

Hey, and did you know it's only 279 miles from Heathrow Airport to Dublin? It's well worth it just for the Guinness and the crack. The Irish are the salt of the Earth and it's a beautiful country. Who remembers The Nolan Sisters? Come on, tell me you wouldn't give them one, or Dana? Irish girls are beautiful, they really are. Who was that one who sung 'Nothing Compares to You'? She shaved her hair off, fuck knows why. Whatever happened to her? And Girls Aloud - wow, hot or what?! I see Britney Spears is getting some stick with her comeback. Fuck me, she's had two kids, so give her a break! It takes it out of you, you know. The body is never the same. How can it be? Britney is still a good 'un in my book.

15 September 2007

I got the magazine story today that my ex-wife did. £500 she got for it. And that's the biggest load of shit I've ever read. Sad, sad woman. I'll not even bother going into it. I can't anyway, I've already wiped my arse on it. Move on.

I got a letter off mum, one off Keeley Thompson and one off my buddy Ronnie Fields and Tom Hardy and a cracker off Gemeni in Cyprus with a couple of photos, specials for me, and only me. What a body! Very eatable if I say so myself - and she knows how to look after a man. My sunbed awaits - Cyprus here I come! Yippeeeeee! A spell out there would do me good. Gemeni has long, beautiful blonde hair, the most amazing breasts with strawberry size nipples - the ones you can suck on all day and still not get enough of, her tan is all over, her skin is so soft and alive that it shines, and her arse is delicious, like a peach. Fuck me, I've got a semi on looking at it. Cyprus here I come, and the sooner the better I'd say! Am I lucky or am I lucky, you jealous fuckers?! Now I know why I'm in jail - they're envious of me. Sad mother fuckers, grow up and live! Get a life! Get your own pussy and stop drooling over mine! And no, I won't let you pervs see my photos of Gemeni, coz I know you lot - you'll try to beat me to it! "I shagged Bronson's bird. I gave Bronson's bird a good seeing to! Blah, blah, blah." Well, fuck off, she's my pussy! Me-fucking-ow!

Here's a mind-blower for you: male deaths in 1999 in the United Kingdom (all ages): circulatory diseases, 119,730; cancer, 78,810; respiratory diseases, 48,910; injury and poisoning, 12,372; Infectious diseases, 2,103;

and other causes, 38,443. A total figure of 300,368, and the number of female deaths was 331,694. That's a lot of coffins. Don't it open your eyes? It does mine. Rest in peace, my brothers and sisters.

Hey, here's Buckingham Palace's telephone number, so you can give my landlady a call: 020 7930 4832. Her private secretary is Sir Robin Janvrin. Just remind her I've been in her establishment for three and a half decades and I've never had a Christmas card or a rent rebate. Tell her I'm paying with my life, and it's very costly.

Did you know Ojos del Salado on the Argentina/Chile border is the biggest volcano on our planet? It's 22,572 feet high and it erupted back in 1981. That must be due to blow again, and when it does just make sure you're well away from it. It's only 6,000 feet shorter than Everest. I suppose we can be thankful that Everest isn't a volcano. Imagine that blowing! Fuck me.

I don't 'arf teach you a lot of things! This book is full of amazing facts.

I wonder what the world's biggest cock is? I did read some years ago about a geezer in the USA who calls himself 'The Human Bull'. He had a 14-inch erect cock and all the porno girls couldn't take it! Imagine that in between your legs, girls. Could you take it? Would you want to try it? I bet some of you would, coz you all say bigger is better, but imagine if he slipped and rammed it up your arse! Ouch! I bet you wouldn't be able to walk to work the next day. You'd look like one of those bandy cowboys who's just got off a horse after three weeks in the saddle. What about those little two-inch cocks? I bet you girls piss yourselves laughing! You must do. Come on, be honest. If a geezer pulls you in a bar, you get to his flat and a two-inch prick is facing you, it must be the let-down of all let-downs. And if you say to him, "Don't worry, size don't matter," you're a lying bitch!

It's a fact of life that you men with a two-inch dick are freaks. You may as well go and put your head in the oven. A real woman can't live with that for 30 years. Face it boys, you're a joke. It's like a woman with three tits - it's not normal. Two inches?! Ha ha ha! You freaky fuckers!

Blimey, where did all that come from? Crazy or what?

Zoroastrianism? Come on, what does that mean? You don't know, do you? I've got you! Well, it's a religion. Zoroastrianism teaches that there is but one God, Ahura Mazda (the wise Lord). There are about 150,000 Zoroastrians worldwide. I wonder why? But, then again, who gives a flying fart! I prefer a plate of fish and chips myself!

It turns out that one of the robbers shot dead was Mark Nunes, 35. He'd served time for another armed blag! So on Thursday the Old Bill blew him and his mate away. They were lying in wait for the robbers, so to whoever grassed them up: live with it, you cunt! Two stiffs on your head. I salute Mark Nunes. He lived and died doing what he did best. You can't knock the guy. He chose to be an armed blagger, just as the Old Bill choose to be Old Bill. It's a job! And, if you're lucky, it pays well, very well. But at times it ends up with a lot of porridge or a hole in the nut. My respect goes to the Nunes family and the other family. I'll leave it at that or I'll be accused of glorifying crime, which I never have, nor ever will. It's a mug's game, believe me!

I've just found out the 2001 sales figures for Sunday newspapers: *Express*, 899,977; *Independent*, 252,672; *Mail*, 2,328,604; *News of the World*, 3,899,417; *Observer*, 453,095; *People*, 1,372,032; *Mirror*, 1,865,943; *Sport*, 195,768; *Telegraph*, 794,653; *Times*, 1,361,281. I bet you never knew that! I find it hard to believe that the *Sunday Sport* sells 195,768. I never realised there were so many lunatics in the United Kingdom. Sadly I'm one of them! I fucking love that paper. It cheers me right up; it's full of nutters.

Did you know the £1 coin was introduced in April 1983 to replace the £1 note? That's 25 years ago! Unbelievable! I miss the old ten-bob note myself, which is now a 50-pence coin. I preferred the notes, coz who really wants a bag of coins when you can snatch a sack of notes?!

16 September 2007

Well, I've slept on it and I've decided for the FIRST time in 33 years to put my side over on how Irene, my first wife, disappeared. The reason for my change of mind is simple: the bitch has gone too far with taking the piss out of me. So it's my turn to put my side. All my books have only ever said good luck to her; not one bad word have I said. But still she tries to buy me with lies. She's even been on the *Trisha* show talking bollocks. Read the latest story, which she sold for £500. Five hundred muggy pounds and she sells this shit! I could understand if it was £50,000, but £500?! Do me a favour! Cheap! Even Saira, my second wife, gets more than £500! So now let's see how you like your name put through the mixing machine ...

Pick Me Up Magazine
DADDY DEAREST
All mums know you have to let your kids make their own mistakes. But what if your son wanted to meet his dad - Britain's most violent prisoner? Irene Dunroe, 55, from Cheshire, reveals a sickening dilemma ...
It was the conversation I'd been dreading for the past 26 years. 'Your dad's been in touch,' I told my son, Mike. 'He says he wants to see you.'
'Really?' he gasped.
Despite everything, I saw his eyes sparkle. After all these years, he still wanted his dad's approval.
We rarely talked about Mike's father, and was it any wonder?
After all, he is the notorious prisoner, Charles Bronson, 54.
With the exception of three months, he'd been in prison for the past 33 years.
He was jailed in 1974 for armed robbery and, after violent attacks on fellow prisoners and jail workers, his sentence kept being extended.
Mike, 29, hadn't seen his dad since he was a toddler. He was 15 before he realised who he was, when a girl at his school had mentioned the similarities between them.
'I knew my dad was in prison, but I didn't realise it was him,' Mike had said to me, shocked.

After all, Bronson was always in the papers and had been branded 'Britain's most violent prisoner'.

Imagine the shame.

Not surprisingly, he hadn't wanted me to tell him anything else about his father.

But now, 14 years on, it was time for him to know the truth.

'I can't let you go and see him without telling you everything I know,' I said.

So I sat him down, and started from the very beginning.

When I first met his father, it was 1969 and he was called Michael Peterson. He changed his name to Charles Bronson five years later, when he got involved in boxing. His promoter gave him the name.

Mick, as I called him, was so different from any other boys I knew. He always wore tailored suits, had perfectly-groomed sideburns and a cockney accent.

We started dating and, eight months later, in December 1970, we married at Chester Registry Office.

I was four months pregnant at the time.

Mick had always liked a drink, but as the years went by, it became a big problem.

'He would disappear for days, and come back drunk and covered in bruises,' I told Mike. 'Then he'd wreck the house.'

But a few hours later, he'd be back to his charming old self, putting Mike on his shoulders and playing daft games with him.

'It was like living with Jekyll and Hyde,' I shuddered.

'Didn't you try to stop him drinking?' Mike asked me.

'Yes, but it didn't make any difference,' I sighed.

I'd thought about leaving him, but I was young and naïve.

Then in February 1974, Mick went missing. He went out one morning and never came back.

After he'd been gone for a week, I was frantic.

Then police raided the house looking for him. Ten police officers stormed in, while Mike clung to me, crying.

'You were only 3, but you were scared stiff,' I said.

'I remember that night,' Mike gasped.

'I was terrified the policemen would take me away.'

Shame cut through me. That had to be one of Mike's earliest childhood memories.

A week later, police told me that Mick had been arrested for armed robbery.

He's robbed a tobacconist shop in Little Sutton, Merseyside, with a sawn-off shotgun.

The next day, I went down to Ellesmere Port Police Station so I could see him on my own.

'Why?' I cried.

Mick just shook his head, and looked down without answering.

That summer, I ran out of Chester Crown Court in tears.

Mick had been sentenced to serve seven years in prison.

I was only 22, with a 3-year-old son. How was I going to cope?

I only went to see him a couple of times. I found it too upsetting.

He was supposed to get out after three years, but his sentence was extended after he got into a fight with another prisoner.

Every time it looked like he'd be released, he got into more trouble.

He even held prison sieges and rooftop protests.

'Can you imagine?' I asked Mike. ' Every time I switched on the news and saw a bearded man standing on top of a prison roof, I felt sick with terror. Because even though I'd stopped going to visit him, I could still see the madness creeping in.'

Finally, five years after he'd been sentenced, I wrote to him.

I want a divorce, I told him.

I can't wait my whole life for you.

My solicitor confirmed he'd signed the papers.

Just like that.

Two years later, I married David and we had two children, Leicia, now 30, and James, 28.

'Every so often, I'd see your dad on the news,' I told Mike.

He'd started writing books on poetry, as well as his life story.

'It's rubbish, though,' I said coldly. 'People are only interested in him because he's dubbed Britain's most violent criminal.'

Over the years, he's been involved in 10 jail sieges, attacked 50 prison officers, and caused £500,000 worth of damage in rooftop protests.

Mick was transferred from prison to prison, often placed in solitary confinement and high-security cells.

He's been moved 150 times.

'Is that any great claim to fame?' I asked Mike.

'He's happy to court publicity but he's not been in touch with me for the past 26 years.'

Until now.

Mike's friend, a man named Ray Williams, had called to say he wanted to see his son.

Crunch time.

'Now you know what kind of man your father is, are you still going to see him?' I asked.

Mike stared at the floor.

Please say no …

I couldn't bear for him to be let down like I had been.

'Yes, I am,' Mike whispered.

I sighed heavily.

Mike was a grown man now. He was a chef and lived in his own flat. How could I tell him what to do?

So two months later, in March 2000, Mike went to visit his father in high-security prison.

All that day, I was out of my mind with worry.

I must have wiped down all the kitchen surfaces a hundred times, until … 'Dad cried and hugged me,' said Mike over the phone.

How touching. Not!

This thug, this career criminal, had done nothing to earn his son's respect, and now here he was crying over him?

What about the 29 years I'd spent raising him, while Mick did everything he could to make sure he stayed in prison?

But Mike didn't notice my resentment. He was too busy gushing about his new hero.

'Dad wants to open a restaurant,' he said. 'When he gets out, we can run it together.'

No. No. No.

'He's never getting out,' I'd wanted to scream.

'These are all nothing but pipe dreams.'

But instead … 'That's great,' I said, weakly.

From then on, Mike and his dad were in regular contact.

Mick would send long letters about plans for their prison-themed restaurant, and he'd also phone Mike from prison every week.

Six months later, I was having a cuppa with Mike in his flat.

I could tell something was up by the way he kept fiddling.

'How's your dad?' I asked.

'I don't know,' he said, quietly.

'I haven't heard from him for about four months now.'

I looked at my son's disappointed face, and anger surged through me.

It was one thing attacking prison officers and letting me down.

But his own son?

A month later, I switched on the TV and there was a news report about how Mick had married Saira Rehman, a Muslim woman, who'd read about him in the newspaper and had started writing to him.

He had even converted to Islam for her, and was calling himself Charles Ali Ahmed.

He was also now famous for his bestselling books, including Solitary Fitness, in which he boasted about doing 2,500 sit-ups a day in his cell.

Sick! Why were the publishers giving him shelf space?

I hesitated to tell Mike, but he'd already seen it on the news.

'He's obviously got more important things to think about now.' Mike shrugged.

I knew he was devastated.

But there he was, no 'I told you so'.

As a mum, you have to let your children make their own mistakes.

And you owe it to them to be there to pick up the pieces when they need you.

And surprise, surprise, four years later, we read in the papers that Mick and Saira had got divorced.

'Marriage is for muppets,' Mick had said.

'He is nothing but an abusive, racist thug,' Saira reportedly said.

Whatever the truth, we were both well out of it.

Then, 16 months later, in 2005, Mike got a letter from his dad.

I'm so sorry, son, he'd written. Please come and see me.

'What do you think?' Mike asked.

I was done with holding back.

'You know what he's like,' I warned.

Two months ago, Mike went to see his dad again in Wakefield Prison, where he's serving life for taking a jail worker hostage.

But now Mike takes all of his promises with a pinch of salt.

Being with Mick was like being near a hurricane; energetic and powerful, but also highly dangerous.

People still stop me in the street to ask about Charles Bronson.

They're fascinated by his story.

Ironic really, because he's caused a lot of heartache and pain.

The really interesting man here is my son, who, despite living in the shadow of his
violent father, has gone on to achieve great things.
He's 35 now, and a talented chef.
He works very hard at his job and that makes me so very happy and proud. Surely
that's worth a million more headlines?

Once upon a time ... I first met Irene Kelsey in The Bulls Head in Great
Sutton, Ellsmere Port, back in 1969. She gave me a blow job in the ladies
toilet, which blew part of my brain out of my left ear. I've never been the
same since! She was older than me, so you could say I was her toy boy, her
plaything. And I make no bones about it, I loved her to bits. I idolised her.
She was the most beautiful, sexiest girl ever, a dream come true. How lucky
could a man get? She was a raving nympho. Ten times a night was not
enough for her, she wanted shagging 24/7.

Sure, it was brilliant, but you can get sick of too much pussy. She loved it
in public, on buses and in car parks. Once at the pictures she got on my lap
and fucked me silly until the manager came over and told us to stop or get
out. That's how it was! It was brilliant! But I actually got bored of it. I was a
young guy and I felt trapped. Her brother Rodney was a plonker, but her
two sisters Janet and Pauline were angels. Her dad was a total nutter and
her mother was lovely. Wedding bells soon arrived, and her dad stopped her
mum coming. So her parents did not come to the wedding because her dad.
What a start to the marriage! But that's life. Did I give a fuck? No!

At this time I was working as an industrial painter, with a bit of villainy on
the side. Life was sweet. But Irene, I think, was losing it a bit. I came home
one night early - well, early for me, about elevenish. I walked down the
pathway and peeped through the window net. The light was dim and the
TV set was on, but what I saw shocked me. Even today I think about it coz
it was insane. Irene was spread-legged on the settee, ramming a cucumber
up and down you know where! I couldn't believe what I was seeing. As I put
the key in the door I made a bit of noise, believing she would jump up and
sort herself out. But I was in for another shock, coz she just smiled at me and
carried on! And like a prat I stayed and watched. That was the start of
madness for me. She got worse with time. Me, I actually felt quite sick, coz
it's just not my cup of tea. It don't turn me on, it actually puts me off. If my
cock is not enough, how's a piece of fruit or veg gonna help?

Another time I brought a drinking mate home and she sat next to him. All
she had on was a nightie. From where I was sitting I could see her muff, as
Irene had a big bush. I said, "Fancy a drink?" They both said yes, so I got
up to get some glasses and when I came back I noticed my mate had a
fucking big hard-on and Irene looked like the cat who'd got the cream. My
mate's face looked guilty!

"Hey, come and look at what I've got in the kitchen," I said to my mate.
He followed me in and I stuck my sawn-off shotgun in his mouth, smashing

out some of his teeth, "Fuck her and I'll blow your head clean off!" That was the beginning of our mad marriage. As much as I loved her, I was feeling like a fly in a spider's web and it became pure insanity.

I would fall asleep being sucked off and I would wake up being sucked off. A man only has so much spunk. Once Mike was born I thought it would change, but it got worse. I was becoming the cucumber! I felt like a slave and I was getting fed up of it all: the arguments and the mental pressure. So I went out a lot and came back less. We had a nice house, nice furniture and a nice car, but all she wanted was cock!

I'll never forget one night, at Christmas time. The day had been great: Mike was spoilt rotten and we all had bellies full of food and drink. But once Mike was put to bed it started! She put some records on and started stripping off. I really wasn't in the mood, and then she did something I didn't like. She got a banana out of the fruit bowl, stuck it up her fanny and said, "Come and get it out." She got down on all fours with her arse up in the air and I could see this banana in her fanny! That was it for me! It just made me wonder what the fuck I was doing there.

I left for a spell. This time I drank a bit and played a lot of poker. I collected dosh for club owners and money lenders and got into robberies. I was what you'd call a nasty bastard and I make no excuses about my behaviour.

Whether Irene was getting cock when I was away I'll never know. I never wanted to know. But our sex life was now reduced to a blow job. I didn't want to shag her. Sometimes she wanted me to wank all over her coz she had this thing about being sprayed with spunk. She even used to talk about what it must be like to have lots of men do it at the same time. My time with Mike was the best of my life, but my last year with Irene was misery. It had taken its toll on me and that's the whole truth, but it's something I've never said because:

1. She's my son's mother;
2. She's my ex-wife; and
3. I don't believe in doing kiss and tell stories.

But I've now had a fucking gut full of her lies!

So, in 1974, I'm nicked for armed robbery, guns and violence. I deserved all I got. I'm not crying about it, nor am I bitter, I deserved it all and more. In 1975 Irene visited me for the last time with my son. In 1976 she divorced me and she met David. Then she stopped my parents from seeing my son. My head was by now blown inside-out. I went on a spiral of madness, I even got certified insane. My whole world caved in.

So I've never seen Irene since 1975. She married this David, whoever he is, and she had two more kids. It was in 1997 that I met my son Mike. Sadly, he was on smack, and our first visit upset me as I'm anti-drugs. Mike will be the first to admit he was a mug. He let all my mates down, he showed me up, he insulted good people. At one night show Dave Courtney had to chin him. The chaps all told me why, and Mike again told me it was his fault.

I saw Mike last month and he's off the drugs and had put on weight, it was a great visit. I was so proud of him. Then I get this *Pick Me Up* magazine, full of shit and lies. Why? For what reason? £500! What have I done to warrant such slander? Me, cry? I have no tears left to cry, my heart is empty. I never let my son down when he came back into my life. I've done everything to help him and still will.

Why hasn't Irene said she's divorced again and double bitter. And she now works in a sex shop - how surprising! Let's hope she's got a 12-inch black member and her fanny juices are flowing. Whatever. Get on with it and fuck off out of my life.

Let me leave you with 1976, the year she left me, the year I did cry. I cried so hard my heart smashed to pieces. That same week my granddad's house blew up and killed him. This is how I found out Irene had cut me out.

I was in Wandsworth block on HI and I'd just attacked three screws outside my door. Why? Well, I could say, why not? They were all big bully boys, forever kicking the shit out of cons and intimidating us and I'd had my lot.

Once the bell went and the rest of the boot boys arrived on the scene, I was seriously smashed up. I was left in the strongbox naked and in a body belt. Blood was pissing out of my head, I'd had a tooth kicked out and my entire body was covered in bruises. I felt fucking great. That's how I used to get in them days. My brain would explode and I would later feel relief. I really was a complex sort of guy, but it was a ruthless system. It's how it was and still is in some blocks. You'd get a bunch of screws with power and they'd come on heavy and bully us. When your door unlocks and there are ten of them and only you, what do you expect? Tea and toast? It's brutal!

So I was lying in the box on planks of wood embedded in concrete. I couldn't even scratch my arse.

I heard some steel-capped boots approaching. The first door unlocked and then the second. A big, tall screw stood there with a large brown envelope. He smirked and threw it at me and growled, "Even your wife don't love you," and then slammed the door. I thought, fuck me, what's he on about? I managed to manoeuvre it about and shake the contents out, and then I saw it all: divorce papers! Yes, I broke up, I was smashed, it was all over, and it was the start of my destruction. Yes, I deserved it and, yes, she did the best thing. Not once in the 31 years since have I been bitter about it. She has a daughter who's 30, so work the dates out yourself, etc.

And now she's divorced again, but it's me who gets the scorn - me - when, like the man I am, I took it all. I was brought up not to be nasty to women. I am pure old school in that sense, so do I have to keep getting these women selling me out to national magazines and TV chat shows? It's lie after fucking lie.

People can see right through it now. It's just, fuck Charlie, who cares. She's poisoned my son, and that's probably why he ended up a smack head. She cut me out of my boy's life, she stops his grandparents from seeing him, she remarries and then fucks that up, and now she has the nerve to blame me for that too.

Irene, grow up and live your life. My life has fuck all to do with you. All you are to me is a fucking leech. You'd sell your soul for a night out on the piss and a big fat cock, so fuck off and enjoy it.

If you want to come clean, then say it all: how when I was arrested I had 12.5 grand hidden in the house - a lot of dosh in 1974 - and you had all that. Tell them how you used to watch me leave the house with a sawn-off shotgun and masks and gloves. Where did you think I was going, a cowboy party? You knew I was a villain, you knew I lived a very dangerous life, so why are you being all squeaky clean and playing poor little Snow White?

Yeah, I went away a lot, but you got your registered mail with dosh in. You had your nice clothes and good living. You probably had more cock too when I was away. I really don't care if Luton Town Football Club went through you and scored a dozen hat-tricks. You killed me off in 1976, but you're still pissing on my grave! You even have the cheek to drag up Saira. You're just a nasty, bitter and twisted old dragon.

My son is my son. He will always be my son. But he's been kept in a shell about my side. My side has never been told. Well, it has now. And if you want more of it to come out, then I will reveal more, as this is only the top of the cake. You know that there's a lot more I could say and I will if you continue to rubbish me off in magazines. If you want it all out in the open, then let's get it out and sell it, but unlike you my dosh will go to charity. People know who and what I was - a vicious, nasty bastard - and I make no excuses. It's what I was, but you forget, Irene, that it's a lifetime ago and I've moved on. Now you're divorced, kids have grown up, and you're alone, so it's you who's back to the beginning. My beginning started the day you fancied another marriage. You've had 30 years of cock and marriage. You've had your cake and eaten it, and now you're sick.

Me, I'm happy in my own way, in my own world, and I could be free soon. If not, then that's my life. I'll not end up blaming anyone for my downfall. I don't regret even marrying you - why should I? I love Mike. It's time you moved on. Surely you can get another cock? But do yourself a favour, Irene, and do something with your eyebrows, coz they look like big caterpillars and it looks weird. Apart from that, you've kept yourself in good shape, but try to smile a bit. Be happy and enjoy what's left. And stop treating Mike like a little boy, coz it's pathetic.

Realise now, you and me are over, there are no feelings left. I really don't even think about you. Obviously I wish you well in life - I would never wish you bad luck - but stop burying the man who freed you. Be thankful that I live my life with a strong code of honour.

To me you were a gangster's moll. You loved the excitement, the danger!

You loved it all. If you wanted different then you should've married a fucking wimpy husband and lived a boring life. You chose to be my partner, I chose you, so what's the regret? I still have some memories. So why don't you just stop the stories, sell your vibrators and party all the way to Disneyland. And yes, I did say marriage is for muppets! But keep your face out of my biz. Don't step where you can't walk, stay on your own pathway of life. I'll leave you with one thought, a distant memory!

The day you came home early from the shops and you caught me in the kitchen sawing off a shotgun barrel, you looked at me with those eyes that said, "I never seen that". Well, that was the day you could've, should've, left me. You knew then what I was, you know now what I was. Sure, I lost and fucked up big time, but who's crying? Look in the mirror, Irene, and get them eyebrows sorted.

Do you know something? I'm now of the opinion that my belief in being the gentleman to women is all shit, like opening the door to them or being good mannered. Why? They all want this equal rights shit. I'm now going with the times. I'll never be like I was with women. coz all I ever get back is the blade in my back. I'm seen as Mr Softy. Yeah, we can do what we want with Charlie. Let him rob the banks, and we'll spend his loot and then fuck off later! Yeah, sure! Look, girls, accept me as I am or go find someone else. Maybe I'll find a young girl who's a villain, so she can rob the banks and I can live off her! Then when she goes to jail for 20 years I'll play the innocent party.

Poor Charlie, I never even knew she was a criminal. When I seen her with that gun I thought it was a silly party thing. And all that money - I thought it was Monopoly money. Honest, I didn't know anything. I gave that nasty woman the best years of my life. Now she's gone to prison for 20 years and I'm all alone. Why me? How cruel can she be? Never mind, I'll get by ... blah, blah, blah! Yeah, I'll play that card next time.

We have to get with the times, coz it's dog eat dog. Men and women are equal and that's how it is today. Sad but true. The sweet and tender loving has dried up. They're now tough cookies, hard as nails, bent as a boomerang, nasty and bitter.

Come on, tell me, what are the top ten ranks of the British Army? Come on, what's the answer? 1. Field Marshal, 2. General, 3. Lieutenant General, 4. Major General, 5. Brigadier, 6. Colonel, 7. Lieutenant Colonel, 8. Major, 9. Captain, 10. Lieutenant. Stand to attention!

Hey, Irene says my books are shit! Well I say that my books are full of knowledge, especially considering that I write them in a fucking zoo, in isolation, with four walls and two doors to cut me off from the real world. Shit! Did you really know the top ten ranks in the Army? Did you fuck. You sure do now, so you've learnt something, and life is all about learning.

Did you know that in Saudi Arabia a woman can divorce her husband if he does not keep her supplied with coffee? How fucking mental is that? And they say I'm nuts!

Hey, you'll love this. A jury in Kentucky, USA, recommended to the judge that the convicted robber and kidnapper should be sentenced to 5,005 years. The judge thought that was a little harsh, so he sentenced him to 1,001 years instead! Who's fucking nuts here, the jury or the judge? It's mind boggling. Don't be a robber in America.

'Tschekan'. Well, what is it? Come on, what does it mean? I'll tell you. It's a Russian war hammer with a blunt steel head. I once had one and it's lethal! How about 'Tuagh-gatha'? Well? You don't know, do you? You haven't got a clue. Well, it's a Scottish battle axe. Here's another one - Kheten'. That's an Egyptian two-handed axe with a bronze head fitted into the wooden shaft. Let's put it this way, you wouldn't want it in your crust! It's awesome.

1952 was the year I was born, and it was also when the first jetliner service was launched - the BOAC De-Havilland comet flight. It started between London and Johannesburg. Not a lot of people know that! Come on, have you ever had a shag up in a plane? It's something I want to do. They say it's brilliant. Imagine if you were to crash - what a way to go! Magic! I wonder just how many are in the Mile High Club. Sadly I'm not, but hopefully I will be one day.

I wonder if the pilots get a blow job up there! I bet they do, don't you? If Bill Clinton can have it then why not our pilots? Why not any professional worker? It's all about enjoying life, gays or straights. What's a blow job between friends?! Come on, think about it. It should be all part of your job description. Get your unions onto it! Get it made a legal part of your contract: one blow job a day or all out on strike. Now wouldn't that make work more enjoyable? Let's not forget women's equal rights, so some pussy eating too! It's only fair. What's a 69 between workmates? That could be a job for me later: a union rep. I'll sort all this out, so vote for me. I'll make our workforce strong again. We will rise to greatness!

In 210 BC Qin Shi Hung died and was buried with 7,500 archers and soldiers in a massive tomb. Fucking loonyology at its very best! Isn't history insane? It's like Robin Hood and his merry men, running around in that wood in green tights and feathered hats - were they all shirt-lifters? Come on! Something don't add up there, does it?!

Did you know there's a tribe of Indians in the Amazon who have what they call 'Love Monkeys'. To us it's called bestiality, but to them it's a love monkey. Imagine that - a fucking monkey for a shag when the wife's got a headache! It's just unfuckinbelievable! Dirty bastards. Leave the poor monkeys alone. I bet you bunch of savages wouldn't pick on a bear or a gorilla, coz they'd probably shag you. Yeah, you're all brave with a monkey, you pervos!

Newsflash exclusive: the two screws involved in the £300,000 drug ring just copped six years and four years. They both broke down in the dock. Who said big boys don't cry? Do your bird, you pair of wimps.

One was a former Rugby League player turned screw. Well, it takes all sorts I suppose! But the crime's the easy part, it's the bird that's hard. The other blagger who was shot dead the other day was Andy Markland, aged 36. The third guy has been charged with attempted robbery and firearms. They should let him go now. If it's not enough to lose two buddies, then what is?

Hey, get on this one for a record breaker. Sean Wozencroft scoffed a raw onion in 60 seconds in Newent this week in Gloucestershire. I bet his eyes were running!

Here we go again with the next story! Who says it don't happen? it's only human nature, so of course it happens. I bet the hubby ain't too happy!

September 2007, The People
A woman prison guard was filmed having wild sex with one of her old inmates, The People can reveal today.
Married Jacqueline Pegg, 40, was caught on camera romping with violent robber Bradley Tomkins - who is just 24.
The film - shot on the ex-con's mobile phone - shows the warden doing a raunchy striptease before performing oral sex and other kinky acts.
At one stage, the sultry brunette even says her own name before grabbing her young lover's manhood.
Tomkins first met Jacqueline while he was serving a four-and-a-half year term for aggravated robbery at Swinfen Hall Young Offenders' Institution in Lichfield, Staffs. He claimed the pair, both from nearby Tamworth, openly kissed and flirted in his cell during his stretch.
Tomkins - who said he did not know she was married - told The People: "She would always come to my cell and we just couldn't stop it.
"She would brush past me as if she was trying to turn me on and sometimes pinch my bum.
"We'd have this game where she would bend over for me and I had to guess whether she was wearing a thong or not.
"Sometimes she would say, 'Actually, I'm not wearing any underwear'. She was really fit for a woman of 40. You could tell she looked after herself because she has a great body."
Tomkins - whose fellow lags included Learco Chindamo, the brute who killed London headmaster Philip Lawrence - went on: "I knew it had got out of hand when I came back from the gym one day.
"I was wearing my vest and pouring with sweat. She told me, 'You look so hot - I wish I could get all steamy with you.'
"I was near my cell and I know for a fact she would have had sex with me there and then.
"But I didn't want to in case we got caught."
Tomkins claimed he once hit a fellow con for yelling abuse at Jacqueline.
He said: "He was bang out of order so I laid into him.
"She was thankful and gave me a warm hug afterwards and whispered in my ear, 'Thank you, my little Tamworth boy'."
Tomkins insisted he did not bed Jacqueline until he was released from Swindon Hall

and they bumped into each other at a pub in Tamworth.

He said the sexual chemistry kicked in instantly - and they raced to a pal's house for the kinky romp.

Prison chiefs will be shocked by the claims because they could seriously jeopardise security.

But Tomkins said: "The thing that worries me most is not the security - it's the fact she was married.

"I would never ever have kissed her if I'd known that.

"I may be a criminal - but I am not a home-wrecker."

Jacqueline - who is married to husband Stuart - told The People last night: "I'm going to lose my job over this."

And a Ministry of Justice spokesman said: "If a member of staff is found to have breached the code of conduct, the likely outcome is dismissal."

Who remembers Manfred Mann, a pop group in the 1960s? Well, the singer Mike d'Abo had just become a dad at the age of 63! Not bad, eh? See, you always get the news in my book! It's full of facts.

Hey, I'll tell you who's a fucking hero - Lee Henderson. He climbed Mount Snowdon in a medieval armoured suit for charity. Imagine that! Awesome! Good on ya, mate! That took some doing. I bet that's a first, and probably a last too!

Hey, here's a little tip for you ladies in the kitchen having problems with flies. We all fucking hate flies, especially near our food. Well, here's the cure. Get some lavender and keep it in the kitchen, coz flies hate it. You'll never see a fly on lavender. Why? How the fuck do I know - ask the fly.

I see the kids' new maths teacher at Lambert Haileybury School in Bracknell, Berkshire, is Colin Croft, ex-West Indies cricket star. I bet they're bowled over! It's not too far from Broadmoor Asylum either.

Here we go, more mothering the nonces. That's how they run these shitholes. This wing will be full of the nonces. They have such an easy time.

News of the World
By Carole Ye Maung
Langham 'Living in Fear'
Disgraced TV star Chris Langham has struck up a close jail friendship - with a twisted Paedophile. The Bafta-winning actor, convicted of downloading horrific pornographic images of children being abused, has become inseparable from fellow sicko Terry Hoath. An insider revealed: "They go everywhere together just like Tweedledee and Tweedledum. They're getting closer because Langham has been having such a hard time coming to terms with prison life. At times he has been suicidal. He is aware that quite a few of the other inmates want to rip him apart for what he has done and is absolutely terrified." Like pervert Langham, married Hoath was arrested as part of Operation Ore, the massive police investigation into child pornography on the internet. A court heard how the bug-eyed beast fantasised about raping and killing a child and hoarded thousands of kiddie porn images. He was caged for five years. The revelation

of their bizarre friendship comes after a judge sentenced father-of-three Langham, 58,
to ten months on Friday. He will be free in less than four. And today the News of the
World reveals the fist picture taken behind bars of the star of comedy dramas Help and
The Thick of It - on his jail ID card. He and Hoath are housed on Block 4, the
despised "vulnerable prisoners' block" of Elmley prison on the Isle of Sheppey, Kent.
Since Langham's conviction last month on 15 child porn counts, the pair have spent
hours working out together in the prison gym. Langham, now Prisoner VH59990,
looks gaunt on his ID card. Our source added: "He has lost more than a stone and is
often heard crying our for the 'Block 4 listener' - who is like a Samaritan - to come
and talk to him. However, Hoath is always there as a shoulder to cry on. He is enjoying
the kudos among the other sex offenders of having Langham as his new best friend.
To them he was a big cheese. He was boasting he wouldn't get a long sentence because
of his celebrity status - and he was right!" The star's pal will disgust his wife Christine,
still reeling over his sick internet activities at their farmhouse near Cranbrook, Kent.
She continues to visit him in jail.

Thirty years ago they would've had a fucking good seeing to and left prison terrified. Now they walk out of the gates proud. I'd send the scum out in a wheelchair; better still, a body bag! Zip them up and take them straight to the crematorium. Burn, bastards, burn. Save our kids!

Here's a sad story. A devoted old couple died on the same day. Alexander Gray, 74, died of a heart attack in the morning, and then Doreen, 73, collapsed and died hours later. What a tragic end! But I guess they were born to live and die together. I think their family can be proud of them, and in some respects I suppose it's a happy ending for them. Rest in peace Alex and Doreen.

I knew a man in Durham Jail, who was a brilliant pickpocket. He used to go around the dog tracks all over England and dip the pockets. Well, I suppose he wasn't so great, seeing as he was serving three years!

This new DNA technology forensic science is beyond belief and it's catching criminals for crimes that took place years ago, like the monster Stephen Shepherd.

In 1981, Shepherd broke eight ribs of 82-year-old Vera Waring, injured her neck, throat and nose and sexually assaulted her. She died of a heart attack. Vera had been the organist at a church in Co. Antrim, Ireland, for the previous 25 years - a lovely old lady. But the perpetrator wasn't caught. It wasn't until 20 years after her death that a DNA match was found with Shepherd. It was a billion to one that it was him, yet he still says he's innocent! Cunt! He got life with a tariff of 14 years. Fucking rot in hell, Shepherd, you monster. I bet you thought you'd got away with it, eh? Well old Vera came back and trapped you, you big brave bastard. You sexually assaulted her and broke eight of her ribs. Somebody needs to slip into your cell and smash your fucking ribs in. You deserve to leave this planet screaming.

Rapist Steven Snowden was convicted in 2001 of a rape he did in

Cambridgeshire in 1991. Ten years had passed, but then he nicked a bottle of Scotch from a shop and, Bob's your uncle, his DNA matched that found at the rape scene in 1991. He copped 12 years!

In 1977, Mary Gregson's body was pulled out of the River Aire in West Yorkshire. She had been beaten, sexually assaulted and strangled. She was a loving mother and wife to an 11-year-old son and a lovely husband. That boy is now 41 years old. Then in 1999 they nicked a van driver called Richard Lowther and his DNA matched. At Sheffield Crown Court in 2000 he was sentenced to life. I bet that cunt is on his way out now, coz them scum don't actually do life. Some get out early. Watch out Lowther, coz I'm sure Mary's son would love to bump into you and have a private chat. I bet your last seven years have been cushy, with a TV, nice bed, good food and gym. But I hope you've got it all to come later. You worms always get your just desserts in the end. Believe it! You can't go around killing and noncing people's mums and daughters and not expect any comeback. Guys like you think you're smart, but when your time comes you'll shit yourself and beg for mercy. That's your end, Lowther - a shitty pair of pants - and the sooner the better!

From 1960 to 1969 here's the top 10 for the greatest number of weeks in the pop charts. I bet you can guess who's no. 1: The Beatles. It just had to be them! Whether you like them or not, they were the true guv'nors! 1. Beatles, 307 weeks; 2. The Shadows, 204 weeks; 3. The Hollies, 233 weeks; 4. The Tremeloes, 191 weeks; 5. The Bachelors, 187 weeks; 6. The Animals, 184 weeks; 7. The Rolling Stones, 181 weeks; 8. Herman's Hermits, 177 weeks; 9. Manfred Mann, 176 weeks; 10. Dave Clark Five, 154 weeks. Incidentally, the Four Pennies were at no. 30 with 56. They had a hit with 'Juliet', a slow romantic one, and I can remember it like yesterday coz I was at a party dancing with a girl called Julie - ironic or what?! We had a real slow crutch-rubbing dance and I got a fucking big hard-on. I was about 13 years old. It was fucking brilliant! Later she pulled me off. That's a memory! Memories like that never leave you. Fantastic. But the Beatles in the 1960s, you've gotta give it to them, they were special! And 307 weeks in the charts says why.

Hey, did you know the average woman shaves off 4lbs of fanny hair in a year! Add that up over 50 years - mind-blowing! Talking of beaver, My ex-wife had a fucking rain forest! She must've had the hairiest fanny in the UK! In them days I don't think the Brazilian was about, so it was just bush.

Hey, here's a memory that takes me back. One day I was preparing to go out on one of my missions where I would be gone for a few days, and I was packing my holdall in the bedroom with her in bed watching me. This would've been 1973 time. She watched me pack up a boiler suit, gloves, a balaclava, a sawn-off shooter and a box of shells.

"Off again are we, Mick?"

"Yeah, I'll be away for a spell."

"What's all that for?"

"I'm going to a fancy dress party and I'll dress up in the car later."

That's how it was, how I was, how she was. But she didn't ask questions when she spent the dosh. When I was away she could've been shagging the milkman for all I knew.

One morning I got up and heard a noise out in our shed. I thought it must be rats or a cat. I went out with the bread knife, to find it was a fucking tramp! Apparently he'd been sleeping in my shed for weeks. It's strange really, coz we lived in a cul-de-sac and the neighbours had been chatting about a tramp who'd been spotted coming and going at strange times around our area, and people's milk had been nicked off the doorsteps.

"Oy, cunt, what's your game?"

He froze, probably due to the bread knife and my bulging eyes. He was an old man with a long grey beard - a proper old tramp, harmless.

"Fancy a mug of tea and some toast?"

He just looked confused, like a lost dog!

"You stay there grandpop, I'll sort it."

So off I went to the kitchen and sorted it. He was made up.

"Look, if you want to kip down in my shed, then don't let nobody catch you or see you. Come late and leave early. But if I catch you at any other time I'll cut your fucking head off. And don't piss or shit anywhere near my place or I'll shoot your legs off. Okay?"

He nodded. He never did come back.

Who remembers 'Toast Toppers'? They were little tins of paste-like stuff that you heated up and put on toast for a snack - bacon flavour, beef and curry, sausage, etc. Anyway, I came home one night and Irene was watching some shit on the telly.

"What's for tea, babe? I said.

"Toast toppers," she replied.

"What?! Fucking Toast Toppers?! I'm a man not a fucking mouse! I want a cooked meal."

What a row we had about that! She never had a fucking clue about cooking. Toast fucking Toppers! Come on, after a hard day's graft, I need more than that.

I took her and Mike to Chester Zoo once and she came very close to sharing the polar bear pit. How I refrained from picking her up and slinging her in I don't know. Moan, moan, fucking moan! It drove me mad.

Here's a funny thing - shopping. We once went shopping - not my thing, but one has to try. I was pushing the pram around the supermarket and she was pushing the trolley, just a normal couple doing what a normal couple do I suppose. I bent down to pick up some cereal and a gun fell out of my overcoat. That was it, she never ever took me shopping again! It was an accident! I just wasn't cut out for that married life shit. I found it hard, but it was causing me a lot of problems. I was a criminal, that's what I was, and our worlds just did not mix. I enjoyed living on the edge, in the fast lane, but with a small boy and a wife and responsibilities, it's like having a chain around your neck. I was drowning big time.

Now I'm older and more mature and sensible, yeh, I could handle it all; back then - no way! But my time with Mike was brilliant - the best memories I'll ever have. I always used to bring him gifts home after my missions away: toys, clothes, all sorts. My time with Mike was precious to me - beautiful times, never to be forgotten. Even Irene was lovely. I truly don't have any bitterness or regrets. Why should I?

Life is only what you put into it and I've given it my best shot. Back straight, stiff upper lip and march on. I fucking despise the whingers and the 'I told you so' brigade, the regretful cunts: I should've done this and that; I should never have let you shag me, etc. To me life is moving on, so enjoy what you have and have a laugh. I can close my eyes and see beautiful things, especially in the bedroom, so why put a black cloud over it? Be thankful - I am! If some people had their wish, I'd die in jail. I may never be in a bedroom again with a beautiful woman. I may never do all that again, so my memories are priceless. Irene, take a step back and think. Was it all really that bad? Didn't we laugh? Wasn't it a mad journey? Grow up, it was fucking brilliant!

Am I missing something here with this next story? Or am I silly? How the fuck can this slag stand by this nonce?

The Sun
Exclusive by Anthony France
The wife of vile Jehovah's Witness paedo Michael Porter vowed to stand by her man yesterday. Porter, 38, who abused a baby and 12 other young boys, was released by a soft judge last month. The Sun tracked him down to his new home, near where he strolled hand in hand with loyal wife Joanne. The couple mingled with shopper s- including children - in Edgware, North London. A family friend said: "Joanne says she married Michael for better or worse. He is a changed man and she is proud to be seen out and about with him. Her love will save him." But a shocked mum who saw Porter out shopping said: "He should be swinging on the end of a rope, not walking the streets as a free man. He's a disgrace." Porter is still a Jehovah's Witness and calls at the homes of local people unaware of his sick past to promote the faith. Joanne's loyalty mirrors that of the wife of disgraced actor Chris Langham who was jailed for ten months on Friday for possessing child porn. A judge showed mercy after reading a moving letter from the star's wife Chrissie, 54. Porter - a ministerial servant to Jehovah's Witness church elders in Clevedon, Somerset - molested boys by putting his hands down their trousers in 'playfights'. One victim was interfered with as he slept in bed while another woke to find Porter on top of him. He abused the boys - aged from 18 months to seven years - when he was trusted to act as a babysitter, take kids camping and host sleepovers. Porter - supported in court by Joanne - carried out the attacks over a 14-year period in the 1980s and '90s. Judge Tom Crowther caused outrage when he spared him jail for 24 counts of indecency after hearing he had undergone therapy.

He gave him a three-year community rehabilitation order at Bristol Crown Court, banned him from working with under-18's and put him on the sex offenders register. The judge said "personal" issues in Porter's childhood made his actions "understandable". However, Porter's own sister Tina Hughes, 40, branded the judge "rubbish" and disowned her brother. She said: "He's an evil monster with no soul. He's not human. The fact he is flesh and blood is irrelevant to me. To me he is 6ft under. Dead." The Attorney General is considering whether to appeal against the sentence.

Don't she have any morals at all? How can she lie next to this piece of shit and not feel dirty? A Jehovah's Witness?! Don't make me sick! He's just a nonce; a fucking smelly nonce who destroys kids' lives! And she's standing by him. How can this be? Or is it me? This cunt should be locked up to rot! It truly does make me sick. This is a classic case of madness. Loonyology's not the word - it's sick! To think of him walking down the street, all proud and respectable. Watch out, society; watch out, public! It's your kid next, then who's to blame? It don't even happen to us, yeh! Believe me, it does. And it will.

Have you heard the one about the geezer with no arms or legs lying on the beach? Three women came up to him and felt really sad for him.

The first woman asked, "Have you ever had a cuddle?"

He said, "Never."

So she gave him a good, long cuddle.

The second woman asked, "Have you ever been kissed?"

He said, "Never."

So she gave him a good kiss with tongues.

The third woman asked, "Have you ever been fucked?"

He looked at her with puppy eyes and said, "Never."

She said, "Well you will be when the tide comes in!"

Three words, six letters, one question, guaranteed to destroy a man's confidence - is it in?

I was involved in a serious accident in my motor. I ploughed into three hoodies on a zebra crossing. I was only doing 85mph. But the Old Bill have been brilliant, considering one went through my windscreen, one dented my bonnet and the other prick got knocked up the road 200 yards. One's been charged with breaking and entering, one for criminal damage and the other prick for leaving the scene of an accident. Sweet!

Hey, you've got to admit that you taxpayers pay untold millions every year over us criminals. But you don't half get your money's worth! Here's a bit of Bronson philosophy for you: depression is a state of anxiety without the enthusiasm.

Well, believe me it's not like that in max secure. The only prostitute you'd see is a big, fat, hairy-arsed faggot eying you up in the bathhouse. That's your lot.

18 September 2007

Mark Fish visited today. On his way here he got a call. Two of his best pals - Nigel Slater and Steve Saunby - were on that crashed plane that went up in flames in Phuket, Thailand. They died along with their wives. In fact Steve had only just married Susan Howells 24 hours before the crash. How sad is that? Mark was gutted coz his mates are his family and so he had lost two brothers. Both Steve and Nigel were in the pub game and were respected in the Lincolnshire area, so my respects go to the families. They died along with 85 others - a sad day for all.

Mark looked his pukka self, suited and booted. His ties alone cost more than a screw's weekly wage. The screw who walked him over told him it's time I moved on. Mark said it should've happened years ago. All the screws, well most of them, tell my visitors the same thing. Pity they don't tell the no. 1 governor that or demand I move on.

Mark always tells me a cracking story. We were having a laugh about *OK Magazine*. He was in it again, at a show, along with Dave Courtney. But for some reason Dave's photo wasn't in it - and Dave loves his photos. Mark, some years back down in a club in Brighton, chinned Jim Davidson. Jim had been on the piss all day and he was getting silly. He didn't know Mark Fish or have any idea who he was, but he soon found out!

Yeh, it was a good visit, despite the bad news, but life must go on. Look out for Mark, coz he'll be playing a part in my movie. He's the one with the psycho eyes!

There's a screw here, Mr Clayton, who won the title of Yorkshire Strongman last Saturday. He's into all that bodybuilding stuff. He's 56 and does himself proud! He's probably the strongest screw in this jail, but also one of the decent ones. His type are all the same: generally a good lot, and they don't have to pretend they're hard, they are hard. They're disciplined, hard workers in the gym, fitness fanatics, and when a man is winning titles at 56 years old that gets my respect. There are screws here half his age with arses like balloons, and bellies like dart players, and that's only the female screws! Yeh, respect to the guy. Top man! But fuck paying his food bill for the week!

Mark Sharman sent me a parcel of clothes in today - sweat tops, etc. - but I can't have them. That's the name of the game. But I did get the Chubby Brown tapes! He's a funny fat fucker, he is; not Mark, Chubby Brown. Hey, when life gives you lemons, make lemonade. And always set the trail, never follow the path.

I got a load of mail today! Di Brown, Keeley, Mum, Mark Emmins, Leyton Frayne, and some cunt called 'Buzzer' from Liverpool. He wants a signed photo! Fucking Buzzer?! What is he, a fucking vibrator? A photo? I don't think so, do you? What sane geezer calls himself Buzzer? And what's he want a photo of me for? Fucking buzz off! Weirdos!

'Honey catches more flies than vinegar'. I like that saying. The sweet things in life are the best! Are they? Remember this: what is popular is not always right, and what is right is not always popular. How true is that?!

I called up Keeley tonight. She's lovely - full of life, full of dreams. I've just sorted her a job out to put a few quid her way. Christmas is creeping closer and the goose needs fattening up.

All you need in life is the three Ds: Desire, Discipline and Determination. Fucking let me out and I'll show you how to do it! I'm raring to go, I need it so bad. Top gear and off I go, you won't see my arse for smoke. Build bridges not barriers, that's what I say, how about you?

19 September 2007

I called Mark Emmins tonight. Top geezer! I always like a chat with Mark. He gets things sorted. Too many are all piss and wind. If people just did what they said, what a much better world it would be, eh?

I had a great day today: double egg, chips and beans and a mug of sweet tea - lovely jubbly! You can't beat a good old-fashioned English meal.

I see OJ Simpson has been arrested and charged with armed robbery. How the fuck he ever got off that double murder charge years ago is beyond me. One law for the rich, another law for the poor. How fucking true is that?

There's a book just come out that's worth a butcher's: *The Battle for Japan 1944-1945* by Max Hastings (Harper Press). If you really want to know about brutality and inhumanity then get a copy. Fuck all these silly psychologists who say forgive and forget. These Japs were fucking animals to our boys in the POW camps. How do they forget? Some watched their best mates being beheaded. There was no humanity for our boys, only hell. The Japs were ruthless, sadistic bastards. They hated and despised tall prisoners coz they're mostly short-arsed twats. Yeh, that was a war that was.

Hey, since 1997 8,555 prisoners have gone missing from prisons in England and Wales! Most have just absconded from low cat. jails. They just walk out and go for a stroll and don't come back. You'd think they would at least nick the governor's car, boring bastards!

Did you know that congenital syphilis can cause a saddle nose? Fact! And Cushing's disease causes a moon-shaped face. I bet you're thinking: here he goes, he don't half come out with some bollocks, but it's all facts. Would I say it if I wasn't right? The human face has 100 muscles in it - no wonder at times it aches!

I had a mental dream last night. I woke up early - must've been about 4 a.m. - and had a fucking big hard-on. It was that hard it bloody hurt, but the dream was mental. I was on a slab in the police morgue and I was surrounded by officers all arguing amongst themselves about my hard-on.

"It's impossible," they said. "How can he be dead with that fucking lob on?!"

One was pulling it about and saying, "It's a beauty!"

Then one woman said, "Don't touch it without a glove, you don't know where it's been."

A bloke responded, "I bet I know where you'd like it to have been."

A poofter said, "I bet its a good 7-incher, probably 7½."

"Look at the helmet," one said. "It's lovely and shiny."

"Fuck me, it's my dick you lot are going on about. I'm alive, I'm not dead," I said, but nobody heard me.

Everybody then fucked off, but the poofter sneaked back on his own and pulled something out of his pocket. I couldn't see what it was, but he then rubbed a load of jelly stuff all over my cock.

"Oy, fuck off!" I said.

But could he hear me? Could he fuck.

Then he got his trousers off and his pants and straddled over my bell end and - whooooshhhh! - it went right up his jacksie!

"Fucking get off, you prat!" I shrieked.

Could he hear me? No. He just kept bobbing up and down making silly noises: "Oooh, ahhh, oooh, God, oooh!"

"Fucking get off, you faggot!" I kept shouting.

But what woke me up was the dirty bastard was having a wank at the same time. I shot up in fear and found it was all a dream. How mad was that?! The very thought of it makes me feel sick. What the fuck is all that about? It wasn't a dream, it was a nightmare. Loonyology or what?!

Anyway, what is a dream? What does it mean? Have you ever been running or falling in a dream and you wake up just in time, with your heart almost exploding?

What about the good old wet dream, when just as you're about to shoot your load you wake up and it's spurting all over the sheets? What a fucking waste! All YPs (young cons) can't help the wet dreams. Come on, how many make a hole in the mattress? Come on, be honest, we've all done it. It really is a lonely old journey in this game. In fact it's mucky and sticky and very, very insane. We should be out shagging for real, not in dreams!

What about all the cons in two-up cells or three-up cells? imagine that! That's madness. Hey, stay out of jail. Live your life, don't waste it!

Do you know something, when I look back over the asylum years, when they pumped me with drugs that stopped me getting a hard-on? I wonder if I could now take them to court for loss of masturbation time? Surely it's my human right to be able to have a wank? Who's got the right to pump any young man with drugs that have such bad side effects. In fact, how do I know now if I'm not sterile? Possible? I could be in for a massive claim here. Must call my lawyer. The fucking wankers are not getting away with this, it's my dick, and I'm entitled to bash my bishop when I fancy it. What a liberty! It's loonyology!

My shagging days are over
My pilot light is out
What used to be my sex appeal
Is now my water spout
Time was when, on it's own accord
From my pants it would spring
But now I've got a full-time job
To find the fucking thing
It used to be embarrassing
The way it would behave
Cos every single morning
It would stand and watch me shave
Now as old age approaches
It sure gives me the blues
To see it hang its little head
To watch me tie my shoes!

Here's a funny thing from years ago, back to 1972. I'll never forget it. I had just come out of the Grace Pub in Ellesmere Port at about 10 p.m. time, wearing my black Crombie, and went to the public telephone box to make a phone call. So there I was, making the call, no drama, all sweet. I actually felt good, but then I clocked three lads outside the box all clocking my way. I smelt trouble. When you're in my game you have a sixth sense; it just hits you. They were up to no good, and I was their target. I put the phone down and stepped outside, and they started to make their move on me. In less than five seconds I'd pulled out a sawn-off from under my coat and fired it over their heads. You should've seen the fuckers leg it! By the time people had come running out of The Grace and the houses nearby, I'd gone.

That's how I dealt with situations in them days. It worked every time. Nowadays, sadly, they just shoot you in the head. In my days, you at least got a warning! Nobody ever got two warnings from me - never needed to. Life's to short to go around issuing numerous warnings. One, and only one, then you fucking get it, simple as that. Like them three were gonna do something to me! The slags!

I think I've just read one of the saddest stories of all time. Last month Natasha Coombs, 17 years old, died tragically on a railway track. Then this month her 40-year-old mother went to the same track and jumped in front of a train. Why? How? What a sad old world it is! The husband, Gary Coombs, now has to live on with two ghosts and two memories. How must he feel? How does he go on? How could any man face that? A loving family just destroyed! Mum and daughter, together in life and death. It just blows me away. I actually felt so sad when I read this today that it's put me on a downer! What must've been going through their minds? Was life really so depressing? Hey, and let's not forget the poor old train driver. How do they cope with such tragedies? It's an all round sad, sad world. My thoughts are with Gary - my sincere condolences to you, mate.

The Sun 20 September 2007
Guards Caught Kipping under Prisoner's Bed
Dozy pair sacked for hospital gaffe
Exclusive by Tom Reilly and Simon Hughes
Two prison officers have been sacked after falling asleep under a prisoner's hospital bed. Doctors complained to prison bosses after catching Fred Cronk and Darren Porter snoozing. Cronk and Porter had handcuffed the offender to his bed frame before pulling out sleeping bags and dozing off. An insider at Medway Maritime Hospital in Gillingham, Kent, said: "These guards were incredibly stupid - sleeping on the job is immediately a sacking offence. They also chained the lag to the bed when the rules state that one of them should be attached to the prisoner at all times. The doctors were clearly concerned about their safety and that of other patients given the fact the officers were asleep. Although he was handcuffed to the bed he could have tried to escape while they dozed. They had clearly planned their nap - they'd brought a sleeping bag." The incident involving Cronk, who has worked in the prison service for 23 years, and Porter is believed to have happened last month. The guards, who both worked at Rochester jail, were being paid £15 an hour overtime and had volunteered to do the watch. It is thought doctors called Governor John Wilson to complain. The two officers were called into his office and sacked. A Prison Service spokesperson said: "Officers investigated for unprofessional conduct may face disciplinary proceedings including dismissal." It is understood the two officers may appeal.

There, both caught out, bang to rights! Two lazy piss-takers! Now get your cards and fuck off!

Who needs screws like these pair of muppets? They're just a pair of prats. Go and get a job on a building site, you mugs, and take your sleeping bags with you.

In 1976, I had just arrived on the Winchester block from Parkhurst for chinning a screw, so I had the big boys committee waiting specially for my van to arrive. There they were, 20 deep, all shaven heads and big steel toe-capped boots. All strong members of the POA, lots of them at this time were also members of the National Front. They were basically thugs in uniform hiding behind a 20-foot wall.

As I stepped off the van, cuffed up to two Parkhurst screws, one said to me, "You're in for it here, son."

I replied, "Oh yeh, what can they do to me that hasn't already been done? Are they gonna kill me then?"

We marched to the block where I was uncuffed and read the rules. I thought I might as well start off on the right foot, so I nutted the screw who was in my face giving it the big bollocks. It was worth the kicking I got. It felt right and good to me.

Years later, around 1995/96, a screw in the block kept looking at me with a smile and a friendly nod. "Alright, Charlie?" he said.

"Yeh, not bad boss," I replied. I'm always polite to decent screws.

"You don't remember me do you, Charlie?"

"No, mate," I said.

"Well, I was one of the committee waiting for you in the 1970s and, believe me, you made my day when you nutted big mouth. He had it coming. Nobody liked him."

It made me smile that! That's how funny jail is. Even screws are funny cunts. They may work together, but lots don't like one another; in fact they hate each other.

Apparently this cunt with the mouth that I nutted was a serious bully boot boy and he'd got his marching orders years ago. He was a friendless fucker. I'm not a bad judge after all! On paper, in my file, I'm a nasty bastard. But am I? My file on these fuckers is bigger than their file on me, and mine is the truth. Who guards the guards? That's what I keep asking. Who guards them? Will we ever know? Never!

21 September 2007

The governor did his rounds today and asked how I am. How am I? How would you be serving a life sentence with a three-year tariff? Not to mention the fact that I'm now four and a half years over the tariff! How the fuck would you be? The more I think about it, the more it winds me up. It really is a fucking liberty.

I got a letter from Joyce Connor. She's been on Canadian TV, taking part in some documentary on her. I saw monster Miller today. It made my day, coz I only have to see that ugly cunt and I feel happy. Ugly is not the word for him, he's grotesque; a living, breathing, walking monster. Why don't they shoot the bastard? Why do you taxpayers put up with him? Start voting for MPs who'll bring back hanging and stop voting for soft prats. Vote for real men who'll stamp on these filthy beasts. And don't forget to vote for Mark Fish for Lord Mayor of Scunthorpe and Dave Courtney for Lord Mayor of London and me for Mayor of Luton. Watch us clean up the streets. Vote for sanity, vote for us! As Mark Fish says, vote for me, you know it makes sense, nudge, nudge, wink, wink. Vote for men not mice!

Just clock all them MPs in the house and listen to them debate. Do you really respect them or trust them? They're a bunch of fucking muppets! All but a handful are lying, evil, two-faced rats! Vote for real people, your own sort. You can bet your arse that if I became an MP I'd fight for the real people, the salt of the earth. I'd look after you right, girls, and you clubbers and gamblers. And all you low-paid workers would be sorted, as priority, coz you're the cream. Fuck all them wealthy fuckers - the taxman will sort that lot out, it's the real people I care about! Think about it, get me in there, trust me. Vote with what's in your heart, not with what's in your brain. Most of what you've been fed for so many years is just shit, so think on!

If all the lunatics had voted me as their union rep when I was in the asylums, where would we have been now? Instead of slagging me off when I was pulling the asylum roofs off, you could've been up there with me, fighting for loonyology. You all shouted nasty things at me, which was very hurtful. But I was fighting for you, for us. I was your main voice. I was the white Martin Luther King, but I fought for all madmen, black or white, even Chinks and Japs. I stood up for you all!

There will always be an asylum. England! Fly the flag. Yippeeeeeeeeeee! Yahoooooooooo! March on, lads, with or without me. Loonyology can become worldwide! Send all donations to me. Trust me. Nothing under £50 or don't bother! I don't fuck about with peanuts. I need big bucks so I can sort our loonies out with all sorts. The mad women will get a blow-up doll off me! The gay lads will also get one. I'm not homophobic. The heteros will get a blow-up doll of Bonnie Parker, coz we love Bonnie. No disrespect to Clyde Barrow.

Yeh, I need the dosh to sort it all out. I need the votes. I need you. You need me. We need each other. This is family. Blood is thicker than vodka, but it's not as thick as treacle. Come on, wake up, I love you nutters, so start loving each other. Let's all laugh in the face of adversity. No more tears or depression, this is party time, with balloons and jelly and ice cream, and sawn-off shooters and axes. It's our fucking party, so we'll do what we want!

Broadmoor here we come to liberate. We salute you loons. Phew! I need a lie down. It's all got to me and I'm feeling very emotional. Just vote! And don't forget the dosh! No cheques; cash, registered post. Trust me.

Sadly, since starting *Loonyology*, some old friends are no longer in my fight. I've always moved on from people who see things that I don't see. I can't be false with people, so I just say "sweet" and move on. It's pointless having a corner man in a fight who has a different fight going on in his head. You just can't win. Like my old mate Tel Currie. He knows why I cut off and so do I, and that's all that matters. He believed in something that I didn't. We could never agree on it, so we moved it on to a new level. He's just not in my corner no more. It's my loss, but that's how it is and I wish him well. I'm not about to come out and blow his head off, but I won't be coming out to have a pint with him either. That's showbiz for you. But thanks for his input to *Loonyology*.

Take Harry Marsden too. To me Harry is a living fucking legend. I always said he was the Frank Frazer of the north. In fact he probably attacked more screws than Frank did over the years. Harry was a serious handful in the 1960s and '70s, and I mean a violent fucker. He was only a small man, but he had the heart of a lion. He was fearless, scared of nobody. In jails like Armley and Durham he was a gladiator! The same guy got out and turned his life around and made good. But we fell out over third parties causing shit. Harry won't back down and nor will I, so it affected the fight. He believes in his way, me in my way, so we moved on. It's sad when that happens; it's like losing a brother. But that's how life ends up, and a 30-year friendship can get sucked into oblivion over other people's shit.

Another example is my old pal big John Beeching. He knows who's poisoned our friendship, and only him and me need to know, We were solid brothers, but then became like leaves in a storm and it's gone. He blew one way, me another, again over third-party shit. That's life. It goes on, but it don't come back. My fight is the same fight - freedom! I'll only stop when I'm free, or dead! The whole world can blow me away, but I'll still go on alone, and win! Yep, that's the journey. I do hope you're enjoying this ride with me. I bet you're wondering what's next. Yeh, so am I!

Did you know a camel's tongue is 20 inches long? That's some fucking tongue. I bet your wives and girlfriends wish you had a tongue like that. It'd be like kissing a fucking chameleon. Yeh, I bet every woman would dream of a tongue like that!

Did you know there's a beetle in South America that eats animal droppings? Dirty little fucker - a shit eater. I'd like to get one of those man-eating dragon lizards and slip it into Huntley's cell. Imagine that - 3 a.m., he's fast asleep dreaming of little girls - gulp - problem solved. Easy.

Did you know that a sperm whale has a 14-pound brain? Well, did you? I know some people who haven't got a brain at all. Too many to mention, plus I don't want to give the brainless bastards a page in my book. Fuck of.

22 September 2007

I had a great visit today off Chris Cowlin - our first meet up. He's a top geezer and is Apex Publishing's main man. Without him there wouldn't be *Loonyology*. He and his colleagues believe in it and me. So I say a big cheer for Apex Publishing! Hip, hip, hooray! Hip, hip, hooray! Hip, hip, hooray! But I don't think Chris was too pleased with the visit situation. For him it was like a day out at London Zoo. Well, that's all it is - a cage. There can be no other word for my surroundings.

Hey, I must be getting slow - I only did 90 press-ups in 30 seconds. Old age is creeping in. But it still blew Chris away. Anyway, thanks mate for supporting me and having faith in *Loonyology*.

Can somebody tell me this: why should the devil have all the best fun, the sexiest women, the nicest clothes, the best food, the hippest parties, the fastest cars? You name it, he has it. What do the angels get? A cloud and a fucking harp. Can you really see me plucking a fucking harp? Can you? Give me a Harley any day or a fast car. I want some of the devil life, don't you? A fucking harp? Do me a favour.

Did you know there's a giant butterfly in South America called the Angel? I bet it don't play a harp though. Did you know at the bottom of the ocean there's a crater seven miles deep? Imagine what lurks down there: a new world of monsters in pitch black. So you don't see them but they see you. You just bump into a giant mouth and you're swallowed up. Just what could be down there? Don't it make you think? Seven fucking miles! The ocean is a world undiscovered. Let's go down and see ... who's coming? What a journey that would be, what an experience - a bit like my art. It makes your heart pump faster - brilliant. The unknown; the not knowing what's around that bend, what's next. Yippeeeee! That's living!

Danny Archer knew what was around the bend back in 2005. He got sentenced to life for murdering Nasra Ismail. He chopped her up, put body parts in a suitcase and dumped it in the Regents Canal in north London. Life for him will probably mean life, coz he's in his mid-50s now. But guess what? He's to marry his pen pal, Christine Travis. Hey, Christine, are you sane, or just out for a laugh? You can't possibly love a guy who cut up a girl like he did. How? They are to marry at max secure Full Sutton Jail. Choke on the cake, you pair of clowns. Who's the best man - Jack the Ripper? Who's the bridesmaid - Rose West? Poison the cake and let's get rid of the nutters. This sort of wedding ceremony gives loonyology a bad name. There'll be no pussy stroking or licking (not in Full Sutton) and all you're gonna drink is lemonade. Marriage? Do me a favour. Don't bother sending me a slice of cake, coz I'm not interested. I just hope it's laced with cyanide.

Talking about bridesmaids, Maureen Cameron, 92 years old, was bridesmaid to her great- granddaughter Jessica Preston. Surely that's a world record. How brilliant is that?! Good old Maureen, we love you! I do love a nice story. It brightens up the whole day.

Latest news flash, exclusive: The prison screws are to get a rise. Men and women will be issued with stilettos! (you get it from *Loonyology* first). I see Lew Yates has written a book on his 'Fight Game'. He calls himself the True Guv'nor. He seems to think he had the better of the fight he had with Roy Shaw 30 years back till it got stopped. He should think again. Roy's now 72; Yates is 62. I'd still back Roy to beat him today. Yeah, at 72. Roy's a winner, see. He don't know how to lose. Who's Yates? Who's Shaw? Every fucker knows who's who and who's done what.

Talking of jokes, Quasimodo is running down the street with a dozen kids chasing him, shouting and screaming at him. Quasimodo stops and shouts: "I've not got your fucking ball!"

24 September 2007

There was a TV drama on BBC 2 last night called *Stuart: A Life Backwards*, all about a drunk and druggie played by Tom Hardy. It was a powerful performance and I reckon Tom will get an award for it. *Stuart* is a true story. His life was so fucked up - society and prison let him down. When he was 11 years old he got put in a home, and even in there he was abused. The house master was shagging his arse.

It's a fucking disgrace what went on in those kids' homes in the 1960s and 1970s and, it seems, even today, coz I keep reading about it. It's out in a book too, so go and get a copy and open up your eyes. I guarantee you'll fill up and get a lump in your throat. Also you should write to the BBC2 producers to demand that they show it again and vote for Tom Hardy to get an award for best actor. He is fucking awesome. I've just called him up to say "You're the Guv'nor". Incidentally, I knew of Stuart Shorter before all this and his mother has my art tribute hanging up in her house.

Stuart ended his life by diving in front of a moving train, so I'll make it 200% clear now. All you mother fuckers in them homes and jails who abused Stuart, you cunts had better be able to live with the fact that your treatment, bullying and abuse actually pushed him to an early death. So how does that feel, you cowardly pieces of shit? Stuart may well have been a down-and-out, but he had a good soul and a good heart.

Let's have a cheer for our Stuart. Hip, hip, hooray! We salute you, son, and now you're free from all your pain. Good luck wherever you are and I'll put my arse on it not being hell.

I got a letter off Terry Turbo today. He's a top geezer. Who? Well, you'll probably know him as Terry Stone or Terry Pettit and if you don't know him now then you're not of this planet. Hey, this guy's got more fucking names than I have. You'll know him from *Eastenders* or *The Bill*. Got him now? He's just played Tony Tucker in *The Rise of the Foot Soldiers*. You must know him now. What are you lot, fucking mental? *Ten Dead Men*, *Rollin' with the Nines*, *Hell to Pay*: he's been in all these movies, and also *Baby Juice Express*, *One Man and His Dog*. Argh! Fuck it. I don't give a flying fuck if you know him or not. To me he's the dog's bollocks at films and, unlike most tough guy actors, Terry is tough; a real tough cookie. Not like them prats the Mitchell brothers in *Eastenders*. They make me laugh. Have you seen that little fat Phil Mitchell? He's about as tough as a packet of crisps. I swear I could do that fat fucker with both my arms tied behind my back. I'd nut him to Disneyland. There's tough guys and there's tough guys and, take it from me, 90% of those tough guy actors are pussies. They might look the part but that's all. Terry came up through the ranks and made good. I respect the guy. We all do. Respect to the fella. Nice of him not to forget me.

I had a good jog on the yard in the rain today. It was lovely and fresh and my skin felt alive. I probably ran about five miles and it felt good. I had a good shit before I went out. There's something about a shit - you always feel lighter, faster afterwards A good shit is still the best thing in the world. Always check your stools. I always do. I don't want to die, see, not yet. A good stool means a healthy body, and my stools are the best. I may even sell them on eBay. Why not? People will buy anything on eBay, so why not a good healthy stool? I'll get my agent onto that.

I was sad to hear that Marcel Marceau died over the weekend. He was the greatest ever mime master of all time. He was only 84 years old. I remember seeing him at the London Palladium as a boy. Even then I thought he was magical. He was a French Jew who survived the Holocaust. His father died in Auschwitz death camp. This guy was a legend and will never be forgotten.

What a guy. R.I.P.

I got my spin today - cell search and strip-off. They used a metal detector and spent a good hour searching my cell. They found fuck all. There's nothing to find, that's why. What do I need? Fuck all. Unless you've got a 30-foot ladder handy. It's all part and parcel of prison life. You get used to it after so many years, or do you?

I also got a letter off my old buddy Ifty today. He's a top chap.

The soup today was thick, like a stew, and tasted nice. I had some big lumps of meat in mine. Fuck the veggies, let 'em starve. What's that veg diet all about or, even worse, the vegan one? They walk about like stick insects and look like POWs in a Jap camp. What's it all about? Somebody tell me.

Did you know that on 13 April 1989 there was the first ever strike by court judges? Lock 'em up, I say. Disruptive old farts.

Did you know that the original prison at Bristol was built on a budget of £60,000? Try that today. Now it'd probably be more like 6 million bucks, if not more. But, then again, it was back in 1816, although £60,000 even then must've been like 60 million today. Fuck me, my head is starting to hurt.

Did you know that there was an old owl who sat on Parkhurst roof for years. I say 'was', as I accidentally hit it with a slate when I was up there. Unfortunately I took its fucking head clean off. Those prison slates are sharp.

In June 2003, Shrewsbury nick was the most overpopulated jail in England. It held 344 inmates and it should've held 183. Work it out. So where did they put them all? Some were three to a cell. Imagine that on a 'curry tea' day. Get me out of here!

Did you know that the cons in Garth Jail work on renovating wheelchairs? Yeh! Well done, lads. That's a worthwhile job, so respect to you. Who said cons are all bad?

In 1977 at Acklington Jail in Northumberland the prison chaplain booked a band to come in and do a show for the cons. It was a punk band called The Upstarts. They played 'Borstal Breakout' but changed the words to 'Acklington Breakout'. The chaplain was mysteriously transferred to Dartmoor four weeks later! I wonder why?

Did you know the most expensive fur in the world is that of a sea otter? And, speaking of fur, get on this. Richard Burton spent 52k on a mink sable coat for Liz Taylor in the 1960s - 52 grand in the '60s! Fuck me, that's a case of more money than sense. You could buy a house for 10 grand in them days, so that's five fucking houses. It's loonyology. It's all nuts to me. What about you?

Hey, and get on this for a mad one. Starfish. You know, them sea creatures with five arms. Did you know they can push their stomachs out of their mouths. How? Or maybe that should be why? Fuck knows - but they can.

The ancient Assyrians could swim for 20 minutes underwater by breathing from goat skins full of air. Now that to me is brilliant. Stuff like that just blows me away. Amazing. I hope you're taking this all in, coz there'll be questions later.

Did you know that more people are killed by accidents in the home than on our roads? And 95% of these accidents happen to old people over 65. It's truly scary. So be careful everyone, especially you old folks. Stop and think what you're doing.

I remember one old con in Parkhurst hospital wing in the 1970s who'd had a few strokes. I used to call him 'Lightning'. Talk about slow! It took him half an hour to walk from his cell to the recess. I often used to pick him up, run with him to get his water, and then run back with him. He loved it. He once said to me: "I wish I had a son like you." I used to get him lots of treats: books, mags, sweets. I just enjoy looking after people. He got life at the age of 50 for two shootings in the 1950s. He was a character was Lightning, a lovely old chap. If anybody fucked with him they fucked with me. So nobody fucked with him. Nobody was that mad - unless they wanted their throat ripping out. Not too many fancied that though. Would you?

25 September 2007

It's been a brilliant day today. Miller got bent up again. The riot mob went into him with shields and put him in the box where the monster belongs. I was shouting through the door, "Give the paedophile a kick in the nuts from me, sling him in the van and fuck him off. The unit would smell better without that cunt." Yeah, that made my day that did.

The screws told me that my son Mike will be up Saturday to see me. That's great news. We need to chat about his mental mother selling insane stories to the mags. I love my son. I owe him. He's what counts and - guess what? - he loves me too. But his mother is now a parasite in my eyes. That's how it has to be now. Fuck that. So many have sucked off my life, it's a wonder I've got anything left to suck off. Talking of sucking, I'm dying for a blow job. Hopefully soon. But who will give me my first one? Yeah, I bet you'd all love to know. Well fuck off, coz I'm saying nothing, and nor will she.

Have you ever wondered why you never see baby pigeons? Well, have you? I'll tell you why. Baby pigeons don't leave the nest till they're 35 days old and by then they're fully feathered and as big as their mother. I bet you never knew that. So next time you're in Trafalgar Square, check it out - there'll be no baby pigeons.

Tim Brady has just been nicked doing 172 mph in his Porsche 911 Turbo. This is the fastest ever speeder caught on our roads. 102 fucking mph over the limit - not bad, eh?! That's what you call moving. They jailed him for ten weeks and banned him for three years. I suppose he could always apply to be a pilot.

Did you know there are three types of frogs in the UK? The common frog, the edible frog and the marsh frog. Hey, and frogs have teeth, toads don't. And did you know every time they swallow they blink? All interesting stuff.

There was a loony in Ashworth Asylum who looked like a frog - big, protruding, bulging eyes. He looked like a reptile freak.

I said to him one day, "Hey, Froggy, have you ever had a shag?"

He said, "No."

"Have you ever had a blow job?"

"No."

"Have you ever been wanked off?"

"No."

"Fuck me ... Have you ever felt a pussy?"

"No."

Now how sad is that? He was in his forties. But, then again, what bird is gonna go near a fucking frog? There's a lot of lunatics like that who've never had a lover. Even gays would give him a wide birth. What gay bloke's gonna shag his frog-faced arse? I suppose it's sad really if you dwell on it. It's just a lonely, sad existence. Oh, and he was in for arson. He set fire to a bed and breakfast place and two people died. What can you say? The frog-faced loony was well fucked. Just another lost soul.

Hey, I've just had a crazy thought about Marcel Marceau. What would happen to the two-minute silence out of respect? How would that work with him? Two minutes of noise? Is that a blinder or what?! It just came to me. Oh well, I did try to make you smile. It's just a bit of good old British wit. In fact it's fucking magical. Even Marcel would've smiled at that.

I got a dozen letters today. One of them was from Susan May. She's another miscarriage of justice. She got lifed off over a murder she didn't commit. It's a sad old story. Although she's free now she still has to fight it. She spent years inside - all wasted. It's tougher for a woman, it really is. Anyway, she's free now and doing well and we are all proud of her. I woke up this morning dying for a piss - bursting. I'll have to cut down on my liquid intake. Have you ever had a piss where it goes on and on and on - a never-ending piss, like an elephant? Don't it feel good when it's over? Relief.

I also got a letter from Jillian Lofts, who sent me in a couple of photos of the Krays' grave and my plant pot on it with a card saying:

To Ron and Reg
Even though I can't be here in person I'd like to pay my respects to you both. I miss you
both very much. You were two great friends of mine. God Bless you both.
From Charlie Bronson (Mick Peterson)

At last they're both together - wherever they are. It was so nice of Jillian to sort it for me. I do respect such loyalty and kindness. I can't believe Ron's been gone for 12 years - so long ago. So much blood has been spilt since then, a lot of it mine too. In fact I don't think I've got any left; I'm on empty. I'll soon fill up when I'm back out, and then I'll pay my respects to the twins in person.

LOONYOLOGY

Well, it's not far from the end
Nothing lasts forever
It's like a candy floss
Blowing away in a storm
Nothing lasts forever
Nothing
One day the sky will fall in
Then we will all be the same
Crushed and broken
But Loonyology I hope has opened your eyes
Made you wonder
Are you mad or are you bad?
Are you happy or are you sad?
Who are you and where are you going?
Better still
Where the fuck have you been?
Or is it a secret
A skeleton in the closet?
Are you a midnight creeper
Two separate lives
One a husband and a father
The other a gay cottage queen?
Who knows
You could be the latest serial killer
Or jack the stripper
Fuck the ripper
Whoever you are
I've let you into my world
Into my darkest dreams
I hope you've enjoyed the ride
And your heart feels good
Loonyology will see you through
The madness is a blanket of comfort
A protector
Don't fight it, it's your best defence
Use it to your own benefit
It's kept me alive for all these years
It's made me shine
I'm alive and kicking
I'm gonna kick a hole through the door
I'm coming home
Back to some sanity and peace
A plate of fish and chips and mushy peas
Salt, vinegar, and Daddies Sauce

A loaf of fresh home-made bread
A large pot of tea
A china mug with a real spoon
A real knife and fork
A real table and chair
Freedom
Life's the ultimate challenge
We all have to do what we do best
To survive
So what are you gonna do?
How will you do it?
Loonyology

Hey, the next time you're nicked and in the police interview room and you're getting fed up of them silly questions, start shouting, "Stop! Don't hit me again! Stop! That hurts! Stop! Help!" They'll soon stop the interview. Remember it's all taped nowadays. You may get a slap back in the cell later, but the interview will soon be over. There's always a way to mess up the system. The system is a well-greased machine, but all machines break down. You only have to come up with the spanner to loosen a few bolts and nuts. If you're so determined to beat a wrap, burn your fingerprints off with acid. That'll fuck 'em. Act dumb if you're on a serious charge, say murder, and you're bang to rights. Is it not better to get a manslaughter charge on the grounds of diminished responsibility or coz you're too insane to stand trial? Would it not be better to spend 10 years in a cuckoo farm than 30 in jail?

Only you can decide that, but loonyology can come in handy in terms of legalities. It could save your arse. A madman is a patient, and patients are treated and cured. There's a big difference between murder and manslaughter, one hell of a big difference. The insane world always comes out on top: "Please, nurse, can I have some more apple pie?" Whereas the cons say: "Give me some more porridge, cunt."

I've lived in both environments and the mad world is exciting. Not that I like it, coz I fucking hate any locked door closing me in. But, at times, I do miss the loonies and all the laughs. Every day was Disneyland, but with a spot of violence creeping in. It keeps one alert.

I was on a visit one day in Ashworth Asylum when I clocked a loony sitting at a table with a very large woman visiting him. He had his dick out. Now this was one big, fat woman. I'm not being nasty, but she was grotesquely ugly and looked like a hippo on heat. She actually put me off my choc bars and milkshake. I said to my two pals visiting me: "Look at that over there." So there we were, the three of us, clocking them two and then - bang - it took off. She put her hand in her knickers. He was pulling himself off and she was fingering herself as they both looked into each other's eyes. It was fucking gruesome. Laurel and fucking Hardy. My pals couldn't believe it;

they were shocked. Me? I've seen it all before. But I must admit she was fucking ugly. But this is loonyology. It's brilliant.

There was a loon in Rampton who used to have a wank in the TV room in front of all the other loons. That was, until I arrived. He soon stopped it when I accidentally tripped up and spilt my mug of hot tea over him. You should've heard him scream.

Who remembers Gary Numan, the pop singer in the 1970s and '80s? He was strange. His music was so unusual it used to give me a fucking headache. Anyway, this nutter used to go mad every time his music came on the radio. He would strip off bollock naked and run around the ward with a big hard-on shouting, "Gary, Gary, Gary, Gary." Then 20 more nutters would all be shouting and screaming. We would all be laughing. I was fucking crying of laughter. This is loonyology at its best. It's brilliant. It's just pure madness. This nutter would do it in Tesco if he could. He really was in the right place. Could you imagine seeing that in your supermarket? What would you do if you saw that? Think about it. And this loon was a 6-footer, 18 stone and hung like a donkey. Imagine that running down the meat counter shouting, "Gary, Gary, Gary." Come on, what would you do? Now that's the question: "What would you do?" Believe me, you've not lived till you've seen and lived with such madness. It's fucking brilliant, it really is. Gary Numan has a lot to answer for. Whatever happened to him?

Yeah, I've seen it all, so when you see me with a smile or see me laughing you'll now I'm getting a flashback, a memory of madness. I'm happy inside myself, I really am.

"Hey, look at this," one loony shouted. Then he dropped his pants in the middle of the TV room, lit a match, held it to his bent over arse and farted. Whoosh! It was like a flame thrower. He got in a lot of trouble that day, coz loons aren't allowed matches. But it was so funny. It would've been even funnier if it'd blown back and burnt his balls off or burnt some other loon's face - or, better still, a screw. Now that would've been legendary.

I'll tell you something, until you've heard the screams of a burning cell and smelt the con's burning flesh you've never been to hell. That's hell come alive, believe me - unless it's a dirty nonce or a filthy grass, and then it's heaven. We all love a toasted wrong 'un.

I see the CPS is deciding whether to charge Robert Black with murdering 13-year-old Devon girl Genette Tate, whose body has never been found after almost 30 years. Black is a triple child killer serving natural life, and the scumbag is here. You can smell the bastard on a windy night. His evil stink travels through the prison corridors.

Hey, this place is truly hell on earth. What the fuck am I even doing here? Now do you understand why I'm in a sodding cage? How could I ever live in the same area as Black and Huntley and Cooke and the like. Could you? Would you? Should you have to? Black is a reptile on legs. He should be the one in the cage, not me. But what if he's charged with Genette's murder -

what then? Another life sentence? What's the point in that? The best thing that could happen here is for Black to be honest for once in his life and say if he did it and, if so, where he buried the body, so her poor parents can at least give her a humane and proper burial. That's the least he can do. But these sorts of scumbags get a kick out of being in control of it. Evil. Fucking torture the bastard. I'd soon find out where he put Genette and any more kids. Then I'd rip his eyes out so he'd live in darkness till the day he died.

Imagine a blind man in Monster Mansion, never knowing who's gonna jump him in the shower or canteen queue; never knowing who's behind his cell door with a home-made knife - some gay serial killer ready to shag his arse off and strangle him on ejaculation. Imagine that! That's what all these child sex killers deserve. Fuck their human rights. Let's get the truth out of them once and for all. Let the SAS have them for a week's interrogation. We'd soon know the truth then, wouldn't we?

26 September 2007

The Woodhill van arrived today, full of screws to take Travis back there. I was having a chat with three of the screws and they asked me if I'd like to go back there. I said, "I'd go to Mars if it meant me getting out."

I called up Mark Emmins today. He does me proud. He's a top buddy. We think the same. Once I'm out me and him will be millionaires in six months. He'll be on my roadshow. He's got a good biz brain. I've a lot of respect for the man. He don't just talk the talk, he walks it too.

I had egg, chips and beans tonight, with an extra bowl of beans. It'll be windy later.

That fat, scruffy cunt Miller moved back into his cell. Now if that'd been me - or any of the rest who got bent up and put in the box - we'd have been slung in the van and moved to a worse shithole. These governors just love a nonce. Why? If you know, tell me, coz I can't work it out.

I'm on a visit tomorrow. Cherri Gilham's up. We always have a laugh. No wonder Benny Hill had her on his *Hills Angels* show. She's just brilliant. Then on Saturday my son Mike's up. It'll be a great couple of days. I don't do bad here for visits.

I'm feeling lucky, I sense some luck on its way - just a feeling I've got. Let's hope it's my legal team. What an Xmas box that would be - more for my mother than me, and for my son. It's time we had a pint together. I'll sort his mum out a big four-foot wooden spoon so she can get on with her stirring. If I won 10 million on the lotto I wouldn't buy her a penny chew, and I'm the sort to win it. That would put it right up Prison HQ. How jealous would that lot be? Cunts. You see their faces when my movie comes out.

27 September 2007, The Sun
A woman was locked up and "lost" for 70 years after being wrongly accused of stealing 13p.
Jean Cambell, 85, was "certified" indefinitely in 1937 over claims she had taken the cash while cleaning at a doctor's surgery.
The money was found - but Jean still spent 70 years in a maze of care institutions.
She was "found" when brothers Alan, 66, and David, 63 - who thought she was dead - read a letter sent by a care home to their mother, who died 25 years ago.
David said: "I was about to throw it in the bin when I saw a name in the corner - Jean Cambell. I rang and they said our sister was there."
The two brothers travelled from their home in Liverpool to see Jean at the home in Macclesfield, Cheshire. Staff warned them she was deaf and may not remember them. David said: "We were very nervous. We wrote on a piece of card 'Hello Jean, we're your brothers'. But she took one look at us and said, 'Hello Alan, hello David' - and flung her arms around us."
He added: "Nowadays there are appeals - but back then a doctor could sign away a life with the stroke of a pen. They basically locked her up and threw away the key and she was stuck in the system. She just got moved from one institution to another. What a waste of a poor girl's life."
Jean had a stroke after meeting her brothers, believed to have been sparked by the shock of the reunion. She is said to be recovering.

If that story don't put a lump in your throat then nothing will. It's tragic and it brings back a lot of sad memories for me of my time in the asylums. There were hundreds like Jean who'd been forgotten. Hundreds. Victims of a shit system; a cruel, nasty, evil government that stood back and allowed it to happen. Jean had her life stolen from her, and for what? Thirteen fucking pence. Her life has been institutions.

What a fucking despicable, evil planet this really is. Now can you understand why I tore off the roofs and fought this shithole of a system? Now can you understand loonyology? Now can you understand how upset I get? This just puts it all into perspective. Locked away for 70 years. Jean Cambell is a product of the system. And that 13 pence was found; she never even stole it. She was a child and this country stepped on her life. It's shameful. If that was my sister I'd go to war. There'd be murders over this. Hang your heads in shame, you dogs. The doctors, the social workers, the guards, the governors, the MPs. Look in the mirror, you cunts, and let's find out how many more Jeans are still locked away in secret. This is Britain not Russia or China. Now see what I've been battling against for all these years. JUSTICE!

This could well be my next project 'The Lost Souls'. Watch this space. I've got a lot of research to do, but someone's got to expose it, so why not me? I'm gonna have to get out quick so I can get hold of the documents. Can you see this lot letting me research this for a project? Yeah - look at that pig flying!

I see the Sex Pistols are back: 17 November 2007, Manchester Men Arena, 30th Anniversary 'Never Mind the Bollocks' tour. Yippeee! They're the fucking bollocks, believe it. 'God Save the Queen'? The Pistols are back! Yiiippppeeee!

29 September 2007

Cuntly ... ooops sorry ... Huntley tried again yesterday to top himself - or did he? Today I was chatting to a screw, who will remain nameless coz he's a half decent screw who gives me the rundown on what's going on. Well Huntley apparently took an overdose 'again' - third time now. But before he took it he called his family. He knows calls are listened to by security, even more so with him being high profile. It's the same with my calls, and often mine are cut off - for obvious reasons. Anyway, he makes the call and then tells a screw: "Sir, I've taken an overdose." Then he's rushed to Wakefield Hospital to be pumped out and then driven back. It's all in the papers today and on the radio.

Now is the cunt having a laugh or what? Why phone? Why tell a screw? This is just a case of pure attention seeking and he's first class at that. Poor little me, or should I say poor fat me, coz he's now a fat cunt that stuffs himself with sweets and chocs and cakes and don't work it off. He's got three chins now and a fuck of a belly.

Huntley is a total joke and it's time the prison bosses stopped bending over for him. He's a nonce child killer and all he's had since the day he came away is a soft ride. Put the fat nonce in a cage like me so he's isolated. Close his visits. Give him liquid medicines, not tablets. That way he can't save the pills up. It don't take Einstein to work it out. If you say: well, what about his human rights? Well, what about mine? Why can't I mix or be in a proper cell or have a real job? Where's my fucking rights?

All Cuntly ever does is abuse his human rights. The screw also told me it probably cost the taxpayer five grand yesterday just to rush him to hospital. You lot out there paid for it, you mugs. This cunt is laughing at you all. He's bang on the front page again. No doubt someone is selling their exclusives. If I was Huntley's parents I would disown him. Wake up, Mr and Mrs Huntley, your son is a filthy double child killer who can't even top himself coz he's a spineless prick. You gave birth to a born coward.

All the screws here despise the fucker, and all the cons hate him. Even other nonces hate him coz he actually believes he's a celebrity, someone special. And it's all the governor's and HQ's fault for spoiling the toerag. Give him some of what I've had. Then let's see the real rat grovel. Then we may see him top himself. I say double him up with Maudsley for the night or let Fred Lowe work on him with a chainsaw. In fact I could do with a punchbag.

Huntley, wake up and smell the shit. You're full of it. Oh, and he left a silly suicide note full of self-pity and blaming everyone but himself. Now the muggy psychologists will be giving him some sweet and tender loving. Poor thing. Tell us about it. It makes me feel fucking sick

Hey, did you know the lacrimal glands are where our tears come from? Can you cry for Cuntly? I wonder.

Have you ever heard of Arthur's Seat? Well, it's an extinct volcano that overlooks Edinburgh city. A fucking volcano?! Come on, how many of you knew that?

Lobscouse. Do you know what that is? Come on, do you? It's Liverpool stew, a favourite Scouse dish.

You stick with me and you may learn things you'd would believe.

Cuntly, fuck off and give us all a rest as you're boring us now.

Oh, get on this. As he was being wheeled out to the van waiting to take him to hospital yesterday the entire nick were shouting out of their cell windows: "Die, you bastard." Sadly over here in the seg unit we're cut off. But what does that tell you? Everybody hates the coward. Even Howard Shipman done a good job of his suicide. It says it all. Now fuck off, Huntley.

Did I ever tell you the time in Risley 1969 when I stopped a hanging? Yeah me! I was in a large cell containing eight of us. We were all cleaners, all young tearaways. We didn't give a fuck about ourselves or anyone else.

There's a lot of bullying on a YP wing, all trying to be the Daddy. Then the screws don't help by bullying us. It's just a violent existence of dog eat dog. I was 17 years old, but an old 17. I've always been old for my time as I associate with older friends. Anyway, this Jock in our dormitory was Mr Big Mouth. He wanted it all his way or no way and he started on the new lad who was very timid and scared.

Next thing we were all having a kangaroo court on the lad and it got out of hand when Jock started ripping up a sheet to make a noose. Even I was getting edgy. It was just getting madder and madder.

"That's it. Enough!" I shouted. "Fucking grow up!"

Then I said to Mr Big Mouth, "If you want to top someone, do it to a screw in the morning, you Scotch cunt."

He replied, "Why don't you?"

I said, "Because I don't want to top anyone … yet."

"What do you mean 'yet'?" he asked.

I said, "Well, if I get the urge to, I'll fucking take you out when you're asleep."

That was it, it kicked off. I must admit he put up a good fight but I really busted him up big time. We both ended up in the punishment block. But I did save that lad, coz if we'd all been weak we could've all topped that lad easily.

That's how things can blow up in a jail, and more so as a YP. And, believe me, the screws wouldn't lose any sleep over it either. They love it coz they're sadistic fuckers. Who says so? Well, ask Jim Dawkins for one. Why do you think he threw his keys in? Coz he's not a coward.

Letter written to me on 17 September 2007 from my ex-wife Irene (after her magazine interview):

Dear Charlie,

Thanks for your card. I told Mike I couldn't face visiting you in prison, I just couldn't. I went to see Mike when he was in all those years ago and I vowed I would never visit anyone in prison again. Mike said you should be out next year, which I'm really pleased about, because you deserve to be out and living a normal life. I'm dead glad that you'll take Mike with you when you come out because he does need you, he's missed you so much, it would be great if you could open that prison themed restaurant you spoke about. Mike is a fantastic chef he really is. It would really take off, you'd make a fortune.

So when you come out we can have a nice chat.

I hope your campaign goes okay and that you do definitely come out. I would love you and Mike to be together, he's so like you, you know.

I haven't seen much of him lately. I think he's got a new girlfriend and he's been staying with her in her house.

Well take car, look to the future and stay strong.

Love Irene x

She's either lost the plot or she's forgotten she did the mag story. Whatever. It's for all to see what a two-faced, lying, cheating bitch she really is - all for 500 poxy quid. And the truth is: do I really need this crap? Does it help me get out? Does it fuck. Mike's my son. She's just a traitor. She can go on *Trisha* and sell her story, but she can't come and tell me to my face. In a nutshell - go suck a lemon.

To all journalists: next time you even think of doing a story with this nutcase, remember this story and letter and then decide, coz it could well be libel. Her letter has exposed her as a liar, all for 500 quid. Sad, sad bitch.

This guy Mark Cook must be the unluckiest fella alive, or lucky to still be alive. He's had two motorbike crashes, fell off a pier into the sea, survived a lorry crushing his car, and fell 25 feet down a lift shaft, landing two inches away from a two-foot spike. Is he lucky or unlucky?

The Indian Lizard man Mukesh Thkore eats 25 live lizards for breakfast. Can you fucking believe it? It's fucking loonyology at its best.

Who remembers The Shadows - Cliff Richard's band in the 1960s? The drummer Tony Meehan died recently. He was only 62. A nice chap.

30 September 2007
PETS FOR JAILBIRDS, The People
Cats and dogs for lags in bid to stop suicide behind bars
Prisoners are being lined up to keep pets to cut down on suicides behind bars. Watchdogs reckon looking after cats, dogs and other pets will stop depressed cons killing themselves at the rate of two a week. Prisons and Probation Ombudsman Stephen Shaw said: "It is not just relationships with other human beings that are fractured when you go to jail. The intensity of our attachment to animals can

mean losing touch with them is almost as hurtful as losing touch with family." He adds in next month's issue of prisoners' mag, Inside Time: "Having a pet to look after and train has a genuinely therapeutic effect." Some long-term cons are allowed to keep birds, like Burt Lancaster in the 1962 movie Birdman Of Alcatraz." Mr Shaw, who investigates prison deaths, cites pet projects working in US jails. He added: "America claims remarkable results for a programme linking problem youths with problem dogs." Mr Shaw says studies show pets for prisoners "reduced violence, drug abuse and even suicide". Maureen Hennis, chief of charity Pets as Therapy, added: "The benefits animals can bring are huge. Just stroking a dog in prison would bring down stress levels and reduce the suicide rate." But Norman Bernnan of the Victims of Crime Trust blasted: "This is nonsense. When people go to prison they forfeit rights and having cats and dogs makes a mockery of the whole system."

I'll have a horse, please, so I can ride it around the exercise yard. Thank you, Governor!

I see former professional tennis star Chris Turner has just copped seven years for a heroin racket. He admitted at Nottingham Crown Court to possessing 5kg of heroin. Such is life. If you play with fire, you get burnt.

Here's a blinder! Burglar Jamie Lacey entered a house in Brisbane and got caught playing with a sex toy. He left his DNA on the toy and got nicked two years later, copping 12 months' community service. How fucking insane is that? Pervo or what? Fancy going on a job with this prat! While you're doing the safe, he'd be having a wank in the knicker drawer. It beggars belief!

Hey, did you know that the Chuckle Brothers have been doing their act for 25 years? Do you think they're funny? I think they're about as funny as getting your cock caught up in your zipper.

Get on this. In 2001 at Usk Prison a 32-stone pig attacked a screw and two cons jumped in and saved him. The prison farm where they worked rewarded them by releasing them a month before their time. Fuck me, the things cons will do to get out! Some screws need attacking by a 32-stone pig.

Did you know that a full-grown elephant drinks 50 gallons of water a day and the trunk can suck up 1½ gallons at a time? Some parts of their skin are an inch thick, but it can still feel a fly land on it. They're amazing animals, but don't fuck about with them, coz you definitely don't want to upset an elephant! In fact, that goes for me too. Don't fuck with us!

I'll tell you what's magical - little six-year-old Archie Gray from Salisbury. He's a black belt in Taekwondo, which he's been doing since he was three years old. That to me is brilliant. Only six years old - wow! What a kid and what an achievement! I bet his mum and dad are so proud! Well done, Archie, you're the gov'nor!

I see Anne Robinson, the 'black widow' of *The Weakest Link*, is getting divorced. Who says it don't pay to be mean and nasty? This is a £60 million divorce! That's a lot of dosh - sacks loads!

Student Sam Wakeling has just smashed the world record on a unicycle. She rode around a track in Aberystwyth for 24 hours and travelled 282 miles. I bet someone had a sore arse! Not bad though, is it, 282 miles on a fucking unicycle? Some lazy fuckers couldn't do that on a real bike. Well done, Sam! You're a world champ now! 'Respect'. And you did it in my mum's birth town. So congratulations.

Did you know that in the last 12 months 113,445 old age pensioners have gone bankrupt coz they've been taking out loans to pay off bills? What sort of fucking shithole country are we running here when we can't even look after the old folk who won the war for us? We won the war? Did we?

East Sussex, Beachy Head cliffs. I'm sure you all know the place or have heard of it. It's where the suicidal people jump off! Well, since 1965 500 have dived off and 500 have died - 500 in 42 years! That's a lot of people. How sad is that? Why do they do it? What makes them do it? Could you see yourself doing that? Or were some pushed?! I wonder! If you're feeling depressed, stay clear of Beachy Head cliffs. Do yourself a favour. Have a cup of tea and a slice of cake and go to bed for a nice warm kip. Don't be silly. Life's too short to jump off a cliff, especially if the tide's out ...

I've just heard Miss Moneypenny's dead! The lovely Lois Maxwell. She made it to 80 years of age! Lois was in 14 James Bond movies, and a right hot cookie she was too. She was in the first Bond movie, *Dr No*, in 1962 with Sean Connery. Let's face it, Sean was the best Bond ever. Did you know that all the bond movies have grossed over 2 billion quid? Two fucking billion! Anyway, Lois Maxwell has gone, and I'd like to say we all loved you, Miss Moneypenny. God bless your soul. R.I.P.

Hey, here's a funny thing. In World War II all the poisonous snakes in London Zoo were put down. Why? Well it's obvious, isn't it? In case the zoo got bombed and the snakes escaped. We had enough slippery, poisonous fuckers to take care of with the Germans. Sad though eh? Still, that's war for you - no one is safe!

I knew a fella in east London who kept reptiles: pythons, boas and them ugly-looking lizards with big, stupid eyes. I always felt itchy when I went round his drum, coz they were crawling all over the place. One snake was 18 foot long. He used to get rabbits and mice from the pet shop and let them loose in the flat. What a fucking dive that was. But this guy was a top armed robber in his day. He just got off on watching his snakes kill and swallow them rabbits and mice. It was fucking mental! He would sit there supping cans of beer, puffing on his fag, and be in a trance watching it all go on around him. It freaks me out! But that's life. We're all mad in our own way. He was just a bit madder! But he was an excellent blagger - fearless. I often wonder what happened to him and his reptiles. He'll remain nameless, simply as he was one of my best partners. I bet he let them slide into the sewers. You'll be amazed at what's been let loose down the London sewers -

even crocodiles, and they grow fast. Fuck going down there! There's stuff down them tunnels of shit you really don't want to know, believe me!

I hear on the grapevine that Ian Tucker has just copped a 6½ year stretch for possession of a loaded gun. He's a good pal of Dave Courtney. From what I hear, it's a right fucking liberty as some prat put it in his garage and never told him, so he didn't even know the gun was there! There were no prints on it, fuck all. I hope he's slammed an appeal in! He should win that. But it's the same old story. If your face don't fit, then you're guilty. If the Old Bill want you bad enough they'll plant the gun themselves. With a bit of form what chance have you got? That's my one big fear in life - getting fitted up for something I've not done. Can you imagine me in jail doing 30 years for a crime I didn't do? Every fucking day they'd have to pick me up and carry me behind the door. How the fuck can any sane man accept it? It's gotta be your worst ever nightmare! Well, apart from me and Dave Courtney chasing you down an alley with chainsaws - now that would soil your pants!

I'll tell you who's a lucky bleeder - Luigi Petroni, the skydiver. He jumps out at 2,000 feet, both his parachutes fail to open, he's dropping fast and he's fucked. This is in a place called Medulin in Croatia. Crash! Thud! Bang! He's out cold. He awakens in hospital - alive, no injuries. Can you believe that? He survived 2,000 feet! Phew! Amazing! It's fuckinmentalphobic if you ask me. We salute you, Luigi. You're the man!

Yareeee! Yahoooo! Yippeeeee! Yeeooowweeeee! Fuck me, I've just had a book sent to me from Tom Hardy - *Stuart: A Life Backwards* by Alexander Masters! Remember the BBC2 programme I was telling you about earlier? I'm off for a read! I'll be back ... maybe. If not, then I doubt you lot will miss me! Then again, I won't miss you either!

CHAPTER 16
MUGGED UP AND SCREWED DOWN ... OR VICE VERSA!

Hey, did I tell you about the day I nicked a snake from a pet shop and pushed it into a postbox? I often wonder what the postman did or whether the snake managed to get out. That was 40 fucking years ago and I still wonder about the outcome. Better still, I still wonder why. Why do we as kids do these mad things? For what reason or purpose? It's just fucking mental, senseless, but we do it. Who can remember that first sweet you nicked from the sweet counter? I can, can you? That first ever sweet. I bet we all did it, or attempted to at least. Some got caught, some lost their bottle and others progressed to bigger things, but that first sweet was the ultimate test. And have you noticed they taste better when they're nicked, free? You nicked it, you took the chance and you won. It's that simple. Well, let me tell you, that buzz of adrenalin never goes away, whether it's a sweet or a Rolex watch or a 50k sack of loot. It never disappears; it's there till the day you die. It just becomes more dangerous and leads to greater consequences if you're nicked. Age can become the burden. It all ends up a gamble on life and death. My buzz has dried up; it's all over for me. Fuck the sweet, fuck the Rolex, and give me freedom any day. Nothing's worth all this shit, believe me. Nothing. But it was good once. I did love a sweet. I had sackfuls.

If it wasn't for grasses half of us would never have ended up in a police cell or in front of the judge. As a kid it's a truly frightening experience, and it was especially so in the 1950s and '60s. It was very regimented and disciplined in that era - the stiff upper lip mob. They all believed in punishment, and strict punishment at that. The 'don't fuck with us' firm will teach you pricks a lesson. Yeah, sure. To me they were a bunch of bullies, fucking idiots. Every clout around the head, every kick in the nuts, I never forgot any of them. And when I came back at them they never forgot either, God be my witness. But it was fun to be in that era. It was like a game of ping pong. Some you win, some you lose.

Hey, did you know a Korean table tennis player died when the ball hit him on the temple? A fucking ping pong silly ball took him out! Can you believe that? It just goes to prove that ANYTHING can kill you. Anything and anybody. You can drown in a tablespoon of water. Anything's possible. Don't doubt nothing. Keep an open mind.

I remember once on Wandsworth yard I watched a con - a grass - get his throat cut. Dozens of us knew it was going down, it was just who got the short straw. Grasses just were not acceptable in the '60s and '70s. Now the jails are full of the cunts! Grasses fell and we just stepped over them as if they weren't there. To us they were bags of shit.

In 1974 up in Walton - now that was a tough jail that stood no shit with grasses or nonces - there wasn't a week went by that one wasn't served up in the bathhouse or found in the recess. It was brilliant. We sniffed them out like bloodhounds and then ripped them up like bits of meat. Jails had no gyms in those days! The old local jails had fuck all. It was all bang up. So we were full of energy and tension and ready to explode. It was just a violent era. It was all part of the journey!

It don't matter who or what you are or what life you lead, you will one day get mugged off big time. We all get it - some on a big scale, some on a small scale - and there's fuck all you can do about it unless you take the law into your own hands. Unfortunately, for men like me who are shut away and who are in the news, we're a magnet for the cranks who want to ride the limelight, and the story you're about to read comes no madder.

Tracey Pearce, a married woman with two sons and two dogs, came into my life out of the blue. She lived in a nice house in Hemel Hempstead and was just a normal nice lady - or so it seemed. She wrote to me, although I didn't actually know her. This was maybe back around 2000 time. Then the visits started up. Her letters also hotted up. She wanted to suck my cock and do naughty things to me. No problem, I can handle that. But what I can't handle are the lies, and her lies caused me a lot of shit. So be warned now, this is what can escape from a mysterious woman: hell. Tracey organised my wedding day to Saira - well, we both sorted it out - and if I say so myself we did a good job. So for that she done both me and herself proud. Then it started to go funny. She became obsessed with me. This was at a time when I was up against the system, which was fucking about with my visits and playing silly games. I needed support and trust, not a mentalist woman obsessed with getting my cock in her fat face. I devised a plan, a simple plan, but it turned into a fucking nightmare. My visits at this time were behind my cage cell door, so visitors would sit outside the door as if it were a zoo visit. It was inhuman. So I made it clear: let's expose it. And the best way to do that would be a photo of the cage. I thought, let the British public decide if this is normal. I was the only con in the UK to have visits like this.

So that was the plan: smuggle a small camera in and get it done proper. A coat, a buttonhole, hand in pocket, click, click, click, sorted. I even had a 10k deal with a Sunday paper for three photos of my caged visit. Tracey jumped at the idea, so that was it; deal done and sorted. I arranged for her to come with my Loraine and Andy, which I felt would make it easier for her as they would provide the necessary cover. So that was it - easy. On the day of the visit it went down as planned and worked a treat. Tracey stood close to the cage door with her hand inside the jacket pocket clicking away and I was looking through the bars and grille at a buttonhole. Magic. The easiest 10k ever, plus the best way to expose the system. I must also add that at this time I had recently been smashed up in another jail and moved there to the cage to get isolated. I was covered in cuts and bruises, so the photos would also show the brutality. Two birds with one stone, as they say. Job's a good 'un. I must make this 201% clear now: Loraine and Andy knew nothing about any camera at that point; they only found out later. So we had a nice chat, visit over, all sorted - well, so I thought. However, the shit was about to hit the fan, big style.

I was mysteriously moved to Whitemoor seg block, but managed to get a call out to Tracey. All seemed sweet. She told me the snaps had come out perfect and would be in the paper soon. I told her to give my mother a couple of grand and save the rest for a rainy day. Two weeks passed. Nothing. Three weeks. Nothing. Even the paper was confused. After four weeks I called again. Then the bombshell.

"Sorry, Chaz. I just pretended to do it."

"What?!"

"I didn't do it. I pretended."

"There was no camera?"

"Sorry, Chaz."

Next thing she wrote to me in detail about the whys and hows, etc. Obviously that letter was photocopied by security and put on my file. Every fucker knew. It mugged me off most of all to the papers. I was the mug. I had been mugged. But why? Well, it's like this. Some people want to mix it and act it, but it's a front. They're just actors, pretenders. Tracey Pearce wanted to do it. She asked to do it because she wanted to help a man in a hole and to expose what was going on. But when it came to it, she couldn't do it. Now that's okay, but come clean and say so. If she'd said, "Look, Charlie, I can't do it," I could've lived with that. I'd had someone else in mind to do it, but she'd insisted: "Let me do it, Chaz. Please, please let me do it. It's easy."

So who's been mugged off on a scale like that? Who could've foreseen that coming? I let the mad loony into my life, into my family, into my circle of friends, all to be mugged off. It really does rip your heart out. Imagine how I felt; try to picture it. It smashed me up. I must confess now, if she'd been a he, it would've resulted in a midnight visit and being taken away for some serious teeth extractions. Believe it. What saved her from that fate was the fact that she was a mother. I had to put some sanity into the problem. Basically, she's a fat, ugly, lying bitch who wormed her way into the life of an infamous prisoner, feeling that it would inject some excitement into her boring mental life. And, no, she never did get to suck or caress my cock. And, to top it all, five years later her eldest son got lifed off for murdering a kid. So the evil must run in the family. Now she can visit her monster son for 30 fucked-up years and live the life of a prison visitor.

So there you have it. Even Charlie Bronson gets mugged off. But shit like this only makes me stronger. It's better to find out the truth quickly than to live in cuckoo land forever. To me a lie is a lie and friends don't need to do that. There are enough lying bastards inside without more outside. Let's hope Tracey Pearce chokes on a big fat cock and her child killer son tops himself. It would be a better world.

Like in any occupation, you get the good and the bad and the out and out cunt of a toerag. Take a dentist. I've had some brilliant ones, but some were made like butchers. Well criminals are no different. Unfortunately some give us a bad name, the same as a dentist. Three bad dentists don't make 300 others bad. Get my drift? Believe it or not, a lot of villains are a very decent lot. You could take them home to meet your granny and they wouldn't smash in her back door and raid her jewel box. They live by morals. Just don't fuck about with their feelings or you could end up with a big hole in the head. Would you play Monopoly with a polar bear? Or go swimming with a white shark? Would you fuck. So don't fuck with the unknown.

Talking of the unknown. It's time everybody got to know Bradley Allardyce. Who? Yeah, I'll tell you who. This long, skinny streak of piss, that's who. This is the lowlife cunt who sold Reg Kray out on his deathbed and you're all gonna know it, as it's time to lay the cards on the table for all to see.

Reg met this faggot in jail and helped him a lot, although everybody knew what he was: a fucking smack head, a total fucking prick. He would do anything for a bag of shit. All Reg did was help the cunt out with his debts. If it weren't for the Kray name, Allardyce would be full of holes as he owes half the jail. Some of the old faces warned Reg: "Don't have it with that mug, he's nothing but trouble." Anyway, I'll cut a long story short, coz it still winds me up even thinking about it all. Do you all remember the photo of Reg on his deathbed with all the tubes coming out of his body? Well, that was down to Allardyce. He took those photos without anybody knowing and then sold them to the press. He sold Reg Kray out. He wasn't content with sucking him dry when he was alive, he wanted the air out of the dying man's lungs. And, to top it all, our old friend and lifelong friend to the Krays, Wilf Pine, was blamed for that photo. Can you believe this shit? Wilf Pine is one of the most loyal men on earth and he'd stood by the twins from day one. Then a skinny fucking smack head slips in and causes all this shit on a man's deathbed. So, with Reg buried and gone, life goes on and Allardyce is back to being a nobody the moment the dirt hits the coffin, but he's not forgotten. Down an alley late one night there would be many who would enjoy disfiguring his boat or ripping his throat out. But that's wishful thinking.

Next thing - bosh! He was nicked over a street mugging and murder and lifed off. He's not even a Cat A, he's a Cat B and went straight to Swaleside. Now who's more of a danger to the public, me or him? He's the smack head and killer and he's in a Cat B. So why the fuck am I still in a Cat A unit? It's total fucking bollocks to me. Anyway, this Allardyce is now giving it large as if he's one of 'the Firm' and gullible cons swallow it. Well, take it from me, he's a total cunt. And he's the one cunt that I truly hope gets fucked up good and proper. Next thing he'll be writing a Kray book. He even sold some stories that he was Reggie's jail lover. We all read it in disbelief. What else will this slimeball do for dosh? Has he got no morals at all? I'll have a copy of this book sent to him. Let's hope it hits a nerve and the cunt does the decent thing. Top yourself, you cunt. You may have had Reg over but you don't have us over. You're a murdering, faceless, gutless, spineless, 6 foot 3 inch, skinny, smack-headed sleazeball. Hey, that's a good title for your book. All you gotta do now is pretend to find Jesus, lick some arse, clean some boots and get early parole - should be a piece of cake for you. But, you'll always have to look in the mirror to see what you really are and how you disgraced Wilf Pine. You couldn't even clean Wilf's shoes. We all fucking spit on you. Wouldn't it be funny if I ended up on Cat B in your jail and I was in the next cell to you. What then, Allardyce? What do you do then? Come at me with some of your muggy mates? You've never been up against a man like me. I truly am your worst ever nightmare. I only come alive when it's ten coming at me. You could rush me with a mob all tooled up and I swear I'd damage most of you. My inner madness comes alive. That's how I survive; how I've lived for all my life. The danger zone is my sweetest heaven. The more I'm stabbed the more you bleed. I'm the only guy like it. I can't be killed off.

I remember walking down a subway in cold, wet and cloudy Luton at 3 o'clock one morning and eight muppets were coming towards me. I took my shirt off and ran at the cunts. They all legged it. That's the story of my life. I don't need a tool. I am the fucking tool and cunts like you only find out when the shadow disappears. You're a lifer now. You're in the web. Reggie Kray had 32 years of it and survived. You're probably on your knees now sucking someone's dick. Cunt.

Another Kray parasite is the one and only Steve Wraith, a total and utter joke, now a big name up north. Let me put it right. Wraith was a young lad collecting autographs. He managed to get the Krays' and that was his nest egg. So he wormed in over the years. I must add that he actually did visit the Krays and in later years put a few bob their way, so he's not all bad. But as soon as they're both dead, what does he do? He starts sucking (selling them out). He even taped Reg Kray's phone messages and sold them. He even sold the funeral service brochure. That fucking eBay has a lot to answer for: people are selling their souls on it. Wraith is now an established biz man up north. But he's not a villain. He don't have our code of honour. He don't know how we work. He wouldn't have the bottle to go on a bit of work. He made it to the top by acting and selling out the Krays. My best mate Tel Currie gave him a well-deserved right hook at a boxing show and Tel was seen as the bad guy. Wraith is now surrounded by guys who seem to think he is a true villain. The Gangster Myth.

Hey, I've been around for ever, I've done it all and even I'm not in that league. I'm not a gangster. Come to think of it, I don't want to be. Wraith's a fucking actor, a good actor at that, and he's a cunt in my book. The whole world's gone acting mad. Where are all the real villains? Come out and save us from this madness.

Talking of real men, I called Dave Courtney recently and Freddie Foreman was with him. So I had a couple of minutes' chat with Fred - our first contact in almost 20 years. It made my fucking year. Yes I get calls - they stick the phone under my cage door. It's like my office phone. Obviously it's all taped and monitored. Fuck me, I have to pay for it out of my canteen, so I don't make that many. A call to me is worth five Mars Bars and, as much as I love Fred and Dave, I love a Mars better. It helps me work, rest and play. All these new choccie bars can't touch a Mars. It's still the best. A Snickers comes a good second, but only coz of the nuts in it - protein. I call my mother as often as I can. She's always worth half a Mars to me. I just like her to know I'm alive and well. Not that she worries anymore, as she knows I'm a chilled-out guy now. Yeh, always remember that not everybody is all they make out. And sadly you may not find out till it's too late. It can and often does cost a life or 30 years stuffed up your arsehole. It fucking hurts.

While on the subject of the Krays, I remember once in Parkhurst hospital wing we all used to have association up in a big room above F3 landing. Them days in Parkhurst our association was for three hours from 6 p.m. till 9 p.m. There'd be a dozen or so of us, including the Kray twins, Colin Robinson, Nobby Clarke, Ray Gilbert, Johnny Heibner, Biffo and Chilly-Cubby. We could watch TV, play cards or just sit around and chat. The screws used to drop us out, as they're always a bit weary when there's a few cons out at the same time. They're only brave when its ten onto one. I noticed that Ronnie was missing, so I went into the recess to see if he was there. And there he was, puffing a roll-up and looking at the sky through the bars. He was in a dream state, deep in thought.

I said, "You okay, Ron?"

He turned and said, "Look at those beautiful stars. Look. Nobody can tell me there's not another life up there."

I said to Ron, "Yeah, you're spot on."

He was a deep man, a very thoughtful man, but he could change in an instant. Nobody messed with Ronnie Kray. He chinned a screw one day because he coughed near him. He hated germs. He hated ignorant people and he despised a nonce. He attacked a rapist once in the recess. He just kept on punching him, busting his body up till he was broken up inside. It was Ron's way of escaping his own depression. But no man can escape himself, and Ron finally lost his way and went insane.

I was in Broadmoor when the twins' mother died. She was buried on 11 August 1982 at the family plot in Chingford Mount Cemetery. That was it for Ronnie. I honestly believe that he died with her. No doubt you'll all remember the twins being at their mum's funeral. Broadmoor and Parkhurst made sure that their biggest screws were cuffed up to them so as to make them look small. They always do that. It seems to be the system's way to belittle the cons. The screw who was cuffed to Ron was big Roger Russell, who's a good 6 feet 8 inches tall. He was a charge nurse at Broadmoor. He was, in fact, a good professional footballer in his day. He looked very embarrassed that day at the funeral, coz it's not his game to belittle anybody, let alone Ron Kray. But that's how it is and how it will always be. I still miss Ron and he's been gone for 12 years now. They're all in the family plot, lying together - free at last.

I remember once Ron gave a cleaner a watch as a gift and the cunt tried to sell it for tobacco. I chinned him, took the watch and gave it back to Ron. Ron said, "Fuck off. You have it." That's how he was - crazy. Ron idolised Joe Louis and Rocky Marciano. They were his ultimate fighters. Every time they flew to the UK the twins laid on limos and hotels for them. They even got Joe Louis to go to Broadmoor to see Roy Shaw. That's how it was in the 1960s: everybody looked after their own and respect was the game. You either lived by a strong loyal code or you got your legs crippled. It's as simple as that.

The Kray brothers only ever fought altogether once on the same fight bill, which was at the Royal Albert Hall on 11 December 1951. And guess what? They all won. Like I keep saying, they were all winners, born fighters. Charlie, Ronnie and Reggie were true old school, men of honour - and anyone who says different, come and see me later!

Ron Johnson, an old buddy of mine, was on the same bill too. Believe me, all the class fighters come out of Bethnal Green, and some good blaggers too. It's no joke that E1 London just bred good fighters and good armed robbers. It's a fact of life. Luton don't do bad either!

Did I ever tell you the time I cracked up a governor in Wandsworth and said, "You're under arrest."

"What?!" he said, in shock.

"You're under arrest."

"What the fuck are you on about?"

"I'm making a citizen's arrest and you're nicked."

He went on to say something else and I just chinned him. Bang! That cost me 120 days' remission and 56 days in solitary.

Months later he asked me, "What was all that about?"

I said, "Don't ask me, Gov, it's all insane to me."

Loonyology at its very best.

There was a screw in Brixton who told me he'd give me £50 to chin a fellow screw. Can you fucking believe it? What a cheek. I took the £50 and chinned him. Fuck off and chin the screw yourself, you gutless cunt. You couldn't make this shit up. How can a man escape this madness? I was having a good old-fashioned ham shank one night in Leicester chokey's 14 block and a big moth flew in the window. It was a beautiful moonlit night with a lovely breeze of fresh air and I just felt like a wank. Would you believe the fucking moth landed on my bell end? Now what's the odds of that happening? You would get 1000:1 at William Hills for that. It's amazing. But for all you psychics, why did it happen? Yeh, that's the question. Strange things do happen in jail. It's just unexplainable; a mystery.

There's some decent screws in Wakefield. There was an old screw here called Terry Maguire. He was a top geezer and a right funny fucker. He only retired last year. He once escorted me to one of my trials down at the Old Bailey and he was so in my corner that he asked my QC if he could be of help to my case. Yeah, he wanted to speak up for me, to tell the judge that I'm not all bad. That's the sort of screw you can't but respect. Lots would rather kick you when you're down. So when a decent screw comes along I always show them respect. They deserve it. There's a few good 'uns I get on with here: Mr Appleyard, Mr Marsden, Mr Wright. They treat me okay. There's one here called Dicko Dickson. He's fucking mental but a right top geezer and another funny fucker. He's always got a good story and he cheers the place up. I've known one screw here, Les Farrell, for 30 years or more. People forget that we all grow old together, cons and screws. There's the women screws too. Some are just really nice people, simply doing a job. There's Ms Walker. She's 43 and as fit as a fiddle. She's fitter than most 23 year olds. She's bang into her fitness and trains all the time. Then there's Little Davina. She dyes her hair pink. I knew her dad years ago in Lincoln Jail. I can go on and on and on. There's Big Pat, a 22-stone caravanner. He's always going on about his caravan, but he's a character and always happy. Then there's Cara. She looks like the bird in *Coronation Street* who runs the knicker factory. She's brilliant; always laughing; a top-class woman. It's like a big fucking Wendy house, it really is. It's mental. Then there's old Jim. He's been a screw on the unit for eight years (a long time to be on a unit). He's just pure old school; always singing; always up to something. That's how it is on a little unit. We all grow old. Sure, they all go home at the end of the day, but they're all back the next day. It's a factory, that's all it is. It can either be a hateful factory or a peaceful factory. Either way, it's gotta run. I've done well here if I say so myself. I'm like an adopted Yorkshireman. Maybe it's soon time to move on before I start talking like them. You can kill a man with kindness you know. I'm too young to die.

And there's some memorable screws from the past too:

* Lorraine Carroll. I called her wonder woman. She was a screwess I met in Winson Green Jail in the early '90s. All she ever did was train. She was a true fitness fanatic, and a fearless woman. I had a lot of respect for her. She even gave me a bollocking once after I grabbed the doctor in a neck hold. That's the sort of screw she was. She called a spade a spade, and there was no back-stabbing, it was all to your face. I used to tell her she was in the wrong job and that she could make a fortune as a bodyguard to the stars or a personal trainer. She had a stomach like a six-pack, plus she had the looks. I'd like to think that she moved on to better things rather than stay as a screw in a shithole. What sane person wants to work in a jail for 30 years? That's 30 years without parole.

* Bob Richards, Another screw I've known for years. I first met him in Brixton 20+ years back. The last time I saw him was in Belmarsh about ten years ago. He's the same now as he ever was. He was a proper skinhead in the '70s and '80s: the Crombie, the Dr Martins and braces. Smart. Let's face it, the skins were special - even the music was spot on. Plus they fought a good fight. Once a skin, you never lose it; it's in your veins. The Union Jack is tattooed on your heart. You die a skin. Bob's a laid-back sort of screw, but don't misread his good nature coz you could be in for a shock. I call him Bob the chair, as he's forever sitting on his fat arse. Sometimes I think he's glued in that chair. Top geezer.

* Bill Peacock. This screw was in Broadmoor in the '70s and '80s. He was ex-Army. He was no more a nurse than I'm a spaceman. He was there solely for a wage packet. He didn't give a flying fuck. One day he kicked a fellow screw in the nuts. We all saw it, and it was the funniest thing I'd ever seen. Sadly it cost Bill his job, and he was gone. The screw he kicked was a dog. He went running off to grass Bill up like the maggot he was. Even the other screws were gutted that Bill got the boot over it. Personally, I'd sooner have men like Bill Peacock lock my door than pretend plastic nurses who are just screws in size 10 boots working in a cuckoo pit. There's no pretend with guys like Bill, so you know where you are. There's too many screws up their own arses pretending to be something they're not. False fuckers. At least Bill had done his bit in the forces and was a proud man, not like the worm he kicked in the nuts. Respect to you, Bill.

Get on this one. The only living creature on the planet with one eye is a fish called cyclops.

Did you know a flea can jump 80 times its own length? That's equivalent to a man jumping over St Paul's Cathedral. Fucking mind-blowing.

There was a screw in Winchester nick in the 1980s that we called Mr Magoo - like that cartoon character who's as blind as a bat and keeps bumping into things. The old cunt even looked like Magoo. Even the other screws used to call him it. When he was on duty we used to get away with murder. How the fuck he ever kept his job is beyond me. You could nick anything from under his nose. There was another screw in Wandsworth in the 1970s who liked to watch cons having a wank through the spyholes in the cell doors. He used to give them ½ oz of baccy for it, which was a lot to a con in them days. You'd be amazed at how many ounces of tobacco he paid out in a week (especially when he was on nights). Fucking pervo. It makes you sick to know that screws can do this sort of thing and enjoy it. Every time the pervo came to my door I gave him a lot of verbal: "Go on fuck off, you nonce. Get away from my door." He never did nick me, so what does that tell you? I wonder why. I know for a fact he got moved to Dartmoor over it all (nothing stays secret in jail). What sort of man wants to watch another man jerk off? Now if it was a screwess - all day long. It's a funny old business. Takes all sorts.

There was a baby killer down this block about 20 years back. He was a right evil fucker: lanky, skinny cunt, ugly - you know the type - monstrous. Fair play to the screws, coz they gave him hell. They used to make him stand in the corner of his cell all day long and look at the floor. If his eyes looked up they bashed him. I say well done screws. That's how baby killers should be treated. This block was famous for giving out kickings and, don't worry, us robbers got it too. I had my fair share in the 1970s, but when these cages opened up we were sort of left alone, just isolated and forgotten. The screws are now more laid back these days, but I'd like to think that some monsters still get a bit of the old treatment. I hope these screws aren't getting too soft in their old age. A week never used to pass by without a few screams. Nowadays it's more of a yelp. A quick bend up and it's all over. Big deal. It's fucking boring.

Did you know Al Capone was one of the most hated men in Alcatraz? No fucker liked him. People need to understand something. Just because you're a face, a somebody outside, it don't mean you're special inside. We're all numbers; we all live in a hole; we're all lost. There are no winners inside. How can there be? The guards see us all as the same. Okay, some guards will take a deal, coz every man has a price and any man can be bought. But you're still a convict, still a number, even if you manage to buy some extra goodies. The Kray twins spent thousands during their years in Parkhurst. Their vodka would come in regular. Some screw probably made more out of the Krays than they did with their wages. Jail is jail, and people who say it don't go on are mentalists. Of course it goes on. Prisons are communities, worlds behind walls. You'd be amazed at what goes on. Okay, it's not on the scale it once was. That's because a max secure jail is now double security - even the screws are searched when they enter - whereas in a less secure jail they can just walk in with bags of goodies: drugs, steroids, booze. Fuck me, the visitors can throw stuff over the fence. That's why cons hate the max secure jails, coz it's bloody hard to get anything in nowadays. Look at some of these 'open jails'. Prostitutes sneak in and sneak out before roll check. No wonder they're all fucking laughing. They're holiday camps, a rest from the stresses of life outside. Let's go inside for a piss-up, lads. Party time! Yahooo! Yippeeee!

I remember once in the Scrubs finding a young screw crying - real tears; really upset. Fuck knows why. I went up to him and said, "Mate, don't do that. Pull yourself together." Now if I was a nasty cunt I could've had a right laugh there. Hey, I felt for the bloke. I don't like to see that sort of thing. I found out later that the screw left his job with a nervous breakdown. That's how it is. Some are not cut out for the job. Others fucking love it - the power. You can see the ones who love it: the John Wayne walk; the Travolta gum chew; the Brando eyes. They become their dream. I'm a tough guy. Look at my polished steel toe-capped boots. I work for the Queen. Look at me. You gotta laugh at their mentality. And they're in charge of my life! Half the prats can't even look after their own life. Hey, don't get me wrong, I'm not a screw hater - never have been, never will be. But what I have noticed over the last 15 years is there seem to be a lot of gay screws, both lesbians and homosexuals, and they don't give a fuck who knows about it. I've actually had one gay screw make a pass at me in Belmarsh (well, it was sort of a pass). He said, "Charlie, you've got a lovely body. You're heavenly candyfloss." Then he wiggled away. I was stunned; in shock. He fucking fancied me. You can't make it up. And it proves how I've changed during the course of my journey, coz 20 years ago I could never have accepted such madness. Who could? Nowadays I just smile it off. I could walk into a gay bar now and feel okay as I know my own sexuality. They're harmless to me. In fact a lot of gays are decent geezers. I've no problem with them, especially the lesbians. They're fucking lovely. There's something about them dykes that turns me on. The thought of two hot, wet, juicy pussies together does it for me. Yeeooooow, yippeeeeee!

I had a shit one night in a newspaper while in Walton, parcelled it up and waited for the security screw to pass below my cell window. I was 20 feet up. Bosh! I slung it out and hit him on the hat! "You little cunt," he shouted. "I'll fucking kill you!" All the lads jumped up at their windows and a good hundred of us all started singing 'Rudolph the Red-nosed Reindeer'. It was brilliant. Great times. Brilliant memories. Who's he gonna kill? All 100 of us? This was real porridge. That was loonyology. In those days we all stood as one - the days when cons really were cons. And most of the screws were militant hard-core union con-haters with steel toe-capped boots and notches on their batons.

I was once dragged off a visit in Wandsworth because I pushed a screw. Just pushed him. But he did smash into a wall and it knocked him out. Still … They soon knocked me out later, and an eye for an eye. It's all part and parcel. You have to be prepared to accept it if you give it out! I'm probably one of the few, or maybe the only one, who's jumped on a dog. Yeh, why not? It's all in a day's work. I was bored and I was fed up of this dog snarling at me! The dog handler was egging it on, trying to intimidate me and rattling its choker chain. Fuck it, I thought, and leapt on it. They're not so tough when you attack them: all that barking and snarling turns to a whimper! I'm just not afraid of dogs. I've got teeth too! Fucking bite me and you'll get bit back, end of!

I broke two toes in the Scrubs. I kicked the door so hard I heard them crack. Fuck me, it's a killer when you damage your toes - stops you dead in your tracks and fucks up all your training for months after. Best not kick doors.

Some lucky screw got £500 off me in Parkhurst. I used to keep my dosh rolled up in my hollow-tube bed frame for a rainy day. Well, it turned out to be his rainy day. Every month the security search screws came round to spin the wings and cells looking for tools, drugs and hooch. Back in 1977 £500 was a lot of dosh and they had away with it. What could I do? "Hey, Gov'nor, the screws have nicked my dosh." I'm not allowed it, am I. The cunts had it and life goes on. My fault. That's life. Greedy fucker! It's all about swings and roundabouts in this world in or out of jail. You must be shrewd.

Did I tell you about the time I kicked a screw down the stairs. It was an accident, of course, but he said that I did it on purpose. The fucking nasty prick was trying to get me into trouble. What's wrong with these screws? They'll do anything for a bit of sick leave. As if I'd kick a screw down the stairs on purpose! Still, he was a fat, lazy cunt.

Talking of stairs, I used to run up and down the stairs in my army boots in Leabank Flats in Marsh Farm, Luton, to keep super-fit - all 18 flights, and wearing a rucksack containing three breeze blocks! Who needs a lift? Now that a real man's workout. You ain't sweated till you've done that. Your legs are burning up, your heart's on fire, it's brilliant. That's freedom. It's heavenly. Follow it up with a long soak in the bath, a dozen egg whites, two pints of milk and a massage, then finish it off with a good shag. That's truly life at its best. That's living, believe it. And I'm having some of that just as soon as I fly out of these pissholes. And to all them cunts out there who've mouthed off, saying Bronson's buried, he's finished, he's an old man, a has been - boy, oh boy, I've not started yet. As for them little pricks running about with those hoodies on and popguns, mugging old ladies and kicking in single mothers' doors, stay well clear of the Bronson Manor, coz I'm one dude that gets it sorted in the shadows. Don't even think of stepping on my face. I'm out of hell. I'm not playing games with no fucker.

We need some respect and sanity back. There's no place on this planet for ignorant, psychotic, muggy little spunkbags. It's time for the truth. Grow up and be a man. Real men don't mug old ladies, not in my world, and leave our kids alone. Amen.

CHAPTER 17
OASYS IS NO OASIS

OASys Assessments
Whilst at HMP Wakefield your offender supervisors will be Officer Michelle Taylor and Officer Angela Walton. Your seconded probation officer will be Michelle Lowe.
You are due an OASys assessment (information attached). This will be carried out by one of your offender supervisors. It is an important document that provides relevant agencies with an accurate risk assessment.
To enable an accurate report to be completed you will be given the opportunity to be interviewed. This interview could take up to 2 hours to complete. During the interview you will not be expected to discuss your offending. The interview looks at other aspects of your lifestyle prior to custody, i.e. accommodation, work history, etc.
When we arrange a date for your interview you will be informed beforehand to give you time to prepare. This interview will be conducted by one of your offender supervisors and Michelle Lowe.
Regards
Officer Walton and Officer Taylor
RAM Team 4

I got this today and this is the sort of stuff that proves what a load of old bollocks this system really is. It's just mental, insane, loonyology. Now if I say "Fuck off" I'm then down as anti-authority or antisocial or that nasty fucker Bronson. But if all the cons had said 'Fuck off' years ago then none of this nonsense would now be here.

OASys is just another way of delving into your family and private life. They want to know everything, even where you buried your loot. Let's all fucking wake up and get real, especially in my case and cases like mine. We are all max secure cons. We are or were professional villains. We were young men when we chose to be villains. That was our way of putting bread on the table. All our associates were villains. All our life was crime and we fucking loved it. It's then up to us whether we cut loose from it all. Some of us do, some of us don't, some of us can't. I'm one of the lucky ones coz I don't have to do any more crime. I'll earn more with my gift of life than I would with crime. I'm one con who can honestly say I'm rehabilitated, coz I know cons older than me who are still dreaming of the 'Last Big One'. They're fucking nuts but that's their goal - that last job and then retire. Disneyland shit. These diehard cons are ruthless and I love 'em all, but I'd prefer my art or some after-dinner speeches or a blue movie. I'm fed up of eating porridge.

So I suppose I should explain what OASys is all about. Fuck that, it's too boring, so here's the official description. It just proves how fucking hypocritical the system now is.

HM Prison Service
Notice to Prisoners
No: 016/2006
Subject: RAM NEWSLETTER - OASys
Originating Department: SENTENCE PLANNING

What is OASys?
OASys is a national system for assessing the risk and needs of offenders before, during and after sentence. OASys is a dynamic process that has a central role to play, it is an open process and the offender will be made aware of the information contained in the document with the targets set during the sentence planning process to reduce the risks of re-offending.
Sentence Planning: The aim of sentence planning is to ensure you make the most of your time spent at HMP Wakefield. A sentence plan will assess your needs and set targets for you to achieve both in custody and on licence when released.
Who has OASYS?: All adult offenders serving sentences of 12 months or more (with at least six months left to serve). All young offenders who have at least one month left to serve.
When will I have my OASys completed? Normally within two months from the date you were sentenced (if you are serving less than four years) or three months if you are serving more than four years.
Who will do my OASys? An Officer from the Resettlement Team will see you and arrange an interview. They will write your OASYS based on your interview and evidence from outside probation, CRATS, place of work, etc,. and the self-assessment questionnaire.
How often will my OASys be reviewed? If you are an adult serving more than four years or more, every 12 months.
Why is the OASys document so important? Your involvement in the preparation of the OASys document is important. The OASys system is an open process, which means that you will be able to see, discuss and comment on what has been written about you.
Does OASys affect my category? Targets are set for you to achieve on your sentence plan. At the review periods the offender supervisors will see what you have achieved against these targets and will make recommendations based on risks. These will be discussed with you at the time of your review.
If you have any further questions please speak to the Offender Supervisors from the Sentence Planning Department.
D R THOMPSON, GOVERNOR, 10 March 2006

OASys
OFFENDER ASSESSMENT SYSTEM
INFORMATION FOR PRISONERS

What is OASys?

It is a computer-based offender assessment system. It is used to assess the risks, needs and targets for all offenders.

RISKS:
Of harm to others
Self harm
Escape and control
Public protection issues

NEEDS: How can we help you stop offending, by looking at:
Current offence
Offending history
Social factors - accommodation, education, employment, financial management, lifestyle, family links
Personal factors - emotional well-being, thinking and attitudes

TARGETS: What we plan to do about these risks and needs, based on:
Work done in the past
Motivation
Offending behaviour programmes
Other interventions needed to reduce the likelihood of re-offending

SAQ: Self Assessment Questionnaire

This is an opportunity for you to record your views and comments on how you see your life. It is intended to show how you see yourself. It is completed on paper (with help if required) and entered onto the system by the assessor.

INTERVIEW: The assessor will need to interview you prior to compiling the OASys document. This is also a good time when you can make further input into your OASys.

DISCLOSURE: OASys is an open document, so information it contains will normally be shared with the offender, except where such disclosure may cause harm.

Get on all that computerised OASys shit. Now it's no secret. I despise anything like this. I rarely indulge or put any input into such stuff.

Risks: Unless you tell them things then it's all guesswork. They think it up and thinking is dangerous, coz what they think becomes your label for life. If you don't say fuck all, then how can they know?

Needs: How they can help us to stop offending by looking at our offending history? Yeah, sure. Well, it's all shit. I know why I robbed - I wanted loot. Would OASys give me loot? I didn't wish to work. Robbers don't work, they rob. What's so difficult to understand about that? It's common sense to me.

Social factors: They've even got the cheek to put in family links. They've tried to smash my family contact for years. Why can't people wake up? They really don't give a flying fig about family contact. Why should they? They've got their own families to worry about, so let's be perfectly honest about it all. What've our families got to do with anybody? It's private, personal. My family is my family and I'm very particular concerning whom I speak to about my closest family. I don't even live with my family when I'm free. My philosophy is that a man must move on in life, earn the dosh, look out for the family and just stay on top of it all. Real men don't sit on their fat arses in one spot.

Disclosure: Get on that bit. The contents will 'normally' be shared with the con. Well, let me tell you now, in cases like mine half of it will be kept secret, coz half of it will be lies (made-up shit) and they won't want me to see that. It's fucking obvious to me you're not gonna see all of it. Plus the Old Bill will no doubt want to add their input to it all. Why can't people fucking open their eyes? This sort of stuff is for prats: domestic crime, white-collar crime, tax dodgers, nonces. It's not for villains. How can it be?

SAQ (Self Assessment Questionnaire): More bollocks paperwork. What for? Why waste your time? It's senseless. I'd sooner do a cartoon, coz that's all it is - one big cartoon.

Targets: What they plan to do. Work done in the past. Well, what if you haven't worked?

Motivation: What the fuck do they know about motivation when they're in a two-bob job themselves? They're not exactly Mensa members are they?

Offending behaviour programmes: That sounds posh. Look, the facts are really so simple. Stop your crime or come back to jail. Only you can decide that, not a bollock OASys committee.

Years ago before computers it was all boxes and boxes of prison files. Now it's all on disk. My boxes of files filled up a van. I really don't need all my biz on a disk. I don't want to end up like Joe Public: dying and the taxman sucks 40% death tax on his will. Fuck that.

When I die no fucker nicks my dosh. It's for those I decide to give it to. I'm not paying no fucker 40% of my dosh. Fucking wake up. Stop discussing your private life with strangers. Even the bank manager will grass you up. If you go into a bank and deposit 50k in cash I can assure you you'll get a visit off the fraud squad. You'll probably have it confiscated - money laundering. People deserve to lose it coz of their own fucking stupidity. Wake up now before you end up with a sore arse. You're being shafted - or maybe you enjoy it. Don't forget the Vaseline.

To me it's all shitty psychological crap; putting your life in a tick box. All for some prat to think they have you ticked off. Cunts. My opinion though, for what it's worth, is that all cons should do it, coz if you don't these control freaks will still do it on you and it will be more lies. So do it. By doing it you at least get your side over and your views heard. You can challenge it too.

This OASys stuff just proves all I say. It's loonyology. It's pathetic. 99% of the OASys report is bollocks. The questions are bollocks. The whole layout is bollocks. But it's how prison is today: the label, the tick in the box. As if you're ever gonna tell them where you've buried your dosh, or tell them your personal plans and dreams. Coz, believe me, these people would sooner release you with 50 quid in your pocket and stuff you into a hostel for no-hopers - so they can control your every move. Anyway, fuck it. OASys - kiss my arse.

Did you know Amnesty International has recorded 120 executions in Iran this so far this year (by August 2007) That's some necks stretched. I was out in the yard today and watched two ladybirds get it on - crazy. I also saw Fred Lowe, my next door neighbour, walk past my door - still as fat as ever. I was gutted to hear that Cliffy Hobbs was caught and flown back from Spain in cuffs. He had it on his toes in 2003 from a prison van. They're gonna slam him up in max secure for a few years. They'll want their pound of meat off him. If I had to put dosh on it I reckon he'll now be on the max secure unit in Belmarsh. Anyway, fuck Spain. They're now working for our flying squad. Fuck 'em.

I was once asked where I would head for if I ever had it on my toes. Well, it wouldn't be Spain, that's for sure. I'd jump a cargo ship, head for South America, grow my hair and beard long and hit the jungle. I'd find me a tribe of loonies and settle down with 14 wives and just knock out as many kids as I could. Once I'd got 100 sons I'd return with my boys. There'd be a lot of us all with shaven heads and handlebar tashes and shades. What a force that would be: The Bronson Family. Who the fuck's gonna take us on? Fuck the flying squad. We'd be the flying squad. Only joking. I'm anti-crime, remember? Fuck it, I'd stay in the jungle.

I see those two Asian lads who killed the Leeds copper, WPC Beshenivsky, in 2005 have now been charged with stabbing a con up in Frankland Jail. Those two, Muzzaker Shah and Yusuf Jama, are already serving life and 35 years, so what's a judge gonna give them for a stabbing? As if they give a flying fuck. I would say to them, though, slow down coz you'll come unstuck if you keep stabbing cons up. You've only just got your life sentences; you've a long way to go. They were here for a spell on remand. Slow down, boys, or you'll be heading for a big hole. I started out like you. Look where it's got me. The fucking bone yard. I am the criminal zombie. You really don't want me in your dreams.

I got this letter today, from Dougie Graham, the governor of Woodhill:

Dear Mr Bronson,
Following our brief conversation on 6 August 2007, I thought I would confirm my understanding of that conversation in writing.
You stated that you wished to progress out of the unit at Wakefield. Your view of your behaviour in the last 7 years was that you had behaved yourself. You were no longer a violent person. You did consider that you needed to see Psychologists or other members of the multidisciplinary team.
I stated that I considered that you did need to engage with the multidisciplinary team

and that you had caused significant damage to people and property in the prison system. Therefore there was a need for you to be assessed before progressing from the unit. I also pointed out some more recent incidents, although you did not see those as important.

You were adamant that you were not willing to engage with the multidisciplinary team available at Wakefield. I reminded you of Mr Atherton's offer for you to start VRP at a one to one level, and you firmly decline this.

Clearly my and your views of your position and possible progression were at odds and at this stage I told you that we were at an impasse and the status quo would therefore be maintained. You felt this was effectively leaving you on the Wakefield unit forever. Given your and my position at the moment I do not see you being moved elsewhere.

I undertook to discuss your case more widely with other professional in the CSC and consider whether there were any other reasonable options in terms of your future management. This may take some time as I shall also be requesting that your records are looked at to ensure that the information considered is as accurate as possible. You will be informed in writing of any future decisions so you can share these with your legal team.

In the meanwhile I think it is important that you consider the possibility that any move is likely to take place only after some kind of assessment and your participation in this will be necessary. This is not "blackmail" but simply part of the risk management process applied to all CSC prisoners' progression through the system.

This geezer here is the no. 1 governor of the CSC system. He's in Woodhill. He's a big fish, or what I call a shark. You can see for yourselves his view on it all. I call it 'blackmail', he calls it 'assessment'. I say they've had seven years to assess me every day that the screws unlock my door. It's the screws who know me best. It's these reports that count. So am I never gonna be moved on? One sure thing is that I'm not playing silly fucking games with nobody for brownie points. Fuck all that. I'm a prisoner not a patient.

Hey, I've an exclusive - only got it today. Get on this one. Pull back your ears. Huntley has been caught in the shower up a con's arse, over in the hospital wing. Can you believe that? The screw who told me has never been wrong yet, so it's 100% fact. Dirty bastard. Oh, the con he's shagging is a child rapist serving ten years. So that about sums this shithole up in a nutshell. Help, I'm not a celebrity, but get me the fuck out of here!

CHAPTER 18
OCTOBER - POSTAL BLUES,
NEWS AND INTERVIEWS

Remember this name: Peter Guest. He's the official Bronson firm photographer. He'll be doing all the art photos for my *Con Artist* book. This guy is the dog's bollocks. You don't have to believe me, just wait till you see it. Seeing is believing. This is the next David Bailey. We only have the best on this journey and he is the best, okay? He will photograph me as I walk to freedom. That's the snap everybody wants to see, apart from Prison HQ. Don't worry, I'll send them an extra large copy. I'll make them slags sick. They must truly hate my guts, eh? The gutless toerags. I don't even hate them anymore, I actually pity them. They're the saddest mother fuckers I can think of. Oh well, let them do what they do. Loonyology takes care of itself. I'm driving this one - no brakes. Fuck me, I've not even got a steering wheel. And there's only one gear - fast. Get out of the way or get mown down.

I'm off for a cuppa now. Two tea bags, coz I fancy a strong one. I've got a packet of custard creams and a book to read. I feel good - happy - fuck knows why. It should be a crime to feel so good inside - or am I just mad?

1 October 2007
You'll fucking love this one! The Giant Sex Beast, 22 stone Richard 'Fatso' Andrews, now claims to have given his Co-codamol painkilling tablets to Huntley. This piece of shit Andrews is another nonce. It's the kettle calling the pot. Unfortunately he's only serving a ten stretch and will get released. But you can't miss the toerag, coz he's 6 feet 7. Throw a bucket of shit over him and he'll soon fuck off. All he does in jail is get depressed and cut his arms up (another attention seeker).

What a fucking place this is! Giant nonces trying to get famous for helping Huntley to die. He's even admitted it! That's how brain dead Andrews is. That's fucked up his jam roll (parole). Fucking get me out of here.

Hey, three cheers for Great Granny Doreen Beal, 75 years old. Some prat nicks her purse in the street in Swindon, she shouts out "Stop that thief!" and a woman passer-by grabs the bugger with Doreen and they hold him till the Old Bill arrive. I told you, these old girls are ruthless - even the German bomber couldn't beat them. They're a national treasure. We all love you, Doreen.

Did you hear about Camilla Chignoli? She kept nagging her dad

Adacberto to stop smoking. He'd enjoyed a fag for 40 years. "Stop Dad. You must stop. It will kill you!" You know how the Italians are - very sensitive and they get very emotional. Guess what? He shot her dead. Now he smokes in peace in a max secure cell. What a mental old world this is, eh?! It's all loonyology - crazy.

3 October 2007

I saw my mum and brother and Di yesterday. It was a great visit. We had a laugh. Mum looks great for 76 and we're all proud of her. She'll get to 100 easy. So long as she's still alive when I get out, that's all that counts to me. I called Mark Fish tonight. He's been in touch with my lawyer and it's all looking sweet. Let's hope so.

There's a geezer down in Bognor, West Sussex called Brian Croucher, who's making a Doctor Who Dalek out of matchsticks - half a million of the fuckers. Half a million matchsticks?! A Dalek?! Now is that bloke nuts? Or a genius? He's sure got lots of time and patience. Good luck, mate. Rather you than me. I couldn't do that, even if it meant my life on it. I just couldn't do it, especially a Dalek. Why a Dalek? Why not Dolly Parton?

Did you know that a giraffe's heart is nine times bigger than a human's? I suppose it has to be big so as to pump the blood up that fucking big neck to its brain. Weird things them giraffes, don't you think? I could do with one of them out on the exercise yard. Up, up and away! Yahoooo! I'd be up its neck before you could say Robinson Crusoe. Anyway, fuck Crusoe. I don't know why I said him. I bet he was shagging that Friday's arse. What do you reckon? Just them two on that island. Come on, something must've been going on. Me, I'd have dived in the ocean and shagged a dolphin. As for that Friday geezer, I would've eaten that fucker. A weird old carry on that.

4 October 2007

I just had some good news today. Danny Hansford has now confirmed that all the dosh is on the table. The movie is gonna happen. Hollywood here we come. I also called up my buddy Al Rayment. We pulled a blinder off. He had a reporter round his place from a Hull newspaper. My first interview for years was on tonight. That's how to pull it off. Simple. So fuck you lot up in HQ. I've fucked you again. That's why they hate me: coz I always get things sorted, coz I've got true pals, coz my side of this story will never be buried. Even when I'm dead there'll be people still fighting for the truth, coz we have fuck all to hide. This country is supposed to have free speech, so why can't I call up the media myself? Just what is HQ afraid of? Anyway, I'm made up with the interview. It'll be in print next week. I'll have a copy sent to the Home Secretary, coz I like to be honest. Unlike them cunts doing their bit in your back, my sort like to do it in the front. We like to look into the eyes before we hit you with some true facts.

Hey, did you know milk chocolate wasn't manufactured in the UK until

1905? It was invented in Switzerland in 1875 by adding cream to a chocolate mix. And get on this for a bit of loonyology: in the 1600s drinking chocolate was very fashionable throughout Europe, but people were warned that too much would cause Negro babies. Can you fucking believe that? No wonder the cunts thought the world was flat and the moon was made of cheese. Talking of cheese, I had a nice cheese salad for tea tonight. I made two sandwiches and a nice mug of hot, sweet tea.

Now for the sad news I learnt today. My old buddy Ronnie Easterbrook has been brought over from the hospital wing and is on the other side of the unit in the seg block, and he's not eaten fuck all for five days. I've pulled the PO and Governor to see if I can have a chat with him in the closed visits room. I've explained I've known the man for over 30 years, and they're looking into it. I don't like to see a good man starve himself. So watch this space, coz I'll keep it updated.

There's a fucking postal strike tomorrow, so it's gonna be like Xmas - no mail. I feel sorry for the OAPs waiting for their mail and cheques. Let's hope it soon gets sorted, as it's a boring day in jail without news.

I had a nice workout today and a lovely jog on the yard. The sun was out but it was chilly - just how I like it. I was jogging around Lincoln seg block caged yard some years back when I came across an injured pigeon. You'd be amazed at the number of bird accidents in the razor barbed wire: legs ripped clean off, wings torn, terrible injuries. This poor sod was in pain, coz its wing was twitching and its beak was trembling, plus it had that look of death in its eyes. Sorry buddy. I snuffed it. I can't watch an animal suffer ... only a nonce.

I was on the yard one day up in Hull Jail in 1975 and I found a fucking toad. Yeah, a toad. How? Where did it come from? I've not a clue. Probably the drains. I just don't know. Anyway, when it was time to come in I slipped it in my pocket and then slipped it into the screw's jacket pocket. Later on I could hear from my cell loads of laughter coming from the screws' office. I found out later that the screw almost had a fucking heart attack when it jumped out on him. That's prison life for you. You just never know what tomorrow will bring. Sometimes it's better not to know.

I was up in Durham block back in the 1980s when the screws set me up big time. They let me out to get some books from the library. As I was walking down the landing a Geordie cleaner, a right screws' tea-boy cunt, was coming towards me. I smelt a rat so I chinned the cunt there and then before he got to do the screws' dirty work for them. That's the sort of strokes they pull. Well, it don't work with me. They did the exact same with Big Ferdie Lieveld, but four cleaners attacked him with bars. Them sorts of cons are known as 'Maggots' - screws' pets. They'd do anything for some jam roll - even suck a cock or ten.

You really do have to spend a bit of time in jail to see how it all works. It's really quite fascinating. It sure is an eye opener. There was one con (who will remain nameless), who was good at making fire bomb devices and explosives with timers. Fuck me, he was a dangerous fucker. We would all bang up, the screws would go home, so there'd just be the night clockies on (skeleton staff), and then at 11 or 12 p.m. - BANG! The fire brigade would be rushed in. Now that can be dangerous. Prison is full of clever people. We all have a speciality and we can, and often do, learn from it all. It's really an encyclopaedia of criminality, a learning college of crime.

Hey, I bet you can't tell me what the human bone is composed of? It's crystals of calcium phosphate and collafen. It's fucking amazing that it all develops from sperm. Don't it freak you out to think about it? It's just amazing.

Hey, I'm gonna get rid of a myth. The red flag to the bull is all shit. Bulls are colour blind and, to add to that, when a bull does charge it closes its eyes. So much for red flags. Hey, come on all you lot who go to Spain for your holidays - who's seen Sticky Vicky? Come on, be honest. If you've ever seen her in the clubs performing you sure won't ever forget her. She's been doing her act for donkey's years. She's now in her sixties and is still pulling a string of razor blades out of her fanny and taking beer tops off bottles with her arse. She's a fucking legend, and at 65 she's in good shape. What a strange act. What a strange woman. That's what legends are made of - strange people.

What about those pole dancers? They must get pussy burns sliding down them steel poles. I just couldn't enjoy my meal watching that sort of thing. Not my scene that. The only pole I want to see them slide on is my pole - up and down at 20 mph. Fuckinfantastical. Yippeeeeee.

Did you know that Mafia boss Eugene Palermiti used to wrestle with killer pit bulls for fun at his home in Bari, southern Italy? One of his henchmen said: "He's fucking mental, but don't tell him that or he'll waste us all."

Hey, get on this. Ten-year-old Huang Li is training to swim the English Channel with her ankles and wrists tied. Now is that loonyology or what? Personally I can't really work out why. What's the point? Isn't life crazy - full of amazing people? Where would we be if we were all like that Gordon Brown, or that Tony Blair, or George Bush? Imagine a world full of boring fuckers. What a sad thought. Bring on the dancing girls I say - knickerless ones at that.

I'll tell you who was a tough lad: Dave Cross. He was a pal of mine in the 1960s. His life was cut short at the age of 17 in a motorbike smash. What a tough cookie he was. Even at school he was a handful. Shoulders like boulders and fearless. He was one of those boys who grew up fast. Some would call him a man before his time. But I'll tell you now, if he'd lived on he'd have been somebody high up, coz he had it all. What a waste of life. I still think of Dave all these years later. Terry Brown was another top lad at my school, Icknield Secondary Modern in Luton. Terry could have a serious punch-up. On our last day in school in 1967 he got a big spanner over his skull. He must've lost three pints of blood and he was still laughing all the way to Luton and Dunstable Hospital to get it stitched up. I remember one lad at my school, a right teacher's pet sort of twat. He grassed me up one day, so I planned a nice big treat for him - only what he deserved. I tied him to the school railings, stripped him off and slung a pot of yellow paint over him. Why not? All cowards need that. He fucking ratted on me, and do you know what about? He said I was getting a blow job off ***** (I'll not say her name) around the back of the bicycle shed. Well, for starters, I wasn't. For seconds, I wish I had been. For thirds, she was bloody gorgeous, the best-looking girl in the school. And, lastly, I had no chance, coz she hated me. So it was all bollocks anyway. I fucking hated school. Real education starts on the street - believe it.

Did you know that Joey Chestnut ate 66 hot dogs in 12 minutes at the Coney Island speed-eating contest? I wonder if they had onions on and sauce. 60 fucking 6! That's some eating. In fact it's a world record. So if you wanna break it, then good luck.

Hey, get on this. The world's most expensive house is up for sale in Colorado - 67 million bucks. Er ... I'll think I'll give it a miss myself. Not my cuppa tea. I prefer a caravan. Flash fuckers. Who wants a 67 million pound house? What for? It had to be in America. Big-heads. That's nothing. What about a ten grand bottle of Sputnik Vodka in a hand-made diamond-encrusted bottle? Come on, I want a drink not plastic surgery. Who's gonna buy a 10k bottle of vodka? You'd be amazed at how many would. More money than sense. Ten fucking grand for a drink. Do me a favour.

Did you know that an octopus has three hearts? I bet you never knew that!

When a girl called Ro Cham H'pnhieng was nine years old she ran into the Cambodia jungle. Nobody saw her again until she was 27 years old. She couldn't talk and she acted like an animal. Her own family could barely recognise her. Ten months later she ran back to the jungle and hasn't been seen since. All I can say is: good luck Ro Cham. I personally think that you're a lot happier and freer with your way of life. It must be lovely. And who knows? There could be a wild man of the jungle who's with her. Maybe that's why she ran back in. Something tells me that Ro Cham is happier where she is.

Did you know there's twice as many chickens on this planet than humans? We really do need to start eating more. I could do with a couple now. I'm fucking starving.

6 October 2007

Them fucking wankers - postmen. They're spoiling my days with their muggy strikes. Fucking liven up, you cunts. You greedy fuckers. Sack the lot of the lazy sods. There's three million people on the dole who can do their job. Liven up.

I see Evander Holyfield fights Sultan Ibragimov next week for a world title shot. Holy's an inspiration to the boxing world, one of my all-time legends. I don't think people realise how long this guy has been around and all that he's won. He's fought them all over and over. Total respect to the man. I salute him. And his training is second to none. Fuck knows how old he must be now, but he can't be that far off me.

Amir Khan fights Scott Lawton tonight. Let's face it, Khan is a born champion. He's got it all and he's a genuine young chap. He's just pumped in 700k of his own dosh to open a new boxing gym in his town of Bolton, to get the kids in off the street and teach them boxing and self-discipline. We salute you, Amir, you're a top geezer. Max respect.

Yeah! Fuck you, postmen, ruining my weekend. I enjoy some letters on weekends - it's my contact from the outside world. I've gone right off you lazy fuckers now. What have I ever done to you lot? What have the British public done to deserve it? It's always the innocent ones that have to suffer. Do you think the government gives a flying fuck? What a load of bollocks. You'll all end up like the miners and dockers and steelworkers - out of a job. All you're doing is losing a day's pay and pissing us all off. Cunts.

England beat Australia today at the Rugby. Well done, lads.

I woke up this morning at 4 a.m. to the chimes of the clock. Wakefield's an old-style jail with a clock tower and the clock chimes every hour. You can hear it all over the jail. I lay there still with a big hard-on. I thought, shall I give it a pull or shall I not? I decided not to and drifted back to sleep, but I still had a hard-on when I awoke at 6 a.m. I got up, had a good piss and then climbed back into bed and lay there for half an hour thinking. It was so peaceful, warm and cosy, with a breeze coming in through the window. At times like these I actually feel happy. It's like I'm not here. I'm just free in spirit. The only thing missing is a woman next to me. That's all that's missing: the smell and taste of a woman; that special touch; the heat; two bodies into one, melting into each other's skin. It must be magical in jail if you're gay. It must be heavenly, especially if you're sharing a cell with another gay or a bi. It must be a dream come true. It's fucking murder for us heteros. Surely it's a case for Human Rights. Fuck wanking. These days I prefer a cheese roll or a slice of cake.

Those fucking postmen. Where's my mail, you twats?

Fucking Rice Krispies today, plus two bread rolls - that was it. For dinner I had a fry-up and for tea I had a pork pie and salad. A fucking rabbit would eat more than I've had today I'm sure. I don't 'arf miss my grub. I love fish and chips, but I'm really a steak man, a Sunday roast man.

Monster Miller was moaning about something today. What's he got to moan about? He should be thankful it's not the 1960s, coz the cunt would've hung. In fact he should've hung. Problem solved. There'd be fuck all to moan about then. What a fucking boring day I've had today. I hope Amir Khan wins later.

Khan did it! He stopped Scott Lawton in Round 4. This was Khan's 14th pro fight. We're all watching a boxing legend in the making. This guy will be as big as Ali was. He's fucking brilliant and still only 20 years old. By the time he's 25 he'll be the greatest pound-for-pound puncher in the world and hold all the titles.

Who remembers Chantelle out of *Big Brother*? Personally I thought she was bloody gorgeous. Well her mother Andrea Sinclair was strangled and mutilated 20 years ago by psycho Keith Pollard. Guess what? He's up for jam roll soon. Chantelle was only a baby when the beast killed her mum. Let's be honest, who wouldn't have put the noose around that fucker's neck and shoved him through the trapdoor?

Hey, did you know 50 Cent, the rapper, survived nine bullets. Nine! Now that's what I call a lucky guy! And Jay-Z, another rapper, wears a diamond-encrusted chain worth 2½ million bucks. The rapper guys don't do it by halves, but they give me a fucking headache. Bring back soul and Tamla, I say, instead of all that bollocks.

That Danny Dyer, the cockney actor, is fucking awesome. He's gonna be around for a long time, so you'd best get used to him. He's up there with the best in my book, coz he's a mad fucker. I like Danny.

Did you know that Britain's tallest man is Neil Fingleton, at 7 foot 7, and when he goes out for a drink he needs 24 pints to get merry? Fuck getting in a round with him. 24 pints? Do me a favour. That's three fucking gallons. It's cheaper to fill the motor up. Guess what he has for breakfast? Come on, you'll never believe it. A packet of sausages, seven slices of bacon, a tin of tomatoes and three platefuls of waffles. He's not fucking staying at my drum.

I bet you keep asking yourselves: "How does Bronson know all these facts?" Well, let's just say - I do. So don't be fucking nosy, okay.

A husband says to his wife, "How about we try a new position tonight?"

She answers, "Yeah, why not? You get to the ironing board and I'll lie on the couch farting and watching telly."

When it comes to a real legend, this French guy will take some beating - Pascal Payet. Who? You may well ask. He copped a 25-year jail sentence, but in 2001 in Luynes Prison his pals hijacked a chopper and flew him to freedom. Up yours, frogs, I'm going home early. Sadly they caught up with him. There's always a snake in the grass with a few frogs. Guess what? The chopper came back for him, this time at Grasse Jail. It landed on the fucking roof of the nick and off he went again. Sadly four months later they pounced on him in Barcelona. He's back in max secure. But something tells me we won't have heard the last of Pascal Payet. What a legend. We salute you. Max respect. As La Cosa Nostra would say - you're a brother, we love you.

There was a French lunatic in Rampton Asylum in 1978 when I was there. He believed he was God. They're all the same them frogs. They've gotta go one better than us Brits all the time. Why not Jesus or the Pope? Why God? That's the frogs for you.

I remember a Polish loony in Ashworth who'd strangled his mother-in-law and his wife. Fuck knows why, but he thought he'd done society a favour. He used to speak a little English and he'd say: "I did it for England. They were witches." The Polish prat. They're a funny lot the Poles.

I've met 'em all, from all corners of the world. There was a Mohican in Wandsworth Jail in the 1970s. He looked like Billy Two Rivers, the famous wrestler in the 1960s. But this guy was nuts, and I mean nuts. How the fuck he never got certified mad is beyond me. He got a good kicking in the recess one day from three of the 'Faces'. They really laid into him over a debt he owed them. You don't fuck with the London Faces - in or out - coz you'll undoubtedly get served up good style, especially if you're a mental Mohican.

"Bronson visit," the screw shouted as I was on the exercise yard in Wandsworth. He also called three more names out. As we got in off the yard this muggy screw said to me, "Do up your shirt button." It was how he said it more than what he said. Bang! He was out cold before he hit the deck. That was my visit fucked and it cost me 120 days' remission and no bed for 56 days. Cunt. What was I supposed to do? What would you have done? Later, an old screw told me in private that it couldn't have happened to a better screw. Apparently no fucker liked this cocky, arrogant screw, so I'm not a bad judge am I?

I often used to think: why me? Why is it always me who's banging them out. 99% of other cons never end up in the chokey. Why is it always me? I guess I'm just more sensitive and I take things too personal. That's what it must be, or I'm just not normal. Still, that was then and this is now, and it's now - today - that counts. But I look back with a big smile, I really do, and I'm still alive. It's fucking wonderful. Loonyology.

8 October 2007

My outside probation officer was up to see me today - our first visit in two years. What does that tell you? She's a nice woman, but to me it's just a total joke. We sit behind bars in separate rooms. Years fly by and fuck all changes. She's my probation officer, so is there any point to it? We had a chat and I gave her one of my artworks. She travels back to Luton and I'm stuck up here in a zoo. I'll probably see her in another two years. That's how it works. This is the penal system: a fucking joke.

The muggy postmen are getting right up my nose - another strike today and tomorrow too. There's millions of letters piled in a mountain. Some are mine. Get back to work, you lazy fuckers, and sort my mail out.

I see a cop in Wisconsin, USA, went berserk over the weekend. He shot dead six teenagers and then one of his own firm shot him dead. It's like the Wild fucking West over there. But how sad is that, when a cop goes nuts and shoots up the town? Why shoot six innocent kids? The guy must've been two cans short of a six-pack. And get on this: his middle name was Peterson. Tyler fucking Peterson. Of all of the names, it had to be my fucking name. I hope he wasn't a distant relation of mine. Cunt. Anyway, the madman is history. His brains leaked out of his head. No fucker will miss him. My condolences to the families of the victims.

Yeah! You postmen get back to work, you cunts.

I called Keeley tonight. She's a hot cookie. I said to her, "Imagine us in a big black hole, with no light, only touch and smell, and you stick your tongue into my mouth." Do you know what she said? "Lovely." That's what you call a hot chick. She's got lovely legs. Perfect. She's a nice girl, Keeley. My special friend.

I had a baked spud and cheese for tea and a passion fruit. A fucking silly passion fruit. What's that all about? Give me a good old apple any day or an orange. Passion fruit? Do me a favour.

I've got a visit tomorrow from Gregg Rickell. I'm looking forward to that. Every day's a birthday for me, it truly is.

Great bit of news: that triple murdering monster, Hughes, who vanished from jail has been found - dead. He committed suicide in his car down a farm track in Belper, Derbyshire, 24 hours after he went missing. Why didn't he do that years ago? Why wait 11 years to do it? They're all the fucking same these child killers - gutless and spineless. Anyway, here's one that's gone for good! Good riddance!

I got this memo today:

Memo:
CSC UNIT Manager
8 October 2007
Prison Number: BT1314 BRONSON
Keeley Thompson
The above named has NOT been approved by the Home Office for the approved visitors scheme.
SECURITY DEPARTMENT

Note: they NEVER give a reason! It's all about control. I've now lost count of how many people they've refused to let me see - dozens, if not scores - and no one is EVER told WHY. No reason is given, because there is no reason. Or is there?

You decide. Make up your own minds. I already have.

I bet they don't put this sort of control on the OASys report. How they enjoy fucking up contacts and relationships. Cunts.

October 2007, The Sun
FORENSIC GIRL PERV IS CAGED
A pervert police worker caught trying to groom a girl aged 12 over the internet got 18 months' jail yesterday.
Sick Paul Rogers, 37, posed as a 14-year-old girl to befriend "Katie" - who was actually an undercover reporter.

The former Met Police forensics expert said he wanted her to meet his "male cousin",
dress him in her bra and knickers then spank him.
They met at a park in south-east London where he offered the 20-year-old female
reporter £100 to "do rude stuff". Dad Rogers of Southampton, Hants, denied sexual
grooming but was convicted last month at Southwark Crown Court.

Now this is what you call a real pervo. Imagine this fat twat living next door to your teenage daughter, and he worked for the Old Bill. Cunt. You never know who's who today. If I bump into this pervo I'm gonna give him a well-deserved slap. Fucking nonce. It's a funny old world.

Hey, did you know it takes 30 Broadmoor screws to change a light bulb? It's a fact. I counted the lazy fuckers. I'll tell you who's in for a nice few bob's compensation: Ryan George. Get on this for a prison blunder. HM Prison Brixton locked him up in a bunk bed cell and put him on the top. Ryan was an epileptic. He had a fit and fell off onto his head. Bang! The poor sod is now in a nursing home 24/7 brain damaged. Ryan's dad sued the Home Office and at court Lord Justice McKay ruled that deficiencies by prison staff amounted to negligence. Let's have three cheers for Judge McKay. See, they're not all wankers. What sort of prat puts an epileptic on the top bunk? They knew he was epileptic. Let's hope Ryan's dad gets a million bucks so he can look after his son. This is just another case of silly screws with tiny brains. They think they're smart. You can put a uniform on a monkey and it thinks it's clever. These screws who allowed Ryan on the top bunk should have to take an IQ test. I bet the result would be the same as the monkey's - if not less. Oh well, live and learn I say. But it's cost Ryan his life. He's now a very sad case.

8 October 2007, Hull Daily Mail
Exclusive interview with Britain's 'most dangerous prisoner'
Charles Bronson: I'm so sorry.
In short, Charles Bronson, the man considered by many to be Britain's most dangerous
inmate, has spoken to the Mail about his regret over taking a teacher hostage at Hull
Prison and his dream of being released back into society. Bronson, 54, speaking from
his isolation cell in high security Wakefield Jail, claimed he is a reformed character.
The man dubbed Britain's most dangerous prisoner today apologised for taking a
teacher hostage at Hull Prison in his first ever interview from his cell. Charles
Bronson, who is serving a life sentence for taking Phil Danielson hostage in 1999,
claimed he is a changed man and poses no threat to the public. In an exclusive phone
interview with the Mail, which can be viewed on our website today, the convicted
armed robber and serial hostage taker claims:
He is sorry for taking Mr Danielson hostage.
He accepts he deserved to be punished, but claims he should never have been jailed for
life.
He is a reformed character and is "anti-crime".
He dreams of living in the country in a home painted in all the colours of the rainbow,

My life, I'm stuck in a cage, a special cage in Wakefield prison. I'm in this cage 23 hours a day. I'm isolated, year after year after year after year. I'm not allowed to mix with nobody - no one ever ****** sees me. "What the public don't realise is I've been out of trouble for seven-and-half years. I should be on a wing mixing with people and I've proved myself in the last seven-and-half years. I've changed. I'm anti-violent, anti-crime, anti-drugs, I'm anti-everything. There is no way in a million years I would ever commit another crime because there's no reason for me to. "I'm an author: I've wrote 10 books. I've got awards for my art. I'm an artist, I'm a poet. Does that sound like Britain's most dangerous man? Over the last 20 years - even though I was a nasty ****** - I've probably helped raise two, three hundred thousand pounds for children's charities. The public never hear things like that. I still help people from a cage. I probably do more for charities than most people outside ever do."

AL: "What were your experiences like when you were in Hull Prison?"

CB: "Fantastic. When I was on the Hull special unit, I was doing my own cooking, wearing my own clothes, I had open visits, treated decently. When I arrived, the Hull Prison HQ boss, he actually said to me 'You're going to be here for five years Charlie', I said 'All right, nice one mate. I'll get my head down.' A couple of weeks later they told me to pack my box. They said, 'We're closing the unit down.' You must remember that that's what set me off. If I'd have been left there like I was told I was going to be left, the incident would never have happened."

AL: "So, if you had remained where you were, you feel you would be a free man now?"

CB: "One hundred per cent free, coz I was doing my time nice and easy. Since that incident I've been thrown in a dungeon and forgotten about."

AL: "What is the current situation with your appeal?"

CB: "As it stands, there is a case going on at the end of the month in the House of Lords - three cases are going up. Now if them lads win their cases, it affects 7,500 people who are serving life sentences who haven't murdered with short tariffs. There is 7,500 of us and if these three people win their cases then we are being held illegally. What you've got to understand is this. When I got this life sentence, my tariff was only three years - I've now served eight years of that sentence. So I'm actually five years over my ****** tariff."

AL: "So is that where the anger comes from?"

CB: "There's frustration and anger: they're sucking my life away. If I was Charlie Smith I wouldn't be in this situation, but because I'm Charlie Bronson … The media don't treat me fairly. I've never spoken to a journalist myself, everything is always leaked or from an anonymous source. If anything happens in a jail and I'm in that jail, you can guarantee the press will use my name - you can guarantee it."

AL: "If your voice was heard, do you think people would have a different opinion of you?"

CB: "If I got out tomorrow I would go on a tour and I would go round all the schools, all the youth clubs. If I could I'd go into YP jails (young offenders' institutions) and I'd tell the kids, 'Think about what you are doing, pack it in now, stop taking your drugs, crime is for mugs'. I would turn a lot of kids away from crime. I would love to do something like that and it is off the back of my experiences in prison."

AL: "Have you always been treated poorly in prison?"

CB: "No, no, no, I put my hands up, I deserve all I got. I'm not one of these people called "rainbow cottage."

In February 1999, Bronson burst into a classroom at Hull Prison where Mr Danielson, then 37, had been teaching. The convict tied a skipping rope around his neck and tugged him around at knife point, holding him hostage for 44 hours and leaving the teacher in fear for his life. Bronson, 54, who is in solitary confinement in high security Wakefield Jail, has staged nine roof-top protests and taken a total of 11 hostages. He has spent 28 of his 33 years behind bars in isolation and is due to have a parole hearing next year. He said: "Since the incident in Hull, I've been in no trouble at all. Let me explain, all the time me and Phil were together, I never harmed that man, not a hair on his head. I made him cups of tea. What I done, I should never have done. I put my hands up, I'm guilty of it. But, what you've got to understand is, I was under extreme provocation." Despite apologising for what the rest is not here.

Charles Bronson interview: Infamous prisoner on his remorse, how he has changed and his desire to live in a rainbow-coloured cottage.

I was a proper nasty villain - armed robbery, the lot. But now I'm a poet and an author.

Charles Bronson is one of Britain's most notorious prisoners. He has spent 28 of his 33 years behind bars in solitary confinement. He has never given any media interview, until now. He spoke to Adam Lovell from his cell in Wakefield high security jail. Here is the interview in full.

Adam Lovell: "How are you doing?"

Charles Bronson: "I'm sweet as a nut, boxing clever, you know. Since the incident in Hull I've been in no trouble at all. Let me explain, all the time me and Phil were together I never harmed that man, not a hair on his head. I made him cups of tea. What I done I should never have done. I put my hands up, I'm guilty of it. But, what you've got to understand is, I was under extreme provocation. When I landed in Hull they told me I was going to be on the unit for five years, this is the top people from the headquarters. "The next minute they told me to pack my box and I'm going back into some dungeon - back into solitary confinement - and I couldn't accept it. Me and Phil, we had a bit of a difference over some of my art. He'd actually said a few bad things about my art, nothing (too) bad, but just criticism. "When I grabbed Phil, like I say, I never hurt him."

AL: "Many people could consider your apology to Phil Danielson just a ploy to receive lighter sentencing."

CB: "Even though I put my hands up. I should have been punished for what I did. But there is no way I should have received a life sentence."

AL: "So you don't feel the life sentence was justifiable?"

CB: "Of course it wasn't justifiable. Let me put my cards on the table. I've been in prison since 1974 - 33 years all, barring 69 days of freedom. "I was a nasty ******, make no mistake about it. I was a proper nasty villain - armed robbery, the lot. But most of my problems have been in prison. I've taken nine prison roofs off. I've taken 11 hostages. I've never cried about my punishment. But now I'm almost 55 and I haven't been in trouble now for seven-and-half years, but I'm still treated as Britain's most dangerous man and that is totally ridiculous, pathetic nonsense."

AL:" Is the Bronson the public know a fair reflection of who you are?"

CB: "Not at all. They don't know who I am. This is what I am trying to say to you.

*who cry about it. What I did was ****** out of order. I was a nasty criminal. You can't go through life robbing people. I was an armed robber, a dangerous man, and I deserved to come to prison. But when I came to prison I was a young kid, right, and I did not like what I saw. There was a lot of bullying going on in the '60s and '70s. There was a lot of young kids hanging themselves, especially in Hull, you know. It was terrible and I didn't like what I saw. And I used to fight for cons' rights and I became a prison activist and they didn't like me and that's why I was moving all round the country, year after year after year. That's why I got certified 'mad' - I was never 'mad', but they sent me to Broadmoor because prison didn't want me."*

AL: "So you are planning for release then?"

CB: "I believe I will get out on legal technicalities within, I would say, hopefully this year."

AL: "When you get out, do you have plans?"

CB: "I have a lot of plans, yeah, a lot of plans. I'm gonna do a lot of art shows, because my art sells for hundreds and hundreds of pounds, I'm going to after-dinner speeches, I've got a movie coming out next year - my life story in a movie. I've got another book coming out next year, so if I do get out in the next six months, a year, it's just all going to fall into place. It's lovely. As far as crime is concerned, I am totally and utterly anti-crime, I don't want to know anything else about crime."

AL: "Where do you want to set up after prison?"

CB: "First of all, I'm going to get myself a caravanette, you know, them mobile homes. I'm getting one of them, but I would like to end up in a nice little cottage right out in the country and I'm going to paint it all the colours of the rainbow and I'm going to call it Rainbow Cottage. That's my dream and I'll be sitting out in the garden in the sunshine doing my art."

AL: "Do you often think of that time?"

*CB: "All the time. See, a lot of people might think I'm institutionalised. I can't be institutionalised because I ****** hate prison. I don't like prison, I ******* hate it. I despise it, everything it stands for: I hate it, so how can I be institutionalised? The system is the people who are institutionalised. The screws are institutionalised. I ****** ain't. I've still got a life out there, I've got a future, I've got a goal, I've got a dream to live out."*

AL: "You mentioned your charity work. On a daily basis, how are you involved with that?"

CB: "I get sack loads of letters every week, people saying, 'Can you send my granny a piece of art?' or 'Send me this so I can sell it on eBay'. I'm always helping people to get a few bob to help their charities."

AL: "If there was anything you could say to anyone who you are not in contact with, who would it be and what would you say?"

*CB: "I would say to Brown, the new Prime Minister, get my file, open it, look at it and do something about it because what is happening to me is a ******** liberty."*

AL: "Is there anything you would say to Phil Danielson?"

CB: "He knows because I've already said it to him, but I am very, very sorry for what happened. I am sincerely sorry. I can only say sorry so many times. It shouldn't have happened. It was more down to frustration than anything else, but I am happy to say I never harmed that man. "My sentence should have been about three years for what

happened. All my other hostages, I don't give a **** about. They deserved everything they got, I'm not interested, but Phil Danielson was an innocent man in the wrong place at the wrong time. It's sad it happened, what else can I say?"
Convict upbeat and jovial during chat.

Charles Bronson was interviewed by the Mail over the phone from his *14ft by 8ft cell in solitary confinement in HMP Wakefield high security prison.* From this cell, where he spends 23 hours of every day, he spoke of his regret over taking a teacher hostage at Hull Prison and his dream of being released back into society. The Mail's Adam Lovell travelled to North Lincolnshire to meet Alan Rayment, who calls Bronson his mentor. A bilateral amputee who has hand-cycled across Vietnam, he is in regular contact with Bronson and claims the convict has helped him with his physical and mental fitness. After arriving at his family home at 5.30 pm we were expecting the call at 6.15 pm. The first 15 minutes were spent checking and double checking the recording equipment to make sure there would be no problems with capturing the first interview with one of Britain's most notorious criminals. Bronson took everyone by surprise in ringing half-an-hour early. The line, coming from deep within the confines of HMP Wakefield, was broken and hollow-sounding in the empty cell. Bronson, however, was not. Surprisingly upbeat for a man locked away in isolation for 28 of the 33 years he has spent in jail, Bronson was jovial and entertaining. He sounded animated and deliberate. During the 20 minute interview it became clear he still has hope of being released, even claiming he could be out within a year. He denied he become institutionalised and claimed he posed no threat to the public. The Ministry of Justice has confirmed Bronson will be considered for parole again at a hearing next year. It will be for the parole officers to decide if he can be trusted.

33 years in prison, 11 hostages taken: Born Michael Peterson on December 6, 1952, the former boxer's name was changed to Charles Bronson by his fight promoter in 1987. He was born in Luton, before moving to Merseyside and later Ellsmere Port. Bronson was first jailed in 1974 for seven years after being convicted of armed robbery. He has spent 33 years behind bars, 28 of them in solitary confinement. Bronson has never killed anyone, but has staged nine roof-top protests and taken 11 hostages. He has not been allowed to mix with other prisoners since taking teacher Phil Danielson hostage for 44 hours at Hull Prison in 1999. In 2000, he received a dis-cretionary life sentence, with a three-year tariff, for the offence. His appeal against the sentence was denied in 2004. He has spent time in more than 120 different prisons. In 2001 he married Saira Rehman. He converted to Islam and was also known as Charles Ali Ahmed. He and Ms Rehman have since divorced and he has renounced Islam and the Ali Ahmed name. While in prison, he has developed an extreme fitness regime and claims to regularly perform 2,500 press-ups a day. He claims he can do 90 in 30 seconds. In 2002, Bronson published a book, *Solitary Fitness*, detailing an individual training process with minimal resources and space. For the past 10 years, Bronson has occupied himself by writing poetry and producing pieces of art and has published 10 books. Bronson, known to his friends and supporters as Charlie, is still a category-A prisoner and is now at HMP Wakefield, one of the country's toughest prisons.

'I've suffered terribly since hostage ordeal.'
Teacher Phil Danielson told the Mail he had been haunted by his ordeal of being held

hostage by Bronson. Bronson is said to have been angry after the art teacher criticised his work in prison. Mr Danielson told how one minute he was teaching, the next he was lying on a snooker table with a home-made spear being held to his throat. Speaking in 2000, he told the Mail: "It happened so quickly I didn't even know who had done it initially. It wasn't until I opened my eyes that I realised it was Bronson. I really thought I was going to die. He said to me, 'You better take your last breath, 'cause this knife is going in you'. My mental state has since suffered terribly. I have had terrible nightmares and I have been diagnosed as suffering from post traumatic stress syndrome."

Mr Danielson returned to work two months after the incident, but later had a breakdown.

Tomorrow's Mail: Why I take my family and kids to see my friend and mentor, the man dubbed 'UK's most dangerous inmate'.

9 October 2007, Hull Daily Mail
Behind the headlines: The fundraiser who has struck up an unlikely friendship with notorious criminal and hostage-taker Charles Bronson.
Why I take my family to visit Britain's most infamous prisoner.
Armed robber and serial hostage-taker Charles Bronson is one of Britain's most notorious inmates, but to charity worker Alan Rayment he is a friend. Adam Lovell reports.
Alan Rayment thinks nothing of taking his wife and parents into Wakefield high security jail to visit the man the national media call 'Britain's most dangerous prisoner'. Mr Rayment has been friends with Charles Bronson for years; they write and speak regularly on the telephone. Mr Rayment of North Lincolnshire is a community sports coach with the Humber Sports Partnership. He has overcome the loss of both his legs, caused by leg ulcers and MRSA, to compete 300-mile treks on a hand cycle and numerous races and triathlons, raising tens of thousands of pounds for charity along the way. He claims he has been helped by Bronson who is serving a life sentence for taking a teacher hostage at Hull Prison in 1999. It was Mr Rayment who set up the exclusive interview with Bronson in yesterday's Mail. During the telephone interview - the first Bronson has ever given - he apologised for taking Phil Danielson hostage more than seven years ago, but claimed his continued incarceration is unjustified. Mr Rayment said Bronson, who has staged nine roof-top protests, taken 11 hostages and spent 28 years in solitary confinement, has helped him with his mental and physical fitness. He said: "Charlie has helped me immensely with my training. Being a wheelchair-user, I find it hard to get rid of my belly and in 2001 I was almost 16 stone - I'm 11-and-a-half stone now. He's put me in the right direction of what I should be doing. Charlie is the master of press-ups, he's taught me clap press-ups and many others. I never thought I could do press-ups, but I've adapted them with a medicine ball after direction from Charlie. It's taken a lot of hard work from me as well. It's really hard work, the training I do, but you've got to look up to the guy there because he is fit as a fiddle. Charlie's ways definitely work." Mr Danielson is living abroad and the Mail has been unable to contact him to inform him of Bronson's apology. But, speaking in 2000, he said his mental state had "suffered terribly" after Bronson held him captive for 44 hours with a skipping rope around his neck. Despite

that, Mr Rayment said he had no hesitation in befriending Bronson, 54. He said: "I came across Charlie in 2003. A good friend of mine who I used to work with had read many of his books. I wanted to meet the guy and know what he was going through as a person. In 2003, he designed my mate a Christmas card and I said, 'Do you think he would draw me one?' - just to be the envy of all my mates, having a Christmas card that was personalised for me from Charles Bronson. A month later a card came through and it was unbelievable, the detail on it. Me on the wheelchair, it was absolutely cracking. I then returned a letter to say thank-you and it spiralled from there." Mr Rayment began writing to Bronson more frequently and then speaking on the phone before a visit to HMP Wakefield in 2004. He said: "I used to include letters about my charity work, races I'd done and what marathons I had coming up, then we started writing every month." As the letters and the phone calls continued, and after several interviews and much correspondence with prison authorities, Mr Rayment was passed to make his first visit. He said: "I've been passed to see Charlie since 2004. My first visit was at Wakefield, December 29, that year. In total I have been to visit him 11 times. The first thing I did was jump up on the table, put my hand through the bars and shake the guy's hand. It was great to meet him." Mr Rayment has since taken his mother Peggy, father Malcolm and wife Natalie to see Bronson. He said: "Me and Natalie have been once together. I took Mum and Dad recently. It's not the best of places to go, I'm sure prisons everywhere aren't the best places to go. You have to go through vigorous checks, fingerprints and all that, but it's different when you visit Charlie - you have to go through so much more. You've got to go through a courtyard, many locked doors and when you get to Charlie's front door to go into the unit, it's quite daunting. It certainly was the first time, knowing what was behind that wall. When you get into there, you sense a cold, damp feeling as you get into the visiting room, then when you see Charlie, you're in one prison cell and he is in the other. The first thing I did when I visited him was put my hand through the bars and shake his hand."

Despite the intimidating surroundings, Mr Rayment has every intention of continuing his visits. He said: "It's good for both of us to continue the visits. Hopefully, one day we won't have to meet through iron bars. When we go we take a flask of hot water and Charlie makes us tea, it's like we are going to his for a cuppa. I'd love to one day go for a pint in a pub with him. I believe the man should be, and one day will be, free.

9 October 2007

A fucking old loony day today. Some prat of a screw from over the hospital wing came over and was giving it the 'daddy big bollocks' with Big Robbo. Robbo don't take shit off nobody, least of all a cunt of a screw. Robbo knocks 'em down like skittles when he goes. Some screws work alongside the likes of Huntley and they come over to this unit and think it's the same. Well it's not. We don't like muggy screws who think they're so special. They're just cunts. You can always tell the mugs by the way they slam your door, adopt that cowboy walk and chew their gum. They're basically idiots. Outside they're faceless prats. Even other screws laugh at them and they're always the ones with the biggest butts and biggest mouths. You know the ones. All you gotta do is stand outside any jail in the UK and you'll see 10% of them marching in. Give them a shout from me! "Charlie says you're a cunt. Get a life, you mug." If one of them ever walked into my boozer or club with their attitude, believe me they wouldn't last five minutes. They'd be laughed out of the door. Anyway, this prat got it off me and Robbo big time. "Get back over the hospital, you mug, and tuck Huntley up. Fuck off from our unit, you prat. Go on and play chess with your mate Huntley." He soon fucked off with a red face. But these sorts of low-life screws are brave when we're in a cage. And the only time they're brave is with ten guards behind them. They're fucking little boys in uniforms. A real screw don't behave like these mugs. Cunt.

I got Terry Turbo's book sent in today: *King of Clubs*. I'm pleased to see Wilf Pine's done the foreword. It looks a great read. I'll get into it Sunday, my day of rest. The post is gradually creeping in, some of it two weeks old.

Now, let's see what's what. Let's all have a laugh. Hey, did you know there's a woman in South America who's got a 5-inch clitoris? Five fucking inches! That's frightening. Imagine waking up with that thing sticking in your face! Come on, that's fucking scary. Looooonnnnyoollogggyyy at its best. I'd love to see it though - just a peep. Wouldn't you?

I know a woman in Luton, who will remain nameless, who's such a nympho she actually scares me. Well, maybe 'scare' is a bit over the top, but she freaks me out. I met her in the Moakes pub in Marsh Farm. She had one of the flats in Leabank's, and guess who got an invite? Now I'm no prude, but the woman actually embarrassed me. So get a load of this. From the boozer to the flat is a ten-minute walk. At the time I was 36 and she was 40. We liked the same music and we were a good match. As we walked along she put her hands in my overcoat and squeezed my balls. Fuck me, we'd only met an hour before. I was fresh out of jail and my balls were full of Dairy Milk Cream Topping. Anyway, we made it to her drum.

Then she knocked me over when she said, "Do you mind if I invite Dave round?

"Dave? Who the fuck's Dave?" I asked.

"Oh, he lives in the flat above mine."

"Well, why invite him?" I said.

"Coz he likes to join in."

"WHAT! Are you fucking nuts? Do you know who I am? Do you fucking realise who you're talking to? What the fuck do you think I am? A pervo? I'm here to fuck you not play games."

"Cool down," she said. "Chill out. You'll like Dave."

Anyway, one thing led to another and we got down to it. I fucked her over the settee, on the floor, on the bed, all over the flat. She loved it. So did I. And I've got to say, she was brilliant. Believe me, these middle-aged birds know what it's all about.

Then the doorbell went. It was Dave. I heard his squeaky voice before I saw him. He looked like what he sounded like: a prat. He was about 5 feet

5, skinny and very timid, about 50. "This is Dave," she said. He stuck his hand out to shake mine. I gave it a miss. Then - bang! - the madness began. Now at this time both me and this woman were in dressing gowns, naked underneath. This skinny prick Dave had a tracksuit on. She led him into the bedroom and told him to sit in the corner like a spoilt, naughty boy.

"Come on, Charlie. In here and show Dave how it's done."

So there I am, giving her one doggy-style over the bed with this nutcase watching. At first I felt uncomfortable. Then the madness took me over. I thought, fuck it, enjoy the moment. All my mates back in the asylum would cut their arms off for this. Wouldn't you? The only problem was I was fucked. I couldn't shoot my load with that prat watching. My dick and her pussy got so sore coz it went on that long. In the end I pulled out with a big hard-on and she gave me the best blow job I've ever had - him still watching. I actually felt sorry for him.

Then she said, "Hey, Dave, don't you fancy a go?"

"Fuck off. He's not touching me."

"Why?"

"Coz he just watches. He loves to watch."

I thought, how fucking mental is this planet? Sometimes I just think it's me. I just attract these nutters. They seem to come to me no matter where I am, or what I do. I'm drawn to them and I'll say now, I cherish these moments. They're lasting memories for me. And once you've stepped into madness you can't escape it. This is what I call harmless madness. She loved it. He enjoyed it. As for me, it was the fuck I needed. My Uncle Jack told me later that the whole estate knew her. She'd actually spent time in the local asylum. It was rumoured that she invited up to six men to some of her sessions. SIX. But I'm telling you now, she was a lovely, happy, sexy soul; a true nympho and with a good body for her age. She had this thing for rubbing her clit as you did her doggy-style. One dirty, hot, sexy bitch - and the language! Bloody hell. "Fuck me ... fuck me ... faster ... you fucker ... you ugly fucker ... pump it up ... fuck me ... you cunt ... you fucking cunt ... fuck me." Okay, yeah, yeah, okay, what do you think I'm doing here? Playing monopoly? It can go on a bit.

Anyway, get on this. I bumped into Dave a couple of days later getting into the lift. His eyes shot to the floor. He looked all guilty and embarrassed. I put my hand on his shoulder and said, "Cheer up, mate." I got chatting to him and he came round. He invited me up to his flat for a coffee, so I went. What a fucking dump. I said, "Get a fucking grip, mate. What's up with you? Get a life. I've seen cells better than this shithole." Anyway, I had a chat with him and basically he was just a lonely soul. He had fuck all and it turned out he'd been paying the nympho 50 quid to watch for years. What a sad old world, full of sad old people. You couldn't make it up if you tried. I guess that's how life is for lonely souls: shit.

I'm just reading my local *Luton News*. Two toerags - John Cole, 41, and Arif

Ullah, 32 - were caught selling drugs on the streets near school kids. Cole copped a six stretch and the other prick got four years. They should've got life for selling smack to kids. If you pair of cunts ever bump into me either in or out, stay out of my way coz I despise scum like you, and it's twats like you who get parole. When you two grow up you'll see what harm you do. Would you be happy if it was your kids buying drugs off two grown men on the street? You're about on my fucking patch, giving Luton a shit name. You're 41, Cole. Grow up. If you wanna be a criminal then do something worthwhile. Don't ruin innocent lives. Luton was once a great town, full of characters and a great place to live. Yeah! You're now inside, so you'll be getting counselling for your own drug addiction. You'll have all the probation and psychology on your side. Believe me, you should've got 20 years, the misery you cunts deal in. I get sick of reading about my town going down the drain and it's me who's the danger, not you fuckers. You fucking wankers. I've done your sentence in a straitjacket. I've done longer sitting on a chamber pot. It's a fucking joke. Pray you never sell drugs to my family in Luton, as I've still cousins there, coz I'd hunt you down, inject you with petrol and show you a hot time. God believe me. Six poxy years.

I phoned Giovanni, my lawyer, up tonight. He had a close call out in Bagdad, Iraq. He was 30 yards away from a bomb when it went off. It actually blew him up in the air. This guy is fearless. He lives and works among danger all over the world. It's why I love him. It's why we all respect him. Back in 1974 I had a real prat of a lawyer. He was fucking useless. One day in the prison interview room in Risley I grabbed his ear and squeezed it till he screamed. I told him if he didn't smuggle me in a box of Dairy Milk chocolates and an angel cake I'd rip his fucking face off. I never saw him again. Some people just can't take a joke. I remember another one I had in the 1980s. I set fire to his trouser leg. All in a day's laugh. At one time no lawyer would entertain me, especially after I took one hostage. Nasty fuckers. Surely that's victimising me? Racist fuckers. Racist to us Luton lads. Anyway, I'm now with Giovanni till the day my brain dries up and my heart explodes. We have 'respect' for each other. 'Family'. Yeah, that's what Giovanni is to me - family. If you fuck with him, you fuck with me. So don't do it. Please stop and think. You really don't want to have me as your nightmare.

This fucking postal strike is still holding up my mail. Odds and sods are trickling through, but I'm getting fed up with it now. You lazy cunts, get back to work.

Hey, did you know that the flu epidemic back in 1918/19 killed off 200,000 people in England and over 5 million in India? That's a lot of stiffs.

I'm dying to go on that Jeremy Kyle show. You lot know you're dying for it too. I just want to put my side over. Fuck the dosh - I'm not interested. I just want my side out there in the open. Hey, I'm really not a bad bloke. I've got no horns. I'm just the same as you. I wonder if my first wife would come on too? Then Jeremy could decide who's the lunatic. Let ten million viewers see who's the liar. We could both do a lie detector test. I'm up for all that, coz I've got fuck all to lie about. Every fucker knows what and who I am. I've nothing to act for, but I'd love to get that parasite of an ex-wife on TV so we can all have a good laugh at her eyebrows and find out why she sold that story to the mag. Let's plan ahead. Let's get it sorted. Come on, Jeremy, or I'll get Trisha to do it. I'm not hanging about.

I had a cell spin today. The security screws, known as 'the burglars', raided me. One of them, a young flash cunt, walked like he'd got something stuck up his arsehole. He was a right muppet. Nine out of ten screws call me Charlie, but with this cunt it was Bronson. So my reply was: "Okay, Guard, Jailer, filthy fuck-face screw." I've no time for his sort. Even the others laugh at him. Needless to say, they found nothing in my flowery dell. I don't need a tool or bags of drugs. I'm clean, crystal clean. I also had a great workout today, I really did, followed by a good hot shower. It felt lovely.

Hey, get on this. I've had a really filthy thought. Imagine this for a record. Pay three slappers for a night of fun. Get one on her knees over the bed, the second one over her with her arse sticking up, and the third over her. So picture it: three arses on top of each other, three pussies winking at you. You give no. 1 a few pumps, pull out and into no. 2, then out and into no. 3, and keep doing it fast. Pump, pump, pump, out, in, pump, pump, Yahooooo, pump, pump, out, in, pump, pump, ride it cowboy, yahoooo, yippeeeee, pump, pump, pump. Tell me, has it been done? It's possible. What would it be like? Fucking fantastic. Loonyology or what? Could you imagine that? Could you? Would you? I'm gonna do that and get it filmed. You wait and see. I'm definitely gonna try that. Why not? You're only jealous. You boring fuckheads. That's what I call excitement, unusual, kinky, sensual, greedy. Okay, so I'm greedy, so what? Three wet, hot, sticky, steaming pussies. That's the dream.

Get on this. Twelve bottles of Romanee-Conti Burgundy (1967) sold for 58k this week at auction. 58 fucking grand! It's fucking mental. Some people have more cash than sense. And in Claridges London Hotel they're selling a bottle of water for 50 quid!

Did you know that if you add up all the numbers on a roulette wheel it comes to 666? It's why they call it the devil's game. Be warned.

Did you know that a male Hollywood star played a female in nine movies. I bet you'll never guess who it was. Come on, have a guess. Have a guess, you boring fuckface. I bet you haven't got a clue. Come on, who was it? Well fuck off then, I'm not saying - not yet. Keep guessing. I'll give you a clue - very hairy.

A snake goes into a pub and asks for a pint of beer.

The barman says, "Sorry, mate, I can't serve you."

"Why not?" the snake asks.

"Coz you can't hold your drink."

Okay, I'll tell you who the male actor was who played nine females - it was Lassie!

Talking of dogs, there was a dog handler in the Scrubs that I'm sure was shagging his dog coz the dog walked funny. All the cons used to shout at him through their bars, "Leave the dog alone, you fucking beast." "Stop shagging that dog, you slag." Believe me, it just walked strange. What are we supposed to think? Just coz a screw wears a uniform and works for the Queen don't mean he's not into bestiality. Let's face it, a lot of screws couldn't pull a bird if they tried, and some of those Alsatians are good looking - better looking than some of the birds that stumble out of the clubs on a Saturday night, pissed and falling in the gutters.

The ugliest bird I ever saw was in Broadmoor. She had a neck like Tyson, little piggy eyes, four chins, rugby legs and massive thighs. Believe me, you wouldn't have touched it with a 30-foot pole. It must be sad for girls like that. They must die virgins. But, then again, they do have their dildos and some of the dillies they found in Broadmoor were huge. Put it this way, if you were to walk down the street with one, you'd get nicked for carrying an offensive weapon. These loony birds just like big ones. The canteen shop sold a lot of bananas and cucumbers in the asylum too. On canteen day the girls all had a smile. Hey, some of the male loons had smiles too, believe me. It's a funny old world in them places.

For a short time I was in Gloucester House, which was supposed to be one of the best wards in Broadmoor. This was 1979 time. There was a full-size snooker table there and I was having a knockabout one day when a loony walked in and put a sandwich on the baize. Why? What reason? What purpose? I whacked the cunt with the cue and then dragged him into the corner of the room and put him in a chair. He had a lump on his head the size of an egg - or a snooker ball. He was out cold for ages. I thought, fuck me, I've killed him. But he came around and went on his way. What can you say? Outside, I'd have broken both his arms and legs. No fucker does that to me. It's a piss-take. It's a challenge. How can you do other than serve him up? But this is Broadmoor, this is the big house. These guys are a special breed, they're unique. It took me ages to realise it too, but once I did I found a new way of dealing with such eccentric behaviour: meet madness with madness. Do unto them as they do unto you. Hit them with their own magic. What I should've done is pick the sandwich up, take a bite and then say, "Not enough cheese in it." Spook them, throw them off, amaze them, humour them, pacify the fuckers.

One day I put three aerosol cans in the oven. You should've heard the explosion. That woke them up. Another time I got three big earthworms out of the garden and put them in the soup urn. Nobody complained, so some loons must've eaten them. There was loads of budgies in Broadmoor chirping away. It was like a fucking giant aviary. Some of the old loons used to walk around with them on their shoulders. It was lovely to see all these characters - real old characters that I loved. There was a horrible, nasty, youngish screw who used to try to make if difficult for some of the elderly loons. We soon sorted that cunt out. Every day we drove him mad. He soon applied for a move to another ward. On one occasion I bumped into him accidentally with a bucket full of slops and he ended up with shit and piss all over him. He was spewing up as he ran off screaming. All the loons were laughing. It was an accident - trust me. I used to throw eggs at him too. I drove that cunt mental. I did that for the old boys. He was just a little cunt with a bit of power and it went to his head (like it has with those postmen - get back to work, you prats).

13 October 2007

I got three letters today. They're still trickling in, but I've got a sackful to come. One was from my good old buddy Alfie Lodge. Back in the 1980s Alf was the no. 1 armed robber in Wales, a top blagger. He did a spell with me in Long Lartin Jail. He made a good drop of hooch too.

England fucked Estonia today. Wright Phillips scored first, then Michael Owen, and then an own goal by one of the Estonians. That about sums that victory up for the lads. Yahoooooo! Yiiipppeeeeee! "We are the guv'nors, we are the gov'nors, don't fuck with us. We're on track now for the next World Cup. Watch us go all the way. Rooney, Rooney, Rooney! Owen, Owen, Owen! We're on our way for real, you'll see. Hey, and the England Rugby lads stuffed it right up the frogs today. What a great day for us English, and to top it all I had a lovely curry today and a bottle of orange squash. All that was missing was the vodka. Fuck you postmen.

Pablo arrived from Woodhill CSC Unit. I last saw him in Full Sutton seg block last year. He's a top geezer - a Londoner serving a ten stretch. He's done most of it in the blocks.

Old Ronnie Easterbrook is still not eating properly. Life just rolls on as ever. It's all slow. Oh, and Giovanni is taking on Charlie Richardson's case of 40 years ago when he copped a 25-year sentence. Giovanni says it was an injustice. Well, we all knew that when he got it. It'll be very interesting to see how this case gets on. Charlie served 17 fucking years of that, and that was when prison was a prison not a fucking Wendy house like it is now.

14 October 2007

Get on this. The *Sunday Sport* paper. The Governor told the screws to cut out two pages of the *Sunday Sport*, so we got a paper that's been censored with two pages removed. I'm told it's because there's something in it about the cons here. I'm also told that I'm mentioned, so my argument is, if so, why stop me seeing it? Also, if it's libellous, how can I take legal action if I'm not allowed to see it? Am I missing something here? Is this illegal? Everyone in the UK can read it except me. Obviously I'll find out exactly what it is. They don't call me the Daddy for fuck all. But how pathetic is this? How fucking childish. Now see what I mean about control? Everything is censored, even my mind. Cunts. Even an old screw told me it was bollocks, but once the Governor says cut it out it has to come out. So there you have it. The *Sunday Sport* has been stopped. Somebody notify the editor. I'm sure he or she won't be happy. What a fucking joke! Even Hitler never cut out pages. Who the fuck do they think they are? And, to top it all, I've paid for that paper, so it's my property. So there you have it. They're destroying my property, are they not? Watch this space, coz this is far from over.

I had a lovely roast chicken dinner today. The spuds were golden brown and the gravy was good too. I really enjoyed it. You'll laugh at how I eat my Sunday nosh. I lay out my table, stick a tissue in the front of my T-shirt (like the posh fuckers do) and just pretend I'm at a posh banquet. I eat slowly and look around my cell as if to nod at people. I sip my wine - well, water, but I pretend it's wine. At 400 quid a bottle I may as well enjoy it. That's my Sunday lunch. Pass the salt please. How was yours?

I hope the mail is back on tomorrow. Come on, lads, get back to work. I suppose they'll all get overtime now for sorting the piles of old letters out first. I'd give them a kick in the nuts myself. That's all they deserve. Lazy fuckers.

I heard that Jennifer Rush song today, 'Power of Love'. What a beautiful song that is and what a voice she's got. I think I'll have that playing at my homecoming shag. Well, one of them anyway. It just stirs my loins that one every time I hear it.

Oh well, a new week starts tomorrow. I feel lucky. Fuck knows why, but I do.

15 October 2007

I just knew today was gonna be a lucky day. Monster Miller got bent up again. The heavy mob went in and wrapped him up like a kipper. I was shouting, "Hit the cunt in the solar plexus, put him in the van and get rid of the nonce." Sadly, he's still here, but it was a bit of excitement for the day. I fucking love it when they bend him up. We all do. Ten or 20 years ago the screws would've given him a good kicking. Nowadays it's just a bend-up and the odd slap. Pathetic if you ask me. Bring back the birch, I say.

Did you hear about the 99-year-old lady out in Poinciana, Florida? Some toerag raped and killed her. Edith Macalla had survived almost 100 years on the planet only for her to be taken out by a fucking psycho sex monster. Her 77-year-old daughter found her. How sad is that? When they catch the bastard they should fry him in the chair. What sort of human could rape an old lady? I'll tell you - a fucking monster. Wake up world. It's happening every single day. You know it; we all know it. Some cunt of a head shrink will say, "Oh, but he's sick, he's got this, he's got that, he should be treated." Well I say, "Fuck off. He's a monster. There's no excuse. Cut his bollocks off."

I see Michael Carroll, the Lottery winner thug, and his girlfriend are having a baby. Nice one. I hope it settles him down. Mick has sent me cards and some of my mates know him well. He's a nice chap, but the media love to write him off. They're just jealous. What of? Well, nine million bucks for starters. Mick's okay, so give the guy a break.

I called Tom Hardy tonight. We always have a good in-depth chat about life. He's a heavy sort of dude, a serious thinker, and he's my cup of tea. You learn a lot from Tom. He's 30 years before his time, if you get my drift. We both like chess and Scrabble. One day we'll play a game or two - loser cooks a Sunday roast. I'm fucking starving and I always play to win. Can you see me cooking Tom a roast? Can you? He don't realise what he's up against. Chess - I'm a grand master. Scrabble - I'm a word freak (I love words). My only problem is that I can't get a game, unless I play myself.

I got only two letters today. There'll be a sackful one day this week, you'll see. I had a cheese salad for tea - a nice lump of cheddar too, which made me four sandwiches. A pickled onion would've been nice. One can dream on. Life's a dream. We all have to dream. None of us can ever be contented, can we?

Yeah, I'm feeling good. This week feels lucky. I've got a tingle in my body, a sense. I'm having an early night tonight. It's 8.30 p.m. now and I'm just about to have a strip wash. I always wash my bollocks, arse and feet before bed. Cleanliness is next to godliness, so I must be in heaven. I give my Hampstead Heath a good brush too, and then lights out and back to the world of dreams. Isn't life wonderful? Well, isn't it? Goodnight.

16 October 2007

Got a load of mail today, some of it 15 days old. Two fucking weeks old - what a farce. I hope the postmen are reading this. You cunts, fucking about with our mail.

I was speaking to a decent screw today (who shall remain nameless). Poor old Ronnie Easterbrook is very weak and poorly now and he's still not eating. It's sort of put me on a downer. An old man like him should not be doing this, but it's his way of saying, "Fuck you lot." I predict that he'll soon be taken to an outside hospital, as he can't even get out of bed now. All these monsters in this hellhole who I'd love to see starve to death, and it's a real legend doing it. Let's face reality here. Ronnie was one of the best armed robbers to come out of east London in the last 50 years and that man has my utmost respect.

I'm just in the mood to expose some more Wakefield monsters now:

* Andreou Anthia. This Cypriot cunt got nicked a few years back in north London - the Nash brothers' manor. He was lucky they never got hold of him before the cops. Johnny Nash would've hit the cunt so hard his nose would've disappeared into his skull. Anthia raped 15 women and copped life with a 25-year tariff. He's up on A Wing walking about like King fucking Kong, as if he's some sort of celebrity. All the other nonces look up to him.

What a sick jail this is.

* Peter Cunliffe. This piece of dog shit copped a 15 stretch back in 2005. He's a serial sex offender. He was actually out on bail for a previous sex attack when he violently raped some others. He likes little girls. He's only in his early twenties now, so he'll be free at 30 - if not sooner. Right now he's up on D Wing. He loves the gym sessions and body building. He gets a good wage, so he can buy all the best food and supplements. Watch out, girls, coz Rambo's coming out - unless he ends up in a real jail where real cons will break his fucking legs or drop 200 pounds on his nonce head in the gym.

* David Harker. A right fucking beast. He's up on D Wing with Cunliffe. Two peas in a pod; two cheeks of the same arse. Harker killed a mother of four nine years back and her head and limbs were never found. Some say he ate her. Whatever, the fucker went past the limits of humanity. He drove his mind straight into a one-way road to hell. Now get on this for a twist of madness: the woman he killed was Julie Paterson - almost my name. Well Julie's fella, Alan Taylor, couldn't take it. He went mad and killed somebody just so that he could come to prison and bump into Harker. Now that's what I call loyalty. So Alan gets a life sentence and then - guess what? - he topped himself. What a turnabout. This whole case stinks of madness, and who suffers most? The four kids. Harker's got a lot to answer for. Fuck me, is he gonna burn.

* Deepak Bouri. This toerag smashed Lisa Spence 80 times over the head with a hammer. She was an East End girl, only 20 years old. Her head was like a crushed tomato. What sort of animal could hit a young girl 80 times? Well, Bouri could and did. I hope he serves 80 years, but he won't. Cunts like this are model inmates. He's the screws tea boy. "Yes sir, no sir, three bags of shit sir?" Yeah? Trust him with a hammer. Cunt.

* Viktors Dembovskis. This Latvian beast raped and killed Jeshma Raithatha 17 years ago. She was a beautiful young girl with all her life ahead of her. And guess what? He was allowed into our country even though he'd committed multiple sex crimes in his own country. The Government let in a beast and it cost a young girl's life. What have you got to say about that, Prime Minister? If it was my girl I'd bring a private prosecution against you for allowing it to happen. This cunt is up in D Wing. He's got a lovely, warm, cushy cell and loves to cook up a favourite Latvian meal. I'd cook the cunt a meal - fucking poisoned mushrooms with an arsenic omelette. Shall I continue? There's hundreds more.

* Ronald Cole. This gutless fucker got four years for raping a woman whilst her baby slept nearby. Four poxy years. After he was released - guess what? Yeah, you've guessed it - within two days he'd committed a carbon-copy rape. And can you believe this - this time he copped 14 years? Why only 14 years? Why not life? Surely this prick is a danger to society. He's fucked up two women's lives. How many more? He'll probably kill the third victim rather than chance capture. The system is creating a potential sex

killer. Ronald Cole is a monster.

    * Dominic McKilligan. This slag likes young boys. He sexually assaulted and killed an 11-year-old boy up north and copped life in 1999. He had a previous for it. Once a nonce, always a nonce. He's up on A Wing with all his lovely nonce pals. A screw told me that when a little prisoner arrives who looks and acts young all the nonces try to get into him by offering him all sorts of goodies. Next thing they'll have a pair of shorts on him and start up a romance. Well, what do you expect in a monsters' paradise?

    I reckon that's enough for now. I'm sick of exposing these cunts. Some may get off on it but, take it from me, this place is full of them. These are just a handful and for me to be associated with these monsters is just an insult, but the papers continue to do so.

16 October 2007, Daily Mirror
by Jeremy Armstrong
Charles Bronson S2 006
Britain's most violent prisoner, the 54-year-old is a lifer. Served 32 years - 28 in solitary confinement because he is so dangerous. He was jailed for an armed robbery in 1975 but given life after taking an art teacher hostage during a siege in Hull Prison in 1969.
Infamous hardman Charles Bronson, 54, is caged in a segregation unit near the perimeter wall.
He carries out cleaning duties naked, save for his £200 designer specs, and boasts he is Britain's "No. 1 hostage taker", having served time in 120 prisons, staged eight rooftop protests and assaulted 20 officers.
Robert Maudsley, 54, his neighbour, earned the nickname Hannibal the Cannibal because he ate the brain of an inmate after killing him.
He has spent 30 years, a UK record of more than 10,700 days, in solitary confinement and is so dangerous he has cardboard furniture in his cell, but enjoys classical music and art.

    What I'd like to ask him is: "Who told you I do cleaning duties naked or is this in your own pervo dreams?"

    1) I'm in solitary.

    2) Even if I wasn't, how could I sweep up naked with women screws about?

    3) Why are you trying to label me as some sort of pervo?

    Why do journalists make up this shit? Coz it sells papers? It's sensationalism at its best. When I get out, Jeremy, you come and see me and I'll give you a story of your lifetime - without you having to make shit up. I've got stories that will make your spine shake, but if you carry on lying about me you may well end up with a snapped spine. Oh, and Maudsley has never painted a picture in his life. All he is, is a fucking lunatic and if he got hold of you, you wouldn't have a brain.

    Maudsley is the original Hannibal Lector. Hopkins is only an actor;

Maudsley is for real. When he wasted the two cons here in the 1970s, after it was all over all he did was laugh. He's still laughing today. On a silent night he often breaks into laughter. He's a strange kettle. He once shouted out of the window at 3 a.m. at the top of his voice: "I want a brain and heart curry tomorrow or I'll rip a screw's throat out." They opened his door the next day with shields and dogs. Loonyology at its maddest.

I called Al Rayment today. He's meeting with Frank "Know what I mean, Harry?" Bruno next week. Oh, I almost forgot: I had a lovely shepherd's pie today, just like granny used to make - and hers was a plate of shit too.

Some people in different parts of the world believe we come back as animals. If this is true then I want to come back as a Bengal Tiger. Why? I'll tell you: it's the most beautiful beast on the planet. Fuck the lions, this is the real king. Look at it, look at the markings: that face, those eyes, it's whole presence is one of 'don't fuck with me'. This animal is ferocious and proud and very gracious. It's a killing machine, it's strong, it's fast and it's very, very unpredictable. It's just brilliant. It's what I would love to end up as in the next life and then, by God, don't dare fuck with me. I would defo be a maneater, make no mistake about it. You fuckers have hunted the tiger for centuries, so it's time the tiger hunted you pricks for real. Pray I don't come back, coz it'd be the worst fucking nightmare you've ever had. Leave the tigers alone, you cowards.

Talking of gracious things, did you know that the lovely Barbara Windsor is 70 years old? Don't she look great? Good on ya, Babs. Keep it up.

What about the devil-crazed knife lunatic who stabbed the vicar, Rev. Paul Bennett, 22 times to death. He wasn't messing about. Geraint Evans just got a 7-inch blade and did the devil's work. That's what religion does to your brain: it screws you up. He did it right on the church steps in broad daylight. What a crazy world we live in. Guess what? He's been sent to a secure mental hospital for the criminally insane. Watch out, hospital chaplain, coz you could be next. I bet Evans won't be in the Christmas choir.

Oh, and congratulations to Anne Enright, who just won the prestigious Man Booker Prize for fiction. She won it with her novel called *The Gathering*. That's a nice 50k bonus for her. Well done, Anne. You beat a lot of favourites to win it. You've got the luck of the Irish.

Memo
CSC UNIT Manager
18 October 2007
Prison Number : BT1314 BRONSON
Tom Hardy
The above named has NOT been approved by the Home Office for the approved visitors scheme.
SECURITY DEPARTMENT

Here's another example of victimisation, with no reason given. Tom's an actor, a man who lives his life decent. He's a respected man with no criminal past, but they deny him a pass to see me. Why? Because it's control. The system don't want me to have visitors. If they had their way, I wouldn't even be able to see my mother. They want me cut off from the outside. They're afraid of what the outside will see. They're ashamed. They're full of hate and evil. Me, I expect it all the time, but Tom is gutted. He feels he's been abused, humiliated and victimised. Maybe he should challenge it? Maybe he should sue the bastards for victimisation. But one thing's for sure - he's now found out just how prejudicial the penal system is, without even entering this world. There is no reason. There is no excuse. It's just pure madness.

"Sorry, Tom, but the only way you'll ever see me is if I walk free or if I fly over the wall."

"It's not your fault, my friend. Piss on them. They're fucking hypocrites."

Even the screw who came to my door said he was shocked over it. It's down to some little, four-eyed, skinny office prat with a bit of power. Let's fuck with Bronson. But the truth is, you actually fuck with yourself. You mugs!

18 October 2007

I got a pile of letters today, but one saddened me. My old buddy Tony Hunt from Birmingham has been diagnosed with cancer of the pancreas. He's been given only months to live. Months. That's heavy shit. The end is near. A sad day. I paced up and down my cell for a good four hours just thinking how sad life really is. It can go dark in the blink of an eye and then it's all over, curtains. I actually feel a bit angry today, coz my life is being sucked dry, and for no other reason but evilness. I don't know how much longer I can accept this shit and the lies, coz that's all it's been for the last six years - one big lie. They're sucking me to death. One up on that, I can't even see my friends, and they won't even give a reason. There is no reason. I feel I may give up hope of ever getting out and go back to my prison activist ways. I was happier then, I really was. What's the sense in playing a game you can't win? It's fucking madness. I just hope this legal matter soon resolves so I know exactly where I stand, coz today I'm getting some very bad vibes going through my brain. I'm not happy. I won't even be allowed to see my buddy Tony. My family and friends are dying and I'm not allowed to be there for them. Year after year after year I'm just being sucked deeper and deeper into the giant abyss. A man can only absorb so much. Believe me, I would prefer to be laughing in a dark room with nothing than live in Disneyland forever. Fuck Mickey Mouse and Donald Duck, and bring on the chainsaw. Stay strong, Tony. Fight it. I could still make it out. I've gotta sit cool - for now.

Another case of the pen being mightier than the sword is when Jason Webster killed Rebecca Love. He stabbed her in the throat with it. He's now in jail for life. If you see him with a pen, knock him out. Don't take chances. Life's too precious to fuck about with. I wonder how long he'll serve? I bet not as long as me.

I called Chris Cowlin tonight. We had a good chat about *Loonyology*. He's more than happy. So he should be, as he's sitting on a no. 1 best-seller with this book. This is not just a book, this is my soul. This was meant to happen. Believe it.

Hey, did you know there's a convict in a Russian jail who ate one of his legs while in solitary? A fucking leg. How the fuck can a man eat his own leg? Surely the food's not that bad? Anyway, he ate a leg. How or why is just bollocks to me - loonyology gone fucking mental. Hey, if he can eat his own leg, what would he eat if he was in a two-up cell? Or a three-up? He could cut the prison population in 20 years. What a nutter.

I was jogging in the yard today and tripped and banged my head. I'm getting dizzy in my old age. I need to move and see some grass. How many more years have I got to be in a fucking fishbowl, swimming around and around? No wonder I get dizzy and confused. It's like living inside a cuckoo clock. How the fuck do you factory workers cope, with the same old shit for 40 years? No wonder you're all nuts out there. You must be.

I said to a young screw today, "Don't worry, mate, you've only got another 30+ years of opening and shutting doors."

He looked at me and said, "I enjoy my job, Charlie."

So I said, "Yeah, and pigs fly."

How the fuck can a man enjoy locking up people for 30+ years? It's not normal, is it?

The screwess Ms Walker was on today. She's a lovely woman. I know when she's on even before my door's opened. I can smell her. She wears a lovely scent. When she's on it's always a nice atmosphere. She's got a nice way about her - a good, decent woman.

There was one woman screw down here four years ago, who had a pair of shoulders on her like Arnie and a neck to match. One day I heard her fart and I said to her, "Bloody hell. I bet that's ripped a hole in your trousers."

It was one of those farts that seem to rebound - disgusting.

"Oh, I was on the lagers and curry last night, Charlie."

Yeah! I thought, you fat slob. You gotta laugh. If you take it all serious you'll need brain surgery.

Oh well, I'll have a thought for my pal Tony and his lovely family. And I hope Tom Hardy complains over being knocked back from visiting me. It's victimising you, Tom. Don't fucking accept it, mate, I wouldn't. Get your MP on it or a lawyer and sue Prison HQ. They're making you look like a criminal. Find out WHY. It's all very eerie; top secret shit. Just what are these cunts afraid of, I wonder?

The most beautiful things in life are free. That must be why I'm just ugly. There's a screw here, Mr Burrell, a small guy in his 50s, but a decent chap.

I've known him years. He's just got a smack in the face, which bust his nose. Some con attacked him. It all goes with the job. But the con couldn't have picked a smaller or more decent screw. I suppose he had his reasons. Maybe he don't like little screws. Maybe he just don't like any screws. Whatever. that's Mr Burrell on the Tom and Dick. We won't see him for a few weeks or, if he's got any sense, a few months. They know how to milk the sick leave. Some get a button ripped off and they're three months on stress leave. You gotta laugh. It's a crazy job for crazy people. Could you do it? Would you fucking want to do it? I'd sooner watch the grass grow.

Hey, did you know that there's a guy in Arizona who can stick his head up his arse? Pity George Bush couldn't do that. Is he real or is he one of the muppets? I used to think that Ronald Regan was a muppet. They're all muppets them politicians. They're all up each other's arses. Would you trust them with your life? Would you fuck.

I went out to a party in 1974. I never went back home. I'm still partying. This is some fucking party. No booze, no women and shit food.

Hey, get on this for a sausage. The world's longest was 35 miles long and weighed a staggering 15.5 tonnes. It was made in Sheffield in October 2000. Now that's what I call a sausage.

And get on this for a laugh. Calderdale Magistrates Court in Halifax gives out puzzle sheets to convicted cons as they await sentencing in the cells below. Talk about left wing Liberal twats. How pathetic is this one? You couldn't make it up. They'll be whipping us next with lettuce leaves. You can stick your puzzles up your arse. I'll do my press-ups and take my bird on the chin, you daft bastards. Fucking puzzles?! That's the last thing a man in the cells below a court needs. Puzzles? Do me a favour.

Anyone for Scrabble? Fuck playing with Paul Allan, coz he's just recently won the UK Championship. He's the new Scrabble Guv'nor. Get on this. He got a word out called 'ai' - it's a kind of sloth. What chance have you got at playing him? They make words out of words. They're brilliant. Congratulations, Paul. Well done, mate.

22 October 2007, The Sun
LAGS DRUG SMUGGLED ON STAMP
A deadly drug nearly 80 times stronger than heroin is being smuggled into prisons under postage stamps.
Fentanyl - nicknamed The Bomb - has led to the deaths of hundreds of addicts in the US.
Security staff discovered patches of the powerful opiate under stamps sent to a lag at HMP Leicester.
A warning was sent to every prison governor in Britain alerting them to the smuggling ploy.
A senior Prison Service source said: "We are very grateful to our staff. It is very difficult to smuggle drugs into jails, but prisoners will always come up with ingenious ways."

Fentanyl is used by surgeons as an anaesthetic and for pain relief - and gives junkies a super- charged hit.
But it is also extremely toxic. Lab technician Dean Norton, 24, of Castle Donington, Leics, died last year after being bitten by rats he had tested the drug on.
Last night an insider at Category B Leicester jail said: "This is a worrying development - God knows how much has got through in other mail."

This about sums up our jails as they are today. The cons have given up trying to escape. All they need is their drugs and they sleep their bird away. How fucking sad is that? Most of them haven't got ten press-ups in them. It really does break my heart. All my years of battling through this system and for what? Was it worth the fight - fighting for cons' rights, fighting for better conditions? Was it fuck. I've lost my life for a bunch of druggies. How fucking sad is that? I'm really now wanting to walk out from all this shit, I really am.

23 October 2007

The screw who got punched up, is back on duty today. The con who did it never got nicked coz he's been certified mad and is waiting to go to Broadmoor. That's the only good thing about being crackers - they can't nick you, coz a madman is not responsible for his actions. So the million dollar question is: "Why the fuck is the madman here?" He's waiting for a space in Broadmoor and has been waiting for the last six months. The screws here are screws not nurses. They're not trained to lock up nutters. Again this is the system proving to be what it is: a load of bollocks. It's run by lunatics. The system is the problem, and it always will be.

Here's another example. Yesterday I put in an official application with a page to the governor. Read it:

P/O Governor CSC Staff
I've known Ronnie Easterbrook for over 30 years. Whether the system accepts it or not, he is a legend, an old school villain with serious morals and a code of honour.
I truly believe he is set to die on his latest protest. I just sense it's his final way of saying "Fuck you" to the system. His death will put a bad stigma over this jail for many years. You're not dealing with a Shipman here - nobody gave a fuck about him, the same as Fred West.
You're dealing with a 75-year-old con who probably should not even be in a max secure jail. It will end up a disaster for all concerned. The day you carry him out in a body bag will be a shameful day, a very sad day for many.
I believe I could change his mind. He will listen to me, whereas he won't listen to you! I will try my best. Only because I respect him and admire his strong will. I believe he could still get out. There is hope for him (but he thinks different). I suggest putting a chair in his cell so I can go in and have a chat - just him and me, as old friends. 'A bit of trust'. Otherwise I doubt he will talk with screws in his cell. He's a very proud, stubborn man. I would like to think I can change his mind before it's too late. Even

now, he has probably fucked up his kidneys. Please consider my request.
Charlie Bronson, 22 October 2007

The response was "No". Well, there you have it from the no. 1 governor's own mouth - NO. What does this tell you? He's a cunt, a totally gutless fucking prick. He knows Ronnie Easterbrook would listen to me, he knows we go back 30+ years, he knows I'm upset over it all, and yet he stops me from seeing him. Why? Because I'm on this CSC fucking piss-take unit, while he can sit back and watch a 75-year-old man starve himself to death. What does this add up to? Madness. It's so insane it's untrue. Now you can understand how I've spent all my years in trouble. These cunts drive a man mad. It's senseless, it's pathetic and it's bloody inhuman. Even the screws have said it's bollocks not to let me have a chat with Ronnie. He's now in his bed 24/7 and I'm told he looks ill - and it goes on.

If this man dies, then I would say to his family and close friends outside: demand a public enquiry! Demand I be called to give evidence. Because the Governor could be responsible. He knows fucking well that I could stop this. Plus, why is a 75-year-old man being left to die in a seg block when he should be in the hospital wing being monitored by nurses? I rest my case - for now.

I got some photos sent in off Keeley today of Al Rayment's show in Doncaster. She's a hot, sexy cookie. I called her tonight for a chat. I always get a hard-on when she talks. I can't help it. It's how it is. What can I do? She's just lovely. What's a bloke supposed to do in a cage, forget about pussy? Life's not like that is it? I wish it was. Anyway, she's a lovely friend.

I had a nice cheese salad for tea. It was a big lump of cheese too, which makes a change from the usual wafer-thin slices we usually get. I used to go out with a bird who lived on cheese. It's all she fucking ate. When she farted it smelt cheesy.

Ain't women weird? Don't they have some strange ways? But they're all still special in their own way. What would we do without them? We'd be fucked, truly fucked.

Hey, the postmen have agreed to a new deal, so they're all happy again. Who'll be the next to strike? I think the nurses should all walk out until they get a £500 rise. They deserve it. They should all be on a £1,000 a week. They're the true angels. Fuck the postmen, that's a muppet job. It's our angels we should be looking after. Don't you agree?

I would've made a good nurse: "Oy, cunt! Take your medication or I'll snap your leg in half."

There was a male nurse in Parkhurst in the early 1970s who got caught in a con's cell giving him a wank. Can you believe that? The jail tried to hush it up like they always do, but nothing is kept secret in a max secure jail. The wanker screw vanished and so did the con. They probably got married and lived happily ever after. Cunts. They give a jail a bad name. Fuck me, there are standards to live up to.

That Parkhurst was a funny old place, it really was. The memories I've got still amaze me. They crack me up sometimes. It's forever. They never go away.

Hey, did you know that a leech has three jaws? Can you believe that? Why would any creature need three jaws? No wonder they're greedy bloodsucking twats. Image a couple of them on your bell end. Ouch! Now that would hurt. That would be a mad torture - to force someone to swallow a dozen big swamp leeches. They'd suck you dry from the inside out. Yuk! Nasty!

What about them lizards that dive on you from the trees in the Borneo jungle, rip off bits of flesh and then jump off again. They fuck off with lumps of your face! Fuck that - think I'll give it a miss.

I fancy a nice beach holiday for a month - soak up some sun and get plenty of shagging done. One can dream. That's all it ever is - a fucking big dream. But at least I've got a dream. Half the cunts in this shithole don't even know what a dream is. They're buried, forgotten. Their souls are burnt to a crisp. Hell's frozen over - they're refrigerated. You can hear their bones rattle on a windy night.

25 October 2007

Ronnie Easterbrook moved back over to the hospital. They took him over in a wheelchair coz he was that weak. Once over there he started eating. That's showbiz for you.

Mark Manson got a life sentence back in 1992 for bashing a woman up and drinking her blood. Yeah, a real-life fuck of a vampire nutcase. He had it on his toes this year and grabbed an old granny hostage. I tell you, these vampires don't fuck about. In the old days we'd spear them with a silver cross and exterminate the fuckers, but at Basildon Crown Court he copped four years. Lucky vampire; unlucky granny.

That little pervo Rampley just got released from jail but within half an hour he'd harassed five women. Five in 30 minutes - can you believe it? When the Old Bill arrested him he said, "Sorry. I've got a problem." He was given another two years for breaching his sex prevention order. Why bother letting the cunt out? When is the system gonna wake up and learn the facts? These sorts of monsters can't be cured. Okay, it wasn't serious, but he's upset five people. He's a fucking nonce. He don't know anything else. To him it's only natural. Wake up system, fucking wake up. Treat these nonces like you treat the villains - 'harsh'. They do love a nonce in the system. I wonder why?

I see Finance Director Sharon Bridgewater just copped a five stretch for a £2 million scam. Two million bucks and five years. She'll probably serve two years, so that's a million quid a year. Who says crime don't pay? She lived the life of a movie star. She had it all. Good luck to you, Sharon. They'll probably make a movie of your life later. You lived the dream, sweetheart. You had the bollocks - sorry, pussy - to do it. Whatever, she did it. Two million bucks.

Beautiful. Imagine it. All them fast cars, the best hotels, the best clothes, everything you can dream of. Was it worth a five stretch? Was it? Come on, don't be daft - two million quid?!

My buddy Big Pat Jackson was 28 stone and he lost 10 stone in one year. Ten fucking stone. That's the size of an average man he lost. I'm proud of him. That's what I call willpower, pure determination. Big Pat's an inspiration to all fat people. We salute you, my friend. Ten stone disappears - awesome. In my book you're a legend and don't you forget it either.

28 October 2007, Sunday Star
JAIL NUT: MY ROUTE OUT
Jail maniac Charles Bronson reckons he could be on his way to freedom.
The man dubbed Britain's scariest prisoner says a legal case next month may pave the way for his release.
And the Court of Appeal hearing could also affect thousands of dangerous criminals, including rapists, paedophiles and violent thugs.
Sex fiend David Walker and attempted robber Nicholas Wells have both served recommended minimum terms under the Imprisonment for Public Protection scheme, introduced in 2005.
The scheme means that at the end of the minimum term, inmates can apply for release on the grounds that they are no longer a danger to the public.
But the pair said they were not given the chance to go on reform courses which would have shown they had changed their ways.
They won their case at the High Court in July, which condemned the indeterminate sentences as "arbitrary, unreasonable and unlawful".
The Government will fight the ruling at the Court of Appeal on November 20.
If the appeal fails, up to 12,500 criminals could be back on the streets. And even inmates as notorious as Bronson, 54 - who has spent 33 years in jail, including more than 22 years in solitary confinement - could benefit.
Bronson, serving life for kidnapping a prison teacher, has staged eight rooftop demos and taken hostages ten times.
From his cell in Wakefield top security jail, West Yorks, he said, "There is a case going on. Now, if them lads win their cases, it affects thousands of people who haven't murdered who are serving life sentences with short tariffs. If these people win their case then we are being held illegally."
Campaigners also say the law should be changed.
The Prison Reform Trust's Geoff Dobson said: "The indeterminate sentences were introduced to tackle a small number of dangerous offenders. But it is clear that they are being used for relatively minor offenders and the prison service is struggling to cope. This has become a ferocious and unjust law."

Yeah, you won't be calling me a nut when I'm out and you want the story. Then it'll be "Mr Bronson" and a nice thick wad of crispy £50 notes in my hand. My only gutter is getting out on the back of David Walker - a sex fiend. That sort of puts a bad smell in the air for me. How fucking mental is that? But, that's how the cookie crumbles. Once the floodgates crash open there's 12-12,500 of us rolling out. What a fucking party. Who said dreams don't come true? Or nightmares. I bet Prison HQ are shitting it! One good thing though, it helps with prison overcrowding. So in one respect we'll be doing HQ a favour. All those empty cells ... Have a nice day...

Hey, did you know that 'Please Please Me' was The Beatles' first no. 1 hit record back in 1963? That's 47 years ago. Can you believe that? Almost half a century ago and I can remember it. Can you?

Get on this one Britain's first atomic bomb exploded in the Pacific in 1957. I bet you never knew that! How are we allowed to let off atomic bombs in the beautiful Pacific?

Did you know that it was only 80 years ago, in 1928, when women got to vote? Amazing. Until then they were regarded as second-class citizens and weren't allowed! Why not? Who said they couldn't vote?

In 1912 the great *Titanic* went down, so she wasn't so great was she? How do I know all this? And why do I keep slipping these facts in? I'll tell you why. Some people think I'm crackers, but I'm not so mad if I know all this, I'm a clever bastard.

Did you know that in 1913 D.H. Lawrence wrote *Sons and Lovers*? Read it - it's a classic. I read it while I was in Wandsworth seg block back in 1976 and enjoyed it. It passed a couple of days.

It was 1865 when Lewis Carroll wrote *Alice in Wonderland*. I read that in Wandsworth seg block in 1976 too. That was a year I read some classics, and I'd never read those sorts of books before - no interest. But when you're stuck in a concrete coffin you'll read anything to pass the time, and I'm glad I read those - classics.

I bet you don't know this fact. In 1917 Ernest Rutherford split the atom. The only things I've ever split are a nice juicy fanny, a watermelon, and a juicy peach or two. He was a clever fucker that Rutherford. Who would've thought of splitting the atom? Would you? I bet you don't even know what a fucking atom is, do you?

Hey, it's time to test you, so come on, who wrote *Treasure Island* and when? Come on, who wrote it? It was Robert Louis Stevenson back in 1883. Can you believe that? Tell me who hasn't read it! We all have, ain't we? What a read, what a book, what a great author!

Here's two classics for you. In 1876 Alexander Graham Bell sent his first voice message. He just had to be called Bell, didn't he?! 'Ding dong'. Why not Smith or Bloggs? And in 1878 Joseph Wilson Swan invented the light bulb. What a great invention that was! Well done, mate. Not really that long ago is it, 1878?!

Did you know that in 1877 Queen Victoria was proclaimed Empress of India? Why? I don't understand that, do you? What had she ever done for India? Somebody tell me!

Another tester for you: who's William Booth, and what's he famous for?

No, he's not a mass killer, or a lunatic, or some psycho in Parkhurst! He's the original founder of the Salvation Army back in 1865. Let's be honest, we do have to salute the good old Sally Army. There was one old boy who used to come in to visit the cons in the block in the Scrubs. He was a nice old chap and he used to do the odd phone call for me. At Xmas time in most jails they bring in the local Sally Band and they're bloody good too!

It was 1807 when 'The Slave Trade' was ended in Britain ... or was it? Maybe in the history books, but not in my book! If you dig deep enough, you'll see what I mean. A lot of laws come in, but they're not always heeded! Slavery was abolished in the British Empire in 1834 ... or was it? I doubt it. In fact, I fucking know it wasn't!

Now here's a fact that'll shock you. Jonathan Swift wrote *Gulliver's Travels* in 1726. I read that as a boy and it's a great book - a masterpiece. But to think it was written almost 300 years ago freaks me out. What does that tell you? It tells me it's magical.

Now I'm gonna freak you all out! This is scary stuff. In 1407 Bethlehem Hospital in London became the first lunatic asylum in the world and it was called 'Bedlam'. Come on, imagine it. What was that place like? You know it must've been hell on Earth: experiments, cutting open their skulls, studying the brain. You know that place was pure loonyology!

It was in 1650 that tea was first drunk in England. The good old pot of rosy lea, brewed up in teapots and poured into china cups with tea strainers, not you're muggy old tea bags. And it was in 1652 that the first ever coffee shop opened in London. I hope you're all learning something here.

Shakespeare died in 1616. Whether you love him or hate him, wasn't he a genius?. I'd say so - for his time.

In 1719 Daniel Defoe wrote *Robinson Crusoe*. Come on, who's not read that? I read that as a boy and then re-read it in Parkhurst back in 1977. If you haven't read it then you're missing out, coz it's fucking brilliant.

Okay, I'm on a roll now, so hold on tight:

1348 marked the first outbreak of the Black Death in the UK. Very nasty too.

In 1133 Durham Cathedral was completed. Now that's old.

In 1117 the first leper hospital opened in London. I bet you've never seen a leper, but we had thousands of the fuckers back then. In fact we had so many lepers that lots got wasted - buried alive! They should do that to the paedophiles. Waste the fuckers I say.

In 1621 the first English newspaper was printed called *Corante*. I wonder if it had a page 3 dolly bird?

In 1634 Convent Garden opened.

In 1710 St Paul's Cathedral was completed.

In 1813 Elizabeth Fry started up the Prison Reform. 'Big deal'. What fucking good has that ever done?

In 1779 the Epsom Derby ran for the first time.

In 1994 the first woman priest was ordained into the Church of England.

In 1982 Pope John II visited Britain. Do we care? I'm still waiting for Santa, so fuck the Pope. What's he gonna bring me? Nothing!

In 1940 the Blitz hit London. Those Nazi bastards.

In 1887 Queen Victoria celebrated her Diamond Jubilee. So what! Who fucking cares? She probably hung a dozen prisoners in the tower for a laugh just to start the party off. Wake up. Get real. This is history!

Phew! Let's slow the pace again!

Do you know what baffles me? The King of Saudi Arabia, King Abdullah! On 29 October he flew to the UK and our royalty welcomed him with open arms. Why? This guy is probably the most brutal king in the world. When are people gonna wake up? Saudi Arabia's human rights are nil. Just making comments about Sharia law will get your head chopped off. One poor sod called Nabil Al-Randan was given nine lashes for employing two women in his restaurant. Women are not allowed to drive or travel without permission from a man. And if you commit adultery, you're fucked - women especially. You'll be stoned to death. As for gays - dig your grave. You go over there with a Bible and see what you get. Their whole way of life and culture are like another planet. So why does he get the red carpet treatment? Could it be his wealth, in particular the oilfields?! We went to war against Iraq for less than the horrors the Saudis do! It's a case of double standards to me. Fuck him. He wouldn't be welcome in my boozer.

Hey, do you know what 'Ectoplasm' means? Well, find out yourself! What do you think I am - a teacher?!

Here's a funny thing about UFOs. Bonnybridge in Scotland is apparently the world's capital for UFO sightings, with an average of 300 a year. Like the Loch Ness fucking Monster and Jocks in kilts with 14-inch dicks and flying haggis, it's all whisky-talking pissheads.

I see Sandra Lester's book is out: *The Ripper Unmasked*. Yeh, she never planned that one, did she?! Another muggy penfriend, followed by a book full of shit. The funniest thing is, though, it will sell. Still - fuck it - it's only the Yorkshire Ripper. I bet he could write a better one on her, though. He wants to sell all her sexy letters on eBay and use the dosh for a party for the loonies. That's how to win against these sicko women who fall in love with caged men. You're fucking madder than the loons. Get a life, you crazy bitches.

31 October 2007

Billy Bristow and his lovely daughter Rachel visited me today! Guess what? Me and Billy haven't seen each other since 1973 - 34 bleeding years. Billy's the brother of Johnny, one of my best buddies ever. Johnny and me were like twins in the 1960s and '70s. It was really good to see Billy after so long. He's a top bloke. Sadly he lost his son Martyn not long back and it's taken a lot out of him and the family. It's never easy to lose someone you love.

Anyway, what a meet-up and chat on all our yesterdays. It was brilliant. And what a treat to meet Rachel. She wasn't even born when I was a nasty bastard. In fact I was in the asylum certified insane before she was born. What a funny old life it is. But what a breath of fresh air it is to meet lovely people!

October 2007, Inside Time
PRISON OFFICERS GUILTY OF MISCONDUCT
Figures obtained by the Guardian, released after months of delay by the Home Office following a freedom of information request, reveal that more than 1,000 prison officers in England and Wales were found guilty of misconduct between 2000 and 2006 for offences including improper sexual relationships and endangering the safety of their jails. Prisons where officers were disciplined most frequently for bad conduct are Birmingham, Manchester, Risley, Belmarsh and Brixton.
One of the two most common offences concerns officers who put the security of the jail in danger. The other involves officers who have been convicted of a crime. Some officers were sacked, while others received a warning because they had committed only minor crimes, Other frequent offences include unprofessional conduct, improper sexual relationships with prisoners and being absent from duty without leave.
In total, 1,300 staff were guilty of misconduct, including assaulting prisoners and other staff, racial harassment, falsely claiming sick leave, failing to obey instructions, theft, and being drunk or high on drugs at work.
A leaked report last year by the Metropolitan Police and the Prison Service suggested at least 1,000 prison staff were corrupt and that a significant number were responsible for bringing mobile phones and drugs into jail.

Oh, surely not! How can this be true? Screws are all lovely people. They're angels. Aren't they? Yeh, like fuck they are.

I hear that Jim Robinson just died. Jim was one of the four men wrongly convicted over the 1978 Carl Bridgewater case. Pat Molloy was another of the four, but he never made it out - he died in Gartree Prison. But they all won their appeals after 15 years inside. Now only two are still alive, and free. Enjoy it. Freedom is wonderful. Have a pint for me.

Another innocent man who recently died was Tony Steel. He copped a life sentence in 1977 for the murder of Carol Wilkinson. After serving well over 20 years for a crime he didn't commit, he won his appeal. But now, at the age of only 52, he's in a coffin six feet under. So did he really win? A man cannot survive for 20+ years in jail for a crime he didn't do without psychological scars. It's fucking bad enough if you're guilty. These men make it out only to die. They're already dead men, their hearts torn up. Their best years have been ripped away by evil cops. Lying, evil pigs! So what's new?

Oh! You must get this book - *The Map of My Life: The Story of Emma Humphreys*, edited by Julie Bindel and Harriet Wistrich. What a bloody sad, lonely life Emma had! Please read it! My eyes just welled up, so if you want a good cry .... I knew her. Rest in peace, angel.

Do you know why women have smaller feet than men? Well, it's one of those 'evolutionary' things. It allows the woman to stand closer to the kitchen sink. It's true.

October 2007, The Sun
My Carrier Lag
A teenager escaped from prison by cramming herself inside a released inmate's suitcase. Helga Schneider, 19, was smuggled out by hiding in luggage the size of a beer crate when her pal, 17, was freed from the youth jail near Hanover, Germany. The girls, both jailed for theft, are still on the run. Schneider had only two weeks left of her sentence. A prison spokesman said: "Our staff will inspect big cases more carefully in future."

Come on, don't we all love a story like this? Even her name, Helga Schneider, sounds magical. It's just brilliant to me. We love ya, Helga. Go for it, enjoy your fame. You're a legend at 19 years of age! I fucking love it. It brought back a memory of Hull Jail in 1975 when a little Irish con called O'Leary (we called him Paddy) climbed into a big cardboard box in the workshop, and some cons picked it up and put it on the back of a wagon that was taking the boxes out. But the dogs sniffed him out, so all Paddy got was a loss of 180 days' remission and a good kicking to go with it! Still, you have to give these people 10/10 for trying. Some make it, some don't, but Helga sure did! Stay free, girl. Respect.

October 2007, The Sun
Lag Buys Own Cell
A lag liked his cell so much that he BOUGHT it. Graeme Alford, in his 60s, served eight years for armed robbery in Pentridge prison, site of Australia's last hanging. The Melbourne jail is being converted into a rare wines depository and the ex-lawyer has snapped up cell 43, from where he was freed in 1980. Alford, now an author, said: "It's an investment."

I don't know about you, but I can think of better things to spend my dosh on! Well, can't you? Once I fly out of my cage, that's my lot. I never want to see another shithole in my life. Can you blame me?

Can you believe it's 81 years ago that John Logie Baird invented television? Now I didn't know that until recently. I thought it was in the 1930s not 1926. We got our first TV set in 1962 - a big fuck-off black-and-white contraption with great big knobs on. It was the shows from the London Palladium era, and Mum and Dad always used to let me and John stay up on a Sunday to watch those (our treat of the week). *Sunday Night at The London Palladium*: Big stars, real legends, glamour, proper showbiz people! Yeh, great memories. Mum would have her big box of chocolates and we'd have our bags of crisps and pop - cream soda, our favourite. The crisps back then had a little blue bag of salt in them and you sprinkled it on yourself! Dad would smoke his roll-ups - Golden Virginia. We were a happy family. Mark was only a baby then. Lovely memories - treasured.

Hey, get on this. The first stone bridge to be built across the River Clyde in Glasgow was back in 1410. Now that's a bit of history for you!

And did you know that in England in 1695 the Government brought out a window tax? Taxing your house windows! Can you believe that? It's a wonder them bunch of prats don't tax a wank! Imagine that - being taxed on every wank you have! And the mad thing is, some people would actually own up to how many wanks they'd had in a week. It's true - they would! Fuck me, I'd be skint if I did that! Imagine how much wanking tax I'd owe them! Fuck 'em, I'm not paying. I've never pulled my cock in my life - I get the prison minister to wank me off. So why should I pay? Fuck off, you wankers.

Who's read T.S. Eliot's *Murder in the Cathedral*? I read than in Brixton Jail in 1988 when I was in the cage. It was a bit heavy going, but I stuck with it and it wasn't a bad read. He wrote that in 1935, and I read it 53 years later - not bad, eh?

Hey! I hope you're all taking this in, coz I'll be asking questions later!

I called my brother Mark tonight. He's a top geezer. We always have a laugh. I can't wait for a night out with him! A good piss-up's what we need, for old time's sake. Mind you, he'd probably drink me under the table now, so it could end up embarrassing for me. Imagine it:

"Hey, who's that over there, Mark, asleep in the corner?"

"Oh, it's my brother Charlie ..."

"What?! Charlie Bronson, Britain's maddest fuck-off psycho? Fuck off!"

Can you imagine that - three pints and I fall asleep in the corner?! I'd never live it down! I think I'd best stick on the pop or a shandy or two, coz I can't be having that - not at my time of life! What if I can't get a hard-on either on my first night? This is serious shit! "Pass the Viagra, love, and hold on tight." Yahooooo! Yippeeeeeee! Yeehaaaah! Lovely jubbly.

An old Luton saying: 'He who wears a bulletproof vest and gets shot in the arse has nothing to complain about.'

An old Broadmoor saying: 'He who sleeps on a bed of nails deserves to be a human tea bag.'

An old east London saying: 'He who eats a vindaloo and shits himself won't eat it again.'

I do love a saying, don't you?

Here's a mad one for you. Now this is insane beyond belief. In 1962 in Oklahoma City Zoo two psychiatrists administered the largest dose of LSD to an elephant. This elephant was a 14-year-old $3\frac{1}{2}$ tonne male. It was given a dose that would make 3,000 people hallucinate. The elephant went mad and fell down dead in a matter of minutes. So why did they do it? Good question! When you work it out. let me know. Mad, sick fuckers.

Did you know that in 1954 a Soviet surgeon called Vladimir Demikhov actually successfully grafted another head onto a dog. The two-headed dog lived for a month with both heads working. Think about it. This was 1954 and it's now 2007. Come on, think. Doesn't it make you suspect that some science laboratory has experimented further - with humans? Think about it carefully. It's fucking scary! What about these top-security buildings out in the middle of nowhere - what do you think they're doing, growing tomatoes? Wake up and get real. It could be your fucking head next. Imagine waking up with my head stuck on your neck. It could be worse - it could be Bob Maudsley's. Food for thought. What a nightmare.

And how about this for strange? I was out on the exercise yard today and as I was jogging around I felt myself floating! I became very light, like I wasn't here. Fuck knows where I was, but I went into a dream state: happy, soul free, totally relaxed, a lovely feeling. My running was like on a new level. Very strange, unexplainable, unreal - but lovely.! Hey, imagine me on LSD! Who fucking needs it?

I called Leighton Frayne tonight. He's a top geezer - a true biz man! They don't come no better than him and his brother Lindsey.

I got a pile of mail today, about a dozen, and some great ones too, full of news from the world outside - what I call the crazy world. I got a strange one from some 'tart' in Wrexham who wants to play a tune on my cock. She must be a strange girl to write such an odd letter, and I don't even know her - not sure I want to either. You gotta be careful in this game. I've been bitten too many times. I rip a lot of these kinds of letters up nowadays. I can smell a nutter.

I get my canteen today - some nuts, Edam cheese, and some choc bars - so I'm sweet for another week. I read the paper today - more shit, more lies. They're now saying bacon causes cancer. I bet there's a Muslim stirring it! Some prat is saying that 'Christmas' should be changed to 'wintertime', coz it upsets the Muslims and Jews. Blah, blah, blah. I was reading about the Japs killing the dolphins and that Heather Mills is crazy. Every fucker's crazy in one way or the other! Who's perfect?

Have you ever had a strange experience like this? I was standing in a busy street, just looking about. In fact, I was actually clocking a Nat West bank, as you do. Anyway, this bus was passing by slowly and I noticed the most amazingly beautiful woman on it. She looked a bit Brazilian. You know the type: those big, brown, sexy eyes, juicy lips, and a tan to die for. Our eyes locked on for those few seconds. She smiled, I smiled, and it was love at first sight. All sorts went through my head. Is this it? Is she the one? Shall I run after her? Shall I hijack a motor and follow the bus? What do you do in a situation like that? I've never forgotten that moment, never forgotten her! This was 20+ years ago, but it's still fresh in my mind. She must now be 50+, maybe 60; maybe a mother with five kids, a big, fat arse, rotting teeth and a fanny like the Mersey Tunnel! It's that memory - a few seconds of pure joy! She smiled for me, and that was a picture to stay forever. I wonder if she remembers me? If she does, she might now think I'm an old, bald-headed, hunch-backed geezer with saggy bollocks and a beer belly, farting my way through life. Hey, I'm not, honest! But back then ... I still say the Nat West looked fitter. It's a funny old world!

Hey, girls, did you know Errol Flynn had a cock on him like a donkey? It's a well-known fact. The girls went weak at the knees for him, and no wonder with a cock like that! It's a wonder they ever walked again!

What a day - living on a cracked dream, living in a bubble of fire. Fuck me, it's roasting in here. I need a beer. I need a woman - some hot sex. That's all I need, all I want. It's not a lot to ask, is it? Us humans are all the same: we all need to rip our souls out and live a bit. Loonyology.

CHAPTER 19
CHOKEY NOSH ...
SOMETIMES LITERALLY!

The prison canteen is a major part of prison life. Cons have gone mad and pulled roofs off and taken hostages over it being fucked about with. You do not mess with a man's canteen. Only the prison governor can stop it.

If you're on report (a nicking against prison discipline) a governor can stop your canteen for a month. Hey, in 1970 I lost my canteen for years. The '80s and '90s were no better. My punishment just multiplied. I had fuck all, but then again I wanted it that way. My philosophy is: if you have nothing, then you can't lose nothing.

Nowadays Aramark does the system's canteen. All jail canteens are run by this mob now. Have a butchers at the list. Clock the prices. I bet Tesco or Asda ain't this dear. Blimey, you've gotta be a bank robber these days to get any canteen. You order it on forms once a week and it comes in sealed bags. Most weeks they get the order all wrong and it's a total fuck-up. I once ordered a Wisdom toothbrush and I got a box of Trill budgie seed. Somebody work that one out!

A lot of the products on this canteen sheet are useless to us on the CSC Unit. Well, we can't have a budgie. Hell, Maudsley would only eat it. Miller would probably try to fuck one. Fred would maybe cut its legs off for a laugh. We are not allowed live pets. Hey, and not even a teddy bear! Miller would fuck that too!

The food products for cooking are a waste of time, as we have no cooker. So it's biscuits and sweets for us. That's why most on this unit have no teeth or the ones they have are rotten.

Years back the canteens were run by the jails. Each jail had its own shop and there was always a dodgy screw! If you dropped him a tenner you was sure to get a bag of goodies. Fuck me, don't you ever think screws aren't 'iffy'. You only gotta look in the car park outside the jail. They've all got nice cars. Some screws are bigger villains than the villains, and the old canteen screw sure made it pay (for him).

Prisons are full of screws on the make. Check out how many have been caught bringing in drugs and booze over the years. But I wish our canteens were still run by the jails. It was so much better that way and we had 'special offers'. Cor ... Broadmoor canteen was like a big shop. They had it all and the shoplifting was incredible! The loons nicked some goodies out of there.

330

I once nicked a big plastic jar of pineapple chunks and another time six big Galaxy bars. We was always nicking something. I once jumped over the counter, nutted the screw and ran out with a box of Malteesers. The only problem is ... there's no place to run. So you're bang to rights.

Parkhurst always had a good, well-stocked canteen. I bet Aramark has fucked that up too. It's called progress - modernisation. I call it bollocks. Leave our canteen alone. Bring the old days back. Hey, have you noticed they say Mars bars are 10% bigger? Are they fuck. They're smaller.

What's more, don't forget it costs a fortune to buy all you would love to get. Well here's the facts. We don't get a fortune on the unit. We get £6 a week (wages) and with that we have to buy phone credit, toiletries, sweets, etc.! It all looks good on the form. I'd need £100 a week to get all the goodies I want. Hey, get on this one (no names mentioned, coz it's a decent screw who told me it in confidence): this jail's most popular purchase up on the wings is number 6,475, Weight Gain Banana, price £5.70. They're all trying to get big and powerful. Keep at it lads, but you'll never get to my level and I do my building on porridge. Fuck the supplements. Fuck paying the mental prices. Wake up. Stop being ripped off.

Now get this for a shock - number 3,634, Porridge Oats. Can you fucking believe that I'm buying my own porridge? A convict buying porridge. That's like a lumberjack buying a tree or a coalman buying a sack of coal. Prison is porridge isn't it? Well, it's not no more. It all went insane years ago. It's now Cornflakes, Rice Krispies and fucking Sugar Puffs. No porridge. Porridge has stopped. I put it down to laziness, so I buy my own. I put some nuts and raisins in it and a spoonful of brown sugar. Lovely. Why can't prisons keep the traditions? Porridge is historic; a part of prison culture. I'll tell you why not. Because it's run by faggots - sick, pathetic people who want to turn us all into whimpering wankers. Talking of wanking, porridge makes your spunk thick and rich (believe me, it does). Rice Krispies don't make me fucking laugh.

I'll tell you what is a good buy - number 3430, Soreen Malt Loaf. It's filling, it's good value, it's good for you. I do love a Malt Loaf. I can eat six of them in one go. Fills you right up. It's also good for the bowel movement. You shit good with a Malt Loaf.

Anyway, enjoy the canteen price list. It's very rare as jails don't like the public to see it. Why? Probably coz they don't want you to see how spoilt we are! Well, the truth is from me. I think the likes of Huntley should not be allowed canteen, and I'd go as far as saying let's all get no canteen if that means the monsters get none. I would willingly fuck the canteen off if it meant none of them got it! But cunts like them would be cutting their wrists and crying about human rights and getting loads of support.

Hey, smoking stops on 1 July. Cons can then only smoke in their cells, but I predict that will be next to stop! Did I ever tell you about when I stuffed a lighted fag out on a nonce's eyeball? Lovely! That's how to deal with the nonces - fucking hurt them. There was a time when the screws gave them a slap and a boot in the nuts. Not no more - it's all human rights now. Am I missing something here or am I not human?

Prison Shop Product Range: Effective from 16/06/2006
ARAMARK - HMP Wakefield

PLU NO.	DESCRIPTION	SALES PRICE
V=Vegetarian Ve=Vegan H=Halal K=Kosher FT=Fairtrade GF=Gluten Free SF=Sugar Free HO=Healthy Option		

TOBACCO

PLU NO.	DESCRIPTION	SALES PRICE
1,102	Golden Blends Virginia 12.5g	£2.34
1,104	Turner's Virginia 12.5g	£2.32
1,106	Turner's Virginia 25g	£4.55
1,110	Golden Virginia 12.5g	£2.72
1,114	Old Holborn 12.5g	£2.72
1,266	Red Bull 12.5g	£1.76
1,272	Rodeo 25g	£3.21
1,275	Rodeo 50g	£6.18
1,278	St Bruno 25g	£4.02
1,284	Clan 25g	£4.02
1,301	Hamlet Cigar	£0.72
1,316	Goldmark 10's	£2.10
1,319	Royals - Kingsize 10's	£2.19
1,340	Safety Matches	£0.11
1,343	Cooks Safety Matches	£0.56
1,346	Flints 9's	£0.50
1,349	Sphinx Papers-Cut Corner-Green	£0.16
1,355	Rizla Papers	£0.22
1,358	Liquorice Papers	£0.35
1,361	G. Hoggarth Filter Tips	£0.74
1,364	Rolling Machine	£1.49

PHONE & STAMPS

PLU NO.	DESCRIPTION	SALES PRICE
1,503	Phone Credit £1.00	£1.00
1,653	1st Class Stamp	£0.32
1,656	2nd Class Stamp	£0.23
1,659	9p Stamp	£0.09
1,662	Airmail Letter	£0.36
1,665	Airmail Stamp	£0.68
1,668	EU Postage Stamp	£0.40

TOILETRIES - SKIN CARE

PLU NO.	DESCRIPTION	SALES PRICE
2,003	Imperial Leather Soap 125g	£0.52
2,006	Knight's Castle Soap 125g	£0.39
2,009	Wrights Coal Tar Soap 125g	£0.91
2,012	Dove Soap 100g	£0.71
2,015	Dettol Soap 125g	£0.79
2,043	Imperial L. Shower Gel 250ml	£2.34
2,046	Spa Body Wash 500ml	£1.49
2,049	Gentelle Shower Gel 250ml	£0.89
2,052	Radox Shower Gel 250ml	£1.99
2,074	Lynx Stick Deodorant 50ml	£2.30
2,077	Imperial L. Roll-on Deodorant	£1.04
2,083	Dove Deodorant Stick 40ml	£2.11

2,100		Palmer's Coco. B/lotion 250ml	£3.21
2,115		Palmer's Skin Suc. Cream 250ml	£4.71
2,141		Imperial Leather Talc 150g	£0.88
2,156		Lypsyl	£1.20
2,162		Gentelle Hand/Body Cocoa Butter	£1.30
2,165		Nivea Cream 50ml	£1.66
2,589		E45 Cream 50g	£1.85
2,632		Johnson's Baby Lotion 200ml	£1.65
2,633		Johnson's Baby Soap 100g	£0.52

TOILETRIES - HAIR CARE

2,203		VO5 Shampoo 200ml	£2.08
2,209		Vosene Shampoo 250ml	£2.08
2,211	Ve	Suma Vegan Aloe Vera Shampoo	£1.69
2,213		Hair Fruits Shampoo 750ml	£0.89
2,215		Head & Shoulders 200ml	£2.29
2,221		Palmer's Coconut Shampoo 25ml	£2.31
2,227		Systeme 2 in1 Shamp/Cond 500ml	£1.94
2,237		Hair Fruits Conditioner 500ml	£0.70
2,249		Carefree Hair Gel 250ml	£0.70
2,255		Palm Coco. Oil formula 125g	£2.65
2,257		African Queen Beeswax	£3.92
2,287		Dax Green 214g	£2.14
2,289		Dax Wave & Groom 99g	£2.01
2,293		Dax Short & Neat 99g	£2.01

TOILETRIES - DENTAL

2,407		Colgate Whitening 50ml	£1.10
2,410		Ultrabrite Toothpaste 50ml	£0.49
2,413		Colgate Total 100ml	£2.02
2,416		Sensodyne Toothpaste 45ml	£2.17
2,418		Mu'Min Halal Toothpaste 100g	£1.99
2,419	Ve	K/Fisher Vegan Toothpaste 50ml	£1.40
2,420	V	Zee Vegetarian Toothpaste	£1.19
2,422		Eucryl Toothpaste 50ml	£1.67
2,428		Wisdom Toothbrush (Soft)	£1.56
2,431		Wisdom Toothbrush (Medium)	£1.56
2,434		Wisdom Toothbrush (Firm)	£1.56
2,437		Addis Toothbrush (Medium)	£0.49
2,443		Steradent Tablets (30)	£1.28
2,446		Poli-Grip Denture Fixative	£3.09
2,449		Dentiplus Mouthwash 500ml	£1.03
2,452		Dental Flossette 100Mtr	£0.99

TOILETRIES - SHAVING

2,501		Mach III Razor Blades 4 Pk	£5.51
2,504		Mach III Razor	£5.69
2,507		Gillette Sensor Excel Razor	£4.66
2,510		Sensor Excel Blades 5Pk	£4.91
2,516		Gillette Blue II Fixed 5Pk	£1.72
2,522		Palmolive Shaving Cream	£1.86
2,525		Umbro Shave Gel 200ml	£1.29
2,534		Gillette Aftershave Balm 75ml	£3.99

TOILETRIES - HEALTH CARE

2,550	Aqueous Cream 100gm	£0.93
2,553	Rennie Tablets 8's	£1.86
2,556	Blistex Relief Cream 5gm	£2.24
2,562	Strepsils 24's	£2.37
2,565	Blackcurrant Throaties 10's	£0.63
2,568	Quinoderm Facial Cleanser 150ml	£3.44
2,571	Clearasil Active Cream 30mg	£4.79
2,574	Polytar Shampoo 150ml	£2.73
2,577	Mycil Ointment 25g	£2.42
2,580	Earex Ear Drops 10ml	£2.90
2,583	Bongela	£2.68

TOILETRIES - MISCELLANEOUS

2,154	Nivea Sun Lotion SPF15	£4.39
2,280	Cushion Hairbrush	£1.50
2,600	Simply Cotton Buds 100's	£0.59
2,612	Davina Nail Clippers	£0.80
2,618	Face Cloth	£0.55
2,621	Sponge	£0.56
2,657	H.S. Luxury Toilet Roll (twin)	£0.79

GROCERIES - BEVERAGES

3,000		Brooks Still Water 1.5 ltr	£0.80
3,001		Sparkling Mineral Water 500ml	£0.36
3,002	Ve	Rubicon Mango Juice 1 ltr	£1.10
3,006	V. Ve	Drink Fresh Orange Juice 1 ltr	£0.94
3,012	FT	Greenleaf Orange Juice 500ml	£1.10
3,014	FT	Greenleaf Apple Juice 500ml	£1.10
3,016	V. Ve	D.Fresh Pineapple Juice 1 ltr	£1.01
3,016	V. Ve	Suncrest Guava Drink 1 ltr	£0.92
3,020	V. Ve	Suncrest Tropical Drink 1 ltr	£0.92
3,027		Rob. F&B Summer Fruits 1 ltr	£1.09
3,029	Ve	H.S. Lemon Squash 1 ltr	£0.75
3,031	Ve	H.S. Orange Squash 1 ltr	£0.75
3,033		Kia-Ora B.Currant & Pear 1 ltr	£1.13
3,035		Kia-Ora Mixed Fruit 1 ltr	£1.13
3,037		Kia-Ora Orange 1 ltr	£1.13
3,041		Diabetic Squash 1 ltr	£0.87
3,052	SF	T/S Dandelion & Burdock 330ml	£0.25
3,054	SF	T/S Iron Brew 330ml	£0.25
3,056		Coca Cola Can 330ml	£0.50
3,060		Fanta Can 330ml	£0.50
3,062		Mountain Mist Flav. Water 330ml	£0.41
3,064		Sprite Can 330ml	£0.50
3,073		Lucozade Bottle Orange 500ml	£0.99
3,082		Test The Zest Cherryade 1 ltr	£0.40
3,084		Test The Zest Orangeade 1 ltr	£0.40
3,086		Test The Zest Limeade 1 ltr	£0.40
3,088	V. Ve.	GF H.S. Diet Lemonade 1 ltr	£0.39
3,096		1.5 ltr Coca Cola	£1.55
3,098	SF	Diet Coke 1.5 ltr	£1.55
3,109		Nescafé Decaf. Coffee 100g	£2.54
3,113		Nescafé Coffee Sachet One-Cup	£0.08
3,115		Nescafé Original 100g	£2.03

3,125		Kenco Filter 227g	£2.36
3,127	FT	Columbian Coffee Sticks	£0.10
3,133		Instant Coffee Powder 100g	£1.23
3,139	Ve	Tetley Tea Bags 40's	£0.94
3,144		Herbal Teas - Lemon & Ginger 20s	£1.15
3,145	Ve	Twinings Herbal Teas 20s	£1.03
3,147	Ve	H.S. Premium Tea Bags 40s	£0.59
3,151	Ve.Ft	Organic Rooibos Tea Bags 40s	£2.00
3,153		Lift Lemon Tea 150g	£1.52
3,155		Malted Drink 400g	£0.90
3,167		Fairtrade Hot Choc. Sachets	£0.20
3,171	V	Cadbury's Drinking Choc. 250g	£1.28
3,174	Ve	White Wave Soya Milk 1 ltr	£0.94
3,176		UHT Whole Milk 500ml	£0.46
3,178		UHT Semi-Skimmed Milk 500ml	£0.46
3,182	V	Marvel Powdered Milk 198g	£1.50
3,184		Freshers Coffee Whitener 400g	£1.93
4,575		Cadbury's Cocoa Powder 125g	£1.25

GROCERIES - TINNED

3,206	V		Ambrosia Custard 425g	£0.85
3,208	V.	GF	Ambrosia Creamed Rice 425g	£0.68
3,212	V		Carnation Evaporated Milk 170g	£0.50
3,214			Nestlé Condensed Milk 397g	£1.35
3,220			Deep Blue Tuna in Brine 185g	£0.76
3,222			Deep Blue Tuna in Oil 185g	£0.76
3,224			Princes Tuna Chunks - Oil 185g	£0.87
3,230			Glenryck Mackerel in Tom 135g	£0.71
3,234			Princes Sardines in Tom 120g	£0.51
3,236			Princes Sardines in Oil 120g	£0.49
3,238			Princes Pink Salmon 105g	£0.75
3,240			Princes Pilchards in Tom 425g	£0.80
3,252			Princes Fruit Cocktail 411g	£0.70
3,254			Princes Peach Slices 415g	£0.77
3,256			V/frutta Pears in Juice 411g	£0.65
3,260	Ve		Princes Pineapple Slices 227g	£0.56
3,270			Morton App/Black Pie Fill 375g	£0.94
3,274			Morton Red Cherry Fill 390g	£1.04
3,286	V. Ve.	GF	H.S. Carrots 300g	£0.39
3,288	V. Ve.	GF	H.S. Garden Peas 300g	£0.39
3,290	V. Ve.	GF	H.S. Processed Peas 300g	£0.26
3,296			Sweetcorn 326g	£0.51
3,298			Princes Mushrooms 285g	£0.65
3,300			Pacchini Chopped Tomatoes 400g	£0.44
3,302			Princes Potatoes 285g	£0.42
3,304			Bat. Red Kidney Beans 415g	£0.45
3,308	V. Ve.	GF	Heinz Baked Beans 415g	£0.55
3,309			H.S. Baked Beans 420g	£0.29
3,312			Chick Peas - Tinned 400g	£0.41
3,334			Plumrose Chopped Ham/Pork 170g	£0.65
3,336			Plumrose Luncheon Meat 200g	£0.62
3,340			Corned Beef 340g	£0.96
3,342			Halal Corned Beef 340g	£1.92
3,344			Princes Stewed Steak 411g	£1.26
3,348			Princes Goulash 410g	£1.84

3,352		Princes Chicken Korma 400g	£1.90
3,354		Princes Chicken Black Bean 400g	£1.90
3,358	H	Tahira Beef Sausages 400g	£1.29
3,360	H	Tahira Chicken Sausages 400g	£1.29
3,362	H	Tahira Chicken Luncheon 200g	£1.40
3,366		Princes Hot Dogs 400g	£0.70
3,372		Steak & Kidney - F Bentos 425g	£1.88
3,374		Heinz Ravioli 415g	£1.11
3,376	V. Ve	Heinz Spaghetti 400g	£0.54
5,057		Nestlé Thick Ster/Cream 170g	£0.58

GROCERIES - BISCUITS

3,500	V. Ve	Crawfords Bourbon Creams 150g	£0.45
3,503	V`	Crawfords Custard Creams 150g	£0.45
3,506	V	Crawfords Choc Digestives 500g	£1.00
3,512	V	Crawfords Fig Rolls 150g	£0.59
3,518	V. Ve	H.S. Ginger Nuts 200g	£0.65
3,521	V	H.S. Coconut Rings 300g	£0.59
3,524	V. Ve	H.S. Fruit Shortcake 200g	£0.55
3,526		Choc. Chip Cookies 200g	£0.59
3,531		Choc. Orange Digestives 300g	£1.09
3,533	V	McVities Rich Tea 300g	£0.71
3,536	V	McVities Digestives 400g	£0.92
3,539	V	McVities Jaffa Cakes	£0.96
3,543		McV AM Forest Fruit Slice 40gm	£0.18
3,548	V. Ve	Hob Nobs 300g	£0.69
3,557	V	Taxi 9pk	£1.09
3,560		Mini Cheddars 50g	£0.39
3,563		Shortbread Multipack 3 x 100g	£0.89

GROCERIES - CEREALS

3,601	V. Ve. K	Kellogg's Cornflakes 500g(v)	£1.73
3,604	V. K	Kell. Crunchy Nut C. Flakes 375g	£1.90
3,610	V. Ve	Kellogg's Rice Krispies 450g	£1.98
3,612		Kellogg's Special K 375g	£2.35
3,616		Nestlé Pick-a-pack Cereal 8pk	£1.18
3,616		Nestlé Cheerios 375g	£1.99
3,619	V. Ve	Weetabix 12's	£1.00
3,622	Ve.HO	Shredded Wheat 12's	£1.55
3,625	HO	Sugar Puffs 320g	£1.84
3,634	HO	M/Flake Porridge Oats 500g(v)	£0.47
3,637	Ve	Ready Brek 250g	£0.98

GROCERIES - SAUCES & JAMS

3,701		Robertson Strawberry Jam 227g	£0.89
3,715	V. Ve	H.S. Marmalade 454g	£0.85
3,723		Honey Portion	£0.20
3,727		Rowse Honey Squeezy 340g	£2.14
3,730	V. Ve	H.S. Tomato Sauce 490g	£0.82
3,732	V. Ve. GF	Heinz Tomato Ketchup 460g	£1.34
3,736	V. Ve	H.S. Brown Sauce 490g	£0.85
3,740		H.S. Salad Cream 44og(v)	£0.79
3,744	V	H.S. Mayonnaise 450ml	£1.46
3,754	Ve	H.S. Mint Sauce 185g	£0.52
3,761		L & Worcester Sauce 150ml	£1.08

3,768		Amoy Soy Sauce 150ml	£0.63
3,813		Encona Hot Sauce-Squeezy 285ml	£1.89
4,776		Pataks Tikka Curry Paste	£1.71

GROCERIES - NOODLES RICE PASTA

3,850	H	Sawadee Chick Chow Noodles 85g	£0.29
3,853	H	Sawadee Beef Cas. Noodles 85g	£0.29
3,856	H	Sawadee Curry Noodles 85g	£0.29
3,859	H	Sawadee Mush & Veg Noodles 85g	£0.29
3,862		Sawadee Spicy Tom Noodles	£0.29
3,865		Sawadee Prawn Noodles 85g	£0.29
3,866		Ko-Lee Noodles - Chow Mein 85g	£0.35
3,867		Munch & Crunch Hot & Spicy 85g	£0.35
3,868	V	Ko-Lee Go Noodles - Hot 65g	£0.79
3,871	V	Ko-Lee Go Noodles - Curry 65g	£0.79
3,877		Pot Noodle - Mushroom	£0.82
3,880		Pot Noodle - Curry	£0.82
3,895		H.S. Easy Cook Rice 500g	£0.69
3,9-5		Basmati Rice 2kg	£2.97
3,912	Ve	H.S. Pasta Shapes 500g	£0.59
3,915		Buitoni Short Spaghetti 500g	£0.83

GROCERIES - SOUPS & PICKLES

3,650	V	C & B Cup Soup Tomato 4pk	£0.68
3,652		C & B Cup Soup Chicken 4pk	£0.68
3,654	V	C & B Cup Soup Vegetable 4pk	£0.68
3,662	V. GF	Heinz Tomato Soup 400g	£0.70
3,666	Ve	H.S. Beetroot 340g	£0.65
3,679		C & B Branston Pickle 360g	£1.08
3,692		Natco Mango Chutney 340g	£1.39
3,698		Natco Mixed Pickle 300g	£1.49
3,699		Natco Mango Hot Pickle 300g	£1.49
3,700		Natco Chilli Pickle 300g	£1.39
4,773		Pataks Korma Curry Paste	£1.71

GROCERIES - HERBS & SPICES

4,016	Chilli Powder 100g	£0.46
4,021	Millstone Chilli Powder 25g	£0.45
4,054	Curry Powder 100g	£0.47
4,063	Ground Coriander 100g	£0.91
4,081	Garlic Powder 200g	£0.41
4,087	Whole Cloves 50g	£0.58
4,102	Millstone Ground Ginger 36g	£0.49
4,120	Ground Cumin 100g	£0.71
4,123	Cumin Seeds 100g	£0.71
4,132	Lion Turmeric 25g	£0.45
4,147	Natco Paprika 100g	£0.55
4,159	Millstone Mixed Herbs 15g	£0.50
4,168	Millstone Thyme 16g	£0.46
4,177	Garam Masala 100g	£0.61
4,198	Natco Basil 25g	£1.05
4,210	Cinnamon Powder 100g	£0.69
4,279	Natco Spinach Leaf 396g	£0.60

GROCERIES - MISCELLANEOUS

3,200		Whit. Desiccated Coconut 150g	£0.72
3,411		Lemon Loaf Cake	£1.19
3,422		Sultana Cake	£1.13
3,424	V. Ve	Flapjacks (Apricot) 4pk	£0.95
3,427		Garlic Pittas 6pk	£0.61
3,430	V	Soreen Malt Loaf(v)	£0.63
3,433	V. Ve	Ryvita Crispbread 200g	£0.64
3,436	V. Ve	H.S. Cream Crackers 200g	£0.29
3,439		Ritz Crackers 200g	£1.05
3,454		Crumpets 6pk	£0.67
3,456		Poppadoms Large Plain	£1.14
3,470		Caster Sugar 500g	£0.84
3,474		Tate & Lyle Sugar 1kg	£0.80
3,476		Canderel Spoonful 40g	£1.34
3,478		Demerara Sugar 500g	£0.89
3,480		Icing Sugar 500g	£0.83
3,667	Ve	H.S. Pickled Onions 250g	£0.79
3,750		Colmans Cheese Sauce Mix	£0.47
3,809		Knorr Cook-in Sweet & Sour	£1.53
3,829		Rose Syrup 250ml	£0.89
3,937		H.S. Self Raising Flour 1.5kg	£0.73
3,940		H.S. Plain Flour 1.5kg	£0.73
3,943		Natco Chapati Flour 1.5kg	£1.60
3,949		Natco Gram Flour 1kg	£1.13
3,958		Cornmeal Fine 500g	£0.43
3,961		Natco Cornmeal 1.5kg	£0.95
4,000		H.S. Table Salt 250g	£0.35
4,030		H.S. Ground Black Pepper	£0.50
4,285		Okra	£0.57
4,291		Fish Masala 100g	£1.01
4,500		Oxo Cubes 6pk Beef 35g	£0.50
4,506	V	Oxo Veg Stock Cubes 12's	£0.94
4,512		Bisto Beef Granules 170g	£1.02
4,521		Skipper Peanut Butter 340g	£1.62
4,533		Shippham's Beef Paste 75g	£0.70
4,539	Ve	Colmans Mustard 50g	£0.71
4,542		Golden Syrup 454g	£0.93
4,563		W.W. Dried Fruit 375g	£1.19
4,569		W/Worths Glace Cherries 100g	£1.15
4,578	V. Ve	Birds Custard Powder 75g	£0.53
4,602		Khanam Veg Ghee 908g	£1.79
4,611		Red Lentils 500g	£0.71
4,626		Jamaica Sun Ackees 540g	£3.91
4,650		Black Eye Beans 2kg	£2.10
4,692		Caywood's Dried Salt Fish	£1.41
4,697		Sitar Ghanna Masala 280g	£1.49
4,698		Sitar Lamb Kheema 250g	£2.29
4,699		Sitar Chicken Methi 280g	£2.29
4,700		Sitar Chicken Makhani 280g	£2.29
4,737		Spinach Puree	£0.70
4,743		Valfrutta Tomato Puree 135g	£0.49
4,749		Supercook Vanilla Flav. 38ml	£0.55
4,752		Supercook Almond Flavouring	£0.55
4,755		Supercook Chocolate 200g	£0.68

4,785		H.S. Thick & Creamy Yoghurt 125g	£0.39
4,797		Whitworths Semolina 500gm	£0.92
4,812	Ve.HO	Supreme Mango Slices	£0.70
4,815	V. GF	Smash Instant Potato 88g	£0.54
4,842		Chivers Jelly 135g	£0.44
4,875		Ferro Cous Cous 500g	£0.78
4,902		Badam Barfi Box 200g	£1.10
5,030		Suma Soya Spread 500g(v)	£1.20
5,054		H.S. Plain Yoghurt 425g	£0.52

GROCERIES - FRESH

5,003	V	Flora 250g	£0.64
5,012		Stork 250g	£0.36
5,021		Lurpak Butter Spreadable 250g	£1.02
5,033		Eggs 6pk	£0.57
5,063		H/S Processed Cheese Slices	£0.99
5,075		Dairylea Cheese Triangles	£0.79
5,078		Blue Vein Cheese 142g	£1.85
5,081		Vegan Cheese 170g	£1.70
5,093		Philadelphia 125g	£0.99
5,099		Cheddar Cheese 250g	£1.79
5,102		Cheshire Cheese 250g	£1.55
5,105		Singletons Col. Cheddar 200g	£1.24
5,117	Ve	Creamed Coconut 200g	£0.99
5,150		Onions x 3	£0.27
5,027		Garlic Bulb - Single	£0.24
5,213		Mushrooms 500g	£1.11
5,222		Potatoes 2kg	£0.65
5,237		Tomatoes x 5	£0.62
5,246		Pepper x 1	£0.55
5,288		Red Chillies 100g	£0.55
5,297		Green Chillies 100g	£0.38
5,366		Fresh Fruit Pack - Apples x 3	£0.66
5,393		Fresh Fruit Pack - Banana x 3	£0.64
5,411	HO	Lemon - Single	£0.18
5,432		Lime - Single	£0.23
5,447	HO	Large Mango - Single	£0.90

HAND MADE GREETING CARDS

6,003		HMGC Daughter Birthday	£1.95

GREETING CARDS & STATIONERY

6,014		Just to Say Card	£0.61
6,016		Blank Greeting Card	£0.61
6,018		Sympathy Card	£0.61
6,020		Missing You Card	£0.61
6,022		Get Well Soon Card	£0.61
6,026		Anniversary Wife Card	£0.61
6,030		Female Traditional B/Day Card	£0.61
6,032		Male Traditional Birthday Card	£0.61
6,034		Mum Traditional Birthday Card	£0.61
6,036		Dad Traditional Birthday Card	£0.61
6,040		Daughter Trad. Birthday Card	£0.61
6,042		Brother Trad. Birthday Card	£0.61
6,044		Sister Trad. Birthday	£0.61

6,048	New Baby Girl Card	£0.61
6,050	Female Cute Birthday Card	£0.61
6,052	Male Cute Birthday Card	£0.61
6,054	Mum Cute Birthday Card	£0.61
6,058	Son Cute Birthday Card	£0.61
6,060	Daughter Cute B/Day Card	£0.61
6,064	Sister Cute Birthday Card	£0.61
6,066	Wife Cute Birthday Card	£0.61
6,068	Wife Traditional B/Day Card	£0.61
6,100	A4 Refill Pad	£0.99
6,103	A4 Binder	£1.33
6,106	A4 Clear Pockets	£0.05
6,112	A4 Envelope	£0.15
6,115	Envelopes-Sml PK20(5.75"x3.5")	£0.43
6,118	Envelopes-Lrg PK20(8.5"x4.25")	£0.80
6,121	Writing Pad - Small	£0.43
6,127	Biro - Black	£0.20
6,130	Biro - Blue	£0.20
6,133	Pilot Pen Black	£1.71
6,145	Felt Tip Pens assorted 10pk	£0.46
6,151	Highlighter Pen	£1.12
6,154	Glue Stick	£1.16
6,172	Drawing Pins (50)	£0.28

ELECTRICAL
6,306	LE03(AAA) Panasonic Alkaline	£0.62
6,324	LR6 Recycled Alkaline Batt 8pk	£1.49
6,327	LR6(AA) Panasonic Alkaline	£0.62
6,342	LR14(C) Panasonic Alkaline	£1.00
6,348	R14 Panasonic Ultra	£0.66
6,360	LR20(D) Panasonic Alkaline	£0.97
6,367	PP3(9v) Memorex Battery	£1.50
6,376	Watch Battery (No. Required)	£2.49
6,381	TDK Audio Tape Single	£0.96

SUPPLEMENTS
6,400		Garlic Capsules 100's	£1.56
6,406		Cod Liver Oil Capsules 90's	£2.00
6,415		All Rounders Multi-Vits 60's	£1.75
6,424	Ve	Kelp 100's	£1.40
6,433		Vitamin 'E' Wheatgerm 100's	£2.95
6,436		Allsports C150-Vitamin C 60's	£1.67
6,447		Nurishment Drink Vanilla 420g	£1.10
6,450		Nurishment Drink Strawb. 420g	£1.10
6,453		Nurishment Drink Choc. 420g	£1.10
6,466		Elite Protein Strawberry 340g	£5.65
6,475		Weight Gain - Banana 450g	£5.70
6,484		Creatine 120g	£5.97

MISCELLANEOUS
6,527	Fairy Non-Bio Auto Powder 950g	£2.64
6,539	Ariel Handwash Powder 960g	£2.42
6,551	Lenor Fabric Conditioner 1 ltr	£1.10
6,554	H.S. Easy Iron Fabric Cond 1 ltr	£0.99
6,560	Drinking Mug	£0.99

6,563		Dinner Plate	£2.36
6,566		Cereal Bowl	£2.36
6,593		Twin Air Freshener	£0.99
6,602		Incense Stick	£0.05
6,605		Ash Catcher	£1.33
6,629		Playing Cards	£0.69
6,632		Tin Opener	£1.30
6,635		Aviva Wash-Up Liquid 500ml	£0.82
6,641		Flip Flops	£4.50

PETCARE

6,701		Trill Budgie Seeds 500g	£1.49
6,722		Budgie Honey Ring	£0.50
6,725		Honey & Fruit Budgie Bell	£0.42
6,737		Millet Spray 150g	£0.88
6,740		Cockatiel Mix 500g	£0.61
6,746		Iodine Nibbles	£0.40
6,749		Kagesan Sand Sheets 8pk	£1.18
6,752		Hook Feeder Med	£0.61
6,755		Bird Grit 500g	£0.53

CONFECTIONERY

8,006		Tayto Rough Cut Crisps 6pk	£1.19
8,009		Tayto Snack Attack 10pk	£1.09
8,018		Tayto Rough Cuts Salt/Vin. 50g	£0.39
8,024		Tayto Rough Cut Ched/Onion 50g	£0.39
8,116		Snacktime Triangles Chilli 50g	£0.40
8,123	V	Doritos Chilli Heatwave 40g	£0.28
8,178		Walkers Crisps Ch. & On. Std	£0.29
8,179		Walkers Crisps Std - Plain	£0.29
8,180		Walkers Crisps Salt & Vin Std.	£0.29
8,216	V	Advantage Whisps French Onion	£0.28
8,258	V	Bournville 200g	£1.33
8,259		Cadbury's Dairy Milk 250g	£1.66
8,264	V	Cadbury's Crunchie 41g	£0.38
8,267	V	Cadbury's Double Decker 67g	£0.36
8,270	V	Cadbury's Dairy Milk 50g(v)	£0.40
8,276	V	Cadbury's Fruit & Nut 50g(v)	£0.43
8,277		Cadbury's DM Crème Egg 45g	£0.41
8,279	V	Cadbury's Picnic Bar Std	£0.40
8,282	V	Cadbury's D. Milk Turkish 49g	£0.40
8,285	V	Cadbury's D. Milk Dream 45g	£0.41
8,291	V	Cadbury's Buttons(v)	£0.37
8,351		Victoria B/Currant & Liq. 350g	£0.99
8,354		Victoria Fruit Flav. Chews 350g	£0.99
8,357		Victoria Mint Selection 350g	£0.99
8,360		Victoria Mint Humbugs 350g	£0.99
8,366		Victoria Midget Gems 350g	£0.99
8,369		Victoria Fizzy Favourites 350g	£0.99
8,372		Victoria Asst Toffee 350g	£0.99
8,402		C. Rich Milk Choc Raisins 225g	£1.32
8,404		C. Rich Salted Peanuts 400g	£1.29
8,405		Pitted Dates 325g	£0.78
8,408		Country Rich Brazil Nuts 125g	£1.09
8,410		Peanuts & Raisins 400g	£0.89

8,411		C. Rich Deluxe Fruit & Nut 325g	£1.19
8,414		C. Rich Deluxe Tropical 325g	£1.19
8,423	V. Ve	Cofresh Bombay Mix 100g	£0.49
8,438		Country Rich Almonds 75g	£1.09
8,456		Salted Dry Roasted Cashews 40g	£0.68
8,462	V. Ve	KP Salted Nuts 50g	£0.43
8,465	FT	Maya Gold Choc. Bar 20g	£0.55
8,483		Pub Pork Scratchings 20g	£0.49
8,489		Chilli Crinkle Crisps 90g(v)	£0.79
8,492	V	Mexican Jalapeno Sticks 90g	£0.79
8,498		Jannis Cashew Bar 60g	£1.19
8,507		Bikaji Tana Bana 180g	£1.80
8,510	V	Geobars Chocolate & Raisin 35g	£0.60
8,513	V	Sesame Bars 30g	£0.30
8,549		Mars Bar 62.5g	£0.33
8,552		Twix 58g	£0.32
8,555		Snickers Bar 62.5g	£0.33
8,558		Bounty - Milk 57g	£0.35
8,561		Nestlé Yorkie 68g	£0.44
8,567		Fry's Chocolate Cream(v)	£0.47
8,576		Nestlé Kit-Kat Chunky Std	£0.34
8,588		Nestlé White Crunch 32g	£0.41
8,594		Diabetic Chocolate 100g	£1.81
8,603		Dubble Chocolate Bar 40g	£0.60
8,645	Ve	Polo Mints Original Std(v)	£0.26
8,648	Ve	Fruit Polo(v)	£0.26
8,651		Swizzels Fun Gums	£0.10
8,654		Rowntree Fruit Frogs	£0.20
8,657	V	Trebor Soft Mints Roll	£0.35
8,660		Werther's Original Bag 150g	£0.95
8,663		Trebor Extra Strong Mints Std	£0.35
8,666		Chupa Chups Lollipop	£0.13
8,687		Matlow's Giant Refresher Chew	£0.10
8,690		Chew Bar Med	£0.05
8,735		Hall's Menth-lyptus 33.5g	£0.53

CHARITY DONATIONS
9,999		Charity Donation NSPCC	£0.01

Prison grub has changed a lot over the years and there's a good choice. You can have a healthy diet today. Some jails are better than others and some are still crap. I suppose it's the same as some hotels. You don't get 5 stars for a 'Greasy Spoon' do you? Yeah, we've come a long way with the prison grub since the 1960s, and I should know. Personally I think it's too fucking good for these filthy monsters here. I'd give them a plate of dog shit myself with sauce on and a mug of hot piss. It's all they bleeding deserve. In fact, I'd starve the bastards. Wouldn't you? Hey, they do a lovely fruit crumble and custard here on a Saturday. It's just like granny used to make.

To give you an idea, this is my lunch and tea menu for this week:

Sunday:
Lunch: vegetable noodle patty, baked cheddar cheese and onion pie, halal steak and mushroom pie or chicken and sweetcorn pie, with orange juice.
Tea: vegetable fried rice h/m, poached fish, halal roast beef slice and H/R sce, roast chicken leg, egg salad, peanut butter sandwich, ham salad, and ice cream for afters.

Monday:
Lunch: salad bap, cheese and chutney bap, halal turkey bap and ham and tomato bap, with orange juice.
Tea: vegetable hash h/m, jacket potato and chilli beans, onion bhajis, beef chow mein, pasta salad, vegan garlic sausage sandwich, tuna mayo sandwich, and lemon muffin for afters.

Tuesday:
Lunch: peanut butter bap, egg mayonnaise bap, halal coronation chicken bap or corned beef and onion bap, with orange juice.
Tea: hot boston beans h/m, macaroni cheese, halal minced beef rogan josh, battered jumbo sausage, cheese salad, salad sandwich, beef sandwich, and a doughnut for afters.

Wednesday:
Lunch: vegan garlic sausage bap, tuna onion and mayonnaise bap, halal chicken roll bap or pork and apple sauce bap, with orange juice.
Tea: vegan mixed grill, Yorkshire fish cake x 2, halal minced beef and onion pie, chicken nuggets, ham salad, peanut butter sandwich, egg mayonnaise sandwich, and a chocolate muffin for afters.

Thursday:
Lunch: salad bap, cheese and onion bap, seafood sticks in a bap, beef and onion bap, with orange juice.
Tea: pancake roll h/m, cheese and tomato beano, halal chicken leg hot and spicy, beef italiene, corned beef salad, vegan garlic sausage sandwich, pork sandwich, and ice cream for afters.

Friday:
Lunch: peanut butter bap, tuna and sweetcorn bap, halal beef and onion bap, pork luncheon meat bap.
Tea: pasta portuguese h/m, cauliflower cheese grill, haddock in batter, gammon steak, turkey salad, salad sandwich, cheese sandwich, and a sultana muffin for afters.

Saturday:
Lunch: brunch, with orange juice.

Tea: vegetable pizza h/m, jacket potato and cheese, halal chicken steak, pork pie, crab stick salad, vegan cheese and tomato sandwich, halal turkey sandwich, and fruit crumble for afters.

Not bad, eh? Mind you, it isn't always how it should be. On 30 July 2007, after speaking to the governor and the hot plate screws, I filled in a prisoner's formal complaint form stating:

"On Sunday 29 July 2007 for my Sunday roast I had a chicken leg the size of a sparrow, cabbage and four tiny croquettes. It was the tiniest meal I've ever had in 33 years of prison life. It was a disgrace and an insult. Even the hot plate screw was embarrassed and all the unit screws agreed that it was unacceptable. I went to bed hungry. This is 2007 not 1807."

The form asks: "What would you like to see done about your complaint?" I wrote: "Sack the 'Boss Man' in the kitchen and charge him with cruelty. This is Wakefield not Belsen!"
The reply was:

"Firstly accept my apologies for receiving a meal smaller than normal. On the day in question we found that a large number of potatoes had gone off, leaving us with a shortfall for roast potatoes. The only alternative we had were croquette potatoes in all limited supply. The potatoes that we had received from our supplier had a shorter shelf life than we would normally expect. We have contacted the supplier and they assure us this will not occur again. The shortage of cabbage was brought about by a misunderstanding between catering staff and inmates. I heard of this problem the following day and took immediate steps to prevent this happening again, and you should now be receiving the correct portion size. When we purchase chicken legs we buy either 30 or 50 legs per box of a certain size, and on rare occasions some of the legs in the boxes are smaller than they should be. There is not a great deal we can do when this occurs, as we only defrost sufficient chicken for each meal and when this is discovered we have insufficient time to defrost any more chicken. Hopefully you are now receiving meals of the recommended portion size. If you do encounter any more problems with portion size please contact the catering department." 07/08/2007.

What the system don't realise is that this meal is served at 4.30 p.m. on Sundays. Our door then locks up till 8 a.m. the next day. That's 15½ hours with no more food. You wake up eating your pillow whilst thinking it's a Yorkshire pudding. If the portions are how they should be then I've no problem. But leave the fucking sparrows alone, you cunt!
Hey, I read a good cookery book, but I couldn't get my teeth into it!
Talking of teeth. There was a lunatic in Rampton who had only one single tooth in his head, and it stuck out like a rabbit! We called him Bugsy. One

fucking tooth! Can you believe that? Why keep just one tooth? Why not get it ripped out and have a set of falsies? Well, it is a nuthouse so what do you expect?

Hey, I read a great book on carpentry too, but it gave me splinters!

I had a beautiful dream the other night in which Huntley and Brady stabbed each other to death. If dreams come true I bet the service won't last 30 seconds. Just burn the fuckers.

Here we go - another Xmas is creeping up. This is how you tell Xmas from any other time in jail: food - a bit of extra nosh. Fuck Santa and Rudolph and all the fairy fuckers. All we want is some extra grub.

Yippeeeeeeeeeeeeeeeeeeee!

Yahoooooooooooooooooooooo!

Yeeeowwwwwwwwwwwwwwww!

Yabadabaadoooooooooooooooooooo! Happy Fucking Jingle Bollocks!

My worst ever Xmas was in Wandsworth seg block in the early 1970s. I spent it in the strongbox, wrapped up in a body belt. All Santa brought me was a size 10 boot in my head and a truncheon or two across my back and legs. 'The good old days'! Wonderful memories - I don't think so. Another mental Xmas was Broadmoor 1980 in Norfolk House, landing one, where 12 of us were banged up with fuck all (in solitary). I had a paranoid schizoid on one side of me and a manic depressive on the other. Tears, shouts and madness - insanity in stereo. They drove me fucking mental. One was shouting out "I'll kill ya! I'll cut you up into pieces and shag your dead arse." The other one was crying and threatening to top himself. On top of these pair of cunts, the screws were eating all the best of our grub. When they opened my door to feed me, I just dived on them and shouted, "Happy Christmas!" I was bashed to bits and injected. I slept Xmas away in a cloud of confusion! Loonyology at its very best I would say. If you can't beat 'em, join 'em, I say! It's good to see the world through the eyes of a madman! Sure, you'll suffer the consequences for your actions, but when you wake up you'll be one of the chaps. Fuck Santa. Take it from me, he never comes, not to us lot! Why should he? We'd only take him hostage and torture the bearded twat. All this Crimbo looks good on the menu. Take a look for yourselves:

Christmas Day Menu 2007:

Breakfast:
CRISPIES, SCRAMBLED EGG, BAKED BEANS, BACON

Muslim: CRISPIES, SCRAMBLED EGG, BAKED BEANS, HASH BROWNS

Vegan: BRANFLAKES, MUSHROOMS, BAKED BEANS, HASH BROWNS

Lunch:

CHARLES BRONSON

TOMATO/BASIL SOUP & BREAD ROLL

Choice of ORD:
ROAST TURKEY & CHIPOLATA SAUSAGES X 2 OR ROAST BEEF
& HORSERADISH SAUCE
Muslim: HALAL ROAST LAMB CHOP & MINT SAUCE

Vegan: APPLE & CRANBERRY ROAST GRILL

Heo: AS MAIN DIET

YORKSHIRE PUDDING, ROAST POTATOES, BRUSSEL SPROUTS,
GLAZED BABY CARROTS, STUFFING BALL X 2, GRAVY

Choice of:
CHRISTMAS PUDDING & RUM SAUCE
OR FRUIT COCKTAIL OR MELON

Tea

Choice of:
Ord: BAPS X 2 1 X CHEESE 1 X TUNA

Muslim/Veg: BAPS X 2 1 X CHEESE 1 X TUNA

Vegan: 1 X PLATED VEGAN CHEESE SALAD

Heo: 1 X PLATED COTTAGE CHEESE SALAD

Ord: CHRISTMAS CAKE, SATSUMA, ENHANCED BISCUIT 1 X 150 GRAMS,
PACKET OF CRISPS, ORANGE JUICE

Heo: FRUIT X 2, PACKET OF CRISPS,
1 X 150 GRAM RICH TEA BISCUITS, CRANBERRY JUICE

Vegan & Muslim: VEGAN CHRISTMAS CAKE, SATSUMA,
ENHANCED BISCUITS X 150 GRAMS, PACKET OF CRISPS, ORANGE JUICE

Subject to availability

Boxing Day 2007:

Breakfast:
Vegan: MUESLI, VEG SAUSAGE, HASH BROWN, TOMATOES

Veg: MUESLI, HASH BROWN, SCRAMBLED EGG, TOMATOES

Muslim: MUESLI, HALAL SAUSAGE, SCRAMBLED EGG, TOMATOES

Ord/Heo: MUESLI, SAUSAGE, SCRAMBLED EGG, TOMATOES

Lunch:
ASPARAGUS SOUP & BREAD ROLL

346

LOONYOLOGY

Vegan: BUTTERED CORN ON THE COB

Veg: LUXURY VEGETARIAN KIEV

Muslim: HALAL ROAST BEEF & HORSERADISH SAUCE
Ordinary & Heo: CHICKEN BREAST & MUSHROOM SAUCE OR
GAMMON STEAK AND PINEAPPLE

MINTED POTATOES, SLICED GREEN BEANS, JULIENNE CARROTS, GRAVY

Choice of:
GIANT XMAS FRUIT MUFFIN & CUSTARD OR YOGHURT OR BANANA

Tea

Choice of Ord: BAPS X 2 1 X EGG MAYONNAISE 1 X CHEESE, VEG & MUSLIM:
BAPS X 2 1 X EGG MAYONNAISE 1 X CHEESE

Vegan: 1 X PLATED VEGAN TOMATO & GARLIC SAUSAGE SALAD

Heo: 1 X PLATED TUNA SALAD

Ord & Veg: MINCE PIE, ENHANCED BISCUIT/SUPPER BUN,
PACKET OF CRISPS, FRUIT X 1

Heo: FRUIT X 2, PACKET OF CRISPS , CRANBERRY JUICE

Vegan & Muslim: VEGAN CHRISTMAS CAKE, ENHANCED BISCUIT/SUPPER BUN,
PACKET OF CRISPS, FRUIT X 1

Subject to availability

New Year's Day 2008

Breakfast:
Vegan: SHREDDED WHEAT, ½ GRAPEFRUIT

Ord/Heo/Veg/Muslim: SHREDDED WHEAT, BOILED EGG

Lunch:
Ved/Vegan: VEGAN KIEV

Muslim: HALAL CHICKEN KIEV

Ord & Heo: STEAK JARDINAIRE OR PORK CHOP, CHIPPED GAME POTATOES,
PETIT POIS, SWEETCORN, GRAVY

Choice of: JUMBO APPLE & RASPBERRY PASTRY & CUSTARD,
ICE CREAM, BANANA

Tea

347

Choice of:
Ord: BAPS X 2 1 X EGG MAYONNAISE 1 X CHEESE, VEG & MUSLIM:
BAPS X 2 1 X EGG MAYONAISE 1 X CHEESE

Vegan: 1 X PLATED VEGAN CHEESE SALAD

Heo: 1 X PLATED COTTAGE CHEESE SALAD

Ord & Veg: FLAPJACK, MINCE PIE, PACKET OF CRISPS, FRUIT X 1

Heo: LOW FAT YOGHURT, FRUIT X 2, PACKET OF CRISPS

Vegan: VEGAN YOGHURT, FRUIT X2 , PACKET OF CRISPS

Subject to availability

I know what you lot outside will be saying - what you say every Xmas. "Look at the grub them bloody convicts get! It's better than the old folks' home. They get fed better than our boys in the Forces! It's not right. They're spoilt! It's a fucking disgrace ..." Well, let me just say that reading it is not the same as getting it. I'm not saying it's shit, just that you shouldn't believe all you read on a prison menu. And let's face it, would you see a prison chef working in the Hilton or the Ritz? Would you see a prison doctor in Harley Street? Get my meaning? Happy Christmas!

CHAPTER 20
REMEDYING MY IRRITATING
PROBLEMS AND YOURS

Hey, I'll tell you who's a cunt, and he's getting right up my nose. He's been warned off twice, but he's becoming a fucking leech on my jugular. Who? You may well ask! He's an ex-screw who worked in Grendon Prison for years. He just wrote to me out of the blue and sounded a decent sort of chap. He knew a lot of cons that I knew. So I wrote back. Then he wrote back. He started to write bits in my favour! It's all on my website. So I decided I wanted to meet this fella and have a proper chinwag. I got him passed, put on my visit list for the agreed day and sent him a visiting order. And guess what? He didn't show! He gave some excuse like his missus was having liposuction or some shit like that. As if I give a flying fuck what it was. The fact is, we agreed on a day, he was sent a visiting order and he didn't turn up. First visit and last one; that's it for me. Fuck off. My family don't let me down and nor do my friends. So why should he (unless he's died)? So I make it 200% clear: fuck off, I don't want to know you. Then he starts sticking his nose in where it's not wanted and starts emailing people he shouldn't, trying to analyse me, trying to control things, making a nuisance of himself. So he gets another fuck off. He says in an email to Mal Vango (my website genius at the time) "I'll step down, but I only tried to help Charlie."

That should've been the end of it, but no. Four months later he's at it again: getting all technical and making himself and his views all official again on forums and sites and emails. It's as if he can't move on from Charlie Bronson. Some cunts don't know when to stop. So again he had a serious 'fuck off' warning and again he said he'd step down! We shall see. Basically he probably means well, but 30 years as a screw has brainwashed him and he can't see it. He's a fucking boring bastard that's getting on my fucking nerves. He's been saying stuff on forums about me, such as Charlie has got to do courses, he's got to see psychologists, he must jump through hoops. Maybe Charlie don't want to get out. He could and probably will die inside. Well, fuck you. Stay out of my struggle, coz it's cunts like you that I've been trying to expose all my life. You're more institutionalised than I am. You only know one way. My way is not yours. Your way bores me to death. I've proved to myself that I'm not what I used to be. All the screws in Wakefield know it too. I've nothing more to prove by sitting with clowns like you, yap, yap, yapping shit. Actions speak louder than words. My behaviour has spoken for me. Okay?

So let's hope this is the last of him and the psychological shit. Sadly he spent a long time at Grendon, which was built and designed for psychological experiments, i.e. talking shit. So the screws become brainwashed with it. They sit down with the cons and get involved in the cons' past. Why did they rob a bank? Why did they shag a 98-year-old lady? Why did they shoot the cop? Why did they rape the kid? Blah, blah, blah. Then they pass round the tissues and all have a weep. How sorry they all are. That's the therapy. To me it's all a load of old bollocks. They're playing the game and securing an easy ride. 90% in Grendon get parole. They're all fucking lobotomised to me. They lose their spirit and cunts like Joe love it. He sees himself as someone special, like a saviour. Look at me. I hope I get the MBE. But what about the nonces he keeps getting paroled and that get released ten years early only to go out and rape more women and kids. Is that worth an MBE? Wake up and get real.

Let's keep prison as prison, 'us' as nasty bastards who need punishing, and cunts like him as screws. You're a silly, daft bastard of a screw. You must've been to do it for 30 years. I've never met a genius screw in 33 years. All a screw is, is a screw. You're nobody special. Any silly cunt can do a screw's job. So don't ride off my name. It don't work. The day you never visited me was the day I said: "Fuck off". Now let's move on before you upset me. Cunt. And to any other cunt who says Charlie Bronson will never get out, I say the same to you: "Fuck off". Get on with your own lives. Don't worry about mine.

Extract from Petition-them.com website:
Free Charles Bronson, 34 years in prison, 28 years in solitary for a man who has never killed, raped or molested anyone. Message from Charles Bronson posted 18 September 2007:

Ok. Re Chapman, you have got to have the last word "again". You said all this before but this time you end it with more crap.
So you are now to be exposed, as nobody on this planet ever rubbishes me off, especially an arse wipe, and that's all you've been all your weak life, a typical working government official who's got the backbone of a squid and the brain of a pussy. It's you who has constantly said, "If Bronson don't do this or don't do that he won't ever get out, or does he really want to get out? Now we've got your boyfriend "Lewis" saying the same. "Two peas in a pod". You're so far up each other's arseholes you think the world's made of plastercine.
Chapman is a 50-year-old man who rides around in a sports car with his tash dyed. He thinks he is some sort of James Bond on a mission to save us cons. For 30 years he worked with all the paedos and rapists you can think of. Group therapist at Grendon. "The occasional robber may have slipped in" but he loves a nonce. That's his job, a nonce helper, and it chews his brain up. I also have it from good solid sources that he likes a bit of navy cake playing around with the rent boys. Not a big deal as a lot of

Chapmans of this world do a job like his and end up pervos themselves. If you work in a farm you smell of shit! All these years of therapy with nonces have rubbed off on him and I don't want that sort of thing in my life.

He then goes on to talk about "Wyn, John and Glynis" again. What has my biz got to do with him? Who the fuck does he think he is even mentioning my life? But I'll put it right all the same. I've no problem with John. John's a good man I respect. It's his daft missus I don't like, who phoned Wyn up to say I was on hunger strike, then Wyn phoned my aunt up, who then phoned my mother up, who was on holiday at the time (it ruined her holiday over lies). I don't need idiots to start spreading silly rumours but this was personal between me and those concerned.

Why did this prick Chapman even mention it? Simple. He's a nosy git out to stir it up. Would he be doing all this if I was not in a cage? Or if I was in a Cat D jail? Or if I was free? Prats like him would be licking my boots. He says he has no interest in the "Charade". Well I will leave that for you all to decide. All this toerag has ever done is stick his nose where it don't belong (coz that's been his job). He can't let go.

Who is he? He has a wife and kids ... and boyfriends. Why bother with a man in a cage? He is after recognition and fame. "I know Bronson."

Well, he don't know me. He could never know me but he sure as hell wants to! He has even gone down the road of my legal team! But he knows f*** all about my appeal. Let me explain for the final time: my lawyer now is the no. 1 in Europe, if not the world. Who are you going to believe? Him or Chapman? I rest my case. ... and who else believes I don't want to get out and I love my own notoriety?

It's obvious to a peanut the dosh I can make outside (maybe this is what upsets people). The same as my comeback fight against Ricky Horsley. Yes I'm 55 but so what? Would you not make a comeback for £100,000? Plus the DVD sales, plus the media? Who else could do that but me? Mugs like Chapman couldn't make that sort of money in 50 years but I will make it in 1 fight (so who's the clown?) It seems to me that jealousy may play a part in this "Bronson put down". Could that be the truth?

Let's face the truth for once (not a computer screen to have a dig at me). Prison is for punishment ... If I had my way there would be the "birch" not silly therapy. Prison should be tough ... hard and make us think about not re-offending. I'm a man not a patient. I don't want or need silly screws in my face like Chapman trying to make me believe that I'm a statistic. I've got problems I need help. The only ones that need help are the Chapmans of this fucked up world and the MPs who make up all this shit.

I chose to be a villain. I'm not proud of it nor am I ashamed of it. I have paid my debt to society and it's time to go home. I'm walking out of jail, not crawling. Then and only then you'll see the true colours of the Chapmans of this world. He really does need a slap, the cheeky sod, for saying all this crap. Now "Lewis" is jumping on his words. Who are these faceless maggots? Don't they realise how insulting it is to me to say I don't want to get out? Them pair of wimps' way of getting out would be to bend over in the shower. Or polish the governor's shoes. Or be the tea boy. So, when others don't do it their way they see me as a nutter who wants to stay in. Hey! I'm a pussy lover! "I don't get no pussy in jail", so why would I want this life? I enjoy good food and smart clothes. I like a fast car, a party and I enjoy a good punch-up in the ring (so there you have it). I am anti-crime, anti-drugs, anti-violence. What more do I have to say to prove it?

I also have my art to fall back on and after-dinner chats (all this is waiting for me). What's waiting for Chapman? A wife that's just spent his dosh on liposuction and a boring existence. Dreams that are dried up. An internet nerd. 30 years of locking up cons.

He is one of those types who live in regret. He would have loved to have walked on my side, lived on the edge, but his bottle dried up. He had to do the next best thing "control the inside" coz he sure can't control the outside.

If I were outside I would not have time to be on the sites. I'm not interested in it. I prefer to see a man's face rather than his words on a screen. Real men don't need all this nonsense. What's the purpose of it all apart from being nosy? It's very rare that I even get to see this stuff. I've got a website that I rarely get to see. I'm only told bits and bobs. I only think or hope that bits of mine actually go on it. I have to trust and rely on people to do it. My life, my world, is all about trusting people. I have little control on my life. It's why I despise Chapman coz his sort are all the same "Power freaks". That skinny little faggot wants to be the "big shot" when in reality he is a gutless nobody. 3 times he was told to f*** off but he is brave because "Bronson's in a box". It's like a bear being prodded with a stick through the bars. The cat and mouse game. Well it's never forgot Chapman by me. It's a big laugh to you. Keep laughing pal … coz the last laugh is mine. You're just a stirring little toerag making me out to still be a nasty fucker and now you've got Lewis doing it for you or maybe you are Lewis as well? Go and dye your tash and get a life. Put your leather trousers on and go to the village. The boys are all waiting for you! YMCA all the way to Disneyland.
Charles Bronson

Message from Charles Bronson posted 18 September 2007, Michaelson
Ok Sherlock Holmes come out from behind your curtain I've got a picture of you in my head. Bald, skinny, specs and a big nose. Grassing all your neighbours up over petty things. Mugs like you make me feel sick but I'm gonna answer your pathetic questions (more for the stigma you put on my name and loyal friends).

Over the years I have made very little dosh and the little that I have made goes on my art, pens and stamps etc. 90% of the art that you may see on eBay is sold by strangers, "people who write to me to send them an art for their charities". I oblige them as I enjoy doing it. Plus it helps them out. With the other 10% I actually look after my choice of charities, so where you get I'm making a fortune is beyond me (or any of my mates).

I'm now going to give you an example of how I work and sort things out. But, in return, I want to know what you do and who you are.

I have chosen these two simply as both gave me a lot of pleasure in doing them, but I could give you 100 more similar ones and prove every one, so it would be good to see what you have done.

1st one. In 1987 when I was freed from jail I was 35 years old. I had been locked up since I was 21 years old. 14 long, hard years. I walked out of jail with nothing. I spat on the gate as I walked out. A week later I was in the ring (as Charles Bronson)and in 69 days of freedom I had 3 fights (all unlicensed). I was unstoppable. My fight manager, Paul Edmunds, applied for me to turn professional. I was denied this by the Boxing Board of Control - reason: because I was ex Broadmoor. So I could not turn pro. One of my fights was at Bow Royal Theatre. It was a charity night. All dosh raised was for a boy with cancer. I travelled from Luton to East London with no expenses. I fought and I donated my purse to charity. The media asked me why? I said: "No comment" and went back to Luton with empty pockets. That night we raised a sack load of dosh. It was one of my proudest nights (would you step in a ring for nothing after 14 lost years to help a young boy?) Weeks later I got nicked on an armed robbery on James Tubins Jewellers in Luton and ended up back in jail. I got what I deserved, but nobody, especially a little turd like you, will ever take away the good I've done. That's what you call a proud night's work.

2nd. Over the last 40 years I've read so much about the Moors Murders (Brady and Hindley). I actually got lucky enough in Parkhurst in the early 1970s to spit in Brady's face through a cage door. If the bars were not there I would have probably broke his jaw. The sad thing that always stuck in my head was Winnie Johnson, the mother of Keith (her son) whose body was never found to this day. A few Xmases ago I decided to cheer her up. I got a nice few quid together and I asked my mate "Ray Williams" to go and see her with his son "Raymond" who at the time was 12 years old. Little Raymond handed her £1,000 cash from me to have a good Xmas. That for me was a magic day, and for Raymond something he will never forget. That's something a nosy little prick like you will never do and if you had your evil little way you would stop me doing it. Do you ever see an MP doing something like that? Or your friend the taxman? Or mugs like you who just read about people like Winnie Johnson, then do sod all about it?

So what have you done, Michaelson? Tell us all. Let the rest decide who's the rat! I suggest you keep your fingers off your keyboard and come and see me at one of my shows later and ask me to my face. Be a man for once in your life. You don't have to like me but don't you dare accuse me or my friends of tax fraud. I will pay my taxes when I'm out earning a fortune … Ok … Mr Columbo Prat!

Message from Charles Bronson posted 18 September 2007
Lewis, you seem to know a lot about Huntley. Well I've been in 3 jails at the same time as this piece of shit - Belmarsh, Woodhill and here, Wakefield. At each jail he has been spoilt rotten. It took me 29 years to get a TV. He got one on day 1 and his Game Boy shit, bedspreads, curtains, canteen. The reason he is spoilt is down to his threat to commit suicide so they give him what he wants. At Belmarsh he had a lovely "special suite" with his own gym. At Woodhill he had a pad in the hospital wing. You, Lewis, don't know what the fuck you are on about concerning me.

I am held year after year in a special cage. I am not allowed to mix. You can call it all the names you wish, Human Rights, Rule Book shit, it's still solitary and no less. Even my visits are isolated. "Ask Mark Emmins" and you have the cheek to say I don't want to get out. Do you realise how insulting that is to a man like me? I have fought all my life to help weaker cons get their rights and a c*** like you says this. Also my hostages, 2 of them were governors, 1 a solicitor, 1 a teacher, 3 Iraqis, 1 a doctor and 1 screw. So what are you insinuating here? Why have you brought this up? So what's your past? Are you Mr Perfect? What skeletons have you got locked away? I don't deny I've been a nasty bastard but it's my last 8 years that I am bothered about, not toerags like you getting lemon.

Here's a question for you: "Ask Chapman what he is doing with all the video tapes of the prisoners' groups at Grendon?" Chapman has all the tapes at his house. He is no longer employed by Grendon so why is he keeping these tapes? Whatever happened to prison confidentiality? Check this up in Inside Time papers. Chapman wrote it himself. I say he is up to something iffy. Screws don't take tapes home. It is official property. You ask him that. Don't worry about Bronson. "I'm sweet".

One last thing. I predict I'll be released within the next 6 months without all your bollocks therapy and psycho tests. The fact is, I'm not like you wimps. I'm a man, a real man, and all who know me, really know me, will tell all you crazy people that I have changed. You lot are the same as the day you were born - wimps. You're not even has beens. You live and die and you're forgotten about in a week. You're nobodies. Now fuck off.

This is one guy you're not ever gonna see in some shithouse prison hostel working for peanuts and being controlled by a bunch of Chapmans. I haven't survived 3 and a half decades of hell to come out and suck on a toffee apple or spend my life like you prats looking at a computer screen.

Charles Bronson

Message from Ann, posted 20 September 2007
Nice one Charlie. I think most on here know for a fact all the negative chat on here is ex screws hiding under false names, but the public are the ones that count and we all know your freedom is well overdue! Apple pies & Guinness will be waiting for you soon, good luck!

Message from Clare, posted 21 September 2007
Love it Charlie, keep on showing what a bunch of pricks these are, it's hilarious, made me smile when I was feeling crap :) Always have the last word me old china! Clare.

If these latest postings on the 'Free Charlie' forum don't put an end to the prick nothing will. Now fuck off, Chapman. Pray you never have to walk into your nightmare, coz I will turn your hair as white as snow in seconds.

Uncle Charlie's Problem Page

Dear Charlie,
Every time I give my boyfriend a blow job it leaves a terrible taste in my mouth. I do enjoy doing it to him, but I don't like the taste. What can I do?
Sue from Ipswich

Look Sue, you've got to tell him how it is. He can either give his dick a good wash and maybe cover it in milk chocolate, or suck mints as that may help his spunk to taste sweeter, or maybe you could come and see me and suck mine, test the taste and compare it, as I've been told I taste of toffee apple. You're more than welcome to come and try.

Dear Charlie,
I caught my grandmother in the bathroom with a vibrator. She's 93 years old and
suffers with serious chronic rheumatoid arthritis. Now I can't look at her in the same
way as before. Should I say something?
David from Bolton

Dave - I get a lot of these sorts of problem letters. It can't be a nice sight
to catch granny working out with a vibrator. I would give her a pull and
break the ice. Just say, "Hey, Nan, that's a big vibrator you got there. Was
granddad that big?" Something like that should do the trick.

Dear Charlie,
I'm only 17 and I feel I'm a woman trapped in a man's body. I don't know who to turn
to, I feel so depressed and desperate. My father caught me wearing Mum's bra and
knickers and kicked me out of the house. What can I do?
John from Watford

Well, John, you sure have a problem here. Are you sure you want to carry
on living? Coz if I was you I'd want to call it a day. Face reality, John, you've
got a meat and two veg in between your legs not a pussy. It's all in your head,
John. Mind over matter. You must fight these urges. What more can I say
but accept who and what you are and be thankful for your meat and two
veg. Get out there and use them.

Dear Charlie,
Would you go out with me?
Rupert

Fuck off and get a life.

Dear Charlie,
My Dad said he smashed your face in when you was in Parkhurst.
Sid from St Helens

Yeah, he probably did with ten of his screw mates. You tell him he couldn't
do it on his fucking own.

Dear Charlie,
Every time I see a banana I get wet down below. What can I do?
Sally from Doncaster

Well, Sally, this is a strange one. I don't quite know what to say. I'm lost for
words. Send me your telephone number and I'll give you a call. It seems
interesting to me. I would like to go further into this.

Dear Charlie,
What qualifications have you got to be an agony uncle?
Carol from London

Carol - what's it got to do with you? Who the fuck do you think you are, my probation officer or something? I'm trying to help people out of the goodness of my heart and a cheeky bitch like you has to stick your beak in. What's your fucking problem? Cunt. I bet you never gave Deirdre or Marjorie Proops this shit, you sexist slag. Fuck off.

Dear Charlie,
I'm a 45-year-old married man with 7 kids. I'm a prison officer and I work a lot of nights. I came home early last week and I found 3 strange men in bed with my wife. She says nothing was going on. I don't know what to think.
Eddie from Birmingham

You're paranoid, Ed. Stop worrying. Stop treating your wife like a prisoner. Trust her.

Dear Charlie,
My daughter is only 19 years old and she's getting a right bad reputation in our village. She's gone through every man in the village and now she's pregnant.
Irene (address held back)

Irene - well, you're gonna be a granny, it's as simple as that. What do you want me to say? What can I say? Your daughter likes her sex and she's been caught. That's life. The dad could be anybody, but it's not me.

Dear Charlie,
I've got a horrible, smelly discharge coming out of my fanny. What do you think it is?
Annie from Somerset

How the fuck do I know. I once had a horse like that. I shot it.

Dear Charlie,
I'm in love with my next door neighbour. I'm 52 and he's 22. How should I tell my husband? I'm not in bad shape - a bit overweight and a flabby belly and drooping tits, but I can still do a turn.
Bertha from Brighton

Bertha, you don't say if the 22-year-old guy is married or if he needs specs. Look, be honest to your husband. Don't cheat on him. It's always best to be truthful. Good luck. Go with your heart.

Dear Charlie,
I'm a lesbian and I don't know where to go and meet lesbians. Can you help?
Suzy from Wakefield

Suzy, what are you? A fucking idiot? How the fuck do I know where lesbians hang out in Wakefield? What do you think I am, some sort of cunt? Fuck off.

Dear Charlie,
I'm a 37-year-old virgin. I wonder if this is normal?
Reg from Winchester

Reg, why don't you just die?

Dear Charlie,
My husband only ever gives me one doggy style. How can I make him try other positions?
Sandra from Halifax

Maybe it's your face, Sandra. Try using a mask or a sack.

Dear Charlie,
My wife's fanny smells and it puts me off sex. What can I do?
Bert from Brighton

Bert - you haven't said how old she is, coz old fannies do chuck up a bit. There's not really a lot you can do, mate. Some fannies do smell more than others. I think you're lumped with it, Bert. Personally I would swap it for a nice, fresh, juicy one. You wouldn't put up with a smelly car, would you? Well, there's your answer.

Bronson,
I think you're a disgusting man and you're giving out ridiculous and pathetic answers to people who need advice - vulnerable people at that. I am complaining to my MP and I'm having a meeting with the Citizens Advice Committee to see if I can have you prosecuted.
Hilary from Bradford

Fuck off, you old bag.

Dear Charlie,
My husband made a slip whilst we were having sex and it went right up my bottom. The only thing is, I now like it better that way. Is this normal? And is it illegal?
Rose from Liverpool

Rose - as I always say, what goes on behind closed doors is your own biz. What is normal anyway? You enjoy it, Rose, but tell your old man to use plenty of lubrication, otherwise it will play hell on your piles.

Dear Charlie,
Is it possible to be allergic to fanny juice as I always come out in a rash when my girlfriend comes in my face?
Eddie from Luton

Eddie, I see you are from my town of Luton and this, believe it or not, is quite a common thing. You could well be suffering from cuntfacephobia. It's more a psychosis thing - 'mental'. I'm told by good sources it's helpful to talk to the pussy. Just get to know it. Obviously it won't talk back, but pretend it lipreads. So when your girl is asleep get under the blanket with a torch and get to know one another. Give it a try. Let me know how it goes, okay?

Dear Charlie,
I can't believe some of the advice you give out. Surely you're taking the piss?
Howard from Bedford

Howard - do me a favour and fuck off.

Dear Mr Bronson,
I am a devoted Christian and I actually feel that you are causing more problems than you solve. It's very moralistically wrong in how you behave. God will not be happy and God does love you Mr Bronson. Please try to reach out.
Kathy from Ascot

Kathy, nobody loves me, least of all God. Now, if you want to love me you know where I am, but bring a box of condoms, okay?

Dear Charlie,
I'm an 18-year-old lad going out with an 18-year-old girl who's got an identical twin. The other night I stopped over at her place and I ended up in bed with them both. I don't know what to do as I love them both. What would you do, Charlie?
Mark from Ellsmere Port

Mark, you lucky bastard. What would I do? It's more like what wouldn't I do. Come on, son, liven up you lucky sod. How lucky can one guy get? You've cracked it, son. You haven't got a problem. I've got the problem. I want some of that.

Dear Charlie,
My girlfriend left me for another man. She took everything: my furniture, my car and
all my savings. I feel so depressed. What can I do, Charlie?
Rupert from Bradford

Well, with a name like Rupert I don't blame her for leaving. But you've got
to be a man. Stand up for yourself. Get after her. Get everything back.
Smash her lover boy's legs. Put him in a chair for the rest of his life. Give her
a good kick in the cunt. Do what any man would do. Kick some arse, Rupert.
Fucking kick off. Failing that, put your head in the oven. What more can I
say? You've got no money, so you can't even pay me to do it for you. Men
like me 'sort' things like this, but it don't come cheap. You can't expect us to
do it for nothing - we are professional people.

Dear Charlie,
Is it dangerous to wank 10 times a day?
Robbo from Clacton

Well, it all depends on where you do it and who's looking. But if you have
got 10 wanks in you a day, I can get you a job in the blue movies. That's on
the level.

Dear Charlie,
My feet smell. I can't do nothing to stop it. It's now depressing me.
Beth from Leeds

If they're so bad, cut them off. Problem solved.

Dear Charlie,
I'm a 49-year-old ex-miner. I'm married with 3 grown-up sons. My wife of 32 years
keeps hinting for a threesome. We have never done anything like that before. In fact
our sex life has been a bit boring for the last 10 years. I'm afraid I may lose her,
Charlie, if I go ahead with a threesome. What should I do? I must add, I'm a bit
overweight and I've a bad back and I suffer with erection problems. I just can't get it
up no more.
Arthur from Yorkshire

Arthur, It's time to face facts. You're fucked, mate. You have let yourself
go. I'm sorry to say it, but put yourself in your wife's shoes. What's she got
left? You can't even get it up no more. You've got to see it from her end. She
still needs a good seeing to and you're not up to it. Maybe a threesome and
you can watch. Some men enjoy that. Get some 20-year-old stud round once
a week. That could do the trick. But lay down some rules. He can't kiss her.
Give it a go, Arthur, it could work. I wish you well, mate. I know how Maggie
fucked you miners years ago. I feel sorry for you ex-miners.

Dear Charlie,
I'm a young single mum living in Leeds' red light area. I get approached at least a
dozen times a day by men wanting sex. I'm just starting to fantasise about doing it,
plus I need the cash as I'm not working. What's your advice, Charlie? I'm not bad
looking, but I do have serious stretch marks and a big, fat, flabby arse.
Yvonne from Leeds

Some men love a big, fat, flabby arse. They pay for what they like. If you're
actually considering it and dreaming of it, then it's odds on you'll do it. But
be careful, more so for your kids. It's not all chocolate cake and mince pies
in that game. It can get nasty and dangerous. I wish you luck, Yvonne. You'll
need it.

Dear Charlie,
My sister thinks you're brilliant, but I tell her you're just a cunt.
Stan from Chester

Stan, look in the mirror, mate! There's only one cunt, and it's looking at
you. My love to your sister.

Dear Charlie,
My girlfriend always squeezes my testicles hard when she is having an orgasm and it
causes a lot of pain and I sometimes lose my erection. I tell her not to do it but she says
she can't help it. What shall I do?
Jack from Norwich

Simple. Grab one of her tits and twist it and then bite her ear. She will soon
stop.

Dear Charlie,
When I make love to my wife I'm starting to imagine she's our pet Labrador. I can't
help it. It's happening all the time. Am I going mad?
Name and address supplied

Yes!

Dear Charlie,
The other night me and my husband were shagging on the rug in front of the fire when
our cat Tiddles joined in and started licking my bum hole and my husband's balls as
he was shafting me. Is this normal for a cat to do this and is it illegal?
But it was exciting and I've never had such an explosive orgasm in my life.
Now when my husband is at work I let Tiddles give me a good licking. I must admit
I do give my fanny a good rub with a pilchard first. Tiddles loves it. What's your
honest opinion, Charlie?
Mary from the Isle of Wight

Well, Mary, you are a naughty lady, aren't you? What would I give to watch this? Is it illegal? I don't know. But Tiddles is a very lucky pussy indeed! I wonder how many more pussies are getting a lick around the country? The mind boggles. You really have made me think. If you and your husband and Tiddles are ever up for a foursome, I'm the man. The very thought of Tiddles' tongue licking my balls as I'm shafting you just makes me all dizzy. What a vision. Keep in touch, Mary.

It's Mary again. Hi Charlie. I enclose a photo of me and Tiddles that my husband took. You're invited down, Charlie.
Mary

Mary, I'm on my way.

Dear Charlie,
I'm writing to find out how it went with Mary and Tiddles and her husband.
Dave from Lincoln.

Dave, fuck off.

Mr Bronson,
I'm disgusted over this cat saga. I am reporting you and Mary and her husband to the RSPCA. You're a disgrace to all pet lovers.
Humphrey from Lincoln

Humphrey, before I say fuck off, let me tell you about Tiddles. It's not an ordinary cat. It's a fucking tiger - a 2-year-old 12½ stone fucking tiger - and I almost got my bollocks licked off. And I make you 100% right. It's disgusting the way Mary and her husband play sex games with Tiddles. They should both be locked up. It really is disgusting. I only went down to investigate it and I'm horrified at what I witnessed. Tiddles really does have a good lick about. My bollocks and shaft are still red raw. You don't realise how rough a cat's tongue is on your privates. It really is disgusting. I totally agree with you, Humphrey.

Dear Charlie,
You really are a hypocrite. If Tiddles was so wrong, then why was it you got your privates licked? Are you not as bad?
Caroline from Hemel Hempstead

Caroline, how dare you accuse me of being a pervo! I was actually shagging that lunatic woman whilst she was giving her nasty hubby a blow job. It was only then that Tiddles crept up and started licking my jewels. It took me by surprise. I was so engrossed in shafting this bitch that I didn't realise at first what was going on. It took me a good 15 minutes to work it out. Then, and only then, I realised and I felt so ashamed and hurt by it. Please don't think bad of me.

Dear Charlie,
I'm a 42-year-old widower with four cats. None of them will even come near my pussy. I've tried everything: fish, cat food, cakes, even fish fingers. Could you put me in touch with Mary for some tips?
Babs from East London

Babs, I'm in enough trouble. Drop me out.

Dear Charlie,
I'm a 16-year-old girl and I caught my dad having a wank in the shed while looking at dirty mags. He never saw me looking through the shed window, but I now can't stop laughing when he looks at me. Shall I tell him or shall I tell mum or just let it go?
Lisa from Manchester

Lisa, let it go. Dads are only human, but you could maybe slip a hint to dad to put some curtains up in the shed. You must understand that a man's body works different to a woman's. We have to blow our tubes often. As Santa would say - empty the sack.

Dear Charlie,
I'm a gay man who's into S and M. Where can I meet others like myself?
Eugene from Norfolk

Try the Prison Officers' Social Club. They're heavily into all that scene.

Dear Charlie,
Are you married or courting and what does your partner think of your crudeness and insulting behaviour? If you were my husband I would divorce you immediately. You're just a thug with a pen.
Beryl from Swansea

Fuck off, you Welsh dragon. You wouldn't get a chance to divorce me, coz I'd bury you in the fucking garden.

Dear Charlie,
That Tiddles. Wouldn't they have to have a licence to keep a tiger like that?
Fred from Devon

Fred, I'm not interested, mate. I've moved on from that, and so should you. Okay?

Dear Charlie,

I know a girl you used to go out with, Suzie, and you destroyed her life. She's never been the same since you took her to Blackpool for a weekend. She still has nightmares about the big dipper. What have you got to say about this if you've got the balls to?
Bob from Hull

Bob! You're a nosy cunt that needs filling in. I'll tell you about Suzie. She's a mentalist. It was her who nearly made me fall out of the big dipper when she got my cock out and started sucking it as we went down the rush. I was the one who shit myself. So don't give me all your bollocks. You wasn't there. She fell out. I didn't push her. I can't help it if one of her legs is shorter than the other after the accident. You can't hold me responsible. Anyway, who the fuck are you, King Kong? Piss off.

CHAPTER 21
NOVEMBER - CHATTER, PATTER
AND MAD AS A HATTER

Hey, don't take your granny to Chicago, USA, coz 82-year-old Lillian Fletcher, all 5 feet 1 inch of her, has just been tasered by the cops. They used an electric gun on her to subdue her! The old girl has schizophrenia and dementia. That about sums the law up in a nutshell! What sort of man can taser an old woman? If she'd had an Uzi, I could understand it. Just who are the criminals today - the cops or the robbers? It makes you think. If they can do that to an old girl, what the fuck are they doing to the youth of Chicago? The mind boggles.

Did you know that the first apple pie made was in the 14th century? It's a fact. I wonder what the pastry was like? Nothing like my mum's I bet.

Here's something for you youngsters to think about in the YP jails. There are chicks with dicks in Thailand called ladyboys. Once you've had a few beers and a few shorts, you're trapped. What are you gonna do? Look at them? How are you gonna know? So be warned, coz you could be in for the shock of your life. This is loonyology at its maddest!

My friend Mickey Dunne lives out in Thailand. Not bad, eh? I'm going out there later for a couple of months' sunshine. Lovely jubbly. Just what the doctor ordered! I can't fucking wait! Mickey and me go back a long way. He's a top geezer - the best.

3 November 2007
I see Colonel Paul Tibbet just died at the age of 92 - not a bad age ... well, for a mass murderer that is. He killed 140,000 civilians. One drop - bang! - you're dead. He did it from the sky - the atomic bomb. Cop a hold of that. It hit Hiroshima at 8.15 a.m. on 6 August 1945. Japanese women and children were burnt to a crisp, their eyes melted, their skin dropped off, babies melted into their prams; the screams, they agony, the pain. What had they done wrong? Who deserved so much horror? One big bang. Anyway, what's Colonel Tibbet gonna be saying at the Pearly Gates? Will they let him in? Would you? I wonder. He said he had no regrets, coz he was only doing a job. Some fucking job! It reminds me of the Nazi war criminals trial. Their defence was the same: we gassed 56 million Jews, but we were only doing our job. What a fucking job! On 15 August the Japs surrendered - wouldn't you have? Colonel Tibbet's bomb may have stopped the war ... but did it? Can anything stop a war? Do you believe the Japs have forgiven and

forgotten? I bet they'll piss on his grave. Japs are like baby elephants - they don't forget fuck all. Believe me, It's not started yet. When hell freezes over, that's when it'll really start up - when the world goes mad, insanity takes over for real, and no one will survive.

Little Maddie McCann has been missing for six months today. She just disappeared from the face of the Earth. How? Why? Where is she? Somebody knows - some evil bastard; some perverted, sicko paedophile. Or will it remain one of life's mysteries, the unsolved crime, the crime that broke a million hearts. Everybody thinks they know who did it. Some think it was an accident and others think she's still alive. But thinking don't stop a tornado, it just rips straight through your soul. Madeleine may be gone forever, pray all you will. What's gone on is wicked and evil. The world's a sick place full of twisted minds and tortured souls. The ones that hide the truth are the ones who have nightmares, and your turn is next. It may be a year away, even ten years away, but it will creep up on you. There is no escape from your mind - you're a target for your conscience. You're gonna burn in hell; you're gonna scream and scream, you sad, twisted, evil maniacs. Enjoy the end, coz the end is your beginning.

So what's the strength on Heather Mills? Is she a gold-digger, or just a victim? Is Paul McCartney such an angel? Only some beetles have wings. There's always two sides to the story, so why not listen to Heather? She may have a leg missing, but the woman's got a heart. She actually cares about people, and she's also an animal lover. She does so much for charity. She's got a good soul. The media are ripping her to bits, but why? What's she ever done wrong, apart from marry a Beatle? Some say she lost the day she got married; she couldn't win. How could she? It's about money, money, money; piles of dosh a mountain high; too much loot; greed, the green-eyed monster, Fuck the yacht, buy the boatyard; stuff the house, get the castle. It's gone insane. It's not Heather, it's the way we are, the way of life. They're probably a load of jealous twats: she got ... I want ... I can't have .... Grow up and leave the woman alone! She's a nice, sweet girl who crushed a Beatle. Big deal.

There's big bucks for John Terry, the Chelsea captain: 135k a week for kicking a leather ball around, for playing a game. Is it insane, or just pathetic? That's not football, it's robbery. No wonder the fans' tickets are so pricey. You're buying his Ferrari, you mugs. Wake up. Nobody is worth 135k a week - apart from an armed robber. A muggy footballer?! They're now all the same. Rooney is on 100k a week. It's madness gone madder, a complete piss-take. Sir Stanley Matthews will be turning in his grave. What could you do with that sort of dosh? What footballer is worth that? It's like that little short-arse Maradona. He scores a goal against England and it's called 'The Hand of God', so it's allowed. He's God to everybody. Well he ain't to me. He's a cheating, short-arsed little twat, that's what he is, but all the fans love him. What a joke. What a fucking game. It's as corrupt as the Kray Firm.

135k? Do me a favour. You fans are to blame for buying the tickets. If you never paid the extortionate ticket prices, how would they get such wages? You work your bollocks off all week to buy these footballers a rich lifestyle. Half the prats can't even score a goal, coz they're too pissed from the night before. You pay for their parties. Wake up.

Trick or treat - what's that all about? Going around with masks on and scaring people so they'll give you a treat. I got 20 years for that. You'll get an axe in the head off me or a can of petrol and a light. Fuck off.

And whatever happened to Lord Lucan? Do we care? I don't think so. He's a suspect in a murder case anyway, so he wouldn't want to be found. It's a pity that a few more lords don't disappear! What good are they? What do they do - apart from talk shit? It's 30+ years since Lucan vanished and they're still talking about it. Stop looking and forget him. Lord Lucan, who's that? Never heard of the geezer. He don't drink in my pub. Move on and get a fucking life. The clock's ticking, and one day it stops. Who gives a flying fuck about Lord Lucan?! Why do we worry about things that don't matter, or things that don't concern us? No wonder we have nervous breakdowns. Stop worrying and get on with your own lives.

Another one of life's big mysteries - Santa. What a joke. A big ,fat, bearded man coming down your chimney. What's all that about? No wonder the kids are mad. No wonder he's fat if you leave him a mince pie. Why don't his beard catch on fire? What are chimneys for? Why ain't he covered in soot? How can he eat millions of mince pies? Santa? Fuck off. We all know it's dad. Don't you think the kids know that? Stop messing about and get real. I could just fancy a mince pie myself.

It's brilliant, it's magical, Mother Christmas. That's what we all need - a Happy Mother Christmas. Why does it have to be Father Christmas? Wouldn't a Mother Christmas be better - more peaceful and gentle? Don't it make sense? How do we know what Santa's up to? He could be a paedophile, we just don't know. They do say a man with a beard is hiding something, but what?

Having said that, I had a beard. My beard was down to my belly button and hid half my body. It was legendary, infamous. The beard of the century, that's what my beard was. It's now in Canada. I cut it off and gave it to Joyce Connor. She's got it in a plastic bag. Why? Why is the world round? Why not? It's my fucking beard, so I'll do what I want with it! In Canada you need a beard in the winter. All the women have a bushy fanny, coz it keeps them warm. A big, bushy, hairy pussy. Meeeeow. Yeh, that's where my beard is - Canada, and I'm still in the hole, beardless. I should've kept it. By now it would've been to the floor - a six-foot beard. I could've plaited it, made a rope and made my escape. Imagine that! Escaping with a beard - food for thought, thoughts of madness, from the depths of insanity.

Hey, let's all grow a beard. Mother Christmas too. If you can't grow one, then grow the body hair. Let's all go hairy. Bring back the Yeti. We love the

Yeti, wild and dangerous - a bit like the Klu Klux Klan. Lunatics. But don't we all love *Nightmare on Elm Street* or the *Texas Chainsaw Massacre*? Don't it get your juices flowing? Well, don't it? That rush of adrenalin, the fear, the unknown. I bet you look under the bed or in the wardrobe after watching those. And when there's a full moon, there could be a werewolf! I'd rip his throat out, werewolf or no werewolf. Lie under my bed and you're dead, brown bread, history. You'll do your last howl, so stay clear. What about the Mummy and Dracula, and that prat Frankenstein? They're all monsters, locked up in the funny farm.

The real danger is drugs. Crackheads are today's monsters. Fear them. You need to be ready. They'll do anything for a fix, even cut off your head or kidnap your granny. Even Dracula had principles, and Frankenstein had a heart ... well, somebody's heart, but he still had a heart. You can't say he never, can you? All a crack/smack/drughead's got is a big, black, empty hole and they'll drag you into it, all the way to the bottom. You'll never see the light again, never. It's all over. They'll rip your eyes out for a fix and dribble all over your face, like a bloodhound, like a rabid wolf. Pay up and die. You're just a meal ticket, something on the bottom of a shoe. Pay up and bleed. Bleed until you bleed no more. Dry up, crumble and die. The crackhead lives in the shadows - the shadows of Hell. Welcome to the world of nightmares, death and destruction. "Wake up, Dad. You're sweating all over me. Your breath stinks of methadone. There's blood in your eye. You're a fucking zombie. It's too late to die. You died years ago." How insane is that? How much madder can it get? Believe me, a lot. I've not started yet. I'm only in first gear.

Who remembers that freaky old bell-ringer, Quasimodo, the Hunchback of Notre Dame? He fell in love with Esmeralda: Beauty and the Beast. She loved his 10-inch cock, that's what it was. Well, she wouldn't love his hump or his ugly face, would she? Would you? Let's face facts, he was a freak of nature, but he was well hung. That's what Esmeralda wanted - a good seeing to, and Quasimodo saw to that. She loved it. That's why she went back again and again. He rung her bell alright. You'd better believe it. The freaky fucker had some fun, and who can blame him, stuck up in that tower year after year, ringing that poxy bell? What a life. What a waste! So what do beautiful women see in ugly men? He had no money. All he had was a big, fat cock. That's all she needed, all she ever dreamed of, and boy did she get it. Isn't life wonderful, full of lovely characters? I love to see the underdog come tops, don't you? It goes to show that nothing's impossible. If Quasimodo can do it, so can anybody. Even the Elephant Man made a living. He trunked his way around the world, and people paid to see the freak. It's brilliant. He had the last laugh. Good luck to him. Don't we all love a freak? I say bring back the circus with all them beautiful freaks: midgets and dwarf-throwing; two-headed monsters; 'The Lizard Man licks'; 'The Fat Woman farts a volcano'. We'd pay to have a laugh. Fuck political correctness. Fuck the left wing goody-goodies. Bring back the good times, when people were simple and happy, when there was no badness and we just had a good laugh, a roll in the hay. It was brilliant.

I had my first fight at a fair, in a sawdust boxing ring. I got a black eye and a busted lip. But it done me good. That's what real life is all about: a punch in the head. Nowadays it's a whip with a lettuce leaf. It's pathetic. Real men are few, and they're getting fewer. They're as rare as rocking-horse shit. Political correctness has gone mad and is taking over the planet for sure! Don't do this, do that; you can't say this, you can't say that; don't eat that, it's bad for you; you can't do that, you can't even think it. Who the fuck are they to tell us all this? What life qualifications do they have? Who or what are they? They're a bunch of nosy prats, control freaks. Fuck 'em off and do what you do best; do what makes you feel good, not what makes them feel good; do what's right for you, not for them. Who the fuck are those do-gooders? They don't drink in my club. They're up their own arses. It's a sad old world, full of sad old folk trying to change everybody. If it's not religion, then it's morals. I've got my own, and they're with me till the day I die. Get a life - your own life - and stay out of mine. Go suck on a Fisherman's Friend. Go suck Quasimodo. Sling a dwarf or two. Get a life, and laugh till you die. In fact die laughing and laugh all the way to the crematorium. What's wrong with that? Don't throw stones in a greenhouse. And don't shit on my lawn - dog or man - coz I'll make you eat it, every little bit, and then you'll lick the lawn. Go shit on your own lawn.

Now there's a thought. So where is all the shit? Imagine it. Let's say you shit a bucket a week, so four buckets a month, or 50 buckets a year. Multiply that by six billion people. That's a mountain of shit, sky high. Where is all that shit? It must be somewhere. No wonder the world stinks. It's a shithole, one gigantic, huge, enormous shit tip, the world's disease. Sick or what? Don't that make you want to puke up? No wonder there's a race to Mars. They're trying to escape the shit. The powers on Earth are running scared. They know the end is one high explosion of shit and they want out of it before it comes. We're all in the shit, so to speak! What an ending to life. I'm off for a cup of tea and a slice of apple pie. I do hope I've cheered you all up. Have a nice day.

5 November 2007

Joe Calzaghe's done it again. What a champion this guy really is. Brilliant. He beat Kessler and won his two world titles. He now has three - a triple world champion. Well done, Joe, you're the Daddy. Fucking brilliant.

I've another visit on 7 November: my two buddies Ray Williams and Roger Devonshire. So more milkshakes and chocolate cake. I've never had it so good.

Tonight our Toastmaster is Mr Roger Devonside from Europartz, Chester, who has kindly supported Chester Committee of Mersey Kidney Research over the last few years both as toastmaster and helping raise funds with events. One of these events was wing walking! Roger has recently earned his place in the Guinness Book of Records, having soared to the skies 13 times in as many years. Later this year Roger is organising a fundraising event for Chester Committee of MKR at the Slow Boat, Chester. This event will include a wonderful 10 course banquet and entertainment from a great comedian. He has organised many evenings like this, including nights with 'Mad Frankie Frazer', and they have always been a lot of fun. The date has yet to be finalised. If you would like more details, please get in touch with Roger on 01244 390011 or Ann at MKR on 0151 706 3538.
Louise
Volunteer and Member
Chester Fundraisers' Committee

Daredevil Roger is flying without wings for charity.
Businessman Roger Devonside is going loop the loop to support a Wirral charity for terminally-ill youngsters. Mr Devonside is performing a wing walking stunt to publicise Claire House Children's Hospice Sparkling Star Appeal to build a £2m unit for teenagers.
Not for the first time he will be strapped to the top of the Utterly Butterly bi-plane as it flies up and down the River Mersey as he get into the spirit of the appeal theme: Reach for the Stars.
Company director Mr Devonside, 55, who does a lot of work for charity, said, 'I have done it lots of times before but it doesn't get any easier. It's quite terrifying.
'Each time I do it, it gets a little scarier because the pilots know me and they push me further and further: I hope this time he just goes up and down in a loop along the Mersey.'
Mr Devonside, who plays rugby, says he is fit for the challenge. He explained that the only way he could signify to the pilot how he is feeling is to put his thumbs up or down but he doesn't necessarily have to take any notice.
'Last time I put my thumbs down four times, but he just ignored me,' said Mr Devonside, who explained that the Beatles' original drummer Pete Best was coming along to watch the stunt on Bank Holiday Monday, August 25.
'One of the pilots dive bombs and only missed the ground by 30 feet. He puts you through your paces. Three days later I was still having stress pains in my chest.'
Mr Devonside, who lives in Caughall Road, Upton, Chester, urged people to get behind the appeal to build and run a teenage unit at the Clatterbridge-based hospice. 'It's very important for these kids who have all got terminal diseases. They don't come out of the place so their time is precious and we need to make their quality of life as good as possible.'
More than 200 families with children with life-threatening conditions have been referred to Claire House since it opened in April 1999.
A teenage unit is needed because the hospice has found itself dealing with an increasing number of teenagers. They make up 26% of patients but will represent 50% of the intake in 10 years' time. The £2m appeal will pay for the unit to be built and

operated for the first 12 months and is over and above the £1.4m current annual costs. It will include four en suite teenage bedrooms, additional recreation and living accommodation, family rooms and a training and resource area. Former Brookside star and all round TV celebrity Claire Sweeney, who is president of the appeal, said: 'I urge everyone to do whatever they can to make this appeal the success it deserves to be and to make sure that the teenage wing is built as soon as possible so that teenagers who are here today and others like them will be able to enjoy the facilities.'

People can help the 'Sparkling Star Appeal' by giving a regular monthly donation through their bank account, by signing a gift declaration and by taking part in a Claire House sponsored event or challenge. Ring Claire House on 0151 343 0883 for further information.

6 November 2007

My old buddy visited today: Mickey Dunne. Our last meet was in Long Lartin Jail in 1988, 19 years ago. Mickey copped a 15 stretch for a crime he didn't do. He served ten years, then got out and cleared his name. Ten wasted years, all over Old Bill lies! That's the West Midlands filth for you. Who didn't that lot fit up in the 1970s and '80s? So many. Anyway, Mick's a survivor and I'm proud of the man. He's a top geezer in my book.

6 November 2007, The Sun
KIDS IN PRISON FOR HOMEWORK WITH LAG DADS
Kids of seven are being let into a grim prison so their convict dads can help them with HOMEWORK. More than 50 youngsters flood into forbidding Wandsworth once a week for learning sessions.

The Homework Club at her Victorian nick in South West London gives the children vital contact with their dads. And it gives the prisoners - some serving life for rape and murder - an extra incentive to rehabilitate.

The club, the only one of its kind, takes place after normal visiting hours on Thursdays. The kids, all primary school age, go through intensive security checks at the Category B nick to make sure they are not being used to smuggle in contraband.

In the visits hall they get out their spelling books, maths homework and geography projects so their dads can see what they are doing at school and lend advice. The hourly club - an initiative of governor Ian Mulholland - is closely supervised. An insider at the jail, which can hold 1,416 cons, said: "It's amazing to see all these kids, some as young as seven, sitting down with their dads inside a nick.

"Precautions are taken to make sure there is no abuse of the homework classes, to unwittingly smuggle in illicit goods like mobile phones and drugs.

"So far there has not been one case. The children are innocent victims and it's good that they are allowed to maintain some sort of relationship with their dads."

One prison officer joked: "We hope none of the dads are teaching their like how to rob banks."

Mr Mulholland said: "The club plays an important part in maintaining family relationships by providing prisoners with the opportunity to help children with homework.

"Prisoners are fully risk-assessed before taking part. Positive family relationships contribute to the offender's eventual resettlement into the community and to the

development of a purposeful, law-abiding life."
Wandsworth, one of the biggest jails in Europe, was built in 1851 and is surrounded
by high walls topped with razor wire. Many of its original buildings are still in use.

Do you not think Prison is getting a bit silly now? Or am I old-fashioned? This sort of shit makes me feel embarrassed! It's just not prison, is it? Wandsworth to me only has hate-filled memories, and now it's a bleeding kindergarten. It's not sane, is it? Am I really on my own? Am I the man on the moon here? One year the place kicks the fuck out of you, then it lets little kids in to do homework. It just don't add up for me. I can't move on like this - my past won't allow it. Wandsworth was the toughest nick in the UK, second to none. All my memories are now confused. It's a dream. I've dreamt it all. They never did try to kill me off. They never did birch cons or hang them. There are no ghosts there. It's a lovely playschool, with wonderful screws and kind governors. Alcatraz was a paradise, St Quinten is a nudist camp, and Colditz is a beauty parlour. Bronson has gone insane. Wake me up when it's home time! I've had my fucking bellyful. I don't belong anymore. I'm a fucking lost soul. Honest.

I see they caught Salvatore Lo Piccolo in Sicily yesterday. He's the Mafia boss who's been on his toes for 20 years. Forty armed cops rushed him. That's his last daylight probably for the rest of his life, as he's in his late 60s now. Well, nothing lasts forever, and he had a good run. His name lives on in the history books. Respect to the man. Cosa Nostra.

I got the *Loonyology* book cover today, sent in by Chris Cowlin. Apex have done a lovely job on it. And, if I say so myself, it's the best cover out of all my books to date. It's brilliant. And the public who buy it are in for a nice treat. Only the best for you lot, and *Loonyology* is the best. It's a bloody masterpiece. And you'll find out soon how I had to do it. It's a miracle it ever got created.

Rachel Bristow sent me in a big box of art paints today, but sadly I'm not allowed it. So I'll pass it out on a visit and use it when I'm free! See how my lovely friends think of me? I really have got some smashing support. I've had 18 letters this week and it's only Tuesday.

Oh, and big thanks to Tel Currie for sorting out a few bits and bobs on my book cover. Even though we fell out, we still respect each other and I would never slag him off. We just can't see eye to eye on a certain problem. That's showbiz, it really is! You've just gotta move on with each chapter of life. Fuck hanging about, coz you only live the once ... or do we?

I had a nice cheese salad for tea, plus a mug of hot tea with a spoon of honey in it - lovely.

I called Mum tonight. She had a great time at the Blind Beggar Pub on Saturday 3 November. All my mates were there and they all spoilt her. Loads turned up, including Mark Sharman, Mark Emmins, my brother Mark, Gary White, Dave Courtney, Danny Hansford. Tom Hardy, Leighton and

Lindsey Frayne, Stuart Godfrey, Jamie and Darren Godfrey, Redd Menzies, Ron Cooper, Chris Cowlin and John Markey. There are too many to mention, I'd be here till Xmas otherwise, but respect to you all.

Lots didn't turn up, but most had genuine excuses! To Jim Dawkins, Mark Fish, Ray Kray, Terry Stone and Alf Lodge, I know you guys would've been there if it'd been possible. But I also know the ones who didn't show up when they could've. What goes round comes back, I say. If you don't want to see me get out, then it's fine by me, but why pretend? I fucking hate pretenders, coz you never know where you are with them. It's on, it's off, it's on, it's off ... fuck me, it's not even past go yet!

I knew a screw in the Scrubs who was so full of shit you could smell him 50 yards away. I get enough bollocks inside without more of it out there, I really do.

Anyway, it's been a great day and another nice one's lined up tomorrow. It should be a crime to be as happy as I am. How can I be so fucking happy? Is it a crime or what? Or is it just madness? Probably.

Did I ever tell you about the time I was sitting in my cell in A Wing in Hull Jail in 1975? I was just looking out of the window at the seagulls. They're beautiful birds to watch. The way they glide through the air and dive down is amazing to see. They must be the loudest birds we have in the UK apart from crows. Anyway, I was just at peace with myself and I was reflecting on my life. There I was, a 24-year-old man in a max secure jail, caged up away from my son Mike, with years more facing me. Then in walked Charlie Wilson. Charlie was one of the Great Train Robbers back in the 1960s and copped 30 years.

"How are you, Mickey?" he said.

"Yeh sweet, Charlie," I said.

"How you settling in?"

"Yeh not bad!"

And that's how life is in jail. There's always somebody to cheer your day up. My chats with Charlie are smashing memories. I probably know more about the Great Train Robbery than most men alive. Others talk about it, guess it and pretend to know, but I do know. I know about all the great robberies in the last four or five decades. I've lived with the best robbers in our criminal history. I'm not saying it's good! What I am saying is that they all lost - me included. What's so great about ending up inside? Let me tell you the truth. Our door shuts in our face every night. That door stops us loving our life. We are all alone, lost in our own crumbling dreams. 'Great Train Robbery' - they all got nicked. I met these guys inside! And, believe me, it's not glamorous! Charlie Wilson was in fact a gentleman, a really nice bloke, and respected by all. He survives his 30-year sentence and goes out to catch a .45 slug in his brain. That about sums up the criminal world in a sentence: fucking dangerous, unpredictable! Where's the glamour? There sure ain't any in jail!

I learnt a lot from Charlie Wilson and it's stayed with me ever since. Thanks, mate.

I was only on that A Wing for a short spell. I ended up wrapping a mop bucket around a screw's head. I can't think why, can you? Probably an off day. We all get them. That cost me 120 days' remission and I become an expert seagull watcher whilst I served my 56 days' punishment in the seg block. It's all sent to test us. Life's brilliant, it really is!

Who remembers the wrestler called Jackie Pallow in the 1960s? For those of you who don't, let me tell you he was a right flash fucker but a brilliant wrestler. He had this walk about him - like a puppet. His head used to roll about as well as his eyes! He was one of the best in his day. Well, there was a screw in Brixton Jail just like him, except he was a total cunt. He really thought he was somebody, especially with his steel toe-capped boots and peaked hat on. What a total prat. Even the other screws used to take the piss out of him. All the cons used to shout, "Here comes Pallow", and he was so up his own arse that he used to exaggerate his walk even more. Fuck me, he fell down the stairs. They said I pushed him. Me? Why do I always get the blame? How can I help being in the wrong place at the right time. So what if he fell down the stairs, what's it got to do with me? Anyway, believe it or not I never even got a kicking over that. I think for once the screws were pleased with me! Fuck knows why, coz I never did push him. Anyway, if he was half as good as Jackie Pallow, he'd have bounced back up, not go on the sick for three months! Fucking wanker.

10 November 2007

Clock the letter I got today. It about puts an end to it all and proves what prison can do to a mind! This guy's on the edge of madness: one step from the canvas jacket and one push into the padded room. It's sad really, but this is reality for a lot of cons. They go mad, and it's a long road back to sanity. I don't think this guy will make it back, do you?

Letter:
Number: WW5768
Name: Diedrick, Clive
Wing: C-2-07 Pentonville HMP
7 November 2007

Dear Mr Charles Bronson,
My name is Clive George Diedrick. I have a cousin called Tony Diedrick who is convicted of murder. I do not know if you have met him, but he is in the prison system. You might have, as you are a long time in the system.
Charles, you have a friend who I met in a night club M.O.S. in London on 30 April 2000. His name is Dave Courtney. This letter is about Brixton Prison. The staff at Brixton Prison are after the Top 200 crime families. S.O. Westgrath + the No 1 Governor. The Governor + S.O. Westgrath should be killed to save the top crime

families in the world. This is the future but they at Brixton Prison have started it now. The system is called round robin. I will come back to this later on in this letter. But for the moment when you read this letter you need to keep on grassing up this information, no matter how mad it seems.

I am the first person in legal history that has been hooked up to a satellite by an invisible web, inside and outside my body. I know this sounds mad, but it is not. This thing works like this. The Intranet via 2 Boxes on C-Wing Cell 4-01 + Cell 2-21. If you look in the window of the toilets of these two cells you can see a box in each which flash a green light when you think or talk. My body is hooked up to this and the staff are trying to drive me mad and kill me with a heart attack.

The satellite robs you of all thought in your mind. This information is used by the staff of Brixton Prison to get people arrested that are friends or family connected to the top crime families in the world, as one way or another we are all connected to each other, like me to you because of Dave Courtney, who I met in the M.O.S night club on 30 April 2000.

The power point in Education at Brixton Prison is corrupt, the evidence is the print-out of a power point and the two boxes on C-Wing in Brixton Prison. And also the Intranet, the Computer System the staff use. They torture and get information about your friends and crime and make you want to commit suicide. Mr C. Bronson you need to pass the word to everyone you know. This is the truth. I am the first person in history and this is the new death sentence. Please tell Dave as quickly as possible as they are after him and his friends. Also yours. Please get back to me as soon as possible. A prison officer has to get killed. They need to be S.O. Westgrath or Paul McDowell of Brixton Prison. I have written to your book publishers John Blake about this to no avail. They did not get back to me. Round robin is the system.

Yours sincerely, Clive George Diedrick

P.S. I am the friend of Richard Watts a so-called cop killer. The staff, the prison officers call themselves the British Mafia. I have written to all the following to no avail, New Scotland Yard, Kennington and Brixton Police Stations, J. Smith MP / Edward Balls MP / Gordon Brown MP and no help is coming out of them. So Chaz pass the word. The most corrupt is the Prison Service.

I get sackloads of mad letters and most go in the bin, but this one has just taken the biscuit! This is loonyology at its very best! It's the biggest penal corrupt conspiracy of all time! This guy is the next Messiah! Unfuckinbelievable. It's the letter of the year - he's gotta win a prize. Best send it to Broadmoor Asylum, coz he's on a one-way ticket there for sure. This sort of puts loonyology into perspective: it's insanity gone mad! Well done, Clive Diedrick. You really are my star loony. Brilliant. We love you. Keep doing what you do best! You could end up the Daddy of the asylum. They may even make a film about you. Loonyology is never ending.

CHAPTER 22
TAKING LIBERTIES V. GAINING LIBERTY

When you play with scorpions, you get stung; sometimes you die. That's life. If you choose to go down the road of violence, the odds are you'll have a bad ending - a violent, ugly death: a fucking big hole in your face, your brains all over the street, broken bones, black eyes, a toothless grin, scars, scars, and more scars, pain. Your body aches, you can't sleep, your kidneys are bruised and swollen and your toes are black and blue. Your knuckles are broken and you walk with a limp. Your chest is on fire. This is violence. This is how it feels. Enjoy it, you muppets.

I'll tell you who was a nasty, violent, ugly mother fucker of a waste of space - me. Yeh, me. I don't know anyone who was as fucked-up as I was. Thank fuck I grew up and matured. Thank fuck I could see myself before it was too late! Look at me now - who and what am I? I'll let you decide that. But 10, 20, 30, even 40 years ago, you wouldn't have dared to look into my eyes. You would've shit yourself in a room with me. Coz I was one of those men that you could never weigh up. What will he do? It's the unpredictability of mankind. You can smell it! Fear oozes out of the pores. Some have got it, some never will. You smell it before you see it - and then it's too late. You're faced with the unknown - that dark shadow that seems to creep up on you. A crack over the head; a chop to the throat; a punch in the mouth; a kick in the nuts: violence erupts with frustration. You really don't want to go down that road, coz it's fucking horrible. Yeh, I was that nasty fucker. The only excuse I can possibly give is that most of my victims were either other villains or nonces. Fuck the nonces and the villains. Well, I've got my own scars, so let's call it quits. The rest of my victims were innocent people, who didn't deserve to face such a nasty fucker as me. I'd like to treat you all to a night out. Please come to my party - even the Old Bill are welcome! I don't hate nobody, and I hope nobody hates me either. Hate is a horrible thing. It'll chew you up and cause serious mental problems. Stop hating - it's ugly.

Hey, see that Carol Vorderman? Did you know she's been on *Countdown* since 1982? She's 46 now and still in great shape. What a lovely, sexy woman she is - such a beautiful smile. Imagine waking up and seeing her next to you. What a way to start the day off. All men need a woman to wake up to; maybe two women, or even three. Imagine waking up with three! Love: that's all we need in life - lots of love. Don't go down my road. Learn from me, especially you kids: don't do it; stop and think! Me, I'm cured. I did it myself, coz I found myself. Some people find Jesus; I found my heart. It's all in your heart, so search for it and be at peace with yourself. Love yourself, and then you can love others. It's fucking wonderful - and so are you. We all have a heart and the ability to love. Any silly cunt can put an axe in someone's face, but not everyone can pull it out and save the poor sod. Be the one to pull it out. Feel the love.

I want to save people, and I know I can do it - you watch me. I've turned loonyology into something beautiful and I've done it with a smile. Thanks for trusting me. Thanks for reading this book. Thanks for understanding. Thanks for your precious time. You can still hate me and put me down, but I won't hate you. Maybe I deserve to remain a hate victim. Maybe you would sooner me leave prison in a body bag. Maybe you would like to piss on my grave. Maybe this, maybe that. It's your choice. But I'm telling you now, it's a lovely, lovely world. Don't waste it, and remember - it's all one big loonyology ride.

And don't forget, if you have a problem you can write to me: Bronson 1314, CSC Special Cage, HMP Wakefield, West Yorkshire, WF2 9AG, or www.freebronson.co.uk. You know it makes sense ...

Dear Mr Bronson
I have decided to write to you to say it's an outright liberty keeping you locked up. It fucking stinks. I'm going to sign the online petition today and get as many people as I can to sign it also. It's about time this government started to listen. They need their heads looking at, as it's a diabolical fuckin' liberty.
I was given a book this week that you wrote about the twins and what you say is bang on. Reg was a gent. He had the decency to say thank you to me for the support I gave and the stamps I sent him and that meant a hell of a lot to me. He didn't have to say thank you, but he still acknowledged me even though he was Reg Kray. The respect he had shown at his funeral. I was the first person at his cemetery apart from a security bloke and I've never attended a bigger funeral before or since, so he can't have been the totally evil person portrayed or nobody would have bothered, least of all neighbours or people who remembered them in the streets of the East End. I'm going to get some of those stickers and a T-shirt from your site to get people to remember you're still in and want OUT now! Keep the fight up, Charlie.
Conrad Hitchon

Monthly Review
A monthly review takes place and acts as a report, which is submitted to the CSC Selection Committee.
The purpose of the monthly review is to consider progress from the previous month and revise risk management plans/behavioural monitoring targets for the next month.
Each meeting is attended by a number of Multidisciplinary prison personnel whose names are listed on the monthly review form. At each review a maximum of 10 targets are set. These targets are not being assessed at the review, they are to be updated following a discussion about progress. The targets should always be positively framed

and should take the form of a statement. The report is completed by the allocated Chair following the monthly case review. An overall assessment of the month's progress will be reflected in the report with specific comments on the targets set. It should be a reflection of the Multidisciplinary team's view.

On the 25th October 2007 Charles Bronson attended a review.
The meeting reviewed Mr Bronson's last target.
It was written that wing history sheets detailed that Mr Bronson had maintained good interactions with unit staff over this reporting period. There had been four new members of staff joining the unit recently and it was noted that Mr Bronson had engaged with them all appropriately. It was also noted that he continued to make use of the unit facilities, specifically gym and exercise.
The report then went on to say that Mr Bronson engaged with some members of the Multidisciplinary team, Psychology and more recently Probation/Offender Supervisors. He had requested to have monthly contact with his Offender Supervisor, and this will commence in November. The Humber Centre staff noted that their last interaction with Mr Bronson was approximately 1 year ago, when he disengaged from them. It was noted that this had been done in a polite and reasonable manner. The team noted that if Mr Bronson was resolved to move forward then he would need to engage with a variety of different organisations/staff members and should be encouraged to do so. The Humber Centre said they will try to re-engage with Mr Bronson.
The report then states various targets that were set at his last Sentence Planning Board meeting on 8th October 2007. These were to:
Engage with members of his RAM Team - comply with interviews to enable completion of the OASys document.
Engage with the multi-disciplinary team - work towards completing objectives set by CSC operations manager.
Attend CSC review - add input to objectives set at CSC reviews.
Continue to increase awareness of problems related to previous behaviour and lifestyle and develop more pro-social behaviour - re-engage with psychology to explore previous behaviour and develop insight into risk factors.
Continue to engage with CSC regime and activities - continue to attend gym/exercise and comply with all CSC requirements.
The meeting noted that Mr Bronson had engaged in a lengthy interview, to aid in the preparation of an OASys assessment report. This is to be completed shortly. The Offender Supervisor who had completed the assessment noted that Mr Bronson engaged and was appropriate throughout the interview.
It was noted that at his last monthly review, Mr Bronson had made some comments. The team noted that he should be made aware that everything written on the minutes goes to the CSC Selection and in the future he should consider the appropriateness of his comments.
On the report it was also noted that on 15th October 2007, when unit staff were moving another prisoner, Mr Bronson made a comment 'put the beast in his cage'. The unit staff challenged this behaviour. The team also discussed a recent incident where Mr Bronson attempted to pass a newspaper article to another prisoner inside another

newspaper. It was noted that unit staff commented that when challenged regarding this Mr Bronson acted appropriately. It was a concern, however, that Mr Bronson had engaged in an activity where he had breached the unit's rules and regulations in passing on the article in a subversive manner. These discussions brought comments from the team that staff, on occasion, focus on positives for Mr Bronson and were less able to identify negatives. It was noted that this needed to be monitored.

The form then goes on to say if there are any recommendations to the CSCSC and on this one it was stated by the chair on behalf of the multidisciplinary team that: Charlie is correctly placed at this time. It is then signed and dated.

The prisoner then is able to write a comment: 'What a load of old bollocks'. This is then signed and dated by Charlie Bronson.

If this is all they can come up with, i.e. calling a beast a beast (Miller) and sending my buddy Reg Wilson a paper, then it just proves what a farce it all is keeping me in a cage. Britain's most violent man passes a paper and calls a nonce a beast. How pathetic can it get? Well, it is loonyology!

I can produce a sackload of these, but what's the point? It's all fucking mental! Like the system - nuts!

On the 31st October 2007 a Prisoner's Formal Complaint form was filled in. The complaint was:

'Recently you had Ronnie Easterbrook in your seg block who is 75 years old and he never ate nothing for 3 weeks. I have known the man for 35 years ... I made it 100% clear if you allowed me to go in his cell to have a chat with him, I could probably stop this protest. All the screws were for it and agreed to it. So why did governor Thompson stop it? On what grounds ... for what reason? Did he get a buzz out of seeing an old man slowly die? Fortunately Ronnie was moved over to the hospital and began eating, otherwise he would have died in this block.'

Mr Bronson was asked on the form whether the complaint was about bullying. He answered yes.

He was also asked what he would like to be seen done about his complaint:

'The Governor is cruel, evil, inhumane and totally unfit to run a prison ... I want an investigation into his behaviour ... before some old con dies ... This may well be Monster Mansion ... but Ronnie Easterbrook is a good old-fashioned armed robber who I respect.'

The response to the complaint was:

Mr Bronson.
It was noted at the time of your request that your intentions were good but, as explained to you by me at the time, your rule 46 status and placement on the exceptional risk unit made it impossible to allow you to be in Mr Easterbrook's cell with him and he was unable and unwilling to go to an area of the unit where you would have been able to

speak with him. Mr Thompson's decision was appropriate and although staff on the unit were appreciative of your concerns and were themselves concerned for Mr Easterbrook they also understood that it was not possible to locate you in a cell with Mr Easterbrook. Once again I would like to thank you for your concern and your offer to try and assist us.

This sums the system up in a nutshell. They would sooner a 75-year-old man die than let me help. Cunts.

On the 31st October 2007 a Prisoner's Formal Complaint form was filled in. The complaint was:

'Tom Hardy (a well-known actor on TV and movies) has been refused by the system to visit me. He has a clean record and lives a good, honest, decent life. So he has actually been victimised and persecuted for no other reason but evil. Some 'power freak' has made this decision simply to say, 'Bronson only sees who I say he sees'. I want their reason in writing ... so I can then take it to court.'

Mr Bronson was asked on the form whether the complaint was about bullying. He answered yes.
He was also asked what he would like to be seen done about his complaint:

'Who made this decision?
Why it was made.
And why is the system is 'trying' its best to cut me off from my friends ...'

The response to the complaint was:
I cannot disclose the reason for not allowing Mr Hardy to visit you, as it is personal to him. However, should Mr Hardy choose to contact me I will give full disclosure to him. This decision may be reviewed after speaking to Mr Hardy.

Why can't they just be honest? They don't like outside people to see me. They're afraid of the world knowing the truth.

On the 8th October a Sentence Planning Meeting Report was filed
It was attended by 6 personnel & Mr Bronson
An Index Offence Summary and Sentence Details are written - it states: -
'Mr Bronson's custodial history began in 1974 when he received a 7 year sentence for robbery. During that sentence he received a consecutive period of 9 months and was detained at Broadmoor following another offence of violence. He was released in 1992 but 2 months later he committed serious offences including GBH, which resulted in a sentence of 8 years. He then accumulated additional sentences totalling 20 years and also a Life Sentence for 7 separate incidents of attempted and actual hostage taking. He is appealing against his Life Sentence which has a tariff for 3 years.'
It also states Mr Bronson's Pre-convictions: -
'Mr Bronson has numerous convictions for a number of offences. These include

burglary, theft, and possession of weapons. Mr Bronson has spent significant parts of his adult life in prison.'

There was no information on the date of the next parole hearing and no relevant information from the last parole hearing.

A risk assessment is also listed

Identified risks were:

Triggers to Mr Bronson's violent behaviour have previously been identified through activity assessments. These include;

Received rebuffs / knock backs /inability to get own way

Unrealistic expectations of the system / perceiving that the unit is stopping progression

Perceived disrespect / insult / criticism / humiliation / ridicule / people taking liberties / betrayal / unfairness / indifferent attitudes of others

Perceived challenge to status and identity

Feeling threatened by others

Certain groups of people (is hostile towards guest staff, medical personnel, sex offenders, drug abusers, ethnic minorities, 'dirty people')

Perceived lack of response to requests/demands

Wanting to fight other people's battles

Talking about violence

Seeing self as the victim

Other people 'knowing his business'/ loud, officious, direct manner of some staff

Situations that trigger feelings of upset, anger, disappointment, annoyance, frustration, tension, stress, anxiety, paranoia

Disturbances to routine, e.g. sudden regime changes, visits delayed/cancelled, delay in mail, no access to gym/exercise.

Association with other prisoners, particularly those who fear/does not like

The form stated that Mr Bronson had currently no critical risks identified, but it was noted that this needed to be closely monitored because of Mr Bronson's history of violent and disruptive behaviour.

The form stated that the Static Risk was: 'due to his fluctuating level of engagement, no formal assessments have yet been completed'. It went on to say that Mr Bronson is encouraged to engage with the CSC Forensic Psychologist Risk Assessment process, which will assist in identifying static risks as well as assessing his current risk and specific personality traits.

The Dynamic risks were listed as:

Factors believed to underpin and explain Mr Bronson's offending include:

Use of violence

Personality disorder

Lack of insight

Poor emotional control

Hypersensitivity / overreaction to events

Negative rumination / brooding

Need to exert control

Deficits in thinking

Attention seeking - media attention

Instrumental use of violence

Hostile bias / perceived disrespect
Difficulty inhibiting aggression
The factors that heighten risk were noted as: Mr Bronson's previous behaviour and presentation suggest that there may be underlying personality issues that could potentially heighten his risk. The ongoing assessment process will assist in providing further information about such factors.
The factors that lessen risk were noted as: Mr Bronson currently shows positive motivation to progress regarding his location and has had some engagement with probation.
The Protective Factors were listed as:
Good relationships with certain staff
Engagement in physical activity
Appears settled on the unit
Wants to progress/'change his ways'
Clear structuring of expectation / definition of progress
Current environment - no association with other prisoners. High staff:prisoner ratio

The risk of re-offending score was not recorded as there was 'No current OASys available.'
The risk of Harm was also not recorded as there was 'No current OASys available.'
The review of progress was recorded as:
Progress in meeting targets set by the last meeting
In the last reporting period, Mr Bronson's engagement with psychology has fluctuated. Mr Bronson engaged in two periods of psychology sessions but withdrew on a number of occasions.
Mr Bronson has engaged with members of the multi-disciplinary team through attendance at Care and Management plan meeting, though he declines any formal contact with departments such as probation, or the psychiatric in-reach team.
Mr Bronson continues to engage with CSC regime and activities.

In the section headed 'Custodial Behaviour/Record of Adjudications' it is was written that:
Mr Bronson has not received any adjudications in the reporting period. On a few occasions Mr Bronson is reported to have been involved in a few confrontations with other prisoners. He continues to follow the CSC regime and communicates with familiar staff well.

The evidence or risk reduction section noted that:
Mr Bronson verbalises motivation to progress though has not yet demonstrated reduction in risk.

The evidence of continued risk noted that:
Mr Bronson has on occasions displayed continued risk paralleling behaviour through outbursts towards staff and other prisoners.

There were currently no new risks identified.

The Offender's perspective on progress reported that:
Mr Bronson feels the system is not enabling him to progress. He states he feels he has
displayed an appropriate level of good behaviour in the reporting period. Mr Bronson
verbalises motivation to move on and states he is willing to comply with any require-
ments in order for this to happen.

There were currently no changes to his protective factors and Mr Bronson currently
had no changes to the level of risk.

It was noted on the 'Planning for the next 12 months'
Mr Bronson still needs to work on all areas of his identified risks.

The form then goes on to describe the 'short and long term objectives'.

The whole meeting is then summed up with the meeting's recommendations.
'Mr Bronson attended the board and was introduced to the members in attendance. Mr
Bronson was given a brief overview of the RAM process of assessing and managing
risk.
The chair explained that the board members had discussed Mr Bronson's progress in
the last 12 months and asked Mr Bronson to state his views regarding his behaviour
in the reporting period.
Mr Bronson expressed that he felt the system was not enabling him to progress and that
the way he is locked up is inhuman. He stated that he is not the same person as he was
5-10 years ago and that he would like to progress and mix with others to show how he
has changed. Mr Bronson also stated that he feels he is no longer a threat and he gets
on well with staff so he should be moved on. Mr Bronson explained that he understood
that this would not happen easily and proposed he has a transfer to Whitmore for a
trial period of three months. The Chair stated that he understood Mr Bronson's
improved behaviour had been documented and explained that it is necessary for a
structured plan to be put in place in order to show these improvements on a higher
level. The Chair explained the CSC operational manager was currently dealing with
this. The Chair stated Mr Bronson's short term targets. Mr Bronson stated that he is
willing to comply with any requirements that will enable him to complete these. The
Chair explained the importance of Mr Bronson attending such things as CSC reviews
to enable him to contribute and get involved with the objectives set. The Chair
explained that Mr Bronson's specific long term targets would be set on completion of
all his short term targets. The Chair explained that even though Mr Bronson has
expressed views that he would like to be transferred to Whitmore it may be necessary
for him to firstly go to Woodhill as this is part of the process which will enable him to
progress in the future. Mr Bronson stated that if this was the case he would have to
comply, although he does feel that Woodhill would not enable him to progress. The
Chair asked Mr Bronson if he had any further questions. No other issues were raised.
The form was then signed 5/11/2007

Anyone reading this who don't know me would believe me to be a serious

problem, a complete disaster, a total psychological wreck. And this is why I'm stuck in the hole, and probably will be until I'm 1,000 years old on a Zimmer frame. Only my legal team will ever get my freedom! How can I ever win this way, with so much negative claptrap - pathetic psychological profiles that really mean nothing? I am what I am; I've done what I've done. Now they want me to get on my knees and crawl through every hoop. They want to change me and my views and personality totally! I'm my own man; I make my own decisions. Note that there's not one mention of my art or poetry or books. Note, too, that there's not one mention of a cage. They refuse to allow me to mix. It's just solitary, year after year, with no form of progress. So how can I really be tested if I'm held in a special cage and I'm not even allowed to mix with fellow cons? It gets boring and frustrating even going on about it! So I'll let you be the real judge!

Here's a piece from my friend, Jillian Lofts:

Why?
Why is this man still locked away?
It just don't make sense.
They say he's the most dangerous man in Britain,
But he's just a gentle giant.
Why are paedophiles and killers freed?
They only offend again.
Why don't they let this man go free?
He will not offend again.
Why keep him in solitary confinement?
He is not a killer.
He could make an honest living from his art.
Let's give him a brand new start.
If they let this man will see,
And say:
"Why did we keep this man locked away?
What did we gain?
Only a lot of pain?"
Why?

What more can I do, apart from continue with my good behaviour? Until I'm allowed one of the basics in life - mixing with other humans - then it all remains just red tape. And I'm not playing these silly games today, tomorrow, or ever! I'll take my chances with the courts. Law is law, so let the law decide on what's right and what's wrong. I'm sick of trying to explain how one-sided it all is. If the powers that be can't see I'm now an old man who's had enough of prison life, then I'll give up trying to convince them. I don't need their muggy hostels or a silly rehabilitation programme or nosy twats trying to run my life for me. I've got friends and family in my corner:

club owners, pub owners, biz men. I've got a better future than the ones who want to rule my life and control every aspect of it. And that's a fact - and they know it. That's probably what sickens them. If the truth be known, it's maybe why I'm kept isolated away, as otherwise it would crash all their reports on me over the last ten years. I'm really not who I'm portrayed to be, nor wish to be! What's left to say?

Comments on the Administration of Prison Sentences.
(Dr Frank Wilkinson BA; MA; PhD)
There can be little dispute concerning the statement that: 'There are crimes which merit punishment.' The level of seriousness of the crime influences the level of punishment. Serious offences merit harsher penalties with the lower level of crime earning lesser punishment. These are given facts and may be considered to be beyond argument. There are crimes which are so heinous that they deserve the most draconian punishment allowed by the law and that can be regarded as quite right too. And in the law today that means imprisonment. Parliament does not allow harsher penalties.

What requires consideration is the nature of that imprisonment, the purpose, aims and goals. What does a prison sentence represent? Is it retribution or rehabilitation? Transgressors must not only be punished but must be seen to be punished. The English have ever been a nation both vengeful and unforgiving. The reason for that is that the English have never had to seek forgiveness, they do not understand the concept. Consequently when the question of mercy arises it is instantly denigrated by the gutter press. This clearly affects the thinking of the prison service who then consider themselves the instrument of a vengeful nation. Mercy cannot be expected from those who have never had to beg for it.

Lip service is paid to the word 'rehabilitation', meaning that those incarcerated within the prison system will be encouraged and taught to lead better lives upon their release. This is a fine sentiment but unfortunately it does not sit easily alongside retribution. The two are completely incompatible. It is completely unrealistic to expect a dog that has known nothing but kicks for a number of years to suddenly become a decent, well-trained animal.

Retribution is another word for revenge and a prison sentence is, in effect, the prison system, on behalf of the public and society, exacting revenge on the wrongdoer for the crime committed. The more serious the crime, the heavier the revenge exacted.

The question therefore is: 'How far does society, in its guise of the prison system, go in the desire for revenge?' Torture is not acceptable in the civilised world which effectively truncates the list of choices in the methods available for this revenge.

In the British legal system a person may be sentenced to an indeterminate sentence with a recommendation for the Trial Judge as to indicate how long that Advocate considers that the convicted person must spend in prison to satisfy the need for retribution. The prisoner then becomes the property of the prison system which takes over and administers that sentence. The Prison Service begins by designing and providing a 'Sentence Management Plan'. A plethora of 'trained' personnel will then, over the years, oversee all manner of courses and provide 'targets' and 'risk assessments' of the situation. The prisoner will attend numerous boards and meetings, be subject to all manner of soul-searching interviews on the long, tortuous obstacle course which purports in time to alter him, his psyche and character and create a better person who will fit into society far better than previously. The prisoner will be continuously assessed and monitored through the years with further courses added and adapted to suit the needs which will make him a more valued member of the human race. The prisoner will jump through hoops, perform the designated and correct number of cartwheels, suffer the myriad abuses and intrusive prying into both his own life and that of his family, and even his very soul will be scrutinised. The years pass until finally he has done everything asked of him, all risk factors will be low and he will no longer be seen as any sort of danger to anyone. He has taken every course and changed his character so much that even his mother (if she still lives) no longer recognises her son. Wives and children have long since deserted him, of course, the passing of time sees to that, not to mention the fact that he is no longer in touch or even knows where his friends live, or even if they live!

Finally, after everything has been done and every single day served which the Trial Judge recommended BE served, the prisoner reaches the moment when he appears before the Parole Board. The Parole Board find before them an entirely different person to the one who was convicted and sentenced so many years previously for whatever crime it was. The changes are there to be seen in his carriage, in his demeanour, attitude and even appearance. His face has become a well-written page in a book, and time was not the only pen. Age, maturity and the simple passage of time have all taken their toll and these are just the natural changes which come to all. Other changes have come about because of the courses and the experiences of the years in prison.

The Parole Board simply refuses to release him. Hopes and dreams are dashed, albeit couched in acceptable terms, mercy and forgiveness not being part of the programme. Years of work are simply ignored, set aside, and the massive effect upon the prisoner of this disappointment completely misunderstood and ignored. The prisoner returns to his cell and for three more years jumps through hoops and further contorts his character until his next Parole Board hearing. Again, he meets with unfeeling refusal.

We are not allowed to use torture apparently, but there are many forms of torture.

Dr Wilkinson can be contacted at: Dr Frank Wilkinson R60852, Whitemoor Prison, March, Cambs PE15 0PR, www.justiceforfrankwilkinson.co.uk

I met Frank Wilkinson when he was on remand 20+ years ago up in Durham Jail. I read his court depositions and this man got fitted-up big time. He's a totally innocent man, yet 20+ years later he's still Cat A and still in a max secure jail serving life for a murder he didn't commit! Even so, he has studied inside and has all sorts of qualifications, including a PhD. He is also an award-winning artist. But he's an old man rotting away inside. This is a classic example of how a man with a label is forever that label. Make no bones about it, Frank was a very angry man and could frighten the devil himself. He's chinned a few guards and governors in his time. But what about now? Why is he still Cat A? Why have they not allowed him to move on or decategorised him? How would any man be with 20+ years stolen from him, and for what? A police fit-up. Get on his website, write to him and support his fight to get a long-awaited appeal. He really is truly innocent, and it's one on the biggest injustices in criminal history! Read his words! You can see he's a clever, smart, educated man - and he's self-taught too! This is loonyology at its very worst: a man's life being sucked away. It's fucking unbelievable. But I'll tell you one sure thing, you can all put your house on Frank Wilkinson never crawling out or begging. He will walk out tall and innocent or he won't ever get out. Remember Frankie, coz he's the man.

Oh, and I've now had a complaint form reply regarding Tom Hardy: "There is now no reason why this visitor cannot be approved to visit you." Well, isn't that just loonyology in a nutshell?! There never was a reason why weeks ago he couldn't see me! It just goes to prove what this penal system is all about: madness. I can produce a box full of these pathetic complaint replies, each one as mad as the next! I call them 'Disneyland Dreams'. The governor who first made the decision about Tom Hardy not being allowed to visit should have to justify the reason and put it in writing so the real facts can be seen. Some of these prison governors are little Hitlers, troublemakers. Or does all this come direct from HQ in the hope that I'll kick off and they can then all say, "We told you so. Bronson's mad"? Yet all the time it's the system that's mad! Now do you see why Charlie Bronson will never be freed on parole? Can you see these prats ever letting me free? It's never gonna happen. It's why my campaign for freedom will now be conducted in a court of law with real judges, not plastic, gutless, spineless prison governors. I rest my case.

Tom Hardy will be visiting in December! You can all see him in my movie in 2008. Tom will expose this madness on screen. Let the world see the meaning of loonyology, coz I'm now sick of fighting it on my own. It's already cost me 33 years of my life! It's time to sit back and let the no. 1 lawyer in the world do his magic. We salute you.

I hope you have enjoyed this book, tell your friends and family to buy it! For the latest news on me look at: www.freebronson.co.uk

WORDS OF SUPPORT
FOR
CHARLES BRONSON

AVALON ADAMS (SUPPORTER):
It's a sad state of affairs that Charlie is still locked up, what with all the paedophiles and other wrong 'uns walking on our streets!

CHRISTOPHER AGIADIS (SUPPORTER):
The law should not be personal and those who do not intervene are part of the crime.

KELLY ALCINDOR (SUPPORTER):
Free Charlie!!!!!!!

JEFF ALDERSON (SUPPORTER):
Kindly use your good offices and authority to secure the early release of Charles Bronson.

WAYNE ALI (SUPPORTER):
I've petitioned for Charlie every time I could and will continue.

SIMON ALMOND (SUPPORTER):
Read your book, you have it rough, hope you're out soon.

IAIN ANDERSON (SUPPORTER):
Free Charlie Bronson and use his cell for someone that should really be in it. Charlie has done his time 10 times over.

SCOTT ANDERSON (SUPPORTER):
Charles should have been free a long time ago.

SILLINA ANDREWS (SUPPORTER):
How long can this situation go on for?? It's a disgrace. Charlie's done his time ten times over. Enough is enough. Give him his life back. I don't know how anyone can justify Charlie's situation.

KIM ASHTON (SUPPORTER):
Enough is enough.

MICK ASHWORTH (SUPPORTER):
I recall reading the book about his life some time ago and was appalled that such a thing could happen to a human being. Good luck with the petition. www.myspace.com/mickashworth

TONI ASPERILLA (SUPPORTER):
Free Charlie. 34 years' imprisonment for his crimes is out of order.

JONNIE BAILISS (SUPPORTER):
Give the guy a break, enough is enough, this is just cruel.

DEAN BAINES (SUPPORTER):
Solitary for 28 years ain't right, they should be banged up.

NICK BANNON (SUPPORTER):
The justice system sucks - free Charlie.

SUNDEEP SINGH BANWAITT (SUPPORTER):
Every human being is capable of change and we should never ever lose hope for even the worst of criminals, we should never lose hope for anyone because we are all humans. Free him please.

JACQUI BARBER (SUPPORTER):
This is Charlie Bronson we're talking about not Ian Brady or Dennis Nielsen. Give the guy his life back!!

MRS ELIZABETH BARKER (SUPPORTER):
Give the guy a break, enough is enough.

DEBORAH BARLOW (SUPPORTER):
Animals have more rights than this poor man, get him out!

ROBIN BARRATT (AUTHOR AND JOURNALIST):
We live in a so-called compassionate, caring, benevolent, democratic society. Per person we probably give more to charity than most other nations. The government prides itself on its human rights, and the system strives for responsibility, accountability and transparency and yet it keeps a human in jail - in solitary confinement - for close on 30 years. This is not the action of a modern, caring society, but an inhumane world that shuts an ignorant and uncaring door on another human being. After all these years Charlie deserves to be given a new life, a new start. He has more than served his time - child killers serve less time than Charlie, Charlie has neither killed, molested or raped, it is only his reputation and infamy that are now keeping him inside, not the crime or the actions. I have known Charlie for a while; in fact he was the very first person to reply with a short story for my new book. Charlie's life is now his art and poetry, his books and his good causes. He is not a danger to society; he won't maim or kill, or molest children or mug grannies. He won't rip people off, or deal drugs or launder money or sell weapons. He won't steal, or take drugs or puke outside a nightclub at two in the morning, like thousands of others every week. Charlie wants to rebuild his life, he wants an ordinary, normal world where he too can have what the rest of us so easily take for granted - a normal life with his family and friends, a life which he can spend being happy and a life helping others and doing some good, instead of a life wasting away in a tiny prison cell. If we live in a Christian, forgiving, compassionate world where we really do forgive, where we do give second chances, where we really do believe that there is decency and humanity in each and every one of us then show it - stop punishing the already punished and release Charlie now.

EMMA BATES (SUPPORTER):
Only in England could this happen and not get everyone up in arms! Never mind the government, what is wrong with this nation that lets it happen in their name?!

DELIA BATTERSBY (SUPPORTER):
Read the book, fab. Talk about injustice. Free Charlie soon, it's a disgrace but that's England's criminal justice system for you.

CAROLINE BAYFORD (FRIEND):
When I used to read in the press the antics of Charlie Bronson, I used to think what a horrible bastard that is, he was nasty, vicious and uncontrollable - a complete and utter nutter - that's how the press articles come over to me - and I expect to 90% of the general public - unless you actually knew him. It wasn't until Mich and Kitch, friends of Charlie's, moved in next door to me that they opened my eyes to what really was happening with Charlie, and made me sit up and think and delve a bit deeper into what is happening to him, which has made me hell bent on doing all I can to help and support him. Thanks for that Mich and Kitch. He heard through them that I was organising an auction for the Baby Emma appeal and sent me some signed artwork which raised □700, I didn't ask him for it, he did it off his own back. I know people who are loaded with everything they want in life, if not more, and they wouldn't even give the shit off their shoes to help people - because the world has become selfish, take, take, take.

Charlie has been punished enough and he is now anti-drugs, anti-violence and anti-crime, so please give my mate Charlie a second chance in his life and let him create and live to do his artwork in peace and tranquility, and be with his loved ones especially his mother Eira who can't wait to have her son back in her arms again and his sister Loraine who has stuck by him for all his life.

DAVE BEATTIE (SUPPORTER):
Good luck, 100% behind you.

ADRIAN BELL (SUPPORTER):
Enough is enough, this man has been unfairly treated long enough. Free Charles Bronson now.

DIANN BENNETT (SUPPORTER):
It is not right. Don't you think Charlie has done enough? Let this man have a life.

GEORGE BERESFORD (SUPPORTER):
Let him out, he has done more than his time, sex offenders only get 3 years.

MICHAEL BETTS (SUPPORTER):
It's scandalous in this day and age that a man can be locked up for so long, when all he needed was help. We have all let him down and should hang our heads in shame.

ZITA BICKERSTAFF (SUPPORTER):
Good luck Charlie, everyone is behind you 110%.

RONNIE BIGGS (FRIEND):
If anyone knows what Charlie is going through I do. I think they have had far more than their pound of flesh from both of us and many others besides. We look down on Third World prisons and the way they are run but let me tell you, the system here is just as bad. What benefit will they gain in keeping us in these hellholes any longer?

BIG VERN (SUPPORTER):
Free him! He is not a nonce or paedo!

RICKY BIRCH (SUPPORTER):
This man is a living legend!!!!! The system has put him through a lot to say the least but he will never give up!!! His book is the best book I have ever read - a true gentleman!!! Keep your chin up pal!

DAVID BKIINFUEKD (SUPPORTER):
Give him back his life.

DAVE BLOOMFIELD (SUPPORTER):
Give him back his life.

MARK A. BLOUNT (SUPPORTER):
Good luck Charlie, best wishes!

CARL BODMAN (SUPPORTER):
Enough is enough! This man has done his time many times over and should be free. That sicko Webster the baby rapist will be free in a few years. This country and everything about it sucks!

CARINA BONE (SUPPORTER):
Give the man a break, he deserves a chance to have a life.

DANIELLE BONNING (SUPPORTER):
For God's sake, 28 years' solitary. This is vicious especially when so many real violent criminals are released so early. Free Charles.

KEVIN BOURN (SUPPORTER):
Free the man and let a paedo take his place in the prison system.

VICTORIA BOWDEN (SUPPORTER):
Simply he should not be there.

BEKKI BRADLEY (FRIEND):
I first heard of Charlie when I was in jail myself. I was out of control at the time and was spending the majority of my time in segregation. I was always kicking off, assaulting screws, trashing my pad and flooding the place. Some screws made it worse by deliberately winding me up so I would react to them. It was one of these times I was kicking off over something a screw had said and they'd had to mufti me into a safe cell, when one of the screws made a comment about how I was a female Charlie Bronson in the making. I started to wonder who this Bronson was and later I asked a screw who I got along with and he told me all about him. I read one of his books not long after that and it shocked me. I realised then that I had to stop it from happening to me; I had to get out before the system did to me what they've done to Charlie. I didn't want to end my days in solitary, I was only in my early 20s and had my whole life ahead of me. My perception of life totally changed. I started to work towards my release, got back on the wings and was eventually released in January 2005. When I came out of jail it was hard. I'd already been released twice during my sentence and because I was so institutionalised I never managed to last very long on the outside before re-offending. This time I wanted it to be different, but the same feelings of helplessness started to overcome me and I was on the verge of re-offending, when I was offered a place at a specialist college for people with Asperger's (a form of autism). I wasn't diagnosed as autistic until I was in jail and I didn't think for one moment that I would be able to last more than a week. I really went along because I was so amazed to think that some company thought they could control me. I already had it in my head to re-offend: this placement was just a stopgap to pass the time. But it didn't work out like that. For some reason I settled at Tasker House College run by ESPA. I started to enjoy my freedom and I became determined not to resort to my old ways. I joined the student committee, became a peer mentor and started to train towards qualifications in counselling. I wanted to help people like myself. I was asked to join the ESPA Equality & Diversity committee and started to work to ensure that my fellow students understood what Equality & Diversity was. I was then nominated for an award by the college and although I didn't win, I was one of the finalists, but winning does not matter to me, just the thought of coming so far since my time in jail has given me the strength to carry on. I believe Charlie could be in the same position as me, if only he was given the chance. He has spent far too long in segregation; he should be working towards his release now. He needs to be out here, as it's people such as Charlie who could help prevent the young people of today from falling foul of the law. He's done so much good work already, raising money for charities, helping needy kids. He could do so much more if he was released. How can the Home Office justify their behaviour? Even today there are criminals being let off for far worse crimes than what Charlie has done. They say the prisons are full, but what do you expect, when they don't get their priorities right? The place Charlie is taking up could be used for a real criminal, someone who needs to be off the streets. Charlie has never hurt a woman or child and has never killed anybody. Yet there are paedophiles and murderers that are getting away with pathetic sentences and Charlie gets life. How is that fair? So much for this being a just country, what has happened to equality? I am now in the starting process of writing my own book. I believe

my story is one that needs to be told and I'm going to tell it. I aim to let people understand what it's like to be in jail and what it's like looking through the eyes of someone with Asperger's and how as Charlie says "I fell into the hole and how I climbed out!" Charles Bronson could probably do some good work with the youngsters of today; he should be free, instead of letting all these paedophiles go free because of overcrowding.

CHARLIE BREAKER (FRIEND):

"Mad, Wicked, Baby-eating Mass Murderer", "Most Violent Prisoner in the Country". 3 million people read the Sun every day and that is the way 99.99% of its readers picture him. No mention of the years of mental and physical abuse in the hands of the British Penal System. No mention of 23 hr bang-ups, week after week, month after month, year after year for over 30 years. These guys are brandishing him as a monster and stopping his release. Born Michael Peterson in 1952 to his loving mother Eira along with his brother and sister Loraine, he was a small time crook and unlicensed boxer. When he started boxing his promoter gave him a ring name, as is the custom in unlicensed boxing. Hence his moniker Charlie Bronson, not after *Death Wish* as the media would have you believe. As his criminal career progressed he started to rob petrol stations at gunpoint, as a 21 year old, he was arrested for armed robbery and sentenced to 7 years' imprisonment. He had as yet never pulled a trigger or even hurt anyone. Well Charlie was at 21 not yet filled out, so once in the prison he was picked on by the gangs of screws and other tough cons. But nobody was taking liberties with young Charlie, he had a short fuse and attempted to give as good as he got. At every possible opportunity he trained in the gym to build himself up. Life is like that in the nick; either you're labelled "violent" or "victim". His attitude to this meant he served 19 years in many different secure units around Britain, the majority of it in solitary confinement. Sometimes the screws, knowing how he relished every moment of his 60 minutes' exercise, would call him in after only 40 minutes, knowing that he would refuse, so they could see the Mufti squad (riot squad armed with shields and truncheons) come in 15 handed and beat him black and blue. In 1992 he was finally released, but he wasn't ready for the turmoil of the outside world. Charlie being a rebel reverted back to armed robbery again and was arrested 53 days later. Once back inside he was soon placed back in the secure unit for being involved in rooftop protests. He just couldn't seem to stay out of trouble, so he took up art to express his anger. He settled down at the secure unit at Hull and was progressing well with his new love, art. He was sending a lot out to raise money for children's charities; I've auctioned off pieces of his work at my boxing shows for good causes. He'd never been so settled before and the prison governor told him he could do the rest of his sentence there. But in 1999 he went back on his word and said Charlie was going to the dreaded CSU unit at Woodhill. In desperation he took prison teacher Phill Danielson hostage for 44 hrs. During this time he fed and watered the fella, even had cigarettes brought in for him (Charlie doesn't smoke). As Phil later testified in court, Bronson did not lay a finger on him, in fact they had bonded in the time that they had spent together. He said that he considers Chas as his friend. He got a life sentence, the underworld was shocked, and he hadn't killed anyone, mugged anyone, raped or hurt any women or children. There have been cases of seriously violent hostage taking where often the offender had received half the sentence. He was sure that an appeal court would see it differently and 5 years later on 1 April 2004 he got an appeal hearing at the London Appeal Courts. Together with Joe Pyle snr, I went to the hearing, and it was a farce. They brought out Phil Danielson, who said what good friends they had become. Lord Justice Rose said he was shocked at the calmness of Bronson and what a changed man he was. CB said that he was now anti-crime, anti-violence, anti-alcohol, anti-drugs, had a job to go out to and just wanted to be a family man, but to no avail. Lord Justice Rose said that he had to go back to prison and let the Prison Authorities decide his fate. Back he went to an 8x10 concrete coffin for 23 hours a day, with its one tiny barred window, his concrete bed, cardboard table and chair, the little hatch in the door where the meal tray is silently pushed through, with 24 hr CCTV watching his every move. How long he be incarcerated like this, nobody knows. In the 8 years since he was lifed off, he has not put one foot wrong with the

Prison Authorities, so surely the time has come, if only to take him out of isolation and release him into the general prison population and enjoy the relative comforts that mass murderers and paedophiles get. I'm in regular contact with Charlie, he is full of remorse for what he did years ago, and he hasn't a bad bone left in his body. The anger has gone with the coming of maturity; all he wants to do is make a life for himself outside doing what he does every day of his life: doing his artwork and using his drawings to raise money for small worthwhile charities. It's 7 years that Charlie hasn't put a foot wrong, he's a changed man, so what more has he got to do for the authorities to see that he is no longer a threat to the public? It is inhumane to treat a fellow human in this manner ... Surely the Government must stop this cruel torture ...

BILLY BRISTOW (FRIEND):
Charles Bronson is a man who has been made an example of by the state for many years, a man who would be better off working with a charity or helping keep youngsters on the straight and narrow. It's time for H.M.P. to let him go. He can now do more good outside jail.

JOHNNY BRISTOW (FRIEND):
"Lets Get Charlie Out!" Charles Bronson should be freed from prison as soon as possible. He has aged now and mellowed out, as we all have as we get older. Things happen in prison due to gossiping and associates; some people react, some do not. Charles is definitely fed up with this regime and will benefit from release, especially now he has some money to live on, and I think he will revert back to his happy self as when we used to holiday at Rhyl when we were teenagers. Charles was no worse than any teenagers walking around the streets today. I'd say he had a lot more respect for his elders, etc. I knew Charles from the age of about 15 to 20 years of age. He was a very true friend and we spent many happy times together doing what youngsters do! Free Charles Bronson I say! It is the system that has made him do the things he has done. Let him out before he's old and grey (like me).

RACHAEL BRISTOW (FRIEND):
Give the man a chance, he's family to us.

JACK STEPHEN BROOKS (SUPPORTER):
Free this man.

DIANE BROWN (FRIEND):
Okay, what can I say about Charlie's situation? I want to try to be objective. I understand that in prison you have to have control and that anyone who commits a crime in prison must be punished. When Charlie committed his last hostage offence he received his life sentence. Also when crimes are committed is it not the case that mitigating circumstances are taken into account? So yes, it was wrong of Charlie to take anyone hostage and now he is kept in solitary and not allowed open visits even though the prison officers walk freely around him and with him.

All crimes are individual and in this case the individual is not a sex offender, a danger to the public or a danger to himself. The prison officers speak fondly of Charlie and say how it is all political keeping him in prison, and they themselves would give him another chance if asked. The situation is a man over fifty who comes from a decent loving family and he is not even allowed to hold his seventy-six year old mother on a visit. When he is not a violent offender, this punishment and being political seems to me to come from the authorities resenting the publicity Charlie gets from being in prison. But the irony is Charlie is only famous from being in prison; the media are at fault, not Charlie. This is a vicious circle and it needs to stop long enough for Charlie to get out of it; at least one last time he deserves another chance. I find it unbelievable that he is kept in such controlled conditions when he has not committed violent crimes. It is unfair to keep him caged; his crimes have been committed in prison and this should be taken into account. The frustration he faces day to day, the media have created

'Charles Bronson', making him into something he is not and as we know most stories in the papers are made up! So why do the prison authorities allow them to be published? It almost makes Charlie a victim. To me Charlie is a funny, kind, loving and intelligent man who I have known for nine years and the friends I have made through Charlie and the pleasure I have had being one of his friends have enriched my life.

We have laughed together and shared stories and I hope it never ends. To me he is a wonderful man whom I hold dear to my heart and I can't wait until we meet in the outside world. He has done a good share of his life sentence and it is time for the people in power to see sense and release Charlie.

ELLE BROWN (FRIEND):
I am 12 years old and I live in Spain. I have known Charlie for a long time, I love him deeply and he is the nicest man I have ever met. I have been to see him and I don't think there is anything wrong with him. He is funny, kind and caring. People who hurt children get treated better than him. It's not fair. The thing that hurts me the most is that he is not even allowed to hug his own mum. If you read this you should do something about it.

JIM BROWN (FRIEND):
My first encounter with Charles Bronson apart from the occasional news story was when my wife Diane, who has long had an interest in the prison system and its inmates, decided to write to him. I wasn't at all happy about that and indeed I'm still not entirely at ease with it. It has been the cause of many arguments between Diane and myself and has placed a strain on our marriage, so as you will appreciate I have no love for Charles Bronson. That being said I try to look at things objectively and I realised that Diane had a real interest in his situation and that the friendship that developed between them was just that, a genuine friendship. Diane has organised a number of events in support of Mr Bronson including a very successful art exhibition at a progressive art gallery in Portsmouth. She has attended many other functions in his support and was at the Old Bailey for his appeal hearing. Through these events (some of which I have attended) Diane and I have met some good people, many of whom I now count as friends. As to the question of Mr Bronson's continued imprisonment that is a very thorny problem. Everybody has a drawer somewhere in their house, usually in the kitchen, into which they put all the things that have no real place, a junk drawer! It is my opinion that Charles Bronson is in the prison system's junk drawer; nobody quite knows what to do with him! He has been in all the usual places such at Wakefield, Belmarsh, Broadmoor, etc., but doesn't fit in anywhere and so to some extent has been abandoned. There are many of Mr Bronson's supporters who call for his release because they see much more dangerous criminals such as paedophiles, rapists, murderers, etc., being released back into society after serving only a few years of a long sentence and in many cases these people re-offend and there is an outcry as to why they were released in the first place! But what people seem to forget is that Charles Bronson does not do his time quietly and that he is a constant thorn in the side of the prison system and continues to break the law whilst in prison, and it is for this reason that he is still behind bars. It is worth mentioning at this point that many of the newspaper reports of Mr Bronson's exploits are wildly exaggerated and inaccurate, often even getting the prison itself wrong. It also seems to me that many of his so-called supporters add to the problem by encouraging him to misbehave, if you check the visitors book on the Bronson website you will often see phrases such as "go on Charlie don't let the bastards grind you down", "keep your chin up Charlie, show 'em who's boss", and so on; fine words from the comfort of your own living room but not really helping to secure his release! I believe it is this encouragement that is a principal factor in keeping Mr Bronson inside. What people should be saying is "bide your time and keep your nose clean". I am personally acquainted with 2 ex prison officers who have had Charles Bronson under their supervision and they along with a number of other officers regard Mr Bronson with an almost fond indulgence and do not regard him as a serious violent threat. That's not to say that he isn't capable of violence under the right circumstances - he is a very tough and powerful man who has no fear of

conflict, but what he does seem to have is an "old school" value and this does him credit. It is my firm belief that Charles Bronson should be set on a path that will lead to his eventual release, but he needs to keep a lower profile and although it may go against his grain he should conform a little more to the system. How he would fare on the outside is another question; his notoriety may well make him a target for people who want make a reputation for themselves by taking on "Britain's hardest inmate" and if he could not avoid such conflict then the probable result of this would be Mr Bronson's return to prison! To sum it up I think that Charles Bronson has done enough prison time, he should fade away and let Michael Peterson take over and work to gain his release. I do not see him as a danger to the public and the fact that many much more dangerous criminals have been released early should at least be reason enough for the Home Office and prison authorities to consider getting him on a programme that with his cooperation will lead to his being released. At least let him see some light at the end of the tunnel! Charles Bronson and I are about the same age and I can feel life slipping quickly by, so I can only imagine how frustrated he must get seeing his slip by. So now is the point at which he needs to save what's left; he needs to help himself from within the system and not rely on what in many cases is unhelpful support from outside. Good luck to you Charlie, this your hardest fight! Listen to your real friends and family; they love you, not what you represent.

RACHAEL BROWNE (SUPPORTER):
Get Charles out and make some room for a real criminal!!!

SIMON BRUCE (SUPPORTER):
Free Charlie, an old school legend, treated worse for the past 34 years than rapists and paedos. The government should be ashamed. Free Charlie.

BULLDOG1809 (SUPPORTER):
Free up the system!!! Let Bronson out, keep a peter in.

CLIFF BURA (SUPPORTER):
How can you live with yourselves? Justice like all the other vulgar dictators taking away a man's freedom, put him in an inhuman environment … just because it is not politically correct to free him.

SIMON BURGESS (SUPPORTER):
I've read Charlie's books and Frankie Fraser's and to me it sounds like the prison screws are the most dangerous animals in Britain.

MICHELLE BURNS (SUPPORTER):
No one should be treated like this.

DAVID BUXTON (SUPPORTER):
Let's have justice!!

IAN C (SUPPORTER):
It's nice to see the British justice system works. Only in the UK can this utter bullish** be done. Free Charlie.

ANGELA CAIRNS (SUPPORTER):
Charles paid for his crime, now it's time he was with his friends and family. He's been served an injustice.

DANIEL CAIRNS (SUPPORTER):
This is such an injustice, this man should be free!!!!!

CAMERON (SUPPORTER):
Inspired by his spirit, good luck Charlie.

J. CAMILLERI (SUPPORTER):
Free Charlie, he has done his time and more! Free him now!

MANDY CAMPBELL (SUPPORTER):
This man has not been treated well. His outside crime was so long ago and he has done his time. Let him free; you have let worse criminals off with a fine. Let him be free to prove himself on the outside.

SIMON CAMPBELL (SUPPORTER):
This is not justice, but a mere vendetta.

DARREN CARR (SUPPORTER):
A travesty ... the British judicial system is wrong!!

HAZEL CARR (SUPPORTER):
Please free Charles, it's time he was given his life back.

KATE CHAMBERLIN (SUPPORTER):
Charles is an admirable man for what he does for our society, yet we seem to have forgotten. Paedophiles can walk the streets yet Charles has to suffer within the system. This stinks.

SEAN CHANDLER (SUPPORTER):
Free him!

ALBERT CHAPMAN (FRIEND):
I speak on behalf of many good people when I say I'm disgusted at how Charlie Bronson is being treated. I'm not just talking about the rascals either. All the good, law-abiding folk I have met think it's barbaric also, so it's not just an underworld opinion it's a public opinion! Good men like Mickey Dunne and Ronnie Brown who served with Charlie in jail have moved on to successful, legitimate lives. Why can't Bronson do that? Because they wont give him the chance that's why. How long must a man serve before he is considered punished? Well, for a sex case it seems not very long at all but for others it's throw away the key time! Oh, what a fine example to the world that is. Also remember, Charlie is NOT mad, he has been certified sane ... have you? Give the man a chance and then the authorities may earn a bit of respect back. Because they certainly have none now!

KAREN CHAPMAN (SUPPORTER):
My prayers are with you.

STU CHESHIRE (FRIEND):
I've known Charlie Bronson for some years now and been to see him at Wakefield prison enough times to know enough's enough! His freedom is long overdue! You wouldn't get away with keeping a dog in solitary the way he is with little exercise! A man that is the product of prison brutality from a bygone age. He gets so much bad press. He's never killed, never hurt women or children. I've done some work with Charlie in the past, donating money to his favourite charity Zoe's Hospice. He loves those kids. He's helped me more than he knows with all manner of things. He looks out for me and gives advice where needed, like a big brother. It's time for a change. He's spent all his adult life behind bars when he has so much to give, so many things he could do. It's about time the past was rectified. I feel Charlie has done his bit. It's time for the prison authorities to do theirs: rehabilitation for him and a release date. It's the least my friend deserves.

ZACK CHISWELL (SUPPORTER):
So much for human rights.

KEV CLARK (SUPPORTER):
It's about time this man was free.

MARTYN CLARK (SUPPORTER):
Let him have some life.

EMMA CLARKE (SUPPORTER):
Free Charlie.

HAZEL CLARKE (SUPPORTER):
Stay strong Charlie x You can beat them!

KATRINA COLLIER (SUPPORTER):
Let this guy go.

JOHN COLLINS (SUPPORTER):
It's simple - why not?

KEITH COLWILL (SUPPORTER):
Charles Bronson would be a better benefit to society out of jail teaching the kids of this world the rights and wrongs of this world rather than rotting in jail. It's almost criminal to keep him in there.

CHLOE CONWAY (SUPPORTER):
Free Charles.

STEVEN COOKE (SUPPORTER):
This man deserves to be helped not caged. Get him out now.

RACHEL COOPER (SUPPORTER):
Free him!!!!

DAVID COTTON (SUPPORTER):
Keep fighting Charlie.

PAUL COUGHLAN (SUPPORTER):
Let him out - start putting nonces away for this length.

DAVE COURTNEY (FRIEND):
Hello people. My name is Dave Courtney and I guess that you would put my occupation down as author and actor. I'm 48 years old and feel I am close enough and have known Charlie long enough to call him my friend. I don't know where to start to say why Charlie should have at least a date for release by now, because there are so many different reasons, apart from the obvious ones such as: he hasn't murdered anybody. Purely on humane reasons, that many years spent in solitary confinement cannot be justified by his sometimes irrational behaviour while in solitary confinement. The way the media portray this man (although we all know they are too proud to do so by the powers that be) is completely wrong. The only reason for doing so is to help the powers that be justify their inhumane and personally spiteful treatment of Mr Bronson and using him as their deterrent to all other prisoners - conform and behave or else. Has been taken far too far now. It don't take the brains of Britain to work out that keeping a man in the extreme conditions that he is in will

and would have an adverse effect, which it has on Charlie. He will be the first to hold his hands up and say that he has not helped himself by some of his antics and has given them far too much ammunition to use against him when justifying their treatment of him. What people must understand is that there are 69 million people in England and only half a million know Charlie and know the truth about how they use all the red tape and confessions in the Masons to just play with his life and try to humiliate and destroy any and all forms of friendship and to squash any form of popularity that he has acquired by his book sales and CDs. The other 68 and a half million believe what they read in the newspapers. He has become a legend and that is I feel the real problem, because they will not allow a man to come out from prison to such a big hero's welcome as he would do and to a certain hero worship by a large amount of people that would very quickly make him a very rich man indeed and that goes against everything they may claim to stand for. Such as you can glamorise crime and crime don't pay, and letting Charlie out goes against both of these so I'm afraid to say that Charlie is now just a pawn in the very political game they are playing with the man's life. Apart from all that, he's a very nice guy, a very funny man indeed. He rang me once to tell me that he had an idea that when he came out we would do a cover tune of 'What a Wonderful World' and call ourselves Chas and Dave. Now that's fucking funny. His many books show he has a talent for telling stories very well and in the stories are so many home truths it's frightening, which proves he is a very intelligent man when giving you his take on things, i.e. the world according to Charlie Bronson. From inside the mind some of his innermost thoughts could be considered as a bit of a cliché, but a good majority of what he says is bang on in my book. His drawings are now world recognised and are fetching good money on various online auction sites. They are extremely detailed and of a very high standard. They are fucking funny as well. I do think Charlie should be given a chance.

SARAH ANDREA COX (SUPPORTER):
This is terrible.

TARA COYLES-GOULD (SUPPORTER):
Get Bronson out. He's suffered enough.

TONY CRABB (FRIEND):
Alright, Charlie son!! Well pleased to hear the rumour was true! You truly deserve it, mate. You mentioned about doing a piece for your book? Charlie, I honestly feel honoured, but what I am about to say are only the facts, mate.
Everyone knows you have been used as a political pawn within the Home Office and the POA. If there was ever any true justice the POA would be inmates and not uniforms. Everyone who has spent long spells in solitary confinement will know their tactics, intimidation, brutality and humiliation. I've known Charlie for almost two decades now so I have been on wings with him and many punishment blocks with him. How that man has kept his principles and standards intact is probably his greatest achievement to date. I have witnessed good, strong lads being absolutely destroyed after being through a fraction of what Charlie has overcome. They say it costs the government almost £3,000 per prisoner per week to reside in many of their establishments? In all the blocks I have been in with Charlie the screws blatantly abused the Home Office funding, i.e. 14 man unlock with riot gear on - every time they put on the riot gear they receive an extra £8.00. I have witnessed them squabbling about who is going to put it on, full well knowing Charlie is not going to be a problem. The POA describe him as the most dangerous man in the prison system! What a fucking joke. Do the British public know there are inmates getting murdered in top security prisons, i.e. Long Lartin, Frankland, Rye Hill, Whitemoor as recently as 2007 and some of the perpetrators are back in the main flow of the prison system - hypocrisy at its worst if you ask me. I'll tell you of an incident way back in 2001 when Charlie was having a peaceful protest due to the treatment he was receiving in Whitemoor block. At the time he was 33 days into a hunger strike, when landing officers decided to get their extra £8.00, all half-cut from the prison mess on a Friday afternoon. I'll

never forget this incident because it affected everyone in the block that day. They decided to rush Charlie at his weakest; he'd lost over 3½ stone and was a mere skeleton of his former self. When they went in Charlie was lying on his bed, because he never had the strength to stand at the back wall as ordered. He couldn't even protect himself let alone defend himself. The assault was over in approximately 5 to 8 minutes and when there's 12 to 14 screws raining blows on you it's a long fucking time - believe me I know. In the assault Charlie's wrist was snapped; not broken, not fractured but snapped for the pure fun of it - so some rejected army coward from Northern Ireland screw could promote his heroism in some dingy little watering hole where lies are often exaggerated. Charlie's never been and never will be a threat in today's society. Charlie was labelled from the over-exaggerated episode in the Hull Unit. He has never killed anyone; in fact I personally don't believe he could. On the wings he was a respected con who was anti-authority. But we are talking the late '80s/early '90s when it was an US or THEM attitude from both parties. You could say the POA lost control of the dispersal system when they were first introduced into prison culture. They were designed to disorientate inmates, make life difficult for us, i.e. put you at the other end of the country so your visitors and loved ones suffered. The then POA was responsible for many family breakdowns, and obviously this would have a reaction with the so-called hard-core of the prison system. Strangeways was literally started by the POA rulings. There were many riots happening at the time but the government told the media to gag it and hush it all up. The only thing you read about the prison system is all negative and anti-inmate. The best comparison it would be fair to say is a zoo full of different animals and creatures, some pleasant and charming, some obnoxious and demanding. But it's only zookeepers that restrain the creatures from showing their original characteristics. The gang culture in today's society is near to boiling point and the government with their policies will not make a blind bit of difference, eventually leading to much civil unrest in urban and built-up cities. This is where a man like Charlie would be so valuable. The youth of today would have heard or read of Charlie's eccentric ways; they would listen. He could inform them of the pitfalls they will incur on their criminal journeys. I myself do a fair bit of advising to young lifers coming into adult jails from YOIs and they always end up on the subject of Charlie, and I tell them what he has had to endure down to pure, simple peer pressure from other members of the prison culture and usually give them a piece of Charlie's artwork. His ability from his Solitude Art is self-explanatory. The fact of the matter is, if you do not express your complaints in some form of protest they will never get dealt with. Well that's how it used to be; going by today's standards the prison service attitude to complaints has progressed with the times. Except in only one case - Charlie's. When they snapped his wrist the whole segregation block went on hunger strike so Charlie could be taken to hospital for humane treatment. This was still not working in Charlie's defence. Eventually it ended up with myself getting on top of a security camera and making my protestations over the disgusting treatment Charlie was receiving. After some negotiating Charlie was eventually taken to hospital and I was dragged through the razor wire surrounding the camera, rolled up like a Swiss roll in a prison mattress to break my fall, taken to the internal hospital and stitched up, then replaced in the box for a day. The two inmates who allegedly helped me received internal punishments, i.e. no canteen etc., etc. That's how much Charlie is thought of within the system and it is that that the POA were worried about, nothing to do with the most dangerous man in the prison system. That is one incident out of many. Is it not about time to bury the old bones in Charlie's case? The amount of money it has cost the public taxpayer is astronomical to keep Charlie in conditions from a Victorian era.

How about the tabloids printing some of the positives Charlie has done? Children's charities, Hospice charities - he is never too busy to help anybody in society, in fact he could stop a lot of crime in his home town of Luton where statistics show that gang culture crimes are on the rise year after year. Serious sex offenders are being paroled and re-offending in less time that Charlie has remained in solitary conditions. People who are the true threats to society are in and out of jail perhaps twice maybe three times whilst Charlie has been used as POA promotion suggesting crime don't pay. How ridiculous and pathetic can one get? But that's what the British judiciary is all about - hypocrisy.

MARK CRABBE (SUPPORTER):
I can't imagine what Charles has gone through at the hands of the system for 34 years. In my opinion the system has failed him and the decent thing to do is to free him. Good luck Charles.

TIM CREES (SUPPORTER):
This government has a distorted view of the term "Justice", when bombers are allowed to walk the streets using our taxes!

PAUL CRIDLAND (SUPPORTER):
Free Bronson.

ANDY CRITCHLOW (SUPPORTER):
Free the man. He's done far too long for so little a crime.

ROB "THE DEVIL DOG" CROSBY (SUPPORTER):
This man should be free!!! The establishment should be out chasing nonces and paedophiles instead of leaving people like Charlie to rot! Fuck the Establishment!!

MATTHEW CUMMINS (SUPPORTER):
How can you do this to this man and give them filthy nonces and paedos a few years then let them roam the streets again?. Makes me sick.

SEAN CUNNINGHAM (SUPPORTER):
Let him out, you c**ts.

TEL CURRIE, SNR (FRIEND):
I have been good friends with Charlie for a good few years now and am proud to call him a friend. It may sound over-simplistic just to say that he shouldn't be in there ... but simply, he shouldn't. What did he actually do that was so horrifyingly wrong that he is locked inside that chamber of horrors they call Wakefield? What did he do to earn neighbours like Ian Huntley, Victor Miller, Robert Maudsley and Roy Whiting (all killers!)? How has he kept it together in that sort of company? Could you do it? So what have we learned? More than anything it's that those with a bit of spirit, anti-authority rebels and mavericks, will NOT be tolerated. They are considered worse threats to society than paedophiles. What does that tell you about politicians and judges?! This is why Charlie is still in a cage, it has become political and frankly they don't know what to do with men like he and Ronnie Biggs. Other rebels like Roy Shaw, 'Mad' Frankie Fraser and Jimmy Boyle - would they have got out if their crimes were more recent? I very much doubt it! Yet, they went on to become successful men in the straight world. Why? Because they were given the chance to show the world they could ... Bronson has not. We all know there have been a lot more infamous characters and heavyweight villains than Charlie released; men like Freddie Foreman and Charlie Richardson were far more involved than Charlie Bronson and they done ok. For God's sake, give him a chance!

LEE DALE (SUPPORTER):
Call this justice?!!

CURT DANFORTH (SUPPORTER):
Honour, respect, free him now!

DAVE (SUPPORTER):
Some people say people don't change. I'm glad I was given the chance to change. I grew up

in Corby, Northants. An alcoholic, I had terrible trouble at school going in drunk, which then led to a life of crime in later years. This led to prison, with me going in an alcoholic and coming out 3 years later addicted to heroin.

In prison (Woodhill) a number of years ago a group of us cons were waiting to get into the gym but had to wait as there was someone from the special unit doing a workout. The prisoner was on his own, with two officers. The prisoner was Charles Bronson. He was the talk of the wing when we got back. During my life of crime I have committed loads of office (no residential) burglaries, ABH robbery, taking taxis from taxi drivers (hijacking).

I know people who have committed worse crimes than Charles Bronson and are walking free. He has never killed anyone but has a life sentence. He deserves a chance. I myself was written off by psychiatrists and doctors. I have been clear of drugs for over 7 years and alcohol. I am a changed man. People do change and I think Charles Bronson has. People can change, I have, and so can Charlie.

MATTHEW DAVEY (SUPPORTER):
Long-term isolation for a man who has been more of a pain rather than a danger is inhuman. Set the man free now!

ADAM DAVIDSON (SUPPORTER):
Free Charlie now.

ANDREW PHILIP DAVIDSON (SUPPORTER):
How could this happen in the UK?

ASHLEY DAVIES (SUPPORTER):
Free Charles Bronson.

BERNIE DAVIES (FRIEND):
Another year passes by and yet more filthy paedophiles and rapists are set free to live among us, among us and our children. Meanwhile, miles away from his family Charlie Bronson will spend yet another year in a concrete coffin. And as usual, apart from the 'few', no fucker will do a damn thing about it.

They may moan about how barbaric the whole thing is, but that's useless unless you are actually DOING something about it! Men like myself, Tel Currie snr and jnr, Dave Courtney, Alan Rayment, Mark Fish, Charlie Richardson, Roy Shaw, Carlton Leach and of course the late Joey Pyle snr and Reg, Ron and Charlie Kray have all proudly and tirelessly worked our arses off for fucking years to get some justice for Chaz. I'm not boasting, but there are so many fakes and bandwagon jumpers and parasites around men like Charlie Bronson, Ronnie Biggs, the Krays and the 'CHAPS' in general that go around boasting how they are all 'best mates with the firm' that it makes me physically sick!

I can tell you that for most of us, our true, staunch, reliable, loyal, tested friends we could count on our fingers and I'm sure Chaz is no different. In fact, he is one of the very best at sussing a wanker a mile away! Point is, his REAL friends, the ones with spine and balls, need to keep the fight going. The plastics and wannabes will always bask in the reflected glory at the benefit and boxing dos but the people who matter know who's who. So let's keep pushing forward and not rest until the door finally springs open and the light shines on an outrageous miscarriage of justice!

GARY DAVIES (SUPPORTER):
Read all the books. Charles Bronson is a victim of the British justice system. It's time to release him NOW!!

BEN DAVIS (SUPPORTER):
Hi Charles, your solitary fitness book saved me from drugs and from myself. God bless you, I owe you.

JIM DAWKINS - EX PRISON OFFICER (FRIEND):
I first heard of Charlie Bronson during my first two weeks' training for the prison service at HMP Wandsworth. He was described as almost a 'mythical monster' by a number of older prison officers, most of whom claimed to have 'rolled around the floor' and 'got the better of him' in a boastful manner as if to try to impress us, the new recruits. At the same time they seemed to be exaggerating these accounts to make us fearful of this man whom they branded the most dangerous man in the prison system. These stories were continued when we arrived at the prison service college where a certain element of instructors again were obviously out to impress us with their own tales of how they 'beat up Charlie' and 'taught him not to mess with them'. I quickly realised that these men had probably never even seen Charlie, much like the men in the army who had been shot by snipers in Northern Ireland but had never in fact been to the country. All these stories did, however, convince most new recruits and many therefore had already formed a biased opinion of Charlie without even meeting him. They were under the impression that this man had to be attacked on sight before he got the opportunity to attack them. Prison staff unfortunately are not alone in judging the man without ever actually meeting him. Due to the way the British media love to report only bad stories, once they have reworded them sufficiently to sell more papers there are sadly many, many people who have an unjustified opinion of Charlie based purely on the one-sided media accounts. I first met Charlie in person at the secure unit at HMP Belmarsh in 1994. I must admit I was nervous about the initial meeting as I had only heard the prison service side of his story. The first time I met Charlie I noticed that he was probably as nervous as I was, as this was his first time in HMP Belmarsh and he was unsure of the reception he would receive. Putting on a brave face I had a nervous first meeting but pushed aside the stories and decided to form my own opinion of the man behind the myth. I quickly built a working relationship with Charlie and within a day or two we had formed a good bond of trust between us. For the month or so that followed I heard his side of the story, which I believed to be genuine as he never denied doing some bad things whilst in prison but I appreciated he was only reacting to some of the brutal treatment he had received over the years. He felt remorse for his actions and even at that early stage wanted the chance to prove he could change. I was surprised to discover what a great personality he had, bearing in mind the years of solitary confinement he had endured. He had feelings, needs and a sense of humour and was highly intelligent and talented. I enjoyed games of Scrabble, helping him with exercise routines and even sat alone in his cell enjoying cups of tea, which he made me! I was of course aware that he had taken hostages in the past but I never felt threatened in any way at any time when I was working with Charlie. There were still officers who would try to wind him up in an attempt to get a name for themselves so they could brag that they had wound Charlie Bronson up. As I mentioned, Charlie will openly admit that he has done some bad things while in prison, but he was sucked into a system that almost needed a myth like Charlie to use as an instructional tool for its new recruits. Yes he has taken hostages, damaged prison property and tried to fight the system in the past, but he has only reacted to years of mental and physical torture by an element of bully-boy prison staff. Since leaving the prison service I have kept in touch with Charlie and met some of his friends who have done so much to keep Charlie focused in recent years. I should make it clear at this stage that the majority of Charlie's friends and supporters are law-abiding, genuine, professional people. Although some of his friends have previous criminal convictions as he met them during his time in prison, Charlie has no intention of becoming involved in any criminal activity. He is in fact totally anti-crime and just wants to get out and help who he can using the benefit of his experience of how much prison and crime hurt all those involved. Over the past few years he has achieved so much when even now the prison service tries to deny him many of his basic allowances. He appreciates that he will need a pre-release programme but is confident, as I am, that given the opportunity to do

this he will react positively, as I found he did when I worked with him. He is in my opinion not a danger to anyone. He has got so much more in his life now: friends like Andy Jones (curator and owner of the Crime Through Time Museum) and I believe some magazines and other media outlets have offered him full-time employment on his release; his writing and artwork for which he has won many well-deserved awards. So the old excuse that he has nothing to get out for if he is released is now unfounded. He loves children and has done much for charity, including setting up his own children's charity; he constantly sends my own three children art and well wishes at birthdays, Christmas etc. There are far more dangerous prisoners in the system that have been released or are on softer regimes than Charlie is. He has psychiatric reports which all counteract the prison service reports to state he is completely sane and focused. All he needs is a chance to prove that he is a different man and is capable of leaving prison and leading a normal life. He could do so much to educate the younger generation about the dangers of wasting your life in prison. My personal experiences of Charlie have all been good, with no exceptions; I have never felt threatened by him and would be more than happy to sign a declaration taking responsibility for him on his release. Both he and his family will always be welcome at my home, as I would have absolutely no reason to feel he would be any danger to my family or me, or to others. He deserves a chance to prove himself and if given that chance I know he will do it to the very best of his ability. He is a good man who has survived some of the most horrendous treatment in an archaic Victorian prison system, but after all he has been through he holds no grudge or any bitterness. He has grown old in prison and the system now owes him the chance to prove that he can go home and live the remainder of his life with his friends and family. The prison service code states that it has a duty to care for people in its custody and help them to lead law-abiding lives upon their release. They have failed to give Charlie this chance up till now and it is time they give him his chance and disregard what I believe is a personal grudge the system has with this man. I am with you all the way, my old pal, through thick or thin. I am always there when you need me, pal, you know that. For more information on my relationship with Charlie, please look at my book *The Loose Screw* published by Apex Publishing Ltd (Telephone: 01255 428500).

MIKE DAZVIS (SUPPORTER):
Has the criminal justice system learnt nothing from the Reggie Kray situation, where he was released 6 weeks before his death? Don't let Charles suffer a similar fate. RELEASE CHARLES NOW.

DE LIBERATE (SUPPORTER):
Keep on punching till the lights blow out!

BRIAN DELVE (SUPPORTER):
Get Mr Bronson out, he's innocent.

MARGIE DEMPSEY (FRIEND):
I have known Charlie Bronson since he was 16 years of age. He went about with my daughter and I trusted him with my life. He is not a nasty man and he is very generous, loves people and life, so I am sure he will be fine when he is released. I am also a very good friend of his mum and know how much she loves him. So please free Bronson.
When I lost my son on 4 September 2000 he sent me a beautiful letter and also helped me with the funeral cost. How can people say he is dangerous? He will be welcome in my home any time. All my family love him.

DEMS (SUPPORTER):
This man is not an animal, he is a human being with morals. Set him free.

ROGER DEVONSHIRE, FRANKIE FRASER AND FRANKIE ALLEN (FRIENDS):
Our thanks go to a man with a big heart, for the great kindness and thought for all the people Charlie has helped. His work has raised money for over 40 different charities. It is a testimonial to his ability to put others in less fortunate situations than himself first. I only hope people will have an understanding of Charles as more sinned against than sinning.

GIOVANNI DI STEFANO (CHARLIE'S LAWYER):
Charles Bronson is in my view a man more sinned against than sinning. He has been given no chance whatsoever to rehabilitate and the prison system has failed miserably to redeem him. Any redemption has come from his own efforts. I condemn the men with dark suits at the Prison Service as those that care nothing about humanity. They strip those they should help not only of their dignity but also of their individuality and create bitterness. Charles Bronson has done his best and for such he should be applauded. When many in prison deal in drugs, alcohol, bullying, Charles Bronson does not pass his time but uses his time a little like swallowing your food or chewing it. The trial imposed upon him a sentence, which in any view was unlawful. Parliament never intended that men such as Charles Bronson serving a discretionary life sentence would remain in jail indeterminately. His 'tariff' was three years. He has served over eight years. It is a disgrace and those at the Prison Service deserve to feel ashamed. Charles Bronson has educated himself and others and refuses to die. Even if the Prison Service kill him, his spirit of freedom and fairness will outlive the men in grey at the Prison Service. I support him and will do all I can to achieve the freedom he deserves.

MICHAEL DI STEFANO (SUPPORTER):
The government have taken the piss long enough. Give Charlie his life back! E la cosa guista da fare!!!

TINY DONN (SUPPORTER):
Free Charles Bronson.

STEVE DOUGHTY (SUPPORTER):
It is impossible for someone like me to appreciate the depths of despair you must have gone through. Your strength of character shines through. All the very best.

ANDREW DOUGLAS (SUPPORTER):
The man is an inspiration; give him another chance at freedom.

SHARRON DOUGLAS (SUPPORTER):
This man should be released now!! Free Charlie!!

CARLY DREW (SUPPORTER):
I think he's done more than his time. If you can find a more articulate, intelligent, sincere man in prison then I'll go and join him myself!

IAN DUGDALE (SUPPORTER):
There should be more with his views.

JOANNE DUNBAR (SUPPORTER):
Call me naïve, but I'm 35 years old and have just found out who Charles Bronson is. Free this man, he has done his time. Men have walked free for worse crimes.

NICK EARNSHAW (SUPPORTER):
Time Charles was out now. The justice system in this country STINKS.

KEVIN EATON (SUPPORTER):
People have done worse and they're walking free. Give this guy another chance.

DAVID ROBERT EDWARD (SUPPORTER):
For a man who has never killed nor raped, free him!

M. ELLISON (SUPPORTER):
Only in the UK. It seems the worse the crime the least the time. 34 years. What a disgrace. Release him now.

ROY ELLOR (SUPPORTER):
Enough is enough. Keeping Charlie in a cage is a crime in itself. Start the rehab and release procedure NOW!

JAN ELVIN (SUPPORTER):
I think this man has now served enough time.

HAYDEN EMERSON (SUPPORTER):
Free Charles Bronson.

MARK EMMINS (FRIEND):
I have become a close friend of Charles Bronson through his website *www.freebronson.co.uk*. I knew of him from years back when the media branded him 'a danger, monster, etc.' and like the majority of the population I believed what was in the national newspapers about him, purely because there was no Internet back then that could show me anything to think otherwise. Now I realise what a destructive, mind-washing weapon the media can really be. On reading some of the legal matters on this website, I became aware of some facts about Mr Bronson that I never knew, things that made me look at Charles Bronson as a human being and nothing like what the media had portrayed him as. I was compelled to write to him, after reading up, and I also spoke with other people that were in touch with him as I just did not know how to start my letter. The strange thing was that everyone around Charles that I talked to spoke highly of him and they were all friendly and happy that I wanted to do this. That letter was the hardest letter I ever wrote as I did not know what to say to a man that had been locked away for this long. I can only describe Charles Bronson in a few words, but these words say so much. He is kind, generous, unselfish, understanding, highly intelligent and compassionate. These words have never been used in a newspaper to describe him, but that is exactly how I see him. He is a man that will put 100% into a project or a friendship; if you are a friend to him, then it's for life. I love the chats on the phone with him every week. He always puts a smile on my face. My wife thinks he is great, as do my children - they speak of Charles like he is one of our family, they understand that he is in prison, and they also understand that he did wrong to be in there. My friend Charles Bronson has been in prison for an incredible 3 decades now, and as he is in solitary conditions I still cannot believe how he manages to laugh and joke and have intellectual conversations on the phone. Any other person would be a vegetable by now. I found this incredible. 33 years is long enough for any person to serve in prison, and the fact that Charles is not a killer, or child or woman abuser just does not warrant the sentence he has served in prisons. I feel that his release would be of benefit to the world. He is not a danger to the public, he wants to live a normal life now, a life that he has been denied for so long, and the only way to see if this is going to work is if he is given the chance out here in our world, a chance that he has been working for for so long now but has been denied. When I write to him or talk on the phone, we talk about places, food, drink, people that we know. We try not to talk about his surroundings and always talk about when he is out, not if! The Prison Service created the monster in Charles Bronson and pushed him over the edge. He has survived the brutality, the drugging, the torture, and has come out of it a better man. I cannot believe that the prisons and Home Office and politicians all pushed this under

the carpet and let this go on. We killed Saddam Hussein for crimes similar to what the prisons have done to Charles Bronson. To sum this all up, Charles Bronson has been a guinea pig, an experiment, an example, a punchbag, and we the British public have just let this go on for 33 years without helping this man, because the media say he is a monster. Unfortunately, the monster is us, all of us, as we sat back and let a man, a fellow human, go through hell and back as we got on with our lives. If our neighbour was kicking the shit out of his dog, chaining it up, drugging it, starving it, we would be outraged and do something about it, but not Charlie Bronson. We should all be ashamed to be human for not acting on his behalf and waiting 33 years to do something. Charles Bronson just wants freedom, nothing more, nothing less. He wants to be with his family, his friends, and create his art and poetry. He has served his time and learned his lessons. Do you really think he enjoys a life in a cage? He never wants to see a jail again. He would like to live a safe, normal life and I truly believe he is 100% ready and deserves his freedom. I regard him as a brother; I have no fear of him around me, my wife, my home or my children. In fact I am encouraging him to come and stay with us for a while when he gets out, as I have sights to show him. I am privileged that I talk with him on the phone; I know his voice, I know his ways, and I know he is sane. I am lucky in the fact that I got to know Charles before I read any of his books. I am reading them now and the books are great reading, Charles Bronson has a violent history, but I take him on what he is now, and it's a long way away from what and who he was. Charles to me is a man with a talent, an artist, a trusted friend; he has a great story to tell. We all have a past and we all move on from it. I know he would be a good messenger for offenders and an encouragement to budding artists. To whom this may concern: let Charles Bronson go free; let him live the rest of his days in peace; let him walk away from the hell of prison life; let him die with better memories of this world than the ones he lives with now; let him breathe real air; let him hold his mother in his arms; let him live. The truth needs to be told once and for all. Free Charles Bronson.

TONY ETHERINGTON (SUPPORTER):
As is stated above, this man has never committed a crime to warrant his huge jail sentence, so let's at least give the guy his later years out of prison.

ANDREW EVANS (SUPPORTER):
Do what's right for once ... as this man has a right!!!

LOUISE EVANS (SUPPORTER):
The time has come to free Charles Bronson.

ANTHONY FARREN (SUPPORTER):
The prisons are too full anyway! Why free paedos when you can free Charlie?!

JANICE FAULKNER (SUPPORTER):
Charles has served more than enough; he is a victim of circumstance.

MARTIN FAZAKARLEY (SUPPORTER):
The way this country is run at the minute, it's no wonder they have forgotten about Mr Charles Bronson's life. Rapists, paedos and murderers with pathetic sentences. Get him free now.

LEE FEWLASS (SUPPORTER):
Good luck, hope you get out soon. P.S. read your books.

CLIFF FIELD (FRIEND):
I met Charlie on his short spell of freedom, at the Halfway House pub on the border of Luton and Dunstable. It was a short time after I'd beaten Lennie McLean for the 2nd time. He came

across as a pretty straightforward guy and was looking at getting into a few unlicensed fights. Years later Charlie and I made contact again through a mutual friend. Due to being back in contact with Charlie I made contact with old boxing friends, receiving visits from Roy Shaw and Johnnie Frankham. The funny thing is, I never ever thanked him for getting these guys to cross paths with me again, but then again I don't think he even expected any thanks. Even now he still comes across to me as the same decent bloke I met and spoke to all those years ago. There is a side of Charlie that the media chooses to ignore ... it is not right, is it? Free him!

RONNIE FIELD (FRIEND):
I have known Charlie for many years in different prisons. The amount of years he has served far outweighs any crimes he may have been responsible for. When you think of nonces, child killers who have committed the most horrific crimes and who go home after half their sentence, it beggars belief that Charlie is still in there and still Cat A.
I have been banged up with IRA bombers in the secure Cat A units, sentenced from anything from one life sentence to eight life sentences, who are all out now. Paedophiles that hunted in gangs and snatched lads off the streets are found guilty of four deaths and get released after nine years even though the police were certain they had raped and killed many more - they go free. Charlie has never killed anybody. I think justice for Charlie is long overdue - release him now!

MARK FISH (FRIEND):
I have known Charles Bronson for a few years now and visit him on a regular basis. In the years I have been visiting Charlie I have not once met a screw who believed Charlie should be kept in the caged animal and inhumane conditions that he still has to endure. Whilst escorting me through a further dozen or more locked doors and gates to get to the dungeons of Wakefield prison and Charlie's cage, after going through normal prison security body scanners, X-ray machines, metal detectors, sniffer dogs, fingerprint recognition devices and mugshots, regular comments made by the screws are: "Charlie is a political prisoner and none of us (meaning the wardens at HMP Wakefield) can understand why he is being kept in this way." These comments are often made soon after leaving the comforts of the open visits canteen where the real monsters - the likes of Ian Huntley and Roy Whiting - are enjoying regular family visits and unassuming, innocent children play and run around (any normal thinking person would cut their fucking throats just for their twisted thoughts). The screws also make comments about the fact that Charlie hasn't so much raised his voice for the past six years and that it is totally wrong what is being done to him. I know the truth about why he is being kept in these conditions, as does Charlie, and more so does the low-life twisted bastard who is doing it behind the cloak of the Government. This vermin knows who he is and is now a worried man because he knows and for the record: we will not stop our fight for justice and an end to this massive wrongdoing. More and more supporters are joining us every day as they come to realise that Charlie is just a human being like the rest of us and not the monster that the Government has 'brainwashed' the British public into believing he is. We will continue until Charlie is rightfully decategorised and then freed - please believe that this IS going to happen. The truth will be revealed and the wrongdoer brought to book! Stay strong, Charlie, you are no longer serving a penance for what you have done but paying for a personal vendetta against you (which is illegal) from a low-life form of evil that fears to expose itself but will get exposed when justice prevails! Stay strong, Charlie, we are on the case.

LEWIS FISHER (SUPPORTER):
He was naughty when he was younger like we all were. He has done his time now. Let him be a free man.

WESLEIGH FISHER (SUPPORTER):
Give him a chance. Put him on an electronic tag and let him out. Been in long enough.

MIKE FORD (SUPPORTER):
The system has taken the piss out of CB for far too bloody long. Whilst terrorist scum get their human rights granted and the red carpet rolled out, this GENTLEMAN is left to rot. Get him out!!!!!!!

FREDDIE FOREMAN (FRIEND):
I don't usually do this sort of thing, reviews, etc., but when my great friend Tel Currie and I had an in-depth chat about it I thought it may be not such a bad idea. Tel (who is more one of 'THE CHAPS' than some of the more well-known 'CHAPS' and I trust his judgement) and I talked at great length about this book and it was not a decision I took on lightly. But the overriding factor I could not get away from is that what is happening to Charlie Bronson is WRONG! He has been left in limbo purely because they don't know what to do with him. These labels they have stuck on him are ridiculous - 'most violent man in Britain' and all that nonsense. I have served time with the best and worst of them, I have seen them all. I could take up this book with a list of the infamous names I have served with. There is a huge difference between a rascal who was anti-authority in his younger days and somebody who is pure evil. Bronson is NOT evil, as this book will explain. I served time with Charlie Bronson and our time together is documented in my books *Brown Bread Fred* and *Respect*. Charlie has calmed down a lot since those days I describe in my books when he really needed help NOT beatings and solitary! Still, he came through it and is a much mellower, articulate and thoughtful man. For all his antics in the past, I can assure you that Charlie has a heart of gold and I mean that sincerely. Is a concrete coffin really the best we can do for somebody like him? The guy is NOT Hannibal Lecter.

ALAN FORSTER (SUPPORTER):
Why doesn't the government want him free? Let him out. He's done his time, so let him go now and give him a chance!

SAMANTHA FOSTON (SUPPORTER):
Free Charles. It is a disgrace that he has been locked up for so long. I believe he is a good man inside who has just had some rough breaks.

CHRISTOPHER JOHN FOTHERGILL (SUPPORTER):
Free the guy. He has not murdered anyone.

JULIE FOX (SUPPORTER):
Let him ooouuuutttt!! Bril artist xxx

FRANKIE FRASER (FRIEND):
Your time does not fit the crime. Let's call it quits and move on to better things.

ROD & ADAM FRASER (SUPPORTERS):
Tomorrow is another day, another day too long. Free Charles Bronson "now".

LEIGHTON FRAYNE (FRIEND):
Charlie and I go back quite a number of years, so when asked to give a contribution on why Charlie should be freed I feel in its entirety I should be honouring such a request, yet the term honoured in my mind dissolves when my true feelings are cloaked with a deep sadness. Therefore my contribution to this book is going to be honest and I am not going to, and will not, bang on and on about why Charlie should be free, but will give my opinion on a system that has failed a man and robbed him of thirty years of his life.

However, just for one moment, look around you, let your thoughts run away for a few seconds, look at your son, your daughter, or even your father and mother. Imagine them locked up within a system that literally treated them like a caged animal, and not only treated them that way but allowed you to visit and view your loved one in a way that is no different than seeing an animal in a zoo. I have no doubt that the animal contained in the zoo would be treated with far more dignity, decency and a greater respect than the treatment given to Charlie, and the way he has to survive under the draconian segregation in which he lives.

I have always known Charlie Bronson as Michael Peterson. It is known that the name Charlie Bronson drives fear into those within the prison system on both sides of the fence, and indeed a borderline fear of love and hate for those that are not familiar with the penal complex. Charlie is fully aware of the crimes that he committed in the past, and without question he too understands that past prison sentences handed out to him were the way it had to go, with no complaint. There is a saying that if you do the crime then you must be prepared to do the time.

It has been said by many that Charlie Bronson is of the 'old school'. What is meant by this phrase? Prisons have changed drastically over each decade, and the prison and prisoners would like to think that these changes are for the better. Years ago if a prisoner attacked a screw he or she would be swiftly taken or dragged to the block (segregation unit) in some cases with a few digs and few boots while thrown into the segregation cell. The prisoner would then go up in front of the governor and the governor would punish the prisoner by a number of means, such as loss of canteen or days/weeks added to the one-third of remission given at that time. These rules at that time would allow a prisoner to earn those days back, of course this being based on good behaviour. In the 1980s these rules began to change: if a prisoner attacked a screw or even another prisoner he/she was still taken to the block and administered a punishment by the governor, but then the police would be called and the prisoner would then be taken to court for the courts to then administer a punishment, even to the point of adding on more of a sentence than the prisoner was already serving. It must be noted here that the prison service is bound by law to inform a prisoner of any changes within the prison system, and this is normally done by giving such notice on the prison's noticeboard and that change of law is then entered into the prison book of Standing Orders. The Standing Orders are the strict guidelines that the prison and prison officers by law must abide by. It must be noted that Charlie, sometimes by fault of his own, gave the prison officers and indeed the governors a very hard time, so what do they do? They section him off to a nuthouse or, as the case may be, a top security mental hospital. I make this point because it's a known fact that Charlie has spent almost ten years in the hospitals regime, and it is the hospital regime that has a totally different set of rules and guidelines within its system. It is also known that Charlie has spent many years within the confinements of the segregation unit, and even today the system that holds him has confined him to a cage, to the point that visitors are sat in one room divided by a hole in the wall, with prison bars between themselves and Charlie. I cannot but wonder, did anyone, such as prison officers and governors, sit down with Charlie and explain about how much the system had changed in the time he was held within the hospital regime?! It has become confusing. From the time Charlie captures and holds hostage a teacher within the prison, he is then whisked off to court, given a life sentence with a three year tariff, and here we are now seven years later and he is still in the cage, with no explanation of why or indeed when he may be freed. He has even been acknowledged by the teacher himself, with him pointing out that he had never feared for his life! To date, there's no explanation from the prison establishment on a date of release, Charlie then approaches the Appeal Courts and they give praise and commend him on his behaviour, and indicate to the Parole Board that he should be seriously considered for release. It was said by the Judge that he had no doubt that the passage of time had changed Charlie and matured him. There is a saying that when sentenced to prison we don't go to prison to be punished, we go as a punishment - I suppose lack of freedom is the punishment, and the prison system has the duty to rehabilitate and reform the individual and to help the prisoner to prepare for their eventual release. This is not the case for Charlie, however. Let's not forget that he has not killed; fighting with other prisoners and prison officers has been the bulk of his crimes. No doubt capturing a prison teacher wasn't a good idea, but let's not forget that the teacher insulted his artwork for which Charlie shows great passion. Nevertheless, even Charlie admits today that his actions weren't the best idea, and openly admits that he has changed and he is a totally different person today. To put into its right perspective, I think what Charlie is saying is that he has matured. Some people will say that he has finally grown up, and I tend to agree, but I hold the prison system responsible for the lateness in his time to grow up and mature. It has done nothing for him, but only treated him like a wild animal. We only need to look at the likes of Frankie and Roy Shaw, as these individuals were taken through a brutal regime very similar to Charlie's and both Frankie and Roy were eventually released, going on to make a success of their lives, and this success outside of crime! Therefore the system can claim that it has had a success with such individuals.

On speaking to Charlie on a visit the other day, it can be seen that he is done with it all; the past is gone. The name Charlie Bronson needs to be left in the prison and Michael Peterson should be allowed to go home to his family, to hold his mother, which the system has denied him for decades. And let the system reflect on the rights and wrongs of it treatment of such an individual, who has never murdered, his only crime having been to fight against a system that had no understanding of how to deal with him.

I can only admire his strength within, because within that little cage that he is kept in he has written eleven books of great success, his artwork is unique within his own right, his poems reflect his fears and emotions about a system that has failed him, and his compassion to help others as individuals and charities is extraordinary. I can only end by how saddened I am with his treatment and I feel the system should give him the chance to grab a little of his life - the black cloak of a wasted thirty years can only but be a reflection to all ...

LINDSAY FRAYNE (FRIEND):
I have been asked to write my views as to why I think Charlie should be released. It would be possible for me to write a thousand-page book, and that would be on how the prison system has failed him and the many judicial laws that have been broken. Charlie, as it is known, has been given a life sentence on a charge of kidnap - a crime that in my view is very different from those of kidnapping outside a prison. I feel if this sort of incident had occurred other than within the prison system, and it was Joe Bloggs who had barricaded himself in the school classroom, undoubtedly the incident would have been viewed in a lesser light, and the courts would have responded with probation or a fine, or maybe just a small sentence. But I am sure that the courts would then have taken into consideration the mitigating circumstances, without the matter being blown out of all proportion. But then this is Charlie Bronson with a long prison record, a wonderful opportunity for the authorities to go to the extreme and use the new laws of three strikes in any crime, and so a life sentence is given. I find it extraordinary that prisoners within the confines of the prisons are placed under the same rule of law of three strikes and a life sentence is given. All prisoners are surrounded by violence, and it's a dog eat dog situation, and that's with the prisoners alone. However, the system sentenced Charlie to life, and the judge gave reference that the sentence given should hold a three-year tariff. Could this indicate that the judge may have viewed such a sentence in a different light if Joe Bloggs had been stood in front of him?! I don't think Charlie would make any excuses on why he did what he did - who would really listen to him? - but there are a number of elements that should have been considered. Surely the teacher in the prison classroom should have been fully aware of how volatile the environment in which he worked was? I wonder if he was fully instructed about insulting prisoners on their chosen craft and the effects and ramifications that insults could hold within the classroom? Prison teachers are chosen due to their unique understanding in using their chosen skill and professionalism to help and guide prisoners that seek skills that are normally hidden in the outside world. A teacher is there in all respects to tease out and develop that skill in the pupil, regardless of any particular teaching environment, but in Charlie's case that teacher's professionalism became unprofessional when instead of good advice the teacher gave an insult. No doubt the teacher would

411

have taken politeness from Charlie as a weakness; 'familiarity breeding contempt'. Of course many will say, "But you don't need to take a teacher hostage and subject him to an ordeal." Of course not, but let's take into consideration that in general these men have been locked up for hours on end, they have years to go before being freed and the last thing they want is to sit down in a classroom, start their work, and then have a teacher insult them on their project. The teacher has always stated that he never feared for his life, yet the system uses threats to kill as part of their case against Charlie. To watch this abuse of power within the legal system and indeed the prison system, surely the Home Office must see that it's not just family and friends that can see and sense this injustice to an individual. If they set out to break the man for his beliefs they would have failed. It's 'time' that has changed Charlie Bronson, as it should be 'time' that has changed the authorities responsible for illegally holding him; it is they who hold him hostage. It must be considered, the talk behind closed doors with those that hold him: "What the hell are we doing holding a man for this amount of time? His pride and strength and courage are beyond our realms. It's time to let him go home. The man is done, he is not your trophy."

People are opening their eyes: technology today informs people with the touch of a button and the blinkers are off. There are questions of why, what reason, and what good is it doing? Many people know the prisoner locked away unjustly is over, and it's time to give Charlie his freedom ...

LEE FRINGE (SUPPORTER):
Typical British justice!! What a joke!!!

REBECCA FRY (SUPPORTER):
It's a shocking insight into this country's justice system.

NICOLE GALLON (SUPPORTER):
Please, please let Charles have his freedom. He is loved by many for the fact that he is a good man who has been failed by the justice system.

ANDREW GASJUB (SUPPORTER):
Enough is enough, let him out and give space to a real molester.

ANTHONY GAWLER (SUPPORTER):
FREE Charlie, an old school legend, treated worse for the past 34 years than rapists and paedos. The government should be ashamed. Free Charlie.

IAN GELDARD (SUPPORTER):
Surely this is enough punishment already?

DOUGIE GENTLES (SUPPORTER):
It's time to free Charlie. It's a crime to keep him locked up.

DAVID GIBBONS (SUPPORTER):
Too much time for a great guy.

DALE GILLIES (SUPPORTER):
Set him free.

JAMIE GILSON (SUPPORTER):
Free Charles Bronson NOW!!

JASON GODDARD (SUPPORTER):
You wouldn't even be allowed to treat a dog like this!!

RICHARD GODFREY (SUPPORTER):
No need. Paedophiles out there. Let him free!

KERRY GOODEY (SUPPORTER):
Free him now!!!

CLARE GOSLING (SUPPORTER):
With u all the way big guy!

ANDREW GOUGH (SUPPORTER):
We are still a backward judiciary system if grandstanding over high-profile prisoners is more important than justice and rehabilitation.

CHRIS GRAHAM (SUPPORTER):
Good luck Charlie, hope you get the justice you deserve.

MIKE GRAHAM (SUPPORTER):
Unbelievable!! The system needs looking at! This must be against human rights!

COLIN GRANT (SUPPORTER):
This is the government that backed the release of known activists from Guantanamo Bay and released hundreds of IRA activists on "political" reasons. Maybe Charlie should go blow up a bus full of people??

DANIEL GRANT (SUPPORTER):
Mix the paedos in with the men. Let's have some fun!

RON GREEDY & CHRIS REID (FRIENDS):
Charlie Bronson we met over 30 years ago and our friendship is as strong today as when we first met.
We believe Charlie should not be kept in prison for life. His offence does not warrant this. People who have committed murder or abused women and children are walking free. Should we ask ourselves where is the justice? Free Charlie Bronson. Your friends always.

STACEY GREEN (SUPPORTER):
It's about time it all stopped.

NATALIE GREENFIELD (SUPPORTER):
Let Charles Bronson be free again.

TIM GREENING (SUPPORTER):
34 years in prison, 28 in solitary, for a man who has never killed, raped or molested anyone. This cannot be allowed to carry on Free him now!

KELLY GREGORY (SUPPORTER):
Free this man!!

MARK GREGORY (SUPPORTER):
Free Charlie, he has done enough time now, let him be free.

ANDREW GUEST (SUPPORTER):
Should have been a terrorist, you'd be out tomorrow.

ANDY HAIGH (SUPPORTER):
Charlie should have been free long ago. He's in wacky nick with all the scum. Free him now.

LISA HALDEN (SUPPORTER):
This is terrible. Like many others have said there are a hell of a lot of people walking our streets that are pure evil.

JAMES HALL (SUPPORTER):
28 years in solitary confinement for a man that's never killed, raped or molested anyone. This is a disgrace. It's time for Charlie to be freed and have his life back. "Free Charlie."

BRIAN HAMMOND (SUPPORTER):
This website has opened my eyes. Yes he has done wrong which he shows remorse for. He has also done more for worthy causes in the UK than the majority of us could dream of.

LUKE HANDLEY (SUPPORTER):
Let him out now!

PHIL HANKINSON (SUPPORTER):
34 years is ridiculous. Terrorists have all these daft rights and this happens to one of our own.

DANNY HANSFORD - PRODUCER OF CHARLIE'S FILM (FRIEND):
I have known Charlie Bronson for the last 3 years or so. I am producing his film and when I first wrote to him I didn't know what to expect. If I'm honest I'd expected some sort of monster after all I had read in the press, etc. The truth couldn't be more different. I have spoken to him on the phone countless times and visited him at Wakefield at least 3 times. I can't judge Charlie on his past but I can since I've known him. He is one of the warmest, funniest and most charismatic men I've ever met. People say to me before I visit him, "Don't you get nervous when you go to see him?" I laugh because I feel so comfortable and relaxed in his presence; it's incredible. If he were sitting in a pub everyone would feel exactly the same way. What you see is what you get with Charlie. There is a profound honesty about him. He tells me every time I see him he has mellowed and does not want a life of violence anymore. I believe him 100% and feel it 100%. When I visit him all the guards at Wakefield prison tell me he should be out. He is causing no problems for anyone and hasn't done for many years now. Enough is enough! Give him one more chance to have some sort of life on the outside before it is too late. If he screws up then so be it, but give him that chance to smell fresh air, eat good food, spend time with his mother, son and friends and experience a life outside of an inhumane cage.
Finally he could do a lot of good on the outside talking with troubled youngsters and inspiring them not to go the same route he has gone. Who would you listen to if you were a disillusioned teenager, a teacher, a prison guard or Charlie? I know who I would. The movie will speak for him - out late 2008/early 2009.

LEE HARDING (SUPPORTER):
Pervs and paedos get it easier than him. How is that fair? Our legal system is wrong. FREE BRONSON.

RAY WILLIAM HARDY (SUPPORTER):
This man has done more time than murderers, rapists - in fact by today's standards he hasn't done anything at all - let him enjoy his life out of prison.

BARRY HARKCOM (SUPPORTER):
Charles Bronson's continued incarceration should be an embarrassment to our criminal and justice system. It's time he was released.

RICCI HARNETT (SUPPORTER):
Let this man paint the world.

JEN HARPER (SUPPORTER):
Stop the torture and give this man his life back. Free Charles Bronson!

JULIE HARPER (SUPPORTER):
Murderers and rapists don't get that long! It's a disgraceful joke!

JACKIE HARRINGTON (SUPPORTER):
Give this man a chance.

GRAEME HARVEY (SUPPORTER):
Enough is enough.

KATE HAYES (SUPPORTER):
Let Charlie have his life back. Stop making an example of him and concentrate on the real criminals and threats to society!!! Be strong Charlie!!!

JAMIE LEE HAZELL (SUPPORTER):
I think it's been long enough, release Charlie, he's no threat to anyone, he's done his time.

DANIEL HENDERSON (SUPPORTER):
Sex offenders and child molesters are out in months!! How is this justice?? Release Charlie NOW!

ALAN HILL (SUPPORTER):
Free Bronson now, Paedophiles and terrorists get treated better and get shorter sentences. The justice system is a joke.

MARK HILLIARD (SUPPORTER):
Free Charlie NOW!!! If we treated animals like this there would be a public outcry.

CHRISTOPHER ALEC HINTON (SUPPORTER):
Be lucky Charlie.

ANDREW HOBDEN (SUPPORTER):
He's done enough punishment.

PETE HOBSON (SUPPORTER):
Give the poor man a break eh!

PAUL HODGKISS (SUPPORTER):
Mr Blair, I'm a father of two children and see Charlie as no harm to the public. This is cruelty that you are doing to this man when he's locked up with scum like Ian Huntley!!!

MARK HODGSON (SUPPORTER):
Politics are the only powers that are keeping Charles behind bars!

CARL HOLDERNESS (FRIEND):
Charlie, how are you doing mate? I wrote to you in February and you sent my disabled kids some lovely artwork (remember Shaun who's autistic? I said he reminded me of John Boy). I've seen all the stuff on you in the *Hull Daily Mail* recently and I am just writing to let you know that your dream of Rainbow Cottage WILL happen one day. I knew then in 1999 that

the situation in Hull nick was that you NEVER meant any harm. The authorities have put on you all your time inside and you never deserved any life sentence. In fact you deserve the Victoria Cross for your courage and standing up for the weaker folk. Hey mate, you're a bloody hero in my house and you're welcome here any day. I'll take any invite to visit the "Danger Man" and tell the Mail it's all made up to make a good-hearted man appear bad. God bless you Charlie.

IAN HOPE (SUPPORTER):
The time has come to free Charles Bronson.

NATHAN HOPE (SUPPORTER):
Free Charles Bronson! Let him live out his years in peace, not a cramped prison cell.

JEFF HOWE (SUPPORTER):
He needs help not incarceration. The system makes him mad.

BRYAN HOWLETT (SUPPORTER):
Unbelievable for a justice system releasing nonces and murderers into our society after a short prison term and Mr Bronson is serving 34 years. Something's very wrong. They still can't break his spirit.

JOANNE HUGHES (FRIEND):
I have never met or spoken to Charles Bronson so he has not influenced anything I have to say.
I am writing this on behalf of my daughter who has been Charlie's friend for nearly a decade, visiting him, writing to him, and talking to him on the phone. He has been nothing but a really nice man and a good friend to her. He has opened so many doors for her to walk through into a world of art galleries, boxing bouts and children's charities, which he does a lot for and never talks about. I think he deserves a lot of credit for it. He is also a bit of a comedian because he always makes my daughter laugh and that's no mean feat. Murderers don't get as long as Charlie has spent in prison. It is time now for people in authority to start seeing sense and start thinking about Charlie's parole. Anyway, thank you Mr Bronson for bringing joy and humour into my family's life. Keep 'em laughing and I will see you on the outside.

IAN HUNTER (SUPPORTER):
Free Bronson.

WAHID HUSSAIN (SUPPORTER):
Free Bronson!! This is meant to be a democratic country. While the real criminals walk the streets of the UK, an innocent man who should have been freed a decade ago is still in prison. What nonsense.

ADAM IBRAHIM & FAMILY (FRIEND):
Charles Bronson, what can I say that has not been written already?
FREEDOM! To the man who's been caged up like a dove which is waiting to be set free. To Charlie the man who wants to walk among us without a care in the world. Walk the hills, lie on the grass and look to the clear blue sky and breathe God-given air that we take for granted.
PEACE! For the gentle giant, no more of slamming doors, echoing through the night and day, keys clanging as the guards walk by.
LOVE! For one chance to be in the arms of his mother where his life began.
Give Charlie what he deserves and let him live the rest of his life with dignity and pride. He has done the time for the crime which happened all those years ago. Charlie will have freedom; he will have peace and love. The fight will not stop until you are that dove spreading

your wings. Keep the faith Charlie as we do. We are thinking of you.

ISHAAQ IFTKAR (FRIEND):

My name is Ishaaq, I am twelve years old, I have never been expelled from school, I have never bullied any kids at school and I try my best to stay out of trouble.

Uncle Charlie has been really good to me and has always told me to stay out of trouble, enjoy your life like kids should and stay away from troublemakers, Uncle Charlie says that trouble-makers don't always get the blame, more than likely it's the ones who hang around with them, so it's better not to have mates like that. Keep good friends who are proud to be good. I listened and did lots of things from uncle and I will always do my best to make him proud of me and for my mom and dad too that's very important, so I am a very busy boy. If Uncle Charlie had not told me about some of these things to watch out for I could have got into a lot of trouble by going round with the big lads, who only want us to do stuff for them, they only pretend to be our mates. I really hope the prison people will stop all these hurtful things by keeping my uncle in jail because he is not a bad person, honest.

None of my friends think he is a bad person and why should they when all he tells us is to be good and my mates think he is so good. We are only kids and we are so frightened to walk down the corner shop at dark because of some men who go around kidnapping kids - they should be in jail, that is who we have nightmares about. Uncle Charlie makes us feel safe; he does not hurt kids. All of my mates and me love his artwork, it is interesting and although we do not understand everything I'd rather look at Uncle Charlie's drawings for hours than play video games.

We really, really hope you come home soon Uncle Charlie. My mates and me are going to give you a brilliant game of football like the one we promised. We have been waiting since we were five years old, how much longer will they make us wait? To all you prison people in charge we say, "Please let Uncle Charlie home and make the world a safer place."

Love you loads Uncle from me and all my mates.

MOHAMMED IFTKHAR (Ifty) (FRIEND):

Please allow me to start by quoting this phrase from Shakespeare's *Hamlet*: "A countenance more in sorrow than in anger". This phrase springs to mind when I think of the powers that be and what they are doing to my friend Charles Bronson, whom they have kept imprisoned for more than 33 years. The bad press that Charlie gets from the media breaks my heart to read, as they do not personally know the man; I do and have done for many years and my teacher has known him for decades. No journalist to this day has risked his or her career by exploring the truth about Charles Bronson. Perhaps they mean no harm and just want to sell some interesting stories, but just like our beloved The Late Princess Lady Diana, Charles Bronson pays the price with his freedom and life. Charlie and I have been friends for over a decade and I met him through my Martial Arts Grand Master Isaac Anoom. G.M. Isaac has been friends with Charlie for absolutely ages, and it was as fate would have it, one day many years ago, we had been doing a Martial Arts Demo in Harlesden, London. After the demo, Isaac asked me and a couple of other students to help him take some of the exhibition equipment used in the demo back to his house, which was close by.

It was there at my teacher's house; hanging proudly in his front room above the mantelpiece I noticed a drawing which captured my attention. I will never forget that day and that moment because I had stepped into a world that I had not known, I witnessed expression through art, I had heard the voice of another human being expressed through his art.

Grand Master Isaac being a very wise man gently closed the door, leaving me in the room, but before he closed the door he said to me, "Ifty if you look closely then you will see that a picture paints a thousand words."

After I had studied the picture and proceeded to leave the room, I became very confused, because the picture described a man who was an artist, and the story I translated was of a fellow human being, alone in a sad world of oppression, a kind man with goals and ambitions who had been pushed into situations that led to situations.

417

When I finally left the room, I asked my teacher how he came by the pieces of art that were signed to him from Charles Bronson. I asked my teacher if that was the same Charles Bronson that had chopped off people's heads and was that crazed lunatic who would attack anybody and anything in his path. My teacher laughed and laughed, "If I was given a pound for every time I heard that then I would be a very rich man." Yes, you are right, I had become a victim of the very same stigma that today I am trying to correct. My teacher asked me, "Did you see this crazed man whilst you studied the art?" "No, teacher, I had seen the opposite and that is why I am confused. The picture reads one story but my little knowledge of this person led me to believe he is dangerous." My teacher explained a very vital point to me. He said, "Every human can become dangerous in a dangerous situation, it's our human survival instincts, and everybody has different tolerance levels. It's really not that difficult to make a comparison; for example, imagine a 6ft 6in, 20 stone strongman lifting heavy weights at a charity event for children - is he a danger to anyone in that situation? No. Now take the same man, picture him in a pub and punch him in the nose. Now is he a dangerous man? Yes, because his environmental instincts kick in, to survive." My teacher asked me, "What do you think is the moral of this story?" I replied immediately as it was so obvious, "Don't punch the man in the nose in the first place." This made me realise that if every man that was likely to defend himself when in danger were to be imprisoned, then most of the human population would be behind bars. My teacher told me that he knew Charlie through Charlie's charity work and as my teacher also helped charities he and Charlie bonded a friendship. I was then introduced to Charlie, and I soon realised that Charlie had been no more than a victim of his environment, situations that led to situations.

However, it also became apparent that his punishment was harsh, imprisoned in conditions that bear resemblance to the Oubliette. The Oubliette was a small prison cell where prisoners were left to die; a secret chamber reached by a trapdoor and shaped like a beehive. There were no windows and the only access was from a trapdoor in the ceiling. Prisoners would be lowered, and forgotten; food would be lowered down from the trapdoor occasionally, but this would not be through an act of humanity, because the establishment knew the starving, dehydrated prisoner would immediately eat the food, thus living longer and unwittingly prolonging the torture. Have we come a long way from the days of the Oubliette in Charlie's case, I beg the question? Norval Morris was a criminologist who in my opinion made many changes to the prison probation service. Mr Morris contributed to the exonerations of many wrongfully convicted prisoners up until his death aged 80. One of his ideas was that considerations of justice forbid depriving people of liberty, or extending deprivations of their liberty, in order to change them.

Another famous quote he made: "It is the belief that what we do to offenders and prisoners matters, that the prison is a microcosm of the social world we inhabit, that how we respond to the suffering of those inside tells us more about ourselves than about them, and that knowing these things makes us better people."

In Chicago on 4 October 2003, Mr Norval Morris ended his last major public talk with "Pass it on, pass it on." That was the echo from his words, but do we absorb and react to the echo of his words or are we simply allowing the echo to reverberate into silence. It is my belief that men like Norval Morris could and maybe would have, if he were still alive, helped to release Charlie from the system that will not release the chains that hold him. It is obvious that there is no point in keeping Charlie locked up, but the system is steadfast in its "dog in the manger" attitude.

Charlie Bronson's injustice draws some parallel to that of Alex Alexandrowicz who spent 22 years in custody protesting his innocence. He wrongly pleaded guilty to aggravated burglary, wounding with intent, in the belief that he would serve a short sentence. At the time he was only 17. From his flat in Milton Keynes, Alexandrowicz fights on to clear his name. He lives alone and it is said that his flat has grown to resemble his prison cell.

The powers that be may well say our plights are "on a hiding to nothing", but far be it from the truth as many cases around the globe come to light and justice is demanded from the masses. Could it be a political motive why Charlie is kept locked up? Somehow I don't believe it is, because the various political parties stand to gain nothing by keeping Charlie locked up; moreover they stand to gain a lot more from releasing him.

While on the subject of the political, how about the story of Chia Thye Poh, a former physics teacher from Singapore arrested without charge in 1966 and jailed without trial for 22 years? Chia was released from prison in 1989 to become Singapore's Sentosa Island's only full-time resident. They say he is forbidden to leave the island without written permission, so is theoretically still imprisoned.

So where are we going with this? Are we are going to help our friend, I ask, or shed "crocodile tears"? In my case it is the former. Charlie has changed so much over the last seven years or so; he has not been involved in any major disturbance. His time and efforts are spent on his art, helping charities, guiding youngsters onto the straight path and dreaming of the day when he can hug his mom, son, family and friends.

I recently went to see Charlie in Wakefield seg unit. For those who don't know, it's a prison that houses a lot of very nasty individuals, who have been convicted of preying on kids and carrying out some very, very nasty murders of young children, amongst whom is that monster who beat two children and their mom to death with a hammer. Ironically, Charlie is kept in a prison within a prison. It's maximum security at its utmost securest, but the child molesters and paedophiles are given rights and freedom of movement that Charlie could not even dream about. On the visit it saddened me to see Charlie caged up like a wild animal, a solitary visiting area unlike the normal visitation areas that everyone else has the use of. A brick wall with a 3-foot square opening with reinforced bars divided us, barely enough space to put a hand through to shake my brother's hand.

After I was fully cleared, fingerprinted, and put through the face recognition system I was led to the canteen where other inmates and visitors sat. At the canteen, a prison officer handed me a flask marked Charlie. The canteen woman filled it up and I was led through another visiting area and then through many more secure doors, across the prison yard area and into another heavily fortified prison area. Then I went through more areas that I just can't remember, until I was led down some steps into the room that I spoke of. I must say the prison officers were courteous to me and from what I could tell they were good with Charlie too. I guess deep inside they feel some compassion for him - what human being wouldn't? Let us get back to the visit and the point. When I entered the divided cell room, through the bars I could see Charlie standing up. He had been waiting for over an hour as there was a bit of a cock-up on my arrival.

"Ifty, what happened mate? I'd been worried that something had happened to you on your drive up. They told me just now there was a mix-up and you had gone to the wrong visiting area ... Don't worry, don't worry, you're here safely now, that's the main thing."

His focus was so much on cheering me up, as I must have been making a poor show of hiding my sadness witnessing Charlie so hard done by. His environment was solitary, the only sounds being the rattle of keys and the odd voices of other prison officers.

"Hey, hey, Ifty, tell me how are my little nephews?" My kids call Charlie 'uncle' and Charlie has always guided them to do the best they can.

"They're okay, Charlie. Everyone sends their love and just wants to see you come home."

During our conversation Charlie said to me witness this and let your teacher Isaac know that I am still doing my press-ups. Incidentally, my teacher Isaac can do 76,000 sit-ups in 24 hours and Charlie can do 163 press-ups in 60 seconds and 93 press-ups in 30 seconds, so the two have always been practising hard on their incredible achievements. I could not believe my eyes when Charlie got up and demonstrated 93 press-ups in 30 seconds, just to cheer me up, and cheer me up he did. I have been connected to fitness and training in one way or another through my entire life and when I saw Charlie pump out 93 press-ups in 30 seconds I was more amazed at seeing this than I did when witnessing our grandmasters in Indonesia doing some mind-blowing demonstrations, utilising the power of Chi. Chi is an invisible force of energy that lies within all of us and when enhanced and centralised can protect the body from blows from swords and so forth. The demonstration I witnessed by Charlie will always be a source of encouragement for me and my students; the thought will stick with me forever.

You know when I left the visit from seeing Charlie I understood some of the questions he asked me, and the things he told me. For instance, what is the weather like, is it windy? How does it smell out there? Many birds about? I remember Charlie telling me he would love to see grass, sit on it and watch it blow around in the wind. Charlie always tells me how he is yearning to spend time with his family and friends, hug his mom, take his son travelling and just spend time doing what we would call the simple things in life, but what Charlie and his son would call the most precious moments of life, spending life together and making up for lost time between them.

Charlie has worked hard for his release and has demonstrated without a doubt that he is a reformed character. The Charlie I know is not the same Charlie you may read of in books that have been written without his consent or in newspaper articles by the press who do not even know the man.

It's to this point that I bring my few pages to an end and my hopes and prayers are for the man who we all so dearly love, the man who has supported and guided kids out of trouble from his solitary cage, and it begs belief what good he could do for the kids and teenagers if he was out. Why do they keep this man behind bars? The man is anti-drugs, anti-bullying, anti-crime. Sure, Charlie has been no angel in the past, but he has put all that behind him. He has paid his debt to society dearly and excessively and now is the time to let him rejoin his family and friends and let him explore his passion for art and to help society with his charities and his guidance for young people to steer clear of crime. Charlie is one of if not the best example for people who are thinking of embarking on a life of crime, because he is so passionate not to let people think that crime pays because he is adamant that it does not.

Keep your chin up, Charlie, we all love you dearly.

SYIED IFTKHAR (Guggy) (FRIEND):
Growing up in this area, which does not really have much going for it, violence and crime fill our streets and affect all our daily lives in some way. We have lost some very good friends while only in their teens and early twenties.

These tragedies make me wonder what future there is for us, whilst violence takes hold of our communities and a tragic event I'd forgotten as quickly as it occurs is only highlighted by another tragic event and so the circle continues. It is almost as if we were living in the world outside of the normal world and the suffering is only known to those who live in it. It makes me wonder what future there is for us, why violence is looked on as a resolution as opposed to a chronic disease plaguing our environment; an enlightened question that not even some probation officers could relate to, but that Uncle Charlie explained year in, year out, to help us relate to the answer, in a way no one else could. Wad and me have always taken notice of Uncle Charlie because he has a way of explaining things to us; his experience in his life is a solid platform to talk from that warrants our attention.

It's clear to me he does not want to see youngsters learn the hard way. He said, "Prison is a terrible place. I do not want you guys to end up in here. I want you all to get a job, get yourself educated. Once you get on your feet you can move to a better environment but don't forget to share your wisdom with the people left in that area, and don't give up on your mates, steer them good too." Wad and I are truly blessed to have an uncle like Charles Bronson. He is a great man who cares sincerely for all his friends and family. Uncle Charlie has never given up on us and we will never give up on him. We all pray and hope that the government will allow uncle home very soon, allow him to share his life with family and friends, surrounded by our love and not the hostility he is under now.

If Uncle Charlie had not told us to stay well away from drugs then I can bet you that is what we could easily have been drawn into. If there's no future for him, then there's no future for us. The justice system would have made a statement in the eyes of the world, stating that it cannot rehabilitate and that the system does not work. On the other hand, as soon as Uncle Charlie is out guiding youngsters on the right path, then the statement will be in favour of the justice system. We will never give up on you uncle. We hope you will be home very soon.

LOONYOLOGY

WAHID IFTKAR (Wad) (FRIEND):

Uncle Charlie is the most genuine person I know. He does not think about himself, he dedicates his efforts to helping and guiding people onto a positive path. That is an amazing quality for a person to have, especially when he himself is so hard done by. Uncle Charlie has helped me and my brother Guggy as far back as I can remember, bearing in mind I am coming up to twenty-one now. He encouraged me and Guggy to get a job and stay away from making the mistake of falling into the clutches of crime, like doing burglaries and robberies and selling drugs. Uncle once told me, "If you'd gone down that path, then you would have made me feel like my time in prison has been for nothing. Because I want you, Guggy, Ishaaq and all of your mates to know one very important thing, and that is that crime does not pay."

One day my uncle wrote to me and my brother Guggy and told us, "Prison smells of urine. You are not kids now, and I have to tell you, you have to listen to me, I want you to know that these places are terrible. There is no glory here despite what you hear. It's a terrible suffering when you're caged up for years on end. I don't want to see you guys ever go down this road, because it serves no purpose, it's only heartache and misery." The same day my dad told me that Uncle Charlie had his appeal knocked back, and he is concerned for all the people he loves never to go through the same trauma he is going through. I have never been so sad and so humbled at the same time. Uncle Charlie does not deserve to be in prison this long, it is not right; it is far too much of a punishment.

Since we were kids Uncle Charlie has been telling me and my brother to do the best we can in life. He will be happy to know that we are trying our best to make our lives better. He always explains how nice it would be on his release to take us guys to visit all the different splendours of the world, even just meet friends and educate our minds. "Education is important." "Look after your mom and dad." "Stay out of trouble." He always writes that in his letters to us.

There has to be some person high up in government who is prepared to make a decision to send Uncle Charlie home. He is not a murderer or something sinister, he is a very caring and kind person who keeps to his word. He helps us stay on the right path and away from crazy stuff. So many of us care for him, we cannot all be wrong. He has done so much good for us from behind those prison walls; just imagine if he was out how much help he could give to society and to so many disturbed teenagers about to go on a path of self-destruction.

Guggy and me will always show you the maximum amount of respect Uncle Charlie, because without your support and guidance we would have not known how to avoid going astray. Thank you.

ZAHRAH IFTKAR (Zah) (FRIEND):

If I could have a wish come true, it would be to see my Uncle Charlie here with us to celebrate all our birthdays, to be here when I pass my driving test. The kindest and best gift I receive on my birthdays has always been from Uncle Charlie. He never forgets and always draws me a lovely birthday card, and more thought, effort and affection has gone into that card than any card from the most expensive shop in the world. What I do not understand is why they always say that Uncle Charlie is dangerous; a dangerous person has no heart, no compassion and no conscience. Uncle Charlie has all these qualities and is the gentlest person you could ever meet. It's such a shame that I have to see my uncle have appeal after appeal turned down; it makes me cry for weeks, as just as I think he is coming home they turn him down. Imagine the cruelty he is going through. You know I think the myth about Uncle Charlie has gone on long enough and it's time it was busted. He is not a monster, he is a kind human being who has people who love him, care for him and pray for him. My mates at college were ashamed of their first reaction when I told them of Uncle Charlie one day; they all pre-judged him on the little knowledge they had of him - crazy I know. However, that is what people have been led to believe; they think he is a monster, a madman, that kind of image. It is when I tell my friends the truth and show them some of his drawings that they then begin to know my uncle a bit better and realise that he is a human being, and that he is not the monster that first springs to mind, but unfortunately that is how he has been portrayed over the years.

421

I appeal to the decision makers, the parole board, the government, to look deep within themselves and look at all the good this man does. It's only common sense that when someone has been in prison for 33 years the last thing that they will do when released is to end up back inside. The life he wants to live is a peaceful life; he only wants to help people better their lives and be an inspiration to do good. There are many positives to why Uncle Charlie should be allowed home.

Please find it in your heart to stop this torment and make many lives better, please. We love you Uncle Charlie.

ADAM IRBRAHIM (SUPPORTER):
Like a bird, let him spread his wings and fly. Free Charlie now!

PETER JACKMAN (SUPPORTER):
Free Charlie now, enough is enough. You can't keep a good man down. We are all behind you Charlie.

STEVE JACKSON (SUPPORTER):
Enough is enough. The man has done his time.

LYN JAMESON (FRIEND):
I first met Charlie in Milton Keynes Crown Court. A friend asked if I would go and support him on his behalf as he was unable to attend. I sat with Charlie's family and friends in the gallery. During lunch I requested to see him, and from that meeting a friendship has developed over 15 years with both his family and friends. Charlie is a very caring man and raises so much money for his favourite charity 'Zoe's Hospice'. His achievement is twice as hard for him with his limited restrictions. I once spoke to a prison officer who said, "I wish I had a landing full of Charles Bronsons."

My personal opinion regarding Charlie is that the system must take full responsibility for what it has done. Isolation for over 25 years has not been beneficial to his well-being. He should have a chance of life outside prison, but firstly he needs to be rehabilitated to mixing and living among others. Charlie has never killed anyone - there are people in the community that have committed far worse than him. Good luck.

EDWARD JARVIS (SUPPORTER):
So much for the British justice system. Nonces and rapists have served less time.

TED JARVIS (SUPPORTER):
My name is Ted Jarvis. I am a chauffeur for many celebrities in London and I live in a riverside flat overlooking the Thames. I have not had the privilege of meeting Charles Bronson but have followed his ill-fated yet well-documented life for a long time and feel that he has been used as a punchbag publicly by the prison authorities as a deterrent to stop other prisoners behaving in such a way. I'm not for one minute applauding Charlie's antics at the beginning of his sentence, but I think that he has more than paid for his earlier behaviour, for how he chose to protest, and if it hasn't already his mental health will deteriorate to such a level that he will not be able to adapt to normal everyday life out on the street, and to keep a man in these conditions is inhumane and cannot be justified just by putting some well-chosen stories in the newspapers. I can see from his website that I am not alone in thinking that Charlie should at least be given a release date to work towards. As you can see by the amount of books he has published, he is a well-established author and his artwork has attracted international interest and is sold all around the world. He is without doubt a natural showman and entertainer, which I feel may have contributed to his past behaviour. I would like to add myself to the ever-growing list of names that are campaigning for Charlie's release.

GRAHAM JENKINSON (SUPPORTER):
This man is a product of the prison system!!! He has never killed, molested or mugged the elderly! He has done more than his time!!!!!

JEREMIAH JEYAKUMAR (SUPPORTER):
Free Bronson. 34 years in prison is inhuman.

BARRI JOHN (SUPPORTER):
Prison hasn't worked, it's time for a change.

EMMA JOHNS (SUPPORTER):
Enough is enough … give this man his freedom.

FRANK JOHNSON (FRIEND):
Questions and Answers:
Q. Who is Charlie Bronson? A. A human being.
Q. Is he a killer? A. No.
Q. Is he a terrorist? A. No.
Q. Is he a rapist? A. No.
Q. Is he a paedophile? A. No.
Q. Is he insane? A. No.
The main reason that Charlie is still banged up in solitary is this country's failure to comply with Human Rights Directives. We have the worst record of complaints regarding prisoners in custody within the European Union.
The killer of Philip Lawrence, the schoolteacher, is due for release soon. His defence team cite his Human Rights; no deportation, so he stays in this country a free man after about a 12-year sentence.
The Stansted Airport hijackers are soon due for release after a short sentence; again the defence team cite their Human Rights, so they all stay here. Miles Cooper, the Kent letter bomber, injures six people with explosives, a possible five stretch, then he walks. Let's add that up: three sentences about 22 years in total for bombers and a murderer, Charlie boy has done that and more, and for what? I'll let you all, judge for yourselves. Human Rights - don't make me laugh. Charlie gets a cheap watch and a pair of glasses replaced after a screw breaks them and the press are making a big deal of it. They ought to be headlining their front pages with the £25 million it's cost us taxpayers for the Stansted hijackers case. Justice? I don't think so. A mob of armed Old Bill kill an innocent young guy on the tube in cold blood and get away with it without even an ASBO. Justice? I don't think so. Guys like Charlie, Ronnie Biggs, Harry Roberts ain't got a chance of justice until the Human Rights of our own are matched to the afore highlighted. Article 3 of the European Constitution for Human Rights states, "No one shall be subjected to torture or to inhuman or degrading treatment or punishment." The prison inspectors are the mob that needs bringing to court; only then will Charlie have any chance of justice. Keep your chin up, Charlie, all the best.

DARREN JONES (SUPPORTER):
Come on, it's about time isn't it?

GORDON AARON JONES (SUPPORTER):
Charles did the crime, and he has served more than his fair share of time. Free Charles Bronson now!!!

JIMMMY JONES (SUPPORTER):
Hello Charlie. I'm a loyal friend of David Courtney and nephew to our late Joey Pyle, RIP. It's a pleasure to sign your petition and I hope the real villains who took your freedom will see the light!

JOHN JONES (SUPPORTER):
He should be a free man.

PHILIP JONES-SPIKE (SUPPORTER):
Free Charlie ... enough is enough!

WAYNE JONES (SUPPORTER):
Why has this man not been released, yet nonces are in next to no time?

ANDREW JOYCE (SUPPORTER):
Disgraceful that he's still inside.

JUDE - TATTOOIST (SUPPORTER):
Evil is a man who takes away the keys from another man's freedom. Good luck, Charlie, love and best wishes to you x.

TEROLIUS KAUPPINEN (SUPPORTER):
Free Charles Bronson.

TIM KELLY (SUPPORTER):
It's time to end this unlawful confinement. Set Charlie free!

JODY KENNEDY (SUPPORTER):
From my reading quite in depth on both side of the fence, this man is now due release.

STUART KENNEDY (SUPPORTER):
Let Charlie out, enough is enough.

JUDITH KENYON (SUPPORTER):
HMP stands for Her Mother's Pussy. Time isn't on our side.

MARK KING (SUPPORTER):
Charlie has done more time than he has ever deserved. Please let the man out now.

ALEXANDER KINNAIRD (SUPPORTER):
Charlie is a victim of the system. His sentence is not in line with the crimes he has committed. He should receive fair treatment in line with other inmates.

STEVE KNAPP (SUPPORTER):
Just read the book *Bronson*. An extraordinary insight into the prison system. How Charles has survived for so long after the Home Office mind games is a testament to his inner (and outer) strength.

JOHN KNIGHT (FRIEND):
The Bronson situation is a total waste of life! What good can it do after all these years? This is not punishment, it's petty revenge by a system out of ideas.

RONNIE KNIGHT (FRIEND):
When our great friend Tel Currie asked if I would write a piece for this Charlie Bronson book, I was more than happy to oblige, even though I don't make a habit of getting involved in other people's books and projects. It usually has to be an exceptional case and Charlie Bronson's case is indeed exceptional! This book will be a great chance for people to get as close to Charlie's thoughts as possible and give a real insight into what keeps this remarkable man going. The amazing thing about Charlie Bronson is that he doesn't just keep going and

survive but always remains positive, looks to the future and cherishes each day. He often comments on how lucky he is! This inspiring outlook doesn't change the fact that what they are doing with him, Ronnie Biggs and others is barbaric! But what do they care? They are all drinking vintage wines and eating caviar in their luxury houses.

DALE KONCZAK (SUPPORTER):
Free the man. This is pure cruelty and outrageous.

EMMA KRAY (FRIEND):
I find it hard to understand a system that complains about overspending and overcrowding, yet keeps a man locked up in such a high security category for so long, a man that has proven he's changed for the better and is ready to move on. Charlie should be released and could even be seen as a success story, from being classed as Britain's most dangerous prisoner, to a prisoner that turned against violence and crime and who took the right steps to being released. The alternative doesn't bear thinking about, the possibility that Charlie would never be freed. But it would show what a two-faced, backward-thinking system we have in this country, one that says that rehabilitation is the way forward, but gives little opportunity to be rehabilitated; backwards in thinking that releasing a paedophile back onto the streets is a safer option than releasing Charlie. I for one know who I'd prefer living on my street, as I'm sure most would agree. I honestly feel that Charlie's ready to be released and is in no way a danger to society.

RAY KRAY (FRIEND):
Like a coin Charlie Bronson has two sides, it's just up to the individual which you choose to believe - the media and prison services version or Charlie's friends and family's version, bearing in mind the media and prison service gain more by keeping him locked away: the media get to continuously make up false stories, portraying him to be an evil man to help sell their trashy 'news' papers; the prison service gain by wrongly justifying their inhumane treatment of Charlie over all these years, and the continuous mistreatment to this day. Or you could believe his friends and family, people that gain nothing but the acknowledgement that Charlie has done more than his time inside and should have been released years ago.

I've been lucky enough to have experienced both sides of the coin, firstly by reading the things that have been printed about Charlie which gave me an image of a man that was physically strong, violent in his actions and aggressive in nature, with little thought for himself or others. But over the years, through corresponding, phone calls and prison visits, I feel that I have gradually come to know the real Charlie Bronson, a man that is not only physically strong but mentally strong, but he had to be to have endured what he has over the years. Now as for being violent, if you kick the most placid dog enough times and provoke it, one day it will turn round and bite, Charlie has been both kicked and provoked many times. As for Charlie's nature, if caring for other people was a crime, he'd be given another 30+ years, as he's done so much for charities that you never see printed, raising money and awareness all from his prison cell. Plus he does care about what happens to himself; that's why he's kept himself mentally and physically fit over the years, keeping himself out of trouble in the hope that his actions will be rewarded in some way, by being decategorised and finally released. One thing I do know is that he genuinely does care about other people, helping his friends, family and even strangers in any way he can.

Obviously some people do deserve to be locked up, but Charlie is not one of those people. I've seen a positive change in Charlie over the years. Back in 2004 when he was up in court at the Old Bailey, I remember sitting in the public gallery listening to Judge Rose when he said that Charlie was a different person from what he used to be. Yet all these years later nothing has changed. In my mind, Charlie is not the evil one, the system that keeps him imprisoned illegally, mentally and sometimes physically torturing him, is the evil one. For every extra day the authorities keep Charlie inside, it's an injustice to him and another day of shame for them.

MATT LACEY (SUPPORTER):
When you see the meagre sentences handed out to rapists and paedophiles, it emphasises the travesty of this case. He has done his time tenfold. ENOUGH IS ENOUGH.

JAN LAMB (FRIEND):
I think it is wrong that Charlie is still in prison. He has done more than his time and he has not done anything wrong in years, so why keep him locked up with paedos/rapists and murderers? He has never hurt women/children or anyone, it's not in him to do that sort of thing. He would be the first to get up and stop a guy if he'd seen him hitting a woman or a kid. You could trust him with a house full of kids and they would be as safe as houses with him; in fact he would be a great children's entertainer. He is a great guy, I have known him for years and he has a great sense of humour. If he were out of prison he could give talks to youngsters about staying out of prisons, etc. He also could have a great career with his drawings, as he is fantastic at it and does a lot of good work. He could teach people on the art of drawing. He is a special friend to me and I love him to bits. He is intelligent, funny and serious when he needs to be. He also has a big, hard cock waiting for me when he gets out of prison. When he was last out of prison in 1987 we had so much fun and I would like to have that again with him. I couldn't find any fault with Charlie as he is so sweet. I trust him with my life and why shouldn't I, as he is very trustworthy and honest and he says what is on his mind which is something I like in people, as there is no point in thinking one thing and saying something else is there? I remember when he was out in 1987 and we were on the beach having a shag when this couple walked past and were looking at us. Why they were looking I don't know, as there is nothing wrong with having a shag when you feel like it. But it was quite funny. We used to do it anywhere we felt like it - in car parks, in the park, etc. - and there is nothing wrong with that is there? We both have a terrific sense of humour and that is good. We were in a caravan and it rocked like hell all the time, and need I say why it was rocking? No, I didn't think so. If we were living together we would spend most of our time in the bedroom exercising; well, exercise is good for you, isn't it? And what better than to exercise in a way that you love, ha ha ha ha. We were great special friends then and we still are to this day and we will always remain special friends until the end of our lives.

PHILL LAMMAS (SUPPORTER):
Would have served less being a terrorist.

LEE LAND (SUPPORTER):
About time he was out!

CARL LANGLEY (SUPPORTER):
People who kill and are terrorists should be in solitary confinement.

MATTHEW LANGSTON (SUPPORTER):
This man should not be in prison. It's manipulation, period!

CARLTON LEACH (FRIEND):
To be honest, I still can't believe we are fighting for this man's freedom. How long must this medieval barbarism go on for? Would Charlie have had more chance if he were a nonce or a killer? My mate Tel Currie (who is like a brother to me and indeed to all the 'chaps') has worked his bollocks off fighting for justice and we are all with him. But will it do any good? Have they already made their minds up? Still, we will keep fighting. This little gem of a book will show you what Charlie is really about. Do you think men like myself, Tel Currie, Charlie Richardson, Ronnie Knight, Roy Shaw, Howard Marks and Albert Chapman would bother with a total lunatic who was a threat to decent people? NO Is the answer.

MARK LEADBEATER (SUPPORTER):
Charlie has served more than his fair share of time, he's paid his debt to society, and so it's time to let the man go! 34 years is 5 times more than he should've served; you get less for murder!

MARK LEE (SUPPORTER):
Release Charlie, he has suffered enough. He's a human being not an animal, so give him his life back, he's served his time!!!!

ROSS LIGHT (SUPPORTER):
Dirty stinking kiddie fiddlers get lesser sentence than this man. Wake up and smell the coffee. Free Bronson.

MISS A. LILLEY (SUPPORTER):
Time to do the right thing and free the man. It's unfair to a man that's not killed anyone. The system is all wrong!!!

DONNA LISLE (SUPPORTER):
Why is it that someone that murders a child gets 4 or maybe 5 years, then you get someone innocent and they bang 'em up for half their bloody life?! Makes me fucking sick!!!

MARTIN LIVELEY (SUPPORTER):
Please release him, or I'll do you.

JOHN ALFRED LODGE (FRIEND):
I first met Charlie in Long Lartin Prison in 1989 on a normal prison wing; I was a cleaner with Johnny Walker of the Birmingham 6. Johnny told me one day that after dinner we would be having another cleaner working with us, who turned out to be Charlie. I worked with Charlie for a couple of months and from that day to this we have got along fine and became firm friends. I have been out of prison for over 17 years and during this time have kept in touch with Charlie through letters and phone calls. Over the years Charlie has sent me a number of his drawings, which have been raffled and the proceeds, which probably amount to several thousand, have been donated to several different charities as Charlie requested. He is a genuinely kind person. There are far more dangerous people living on almost every housing estate in this country, i.e. drug dealers, rapists, paedophiles and murderers to name but a few, and Charlie is none of those.
On a personal level I have not served any time back in prison for almost 17 years, although I have committed a drink driving offence and also appeared in court for being the owner of a dog which killed a rabbit. I think my time in prison taught me to appreciate life and the choices we have. On Boxing Day 2006 I suffered a minor stroke and in order to come to terms with the change it brought to me I needed some counselling. Because of this and revealing my past I was then asked to give some talks to local young offenders about crime and prison life, and to hopefully deter them from re-offending. Some of these lads have come out hunting and fishing with me, and we talk, and they listen to me and I hope I have done some good at stopping them re-offending and ending up in prison.
Charlie would be an ideal person to help young offenders, more than most people I can think of who has had experience of life behind bars. Also now it is time that Charlie's mum deserves some happiness and gets her boy home and is able to see him do some good from the time he has spent inside. I have met Charlie's mum a few times and we chat on the phone. A very nice lady Eira is. I believe Charlie should be given a chance. Show him there is light at the end of the tunnel. Take him out of isolation for a start, as most of the time he is isolated away for no reason. I am 100% sure that given the chance Charlie will do more good outside! Anti-drugs, anti-crime, anti-violence. Free Charlie Bronson now!

JILLIAN LOFTS (FRIEND):
I think the system's all back to front when Charles Bronson is kept in prison while child molesters and killers, rapists and people who murder for no reason are set free only after a few years serving a sentence when everyone knows full well they are going to re-offend. What is wrong with British justice? All the wrong people are kept locked up while real evil criminals are set free. Charles Bronson is not a murderer, he didn't hurt any child or old person, but he's been kept inside for over 32 years. Why? To add insult to injury, he's kept in solitary confinement. This is madness! He has proved in the last seven or so years that he's reformed (the only reason he was violent in prison before is because of frustration of being cooped up, which makes you want to lash out and smash everything up). It don't help that the prison staff deliberately wind up prisoners; just because they wear a uniform, they get big-headed and think they are better than the inmates. But they're not, they are only normal people doing a job for a living the same as a cleaner or office worker. No wonder inmates get the arsehole! Then the inmates get punished further and the press make a big story of it all. Anyway, Charles Bronson has proved himself. He has done a lot for charities, especially for children, and he is more a gentle giant than 'the most dangerous man in Britain'. I would rather be alone with Charlie than some of these young thugs of today who would mug an old lady for a few pence, and all they get is a slap on the wrist!
The reason he's kept locked up is political. The same thing happened with the Kray twins - they should have been released years ago. If they had, they would probably be alive now and doing 'gangland' tours with Frankie Fraser. I've been on one of Frankie's tours and it was great - Frankie is a lovely guy. Also it's madness to keep Ronnie Biggs locked up. He's a sick old man and he should have his last years as a free man. Prisons are overcrowded at the moment, only because there are people in there that shouldn't be - like poor Charlie. Instead of having Charlie in that cage, put some ghastly paedophile in there instead and throw away the key (like they used to do years ago). The general public all feel Charlie should have been freed long ago, I'd be happy for him to be my neighbour - he's not dangerous, just muscular and fit due to all the sit-ups and press-ups he does.
Also I'd like to add that my eldest son, Peter, 28, supports Charlie all the way, and says that he should have been out of jail ages ago. He thinks Charlie's very brave to have stuck it out all these years, and I do too. Charles Bronson is a man to be admired; the way he's being treated is diabolical, but he keeps his head high and lives in hope of freedom - never give up hope. I look forward to the day - and so does Peter - when Charlie walks through that gate with a triumphant smile on his face. Because one day it will happen - the sooner the better! So come on, Home Secretary, free Charlie Bronson now - give him a chance. The prison system is overcrowded, so why keep people in when they don't need to be there? It is sheer cruelty to keep this man locked up like an animal and for no reason. He's served his time and his release date is well overdue. He could make a good honest living out of his brilliant cartoon artwork; it would look great in newspapers and magazines. He's certainly got a good sense of humour! He is also a brilliant writer and he also writes poetry, which would sell well. So wake up, Home Office, and free Charles Bronson now!

BRAD LONG (SUPPORTER):
Time served, free Charles Bronson.

TIM LONGDEN (SUPPORTER):
The British judicial system is a f**king joke.

LISA-MARIE LONGHURST (SUPPORTER):
Surely Charlie's served more than enough time.

KRYSTAL LONGLEY (SUPPORTER):
Good Lord, murderers don't get this kind of sentence. Do what's right, let this man have what's left of his life back.

NIKITA LONGWORTH (SUPPORTER):
Free Bronson. Just read the book, a lot of respect for this guy ... system is sh*t! What about the real sick criminals out there, child killers, etc.? Hope you're out soon. Maybe we could get to see a C.B. art gallery.

CHARIS LOWE (SUPPORTER):
I hope they see sense soon and free you. They let scum roam free while keeping you locked up. Says to me and I'm sure many others that the system is so wrong.

ERIC CLAPTON LOWE (SUPPORTER):
Mr Bronson could and would do great work in the outside world. 34 years - the government should be ashamed. Free Charles. See what good he will do for so many.

DESSY LUDWICK (FRIEND):
This man should now be let out of prison. He's been locked up now for over thirty years, most of this time in solitary confinement, which is enough to make any man go mad - but not Charlie. Yes he's had his days in Broadmoor, Ashworth and Rampton. Yes he has been violent and destructive. But that's now all in the past. Charlie's moved on. He's not violent or destructive anymore and the system knows this. I feel the system doesn't want to let Charlie out, or for Charlie to move on. Why? Because they always bring up the past! They would sooner keep him locked up like a wild animal, throw away the key and forget about him! The system is wrong.

Charlie is now at peace with himself and others and he needs to get back out there to be with his family, more so to be there for his beloved mum and his son Mike, and not forgetting his beloved angel Loraine, his sister. Charlie can and will do good out there. Charlie has got good people out there who can help him in many ways - and I don't mean doing banks, I mean help in making an honest living, living a normal life. Yes Charlie knows criminals, but they've moved on. They've had their days of crime and prison. They're now living normal lives, crime free. They had that chance to make good of their lives. It's about time Charlie had his chance to make good of his life.

Let me tell you, Charlie is a lovely man - warm, kind and caring, with good morals, and a true gentleman, and what a great sense of humour this man has got. Considering what he's been through, 'to hell and back', you wouldn't have thought that Charlie had these qualities, but Charlie has. Charlie is now 56 years old. Come on, he doesn't want to go back out there robbing banks. He just wants to live a normal life, like most of you out there. Charlie could be a bricklayer, he could be a painter, he could get into the boxing game, he could be a writer like he is at present. There are many things that Charlie could do out there - good things, crime free. He could help kids out there, steer them away from crime and drugs, as Charlie loves to help the young. Charlie also loves to do things for charity. Please don't think: Charlie - charity?! He's done loads of things for charity whilst in prison. One that sticks in my mind is about ten years ago Charlie raised money for a ten-year-old girl who had cancer - he done loads of press-ups and sit-ups. She later died from cancer, God bless her. But Charlie raised money to help her in the best way he could. Charlie loves kids, he loves women, he loves old people and he loves animals, and if he could do anything to help any of these Charlie would. Charlie will not find it hard to make an honest living out there and the system knows this, 'the people at the top'.

Give Charlie that chance and let him out so he can move on and make better of his life, and others'.

DEAN LUPTON (SUPPORTER):
It's about time Charlie got his life back. Enough is enough. There are people who have committed far worse crimes and don't do half the time he has. Free Charlie!!!

ALAN LYNAM (SUPPORTER):
Insanity at its worst. People who kill get less time. Whatever happened to human rights? Bronson is a sound man, so let him out. Rehabilitation - you give it to everyone else!!!!

TONY LYNE (SUPPORTER):
FREE THE LUTON ONE!!!! Hasn't Mr Bronson suffered enough??? Let him out now, as he is NOT a danger to society.

KATY M (SUPPORTER):
Free Charlie!!

VIKI M (SUPPORTER):
Prison system is a joke.

MARK ROBERT MACKIE (SUPPORTER):
When you push some men, they push back harder. Charles is one of those men! It is not a crime to stand up for yourself! Free Bronson.

JAMES McCANN (SUPPORTER):
Keep strong Charlie!

STUART McCLURKIN (SUPPORTER):
Free Charlie.

LUCY McDONAGH (SUPPORTER):
Let this man free, he has served long enough.

EMMA McDONALD (SUPPORTER):
Free Bronson and lock up some of the real criminals that are running free and harming people.

LEIGHANN McELHINNEY (SUPPORTER):
Free Charles Bronson.

JASON McKAY (SUPPORTER):
The book, the art ... the man is not an animal, murderer, paedo, junkie but what he is. He is a legend and what he should be is free! Free! Free!!!!!!!

GEMMA McLEAN (SUPPORTER):
Free Charles, he no longer poses a danger to anyone and should be freed. He's done more time than necessary for the crimes he committed.

ROBERT JOHN McLEAN (SUPPORTER):
Just finished reading his book and it is a disgrace he has been put away for this amount of time!

STEWART McLEAN (SUPPORTER):
How can it be that paedophiles can be allowed back onto our streets, but this man, a gentleman, has spent nearly a lifetime in a cage? Sort it out. Free Bronson.

CHARMAINE MAEER: (FRIEND):
I chose to write my feelings about Charles Bronson. I first started to read one of Charlie's books after I had 'hit a low' in life. I was in the media a lot after I gave my story of the abuse I suffered in the British Army; the ten days I was locked away and taken prisoner by the Army

and in basic words 'tortured'. I told my part of my story to the world and it is a day I shall never regret; after all, it was the only bit of justice I got.

I knew what it was like to be a prisoner and I felt that after this experience my life would never change. I could see no way out of the deep depression I was in and I felt I was the only person to be feeling like this.

That is when I decided to start reading about other people's lives. I went to a local book store and the first book that captured my view was one by Charles Bronson. I looked at the book and decided to take this one, and that is what I did. I took the book home and started to read it over the next few days. It was a book I couldn't put down. It was interesting and very inspiring and I already wanted to read more about this man. I started to read more and more about Charlie and I could see what a gifted person this man was. He was a great writer and artist and his work seemed to 'put me on a high' without the need for medication. I was amazed that this man was behind bars and the more I read the more I got angry that he had been in prison for all those years and yet he had such gifts that were astounding. His books and artwork gave me hope that I also may be strong enough to turn my life around, and that I also may have gifts I could use to help and inspire others.

People may say, "But your situation is different", and to that I would answer, "Yes I may not have been in prison, but I was a prisoner." A prisoner is locked away from the world and given no hope that the door may open and they may walk free outside; they can't go where they decide and they can't feel the fresh air on their face. A prisoner is a number, and treated just like that! It seems their name has no meaning and they feel less human than the person that walks free. I would tell anyone to do an experiment for a short time and take a day of their lives and let another human being take their life for a day and lock them up for 24 hours. I would then ask that person to then ask the question, "What is a prisoner?"

I also suffered from Post Traumatic Stress Disorder just like Charles and I know that this is something that doesn't just go away overnight. It is etched in the memory of that person for life. It is bad enough being free and having that condition, but I really don't know how Charles copes being locked away. That is like 'rubbing salt in the wound'. I know that if I was still a prisoner I would truly have 'gone mad' by now. I feel that Charles Bronson holds such a great strength and courage that is very inspiring. It is this inspiration that kept me going. To think that this man has been locked away for all that time and yet he can turn out such a remarkable gift is amazing. I know that he has turned his life around and he has done more than what a free man can do. I know of men who don't do a single thing and they get praise from the highest places. Charles has shown a gift of writing and art that wasn't just for him, but was to help others with his wisdom and inspiration.

What I have learnt about this man brings a tear to my eye. To think that 'monsters' who ruined my life walk free and will go on to harm people and yet they lock Charles up all that time and don't seem able to admit the mistakes they have made, well that is horrendous and horrifying to think that they can take Charles' life for so long and not just lock up a gentleman but also lock up a great skill; it is beyond my thinking. This man is worthy of that title 'gentleman'. He is kind and gentle, and even though people have caused him so much pain he still doesn't hold a grudge and talks like a true gentleman. That in itself is worth a medal. This man can help others in society and he should be free. My God, they have taken enough from him and I admire how calm he remains about it all. It shows how mellow he is just by that. I know if I were in his shoes I would have a temper like a lion. Yet he doesn't; he instead has given people his writing and art and he shows a skill of great communication with people that he could use to help young offenders keep on the straight and narrow. I know they would be able to relate to Charles and he has a way with words that I know they would respect. He has a gift to society and they are keeping this gift from us.

People can be so blind to what goes on in their own country and it seems they want to be like sheep, and what they are told they will believe. It is time people opened their eyes and made their own minds up and not listen to 'small talk'. People need to make a stand for this man and help him, and see how he has helped many. If he is so bad, why does he have friends and support everywhere from people from all walks of life? I am proof of the effects of his books and work. He has inspired me to come out of my depression and write myself. I am now working on a book that will be published about my experiences. I want to thank this man for his gifts that I only wish society could share; he has changed my life. So why should he still be locked away when it is clear he is a better man than some that walk free?

PIERCE MAGUIRE (SUPPORTER):
It's a disgrace how Charles Bronson is still in jail whilst rapists and paedos roam the streets - they should rot in jail. Surely he can be of much more benefit helping youngsters defer from violent crimes?

STACY MAGUIRE (SUPPORTER):
Look at the mess you made when you didn't release Reggie Kray. What he did was a long time ago.

JOE-BOY MAINNIE (SUPPORTER):
Its time to let Charlie out, this is beyond a joke.

CAROLE MANLOW (SUPPORTER):
I'm with you 100%, don't give in.

HOWARD MARKS (FRIEND):
Charlie considers his life as a positive gift not some kind of curse and sees every day as a victory. Now, that's amazing for a man in his position.

LEE MARKS (SUPPORTER):
Let this man make his peace with God.

IAN MASON (SUPPORTER):
Feel so sorry for Charlie. Get him out now.

SUE MAY (FRIEND):
What can I say? If the public read media reports about Charlie then maybe one would think he was mad, bad and violent. Charlie is none of these! Okay, he has been a 'hothead', he has fought the system, but take time to research Charlie's life since he first went into prison many years ago and you will see why he has behaved as he has, and any right-minded person will surely wonder what sort of a system it is that can treat a human being in such a barbaric way. I was wrongly convicted in 1993 and given a life sentence - so began my nightmare journey through the prison system. I first heard about Charlie through another female prisoner in Durham Jail. I began writing to Charlie in 1993. In fact he used to send me his handwritten notes, which I computerised with cartoons and these eventually went into his book *Legends* - a great book of Charlie's memories and recollections of the various characters he had come across in those early years of his journey through the many prisons he was sent to. I know Charlie has 'lost it' from time to time - but he is a product of the system! He has done all his jail the hard way - BUT he is a compassionate and caring human being. Not long after I was sent to Durham Prison, a very hard jail, my beloved mum died. Charlie wrote me a letter and it was on the strength of that letter that I knew for certain Charlie Bronson was NOT a bad man - far from it; foolish maybe at times, but a man with a big heart. I will never forget Charlie's thoughtful words at that time. Since then I have kept in touch with Charlie - oh yes, ticking him off when he gets into trouble (taking hostages, etc.), but having been incarcerated myself for 12 years, I can understand how frustrating and damaging a prison environment can be. I think Charlie knows now that you cannot 'beat' the system. However, the system should hang its head in shame when you look at how Charlie has been treated. You cannot lock an individual up for years in very oppressive conditions and expect that person to 'reform' or to change. Violence breeds violence and cruelty will not make a better person.

Charlie has been treated cruelly. Society needs to be made aware of what goes on in some of our prisons.

Charlie Bronson has great respect for women and children, and he has never killed anyone - yet he is refused release! What kind of society are we when an individual can be 'lost' indefinitely in the prison system? Yes, Charlie's past record can be criticised - but in the past years he has been calm and non-confrontational. Let's start to give him credit for that - for his books and artwork, for his fund-raising too. He deserves a life free from the confines of prison - he deserves to be allowed to regain his life. Charlie could be a 'mentor' to troubled kids on the out!

LEANNE MAYERS (FRIEND):

Hello, my name is Leanne Marie Mayers, I'm from Bournemouth in Dorset. I first learnt about Charlie in the *Inside Time* when I was in HMP Peterborough. I wrote to him and after getting a reply I really wanted to know more about him so I went to the library to get his book *Charles Bronson*. I'm not and never have been one for reading books but his I just couldn't put down. I totally understand what Charlie was going through in his earlier years in prison, as I was quite the same in a way. I've been in and out of jail since I was 16, and I'm now 22. Every time I've come out it's never taken more than 2 weeks for me to be nicked for fighting behind my door with loss of everything. But there comes a point when we say enough's enough and I personally think, well I know, Charlie has come to that point. Rather than trying to help Charlie with his anger or issues with a counsellor or courses, the system just isolates him so he's out of sight, out of mind, so to speak. I can tell from reading his book that he is now in a totally different state of mind and has been for a long time. Charlie is a very kind man with a very big heart and deserves at least one REAL chance. I know it will take time, but by his parole date (2010) if the system actually works with him for a change, I have faith that he will be freed. When he is free he can and will help a lot of young people stay out of jail by working with them. I know this will please Charlie a lot. You see most young people have someone they look up to and like myself Charlie is one of them. Charlie don't want them in and out of jail all their lives like him. He's always telling me to "stay out and win". I'm sure he would persuade a lot of teens it's no way to live, he doesn't want it for no one. With him being so anti-drugs that would most definitely stop so many youngsters turning to drugs in and out of jail. I would love someone like Charlie to be around to put my children along the right path. If only I'd had someone like Charlie to tell me that this life gets you absolutely nowhere, and although I'm in jail now Charlie's influence has certainly given me the push I need to stay out and win. So just think of the influence he would and could have on people if he was out. It's so wrong that years after he done what he done he's still in isolation. When I think of him, at night mainly, I wonder what he's doing. I picture him, such a good man at heart, locked in a cage all alone having his food through a hole in the door. This brings tears to my eyes every time. He needs rehabilitation to prepare him for release, however near or far that is. My heart bleeds for him. Along with this I'm writing to the governor to beg him to begin some sort of process to prepare Charlie for his release, whenever that may be. Charlie has most definitely paid for what he done. It's not fair to keep him in that dark place where he is now. I love you with all my heart, Charlie. I'll never give up on you until I get you out!

MARK MEASURES (SUPPORTER):
Time to let Charlie out.

CHRISTIAN MELLING (SUPPORTER):
He's the perfect guy to go for a pint with. Free Bronson.

JODIE MENZIES (FRIEND):
I'm a horse rider. I don't know anything about boxing at all, but I do know who Charlie Bronson is. He's a good friend of my dad's. We're always getting letters and drawings from him. He draws me special horse cards and likes to hear about my stable work. "Get out in the

433

fresh air and be healthy," he tells me. It's just a shame he can't practise that himself. Hopefully I'll be able to take him to the stables one day. He may not have an equestrian interest but I'm sure he'll enjoy the view of the countryside. It's a better view than brick walls and a thick mesh fence.

REDD MENZIES (FRIEND):

"Over-punished" - if there is such a word then it applies to Charlie Bronson, a man who has been punished excessively in comparison to child abusers, rapists and murderers. Not one of these mentioned offences applies to this man, yet his sentence has been extended further than any person that would have done all three.

We are talking of a man who has, on many occasions, admitted the wrongdoings in his life. He has turned his life around and poses no threat to society. Charlie and myself have written to each other for many years and met on prison visits many times. Our conversations are not that of the next 'bank job' or act of 'thuggery' but genuine conversations no different to any two friends passing the time over a beer at their local pub. He has a passionate interest in his successful charity work, raising large sums of money for many a needy cause through his artwork and exercise regime.

His interest travels further a field with his encouragement of the activities of any people outside the walls of the prison, be it charity walks, sporting events or just life in general. In our society today the release of Charlie Bronson would be somewhat of an asset. A man who would assist people of all ages, colour and creed to stay away from drug culture and its lawless route and health dangers. A man who would help would-be offenders by steering them to develop themselves and express themselves through more meaningful activities. A man with whom women, children and the weak will be safe. A man from whom the strong can learn. A man ... a man who has served his punishment and has earned the freedom he deserves.

SABRING MENZIES (FRIEND):

I've grown up with Charlie Bronson as part of my life. My dad has been friends with him through being friendly with ex-boxers that Charlie has known.

I study 'Sepoy Karate' a mixed martial art, something that Charlie has encouraged me in at many a time.

When I was beaten into 3rd place in an open tournament in Winchester I was devastated. Charlie found it almost amusing. "Learn to walk - then run!! Lose with dignity not anger!! Let losing be your past, make your future stronger!!" I saw these as wise words and have benefited from them. Charlie gives me a lift with my karate, always trying to get me to go one step further each time.

As for what is said of him in the papers, I believe there is more truth in Andy Capp!!!

STELLA MENZIES (FRIEND):

My family have been in contact with Charles Bronson for many years now. His letters through our mailbox are accepted the same as any other friend in any other town. My husband has visited Charlie several times and has always returned home in good spirits. Some while ago I was unfortunate enough to go through some treatment for breast cancer. During this time I received personal letters offering strong support and logical guidance through my trying time.

The support offered was very strong and very emotional; it was also very much appreciated. A madman? A psychopath? My letters gave no indication of any of these. These descriptions are used by the media to make a mundane story slightly interesting. Should Charlie Bronson be freed, and I think he should be, then he would be certainly be welcome in my home with no fear of threat or intimidation.

MICHELLE AND KITCH (FRIENDS):

Ask the question to the over 30s - who is Charles Bronson? Most will say a famous actor from the 'Death Wish' films - correct! But that is not the Charles Bronson, aka Michael Peterson, that Michelle and I have gotten to know over the years. He is not a rapist, paedophile or even murderer. His initial crime was armed robbery - that doesn't justify 32 years at her majesty's pleasure (over three-quarters of that sentence spent in solitary). He did, in 1999, take a hostage during a prison siege, and on reflection his action at that time was not in his best interest. All of us in life have made mistakes - time changes people and Charles Bronson is no exception to that rule. News programmes tell us daily that our prisons are overcrowded. Now it gives the Home Secretary the perfect opportunity to release him. He has paid for his crime, more than anyone else in the prison system, and enough is enough - give him his freedom! I'm sure Charles won't mind that I use a couple of lines to highlight the case for the release on health grounds of Ronnie Biggs from Belmarsh Jail. It was he, over a few drinks in Rio, who told us to read Charles's book and on his recommendation we purchased *Bronson* and we could not put it down. It gave us - average Joe Public, which Chelle and I are - a very rare and unique insight into the life and times of Britain's most notorious and infamous lifer and that book changed our world. And for those that have not heard of it or read it, I am sure it is still available in paperback by Blake Publishing Ltd - please read it today! Chelle and I have every letter from him. I asked if he would sign our book for us. He refused to sign an autograph - he believed it showed emotion and a sign of weakness. This is not the same man today. His signed photos and artwork to raise money for much needed causes around the world. He has changed and the world needs to know this.

It's been a very low time for us. Charles got to hear about it through the grapevine and the next minute we received a beautiful card and letter of support from him, which was gratefully received. Michelle and I look forward to meeting him on the outside. As for the saying "life begins at 40", we hope that Charles will not have to do 40 years before he is released! We will have the Black Russians on ice for ya! On a final note, to be asked to write a paragraph in this book has been an honour and a privilege.

PATTI L. MILLER (SUPPORTER):
This man has overpaid his debt! It's past time to set him free! God bless you Charles.

ROSE MILLIGAB (SUPPORTER):
If he was a mass murderer he would be free by now. That's our justice system for you.

MARK JAMES MONTGOMERY (SUPPORTER):
Murderers don't even serve this long. Free Charles Bronson NOW!!!

ROGER MORGAN (SUPPORTER):
This is absolutely crazy - why is Charlie being treated this way when people who really need locking up are walking the streets? Let him out!!!

AYSHA MORRIS (SUPPORTER):
All the best Charlie. Hope the tit-heads let you out soon.

DALANYA MORRIS (Dee) (FRIEND):
I have known Charlie for over ten years. During this time we have got to know each other extremely well and have become good 'solid' pals. We trust and respect each other and are loyal to one another, which is a rarity in people in this day and age. It is because of this I class Charlie as a member of my family and know that he shares the same views about me. I am also good friends with his mum Eira, who I can only describe as a lovely lady with great strength and spirit. How would I describe Charlie? Positive, optimistic, thoughtful, respectful, caring, intelligent and very creative. You would never believe that he has suffered what he has, and continues to, in his current situation. My pal's situation guts me, deeply. People who have committed murders, child killers, rapists and re-offending paedophiles are walking free on our streets. Yet Charlie, having killed no one, still remains locked away and has done for 33 years. The media love to describe him as the hardest and most dangerous. Regarding

Charlie, what I find to be the hardest are the conditions that he has to endure; the constant everyday struggle to remain focused and positive with a constructive mind rather than a destructive one. Charlie has managed to achieve this through his great inner strength and courage and the love and support of his family and close loyal friends. Despite his loneliness, isolation and conditions that he has endured for so, so many years, Charlie is always the first to greet you with a smile, and with his great sense of humour always ensures that you too are smiling and remain that way! What I find the most dangerous are the penal, justice and probation systems, the systems that control people's lives, and the power that they can have over them. Charlie is still very positive and caring, despite the fact that he has for over 8 years now not been able to feel the warmth and affection from a motherly hug (due to closed visits), yet he remains warm and affectionate. His personality, nature and behaviour have for many years been created and described very publicly. Much of this was done by the media, strangers and people that did not and do not know Charlie. Charlie, however, is not given the chance to speak so freely and publicly, yet who knows him better than anyone - surely that is Charlie himself? If he was given the chance to speak freely and publicly, then people would know the real person, the real nature of him and the real reason for his behaviour.

As a good friend of Charlie I am happy to describe him and his personality and offer him my full support in his bid for freedom. I do not support his bid for freedom because he is my pal, I support him as I believe his case is unjust and unfair. It was due to my strong feeling of the unfairness and injustice that we have become such good pals. Nobody is perfect; we all make mistakes. How we are judged for them and what bigger price we pay for these mistakes are more often than not out of our control. Charlie has made mistakes; he will freely admit it. However, I firmly believe he received his judgement and has more than paid the price for them!! Many others feel this way too, not just Charlie's friends and family but lawyers, screws and strangers; not fans or fanatics but ordinary working-class professional people who are disgusted and appalled by the conditions he endures and the injustice that he has to suffer. Many too would also agree that he has paid the price, yet no one it seems is willing to - or has the courage to - stand up and admit this error. For this reason no one is made to stand up and correct it. For over 28 years my good friend Charlie has been kept caged in solitary; caged like an animal. Yet despite this he is far from being one. If I had to describe Charlie as an animal I would compare him to a giraffe, as they out of all the animals have the largest heart. We know the justice system is wrong, we know it's unjust, unfair and corrupt, yet we don't have the courage to stand up and say so. All the fight for 'freedom of speech' and then we don't have the ability to use it!!!

Evil people that have killed and darkened children's lives walk and associate freely around him, yet his isolation remains. Charlie never has and never will want to darken children's lives. He wants to enlighten and inspire them and he is a great inspiration. They would listen to him; he knows what he's talking about. He has endured it all: physical violence, isolation, starvation, no affection, betrayal … and the list goes on and on. Despite all these adversities Charlie's inner strength has managed to overcome them all and come out stronger and wiser each time. Charlie always remains in great spirits. He loves to laugh and loves to make people laugh. He does this not just with his personality but also with his very creative and humorous art. Although his art and personality remain very humorous, the conditions and the unfairness of his case remain far from that! But because of Charlie's nature, whilst everyone should be thinking of Charlie, he is thinking of everyone! He does art for charity and inspires and supports so many others. He is greatly trying to make a positive difference, not just in his own life but also in the lives of so many others. Many are young people who look to Charlie for advice, support and guidance. This he readily gives and happily too.

Charlie doesn't want sympathy, he never has. During and after visiting Charlie he tries to ensure that you don't feel any pity or sadness for him, although it is very difficult not to. Coming to see my good friend and just having a small window to see him through with thick steel bars in between it is a great pity and makes me too begin to imagine the 'coldness', pain and misery that Charlie must feel. Yet there is Charlie, smiling away happily, pouring me a coffee in between the bars and persuading me to have another one of his chocolate muffins.

After a visit with Charlie you feel lifted, positive and your stomach hurts where you have laughed so much. He has so much enthusiasm and spirit. He is so down to earth and witty - a unique, genuine, good character. I just wish that I could make as many people as aware as the media manage to. I wish that people would take notice, spare some of their time, thought or consideration for Charlie, and his case and conditions that he continues to suffer. Are we all really that wrapped up dealing with our everyday mistakes on the outside that we don't spare the time and thought for others on the inside, severely suffering due to their past ones? We need to support Charlie. He needs to be given the chance to prove his rehabilitation. He deserves association with people, he deserves the chance to prove himself and he more than deserves a hug from his mum. They deserve to spend quality time together - not drinking between bars but leaning against one on the same side!!!

I hope and pray that you get the freedom you deserve and I look forward to the day when I don't need a VO to come and see ya. Stay strong Charlie. Stay smiling ... I'm behind you all the way!

GUY MORRIS (SUPPORTER):
The system is abhorrently wrong letting Charles rot in jail whilst rapists and nonces go free. Sickening!!!

HELEN MORRIS (SUPPORTER):
Let Charlie free. He's done his time. You wouldn't treat an animal this way.

JACKIE MORRIS (SUPPORTER):
Don't let the turkeys get you down. Stoned at the moment, get back to you soon!

MICHAEL MORRIS (SUPPORTER):
Free Charles Bronson, Has this man not proved enough he is no danger to anyone??

MIKE MORRIS (SUPPORTER):
Imagine yourself in his position!

ELLIOTT GEORGE RICHARD MUDDYMAN (SUPPORTER):
I know that you weren't a bad man - I am 14, just read your book, unbelievably incredible.

D. J. MURRAY (SUPPORTER):
Good luck, Mr Bronson.

CHRIS NAPIER (SUPPORTER):
Free Charles. 34 years is terrible. I could do a worse crime than Charles did and still be out of prison before him. Let him live the rest of his life a free man. Do the right thing.

JOHNNY NASH (FRIEND):
I find it revolting that Chaz Bronson is looked at as someone who is a lost cause. Brady - yes, lost cause. Maudsley - yes, lost cause. Huntley - yes, lost cause. Bronson is not one of these. The man is an artist, poet, author, son, father and brother who killed nobody. Why can nothing be done for him?

Look what happened when Jimmy Boyle was released. Chaz can make good legitimate money easily now; crime is over. I find it amazing that people think men like us would tolerate a dangerous psycho running around hurting normal, good folk - we would NOT have it, let alone support the bastard. That's proof enough that Bronson does not come into that league. Who has the right to keep a man in a piss-hole until he rots? Who?!

DARREN NEADS (SUPPORTER):
Get this guy out NOW!!!!

437

LEE PLUG NEVIN (SUPPORTER):
Hey how's things? I don't know anybody that can be as strong as Charles Bronson ... rock on.

DAN NEWMAN (SUPPORTER):
Free Bronson.

STEVEN NEWMAN (aka Lenny McLean) (SUPPORTER):
Do the right thing ....

JENNIFER NEWTON (SUPPORTER):
Outrageous that Charlie is still in prison after all these years. Free him now!

RICHARD MARK NOWELL (SUPPORTER):
Enough is enough. Free Charles.

BRIAN NUNN (SUPPORTER):
Why should a man who has never murdered, raped or molested any man, woman or child be locked away in solitary confinement for so long? If you had killed someone you would be out by now, Charlie.

MIKE O'HAGAN (FRIEND):
In the early '90s BT1314 Bronson arrived at HMP Wakefield and was immediately located in the Segregation Unit. He came in a body belt, which was only used on dangerous and violent inmates. With his past history it was certainly warranted. After a few days in my role as Wing Principal Officer I went to his cell and had a lengthy conversation as to how he saw his future and how he spent his time in solitary other than working out. He didn't know how to, so I gave him a sketch pad and coloured pencils and lots of encouragement. The cartoonist was born. It took over his days and he spent hours working at them. His whole attitude changed. He became positive and we built a rapport, which surprised everybody, including some at the Home Office. He spent several years at HMP Wakefield and never gave me any cause for concern. I was well known to run a firm but fair regime, and Bronson responded to that. His problems occurred elsewhere, with him eventually receiving a life sentence. The national press love to refer to him as "Britain's Most Dangerous Prisoner" but this is not the case anymore. Nobody knows better than him that he has deserved a lot of what has happened to him, but after so many years of good behaviour surely he deserves a chance to prove himself. Contrary to popular belief, he has not killed anybody; he never hurt his hostages. The press never mention the fact that he raises a lot of money for a children's hospice. I know this man better than most in the Prison Service and it is high time he was taken out of his present conditions and given an opportunity to prove he means what he says. I am now retired but we write to each other and I have been up to Wakefield to see him. I have no doubt he no longer poses the threat he once did. There is no logic in him being kept in solitary for this amount of time compared to many prisoners in the system today. He deserves and should be given a chance.

JAMIE O'KEEFE (FRIEND):
I'm not going to begin by comparing different imprisonment tariffs and crimes in order to justify why Charlie Bronson should be released, because that's been done, and although it is a valid and important point it has proved not to be enough to make those in power listen. We all know that those committing sex crimes and murder have spent relatively short periods of time in prison for their horrendous crimes, some not even serving a third of the time Charlie has been inside. So what is it that Charlie has done that warrants 33 years inside so far?
I would like to change your thinking and pose some questions that will make you delve deeper into Charlie's situation to gain understanding and knowledge specific to this case.
The first thing I wish to put to you is, why should we keep Charlie in prison and what were

his crimes?

Most of you reading this won't even be able to accurately answer these simple questions. Write down now exactly why you think Charlie needed to serve 33 years to date. You will struggle with this one. While you're pondering on that I will run some other things by you.

The resources that are needed to keep Charlie locked up in solitary confinement must cost the taxpayer at least £1,000 a week. For this Charlie gets an 8ftx12ft bedsit; no double glazing or basic luxuries like carpets, cable TV, Internet, phone, central heating.

In comparison, on the outside, a man of Charlie's age who couldn't find employment would get his bedsit paid for and income support of about £50 per week, half price bus and tube travel, and could go and lie on a beach all day if he wished. This has become a lifestyle for many people in Britain today.

Then you have Charlie Bronson, who doesn't want the state to finance his day-to-day living, and wishes to work and pay his way in society, but is forbidden to experience life and people due to his confinement in solitary.

Charlie should at least be given the opportunity to work on the outside in a normal job to work towards paying for his day-to-day living. This would give him a chance to reintegrate into the community and prove his worth to society. Let's face it, if a single man on the outside was claiming £1,000 a week to live in the squalor of a bedsit, there would be an outcry from the taxpayers. We would say things like: make the lazy git get a job and support himself. If the lad was physically fit and had not had an unlawful occurrence in over 8 years, then there would be many agencies and companies willing to give him work. So what is the difference between the lad on the outside and Charlie, who's on the inside?

This takes me back to my earlier posed questions. Why is Charles Bronson still locked up? You are still struggling to answer this, aren't you? Yet if I asked you what any of the following infamous names were known for, you could tell me, names such as Myra Hindley, Ian Brady, the Yorkshire Ripper, Adolph Hitler, Gary Glitter, and the list goes on. But you still don't know what it is that Charlie Bronson has done that is so bad that he needs to be in solitary confinement and still has not been released after serving 33 years.

He has for the last 8 years been focusing on becoming a positive role model and works towards inspiring young people to turn their back on prison life and a criminal lifestyle. To put the last 8 years into perspective, I will give you some examples of other people who we trust with our lives and to live among us within our community and how long it takes to reach that status within each profession. Doctor 7 years, dentist 5 years, airline pilot 18 months, fireman 16 weeks, midwife 4 years, bus driver 6 weeks, driving instructor 1-2 years, train driver 1 year, school teaching assistant 1 year, ambulance technicians 20 weeks, school caretaker - no qualifications needed, door supervisor 30 hours, MP member of parliament - no formal qualifications required, prison officer 8 weeks.

All these roles and professions have given people an opportunity to make changes to their lives. We put our trust in these people and know nothing about them on a personal level.

Well Charlie has spent longer than any of these people in their chosen professions proving that he has made changes in his life. His 8-year apprenticeship of being a good role model who has steered away from problems has proved that he is stable and ready to make his contribution to society.

Imagine any teenager being confined to their bedroom in solitary confinement for 8 days, without a computer, no Internet, no phone, no cable TV, no ipod/mp3 player, etc. They would become as lifeless as their surroundings. Motivation and the will to do anything would decrease. That's just in 8 days. It doesn't bear thinking about 8 weeks, 8 months or 8 years. Is this how we prepare people in the UK to create a better society for the good of all? So what is it that they are trying to do to Charlie? I don't have the answer but I can at least help make you think more about it and see how unjust the whole situation is.

Another reason I am adding my support here is that I am very much into positive role models, especially those that have come from, or have had difficult and challenging pasts or experiences and have made positive change. That's how I view Charlie - a positive role model, which is why I was happy for my sons to appear and help him out with the 2007 version of his book *Training in Solitary*.

I am lucky enough to be able to see through the bullshit and unfair representations of Charlie that are more often reported in the media by those trying to profit on his name. My view of Charlie goes back to the '60s when I was a kid growing up in Bethnal Green, East London. It was back in the day when there was no Internet or Blue Tooth, no mobile phones or calculators, no video recorders or personal music players. We had a TV with three black and white channels and a pay-per-view coin box on the back to charge us for watching it.

It was a drug-free environment where we had different role models to the Americanised gangster rappers that the youngsters of today admire. In my days as a child the role models for me were people like Charles Atlas and Popeye, and that's how I see Charlie today - a modern-day Popeye that eats porridge instead of spinach and serves as inspiration for youngsters who want to train in a healthy, drug-free way. It's a part of our lost youth that we all reflect on and wish that was part of today's youth culture. Charlie has more than proved himself to be a good role model for the youth of today. He is anti-drugs and anti-crime and has a lot to offer.

You have had time to reflect on the question I posed at the beginning, so I will finish by asking you to make a list of the pros and cons of whether Charlie should remain locked up. You will soon see that there are no factual reasons that warrant him staying in prison.

TOM O'LEARY (SUPPORTER):
Release Charlie, he's done enough time inside to run the system himself. He's a great bloke with great character. Or at least think about recat'ing him so he's off 23-hour bang-up.

JAMIE OTTO (SUPPORTER):
This man should have been out years ago!!! The Home Office are the real criminal - they have stolen his life!!!

KRISTEN PAGE (SUPPORTER):
I've followed Charles Bronson for years and think he has been treated unfairly for most of his life. He deserves to be free.

MICHAEL PAINI (SUPPORTER):
34 years? It's ridiculous. Anyone would think he's a child killer! Let him out!

SEAN PALMER (SUPPORTER):
The biggest crime of all is being done by the government by keeping this man incarcerated!

BOGMAN BLUEQUARTZ PALMJAGUAR (SUPPORTER):
Mr Bronson is another example of why societies must be governed by all responsible citizens rather than corrupt elites.

MARK PARKER (SUPPORTER):
Enough is enough. Let Mr Bronson out and admit you've made a mistake by holding him for this long.

EILEEN PARRY (CHARLIE'S AUNT):
Charlie Bronson - who's he? Well he's my nephew and no one knows him better than me. He was always in my house when he was a young lad. He grew into a very handsome young man. All the women were after him. Then when he was older he started to go round with the wrong crowd, all older than him. Then the big blow came to our family when he was sentenced to 7 years. We were all devastated. We thought he would be out after 3½ years but it never happened. He's been inside now for 33 years only due to himself. He thought he could beat the system but he couldn't. We know he's been naughty inside but let's be honest, he shouldn't be in there all this time. He's not a rapist, murderer or paedophile. He's never hurt anyone.

He has taken a lot of 'beatings' inside so he's retaliated. That's why he's in there so long. Even some of the screws say he shouldn't be in there. He's done the crime and done too much time. Surely they can't keep him in there forever? He is a very talented man. He can live an honest life just with his art. He would not be a danger to anyone. But they keep calling him 'the most dangerous man in Britain'. I can't see that. What about all these child killers, bombers - that's what I call dangerous. They should never be let out. They should be hanged. But they let them out to do it again. If they treat him with respect he'll give them respect.

His mother is my sister and she is 77 this year. She has lost 33 years of his life. Surely she's entitled to a few years with him? She can't even have a decent visit with him as he's locked in a cage. She can't give him a hug and a kiss. It's disgusting he's locked up like an animal in a cage. For God's sake he's a human being, not an animal. Where's Huntley? - roaming around the visiting room, which should never be allowed, and Charlie's in a cage. Come on, something is radically wrong here. We want him home with us. We're all getting older and we want some special time with him. That's not asking too much is it? He's done more time than a killer; he needs a break now, not in years to come. Let him lead a decent life and be happy and with his family. I can tell you that if he had killed anyone we would not be asking for his release, we would have disowned him long ago. It's heartbreaking for his mum and the rest of us. We have a big family and we would look after him. He wouldn't be a danger and he never has been. If someone took beatings like he has you wouldn't let them get away with it. So come on, let's be civilised about this, Let the man free so he can get on with his life. He doesn't hate anyone. He's a heart of gold. But he doesn't like people that kill or hurt women or children and druggies. He even tells me off for smoking. I wouldn't smoke in front of him, as I know he doesn't like it. There's lots of other things we would catch up on. Be nice to take him out for meals. Something he's missed for years. Take him on a nice holiday. So when they free him from that bloody cage we can do something that's human. We all love him very much. We need him home with us. We can start planning things then. But as it is now we don't know if he'll ever come home. They are surely taking their time. He has kept himself clear of trouble for a long time now. I think he's realised he can't beat them. So why doesn't the government sort his case out? They should sort out all the wicked ones. He's not a bad man as they make him out to be. The media put stories in the papers about him that are completely untrue. Don't know where they get them from. But we phone the prison up and ask about it and they say he's fine, he hasn't done anything. So why do people make these stories up? People read this and they think, oh it's that mad man again. But he's not mad. If he was he would never be able to draw like he does. He has a brilliant sense of humour, very clever. He could make a lot of money. He's very artistic. He would make a very good Home Secretary as he would clear the streets of all the wrongdoers; he'd say lock them up. So they have the wrong man here locked in a cage when there's thousands worse than him walking the streets. Well we are all waiting for the day when Charlie comes home. Let it be soon. He's got lots of cousins born since he's been inside so we'll have one hell of a party. Roll on the day. It can't be soon enough.

God bless Charlie.

SIMON ANTHONY PETER (SUPPORTER):
Free the man now.

EIRA PETERSON (CHARLIE'S MOTHER):
I've not been allowed to kiss or give Charlie a hug since 2001. He's been in prison for a long time, he's done 35 years now. I really think it's time for him to be released now. He's done a crime and done his time in prison. He's never hurt a child or any women and he's always been a good son to me. If only the system would give him a chance to show he could make a new life for himself, live a good life and show people he can do it. I'll always be there for him. He's in Wakefield and they all treat him with respect and he gives them respect. I pray that he will be out soon, before I pass over. He wasn't allowed out for his father's funeral and I thought that was bad on the prison's part. He also lost his brother John and his aunty Pamela, along

with two sets of grandparents. I'm sure he could help a lot of teenagers to keep out of trouble and live a good life. He has written books and is great at art. His IQ is very high. They seem to let people out that should never walk the streets as they come out to commit the same crimes with children and kill again. So why don't you give him a chance to prove himself? I've travelled around the country to visit him. He is always behind bars on my visits. It's about time I could sit around a table on my visits to him. I love Charles and I want to spend some time with him, as I'm in my 70s now. So why not release him soon? I know Charles better than anyone. We have always been close. All the family are there for him as well. So please look into his case.

MIKE PETERSON (CHARLIE'S SON):
Let my Dad out
He's done his time
I want a pint with him
It's been too long
What's the sense in
Keeping him locked up?
What's he doing serving life?
It's a complete farce
Let him come home
There's a lot worse than Dad
Walking our streets
Let the man out.

WILF PINE (FRIEND):
Both myself, Tel Currie and most of the other 'CHAPS' have had our ups and downs with the man the public call 'Britain's most violent man', a man us little mob know simply as Charlie or Chaz. Considering his position and the way he is being brutalised it's hardly surprising he gets frustrated, don't you agree? Most people can just pick the phone up and resolve a situation in minutes; Chaz can't do that, the result being that his imagination festers and tiny things can blow up. People must understand this because not many people could cope with his existence. Why on earth he is being forced to live the life of a fucking nonce or grass is not something that will be disclosed to working-class rascals like us; this sort of thing comes from Sir Rupert and Lord Sebastian at the top.
There are only a few people who really know Charlie and, despite all the claims from wannabes, fakes, plastic gangsters and good weather supporters, there are only a few hard-core friends and supporters! This is a long-term battle, like the one with Ronnie Biggs; it's a constant, intense fight. As far as I know, Tel Currie, Mike Biggs, Mike Gray and Roy Shaw are now Ronnie Biggs' only regular visitors. Compare that to when Ronnie returned and EVERYONE wanted to tell everyone else they had visited and he was their pal. I can tell you, these good weather pals are NOT what we need
now for Chaz, Ronnie or any other prisoner who has done his time or should not be in there at all. WE need a strong, solid, intense, consistent fight.

BEN PLAYFORD (SUPPORTER):
I read Charlie's book on fitness and it was a true inspiration. This man needs release, He is intelligent and can be a role model to many. Much respect, sir.

ANDREW POOLE (SUPPORTER):
Free this man. It is outrageous that he be kept like an animal.

REECE POTTS (SUPPORTER):
This man sits in solitary while paedophiles and child killers are in normal cells, some even with TVs! This is a disgrace.

NOSHER POWELL (FRIEND):
It's a funny thing with Charlie Bronson. Despite the tragic and brutal environment he is enslaved in, he always makes you come away laughing. I don't know how anyone in that kind of hell can make people roar with laughter but he does. Charlie has some good supporters around him and I think at some point he has fallen out with all of them! Ha! Ha!
But here is a man, full of talent for all sorts of things, stuck behind concrete and iron. What good will that do?
I was the main MC and sometimes ref in the golden age of unlicensed. I'm talking from about 1975 to 1986. These were the days when Roy 'Pretty Boy' Shaw and Lenny McLean had virtually declared war and their three epic fights will go down in folklore. There were also good fighters like Cliff Fields and Johnny Waldren who both knocked Lenny spark out cold twice! Nobody wanted to fight Cliff Fields; he was without a doubt 'The Guv'nor'.
Sometimes I think what a shame it is that Charlie Bronson was not out there in the unlicensed circuit. He and Joey Pyle would've made a great team. He looked up to Joe like a dad and he certainly would not disrespect Joe like he may have done some others. Imagine my famous announcement "BRING ON THE LIONS!!!" and having Charlie walking down one side and say Lenny down the other!!! Who knows how good he could've been.
But now he has a much bigger fight on his hands ... BUT one thing's for sure, THERE WILL BE NO TOWELS BEING THROWN IN!

MARTYN PRETTY (SUPPORTER):
He did not actually kill anyone, and seeing as the government always seem to let the murderers and rapists go, why not let Charlie go free?! Free Charlie!!!!!

ADAM PRIDMORE (SUPPORTER):
Where is the justice? He's never killed or committed rape, so let him be free. Murderers do 15 years and rapists do less. Where is the justice?

CLAIRE PRIOR (SUPPORTER):
Stop mentally torturing Charlie.

KENNETH E. PUGH (SUPPORTER):
Good luck! From your first block screw.
Charlie writes: I remember this screw, in Parkhurst seg block. He worked with an old screw, Tom Cotton. Two diamond screws - when screws were screws, tough but fair.

MARK EVERETT PUPLETT (SUPPORTER):
Done long enough in prison.

MARK ANDREW PURVIS (SUPPORTER):
Free Charles immediately.

KIRSTY QUIGLEY (SUPPORTER):
34 years too long. This talented man could be doing so much good work on the outside. Good Luck.

JANIC RAINE (SUPPORTER):
Mr Bronson has been in prison far too long. Free him.

SEAN RAINEY (SUPPORTER):
Let's hope that they do the decent thing and let Charles out.

CLAIRE RAPER (FRIEND):
I first got in touch with Charlie after reading *Silent Scream*. I wrote to him to ask if he would

donate one of his pieces of art to auction for a charity and he replied within 3 days, along with a signed drawing. 8 years later and we're good friends! We write each week and I visit whenever I get the chance. Charlie is a great bloke. I know everyone says stuff like he does a lot for charity, he loves kids and he's a nice guy, but they say it because it's true.

He's not the monster portrayed by the press. He's kind-hearted, generous, warm and humorous. He's always been there for me over the years; he's helped out in all kinds of situations that are too personal to go into. My husband Phil always takes me through to visit Charlie, and I usually take my youngest daughter Lilli with me to see him; she's 12 and she adores him. When she was little she used to write and send him little drawings; now she's nearly a teenager, so she doesn't write very often but she loves going to visit him, even though the conditions we see him in are harsh and unnecessary.

Charlie's changed a lot over the years I've known him. Now he's a lot calmer, a lot more mature. Years ago you could tell by the contents of his letters when he was upset or angry, and sometimes weeks would go by without me hearing from him. When he eventually did write he'd tell me he hadn't been able to get in touch because he'd been in bother for one thing or another and they had taken away his writing stuff as part of his punishment. Now he's so different; he's mellowed with age, he's more open and relaxed.

Now it's time he was released from prison. He's not a killer, nor a paedophile, and he never has nor ever will be a threat to women or children. I would trust Charlie with my life and the lives of my kids and grandkids. In the past he's made some mistakes and he's the first to admit it, but now he needs to be able to prove he's changed. How can he prove it though when he isn't given the chance? He has family and true friends who love him and see the person he really is. He has his art and poetry, he has ambition and dreams, just like anyone else, the only thing he doesn't have is his freedom. Let's hope he gets it soon and that the next book he writes will be about his life outside prison!

Charlie writes: Little Katie - one of my heroes of life. A true fighter and this baby does nothing but smile. It puts life into perspective. Katie, born 17 March 2007, 3lb 14ozs. Diagnosed with Aicardi Syndrome at 2 weeks old. Only affects girls, 300-500 cases worldwide (5 in the UK). Symptoms include cysts on the brain, seizures, scoliosis (curved spine), learning difficulties. There is no cure, only medication to control the seizures, which can occur 20 to 100 times per day. Katie has hip dysplasia and is blind in her left eye. She's gone through more in her short life than most do in a lifetime, but she's a fighter and is a happy, placid baby; she's a blessing.

LILLI RAPER (FRIEND):

My name is Lilli and I'm 12. My mum and dad are friends of Charlie. My mum has been writing to him since I was 5. When I was little I used to write to him and draw pictures for him because he always used to send drawings to me when he wrote to my mum. I go to see Charlie with my mum. I love going to see him because he always makes me laugh, but it's not nice where he is. Everybody else goes in the visiting room but we have to see Charlie on his own and we aren't even allowed in the same room as him, which is stupid because he wouldn't hurt us.

One time when we went to see him we went to get him some milkshake from the canteen. We saw that man who killed 2 little girls. That's not fair that he's in there where all the kids are visiting their dads but Charlie is on his own. We even have to sit on the table so we can see him through the bars in the wall. He always does us good drawings and he's funny, he tells jokes all the time. He helps loads of kids that are ill; he sends his drawings so they can be sold to people to make money for charity. He loves kids. When my brother's baby Katie was born, my mum sent Charlie a photo and he made a lovely picture with it and wrote 'Clare's Angel' on it for her. When he gets out of prison we're going to go to his party and then he's going to come to our house to see us. I can't wait. I hope it's soon.

ALAN RAYMENT (FRIEND):

I have been a regular writer and visitor to Charlie Bronson for some years now. I was introduced to Charlie through a very good friend of mine, Tony Simpson. I wrote to Charlie for many years and I first visited Charlie in HMP Wakefield on 29th December 2004. I was appalled by the way the visit took place. Charlie is kept in a cage, a prison within a prison. We were in one cell and Charlie was in another with bars separating us. I shook Charlie's hand and we got to know each other even more. We both share a passion for fitness and Charlie has given me excellent advice on my own training. I am a wheelchair user I had my left leg amputated in 1997 and my right let amputated in 1998 due to leg ulcers and massive MRSA infection. I have completed many races including the London Marathon in 2004 and I completed the gruelling 26.1 miles in my day chair. In 2004 I carried the Olympic Flame through London. "Pass the flame, unite the world" was the theme of Athens 2004 Olympic Torch Relay. I have completed various marathons, half marathons and 10k races; in 2005 I was the 1st person in the world to hand-cycle 500km from Vietnam to Cambodia, raising over twenty thousand pounds for disabled kids. I am now taking part in triathlons, including open water swimming. Triathlons are extremely hard for people with disabilities to take part in. My next big challenge is planned for 2008. I am going to hand-cycle from Land's End to John O'Groats, 925 miles in 17 days. I have helped Charlie put his *Solitary Fitness* book together. I wrote 12 pages of the book, explaining how reading the book helped.

I visited Charlie in 2006 when he had a recent move to Full Sutton, and what we saw was unbelievable: 20 Mufti squad all with helmets and shields - they had just brought Charlie to the visiting room and they were waiting to take Charlie back to his cell. Charlie had his glasses and watch broken at Full Sutton and he recently received compensation of £185. The press blew the story way out of proportion, saying he had now purchased a designer pair of glasses and had them tinted and it was coming out of taxpayers' money. Yes Charlie received compensation and the money was well spent: £100 went to Zoe's Hospice in Liverpool. Charlie gave his mother, Eira, £50 and he purchased some flowers for a friend that had just passed away - that's the truth. The press do Charlie no favours. They print all this garbage to sell newspapers. Why don't they tell the truth about Charlie? It was recently printed in a Sunday newspaper that Charlie had smashed his cell up - another wrong statement. Where do they get their information from? Somebody is obviously making a few quid by feeding the press this information. We don't expect them to print good reports like Charlie is supporting charities, we do not expect good press, but we don't expect the lies that are printed every time.

I have become firm friends with Charlie and so have all my family. I have read all of Charlie's books and I am passing on the word about Charlie. Every person I talk to thinks Charlie is a killer. so I explain that Charlie has never killed, but this is the impression most people are given after reading the newspapers. I cannot believe what Charlie has gone through physically and mentally, but Charlie still to this day remains positive about his future. He does get frustrated, but who wouldn't, being locked up 24 hours a day? He has no reason to return to crime on his release, as he will make a fortune with his film and books. He could help deter people from crime. Charlie is now looking to the future; he can't turn his past around. What has happened has happened; Charlie can't go back. He has an excellent solicitor, the best in the world. Giovanni di Stefano believes in Charlie's case and we believe he is the man to fight for Charlie's freedom. I have written many letters to MPs and the Prime Minister. You get a response but that is as far as it goes. The letters usually say - "we can't comment" or "I will pass your letter on". I am supporting Charlie's fight for freedom, as I believe it is an injustice what is happening to Charlie. I am no gangster; I don't have a criminal background. I just believe Charlie Bronson has paid his dues and it is now time for him to get on with life outside prison. Free this man, he has paid his dues twice over. Charlie, box it clever, brother.

KAREN REED (SUPPORTER):
I think it's a disgrace. He should have been released years ago.

KAZZI REES (SUPPORTER):
Good Luck Charlie.

GEMINI REYNOLDS (FRIEND):
I wrote a letter to Chaz because I was curious. I had read so much about him and wanted to find out what he was really like. I didn't know if he would reply or not, let alone how our amazing friendship would develop. Since those early days we have exchanged a number of letters and photos and also he has sent me some lovely artwork. Sometimes the letters make me laugh out loud. He has such a great sense of humour, even after all those years behind bars. He has been punished long enough. Everything that I have read from him leads me to believe that he is no longer a danger to society. Chaz seeks a peaceful life. I hope that he is released soon and can get on with the rest of his life. He would be welcome to sip a glass of champagne by the pool here in Cyprus with me anytime.

JIM REYNOLDS (SUPPORTER):
Why is this man being kept like this? He has more than served his time. Let him out. Chin up, Charlie.

MARC REYNOLDS (SUPPORTER):
This guy has served well over the time he should have for such a little crime.

GREGG RICKELL (FRIEND):
Charles Bronson - This is a man that is so complex that the system is scared to do anything with him, so they just choose to lock him away in a concrete coffin and try to forget about him! Except for when it suits them and they need to release a story from time to time to reaffirm his position as 'Britain's Most Dangerous Con'. This is their simple way to keep people scared and make them believe what they are telling them. Most people are happy to carry on this way and go on with their lives, choosing not to be involved, because who would want a monster free? The system has been very good at this and if it wasn't for those of us that believe in Charles Bronson's cause then I am sure he would be denied any contact at all. But unfortunately for them the numbers are growing of people seeing the truth and their negative attitude towards Charlie is going to have to change. How can they keep a man locked away in solitary for so long when the real monsters are being released and allowed human contact?! It's these monsters people should really fear, not Charlie! Charlie has spent years rehabilitating himself because there is no provision offered to him to help. They may say that he has been released before and messed up, but how can they say that, when he wasn't even given a starting chance?! Straight from Cat A solitary to the streets, set up to fail. There is no wonder that Charlie has had such an eventful past - wouldn't anybody who has been put through such anguish fight back against the system that has failed to provide him with his civil and human rights? Even when he has no interest in fighting and is working hard to redeem himself, there is always an obstacle put up to knock him back down.
Luckily Charlie has found his true passion in life, Art. Even this they try to take away, although it raises so much money for charities and touches people's lives! They cannot allow Charles Bronson to be seen to have a human side; they need him to be a monster! I know about this first hand through being a prison officer for three and a half years, I've heard all the glory stories about Charlie and I have even seen real-life footage of this so-called monster. I am just happy that I know the real Charles Bronson and I don't read into the stories that are published. I have seen the real Charles Bronson, the man like me that bleeds, sweats and cries like the rest of us, the man that has emotions and feelings. I know he has no interest in crime when he is released; he wants to continue with his art a free man! Is this too much to ask - to be free and live the rest of your days peacefully and become a successful artist? Because when Charlie is released I can only imagine the art he will be able to create using the correct equipment and using all the colours of the world, a world he is being denied.
Charlie would be brilliant talking to young offenders, as he would be able to give them a true-to-life account of the darkness that is crime and prison life. Who are they going to listen to more, someone with no experience or someone who has lived it? Everyone deserves a chance in life to be free. Let's give Charlie this chance, a chance he has earned! It may be that when

he's released no one ever hears the name CHARLES BRONSON again, or it may be that he becomes a really successful artist. We will never know until that day comes. It's time the Home Office stop contradicting themselves; that's all they're doing. They say murder is the worst crime that a human can commit, but what are they doing if it is not murder? They are slowly taking away a man's life day by day, a man who wants to forget his past and focus on his future. The past is in the past, nothing will ever change the past, but we have the chance to provide a future. Let's take that chance. Charles Bronson, victim of his past, destined for a great future! I don't know of many people who can take it on the chin like Charlie has; he's a born fighter with a heart as big as the world. So many lives have been touched by this man; let's give him a chance to touch so many more. Charlie, I admire your strength and courage and look forward to seeing what you can do as a free man. I know you will do great things. Keep fighting and know we are fighting with you.

DANIEL RIDGEWELL (SUPPORTER):
Let the man out.

TOM RIDINGS (SUPPORTER):
Free Bronson!!! He's a legend in my eyes!

TONY RIDLEY (SUPPORTER):
Let the man go free. He has done his time! Some men can mug an old lady or rape a woman and all they get is a slap on the wrist. What is the world coming to? Let him go!

GAIL RIVINGTON-EDWARDS (SUPPORTER):
Free Charles and give him a chance. There are really bad people walking the streets who have done worse. Let him breathe some fresh air. Free this man.

CHRISTOPHER ROBERTS (SUPPORTER):
The system is a joke! But not at all funny.

JAMES ROBERTS (SUPPORTER):
Charles Bronson deserves his freedom.

CARLA ROGERS (SUPPORTER):
They don't want him free because he will tell the real truth - the cowards should let him go.

TRAVIS ROSE (SUPPORTER):
How can it be called a justice system when 34 years inside (28 in solitary) is far from just?! It stinks!!!! Free Charlie now! The only thing criminal about him is the way he has been and is being treated! Steve Tindle, a guy who raped a twelve-week-old baby, got a lesser sentence! Make scum like that serve a sentence like Charlie's and release him now.

NICOLA LOUISE ROYDON (SUPPORTER):
"Enough is Enough". Where's the justice?!!

PETER RUFFLE (SUPPORTER):
Killers and paedos do less time than Charles. Where's the justice?

TOM RULE (SUPPORTER):
Don't make the same mistake as with Reggie Kray, wake up.

MATT RYALS (SUPPORTER):
Free Charles Bronson.

ANDY SALVAGE (BROTHER IN LAW):

My name is Andrew Peter Salvage (Andy). How do I know Charles Bronson? I am married to the fantastic rock of a lady he calls his sister, Loraine (she's his first cousin, for the record). They were inseparable until 1974 when he was jailed. When I met Loraine I had no idea about Micky Peterson until she mentioned him one day. Now if I had read anything in the papers about the man I might have thought, "What the fuck is he doing that for?" Well, now I know. You see, for 34 years my wife has been to every shithole and dungeon in the country. She has seen and felt his pain; she has seen the aftermath of the drugs and beatings he has had to go through. I myself have only seen 21 years of seeing my wife's pain and anger at the way he has suffered. I know the real Micky Peterson (aka Charlie Bronson), the poet, artist, strong man and funny man. I have been to many prisons over the last 21 years; he even stayed at our house in Luton the last time he was out. I love this man like a brother and I have the utmost respect for him.

I know a lot of you out there write to him and visit him and for that we thank you - your words and support mean everything, not only to Charlie but to the family as well. Some of you travel miles to 'Monster Mansion' in Wakefield where you can spend 2 hours with him. Ian Huntley and others like him are in there and it's frustrating to know that Charlie is being compared to these animals. He has never raped or killed, and he hasn't been in trouble for 7 years or more, so why keep him there? He is no danger to society, when the papers write 'Britain's most dangerous prisoner'. In the last year they have said he's on hunger strike (lies); he wants 10k for glasses that were smashed (lies) - but the guards did stamp on his glasses and that's why he was offered money. They continue printing old photos of him (he looks nothing like that now) and when you try to get in touch with the papers over it you just hit a brick wall.

He is long overdue to be out here with his family and friends; many of his friends will be in this book. God bless you all! If you keep a dog in a cage and poke him with a stick one day that fucker is gonna bite; this is how they treat Charlie. Me and Loraine will never give up on what it takes to free this man. Through him I have met some top people who have been fantastic. The list is massive so to all past (God rest you) and present (you know who you are) we thank you all. In 21 years I have seen lots of changes in Charlie, the ups and downs, the farce of the wedding, the death of his father (God bless you, Uncle Joe), the shit that's in the papers. He has a good lawyer in Giovanni di Stefano, and I know that one day we will be a family again. There is so much I want to show him and share with him - a glass of his favourite drink, Black Russian, and eating one of his stews! He can visit all the charities that he has helped (they don't print that in the fucking papers!)

Anyway, I will end this now the way I end all my letters to Charlie and that is - stay strong, don't let the bastards get you down, we will win and I love you. Your little brother.

LORAINE SALVAGE (CHARLIE'S SISTER):

Never believe 90% of what you read in the papers! I've known Charlie Bronson from the minute he was born, only he was Michael Peterson then. Our mums are sisters born a year apart and we were only 2 years apart. We spent our childhood together as our mums Eira and Eileen always lived virtually next door to each other. There was John (Charlie's brother), Michael and myself. When my parents split up and I was taken away by a wicked stepmother, it was John and Michael who found me. Then John went off to join the Royal Marines when he was very young and that left me and Charlie. We spent all our time together; even when we moved to Ellesmere Port we lived opposite each other. He always called me sis and he was my bruv. We are the same, we know how the other is thinking, even though we are really 1st cousins. I can honestly say that I know him better than anyone else in this world, and he will tell you that himself, and that's why it infuriates me to read all the rubbish that is in the newspapers, 'Charles B the monster' for example. People like Ian Huntley and Robert Maudsley and paedophiles are the monsters, not Charlie. Okay, he's not been an angel but he's no monster.

I've seen him beaten black and blue, fingers and toes broken, beaten so badly that he nearly lost a kidney, but no one reports this in the papers. He's been degraded, stripped naked and forced to wear a body belt, pulled out of his cell in the middle of the night and ghosted to another prison halfway around the country with no warning. Do you blame him for retaliating? If he gets beaten by these animals, he fights back. I cannot begin to tell you how many times he and the family have written to the Home Office to complain about his treatment, but it does no good. When you are locked up 23 hours a day you look forward to your 1 hour of exercise outside, but sometimes the bastards drag him in after 40 minutes; it's his right to have 1 hour but they just don't care. Some of the officers just want to be able to say, "I've had Charlie Bronson." None of this is reported in the papers. I've had other prisoners and officers phone me anonymously to tell me that he's had another beating. The government don't care; they don't want him out because he knows too much. It's propaganda like Ron and Reg and Ronnie Biggs. Charlie is well known for taking hostages - why? I'll tell you why, because it didn't matter how many times he complained, asked to see the governor, wrote to the Home Office, it all fell upon deaf ears. After a couple of months of this with no reply he took a hostage. He didn't hurt him but it made people take notice! 'Charlie the hostage taker' hasn't taken a hostage for over 8 years now. He's been in no trouble and he hasn't had a beard for years (I know because I've got it), but the papers still print pictures of him like that and still call him a hostage taker.

The real Charlie is kind, funny and a gentleman. He is a very talented artist, has a wicked sense of humour and is very old-fashioned in his ways; he'll hold a door open for a lady. He has done loads of artwork to be auctioned for charity and has a lot of good friends who adore him. The prison officers at Wakefield Prison know exactly what sort of person he is. Ask the guards that've looked after him day in, day out, for the last 5 to 6 years. They will tell you the truth. They all think the world of him, have nothing but praise, train with him every day - they are the people who know him now. Wakefield Prison is probably one of the best prisons he has ever been in. Even though it is called Monster Mansion there are also a lot of ordinary prisoners in there that are not monsters and Charlie is one of them!

As I said, don't believe everything you read in the papers. I know him, the family know the real him and so do the guards that have been looking after him the last few years in Wakefield. Don't judge him by what you read - it's not true. Ask Jim Dawkins who wrote *The Loose Screw*. He was a prison officer who has known Charlie and seen the awful things that have been done to him - read his book and read the truth. Another former officer who guided Charlie to do his art is Mike O'Hagan - he believes in him and knows the real Charlie. Another ex-officer called Greg wrote on Charlie's website about the appalling way he was treated and if the officers managed to get a swing at him they were awarded. I rest my case. Don't believe what you read in the papers - you don't know Charlie, I do. Have you ever been certified sane? Charlie has.

Charlie writes: I had two big beards, one went to Canada, which I sent to Joyce Connor, and the other to Loraine, so they both have a part of me.

KEV SANDERSON (SUPPORTER):
Free him and make room for someone who deserves to be locked up!

PAUL SAUNDERS (SUPPORTER):
Enough is enough. Free the man.

ERIC SAUNDERSON (SUPPORTER):
Enough is enough!!

JOSH SCORAH (SUPPORTER):
Great man. Free him.

TOM SCOTT (SUPPORTER):
Enough is enough. If you don't believe me, read the man's books and learn.

ASHTON SEYMOUR (SUPPORTER):
Free Charlie now!!

MARK SHARMAN (FRIEND):
Charles Bronson is a man I have known for over 7 years. To build up a relationship and become firm friends takes more than a letter now and then or the odd packet of stamps. Such friendships are built on solid foundations such as trust, loyalty, honour, and above all respect for each other. We come from totally different backgrounds but we have become friends. I don't need to write several pages on what I have done for Charlie when one word can sum up what I feel for Charlie - 'Brother'.

Now like thousands of other people we see scum in the papers every day: child abuse, rape, murder. Now I have hit on 3 words there: 1) Child abuse; 2) Rape; 3) Murder. Now I will give anyone 10k if they can find any of Charlie's offences that include those top 3.

Let's just look at 2 cases to prove my point as to why Charlie should be free:

1) Several years ago terrorists hijacked a plane full of passengers. These people had done no wrong but did not know whether they were going to die or not. As it happened, the plane landed and these terrorists were put on remand in one of our jails. Now Charlie is walking down the landing and they decide to attack him, but Charlie being as strong as he is turned the tables on them and took some of them hostage. His demands were that they tickled his feet, a cheese sandwich, a helicopter, and if I remember rightly a blow-up doll!! This was a moment that Charlie had to defend himself from these people.

Now get this. Both cases go to court. The terrorists who put 200 lives at risk and have left people mentally scarred get sentenced to 5 years. Charlie makes them tickle his feet and gets 7 years. Where is the justice in that sentence? ... YOU DECIDE.

2) The second point I need to make doesn't make nice reading but the facts speak for themselves. A few years ago a small boy, aged 2, called James Bulger was taken from his mother and marched for 2 miles to a secluded field where he was beaten with bricks and iron bars then raped, then left on a railway line where a train decapitated him. Now the two pieces of low-life shit who did this awful thing get sentenced to 15 years but are released early with a new identity. Charlie takes a man hostage for a few days because he insulted him. Okay, Charlie didn't rape him or hit him with iron bars, but more importantly he did not kill him, but he got a life sentence for this crime and has had no rehabilitation, has had no parole, nor has been moved off Cat A. You tell me which was the worst crime here.

Even the Kray twins only did 13 years on Cat A. Charlie to date has done over 28 years in solitary and 30 years on Cat A. Let me simplify that for you. Imagine being in a room for 23 hours a day with only 1 hour out for 28 years. This is barbaric and needs to be stamped out now. Let's make my stance on this very clear - I would trust Charlie in my house with my wife and kids 100%. No hesitation.

LYNDA SHARP (SUPPORTER):
Charles has shown his compassion. Show him some now!

STEPHEN SHAW (SUPPORTER):
Enough is enough. Let him go.

MARY SHAW-TAYLOR & JOHN BURTON (FRIENDS):
Charles Bronson should be released. It's appalling how he's been cruelly treated from day one. What gave certain prison officers the right to make it bad for Charlie, to keep him longer in jail, provoking him and goading him into anger because they didn't like him? Don't you think the prison system has done enough to him? He's been savagely beaten in every prison he's been sent to. No wonder he lost his temper trying to fight back to protect himself. He didn't stand a chance, like I said from day, one against his attackers. Also the men who beat Charles severely in that mental hospital when he was sent there, surely they should be punished and sent to prison? They were bullies and cowards. If they got the same beating as

they gave to Charles, I'm sure they wouldn't beat anyone else up. All these types of men who ill-treat prisoners get away with it (and you know why) - because they put fear into them so they don't like saying who beat them up. Charles was one of them. He was locked away from everyone until his injuries healed up so there's no evidence of him being beaten up by those certain officers. And to keep Charles in a cage is inhuman. The prison cruelty made Charles what he is today. It's time to release Charlie and leave him in peace. Let him live his remaining years in happiness. Give him his human rights to freedom.

BOYD SHELTON (SUPPORTER):
Free the man for f**k's sake!!

STEVEN SHINTON (SUPPORTER):
End his torture!

DAVE SHONE (SUPPORTER):
It's an absolute disgrace that Charlie is still inside!! After 34 years!! Unbelievable!!

VICKI SIMS (SUPPORTER):
Free him now, he has served more than his time … he isn't a murderer, you know!!! You got my support, Charles.

PHIL SIMPSON (SUPPORTER):
Come on now, a true strong character that could do a lot of good, let him free, he's served enough time for most crimes.

TONY SIMPSON (FRIEND);
How loony do you ever have to be? Well, just to be mates with Charlie Bronson, people say you must be a lunatic. Why? The press and TV make this man a right loony. Why? Because they don't know him; because they hear about a man who kicks off and the official word is the man is a loony. Mmmm, then work out this! If you said to your mate, cook me up a meal and a nice cup of tea and as you were about to eat and drink this well-prepared meal and drink your mate told you that he had pissed in your tea and shit on your cottage pie, would you not go loony and kick off? Mmmm, so this makes you loony. When you make a stand and say, no, you want a bit more time out of the cage on exercise just to feel the daylight on your cheeks and the wind on your face and the PO says, no, you have to come in or else! You say, no, just half an hour more, and then they fetch 12 POs with dogs and pepper spray, would you not go loony? My loony time is running 3 London Marathons at 23 stone, a strongman pulling a 105 tonne VC 10 RAF plane, and a 500k bike ride across Vietnam/Cambodia with Alan Rayment, my mate, double amputee. So when people say to you, you're a lunatic, read these words, write off to the Oxford Dictionary and say this is the definition of loonyology: when you get your ribs broke by a sad PO who wants to make a name for himself or a fat twat aged 50+ who thinks he is 20 and tries to raise thousands for kids charities … end of definition.

MICHAEL JOSEPH SLAVEN (SUPPORTER):
Believe he has a right to be free.

CALEM SMITH (SUPPORTER):
Charlie deserves his freedom.

JOE SMITH (FRIEND):
In the years when Tel Currie was my boxing coach and trainer along with my cousins Jimmy 'on the cobbles' Stockin and Billy Smith, he would keep me updated on all that was going on in the world of the 'CHAPS'. This would also include 'Gypsy' Johnny Frankham (the official King of the Gypsies), a man Tel will not mind me telling you he looked up to a great deal. So

myself, Billy Smith, Jimmy Stockin and the 'King of the Gypsies would always ask Tel what was going on. Mostly, this would concern Charlie Bronson and Ronnie Biggs (the rest of the things we talked about I cannot tell you about, ha!) Christ, we had some wild days, me, Tel, Bill, Jim, Toucher and the boys, even being thrown out of an unlicensed bout once when shots started ringing out all over the place. "Have you checked the kitbag Telboy?" "Yep, Q-tips, towel, bandages, Vaseline, bayonet, Lugar, berretta, duster!" Great days! Only joking (a bit). Anyway, it was pretty obvious that what was happening to Charlie Bronson was disgusting, when you think what other scum have done.

LESLEY SMITH (SUPPORTER):
I first heard about Charles Bronson through a guy at work called Al. I was interested from the start. I firstly read his *Bronson* book and was totally astonished. The book kept me interested and mesmerised. The treatment Charles has received and been through is absolutely disgraceful; they wouldn't treat an animal like that. After reading the book I wanted to know more about him. I got his website address and started looking. I found it very interesting as there are so many articles and stories from numerous people backing Charles all the way ... I even signed his petition to free him, and I don't even know him. He doesn't deserve to be behind bars after all these years. I ask has he murdered? NO. Yes, he's hurt people, but when you read whom and why, you totally understand! I have never met Charles, and would not be afraid of him. He is a grown man who has been to hell and back and deserves to be FREE ... A total injustice.

LIAM SMITH (SUPPORTER):
Human Rights.

MICKY SMITH (FRIEND):
Charles Bronson was originally sent to prison for 7 years for armed robbery, a robbery in which no one was hurt. He has now spent 32 years in prison, 28 of which have been in solitary confinement, where he has suffered physical and psychological punishment and brutality. Not solely due to this punishment has Charles Bronson become a changed man. He has set his mind to greater tasks. He has trained his body and mind with his incredible fitness levels, with which he has beat world records, and that he has also written books on. He has also created some great poetry and some really awesome artwork. I think it is about time he was set free with the accomplishments he has achieved in a small, dark cell. I want to see what he can do with freedom.

STEVEN SMITH (SUPPORTER):
How can the justice system condone its decision to lock up a man who has never killed for life, when paedophiles are returned to society with 'tags' and are able to re-commit vile offences.

TERRY SMITH (FRIEND):
As with all characters that come across as larger than life, we are all sucked in by the gossip, rumours and propaganda that we hear about them. I initially heard of Charlie when I was serving 15 years for armed robbery in the late 1980s. Other long-term prisoners spoke of Charlie as if he was taking on the prison system single-handed. Charlie was portrayed a strong and fearsome man who absolutely abhorred taking shit off the screws. Over the preceding decade in some of Britain's toughest top-security jails our paths crossed several times and it dawned upon me that Charlie was a person 'more sinned against than sinning'. Invariably he was a victim of mind games, maltreatment and brutality from the governor grades and screws. This is because in every jail that Charlie was transferred to the so-called 'hard man screws' in the block would view Charlie as a veritable challenge and threat to their very own mini kingdom, whereupon they would hatch a perverse plot to provoke Charlie into expressing the only language, at that time, that he knew that they would understand and fear: violence. Looked at in this context, we learn Charlie was himself a real and genuine victim and his

healthy obsession with physical fitness and training was his only saviour.

Ironically I first met Charlie in HMP Albany segregation unit in 1990. We were in opposing exercise yards separated by a twelve-foot high wall with razor wire. He shouted to me, "Hey, mate, fancy a game of tennis?", and a medicine ball came over the wall. He added, "If the ball touches the floor, it is one point to me." Despite being in a depressive dungeon of the prison block, during the next 30 minutes I have never laughed so much. He had me in hysterics. It was then that I realised that Charlie was a genuine, warm and endearing person. In 1992 our paths crossed again in HMP Long Lartin where we shared a bucket of prison-brewed hooch together. Again he was hilarious, especially when he did his rendition of 'Amazing Grace', which he performed for Ronnie Kray while he was in Broadmoor. Even with a belly full of powerful prison hooch, Charlie was not the fire-breathing ogre that the Prison Service and media loved to portray. He was like meeting a pal down the pub for a guzzle. He exhibited all the social and communication skills of a man that was ready for release back into society. But here we are, some fifteen years on, and Charlie is still caged like some diseased animal in prison.

In spite of all the abuse and mistreatment that Charlie has had to endure, he has buried himself into his award-winning artwork and writing. He has blossomed like a plant that grows against the odds in the cracks of a pavement. He is a man that should be revered as a rehabilitative success and not pushed away into the darkest corners of society like a leper. They say that you can always measure a democratic society by the way it treats its minority groups and prisoners. The way Charlie has been treated by the British prison system over the last three decades is nothing short of scandalous. He has never killed anyone. He is not some sadistic murderer. He has not maimed anyone. Over the last decade he has done nothing but consistently show us on the outside that he is eminently salvageable and in desperate need of a chance to reintegrate back into our society.

In decades to come, when social historians and criminologists look back at the way Charlie Bronson was imprisoned and caged because the Prison Service could not and would not ease him back into society, they will be ashamed. The time has come to proclaim who are the real criminals here! A man who has spent the last 30 years in isolation in segregation units for relatively minor crimes, or the Prison Service, Probation Service and Parole Board who persistently fail in their obligation and duty in aiding and endorsing his release.

JAMES SMYTHE (SUPPORTER):
Release Charles, he's suffered enough. Stay strong. If enough people sign, you'll be free.

BETH SOUTHERN (SUPPORTER):
Let the poor man have his life back.

GARRY STABLER (SUPPORTER):
This man's done his time. Let him home for his wife and kids.

MARK STAGG (SUPPORTER):
How is this man any danger now to society? He has more than paid his debt and he should now be released.

MARTIN JOHN STANLEY (SUPPORTER):
Free Charlie!! 30 yrs+ and still inside. Murderers out quicker. How is this possible? Good luck, Chas mate.

PAUL STEVENSON (FRIEND):
I first met Charlie in 2002 at HMP Whitemoor Prison. Like everyone else before me, I'd only heard the stories of this man mountain that was to only be unlocked by no less than 8 prison officers in full riot dress with dogs and more officers off to one side. A man so dangerous that he can only be held in specially constructed cells at maximum security prisons such as

Whitemoor, Full Sutton, Long Lartin etc. and the super CSC unit at Wakefield - that's everybody's impression of Charlie, an impression based on hearsay and Chinese whispers spread by prison officers. Charlie Bronson has never taken a life or molested children; he's never mugged an old person. There are men in the prison system who have committed such crimes - evil men, child murderers. These men will walk free when they have served their time because you - the public - have never heard of them. They commit the crime, it will be on the news briefly, they serve 12-15 years for taking a young life and then they walk out of the gates free, unchanged and still as perverted and deviant as the day they were arrested! Yet a man who committed a small crime involving money has to spend his whole life in prison because everyone's heard stories of him due mainly to seedy prison officers selling illegal stories to the tabloids.

Yes, all criminals need to be punished if they get caught. I'm not trying to say otherwise. But Charlie's done his time over and over. I've met the man. He's a good friend of my Nan and Granddad. He's an artist of exceptional standards; he's not mad or psychotic in any way. He's got a mum like any other man - who loves her son. He's a normal bloke. He's got a family who care for him and he is a father himself. If people took the time to stop and talk to him they would all see what everyone else has seen who has got to know Charlie. He can be helped and is not a lost cause. "Okay," you might say, "but it's not up to me to release the man. I'm just a member of the public. What can I do?" Next time you're in front of your computer, click onto his website. The biggest problem I can see as to getting Charlie released is that when a prisoner comes up for his parole, the Parole Board only get to see what's on paper, so you sort of see the picture about what I'm trying to say. The Parole Board are not going to spend the weekend getting to know Charlie before their decision; they don't even have a 5-minute chat. They sit down, read all the years of paperwork - most of which is written by prison officers - and it's this information that they base their decision on.

If you are under any delusion about our prison officers being a professional and honest body of men you're very much wrong. Most of them are ex-traffic wardens and police outcasts. They lie, steal and conspire their way through their careers. I am not saying convicts are all angels with little halos floating above their heads, but that's not the point. Over the years I've lost watches, radios, chains and bracelets. I had a lovely old Cartier watch, which went missing. The only people who came in contact with that watch were me and the officers. I was in segregation, so it was not another inmate, and when I went mad, as anybody would, when I found it missing, I was told that I didn't own such a watch and there was no evidence of me owning a watch. The officer involved contacted his mate, who worked in reception, and got him to write me out a new property card, minus one watch, and they wrote in my file that I was deliberately trying to entice staff into a confrontation over a watch that didn't exist. Had I been up for parole, a statement like that on a prisoner's file would've held me back. Even years later they will hold something like that against you. The watch was in fact a present from my mum for my 18th, a present my mum enjoyed buying me but probably had to save quite hard for. This sort of behaviour from staff is rife and that's just one example that they have been doing that sort of thing to Charlie for years and years and years in prison.

There are procedures for dealing with difficult inmates, so there's no excuse for the way they sometimes treat people. Another example is when I was in HMP Full Sutton. Charlie was in the cell opposite mine. This was the segregation unit in a maximum security prison. So as you can imagine a basic day consists of one hour outside in the exercise yard, which is only about the size of a front garden. It has a 22-foot high fence, which goes all the way around it and is topped with barbed wire. Once you've had your hour out on the yard you get a quick shower and then you are locked away until the next day. There's no need to open the cell for food, because as in Charlie's case they feed him through a special security tight airlock, built into his special cell. This is the routine Charlie has to endure day in, day out, month after month, year after year, and now decade after decade. How that man hasn't lost his mind is a miracle in itself. The strength of mind this man must have is going to waste.

Anyway, this particular day started off like any other winter morning in Full Sutton. I woke up. My alarm clock was the gate slamming shut as the 1st officers arrived for work, so I laid there for a while and then got up and stretched - something I do every morning as it helps to keep you flexible, something that comes in useful in Full Sutton. Then I had a wash at my sink. After this I got dressed, made my bed up, got my book and laid on my bed. My cell overlooked the exercise yards, which we went out on. In any prison, especially a maximum security, the screws do security checks on all the locks. This is carried out 1st thing in the morning. I heard two screws talking and I could even smell the tobacco smoke from their cigarettes while they walked up and physically checked the locks on all 4 yards by opening and shutting the gate. After a while, the same two officers came round to get everyone up and offer some hot water for a tea or coffee. While they were doing this I could hear some of the questions some of us were asking. One of the questions was, "What time is exercise today?" I heard one of the officers say, "Locks are frozen solid and we can't open the gates." Now that might not sound a big thing, but these officers are supposed to be the best trained screws in the country. They deal on a daily basis with some of the most dangerous men in this country, men so evil they really would kill you if you gave them the opportunity and as soon as they had finished would not give it another thought! So you would think the prison officers wouldn't want to unnecessarily upset 50 of the bastards. Little things like that cause a lot of problems and it did. One bloke, a real hard-nosed fella in for a typical murder, a man you would never want to meet, ended up rolling round on the floor with the staff. Then 3 cells along some big Jamaican bloke who was in for rape, murder and drug trafficking - another individual you wouldn't have on your Xmas card list and, for the record has since been released and is living in a small town somewhere in England - ended up punching a screw and had to be restrained.

By now the screws are well fired up, so they open Charlie's door and offer him his shower, which he accepts as he does every day. Remember, the screws are now about 10 handed, with 2 dogs and in full riot dress. I've been watching the whole thing out my cell door. I can see this one officer, a young chap no older than 25, and he is taunting Charlie about the exercise yards, trying to get a reaction from him. They moved into the shower block and as soon as the screws were out of camera shot they set about Charlie and I watched a group of young men in protective riot gear beat up a 50-year-old man. They beat Charlie black and blue, and do you know what excuses they used? They all conspired and said Charlie smashed up the showers. The incident was so bad that when prison inspectors came to visit Full Sutton a month later they could still see the bruises on Charlie's face. Still not a lot was done, as there was no evidence. All the officers consolidated their stories and that was the end of if: no justice, no inquiry, nothing. Of course the officers did their paperwork trick on Charlie's file. I told Charlie I'd give evidence for him and as soon as the officer found out I was off to some faraway hole. I ask you this - if you were walking one day and saw 10 fully grown blokes beating up a 50-year-old man, would you be sickened to live in such a place where that could happen? This sort of thing still goes on every day in British prisons.

My Nan, a frail old lady who's been with my Granddad for 40 years, a woman who has no criminal record, a woman who wouldn't hurt a fly, and my normal, loving Granddad would like Charlie at their table for Xmas dinner. Why would they want Charlie Bronson, 'Britain's Most Dangerous Convict', sitting at their table? I will tell you why - because she's not blind, she can see past the labels, past the tags that the system has given Charlie and see the man he is: a loving father, a loved son and a good, warm-hearted, normal bloke. I promise you, 'Britain's Most Dangerous Convict' is bollocks! That murdering rapist who got released and could be living in your town - now he's dangerous. Justice - shit. It's cobblers. Charlie doesn't want your sympathy. He knows he committed a crime, he knows he had to be punished. So he doesn't want everyone's sympathy, he just wants justice; nothing more, nothing less; just what he is entitled to. That man is not a danger to you or anybody else.

Just imagine if Charlie was released. Think of the impact he could make on young teenagers who have got caught up in gangs and drugs. Imagine the short sharp shock they would get from a talk with Charlie Bronson, the real-life experiences he could put across. Think of the work he could do. The talent he's got in art could inspire other people to get involved. Charlie doesn't want you to like him; Charlie doesn't want you to hate him either. He wants you to make up your own mind. Don't listen to stories or clever articles in the tabloids. Make up your own minds. Imagine if the shoe was on the other foot and you got off to a bad start in life. You had no money and committed a crime to provide for your family - not the best decision you've ever made, but a decision nonetheless. You get arrested. Over the years you're drugged with medication and brutalised by staff. Yes, you gave as good as you got, but you were a young man. Now you are not a young man anymore, you're 50. Your family haven't seen you in 20 odd years. You've got a son who's in his 30s. And, to make matters worse, the whole country thinks you're 'Britain's Most Dangerous Convict'. And we are supposed to have one of the best justice systems in the world. I am giving credit where it's due. Charlie is a real case. 99% of prisoners should be locked up. I am not trying to say otherwise. The system made Charlie into some sort of mascot. But this isn't a joke or something people should turn a blind eye to. This is a man, a human being, and you can help. First make up you own mind, then give him some backing. Do what you feel you can. Any help is welcomed and appreciated.

RYAN (RAZ) STEVENSON (SUPPORTER):
What about those beasts/rapists that only serve a few years? Free fuckin' Charles now!

MICHAEL STRIDE (SUPPORTER):
Free Bronson!!!

TYEA STRINGER (SUPPORTER):
Free Charles!

RUSSELL STUART (SUPPORTER):
His time would be better spent doing a million other worthwhile things. It's sick how the Home Office just wants to ruin his life. They can't do anything right.

MICHAEL STURE (SUPPORTER):
Unbelievable he is still inside.

PAUL SULLIVAN (SUPPORTER):
What a joke. 34 years for what?

NEEDS SWELLBELLY (FRIEND):
It was in the eighties whilst spending some time in one of Her Majesty's Hotels in Scotland, I was reading a newspaper article on a prisoner in England. His name was Charles Bronson. Back in the real world I set about putting my life back together and did a little travelling. Whilst in the good old US of A, I decided to put another punk rock band together, around the same time I read one of Charlie's first books; it was a book about poetry. After reading his autobiography I decided to write a song for the band about Charlie's plight. The band recorded the song for its first demo and I sent Charlie a copy. He replied with a letter and a piece of artwork done by the good man himself. Since then we have been in touch at least once a fortnight by letter and have formed a solid friendship. As time passed, Charlie penned some songs for the band, which were used on the band's first album and single, with Charlie also designing the artwork for the record covers. I have known Charlie now for close to ten years; that's about a third of the time he has spent in prison. I have met Charlie several times and have spent hours talking to him through a window two-foot square with bars on it and have enjoyed every minute. Charlie has to be one of the most respectful gentlemen I have had the pleasure to meet, a true diamond.
For me the real crime in Charlie's case is the fact that being kept in prison any longer will do more harm than good. I have witnessed a lot of change in Charlie and know he is ready for a shot outside of prison. Out in the real world Charlie can put his life in order and put his writing and artistic skills to good use. He could spend more time on his charity work and

maybe do some public speaking; he certainly has a story to tell. For me Charlie's paid for all crimes committed and I'm sure most people would agree. Let's give him the chance of freedom to go home, the chance to grow old with the wind and rain on his face; it's time for sure. He has certainly done enough time locked up, hidden away from his family and friends and the rest of the world and left to rot basically in a place that lets rapists and paedophiles have open visits with friends, family and children while Charlie has closed secure visits. He is not even able to hug his mum when she visits. It's crazy to think that they treat Charlie like a caged monster when the jails are home to child killers and mass murderers and the type of scum who beat up the elderly, the type of scum who need to be locked away for everyone's sake, but Charlie, who has never killed anyone, is kept in solitary in a prison inside a prison. It disgusts me that the justice system can get it so wrong with the treatment of Charlie. It just isn't right. The justice system would like to sweep his life under the carpet to forget he even exists. Well screw that, Charlie has a right, the right to leave behind the ball and chain of prison life and take part in the real world.

See you on the outside, mate.

MARTIN SWINGEWOOD (SUPPORTER):
Free Charles Bronson. 34 years is too long. He is no monster, he is a man.

MARK SYKES (SUPPORTER):
Turn this man free; he's done his crime and his time.

GAVIN TANNER (SUPPORTER):
Charles Bronson for Prime Minister.
Charlie writes: Yes, I would do a better job! Believe me.

ANDREW TARR (SUPPORTER):
Free Bronson!

NEIL TATTERSALL (SUPPORTER):
Come along, you do the crime you do the time, which Charlie has done and some. It's time to set him free.

RYAN DAVID TAYLOR (SUPPORTER):
Would you put yourself in prison for over 20 years if you hadn't done anything wrong?

STEVIE TAYLOR (SUPPORTER):
Justice must be done now.

LEE THOMAS (SUPPORTER):
Free Charlie.

KEELEY ANNE THOMPSON (FRIEND):
I first got in touch with Charlie in 2005. I had read one of his books and on the back of one of his books was his address. I didn't know that much about him at first, only what I had read, but as time passed I started to know him a bit better and found out what he is really like, and I really mean it when I say I have never met such a caring and selfless person. None of the letters he sent me had a shred of self-pity in them. He always seemed so positive and happy and always gave me good advice that I always took in and listened to. He knew I was going through a bit of a rough patch and sent me presents to cheer me up. Here was Charlie in solitary for all these years and here he was cheering me up!

A lot of people who have never had contact with Charlie judge him on what he has done without knowing what he is really like. I feel that Charlie has more than paid the price for what he has done and sincerely hope that he gets released. Keeping him locked away would not achieve anything. It's about time Charlie was given a chance, and also about time he was shown some humanity. God - even sex offenders get chance after chance after chance and a lot of them only ever served a fraction of what Charlie has. Charlie has stayed out of trouble for a long while now. Doesn't that show he is trying? Everybody has got a past and Charlie is no different, only with him people hold the past against him time after time. What if Charlie was your son, brother, uncle, wouldn't you want him to be able to have a chance in the outside world? Well Charlie has got family and lots of friends, people who will be there for him when he gets out. I am very proud and honoured to have Charlie as my friend and will be there for him whatever happens.

WYN THOMPSON (FRIEND):
Charlie should be released. What purpose does it serve? Has no Home Secretary got the balls to sanction his release?! I think not! Therefore it's political, he's the forgotten one. Chas and I are pals; mind, we do have our fall-outs, big style. It all goes quiet for a while, and then off we go again, like brother and sister. He is one of the nicest people I know, genuine, gentle and humanitarian, a loving son and brother. But he doesn't tolerate fools gladly and finds them out in the end. With the goodness of his heart he's given countless works of art away, simply for the asking, only to be informed it's available at a price on eBay! We all want him out of the hole to live his life, doing as he wishes - the world's his oyster. What better ambassador for anti-crime, anti-drugs? He's an eloquent speaker, not a problem, for he speaks from the heart.
If you ever get the honour of meeting Chaz, you're in for a big surprise. Get through the elaborate security, which is daunting. In trepidation you envisage yourself facing what your nightmares are made of. Yet it is no Hannibal Lecter, but a smiley face, big handshake, straight in the eye look of the man himself. I'll tell you, it is two hours of laughing and finding yourself at total ease. Chaz even pours the tea. People who know him love him, respect him; even the screws show him utter respect. And on the way down they tell you what a great fella he is. Everyone I've spoken to all say the same - he shouldn't be here, yet he's vilified. The press do him no favours, same old shit, same old photos.
So in retrospect all I can say is, he's simply the best is our Chaz. He must be to endure all the hardships he's had over 30+ years and still laughing. What a man! Also, to add to this, I'm no silly, lonely housewife looking for a kick. I don't hero-worship no one. But this guy, he's got all my respect. He's done and still is doing what 99% of the population can't. I rest my case!

LUKE THURLOW (SUPPORTER):
Enough is enough, get him out!

JAY TILLEY (SUPPORTER):
Enough is enough!

PAUL ADAM TODD (SUPPORTER):
Free Charlie! Keep strong Charlie.

CRAIG TOLEY (SUPPORTER):
For what Charlie done he does not deserve to die in prison! People who kill and rape people get less than that!

JOHN TRUNDLE (SUPPORTER):
What's this man got to do to start living his life again?

PAUL TUCKER (SUPPORTER):
Free Charlie and hang the perverts.
Charlie writes: I'll drink to that Paul.

REBECCA TURNER (SUPPORTER):
Free Charlie. Just look at all the murderers that get out after 7 years. Come off it. The 'justice' system in the UK really needs reviewing.

STUART ANDREW TYE (SUPPORTER):
Just finished one of his books *Insanity*. God, Chas is more sane than me. Get him out.

ALEASHA TYLER (SUPPORTER):
How much can a man take? We are supposed to have a fair justice system. I don't think so!! Too many years have been stolen. Give him his life back!!

LEON TYRRELL (SUPPORTER):
British justice at its finest. 34 wasted years because one man scares the shit out of parliament!!!!!

SAM ULYET (SUPPORTER):
28 years' solitary, it's time he was freed.

PAUL UNGI (SUPPORTER):
The system fuckin' stinks!! Rapists and child molesters get less! Where's the fuckin' justice?!

KERRY VEITCH (SUPPORTER):
A Democracy you say ... I think not.

GREGG AND ANN VORLEY (FRIENDS):
Charlie should have been freed years ago. We can't believe he's still being treated as an animal. If I treated any of our pets like that the RSPCA would be on my case, yet Charlie's a human being and is being kept in this way by our government.
Charlie has never hurt a woman or a child, yet he's being treated worse than any nonce, rapist, child killer, but why? He's been on excellent behaviour the last 7 years without even being moved to mix with the other cons. Charlie shouldn't even be in jail. He's served his time over and over again. What's up with this country and the system? It's all wrong.
Charlie has proved he has changed his ways; he's no longer violent. He's found a new thing to take up and that's his wonderful art; we have some on our walls with pride. I'm sure he could do the world better on the outside showing off his work, helping donate money to sick kids, etc. He could even learn the younger generation how to stay out of trouble. He sure could do a lot more out than stuck in a cage wasting taxpayers' money. They could use that cage for the monsters that truly deserve it (i.e. Ian Huntley, Brady, etc).
We have been in touch with Charlie after having some of his art. I have also chatted to him on the phone. He's got a great personality and after all these years behind bars and treated the way he has been I'm stunned. Most people would have gone mad, but not Charlie. The papers might say so, but who believes the crap in papers anyway?
Charlie ain't getting any younger in prison and neither is his family on the outside. It's about time Charlie was set free so he can see his mum in her own home, go for a pint with his son that he's never been able to do, enjoy family life that some take for granted. You only have to look on his website petition to see how many want him out - we sure do!
Charlie we wish you all the best on your fight for freedom. We and 1000s of others are right by your side 100% all the way! Enough is enough, time to set him free!! People who hurt kids are treated better! Time to set free!!

LIAM VORLEY (FRIENDS):
Give the man his life back!! (The time is now)!!!!

RYAN VORLEY (FRIENDS):
If Mr Bronson hurt little kids he would have been out years ago. He don't do this, or has he killed anyone? Time to set free, it's all wrong.

KEN WALDER (SUPPORTER):
Best book I've ever read. Stay strong.

COLIN STEVEN WARD (SUPPORTER):
Free Charlie! Don't you think he's been through enough?

DARREN WARREN (SUPPORTER):
If this happened abroad to one of ours there would be uproar. Why don't they start looking closer to home and get this sorted?

LEE WARRINER (SUPPORTER):
Charlie has done more than enough time for his crime.

JAMES WATSON (SUPPORTER):
I think it's all bollocks the way he is treated. Let him free now!!! The system is shit. Nonces get less and they should be hung.

RORY JAMES WEBB (SUPPORTER):
U bastards!

GLEN WESTWOOD (SUPPORTER):
Let him out, you corrupted bastards!

DAVID WHILLIANS (SUPPORTER):
Why this long??? The system is a total joke. Good luck.

GARY WHITE (FRIEND):
I have known Charlie a while now and I like most thought he was a murderer. Charlie is the most honest and genuine person I have ever met, and believe me he is not the monster that they keep in that cage at Monster Mansion. I would rather have Charlie on our streets or living next to me than some that are allowed on our streets now.

LINDSAY WHITE (SUPPORTER):
Free Charles Bronson.

SHELLEY WHITE (SUPPORTER):
This man is a legend and always will be. He deserves a pat on the back not a cage! Set the man free. He's been through enough!

JAY WHITMAN (SUPPORTER):
Free the man.

FRANK WILKINSON (FRIEND):
The main reason Charlie is still banged up in solitary is this country's failure to comply with human rights directives. We have the worst record of complaints regarding prisoners in custody within the European Union.

TIM WILKINSON (SUPPORTER):
Believed all the rubbish until I looked into it further. It is totally wrong what the system has done to this man.

CRAIG WILLIAMS (SUPPORTER):
Release him. Give his cell to the evil who walk our streets!

DAVID WILLIAMS (SUPPORTER):
Free Charlie NOW! There is so much scum walking the streets today. Charlie is a good man at heart and should be free. Keep going Charlie. Don't let the bastards get you down!

GEMMA WILLIAMS (SUPPORTER):
Just read your book. It was fantastic, funny and sad. You wouldn't treat a dog in that way, so why do it to Charles Bronson? He's done his time, so let him free to see what living life is really all about.

GERAINT WILLIAMS (SUPPORTER):
Terrorists get treated better.

GERAUBT WILLIAMS (SUPPORTER):
Terrorists get treated better.

PETE WILLIAMS (SUPPORTER):
Enough is enough. It's time surely to release Charles Bronson after 34+ years. Live and let live as Charlie has!! Good luck!!

RAY WILLIAMS (FRIEND):
I first met Charlie about 38 years ago. Why is Charlie still in prison? Has he killed anyone? No! Has he raped or beat a woman? No! Has he abused or hurt a child? No! What the fuck has he done to warrant being locked up for over 30 years? He has fought the system. Why should they treat somebody like an animal? The chance is they will start acting like one. I will tell you something about Charlie. He would cut his hand off before he would hurt a woman or a child. I would trust him with my life and my family's life. He is and always will be a true friend and brother to me and my family. He has spent over 30 years in prison, most of the time in solitary confinement in a cage. When I say cage - I mean it.
I have visited Charlie in his cage in Wakefield Prison. A cell within a cell. I'll tell you a story about Wakefield. I went to visit Charlie with my son, who was 13 at the time. We were met and escorted to the visit. We called at the canteen to get some orange juice and chocolate for him. The canteen is situated in the main visiting hall. All the prisoners are sitting around tables with their family. Children are running about. Sitting at one of the tables, laughing and joking with his visitors, my son saw Ian Huntley. I said it wasn't him, as they would not allow a monster like that to have an open visit with children in the same room. The prison officer with us said, "Yes it is him and he gets special treatment like many of the other beasts in here." The officer's words not mine! Another time I visited him with his mother Eira and his brother Mark in the cage with 1-inch thick bars and a table between us. His mother cannot even give her son a hug and a kiss. Why? Because they don't think we would be safe. What a load of shit. Is he going to take us hostage? I don't think so.
It has been 8 years since Charlie last got in trouble. Why is he still in a cage? Isn't it about time they started treating him with a bit of compassion? Charlie has had enough. All he wants now is to go home and spend a few years with his mum, while he still can. His dad died and they would not let him go to his dad's funeral. They let Peter Sutcliffe out for his dad's funeral. They let Myra Hindley out to go shopping. They let paedos out after a few years. Why the fuck won't they let Charlie out? I don't know, but surely there is somebody who can answer this question and it needs to be answered as soon as possible. What do you think? Charlie Bronson - man or monster? Some fucker tell me please. Let him out!

CHRIS WILSON (SUPPORTER):
Make room in the prisons for scum and let Bronson out!

JAMES WILTSHIRE (SUPPORTER):
Come on PM. For someone who has been inside for as long as Charlie and what he actually did it's a disgrace!! FREE CHARLIE!

JONATHAN WINSPUR (SUPPORTER):
He's more than done his time! Let him live a free life!

GARY WISEMAN (SUPPORTER):
Free Bronson! The government should be ashamed of the way they have treated him!

LEE WITTY (SUPPORTER):
I've done a good bit of bird myself fella, not as much as u though, so not gonna say all the same anti-government fuckin' shit, but if u need another pen-pal, get Mally to give u my address.

MICHAEL WOLOHAN (SUPPORTER):
It's clear that the justice system has got it in for Charlie. Free Bronson.

CHRIS WOODFIELD (SUPPORTER):
Wishing you the best.

DERI WOODLAND (SUPPORTER):
Free this gentle giant, he's no Ian Huntley. Let him free to enjoy his life.

RACHEL WOOD (SUPPORTER):
They can only hold your body; your mind will always be free x.

JON WOOD-STORTFORD (SUPPORTER):
Free Charlie, Even the perverts are getting released after 3 years to hang about outside the schools again. This country needs to sort it out before it's too late.

MATTHEW WORTON (SUPPORTER):
Free the man who never did anything that bad.

MATT WRIDE (SUPPORTER):
Let's start using some common fucking sense.

MARCUS WRIGHT (SUPPORTER):
Just another lost soul. Aren't we all! Free Charlie! Let him be a free man and enjoy a good cup of tea!!

SHAUN WRIGHT (SUPPORTER):
Totally let down by the penal system.

TRUDY WRIGHT (SUPPORTER):
Why keep him in any longer? He's done his time, now give him a chance!!

VERNON WRIGHT (SUPPORTER):
Good luck Charlie, But if you get out, stay out, ok, running on the beach in rain, wind, snow, whatever the weather. You may be in solitary, but we are all here for you.

JASON YETMAN (SUPPORTER):
Free Charlie Bronson.

HELENA YOUNG (SUPPORTER):
A total miscarriage of justice, free him!

SEYMOUR YOUNG (FRIEND):
My name is Seymour Young. I have known Charlie B for a good number of years. I never met him on the out but times when he would phone D.C. I would be there and answer the phone. So little by little I began to understand Charlie B. Now don't get me wrong, because he is a very complicated man. He is an artist in his own right, a very good one I might add, but all his drawings seem to be based on insanity being incarcerated or just blatantly locked up. But beyond all that I do believe that he is a very intelligent fella that definitely lost his way at one point in his life, or two or three, but who's counting? Bottom line is that in life sometimes shit happens and it's right in your face. That's when you've got to eat it and hope you can live through it. But with Charlie B it's a bit different. They want him to eat it, shit it and live in it. I think he is one of society's forgotten few and there are some; locked away, never to be seen. Who am I to give my 50p's worth? Me, that's who. Charlie B has paid his debt but he's a strange one, so let's just hold on to him forever. This one won't be missed. "Wrong". A lot of people are missing him, people that don't even know him; how kind. Free him, put him on a chain. Oh no, that's not humane. Ok, put him on a tag, let him sign on 5 days a week and if he fucks up well he's straight back to jail. Peace and love.

Charlie writes:

Without exaggerating I would need three more books to put in all the other friends and supporters. It's just impossible to put them all inside one book, but I thank and respect you all for all your magic support. You are stars - cheers! I'll leave you with this: on 12 January 2008 in the *Daily Mirror* there was a two-page spread - you can check it out on my site or the Apex Publishing Ltd site: *www.apexpublishing.co.uk* The journalist was Jeremy Armstrong. No money was put on the table, but £1,000 was sent to Zoe's Babies Hospice, otherwise I wouldn't have done the interview. The reason I am ending this section of *Loonyology* on this story is: could you have seen my two ex-wives doing this? The greedy, selfish, blood-sucking leeches. I rest my case your Honour!
Loonyology is to be enjoyed ... pass the popcorn!

Red hot exclusive! There will be a *Loonyology* Volume 2! You lucky people!

OTHER CRIME BOOKS
PUBLISHED BY APEX:

THE LOOSE SCREW
by Jim Dawkins
£10.00
ISBN: 978-1-906358-01-3

**THE BRITISH CRIME AND
PRISON QUIZ BOOK**
by Jim Dawkins and Dave Courtney
£7.99
ISBN: 978-1-906358-01-3

**WARRIOR KINGS:
THE SOUTH LONDON GANG WARS 1976-1982**
by Noel 'Razor' Smith
£7.99
ISBN: 978-1-904444-95-4

**NIL DESPERANDUM:
"NEVER DESPAIR"**
by Terry Smith
£7.99
ISBN: 978-1-904444-83-1

REVIEWS:

"When the history of modern-day crime is written, the name of Charles Bronson will figure in many chapters. "Loonyology" gives a rare insight into the inside-out world of one Britain's longest serving prisoners. Caged, confused, violent: Charles' 34 years behind bars - many of them in solitary confinement - reveal more about what is wrong with our prison system than is right."
- Anthony France, The Sun (Crime Reporter)

"Told with brutal honesty, this book is a frightening insight into the mind of the man dubbed Britain's most violent prisoner."
- Robert Verkaik, The Independent (Law Editor)

"All directly from Charles Bronson himself, Loonyology is a fascinating insight into the mind of one of Britain's most notorious prisoners, and an opportunity to draw your own conclusions about our prison system and the way we treat those at the very heart of it."
- Sofia Zagzoule, Daily Star Sunday

"Poet, artist, writer, armed robber - there may be no end to Bronson's talents. Loonyology lifts the lid on life as Britain's most infamous maximum security prisoner. Train wreck gripping stuff."
- James McCarthy, Wales on Sunday

REVIEWS:

"Charles Bronson is certainly unlike anyone else in the British prison system. Truly, this is the dark side of the loon."
- Duncan Campbell, The Guardian (Senior Correspondent)

"After more than 30 years in solitary confinement, Charlie Bronson gives a unique insight into life behind bars and how you give meaning to that life - with wit, bravado and sheer bloody mindedness."
- Jeremy Armstrong, Daily Mirror

"Scary reading, this book is as close as we're comfortable getting to Mr Bronson!"
- Jon Wise, Daily Sport (Literary Editor)

"There have been many amazing, brilliant or insane quotes which can be attributed to villains across the world during the past century.
"But none, without possibility of contradiction can compare with the immortal line uttered by Charles Bronson: "'Nobody, no one on this planet touches my pineapples. The only person who would get them pineapples is my mother. They are my pineapples. I paid for them. But I opened that tin of pineapples and I fed him my pineapples because he was a human being the same as me.'
"This, perhaps more than anything else, sums up the enigma that is Bronson. The contradictory stories in the Press which surround him are legion yet here in 'Loonyology' we finally begin to understand the real character, the real man, the real human being behind the media legend.
"The man from Aberystwyth, he says 'yes'."
- Richard Elias, Scotland on Sunday

"Loonyology is a fascinating insight into one man's quest to keep his sanity when everything around him is conspiring to make him lose it. Bronson paints a graphic and frightening picture of the psychopathic criminals he shares Britain's jails with. At the same time, he blows the lid off the most insane aspect of his incarceration: the prison system itself."
- Rick Lyons, Daily Star Sunday (Crime Correspondent)

466